VICTOR A. SMITH

SO-AFY-266

Readings in the
Socio-Cultural Foundations
of Education

Readings in the Socio-Cultural Foundations of Education

EDITED BY

John H. Chilcott
University of Arizona

Norman C. Greenberg
George Peabody College for Teachers

Herbert B. Wilson
University of Arizona

Wadsworth Publishing Company, Inc., Belmont, California

© 1968 by Wadsworth Publishing Company, Inc.,
Belmont, California.
All rights reserved.
No part of this book may be reproduced in any form,
by mimeograph or any other means,
without permission in writing from the publisher.

L. C. Cat. Card No.: 67–17518

Printed in the United States of America

Preface

An educational program reflects the life and conditions of society; it cannot be removed from the social, historical, and philosophical forces that ultimately shape its direction. The educator must be aware of the relationship between education and society; thus, the study of socio-cultural foundations of education is essential in the training of teachers, counselors, and administrators.

The cultural values of our Western world have historically impregnated our ideas with the need for education as a way of perpetuating the democratic way of life. However, during the 20th century we have observed that many of the actualities of our society tend to be in conflict with the very ideals we have proclaimed. The problems of assimilation, acculturation, and equality of opportunity constantly and vividly manifest themselves in the classroom and display the gap within our present value structure between our democratic ideal and the actuality. And the examination and understanding of these problems and others faced by society today—for example, the drive for social status, the role of pressure groups in redirecting educational programs, the advent of automation vs. manpower, and the speed of integration—can be accomplished through the study of the socio-cultural foundations of education. In the discussion of these problems, one needs to apply an interdisciplinary approach—to consider contributions from the fields of sociology, anthropology, economics, political science, history, philosophy, psychology, and aesthetics.

The study of socio-cultural foundations of education should lead a student to a comprehensive interpretation of the issues that are influencing and have influenced society. It demands a familiarity with different cultural values and practices and a self-examination of one's own cultural attitudes. A teacher must develop an empathy for those students whose cultural values and practices may be in complete or partial conflict with the American "middle-class" preferences.

The editors of this collection of readings have attempted to reshape the past concepts of social foundations of education into the present, more appropriate precepts of the socio-cultural foundations of education. The educative processes are usually responses to societal needs, and societal needs manifest themselves in the historical action of the times. With this in mind, the editors have attempted to mingle the past with the present, the theory with the social issues, and the educational hypotheses with the educational practices.

We are aware of the sizable proportion of social science and educational literature which is not included in the present selections. However, in bringing together many of the social and some of the behavioral scientists, we have attempted to develop the kind of readings book that permits the illustration of concepts that demonstrate the interrelationship of the "socio-" and "cultural." By viewing education as an outgrowth of the cultural milieu, the reader will quickly discern that education becomes a beneficial factor only when those to be educated become aware of the controls and limitations placed upon the individual by his society. One becomes "free" to make crucial decisions and develop creative thoughts when one is clearly aware of the socio-cultural foundations from which one emanates. This work has not been developed for the purpose of answering questions; rather, it is intended to be a thought-provoking collection of readings which provides educators with material for ongoing class discussion and personal introspection.

John H. Chilcott
Norman C. Greenberg
Herbert B. Wilson

Contents

---

3   THE SCIENCE OF CULTURE IN EDUCATION

---

4   AMERICAN SOCIETY AND VALUES

---

5 SOCIAL STRUCTURE AND POWER: EDUCATION AS AN INSTITUTION IN AMERICAN SOCIETY

6 SOCIAL STRATIFICATION/ ETHNIC AND RACIAL GROUPS

7   THE FAMILY AND PEER GROUP IN AMERICAN SOCIETY

1

The Social Foundations of Education

INTRODUCTION

Anthropology is a comparatively recent endeavor and is probably the most comprehensive of sciences related to man and his creations. By combining into one discipline the biological and social sciences we see man as a member of the animal kingdom as well as an interacting participant in human society.

Sociology is the study of society—the scientific study of the man-made rules, devices, and mechanisms that provide a cohesive pattern for successful survival and action between individuals living in specific groups.

Obviously, these two sciences are closely related to each other. Since education is the process by which the adult generation enculturates the younger generation, it becomes readily apparent that a knowledge of these two disciplines is directly related to the educative process.

The first two articles that follow indicate the ways in which the findings and research methods of anthropology and sociology can be useful to educators; the third reading suggests that the field of social foundations can bring together the contributions of the social sciences for the educator's benefit.

The durability of a study of the socio-cultural foundations of education becomes evident as we learn how man responds to the cultural patterns (anthropology) practiced by the groups (sociology) in which he participates. Education as a societal institution in America reflects the needs and desires of our society. Formal education attempts to prepare individuals to take their place in this society. Through an awareness of the base upon which formal education is built we discover the importance of the socio-cultural foundations of education.

1-1   SOME CONTRIBUTIONS OF SOCIOLOGY TO THE FIELD OF EDUCATION

Neal Gross

Neal Gross is professor of education and sociology at the Graduate School of Education, Harvard University. He has been the recipient of fellowships from the Social Science Research Council and the Center for Advanced Study of Behavioral Sciences. He is the author of numerous articles and books including "Sociological Analysis of Educational Organization and Professional Roles," "Structure and Function of Small Groups," *Pressure on and the Dilemmas of the School Executive*, and *Who Runs Our Schools?*

The purpose of this paper is to delineate *for the educational practitioner* some specific contributions of sociological analysis to the field of education. We propose to focus on a limited set of substantive sociological contributions that teachers, supervisory personnel, school principals, or school superintendents may find of value in dealing with their work environment in a more realistic and effective manner.

Of the many approaches possible in describing some "practical contributions" of sociology to the field of education, the following procedure has been adopted. Specific contributions will be discussed under three headings that constitute sociological perspectives in the examination of school systems as functioning social systems. The first is that educational relationships occur in the context of a formal organizational setting. Students, teachers, supervisors, principals, and school superintendents interact as incumbents of positions in a social system which has an organizational goal, the education of children. To accomplish this task the work that goes on in a school must be assigned, coordinated, and integrated. Educational practice involves a number of people in a complicated division of labor; this necessitates networks of role relationships within an organizational environment. The second perspective derives from the fact that the basic work of the school, the educational transaction, takes place primarily in a relatively small social system, the classroom. The third perspective emerges from an observation that the sociologist would make about the school as a social system: Like all organizations, it is influenced by forces external to it. The impact of these external factors on the functioning of the school therefore comes under his scrutiny as a focal point of inquiry. It is from these three limited perspectives[1]—the school system as a formal organization, the

From *Harvard Educational Review*, XXIX, No. 4 (Fall 1959), 275–287. Copyright © 1959 by the *Harvard Educational Review*; reprinted by permission of *Harvard Educational Review* and the author.

[1] For other perspectives and an examination of needed research in the sociology of education see Orville G. Brim, Jr., *Sociology and the Field of Education* (New York: Russell Sage Foundation, 1958), and Neal Gross, "The Sociology of Education," in Robert K. Merton, Leonard Broom, and Leonard S. Cottrell, Jr., eds., *Sociology Today* (New York: Basic Books, 1959).

classroom as a social system, and the external environment of the schools—that we propose to delineate some contributions of sociology to practitioners in the field of education.

THE SCHOOL SYSTEM AS A FORMAL ORGANIZATION

A school system from a sociological point of view shares many common characteristics with other kinds of large-scale organizations. Two of these are of special relevance for our purpose. The first is that a school system, like business firms and hospitals, has an organizational objective. It is a goal-directed social system. Second, it contains a network of interrelated positions (for example, teachers, supervisors, and administrators) that are directly linked to the accomplishment of the organizational goal.

According to the "organizational model" for public schools, the business of the school is to impart knowledge and skills to students, and therefore teachers are employed for this purpose. The function of supervisors is to help teachers to do a more effective job, and the formal duties of school administrators are to coordinate and integrate the diverse activities of the school. The incumbents of these positions have certain rights and obligations in their relationships with incumbents of other positions with whom they interact. Implicit in discussions of these aspects of the organizational structure of the school are two assumptions that deserve empirical examination. The first is that there is basic agreement on the organizational objective of the schools. The second is that there is agreement on the rights and obligations associated with the various positions in education. Sociological analysis suggests that both assumptions may in fact be tenuous in many school systems, and that lack of agreement on educational objectives and role definition may constitute major dysfunctional elements in the functioning of the school and may affect the gratification educators derive from their jobs.

The formal organizational goal of public school systems is vague and is characterized by ambiguity. This observation emerges from a comparison of school systems with other types of organizations, for example, a business firm. The formal organizational goal of a business firm is unambiguous: to produce products or services for a profit. Labor unions may fight with management over the distribution of profits, but typically there is no quarrel over the organizational goal itself. The situation is quite different, however, when an effort is made to specify the organizational objective of a school system. "To educate children" is a largely meaningless statement unless the purposes of the education are specified. And here lies the difficulty.

The specification of educational purposes invokes value issues such as the respective responsibilities of the home and the school or the meaning of a "good education." Whether the schools should give greater primacy to the intellectual, social, or emotional development of the child; whether or not they have the responsibility to impart moral values; whether the schools have different obligations to the "typical" and "atypical" child; whether they should encourage or discourage the questioning of the status quo; whether driver education, physical education, and courses in home economics and family living are legitimate or illegitimate functions of the school—each of these is a value question on which there may be contradictory points of view within and outside of school systems. An unpublished Harvard study involving personnel at different levels in eight New England school systems revealed dramatic differences in the beliefs teachers hold about educational goals and revealed that principals and teachers frequently do not share common views about educational objectives. Striking disagreements between superintendents and school boards have also been uncovered in regard to certain educational objectives.[2] Research evidence[3] further indicates that one of the major sources of pressures to which school administrators are exposed consists in conflicting viewpoints in their communities about school objectives and programs. Educational practitioners need to recognize that a fundamental source of controversy within the schools may be related to basic and unrecognized value conflicts over its organizational objectives. These differences in beliefs are infrequently brought to the surface for frank and open discussion. They may constitute basic blocks to effective group action and harmonious social relationships.

The second "organizational assumption," that there is agreement on the role definition for educational positions, also appears to be suspect. Although textbooks in education glibly speak about the role of the teacher and of the school administrator as if everybody agreed on what they are, and many educational practitioners make this assumption, the organizational fact in many school systems may be that those people who work together frequently do not share similar views about the rights and obligations associated with their positions.

Should teachers be expected to attend PTA meetings regularly? Does the teacher's job include the counseling function? What are the teacher's obligations to the especially bright or especially dull child? Or the problem child? What are the teacher's obligations in handling discipline problems? Should teachers be expected to participate in in-service training programs? Does the teacher have the right to expect that the administrator will always support him when parents complain about his behavior? On these and many other phases of a teacher's job there may be considerable disagreement between principals and teachers as well as among teachers.

The findings of a study concerned with the role definition of approximately 50 percent of the superintendents and school board members in Massachusetts revealed a basic lack of agreement over the division of labor between them.[4] On the issue of hiring new teachers, seven out of ten superintendents interviewed reported that the arrangement they desired was this: when a new teacher was to be hired, the school board should act *solely* on the nominations of the superintendent. But only one out of five of the school board members agreed with them. How about the selection of textbooks? Nearly nine out of ten superintendents felt that the school board should always accept the recommendation of the superintendent in choosing a textbook. But less than one-half of the school board members agreed. What about teacher grievances? Nearly 90 percent of the superintendents believed that teachers should always bring their grievances to the superintendent before they went to the school board. Only 56 percent of the school board members agreed. What should the procedure be when a community group wishes to use school property? Nine out of ten school superintendents thought that this decision should be the superintendent's responsibility. Nearly one-half of the school board members, however, felt that these

[2]Neal Gross, *Who Runs Our Schools?* (New York: John Wiley & Sons, Inc., 1958), pp. 113–125.

[3]*Ibid.*, pp. 45–60.

[4]Neal Gross, Ward S. Mason, and Alexander W. McEachern, *Explorations in Role Analysis: Studies of the School Superintendency Role* (New York: John Wiley & Sons, Inc., 1958), p. 124.

decisions should be made by the school board. What about recommendations for salary increases for school system employees? Over two-thirds of the superintendents felt that the superintendent should make all such recommendations. Only one-third of the school board members agreed with them. These findings imply that in many school systems disagreements over the rights and obligations associated with educational positions may constitute basic sources of stress in the school system. They also suggest that intra-role conflicts appear to be "built into" many educational positions.

By an intra-role conflict we mean conflicting expectations to which an individual is exposed as a consequence of his occupancy of a *single* position. Teachers are frequently exposed to conflicting expectations from their principal and supervisors, from guidance personnel and their principal, from parents and administrators, and even from students in their classrooms. School principals are exposed to conflicting expectations from their superintendent and their staff over such matters as the supervision of classroom instruction and the handling of discipline problems. School administrators are confronted with conflicting expectations among their school staff. For example, some teachers expect their principal to make all important decisions affecting their welfare, but other teachers expect to participate in such decisions.[5] In addition, parents and teachers frequently hold contradictory expectations for the principal's behavior in regard to student promotion and discipline practices. It is the school superintendent, however, who probably is exposed most frequently to intra-role conflict. A major source of these conflicting expectations arises from the differential views held by his school board and his staff for his behavior. Whose views should he support when the school board and the staff hold conflicting expectations for his behavior on such issues as the size of the school budget or promotion policies? Superintendents, like school principals, must also frequently deal with differential expectations among the teaching staff. And their most difficult problems may emerge from conflicting expectations held by their school board members for their performance.

To sum up: Viewing school systems as organizations from a sociological perspective suggests major organizational barriers to their effective functioning. We have emphasized two of these blocks: lack of agreement on organizational goals and lack of consensus on the role definitions associated with educational positions.

THE CLASSROOM AS A SOCIAL SYSTEM

Parsons, in a recent paper, presents a provocative theoretical analysis of the school class as a social system from the viewpoint of its functions for American society.[6] Coleman's analysis of the structure of competition in the high school and its influence on academic achievement clearly has implications for isolating forces that influence the "academic output" of the classroom.[7] These analyses, plus those of

---

[5]Melvin Seeman, "Role Conflict and Ambivalence in Leadership," *American Sociological Review*, XXVIII (August 1935), 373–380; also see Charles E. Bidwell, "The Administrative Role and Satisfaction in Teaching," *Journal of Educational Sociology*, XXIX (September 1955), 41–47.

[6]Talcott Parsons, "The School Class as a Social System: Some of Its Functions in American Society," *Harvard Educational Review*, XXIX (Fall 1959), 297–318.

[7]James S. Coleman, "Academic Achievement and the Structure of Competition," *Harvard Educational Review*, XXIX (Fall 1959), 330–351.

sociologists like Gordon[8] and Brookover,[9] suggest the importance of a sociological perspective in examining the structure and functioning of the classroom as a social system.

At this stage of sociological and socio-psychological inquiry on the classroom as a social system, the major empirical contributions of the sociologist have undoubtedly been to draw attention to the sociometric structure of the classroom and to isolate basic sources of strain and tension to which teachers are exposed in the classroom. Sociometric studies reveal that classrooms typically contain "stars" and "isolates," and they have uncovered factors that affect student interpersonal relations in the school class.[10] Of especial importance to educators is the finding that teachers appear to misperceive frequently the interpersonal relationships among students in their classrooms.[11] They do not show high sensitivity to the way children actually react to each other, and they frequently allow their own biases toward students to hinder a correct assessment of the "sociometric facts of life."

A second sociological contribution to the understanding of classroom behavior stems from the isolation of some potential sources of strain for the classroom teacher. One source of stress is the collision between the authority structure of the school and the professional status of the teaching staff. A school system must provide for the coordination and integration of the work of its members. Someone has to assign responsibilities, see that tasks are accomplished, and have the power to sanction teachers and students for deviant behavior. The elementary school principal, for example, as the formal leader of his school, has to make room assignments and final decisions about the disposition of discipline problems. He must also see that the educational experiences of the child in the first grade are integrated with those he receives in the second and third grades. This requires some type of control over the work content and work output of teachers at each of these levels. Their classroom behavior is part of his concern. The authority structure, however, conflicts with another characteristic of school organization—the school is staffed with professional personnel. A professional worker is supposed to have autonomy over his own activities. This implies that the teacher should have considerable freedom in the manner in which he conducts his classes and in the skills and knowledge which he imparts to his students. It is this built-in source of strain that in part accounts for the "social distance" that frequently exists between school principals and their teachers and for the charge—by teachers—that administrators upset "their" classes. The clash between the authority structure and the professional status of teachers is also undoubtedly reflected in the latent and overt opposition of teachers to the introduction of new educational practices.

[8]C. Wayne Gordon, *The Social System of the High School: A Study in the Sociology of Adolescence* (Glencoe, Ill.: The Free Press, 1957).

[9]Wilbur B. Brookover, "The Social Roles of Teachers and Pupil Achievement," *American Sociological Review*, VIII (August 1943), 389–393.

[10]See Lloyd A. Cook, "An Experimental Sociographic Study of a Stratified 10th Grade Class," *American Sociological Review*, X (April 1945), 250–261; Otto H. Dahlke and Thomas O. Monahan, "Problems in the Application of Sociometry to Schools," *School Review*, LVII (April 1949), 223–234; Robert J. Havighurst and Bernice L. Neugarten, *Society and Education* (Boston: Allyn and Bacon, 1957); and August B. Hollingshead, *Elmtown's Youth* (New York: John Wiley & Sons, Inc., 1949).

[11]Merl E. Bonney, "Sociometric Study of Agreement between Teacher Judgments and Student Choices: In Regard to the Number of Friends Possessed by High School Students," *Sociometry*, X (May 1947), 133–146; and Norman E. Bonlund, "The Accuracy of Teachers' Judgments Concerning the Sociometric Status of Sixth-Grade Pupils," *Sociometry*, XIII (August 1950); part 1, 197–225; part 2, 329–357.

A second source of strain derives from the differential norms held by teachers and students for the students' behavior. Gordon's analysis[12] of a high school suggests the differential frames of reference that may be operating in many classrooms. His analysis indicates that teachers expected students to perform in a manner that approximated their knowledge and ability potential. But students' expectations were in part based on the informal social structure and values of the students. He indicates that student stereotypes had an important influence on the "roles" students assigned each other and played themselves, and that these stereotypes therefore affected their role performance. When student-defined and teacher-defined roles and values were incompatible, the net result was strain for the teacher in his transactions with students.

Another contribution of a sociological perspective on classroom behavior is demonstrated by the current work of Lippitt and his associates at the University of Michigan on the "socially unaccepted" child in the classroom. In addition to showing the need for a typology of such children, their studies suggest the powerful group forces operating on the unaccepted child. The major barriers to changing his behavior may be in the classroom, rather than or in addition to forces within the child. This finding has important implications for teachers and also for school guidance practices which are usually based on the assumption that individual counseling is the only way to change a student's behavior. The observation that the attributes and stereotypes of classmates as well as the teacher are barriers to behavior changes is one demanding rigorous exploration.

In addition, sociological analysis strongly suggests that the attitudes and behavior of the individual are strongly linked to those groups to which he belongs or aspires. These reference groups constitute "anchoring points" which have to be considered in inducing changed behavior. For the classroom teacher, the important consequence of this observation is that to deal effectively with a child may require isolating group forces that are constraining his behavior and inducing changes in clique norms and values.

THE EXTERNAL ENVIRONMENT OF THE SCHOOL

A school system does not exist in a vacuum. Its existence and functioning depend in part on its outside world, its external environment. This sociological point of view has many implications for the analysis of school systems.

One implication is that changes in the larger social system of the community materially affect the composition of the student body in a school system, and therefore may require modifications in the curriculum. The heavy migration of the rural population in the South to metropolitan centers implies that many large city school systems need to undertake a critical review of the ability of their school program to meet the needs of the school's changed clientele. The empty school buildings in the center of many cities and the needed new school buildings in suburban areas, associated with the recent "flight to the suburbs," suggest the need for a metropolitan approach to school planning, a concept infrequently considered in educational circles. In short, the educational implications of demographic studies require considerably greater attention by educators.

---

[12]Gordon, *op. cit.*

_II_.   A second aspect of the external environment of public school systems to which
sociologists have given considerable attention is the social class structure of communities. Studies in this area[13] reveal that most aspects of school functioning are influenced
by social class phenomena. Research on social class strongly supports the notion that
teacher grading practices and the criteria which teachers apply to children are related
to the social class placement of the child and the teacher. The mobility aspirations of
children, the drop-out rate, participation in extra-curricular activities, dating behavior,
and friendship patterns are in part accounted for by the socio-economic characteristics
of the child's family.

III.   A third "external environment" factor that has important implications for the
public schools is the power structure or structures of the community.[14] School systems
absorb a large portion of the local tax dollar, and the influence of informal and formal
power agents in the community on educational budgetary decisions is without doubt
a basic influence on the quality of the staff and the program of a school system. It
is not surprising that national meetings of educational administrators usually have
sessions devoted to "techniques for studying community power structure" and that
sociologists are invited to participate in them.

_IV_.   A fourth contribution of sociology to the understanding of the external environment of the schools is the analysis of the basic link between the community and the
schools—the school board. Charters has questioned the assumption, frequently found
in the educational literature, that the disproportionate incidence of school board
members from upper socio-economic strata results in "a conservative bias" in public
education.[15] Sociological research has demonstrated the impact of the behavior of
school board members and of their motivation for seeking election to this position on
the superintendent's job satisfaction and his job performance. The effect of such
factors as religion, occupation, and income on the school board member's behavior as
well as the pressures to which school administrators are exposed by their school
boards have also been examined. These findings lead to the general conclusion that
a crucial, but frequently neglected, variable influencing the operation of the school
is the behavior of the small group of laymen who are its official policy-makers.[16] This
conclusion has had many important ramifications, one of which is the National School
Board Association's current effort to improve the "quality" of school board members.

_V_.   A fifth sociological contribution emerges from the analysis of inter-role conflicts
to which educational personnel are exposed as a consequence of their occupancy of
positions in schools and in other social systems. Getzels and Guba[17] found that

---

[13]For a summary of these studies see Wilbur B. Brookover, _A Sociology of Education_ (New York: American
Book Co., 1955); and Havighurst and Neugarten, _op. cit._ For a critical appraisal of some of this literature see
Neal Gross, "Social Class Structure and American Education," _Harvard Educational Review_, XXIII (Fall 1953),
283–329.

[14]See, for example, Robert E. Agger, "Power Attributions in the Local Community," _Social Forces_, XXXIV
(May 1956), 322–331; Floyd Hunter, _Community Power Structure: A Study of Decision Makers_ (Chapel Hill:
University of North Carolina Press, 1953); Peter Rossi, "Community Decision Making," _Administrative
Science Quarterly_, I (March 1957), 415–441; and Robert O. Schulze, "The Role of Economic Dominants in
Community Power Structure," _American Sociological Review_, XXIII (February 1958), 3–9.

[15]W. W. Charters, Jr., "Social Class Analysis and the Control of Public Education," _Harvard Educational Review_, XXIII (Fall 1953), 268–283.

[16]For a report of the specific findings leading to this conclusion, see Gross, _Who Runs Our Schools?_

[17]J. W. Getzels and E. G. Guba, "The Structure of Roles and Role Conflict in the Teaching Situation,"
Journal of Educational Sociology, XXIX (September 1955), 30–40.

many of the expectations linked to the teacher's position conflict with other positions
he occupies, and that some of these conflicts are a function of local school and community
conditions.

The school superintendent's position is especially exposed to inter-role conflict.
His job and the way he carries it out influence in some way virtually all members of
the community. In dealing with him, members of his church, his personal friends,
members of other organizations to which he may belong, and, of course, his wife and
family, are inclined to identify him not only as a fellow church member, for example,
but as a fellow church member who is at the same time the superintendent of schools.

Some unpublished findings of the School Executive Studies[18] shed light on the
kinds of inter-role conflicts to which school superintendents are exposed. Twenty
percent of the superintendents reported that they faced incompatible expectations
deriving from their simultaneous occupancy of positions in the *educational and religious
systems*. The formal leaders and certain members of their church expected them to act
in one way regarding certain issues, while other individuals and groups expected
contrary behavior. One Catholic superintendent said that he faced situations like this
all the time:

> Sometimes, the situation gets pretty touchy. I want to keep good
> relations with the Church. Don't forget—most of my school committee members
> and the local politicians belong to my church. Take this for example: one of the
> Catholic groups wanted to let the kids out early from school. They were
> having some special meetings, and they wanted the kids to be there. I knew
> that wouldn't be right. It wasn't fair to the other kids. So what did I do? I refused
> to give an official o.k. to the request, but at the time I simply winked at it
> [letting them out early]. I would have offended them if I'd stopped the kids
> from going, and I just couldn't afford to do that. It really left me bothered.
> Should I have stopped it? Legally, I could and I would have been right. But I
> know I would have had hell to pay.

Another superintendent, a Protestant, told the interviewer:

> [My] minister wants all kinds of special favors because I am a
> member of his church. He expected me to turn over our gym to the church
> basketball team. He wanted me to support his idea of giving out a Bible to
> each public school child. He told me that he thought I ought to see that more
> of 'our people' get jobs in the school. None of these are fair requests. I'm
> supposed to represent all the people, and I want to use the criterion of 'what's
> best for the schools,' not 'what's best for my church.' I might give him the
> gym, but it would be worth my job to give in on the Bibles in this community.
> I try not to play favorites, but sometimes it's hard to know what is the right
> thing to do.

Of perhaps as great personal and emotional significance to superintendents
are the role conflicts arising from the expectations of their *personal friends* which are

---

[18] For other findings of the School Executive Studies, see Gross, Mason, and McEachern, *op. cit.*; and
Gross, *Who Runs Our Schools?*

incompatible with those held by other individuals and groups in the community. Thirty-five percent of the superintendents reported conflicts of this kind.

Although some superintendents said that their "personal friends" expected special consideration in the areas of personnel decisions and the allocation of school contracts, more often the superintendents said that their friends expected special consideration for their children. These included requests that teachers be reprimanded for treating their children unfairly, that their children be transferred to a school in another district, that transportation be provided for children who are not entitled to it, that their children be promoted against the best judgment of the teacher and principal involved, and so on. Each of these "special consideration" expectations is incompatible with procedures and principles which the superintendent is expected to follow and which are set by the school board, by the teachers, and by PTA groups. Undoubtedly there are many requests of this kind which superintendents automatically ignore or refuse and which they did not mention in the interview; it is when these requests come from personal friends and when these friends expect the superintendent to make particular concessions, that the superintendents describe them as "role conflict" situations.

One superintendent said:

> [One of the] nastiest aspects of my job is bus transportation. Good friends of mine have the nerve to telephone me, the superintendent of schools, and ask that a bus pick up their children, when they know, and I know, and the bus driver knows, that they live within the one-mile limit. I tell them I don't drive the bus. I'm just superintendent of schools. Talk to the bus driver. They think I'm saying okay, and I guess I am if you come right down to it. Someday I guess I'll get into trouble when someone who doesn't have the gall to come to me goes to the committee and says 'so and so, the superintendent's friend, has his kids picked up. Why can't I have mine?' It's all in the game and sometimes the game is rough.

A third role conflict situation frequently mentioned involved the *superintendency and the father positions*. Forty-eight percent of the superintendents described conflicts of this type.

The superintendents reported a wide variety of situations in which their children expected one thing and others expected something quite different. One superintendent who ·was greatly troubled by problems in this area described his situation in this way:

> You know one of the worst things about this job that you never think of before you get into it is its effect on your children. You don't have time for your children. You have to be out every night and it just isn't fair to them. They don't like it; they resent it. And then the kids have a cross to bear. Either they get especially soft or especially rough treatment by the teachers. And the teachers are just waiting for you to throw your weight around.
>
> For example, my boy has told me certain things about one of his teachers— the way she behaves in the classroom. He's an honest youngster so I have no reason to doubt him, and if I were not the superintendent you can be darn sure I'd raise a lot of cain. But as the superintendent I'm not supposed to invade a

teacher's classroom. So I try to support the teacher even though I know she is in the wrong. I feel pretty mean about this, but what else can I do? I hope my boy will understand the situation better later on.

Eighteen percent of the superintendents mentioned inter-role conflicts stemming from incompatible expectations held for their behavior as a *member of a local community association and as the superintendent*. For example, in many communities certain local organizations to which the superintendent belonged expected him to allow them to use the time of students and staff to achieve their own organizational objectives, whereas the professional school staff expected him to protect the schools from this type of "invasion." School superintendents are exposed to requests for school children to be active in fund raising activities, for the school band to play in parades, and for the schools to participate in youth activities. Local community groups expect the superintendent to facilitate their use of these school resources. On the other hand, many superintendents know that one of the major complaints of their faculty is that this type of activity frequently disrupts classroom activities and planned school programs. This constitutes a difficult area of decision making, especially when the organization in question has a powerful voice in community affairs.

These findings support the proposition that inter-role conflicts stemming from occupancy of positions in the school system and in the environment external to it constitute a basic source of potential stress for the educator.

There are dangers to be avoided as well as benefits to be derived from the closer alignment between the fields of sociology and education. One of these dangers is to overgeneralize sociological research findings that apply to a single case or a small population to American education or American society when there is no logical basis for such induction. Sociologists as well as educators have erred in this respect. A second pitfall is the uncritical acceptance of unverified pronouncements of sociologists as verified propositions. There are many statements to be found in textbooks of educational sociology that are speculative in nature and which are not based on rigorous research evidence. Hunches and speculations need to be distinguished from verified propositions. A third danger is the acceptance of sociological research findings without critical examination of their assumptions, the adequacy of their research methods, and their conclusions. The literature on the influence of social class structure in American education is permeated with each of these, as well as other, pitfalls in the sociology-education mating process. The educational practitioner needs to be aware of these difficulties in his utilization of sociological analyses of educational problems.

These precautionary observations lead to the consideration of the major contribution of the sociologist to educational practitioners. The teacher or school administrator must constantly bear in mind that he is working in a complex environment in which many variables are at play. The forces are multidimensional and his environment, although it shares common features with the situation confronting other educational practitioners, has many unique features. The sociologist, however, usually defines his problem so that he is working with one or a few independent variables (for example, social class or leadership structure) and one dependent variable (for example, academic achievement or sociometric choice), and he attempts to control other variables that may be influencing the relationships he is investigating. Of necessity he must simplify his problem so he can deal with it. He usually assumes multiple causation, but his methodological tools allow him to deal with only a very limited number of the forces that may account for the phenomena he is trying to explain. He never deals with *all* the variables that the practitioner probably needs to take into account in his decision making. Further, the research findings of the sociologist may not be applicable to the particular set of conditions confronting the practitioner. Research findings based on a sample of suburban school systems may not hold for city school systems. These considerations lead to the following point of view about the sociologist's major contribution to the educational practitioner. What the sociologist has to offer is basically a series of sensitizing and analytic concepts and ideas based on theoretical and empirical analysis that will allow the practitioner to examine in a more realistic and more incisive way the multiple forces operating in his social environment. The sociologist cannot make the educational practitioner's decisions for him, nor can the sociologist's research findings based on one population be applied to any educational population indiscriminately. The practitioner's task is to assess the various forces that have a bearing on the achievement of his objectives, assign them relative weights, and make a decision based on these calculations. The basic sociological contribution is to add to the educator's kit of intellectual tools a set of sociological insights and concepts that will allow him to take account in his decision-making organizational, cultural, and interpersonal factors at work in his environment.

1-2   CULTURAL ANTHROPOLOGY AND EDUCATION

F. Robert Paulsen

F. Robert Paulsen, who is dean of the College of Education at the University of Arizona, received his M.S. and Ed.D. at the University of Utah. He has contributed extensively to the *Journal of Teacher Education*, *Journal of Educational Sociology*, *Educational Administration and Supervision*, and *Journal of Social Work*. He studied at the University of Oregon under a Kellogg Foundation Faculty Study Grant, and at the University of Michigan through a Carnegie Foundation Fellowship in Higher Education.

The most significant accomplishment of anthropology during the first half of the twentieth century has been the extension and clarification of the concept of culture.[1] Most cultural anthropologists take it for granted that culture is the basic and central concept of their science. Although there is no total agreement among all professionals concerning a precise definition of culture, there is sufficient generic meaning to indicate a considerable need for this science to be included in any total study of the theory and practice of professional education.

Anthropology may be considered the most molar of the social sciences. Conceiving the largest possible units of society as areas of structural-functional study,

From *The Journal of Educational Sociology*, XXXIV, No. 7 (March 1961), 289–299. Copyright © 1961 by the Payne Educational Sociology Foundation, Inc. Reprinted by permission of the Payne Educational Sociology Foundation, Inc.

[1] A. L. Kroeber, *The Nature of Culture* (Chicago: University of Chicago Press, 1952) p. 139.

anthropologists have developed theoretical tools and techniques for describing and analyzing "cultural wholes." These theoretical techniques may have to be enlarged and refined as anthropologists probe to greater depth in the analysis of modern complex cultures. Notwithstanding, the fact remains that culture as culture is the province and specialty of the cultural anthropologists.[2]

When one speaks of anthropology and education, and particularly what the former might contribute to the professionalization and advancement of the latter, there is need for definition and structuralization.

A basic definition of culture, generally accepted for over half a century, was afforded by E. B. Tylor. Culture was conceived to be that "complex whole which includes knowledge, belief, art, morals, law, custom, and any other capabilities and habits acquired by man as a member of society."[3] Leslie White, in an attempt to develop a more precise definition, has suggested that culture is a class of things and events dependent upon symboling. White states that "the locus of culture has existence in space and time, (1) within human organisms, i.e., concepts, beliefs, emotions, attitudes; (2) within processes of social interaction among human beings; and (3) within material objects (axes, factories, railroads, pottery bowls) lying outside human organisms but with the patterns of social interaction among them."[4]

The word "education" has been used in many different ways. From designations of such general character as the totality of influences that both nature and man exercise on our intelligence to a narrow provincial acceptance of mere verbal ability to repeat scriptural doctrine of fundamentalist religions, students and scholars have formulated philosophical and practical definitions of education and the educated man. It would seem advantageous, however, to consider "education" as more directional rather than as many disparate elements which may or may not produce change in men. Emile Durkheim has suggested that from an anthropological and sociological point of view, education must be more meaningful than many modern educational philosophies suggest. Durkheim stated that "education is the influence exercised by adult generations on those not yet ready for social life. Its object is to arouse and to develop in the child a certain number of physical, intellectual, and moral states which are demanded of him by both the political society as a whole and the special milieu for which he is specifically destined."[5]

Even if we agree generally with Durkheim, it would seem necessary to note that education continues throughout adult-life, and that adults can and do learn in both formal and informal situations. At least, both anthropologist and educator agree that formal schooling should assume responsibility for perpetuating the culture and for directing its positive development.

With these definitional preliminaries, we might then address this brief paper to the question: What insights does cultural anthropology afford the educational leader of the mid-twentieth century? Perhaps more specifically, what principles of anthropology have emerged which have import for the administration of educational programs?

---

[2] John Gillan, "The Application of Anthropological Knowledge to Modern Mass Society," *Human Organization*, XV, No. 4 (Winter 1957), 29.

[3] *Primitive Culture* (London, 1872).

[4] "The Concept of Culture," *American Anthropologist*, LXI, No. 2 (April 1959), 234.

[5] *Education and Sociology* (Glencoe, Illinois: The Free Press, 1956), p. 71.

This study has not been of research orientation into the field of anthropology. The study has not been exhaustive in the treatment of what one discipline might provide in fundamental knowledge to another professional curriculum. At most, it represents an attempt to review some principles of anthropology which seem to have relevance to the study of education.

THE GROWTH OF CULTURE

The history of man from the Stone Age to the present era is a wonderful story of cultural growth.[6] The social inheritance of man might be understood with greater clarity if considered from the eyes of the anthropologist. Indeed evolution in its multitudinous forms, particularly the technological, social, and political, may be viewed in considerable perspective with anthropological understandings. As a single illustration, one might consider the final work of Ralph Linton, who treated the history of mankind with an emphasis on three basic mutations in the determination of the course of human culture.[7] These were: (1) the use of tools, fire, and language; (2) the discovery of how to raise food and domesticate animals; and (3) the discovery of how to obtain power from heat, and how to use the scientific method. Linton suggested that mankind may well be found within the fourth mutation involving the use of atomic energy and the penetration of space before he is fully adjusted to the third phase.

With respect to our own complex society, as well as the primitive, the key to any growth or even the transmission of culture must be an understanding of it. The modern educator, at any level of instruction, cannot afford to neglect knowledge of his total inheritance or the role he plays in building upon it.[8]

THE HISTORY OF EDUCATION

An analysis of the history of education through the eyes of the anthropologist substantiates the fact that educational institutions of the twentieth century are the products of several centuries of cultural growth. The impact of universal education felt in the twentieth century stems from a concept of its possibility during the past century. The culture not only demands its fulfillment in the public schools at the present time, but is now demanding that institutions of higher learning prepare to accept it.

Historically, the individual student sought out the teacher; now the teacher is brought to large numbers of pupils. Teaching became more than tutoring, and the culture demanded teaching skills of greater complexity than parents, tutors, or apprenticeship could handle. Thus, from a primitive pattern affording presents and gifts to a single man one hoped would teach his child, American society has shifted to a pattern of forcing all children, and even adults to learn. More than this, there has been consistent

---

[6] Ruth Benedict, "The Growth of Culture," in Harry L. Shapiro (editor) *Man, Culture, and Society* (New York: Oxford University Press, 1956), p. 188.

[7] *The Tree of Culture* (New York: Alfred A. Knopf, 1955).

[8] George A. Spindler, *The Transmission of American Culture* (Cambridge: Harvard Graduate School of Education Publication, 1957).

effort on the part of the body-politic to equip schools, train teachers, and effect sanctions to make children and young adults learn.

A survey of educational history supports an anthropological thesis that the realistic adaptation of dominant-status adults to new conditions has been more responsible for the development of universal education than the "needs" of children as children.[9] Intelligent cultural patterns may be traced, however, to series of minor changes suggested to children in school, and which are promoted forward when these children reach the adult dominant status.

In historical perspective, but in light of educational objectives, it is possible to trace a reduction in much of the inhumaneness man has manifested to man. This problem has not been completely solved, however, but in a projection of the history of education it is possible to contemplate an increase of interpersonal, inter-cultural, and inter-societal understandings. Certainly, this is a basic need in a world which can be circumnavigated in a matter of hours, and one to which schools should give attention as a means of eliminating prejudice, bigotry, and provincialism.

THE COMPARABILITY OF ALL HUMAN CULTURES

One of the basic emphases of cultural anthropology has been the comparability of all human cultures. This concept has profound implications for education. Although anthropologists have observed that each human culture is unique and embodies a whole way of life for the people within, since World War II there has been greater emphasis upon the "comparability concept." Margaret Mead has summarized an emergent principle. "Each viable human culture, whether that of a handful of Eskimos or of a nation of fifty million people, must be seen as a system which contains provision for all 'normal' human beings who are born within it, with the recognition that, as we make technical and ethical advances, more previously discarded individuals, such as the blind, the deaf, the cerebral palsied, will be included within the communications system of the culture."[10]

Studies of cultural comparabilities have also indicated that a language or mores, or any other part of a whole system of a culture, developed by one group of human beings can be learned by normal human beings in another group.[11] In fact, anthropologists have concluded that people can be shaped in almost any direction. Questions remain chiefly in the area of "control," and how far the direction of cultural growth might be determined by educators, or anyone who presumes to teach children or adults.

PATTERN CHANGE

Concomitant with general knowledge acquired by studying the comparability of cultures has been the mores-specific understandings of "pattern-change." The behavior of people is not haphazard, but conforms to a pattern, and parts of the pattern of

[9] Ralph Linton, "Potential Contributions of Cultural Anthropology to Teacher Education," *Culture and Personality* (Washington, D. C.: American Council of Education, 1941).

[10] "Cultural Factors in Community-Education Programs," *Community Education: Principles and Practices from World-Wide Experience*, The Fifty-Eighth Yearbook of the National Society for the Study of Education (Chicago: University of Chicago Press, 1959), p. 91.

[11] *Ibid.*

behavior are interrelated.[12] It has been concluded, by the anthropologists, that the life of a people may be oriented in many different, yet definite directions, and that while *value-judgments* may not be analyzed with strict scientific validity, *values per sē* seem to be a most important subject for objective consideration.

Whereas, historically, it was assumed that slow educational change was necessary for the welfare of people caught in cultural-lag, it is now suggested that rapid change, in which a whole culture is transformed, may be less traumatic than slow, uneven change. Margaret Mead has stated that "groups, primitive or present, who have a clear, coherent cultural tradition may be able to change their entire way of life in a very few years, carrying the entire community, grandparents, parents, and grandchildren with them, and take on a new view of life in a very few years, provided they are presented with living models of the new culture."[13]

With this possibility, educators find themselves face to face with the question posed by George Counts three decades ago: *Dare the Schools Build a New Social Order?*[14] Although Leslie White and other advocates of the science of "culturology" or cultural determinism would reject any such possibility, the evidence is not conclusive in their favor.[15] Certainly, there is evidence that the culture has controlled to a considerable degree the development of educational patterns. In the context of interaction, however, one cannot deny the influence on culture of new ideas or the power of a dynamic personality.

Essentially, if the educator should attempt to change society, the task would be that of teaching different values, even though many values lie beneath the realm of consciousness. And if education can proceed with full recognition that new conditions of life may be met and new patterns of culture emerge through understanding the real importance of how man thinks and feels rather than how he behaves, there may be greater correlation between the objectives of education and the achievement of the pupil.

The anthropologists have not answered the question concerning whether or not the schools should build a new social order. They have not indicated how much educational effort would be needed to change cultural patterns. They have indicated the possibility.

THE VALUE SYSTEM OF A MODERN CULTURE

An analysis of various values and value-systems in both primitive and modern societies affords considerable insight in understanding the behavior of people. Thus, the utilization of an "ethos approach" may be most important in studying a community or a nation, and ultimately important in developing improved programs of education.

John Gillan has noted that the ethos approach suggests that even complex cultures have a "core" and that once this is understood the other aspects of the culture can, in part at least, be interpreted in terms of it. "The search for a common ethos or basic controlling pattern, or value system of a modern culture, is an attempt to grasp a

[12] Eugene A. Nida, *Customs and Cultures* (New York: Harper & Brothers, 1954).
[13] *Op. cit.*
[14] New York: The John Day Company, 1932.
[15] Leslie A. White, *The Science of Culture* (New York: Grove Press, 1949).

reliable conception of the culture as a whole while avoiding the methodological difficulties presented by large scale complexity of sub-cultural content and integration, and revolutionary change."[16]

Values are the principles of a culture. Even though there are usually differences between what is believed, and what is said and done, some anthropologists have noted that the "ideals" proclaimed by men are in a sense the ultimate value system of a culture.[17] Only by understanding the ideal value system, the emotional intensity man attaches to some values within the system, and the relationship of these values to the behavior of people within the culture, does the culture fit into a pattern and effect closure.[18] A. L. Kroeber has appraised this aspect of anthropological study. "We can act as if our culturally acquired but preferentially held values were absolute, and, in general that is what we do when we have to act, even if we consider ourselves relativists. We do not review the hundreds of other value systems and paralyze our decision, but we use our own value system, act according to it, and abide by the consequences. As human beings, that is all we can ordinarily do."[19]

Values then may be considered permanent and relative. Education becomes the means whereby values might be recognized for what they are, and educators become the agents of interaction in promoting the acceptance of values, which might afford the establishment of a better society in which to live.

COMMUNITY STUDIES AND TECHNIQUES OF THE ANTHROPOLOGIST

The "ethnologizing" of modern national cultures has been a step forward in understanding the behavior of individual man and his group-life. Ethnographical studies of sub-cultures, or of single communities within a nation, are important for teachers interested in developing insights concerning the behavior of children. These community studies have indicated that a method of science can be developed in a study of group-life.[20] And, science without a method is of little merit regardless of the number of data one might collect. Indeed, the collection of data has become indicative of the entire corps of teachers and professors during the past decade. But of what value is the data? How are these data to be interpreted? Anthropology has given some direction in this field.[21]

The ethnographical method has at least developed a means of classifying sources according to time, place, and manner by which information is obtained. Ethnographical studies of community life have provided information showing important "power-structures" and informal organizations operating in society. These studies have also been helpful in determining the real *values* held by people in a community.

---

[16] "The Application of Anthropological Knowledge to Modern Mass Society," *Human Organization*, XV, No. 4 (Winter 1957), 26.

[17] See: Ethel M. Albert, "The Classification of Values," *American Anthropologist*, LVII, No. 2 (April 1956).

[18] A. L. Kroeber, "Concluding Review," in *An Appraisal of Anthropology Today* (Sol Tax, *et al.*, editors), (Chicago: University of Chicago Press, 1953), p. 373.

[19] Kroeber, *op. cit.*, p. 376.

[20] Ralph Linton, "Potential Contributions of Cultural Anthropology to Teacher Education," *Culture and Personality* (Washington, D. C.: American Council on Education, 1941), p. 15.

[21] W. Lloyd Warner, *Structure of American Life* (Edinburgh, The University Press, 1952).

Anthropologists have developed interviewing techniques as a scientific means of extracting valid information from "real" people. The techniques have been clinical rather than statistical, documentary, or of the questionnaire variety. The anthropologist has developed the research technique of "participant-observer" to a considerable degree of proficiency. Conclusions made through the use of these methods of research may be more valid than many other common techniques used by other social scientists.

CULTURE AND PERSONALITY

No other subject has been afforded more deference and investigation by the psychologist and educator than has that of "personality." One can only be impressed with the vast amount of research in both psychology and psychiatry which has promoted a better understanding of the concept, structure, and development of human personality. The anthropologist has related this most molecular of the social sciences, psychology, to the analysis of man's personality as a social being. Personality is an organization which lies behind behavior and within the individual. Values learned in early childhood become persisting forces of personality, and help in the determination of responses to various social situations.

The social life of man cannot be observed in totality if separated from societal means and values, or in separation from the psychological structuralization of the individual.

Thus, any explanation of culture should indicate cognizance at the psychological level. It is necessary to keep in mind that culture as a social fact is constantly impinging upon the development of the individual personality, while, in turn, the causes of cultural phenomena are persons. Thus, personality, culture, and society form systems of integrated "wholes" having real existence only in consideration of each other. The phenomenon of *interaction* again assumes a position of primary importance.

ANTHROPOLOGY AND HUMAN NATURE

It would seem as if the most important contribution anthropology has made to the study of man, his intellectual and physical development, his culture, and his emotional dispositions, is to be found in the analysis of *human nature*. Indeed, the findings of anthropologists give foundation for the proposition that education can improve society by discarding historical concepts of the innate nature of man. Most of what we have previously called "human nature," and upon which culture has been built, is not "nature" at all. Early training and the inculcation of values at an early age has been mistaken for human nature. Linton proclaimed that "we have positive proof that most of the values and attitudes which cause trouble in our own society cannot be innate since they are lacking in one society or another."[22]

Cutting across both science and the humanities, and the social and behavioral sciences, anthropology substantiates the proposition that human equality is possible and valid.[23] Anthropology has thereby denoted additional responsibility to the role

---

[22]Linton, *op. cit.*, p. 12.

[23]A. Irving Hallowell, "Culture, Personality, and Society," in A. L. Kroeber (editor), *Anthropology Today: An Encyclopedic Inventory* (Chicago: University of Chicago Press, 1953).

of the educator. Recognizing the importance of facts in transmitting culture and in suggesting improvement, it has been noted that the interpretation of these facts may be more important. Teachers and professors have a great responsibility in assuming the role of "interpreter."

Ashley Montagu has summarized an anthropological point of view respecting human nature. What anthropology is capable of doing for the student, at all levels of education from the elementary school to the university, is first and foremost to give him an understanding of his own place in the world in relation to the rest of animated nature in all its forms. It is important for the healthy development of the person to be rooted *Why?* in the great tradition—and all its varieties—of humanity. It is the great understanding of what it means to be human that is the principal contribution that anthropology has to make to the human being in process of being taught to be human. And learning to be human, and to understand what this involves, should, it seems to me, be the principal purpose of education to which all else is secondary. It is perhaps only when this has been fully recognized that anthropology will assume its proper place at the centrum of all general education."[24]

In a personal reference, Montagu writes with firm belief that no other subject is capable of humanizing the student as is the study of anthropology. "And by 'humanizing' I mean not only enabling the student to feel that nothing that is human is alien to him, but to remain all his life actively interested in constructively increasing his own and others' understanding of what it means to be human. Today more than ever such understanding has become critically necessary. And I would go so far as to say that of all forms of understanding this will always remain the most adaptively valuable. I know of no other subject which can teach us more helpfully how to understand other societies, or how best to meet their needs."[25]

Undoubtedly, one of the most insidious anachronisms faced by the modern educator has been the faulty interpretation of human nature on the part of many societal groups. Historically, many beliefs about human nature have created "trapped universals" in the minds of men to the extent that the most important species characteristics of man, thinking and high educability, have been thwarted by the time the child enters school. In a vicious circle, man has continued to develop educational programs based upon concepts of human nature suggesting an intrinsic "goodness" or "badness" of himself rather than upon propositions more nearly validated by the sciences.

At first sight, this seems like a hopeless dilemma, for men can teach only what they know, and they have known so little about human nature. Anthropological research has indicated an avenue whereby man might find convergence for his many conflicting concepts of his being.

. .   It has been suggested that "anthropology holds up a great mirror to man and lets him look at himself in his infinite variety."[26] In his mirror, man might see that he is indeed unique, reflecting both biological and psychological propensities affording creative expression beyond cultural necessity. In contemplating his variety, man might *might* adopt humility and perspective, building character without external sanction, which will afford him greater opportunity of "means" to greater opportunity of "ends."

---

[24] M. F. Ashley Montagu, *Anthropology and Human Nature* (Boston: Porter Sargent Publisher, 1957), pp. 3–7.
[25] *Ibid.*
[26] Clyde Kluckhohn, *Mirror for Man* (New York: Whittlesey House, 1949).

1-3   SOCIAL FOUNDATIONS AS A FIELD OF STUDY IN EDUCATION

Richard L. Derr

Richard L. Derr is assistant professor of education at Western Reserve University in Cleveland, Ohio. In this excellent essay he traces clearly the interrelationships of the various branches of the social sciences with the several areas of social foundations of education.

Social foundations is probably at a critical juncture in becoming a distinct branch of study in education. Insofar as course offerings, graduate programs, and a body of literature are accurate indicators, it has been recognized as a legitimate area of specialization since the middle 1930's.[1] Despite this it has failed to attain the status of an original and productive field of study. This has recently led many critics to question the wisdom of maintaining it in departments and colleges of education.[2] At the same time, related fields, whose contributions ordinarily are not questioned, are thriving. Sociology of education is moving forward with renewed vigor, and several other social sciences—social psychology, anthropology, and political science—are developing branches which specialize in the study of the social aspects of education.[3]

As things now stand, "social foundations of education" seems to denote two related things. First, it refers to social factors which inquiries in the social sciences or in education presumably have shown to be relevant to the school's operation. When, for example, the phenomenon of social class is examined by sociologists in a school setting, the social foundations of education is under examination.[4] Again, when philosophers of education analyze conditions in society as they develop and justify views regarding educational purposes and practices, these foundations are being revealed.[5]

From *Educational Theory*, XV, No. 2 (April 1965), 154–160. Copyright © 1965 by *Educational Theory*; reprinted by permission of *Educational Theory* and the author.

[1] Charles J. Brauner, *American Educational Theory* (Englewood Cliffs, N. J.: Prentice-Hall, Inc., 1964), pp. 200–205.

[2] *Ibid.*, pp. 304–305. Also see James B. Conant, *The Education of American Teachers* (New York: McGraw-Hill, 1963) and James D. Koerner, *The Miseducation of American Teachers* (Boston: Houghton Mifflin, 1963).

[3] See Neal Gross, "The Sociology of Education," in R. K. Merton *et al.* (eds.), *Sociology Today, Problems and Prospects* (New York: Basic Books, Inc., 1959), pp. 123–152. Here are some of the major publications in these fields since 1963: W. W. Charters and N. L. Gage (eds.), *Readings in the Social Psychology of Education* (Boston: Allyn & Bacon, Inc., 1963); W. B. Brookover and D. Gottlieb, *A Sociology of Education*, Second Edition (New York: American Book Co., 1964); Charles H. Page (ed.), *Sociology and Contemporary Education* (New York: Random House, 1963); George D. Spindler (ed.), *Education and Culture* (New York: Holt, Rinehart and Winston, 1963); N. A. Masters, R. H. Salisbury, T. H. Eliot, *State Politics and the Public Schools* (New York: Alfred A. Knopf, 1964).

[4] Two well known examples are W. Lloyd Warner, Robert J. Havighurst, and Martin B. Loeb, *Who Shall Be Educated?* (New York: Harper & Bros., 1944) and August De B. Hollingshead, *Elmtown's Youth: The Impact of Social Class on Adolescents* (New York: John Wiley & Sons, Inc., 1949).

[5] See William O. Stanley, *Education and Social Integration* (New York: Bureau of Publications, Teachers College, Columbia University, 1953). Harold Rugg and William Withers, *Social Foundations of Education* (Englewood Cliffs, N. J.: Prentice-Hall, Inc., 1955), is another good example.

Second, social foundations refers to the courses, programs, and literature in education where the results of these inquiries usually are brought together to permit an extensive review of the social aspects of schooling.

There would be no need to disturb this arrangement if the interests of educationalists and the schools were being adequately served. But this is clearly not the case. Social factors are perhaps the most prominent but also the least understood aspect of the bulk of the pressing educational problems of our time. Such social problems as juvenile delinquency, family instability, unemployment, rapid social change, and racial strife constitute critical components of the tasks schools face—among other things—in retaining potential dropouts, providing school experiences which will have meaning today and utility in an unknown tomorrow, and maintaining a staff of able teachers in the slum areas of large city systems.

As various branches of social science develop, this situation will be alleviated somewhat, but far from completely. For even if they were to attain maximum growth, they still would be deficient in two basic respects. First, they do not deal directly with *the* educational problem; namely, what course of action should be taken in such and such type of school situation. The social sciences and especially those branches which study their problems by using data gathered from the schools are an indispensable source of knowledge regarding crucial aspects of the school situation, but they do not and cannot be expected to relate this knowledge to the evaluation of educational policies and techniques.[6] Second, each of these branches focuses—as it must—on only certain aspects of the total school situation; whereas, the decision maker in the schools must have a construct of the total situation.[7] Hence, the study of racial conflict, in metropolitan areas by sociologists and political scientists is not likely to have important utility for school administrators, teachers, and boards of education unless they or specialists in the study of education integrate the various studies and determine their implications—if any—for the administrative and curriculum decisions which must be made.

Educational practitioners and board members do not ordinarily have the time, resources, or intensive training in the social sciences which would permit them to perform this task of application. Thus, it remains for educational researchers.

Philosophy of education, at first glance, would seem to be the appropriate field to undertake this task, since it has had a long-standing interest in the social aspects of education as they pertain to any and all areas of the school's operation; but closer examination reveals otherwise. One of its major concerns is to build a justifiable conception of the ends and means of schools.[8] The aim is to produce a philosophy of education for schools. It is to contain, within one theoretical scheme, reasoned answers to all the major questions of purpose, policy, and technique which must be answered if schools are to operate effectively. The accomplishment of such a far-ranging task requires the utilization of concepts and conclusions drawn from all those other branches of education which have more limited aims. The philosopher of education is

---

[6] Archibald W. Anderson, *et al.*, *The Theoretical Foundations of Education* (Urbana, Ill.: Bureau of Research and Service, University of Illinois, 1951); also see Elmer Eason, "Sociology of Education Is Not Enough," *Journal of Educational Sociology*, XXXV, No. 3 (November 1961), 141.

[7] Eason, *op. cit.*, pp. 141–2.

[8] B. Othaniel Smith, "Philosophy of Education," in *Encyclopedia of Educational Research*, Third Edition, edited by Chester W. Harris (New York: The Macmillan Co., 1960), p. 957.

obligated to *stay on top* of developments in the areas of administration, curriculum, supervision, guidance, educational psychology, social foundations, and history of education. In addition, he also specializes in examining educational questions from the perspective given by the discipline of philosophy. The moral is clear. The existing work load of philosophy of education is much too great for it to assume the major responsibility in education of processing the work of sociology, anthropology, social psychology, political science, and economics.

There is then a need for a branch of study in education which specializes in identifying, integrating, and interpreting that knowledge in the social sciences which pertains to the social dimension of educational decision-making. The simplest way of developing such a branch would be to transform social foundations into an acknowledged discipline with its own corps of specialists, unique contributions to the solution of educational problems, and possibly even its own professional organization. This would be simplest since it would largely involve the extension of existing trends and practices. Most departments and schools of education already offer courses in social foundations, and many contain a graduate program in social foundations which trainees in philosophy of education take in varying degrees. Those trainees who elect to specialize in social foundations probably receive a greater amount of advanced training in the social sciences than specialists in any other area of education. And finally, it should be noted that, in the last two annual meetings of the Philosophy of Education Society, a section in what could be fairly called *social foundations* has met, with several participants expressing an interest in making it a more significant part of the annual meetings.

Specialists in social foundations seem, therefore, to be presented with a rare opportunity to strengthen their area and to benefit the study and practice of education. This opportunity cannot be exploited, however, unless a way is found to utilize social scientific knowledge so that the promise of recognizable gains in the making of educational decisions can be shown. Accomplishing this is not an easy matter; however, a partial answer is given by the recognition that this knowledge describes and explains conditions in nature which the school must take into account as it seeks desired ends. If the school is not well adapted to these facts of human behavior, its goal attainment is likely to be severely reduced. Whether the school is adapted or maladapted will depend largely on the policies it adopts. The contribution of social foundations hence would lie in producing conclusions for the decision maker that such and such policies are likely to be effective because they are well adapted to certain social conditions and that other designated policies will likely fail because they are poorly adapted to these conditions.

The points made in the preceding paragraph will now be stated in somewhat different language and in more detail. Research in social foundations is not likely to be fruitful unless great care is exercised in the choice of the paradigms upon which it is based. Paradigms are models or generalized frames of reference which constitute ways of thinking about phenomena in experience. When analyzed, paradigms can be shown to consist of a few categories of variables and relationships thought to exist among them. Pavlovian conditioning, consisting of the categories of stimulus and response and the conception that the former will produce the latter, is an example of a paradigm.[9] Paradigms are indispensable tools in designing research and in constructing

[9] N. L. Gage, "Paradigms for Research on Teaching," in *Handbook of Research on Teaching*, edited by Gage (Chicago: Rand McNally & Co., 1963), pp. 95–6.

theories, for they provide an entry into the study of complex systems of events. Belanger puts it this way:

> Research in any complex system requires the placement of constraints on the system in order to reduce the complexity to some manageable portion. This reduction of complexity can be accomplished by selecting factors in the system which are of interest to the investigator and which are suspected to be interrelated. The conceptualization of any system as an abstraction consisting of variables (factors) and a network of relations among the variables is frequently termed a *model* or *paradigm*.[10]

Any piece of theoretical or empirical research derives its basic structure from one or more of these underlying conceptions researchers have as to how the subject matter of their respective fields *fits together*. Applied to the problem at hand, the argument is that specialists in social foundations must conceptualize the school situation in such a way that those phenomena which are studied by the social sciences can be fruitfully *fitted together* with the practitioner's task of selecting the best policies for their school. The following is offered as an example of such a paradigm. It focuses attention on three categories of variables and two relationships in the school situation.

A PARADIGM FOR RESEARCH IN SOCIAL FOUNDATIONS OF EDUCATION

I. *Categories of variables:*

1. *Policies:* Generalized courses of action designed to give direction to the major areas of the school's operation.

2. *Values:* Desired outcomes which are or could be associated with the school's operation.

3. *Social conditions:* Culturally patterned regularities in behavior within and external to the school which influence the school's operation.

II. *Relationships:*

1. *Policies* are adopted in order to achieve *values*.

2. Differences in the effectiveness of alternative *policies* in achieving *values* is a function of differences in the extent to which they adapt the school to underlying *social conditions*.

In this paradigm, the school situation is conceptualized for the proposed field of social foundations as one which contains three principal components: policies, values, and social conditions. The school is perceived as having as its basic concern the achievement of a number of values which are or could conceivably be associated with

---

[10] Maurice Belanger, "Methodology of Educational Research in Science and Mathematics," *Review of Educational Research*, XXXIV, No. 3 (June 1964), 376.

its operation. Policies are regarded as the basic means or tools with which the school will make its attempt to achieve these values. When policies are selected which well adapt the school to impinging social conditions, the school—other things being equal—will be freed to realize its desired outcomes. When policies are adopted which do not permit the school to avoid, exploit, or overcome—as the case may be—impinging social conditions, then the latter will interfere with the school's operation and block it from satisfactory achievement of its values.

The paradigm would focus research in social foundations on the problem of determining which of a number of alternative curricular, administrative, supervisory, co-curricular, and counseling policies are most likely to achieve certain designated educational values. Its research would consist of policy evaluation wherein the literature of social science and education, to some extent, would be analyzed and interpreted in order to estimate the inhibitory or facilitative effects of various social conditions on each of a number of alternative educational policies in achieving each of a number of educational values.

Its research would be theoretical in nature. This is to say that it would integrate and interpret existing concepts, facts, and generalizations for the purpose of constructing hypotheses, but it would not test these hypotheses through the accumulation of new data. It is highly improbable that research designs exist which would permit the testing of a hypothesis that, for example, compared two secondary school curriculum policies in regard to the promotion of freedom in American society as this was determined by differences in adaptability to such social conditions as bureaucracy, *anomie*, and urbanization. If and when the testing of such hypotheses became workable, then social foundations specialists could develop the needed skills.

The basic form of these hypotheses would be as follows: If social conditions D, E, F, are present, then Policy A would be more effective than Policies B and C in achieving values X, Y, Z. Hopefully, these reasoned conclusions would be incorporated into the policy-making deliberations of school administrators, faculty committees, and board members in school districts throughout the country. Effective utilization would require a determination of the presence or absence and approximate strength of the various values and social conditions in each individual situation.

On the other hand, the utility of these hypotheses would depend partly on their emerging from an inquiry in which a broad range of values, policies, and social conditions had been considered. Their utility would be narrowed needlessly if, for example, instructional goals were treated as the only values associated with the school's operation. Many factors, somewhat removed from the desired outcomes of instruction, also operate in the actual policy-making situation as criteria for the acceptance or rejection of alternative policies. For example, generally it is held desirable that schools be operated economically and efficiently. It is likely that individualized instruction has received little support for this very reason. Again, the maintenance of faculty harmony undoubtedly influences administrative decisions in regard to policy changes. If actual decision makers are influenced by these values, then social foundations cannot have widespread utility and impact unless it also incorporates them into its own inquiry.

Similarly, the greater the number of relevant social conditions which are examined, the wider the utility of the resultant hypotheses. In some districts, conditions associated with the phenomenon of social class may be especially critical in determining the success or failure of school policies. Where the upper middle and upper class are dominant, a curriculum policy which upgraded vocational training at the expense of college preparation would receive little community support and, therefore, would have little chance of achieving instructional goals as well as other values. In other districts, major social problems such as those mentioned above may constitute the critical conditions to which policies must adapt the school. It is likely that all such social conditions are present in most school districts, but they vary in intensity from one point in time to the next. In any case, social foundations would have maximum practical utility only if it examines alternative policies from as many different social perspectives as developments in the social sciences make possible. Armed with hypotheses regarding the relative effectiveness of certain competing policies in achieving values, policy makers could select the policy most likely to achieve that value or those values which are dominant at that particular time in that particular situation.

Non-social, i.e., psychological, conditions are also operating in the school situation—especially in the classroom—and consequently would have to be considered along with social conditions by policy makers. If educational psychology were to orient itself to policy evaluation, as is being proposed for social foundations, then the policy-evaluation process occurring at the level of the study of education would correspond very closely to that process as it takes place in actual practice. This would be especially true if philosophy of education would, in turn, incorporate the hypotheses of both these fields into its overall evaluation of policies, values, and techniques. For philosophy of education most closely approximates the decision-maker's interest in the total school situation.

None of these hypotheses, whether it comes directly from social foundations and educational psychology or indirectly from philosophy of education, would be foolproof. The behavioral sciences, which are themselves at a relatively early stage of development, would provide the bulk of the data. Thus, the dangers of misinterpretation and over-generalization are high. Precise relationships, between conditions and values or between conditions and policies, will rarely be established by research; hence, estimates and inferences will be made. The sheer volume of variables in the school situation, not to mention the complexity of their interrelationships, will itself generate error in the formulation of the hypotheses. So policy makers will take some risks in basing their decisions on the work of specialists in the study of education. But, and this is critical, the risks are likely to be substantially higher if they were to base their decisions solely on their own deliberations. These conditions of individual and social behavior will be present and operating in the school situation whether they have been identified and appraised or not. Policy makers ordinarily will have some training in the behavioral sciences and are usually inclined to employ their concepts and research findings as they perform their tasks. But their command of this knowledge is not likely to be as disciplined, extensive, and up-to-date as it would be for persons who specialize in applying this knowledge to education. Hence, they are much more likely to overlook important phenomena and, what is perhaps worse, to misinterpret such phenomena than are these specialists.[11]

In addition, misuse of behavioral sciences by specialists in education would be reduced if a division of labor among social foundations, educational psychology, and philosophy of education, such as the one considered here, were utilized in research. For

---

[11] See Aaron V. Cicuorel and John L. Kitsuse, *The Educational Decision Makers* (Indianapolis: The Bobbs-Merrill Co., Inc., 1963), pp. 16–20.

this would afford their respective specialists reasonably manageable tasks in the way of maintaining minimum competence in parent fields.

The school is affected by the social environment within which it operates. Therefore, this environment is a matter about which educational practitioners must become knowledgeable and over which they must be able to exert some control. Practitioners lack the time, training, and resources to accomplish this on their own. Some aid is given by the social sciences and by philosophy of education, but it is spasmodic and limited in nature. A field of study in education which has this as its special concern is needed. Social foundations of education would be the natural candidate to fill this need. Indeed, if it does not shortly show itself capable of making a unique contribution, research and teaching in the social dimensions of education may become the exclusive concern of social scientists. Development of social foundations would be accelerated by the use of a research paradigm which holds the effectiveness of school policies to be a function of the extent to which they adapt the school to both the modifiable and intractable aspects of its social environment.

CONCLUSION

Although history and philosophy have made large contributions to the social foundations of education, other social sciences such as sociology and anthropology should be incorporated into professional education and research in order to assist teachers and administrators in making wise choices from a series of alternatives.

Gross and Paulsen have delineated those concerns of social scientists, such as the classroom and the community as social systems, in which research can contribute to a better understanding of the educational enterprise in America. But as Derr has suggested, the field of social foundations can integrate the various contributions of the social sciences to provide an overall understanding of their implications for education.

Education is necessary in every society to provide children with the skills, attitudes, and outlook on life necessary to participate as adults in their culture. With the advances of science in a complex culture such as our own, we can study education as a social-cultural process, not only to solve social problems associated with the school, but also to determine the cultural limits within which education can operate in our society. An analysis of these limits, together with the determination of the goals of an organized educational system, are major tasks of the social foundations of education.

This book, therefore, can be both a basis for resolving conflicts in education and an aid to students in developing their own teaching goals.

ADDITIONAL READING

Theodore Brameld, *Education as Power* (Holt, Rinehart and Winston, Inc., New York, 1965), pp. 1–9. A plea for education rather than science to solve the problems which face America.

Louis Fischer and Donald R. Thomas, *Social Foundations of Educational Decisions* (Wadsworth Publishing Company, Belmont, California, 1965), Part 1, "Educational Decision Making," pp. 3–127. A thorough analysis of the contributions of the social foundations to educational decision-making.

Norman C. Greenberg, "Social Foundations of Education," *Peabody Journal of Education*, XLII, No. 5 (March 1965), 281–284. An excellent, concise statement on the forces that shape American education and the important role that the social foundations of education play in education for cultural survival.

2

The Science of Culture

INTRODUCTION

The concept of culture, which is the central focus of cultural anthropology, is difficult to define; over two hundred definitions or explanations have been offered. Sometimes it is easier to describe what culture does than to define what culture is. Regardless of the difficulties, social scientists have found the concept of culture most useful in explaining human behavior.

The following readings demonstrate the variety of approaches that can be used to explain culture, the difficulties of defining it, and an internal consistency that emerges in spite of the variant approaches. Some of the selections are quite simple, while others are more erudite discourses. Some of them attempt to explain the components of culture, while others describe what culture does for the individual and the group that share its patterns.

Once the theory of culture is understood, the other factors relating to the enculturation of American children and the conditions that inhibit or accelerate cultural innovation or change will be more clearly comprehended. A basic objective of a course in social foundations of education is an awareness of the factors in society and in culture that influence learning and the acquisition of skills important to survival and self-fulfillment.

2-1   QUEER CUSTOMS

Clyde Kluckhohn

Clyde Kluckhohn (1905–1960) was a leading American anthropologist. He received his B.A. from the University of Wisconsin, studied at the University of Vienna, earned his master's degree at Oxford where he was a Rhodes Scholar, and concluded his formal education with a Ph.D. from Harvard University in 1936. He began his teaching career at the University of New Mexico but soon returned to Harvard, where he spent most of his academic career. He received many honors for his scholarly efforts, among which was the Viking Medal for Anthropology. A prolific writer, he edited a large number of articles, monographs, and books. His classic study *The Navajo* remains one of the finest examples of ethnographic research. *Mirror for Man*, from which this selection was taken, is still one of the best of the popular introductions to anthropology.

Why do the Chinese dislike milk and milk products? Why would the Japanese die willingly in a Banzai charge that seemed senseless to Americans? Why do some nations trace descent through the father, others through the mother, still others through both parents? Not because different peoples have different instincts, not because they were destined by God or Fate to different habits, not because the weather is different in China and Japan and the United States. Sometimes shrewd common sense has an answer that is close to that of the anthropologist: "because they were brought up that way." By "culture" anthropology means the total life way of a people, the social legacy the individual acquires from his group. Or culture can be regarded as that part of the environment that is the creation of man.

This technical term has a wider meaning than the "culture" of history and literature. A humble cooking pot is as much a cultural product as is a Beethoven sonata. In ordinary speech a man of culture is a man who can speak languages other than his own, who is familiar with history, literature, philosophy, or the fine arts. In some cliques that definition is still narrower. The cultured person is one who can talk about James Joyce, Scarlatti, and Picasso. To the anthropologist, however, to be human is to be cultured. There is culture in general, and then there are the specific cultures such as Russian, American, British, Hottentot, Inca. The general abstract notion serves to remind us that we cannot explain acts solely in terms of the biological properties of the people concerned, their individual past experience, and the immediate situation. The past experience of other men in the form of culture enters into almost every event. Each specific culture constitutes a kind of blueprint for all of life's activities.

One of the interesting things about human beings is that they try to understand themselves and their own behavior. While this has been particularly true of Europeans in recent times, there is no group which has not developed a scheme or schemes to

From *Mirror for Man* by Clyde Kluckhohn, pp. 17–37. Copyright © 1949. McGraw-Hill Book Company. Used by permission.

explain man's actions. To the insistent human query "why?" the most exciting illumination anthropology has to offer is that of the concept of culture. Its explanatory importance is comparable to categories such as evolution in biology, gravity in physics, disease in medicine. A good deal of human behavior can be understood, and indeed predicted, if we know a people's design for living. Many acts are neither accidental nor due to personal peculiarities nor caused by supernatural forces nor simply mysterious. Even those of us who pride ourselves on our individualism follow most of the time a pattern not of our own making. We brush our teeth on arising. We put on pants—not a loincloth or a grass skirt. We eat three meals a day—not four or five or two. We sleep in a bed—not in a hammock or on a sheep pelt. I do not have to know the individual and his life history to be able to predict these and countless other regularities, including many in the thinking process, of all Americans who are not incarcerated in jails or hospitals for the insane.

To the American woman a system of plural wives seems "instinctively" abhorrent. She cannot understand how any woman can fail to be jealous and uncomfortable if she must share her husband with other women. She feels it "unnatural" to accept such a situation. On the other hand, a Koryak woman of Siberia, for example, would find it hard to understand how a woman could be so selfish and so undesirous of feminine companionship in the home as to wish to restrict her husband to one mate.

Some years ago I met in New York City a young man who did not speak a word of English and was obviously bewildered by American ways. By "blood" he was as American as you or I, for his parents had gone from Indiana to China as missionaries. Orphaned in infancy, he was reared by a Chinese family in a remote village. All who met him found him more Chinese than American. The facts of his blue eyes and light hair were less impressive than a Chinese style of gait, Chinese arm and hand movements, Chinese facial expression, and Chinese modes of thought. The biological heritage was American, but the cultural training had been Chinese. He returned to China.

Another example of another kind: I once knew a trader's wife in Arizona who took a somewhat devilish interest in producing a cultural reaction. Guests who came her way were often served delicious sandwiches filled with a meat that seemed to be neither chicken nor tuna fish yet was reminiscent of both. To queries she gave no reply until each had eaten his fill. She then explained that what they had eaten was not chicken, not tuna fish, but the rich, white flesh of freshly killed rattlesnakes. The response was instantaneous—vomiting, often violent vomiting. A biological process is caught in a cultural web.

A highly intelligent teacher with long and successful experience in the public schools of Chicago was finishing her first year in an Indian school. When asked how her Navaho pupils compared in intelligence with Chicago youngsters, she replied, "Well, I just don't know. Sometimes the Indians seem just as bright. At other times they just act like dumb animals. The other night we had a dance in the high school. I saw a boy who is one of the best students in my English class standing off by himself. So I took him over to a pretty girl and told them to dance. But they just stood there with their heads down. They wouldn't even say anything." I inquired if she knew whether or not they were members of the same clan. "What difference would that make?"

"How would you feel about getting into bed with your brother?" The teacher walked off in a huff, but, actually, the two cases were quite comparable in principle. To the Indian the type of bodily contact involved in our social dancing has a directly sexual connotation. The incest taboos between members of the same clan are as severe as between true brothers and sisters. The shame of the Indians at the suggestion that a clan brother and sister should dance and the indignation of the white teacher at the idea that she should share a bed with an adult brother represent equally nonrational responses, culturally standardized unreason.

All this does not mean that there is no such thing as raw human nature. The very fact that certain of the same institutions are found in all known societies indicates that at bottom all human beings are very much alike. The files of the Cross-Cultural Survey at Yale University are organized according to categories such as "marriage ceremonies," "life crisis rites," "incest taboos." At least seventy-five of these categories are represented in every single one of the hundreds of cultures analyzed. This is hardly surprising. The members of all human groups have about the same biological equipment. All men undergo the same poignant life experiences such as birth, helplessness, illness, old age, and death. The biological potentialities of the species are the blocks with which cultures are built. Some patterns of every culture crystallize around focuses provided by the inevitables of biology: the difference between the sexes, the presence of persons of different ages, the varying physical strength and skill of individuals. The facts of nature also limit culture forms. No culture provides patterns for jumping over trees or for eating iron ore.

There is thus no "either-or" between nature and that special form of nurture called culture. Culture determinism is as one-sided as biological determinism. The two factors are interdependent. Culture arises out of human nature, and its forms are restricted both by man's biology and by natural laws. It is equally true that culture channels biological processes—vomiting, weeping, fainting, sneezing, the daily habits of food intake and waste elimination. When a man eats, he is reacting to an internal "drive," namely, hunger contractions consequent upon the lowering of blood sugar, but his precise reaction to these internal stimuli cannot be predicted by physiological knowledge alone. Whether a healthy adult feels hungry twice, three times, or four times a day and the hours at which this feeling recurs is a question of culture. What he eats is of course limited by availability, but is also partly regulated by culture. It is a biological fact that some types of berries are poisonous; it is a cultural fact that, a few generations ago, most Americans considered tomatoes to be poisonous and refused to eat them. Such selective, discriminative use of the environment is characteristically cultural. In a still more general sense, too, the process of eating is channeled by culture. Whether a man eats to live, lives to eat, or merely eats and lives is only in part an individual matter, for there are also cultural trends. Emotions are physiological events. Certain situations will evoke fear in people from any culture. But sensations of pleasure, anger, and lust may be stimulated by cultural cues that would leave unmoved someone who has been reared in a different social tradition.

Except in the case of newborn babies and of individuals born with clear-cut structural or functional abnormalities, we can observe innate endowments only as modified by cultural training. In a hospital in New Mexico where Zuñi Indian, Navaho Indian, and white American babies are born, it is possible to classify the newly arrived infants as unusually active, average, and quiet. Some babies from each "racial" group will fall into each category, though a higher proportion of the white babies will fall into the unusually active class. But if a Navaho baby, a Zuñi baby, and a white baby—all classified as unusually active at birth—are again observed at the age of two years, the Zuñi baby will no longer seem given to quick and restless activity—*as compared with the white child*—though he may seem so as compared with the other Zuñis of the same age. The Navaho child is likely to fall in between as contrasted with the Zuñi and the white, though he will probably still seem more active than the average Navaho youngster.

✗   It was remarked by many observers in the Japanese relocation centers that Japanese who were born and brought up in this country, especially those who were reared apart from any large colony of Japanese, resemble in behavior their white neighbors much more closely than they do their own parents who were educated in Japan.

I have said "culture channels biological processes." It is more accurate to say "the biological functioning of individuals is modified if they have been trained in certain ways and not in others." Culture is not a disembodied force. It is created and transmitted by people. However, culture, like well-known concepts of the physical sciences, is a convenient abstraction. One never sees gravity. One sees bodies falling in regular ways. One never sees an electromagnetic field. Yet certain happenings that can be seen may be given a neat abstract formulation by assuming that the electromagnetic field exists. Similarly, one never sees culture as such. What is seen are regularities in the behavior or artifacts of a group that has adhered to a common tradition. The regularities in style and technique of ancient Inca tapestries or stone axes from Melanesian islands are due to the existence of mental blueprints for the group.

Culture is a *way* of thinking, feeling, believing. It is the group's knowledge stored up (in memories of men; in books and objects) for future use. We study the products of this "mental" activity: the overt behavior, the speech and gestures and activities of people, and the tangible results of these things such as tools, houses, cornfields, and what not. It has been customary in lists of "culture traits" to include such things as watches or lawbooks. This is a convenient way of thinking about them, but in the solution of any important problem we must remember that they, in themselves, are nothing but metals, paper, and ink. What is important is that some men know how to make them, others set a value on them, are unhappy without them, direct their activities in relation to them, or disregard them.

It is only a helpful shorthand when we say "The cultural patterns of the Zulu were resistant to Christianization." In the directly observable world, of course, it was individual Zulus who resisted. Nevertheless, if we do not forget that we are speaking at a high level of abstraction, it is justifiable to speak of culture as a cause. One may compare the practice of saying "syphilis caused the extinction of the native population of the island." Was it "syphilis" or "syphilis germs" or "human beings who were carriers of syphilis"?

"Culture," then, is "a theory." But if a theory is not contradicted by any relevant fact and if it helps us to understand a mass of otherwise chaotic facts, it is useful. Darwin's contribution was much less the accumulation of new knowledge than the creation of a theory which put in order data already known. An accumulation of facts, however large, is no more a science than a pile of bricks is a house. Anthropology's demonstration that the most weird set of customs has a consistency and an order is comparable to modern psychiatry's showing that there is meaning and purpose in the apparently incoherent talk of the insane. In fact, the inability of the older psychologies and philosophies to account for the strange behavior of madmen and heathens was the principal factor that forced psychiatry and anthropology to develop theories of the unconscious and of culture.

Since culture is an abstraction, it is important not to confuse culture with society. A "society" refers to a group of people who interact more with each other than they do with other individuals—who cooperate with each other for the attainment of certain ends. You can see and indeed count the individuals who make up a society. A "culture" refers to the distinctive ways of life of such a group of people. Not all social events are culturally patterned. New types of circumstances arise for which no cultural solutions have as yet been devised.

A culture constitutes a storehouse of the pooled learning of the group. A rabbit starts life with some innate responses. He can learn from his own experience and perhaps from observing other rabbits. A human infant is born with fewer instincts and greater plasticity. His main task is to learn the answers that persons he will never see, persons long dead, have worked out. Once he has learned the formulas supplied by the culture of his group, most of his behavior becomes almost as automatic and unthinking as if it were instinctive. There is a tremendous amount of intelligence behind the making of a radio, but not much is required to learn to turn it on.

The members of all human societies face some of the same unavoidable dilemmas, posed by biology and other facts of the human situation. This is why the basic categories of all cultures are so similar. Human culture without language is unthinkable. No culture fails to provide for aesthetic expression and aesthetic delight. Every culture supplies standardized orientations toward the deeper problems, such as death. Every culture is designed to perpetuate the group and its solidarity, to meet the demands of individuals for an orderly way of life and for satisfaction of biological needs.

However, the variations of these basic themes are numberless. Some languages are built up out of twenty basic sounds, others out of forty. Nose plugs were considered beautiful by the predynastic Egyptians but are not by the modern French. Puberty is a biological fact. But one culture ignores it, another prescribes informal instructions about sex but no ceremony, a third has impressive rites for girls only, a fourth for boys and girls. In this culture, the first menstruation is welcomed as a happy, natural event; in that culture, the atmosphere is full of dread and supernatural threat. Each culture dissects nature according to its own system of categories. The Navaho Indians apply the same word to the color of a robin's egg and to that of grass. A psychologist once assumed that this meant a difference in the sense organs, that Navahos didn't have the physiological equipment to distinguish "green" from "blue." However, when he showed them objects of the two colors and asked them if they were exactly the same colors, they looked at him with astonishment. His dream of discovering a new type of color blindness was shattered.

Every culture must deal with the sexual instinct. Some, however, seek to deny all sexual expression before marriage, whereas a Polynesian adolescent who was not promiscuous would be distinctly abnormal. Some cultures enforce lifelong monogamy; others, like our own, tolerate serial monogamy; in still other cultures, two or more women may be joined to one man or several men to a single woman. Homosexuality has been a permitted pattern in the Greco-Roman world, in parts of Islam, and in various primitive tribes. Large portions of the population of Tibet, and of Christendom at some places and periods, have practiced complete celibacy. To us marriage is first and foremost an arrangement between two individuals. In many more societies marriage is merely one facet of a complicated set of reciprocities, economic and otherwise, between two families or two clans.

The essence of the cultural process is selectivity. The selection is only exceptionally conscious and rational. Cultures are like Topsy. They just grew. Once, however, a way of handling a situation becomes institutionalized, there is ordinarily great resistance to change or deviation. When we speak of "our sacred beliefs," we mean of course that they are beyond criticism and that the person who suggests modification or abandonment must be punished. No person is emotionally indifferent to his culture. Certain cultural premises may become totally out of accord with a new factual situation. Leaders may recognize this and reject the old ways in theory. Yet their emotional loyalty continues in the face of reason because of the intimate conditionings of early childhood.

A culture is learned by individuals as the result of belonging to some particular group, and it constitutes that part of learned behavior which is shared with others. It is our social legacy, as contrasted with our organic heredity. It is one of the important factors which permit us to live together in an organized society, giving us ready-made solutions to our problems, helping us to predict the behavior of others, and permitting others to know what to expect of us.

Culture regulates our lives at every turn. From the moment we are born until we die there is, whether we are conscious of it or not, constant pressure upon us to follow certain types of behavior that other men have created for us. Some paths we follow willingly, others we follow because we know no other way, still others we deviate from or go back to most unwillingly. Mothers of small children know how unnaturally most of this comes to us—how little regard we have, until we are "culturalized," for the "proper" place, time, and manner for certain acts such as eating, excreting, sleeping, getting dirty, and making loud noises. But by more or less adhering to a system of related designs for carrying out all the acts of living, a group of men and women feel themselves linked together by a powerful chain of sentiments. Ruth Benedict gave an almost complete definition of the concept when she said, "Culture is that which binds men together."

It is true any culture is a set of techniques for adjusting both to the external environment and to other men. However, cultures create problems as well as solve them. If the lore of a people states that frogs are dangerous creatures, or that it is not safe to go about at night because of witches or ghosts, threats are posed which do not arise out of the inexorable facts of the external world. Cultures produce needs as well as provide a means of fulfilling them. There exist, for every group culturally defined, acquired drives that may be more powerful in ordinary daily life than the biologically inborn drives. Many Americans, for example, will work harder for "success" than they will for sexual satisfaction.

Most groups elaborate certain aspects of their culture far beyond maximum utility or survival value. In other words, not all culture promotes physical survival. At times, indeed, it does exactly the opposite. Aspects of culture which once were adaptive may persist long after they have ceased to be useful. An analysis of any culture will disclose many features which cannot possibly be construed as adaptations to the total environment in which the group now finds itself. However, it is altogether likely that these apparently useless features represent survivals, with modifications through time, of cultural forms which were adaptive in one or another previous situation.

Any cultural practice must be functional or it will disappear before long. That is, it must somehow contribute to the survival of the society or to the adjustment of the individual. However, many cultural functions are not manifest but latent. A cowboy will walk three miles to catch a horse which he then rides one mile to the store. From the point of view of manifest function this is positively irrational. But the act has the latent function of maintaining the cowboy's prestige in the terms of his own subculture. One can instance the buttons on the sleeve of a man's coat, our absurd

English spelling, the use of capital letters, and a host of other apparently nonfunctional customs. They serve mainly the latent function of assisting individuals to maintain their security by preserving continuity with the past and by making certain sectors of life familiar and predictable.

Every culture is a precipitate of history. In more than one sense history is a sieve. Each culture embraces those aspects of the past which, usually in altered form and with altered meanings, live on in the present. Discoveries and inventions, both material and ideological, are constantly being made available to a group through its historical contacts with other peoples or being created by its own members. However, only those that fit the total immediate situation in meeting the group's needs for survival or in promoting the psychological adjustment of individuals will become part of the culture. The process of culture building may be regarded as an addition to man's innate biological capacities, an addition providing instruments which enlarge, or may even substitute for, biological functions, and to a degree compensating for biological limitations—as in ensuring that death does not always result in the loss to humanity of what the deceased has learned.

Culture is like a map. Just as a map isn't the territory but an abstract representation of a particular area, so also a culture is an abstract description of trends toward uniformity in the words, deeds, and artifacts of a human group. If a map is accurate and you can read it, you won't get lost: if you know a culture, you will know your way around in the life of a society. Many educated people have the notion that culture applies only to exotic ways of life or to societies where relative simplicity and relative homogeneity prevail. Some sophisticated missionaries, for example, will use the anthropological conception in discussing the special modes of living of South Sea Islanders, but seem amazed at the idea that it could be applied equally to inhabitants of New York City. And social workers in Boston will talk about the culture of a colorful and well-knit immigrant group but boggle at applying it to the behavior of staff members in the social-service agency itself.

In the primitive society the correspondence between the habits of individuals and the customs of the community is ordinarily greater. There is probably some truth in what an old Indian once said, "In the old days there was no law; everybody did what was right." The primitive tends to find happiness in the fulfillment of intricately involuted cultural patterns; the modern more often tends to feel the pattern as repressive to his individuality. It is also true that in a complex stratified society there are numerous exceptions to generalizations made about the culture as a whole. It is necessary to study regional, class, and occupational subcultures. Primitive cultures have greater stability than modern cultures; they change—but less rapidly.

However, modern men also are creators and carriers of culture. Only in some respects are they influenced differently from primitives by culture. Moreover, there are such wide variations in primitive cultures that any black-and-white contrast between the primitive and the civilized is altogether fictitious. The distinction which is most generally true lies in the field of conscious philosophy.

The publication of Paul Radin's *Primitive Man as a Philosopher* did much toward destroying the myth that an abstract analysis of experience was a peculiarity of literate societies. Speculation and reflection upon the nature of the universe and of man's place in the total scheme of things have been carried out in every known culture. Every people has its characteristic set of "primitive postulates." It remains true that critical examination of basic premises and fully explicit systematization of philosophical concepts are seldom found at the nonliterate level. The written word is an almost essential condition for free and extended discussion of fundamental philosophic issues. Where dependence on memory exists, there seems to be an inevitable tendency to emphasize the correct perpetuation of the precious oral tradition. Similarly, while it is all too easy to underestimate the extent to which ideas spread without books, it is in general true that tribal or folk societies do not possess competing philosophical systems. The major exception to this statement is, of course, the case where part of the tribe becomes converted to one of the great proselytizing religions such as Christianity or Mohammedanism. Before contact with rich and powerful civilizations, primitive peoples seem to have absorbed new ideas piecemeal, slowly integrating them with the previously existing ideology. The abstract thought of nonliterate societies is ordinarily less self-critical, less systematic, nor so intricately elaborated in purely logical dimensions. Primitive thinking is more concrete, more implicit—perhaps more completely coherent than the philosophy of most individuals in larger societies which have been influenced over long periods by disparate intellectual currents.

No participant in any culture knows all the details of the cultural map. The statement frequently heard that St. Thomas Aquinas was the last man to master all the knowledge of his society is intrinsically absurd. St. Thomas would have been hard put to make a pane of cathedral glass or to act as a midwife. In every culture there are what Ralph Linton has called "universals, alternatives, and specialties." Every Christian in the thirteenth century knew that it was necessary to attend mass, to go to confession, to ask the Mother of God to intercede with her Son. There were many other universals in the Christian culture of Western Europe. However, there were also alternative cultural patterns even in the realm of religion. Each individual had his own patron saint, and different towns developed the cults of different saints. The thirteenth-century anthropologist could have discovered the rudiments of Christian practice by questioning and observing whomever he happened to meet in Germany, France, Italy, or England. But to find out the details of the ceremonials honoring St. Hubert or St. Bridget he would have had to seek out certain individuals or special localities where these alternative patterns were practiced. Similarly, he could not learn about weaving from a professional soldier or about canon law from a farmer. Such cultural knowledge belongs in the realm of the specialties, voluntarily chosen by the individual or ascribed to him by birth. Thus, part of a culture must be learned by everyone, part may be selected from alternative patterns, part applies only to those who perform the roles in the society for which these patterns are designed.

Many aspects of a culture are explicit. The explicit culture consists in those regularities in word and deed that may be generalized straight from the evidence of the ear and the eye. The recognition of these is like the recognition of style in the art of a particular place and epoch. If we have examined twenty specimens of the wooden saints' images made in the Taos valley of New Mexico in the late eighteenth century, we can predict that any new images from the same locality and period will in most respects exhibit the same techniques of carving, about the same use of colors and choice of woods, a similar quality of artistic conception. Similarly, if, in a society of 2,000 members, we record 100 marriages at random and find that in 30 cases a man has married the sister of his brother's wife, we can anticipate that an additional sample of 100 marriages will show roughly the same number of cases of this pattern.

The above is an instance of what anthropologists call a behavioral pattern, the practices as opposed to the rules of the culture. There are also, however, regularities in what people say they do or should do. They do tend in fact to prefer to marry into a family already connected with their own by marriage, but this is not necessarily part of the official code of conduct. No disapproval whatsoever is attached to those who make another sort of marriage. On the other hand, it is explicitly forbidden to marry a member of one's own clan even though no biological relationship is traceable. This is a regulatory pattern—a Thou Shalt or a Thou Shalt Not. Such patterns may be violated often, but their existence is nevertheless important. A people's standards for conduct and belief define the socially approved aims and the acceptable means of attaining them. When the discrepancy between the theory and the practice of a culture is exceptionally great, this indicates that the culture is undergoing rapid change. It does not prove that ideals are unimportant, for ideals are but one of a number of factors determining action.

Cultures do not manifest themselves solely in observable customs and artifacts. No amount of questioning of any save the most articulate in the most self-conscious cultures will bring out some of the basic attitudes common to the members of the group. This is because these basic assumptions are taken so for granted that they normally do not enter into consciousness. This part of the cultural map must be inferred by the observer on the basis of consistencies in thought and action. Missionaries in various societies are often disturbed or puzzled because the natives do not regard "morals" and "sex code" as almost synonymous. The natives seem to feel that morals are concerned with sex just about as much as with eating—no less and no more. No society fails to have some restrictions on sexual behavior, but sex activity outside of marriage need not necessarily be furtive or attended with guilt. The Christian tradition has tended to assume that sex is inherently nasty as well as dangerous. Other cultures assume that sex in itself is not only natural but one of the good things of life, even though sex acts with certain persons under certain circumstances are forbidden. This is implicit culture, for the natives do not announce their premises. The missionaries would get further if they said, in effect, "Look, our morality starts from different assumptions. Let's talk about those assumptions," rather than ranting about "immorality."

A factor implicit in a variety of diverse phenomena may be generalized as an underlying cultural principle. For example, the Navaho Indians always leave part of the design in a pot, a basket, or a blanket unfinished. When a medicine man instructs an apprentice he always leaves a little bit of the story untold. This "fear of closure" is a recurrent theme in Navaho culture. Its influence may be detected in many contexts that have no explicit connection.

If the observed cultural behavior is to be correctly understood, the categories and presuppositions constituting the implicit culture must be worked out. The "strain toward consistency" which Sumner noted in the folkways and mores of all groups cannot be accounted for unless one grants a set of systematically interrelated implicit themes. For example, in American culture the themes of "effort and optimism," "the common man," "technology," and "virtuous materialism" have a functional interdependence, the origin of which is historically known. The relationship between themes may be that of conflict. One may instance the competition between Jefferson's theory of democracy and Hamilton's "government by the rich, the well-born, and the able." In other cases most themes may be integrated under a single dominant theme. In Negro cultures of West Africa the mainspring of social life is religion; in East Africa almost all cultural behavior seems to be oriented toward certain premises and categories centered on the cattle economy. If there be one master principle in the implicit culture, this is often called the "ethos" or *Zeitgeist*.

Every culture has organization as well as content. There is nothing mystical about this statement. One may compare ordinary experience. If I know that Smith working alone can shovel 10 cubic yards of dirt a day, Jones 12, and Brown 14, I would be foolish to predict that the three working together would move 36. The total might well be considerably more; it might be less. A whole is different from the sum of its parts. The same principle is familiar in athletic teams. A brilliant pitcher added to a nine may mean a pennant or may mean the cellar; it depends on how he fits in.

And so it is with cultures. A mere list of the behavioral and regulatory patterns and of the implicit themes and categories would be like a map on which all mountains, lakes, and rivers were included—but not in their actual relationship to one another. Two cultures could have almost identical inventories and still be extremely different. The full significance of any single element in a culture design will be seen only when that element is viewed in the total matrix of its relationship to other elements. Naturally, this includes accent or emphasis, as well as position. Accent is manifested sometimes through frequency, sometimes through intensity. The indispensable importance of these questions of arrangement and emphasis may be driven home by an analogy. Consider a musical sequence made up of three notes. If we are told that the three notes in question are A, B, and G, we receive information which is fundamental. But it will not enable us to predict the type of sensation which the playing of this sequence is likely to evoke. We need many different sorts of relationship data. Are the notes to be played in that or some other order? What duration will each receive? How will the emphasis, if any, be distributed? We also need, of course, to know whether the instrument used is to be a piano or an accordion.

Cultures vary greatly in their degree of integration. Synthesis is achieved partly through the overt statement of the dominant conceptions, assumptions, and aspirations of the group in its religious lore, secular thought, and ethical code; partly through habitual but unconscious ways of looking at the stream of events, ways of begging certain questions. To the naïve participant in the culture these modes of categorizing, of dissecting experience along these planes and not others, are as much "given" as the regular sequence of daylight and darkness or the necessity of air, water, and food for life. Had Americans not thought in terms of money and the market system during the depression they would have distributed unsalable goods rather than destroyed them.

Every group's way of life, then, is a structure—not a haphazard collection of all the different physically possible and functionally effective patterns of belief and action. A culture is an interdependent system based upon linked premises and categories whose influence is greater, rather than less, because they are seldom put in words. Some degree of internal coherence which is felt rather than rationally constructed seems to be demanded by most of the participants in any culture. As Whitehead has remarked, "Human life is driven forward by its dim apprehension of notions too general for its existing language."

In sum, the distinctive way of life that is handed down as the social heritage of a people does more than supply a set of skills for making a living and a set of blueprints for human relations. Each different way of life makes its own assumptions about the ends and purposes of human existence, about what human beings have a right to expect from each other and the gods, about what constitutes fulfillment or frustration. Some of these assumptions are made explicit in the lore of the folk; others are tacit premises which the observer must infer by finding consistent trends in word and deed.

In our highly self-conscious Western civilization that has recently made a business of studying itself, the number of assumptions that are literally implicit, in the sense of never having been stated or discussed by anyone, may be negligible. Yet only a trifling number of Americans could state even those implicit premises of our culture that have been brought to light by anthropologists. If one could bring to the American scene a Bushman who had been socialized in his own culture and then trained in anthropology, he would perceive all sorts of patterned regularities of which our anthropologists are completely unaware. In the case of the less sophisticated and less self-conscious societies, the unconscious assumptions characteristically made by individuals brought up under approximately the same social controls bulk even larger. But in any society, as Edward Sapir said, "Forms and significances which seem obvious to an outsider will be denied outright by those who carry out the patterns; outlines and implications that are perfectly clear to these may be absent to the eye of the onlooker."

All individuals in a culture tend to share common interpretations of the external world and man's place in it. To some degree every individual is affected by this conventional view of life. One group unconsciously assumes that every chain of actions has a goal and that when this goal is reached tension will be reduced or will disappear. To another group, thinking based upon this assumption is meaningless—they see life not as a series of purposive sequences, but as a complex of experiences which are satisfying in and of themselves, rather than as means to ends.   *) Conflict*

The concept of implicit culture is made necessary by certain eminently practical considerations. Programs of the British Colonial services or of our own Indian service, which have been carefully thought through for their continuity with the overt cultural patterns, nevertheless fail to work out. Nor does intensive investigation reveal any flaws in the setup at the technological level. The program is sabotaged by resistance which must be imputed to the manner in which the members of the group have been conditioned by their implicit designs for living to think and feel in ways which were unexpected to the administrator.

2-2   THE CONCEPT OF CULTURE   *Failure   Experience*
Leslie A. White

Leslie A. White is one of America's leading theoreticians in cultural anthropology. He received his B.A. and M.A. from Columbia University and his Ph.D. from the University of Chicago. He has taught at Yale, Harvard, Columbia, and California Universities and at Yenching University in Peking, and has served as chairman of the Department of Anthropology at the University of Michigan for many years. Among his many publications, *The Science of Culture* and *The Evolution of Culture* have created considerable discussion among social scientists. Consequently, no statement concerning the nature of culture would be complete without some comment by Leslie A. White. In "The Concept of Culture" Professor White disagrees with Kluckhohn's statement that culture is an abstraction, and then provides some alternative explanations.

Virtually all cultural anthropologists take it for granted, no doubt, that *culture* is the basic and central concept of their science. There is, however, a disturbing lack of agreement as to what they mean by this term. To some, culture is learned

From *American Anthropologist*, LXI, No. 2 (April 1959), 227–249. Reprinted by permission of the author and the American Anthroplogical Association.

behavior. To others, it is not behavior at all, but an abstraction from behavior—whatever that is. Stone axes and pottery bowls are culture to some anthropologists, but no material object can be culture to others. Culture exists only in the mind, according to some; it consists of observable things and events in the external world to others. Some anthropologists think of culture as consisting of ideas, but they are divided upon the question of their locus: some say they are in the minds of the peoples studied, others hold that they are in the minds of ethnologists. We go on to "culture is a psychic defense mechanism," "culture consists of n different social signals correlated with m different responses," "culture is a Rohrschach of a society," and so on, to confusion and bewilderment. One wonders what physics would be like if it had as many and as varied conceptions of energy!

There was a time, however, when there was a high degree of uniformity of comprehension and use of the term culture. During the closing decades of the nineteenth century and the early years of the twentieth, the great majority of cultural anthropologists, we believe, held to the conception expressed by E. B. Tylor, in 1871, in the opening lines of *Primitive Culture*: "Culture . . . is that complex whole which includes knowledge, belief, art, morals, law, custom, and any other capabilities and habits acquired by man as a member of society." Tylor does not make it explicit in this statement that culture is the peculiar possession of man; but it is therein implied, and in other places he makes this point clear and explicit.[1] Culture, to Tylor, was the name of all things and events peculiar to the human species. Specifically, he enumerates beliefs, customs, objects—"hatchet, adze, chisel," and so on— and techniques—"wood-chopping, fishing . . . , shooting and spearing game, firemaking," and so on.[2]

The Tylorian conception of culture prevailed in anthropology generally for decades. In 1920, Robert H. Lowie began *Primitive Society* by quoting "Tylor's famous definition." In recent years, however, conceptions and definitions of culture have multiplied and varied to a great degree. One of the most highly favored of these is that *culture is an abstraction.* This is the conclusion reached by Kroeber and Kluckhohn in their exhaustive review of the subject: *Culture: A Critical Review of Concepts and History.*[3] It is the definition given by Beals and Hoijer in their textbook, *An Introduction to Anthropology.*[4] In a more recent work, however, *Cultural Anthropology,*[5] Felix M. Keesing defines culture as "the totality of learned, socially transmitted behavior."

Much of the discussion of the concept of culture in recent years has been concerned with a distinction between culture and human behavior. For a long time many anthropologists were quite content to define culture as behavior, peculiar to the human species, acquired by learning, and transmitted from one individual, group, or generation to another by mechanisms of social inheritance. But eventually some began to object to this and to make the point that culture is not itself behavior, but is an abstraction

---

[1] Edward B. Tylor, *Anthropology* (London: 1881), pp. 54, 123, where he deals with the "great mental gap between us and the animals."

[2] Edward B. Tylor, *Primitive Culture* (London, 5th ed., 1913), pp. 5–6.

[3] A. L. Kroeber and Clyde Kluckhohn, "Culture, A Critical Review of Concepts and Definitions." *Papers of the Peabody Museum of American Archaeology and Ethnology,* Harvard University, XLVII, No. 1 (1952), 155, 169.

[4] Ralph L. Beals and Harry Hoijer, *An Introduction to Anthropology* (New York: Macmillan Co., 1953), pp. 210, 219, 507, 535.

[5] Felix M. Keesing, *Cultural Anthropology* (New York: Rinehart and Co., 1958), pp. 16, 427.

from behavior. Culture, say Kroeber and Kluckhohn,[6] "is an abstraction from concrete human behavior, but it is not itself behavior." Beals and Hoijer[7] and others take the same view.[8]

Those who define culture as an abstraction do not tell us what they mean by this term. They appear to take it for granted (1) that they themselves know what they mean by "abstraction," and (2) that others, also, will understand. We believe that neither of these suppositions is well founded; we shall return to a consideration of this concept later in this essay. But whatever an abstraction in general may be to these anthropologists, when culture becomes an "abstraction" it becomes imperceptible, imponderable, and not wholly real. According to Linton, "culture itself is intangible and cannot be directly apprehended even by the individuals who participate in it."[9] Herskovits also calls culture "intangible."[10] Anthropologists in the imaginary symposium reported by Kluckhohn and Kelly[11] argue that "one can see" such things as individuals and their actions and interactions, but "has anyone ever seen 'culture'?" Beals and Hoijer[12] say that "the anthropologist cannot observe culture directly . . ."

If culture as an abstraction is intangible, imperceptible, does it exist, is it real? Ralph Linton[13] raises this question in all seriousness: "If it (culture) can be said to exist at all. . . ." Radcliffe-Brown[14] declares that the word culture "denotes, not any concrete reality, but an abstraction, and as it is commonly used a vague abstraction." And Spiro[15] says that according to the predominant "position of contemporary anthropology . . . culture has no ontological reality. . . ."

Thus when culture becomes an abstraction it not only becomes invisible and imponderable; it virtually ceases to exist. It would be difficult to construct a less adequate conception of culture. Why, then, have prominent and influential anthropologists turned to the "abstraction" conception of culture?

A clue to the reason—if, indeed, it is not an implicit statement of the reason itself—is given by Kroeber and Kluckhohn:[16]

> Since behavior is the first-hand and outright material of the science of psychology, and culture is not—being of concern only secondarily, as an influence on this material—it is natural that psychologists and psychologizing sociologists should see behavior as primary in their field, and then extend this view farther to apply to the field of culture also.

---

[6] Kroeber and Kluckhohn, p. 155.

[7] Beals and Hoijer, pp. 210, 219.

[8] One of the earliest instances of regarding culture as an abstraction is Murdock's statement: "realizing that culture is merely an abstraction from observed likenesses in the behavior of individuals . . ." (George P. Murdock, "Editorial Preface to Studies in the Science of Society," presented to Albert Galloway Keller, New Haven, Conn.: Yale University Press, 1937, p. xi.)

[9] Ralph Linton, *The Study of Man* (New York: D. Appleton-Century Co., 1936) pp. 288–289.

[10] Melville J. Herskovits, "The Processes of Cultural Change" in *Man, Culture and Society*, Harry L. Shapiro, ed. (New York: Oxford University Press, 1945), p. 150.

[11] Clyde Kluckhohn and Wm. H. Kelly, "The Concept of Culture" in *The Science of Man in the World Crisis*, Ralph Linton, ed. (New York: Columbia University Press), pp. 79, 81.

[12] Beals and Hoijer, 1953, p. 210.

[13] Linton, 1936, p. 363.

[14] A. R. Radcliffe-Brown, "On Social Structure," *Journal of the Royal Anthropological Institute*, LXX, 1–12, reprinted in *Structure and Function in Primitive Society* (Glencoe, Illinois: The Free Press, 1940), p. 2.

[15] Melford E. Spiro, "Culture and Personality," *Psychiatry*, XIV (1951), 24.

[16] Kroeber and Kluckhohn, 1952, p. 155.

The reasoning is simple and direct: if culture is behavior, then (1) culture becomes the subject matter of psychology, since behavior is the proper subject matter of psychology; culture would then become the property of psychologists and "psychologizing sociologists"; and (2) nonbiological anthropology would be left without a subject matter. The danger was real and imminent; the situation, critical. What was to be done?

The solution proposed by Kroeber and Kluckhohn was neat and simple: let the psychologists have behavior; anthropologists will keep for themselves abstractions from behavior. These abstractions become and constitute *culture*.

But in this rendering unto Caesar, anthropologists have given the psychologists the better part of the bargain, for they have surrendered unto them real things and events, locatable and observable, directly or indirectly, in the real external world, in terrestrial time and space, and have kept for themselves only intangible, imponderable abstractions that "have no ontological reality." But at least, and at last, they have a subject matter—however insubstantial and unobservable—of their own!

Whether or not this has been the principal reason for defining culture as "not behavior, but abstractions from behavior," is perhaps a question; we feel, however, that Kroeber and Kluckhohn have made themselves fairly clear. But whatever the reason, or reasons—for there may have been several—may have been for the distinction, the question whether culture is to be regarded as behavior or as abstractions from it is, we believe, the central issue in recent attempts to hammer out an adequate, usable, fruitful, and enduring conception of culture.

The present writer is no more inclined to surrender culture to the psychologists than are Kroeber and Kluckhohn; indeed, a few anthropologists have taken greater pains to distinguish psychological problems from culturological problems than he has.[17] But he does not wish to exchange the hard substance of culture for its wraith, either. No science can have a subject matter that consists of intangible, invisible, imponderable, ontologically unreal "abstractions"; a science must have real stars, real mammals, foxes, crystals, cells, phonemes, gamma rays, and culture traits to work with.[18] We believe that we can offer an analysis of the situation that will distinguish between psychology, the scientific study of behavior on the one hand, and culturology, the scientific study of culture, on the other, and at the same time give a real, substantial subject matter to each.

Science makes a dichotomy between the mind of the observer and the external world[19]—things and events having their locus outside the mind of this observer. The scientist makes contact with the external world with and through his senses, forming percepts. These percepts are translated into concepts which are manipulated in a process called thinking in such a way as to form premises, propositions, general-

---

[17] Several of the essays in *The Science of Culture* (1949)—"Culturological vs. Psychological Interpretations of Human Behavior," "Cultural Determinants of Mind," "Genius: Its Causes and Incidence," "Ikhnaton: The Great Man vs. the Culture Process," "The Definition and Prohibition of Incest," etc.—deal with this distinction.

[18] I made this point in my review of Kroeber and Kluckhohn, "Culture: A Critical Review, etc.," *American Anthropologist*, LVI (1954), 464–465. At about the same time Huxley was writing (1955: pp. 15–16): "If anthropology is a science, then for anthropologists culture must be defined, not philosophically or metaphysically, nor as an abstraction, nor in purely subjective terms, but as something which can be investigated by the methods of scientific inquiry, a phenomenal process occurring in space and time."

[19] "The belief in an external world independent of the perceiving subject is the basis of all natural science," says Einstein. Albert Einstein, *The World as I See It* (New York: Covici, Friede, 1934), p. 60.

izations, conclusions, and so on. The validity of these premises, propositions, and conclusions is established by testing them in terms of experience of the external world.[20] This is the way science proceeds and does its work.

The first step in scientific procedure is to observe, or more generally to experience, the external world in a sensory manner. The next step—after percepts have been translated into concepts—is the classification of things and events perceived or experienced. Things and events of the external world are thus divided into classes of various kinds: acids, metals, stones, liquids, mammals, stars, atoms, corpuscles, and so on. Now it turns out that there is a class of phenomena, one of enormous importance in the study of man, for which science has as yet no name: this is the class of things and events consisting of or dependent upon symboling.[21] It is one of the most remarkable facts in the recent history of science that this important class has no name, but the fact remains that it does not. And the reason why it does not is because these things and events have always been considered and designated, not merely and simply as the things and events that they are, in and of themselves, but always as things and events in a particular context.

A thing is what it is; "a rose is a rose is a rose." Acts are not first of all ethical acts or economic acts or erotic acts. An act is an act. An act becomes an ethical datum or an economic datum or an erotic datum when—and only when—it is considered in an ethical, economic, or erotic context. Is a Chinese porcelain vase a scientific specimen, an object of art, an article of commerce, or an exhibit in a lawsuit? The answer is obvious. Actually, of course, to call it a "Chinese porcelain vase" is already to put it into a particular context; it would be better first of all to say "a glazed form of fired clay is a glazed form of fired clay." As a Chinese porcelain vase, it becomes an object of art, a scientific specimen, or an article of merchandise when, and only when, it is considered in an esthetic, scientific, or commercial context.

Let us return now to the class of things and events that consist of or are dependent upon symboling: a spoken word, a stone axe, a fetich, avoiding one's mother-in-law, loathing milk, saying a prayer, sprinkling holy water, a pottery bowl, casting a vote, remembering the sabbath to keep it holy—"and any other capabilities and habits (and things) acquired by man as a member of (human) society."[22] They are what they are: things and acts dependent upon symboling.

We may consider these things-and-events-dependent-upon-symboling in a number of contexts: astronomical, physical, chemical, anatomical, physiological, psychological, and culturological, and, consequently, they become astronomic,

---

[20] Thinking, in science, means "operations with concepts, and the creation and use of definite functional relations between them, and the co-ordination of sense experiences to these concepts." Einstein has much to say in this essay about the manner and process of scientific thinking. Albert Einstein, "Physics and Reality," *Journal of the Franklin Institute*, CCXXI, 349–382.

[21] By "symboling" we mean bestowing meaning upon a thing or an act, or grasping and appreciating meanings thus bestowed. Holy water is a good example of such meanings. The attribute of holiness is bestowed upon the water by a human being, and it may be comprehended and appreciated by other human beings. Articulate speech is the most characteristic and important form of symboling. Symboling is trafficking in nonsensory meanings, *i.e.*, meanings which, like the holiness of sacramental water, cannot be comprehended with the senses alone. Symboling is a kind of behavior. Only man is capable of symboling. We have discussed this concept rather fully in "The Symbol: The Origin and Basis of Human Behavior," originally published in *The Philosophy of Science*, VII (1940), 451–463. It has been reprinted in slightly revised form in *The Science of Culture* (New York: Farrar, Straus and Cudahy, 1949); paperbound (New York: The Grove Press, 1958).

[22] Tylor, 1913, p. 1.

physical, chemical, anatomical, physiological, psychological, and culturological phenomena in turn. All things and events dependent upon symboling are dependent also upon solar energy which sustains all life on this planet; this is the astronomic context. These things and events may be considered and interpreted in terms of the anatomical, neurological, and physiological processes of the human beings who exhibit them. They may be considered and interpreted also in terms of their relationship to human organisms, i.e., in a somatic context. And they may be considered in an extrasomatic context, i.e., in terms of their relationship to other like things and events rather than in relationship to human organisms.

When things and events dependent upon symboling are considered and interpreted in terms of their relationship to human organisms, i.e., in a somatic context, they may properly be called *human behavior*, and the science, *psychology*. When things and events dependent upon symboling are considered and interpreted in an extrasomatic context, i.e., in terms of their relationships to one another rather than to human organisms, we may call them *culture*, and the science, *culturology*. This analysis is expressed diagrammatically in Fig. 1.

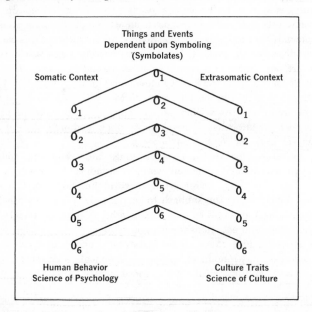

Fig. 1

In the middle of the diagram we have a vertical column of circles, O_1, O_2, O_3, etc., which stand for things (objects) and events (acts) dependent upon symboling. These things and events constitute a distinct class of phenomena in the realm of nature. Since they have had heretofore no name we have ventured to give them one: *symbolates*. We fully appreciate the hazards of coining terms, but this all-important class of phenomena needs a name to distinguish it from other classes. If we were physicists we might call them "Gamma phenomena." But we are not physicists, and we believe a simple word would be better—or at least more acceptable—than a Greek letter. In coining our term we have followed a well-established precedent: if an *isolate* is something that results from the process or action of isolating, then something that results from the action or process of symboling might well be called a symbolate. The particular word with which we designate this class of phenomena is not of paramount importance, and perhaps a better term than symbolate can be found. But it is of paramount importance that this class have a name.

A thing or event dependent upon symboling—a symbolate—is just what it is, but it may become significant in any one of a number of contexts. As we have already seen, it may be significant in an astronomic context: the performance of a ritual requires the expenditure of energy which has come from the sun. But within the sciences of man we may distinguish two significant contexts: the somatic and the extrasomatic. Symbolates may be considered and interpreted in terms of their relationship to the human organism, or they may be considered in terms of their relationships to one another, quite apart from their relationship to the human organism. Let us illustrate with some examples.

I smoke a cigarette, cast a vote, decorate a pottery bowl, avoid my mother-in-law, say a prayer, or chip an arrowhead. Each one of these acts is dependent upon the process of symboling;[23] each therefore is a symbolate. As a scientist, I may consider these acts (events) in terms of their relationships to me, to my organism: or, I may treat them in terms of their relationships to one another, to other symbolates, quite apart from their relationship to my organism.

In the first type of interpretation I consider the symbolate in terms of its relationship to my bodily structure: the structure and functions of my hand, for example; or to my stereoscopic, chromatic vision; or to my needs, desires, hopes, fears, imagination, habit formation, overt reactions, satisfactions, and so forth. How do I feel when I avoid my mother-in-law or cast a ballot? What is my attitude toward the act? What is my conception of it? Is the act accompanied by heightened emotional tone, or do I perform it in a mechanical, perfunctory manner? And so on. We may call these acts *human behavior*; our concern is *psychological*.

What we have said of acts (events) will apply to objects (things) also. What is my conception of a pottery bowl, a ground axe, a crucifix, roast pork, whisky, holy water, cement? What is my attitude and how do I react toward each of these things? In short, what is the nature of the relationship between each of these things and my own organism? We do not customarily call these things human behavior, but they are the embodiments of human behavior; the difference between a nodule of flint and a stone axe is the factor of human labor. An axe, bowl, crucifix—or a haircut—is concealed human labor. We have then a class of objects dependent upon symboling that have a significance in terms of their relationship to the human organism. The scientific consideration and interpretation of this relationship is *psychology*.

But we may treat symbolates in terms of their relationships to one another, quite apart from their relationship to the human organism. Thus, in the case of the avoidance of a mother-in-law, we would consider it in terms of its relationship to other symbolates, or symbolate clusters, such as customs of marriage—monogamy, polygyny, polyandry—place of residence of a couple after marriage, division of labor between the sexes, mode of subsistence, domestic architecture, degree of cultural development,

---

[23] "How is chipping an arrowhead dependent upon symboling?" it might be asked. I have answered this question in "On the Use of Tools by Primates," *Journal of Comparative Psychology*, XXXIV (1942), 369–374; reprinted in White, *The Science of Culture*.

etc. Or, if we are concerned with voting we would consider it in terms of forms of political organization (tribal, state), kind of government (democratic, monarchical, fascist); age, sex, or property qualifications; political parties and so on. In this context our symbolates become *culture*—culture traits or trait clusters, i.e., institutions, customs, codes, etc., and the scientific concern is *culturology*.

It would be the same with objects as with acts. If we were concerned with a hoe we would regard it in terms of its relationships to other symbolates in an extrasomatic context: to other instruments employed in subsistence, the digging stick and plow in particular; or to customs of division of labor between the sexes; the stage of cultural development, etc. We would be concerned with the relationship between a digital computer and the degree of development of mathematics, the stage of technological development, division of labor, the social organization within which it is used (corporation, military organization, astronomical laboratory), and so on.

Thus we see that we have two quite different kinds of sciencing[24] with regard to things and events—objects and acts—dependent upon symboling. If we treat them in terms of their relationship to the human organism, i.e., in an organismic, or somatic context, these things and events become *human behavior* and we are doing psychology. If, however, we treat them in terms of their relationship to one another, quite apart from their relationship to human organisms, i.e., in an extrasomatic, or extraorganismic, context, the things and events become *culture*—cultural elements or culture traits—and we are doing *culturology*. Human psychology and culturology have the same phenomena as their subject matter: things and events dependent upon symboling (symbolates). The difference between the two sciences derives from the difference between the contexts in which their common subject matter is treated.[25]

The analysis and distinction that we have made with regard to things and events dependent upon symboling in general is precisely like the one that linguists have been making for decades with regard to a particular kind of these things and events, namely, words.

A word is a thing (a sound or combination of sounds, or marks made upon some substance) or an act dependent upon symboling. Words are just what they are: words. But they are significant to scientific students of words in two different contexts: somatic or organismic, and extrasomatic or extraorganismic. This distinction has been expressed customarily with the terms *la langue* and *la parole*, or language and speech.[26]

---

[24] "Sciencing," too, is a kind of behavior. See our essay, "Science is Sciencing," *Philosophy of Science*, V (1938), 369–389; reprinted in *The Science of Culture*.

[25] Importance of context may be illustrated by contrasting attitudes toward one and the same class of women: as mothers they are revered; as mothers-in-law, reviled.

[26] "According to (Ferdinand) de Sassure the study of human speech is not the subject matter of *one* science but of two sciences. . . . de Sassure drew a sharp line between *la langue* and *la parole*. Language (*la langue*) is universal, whereas the process of speech (*la parole*) . . . is individual" (Ernest Cassirer, *An Essay on Man*, New Haven: Yale University Press, 1944). Julian S. Huxley (*Evolution, Cultural and Biological*, Yearbook of Anthropology, Wm. L. Thomas, Jr., ed., 1955), citing Cassirer's discussion of de Sassure's distinction between *la langue* and *la parole*, speaks of the former as "the super-individual system of grammar and syntax," and of the latter as "the actual words or way of speaking used by particular individuals." He goes on to say that "we find the *same distinction in every cultural activity*—in law . . . ; in art . . . ; in social structure . . . ; in science . . ." (emphasis by Dr. White).

Words in a somatic context constitute a kind of human behavior: speech behavior. The scientific study of words in a somatic context is the psychology (plus physiology, perhaps, and anatomy) of speech. It is concerned with the relationship between words and the human organism: how the words are produced and uttered, the meanings of words, attitudes toward words, perception of and response to words, and so on.

In the extrasomatic context, words are considered in terms of their relationships to one another, quite apart from their relationship to the human organism. The scientific concern here is linguistics, or the science of language. Phonetics, phonemics, syntax, lexicon, grammar, dialectic variation, evolution or historical change, etc., indicate particular focuses, or emphases, within the science of linguistics.

The difference between these two sciences may be illustrated by citing two books: *The Psychology of Language* by Walter B. Pillsbury and Clarence L. Meader,[27] and *Language* by Leonard Bloomfield.[28] In the former we find chapter titles such as "The Speech Organs," "The Senses Involved in Speech," "Mental Processes in Speech," etc. In the latter the chapter headings are "The Phoneme," "Phonetic Structure," "Grammatical Forms," "Sentence-Types," etc. We illustrate the distinction between these two sciences in Figure 2.

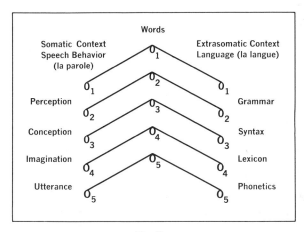

Fig. 2

Figures 1 and 2 are fundamentally alike. In each case we are concerned with a class of things and events dependent upon symboling. In Fig. 1, we are concerned with a general class: symbolates; in Fig. 2 we are dealing with a particular class: words (a subclass of the class symbolates). In each case we refer the things and events to a somatic context on the one hand, and to an extrasomatic context on the other, for purposes of consideration and interpretation. And in each case we have two distinct kinds of science, or sciencing: the psychology of human behavior or of speech; and the science of culture or of language.

Culture, then, is a class of things and events, dependent upon symboling, considered in an extrasomatic context. This definition rescues cultural anthropology from

Definition

[27] Walter B. Pillsbury and Clarence L. Meader, *The Psychology of Language* (New York, 1928).
[28] Leonard Bloomfield, *Language* (New York, 1933).

intangible, imperceptible, and ontologically unreal abstractions and provides it with a real, substantial, observable subject matter. And it distinguishes sharply between behavior—behaving organisms—and culture; between the science of psychology and the science of culture.

✗   It might be objected that every science should have a certain class of things per se as its subject matter, not things-in-a-certain-context. Atoms are atoms and mammals are mammals, it might be argued, and as such are the subject matter of physics and mammalogy, respectively, regardless of context. Why therefore should cultural anthropology have its subject matter defined in terms of things in context rather than in terms of things in themselves? At first glance this argument might appear to be a cogent one, but actually it has but little force. What the scientist wants to do is to make intelligible the phenomena that confront him. And very frequently the significant thing about phenomena is the context in which they are found. Even in the so-called natural sciences we have a science of organisms-in-a-certain-context: parasitology, a science of organisms playing a certain role in the realm of living things. And within the realm of man-and-culture we have dozens of examples of things and events whose significance depends upon context rather than upon the inherent qualities of the phenomena themselves. An adult male of a certain animal species is called a man. But a man is a man, not a slave; a man becomes a slave only when he enters a certain context. So it is with commodities: corn and cotton are articles of use-value, but they were not commodities—articles produced for sale at a profit—in aboriginal Hopi culture; corn and cotton become commodities only when they enter a certain socioeconomic context. A cow is a cow, but she may become a medium of exchange, money (*pecus*, pecuniary) in one context, food in another, mechanical power (Cartwright used a cow as motive power for his first power loom) in another, and a sacred object of worship (India) in still another. We do not have a science of cows, but we do have scientific studies of mediums of exchange, of mechanical power, and of sacred objects in each of which cows may be significant. And so we have a science of symboled things and events in an extrasomatic context.

          The locus of culture. If we define culture as consisting of real things and events observable, directly or indirectly, in the external world, where do these things and events exist and have their being? What is the locus of culture? The answer is: the things and events that comprise culture have their existence, in space and time, (1) within human organisms, i.e., concepts, beliefs, emotions, attitudes; (2) within processes of social interaction among human beings; and (3) within material objects (axes, factories, railroads, pottery bowls) lying outside human organisms but within the patterns of social interaction among them.[29] The locus of culture is thus intraorganismal, interorganismal, and extraorganismal (see Fig. 3).

          But, someone might object, you have said that culture consists of extrasomatic phenomena and now you tell me that culture exists, in part, within human organisms. Is this not a contradiction? The answer is, No, it is not a contradiction; it is a misunderstanding. We did not say that culture consists of extrasomatic things and events, i.e., phenomena whose locus is outside human organisms. What we said is that culture

---

[29] "The true locus of culture," says Sapir (Edward Sapir, "Cultural Anthropology and Psychiatry," *Journal of Abnormal and Social Psychology*, XXVII, 1932, 236), "is in the interactions of . . . individuals and, on the subjective side, in the world of meanings which each one of these individuals may unconsciously abstract for himself from his participation in these interactions." This statement is like ours except that it omits objects: material culture.

consists of things and events considered within an extrasomatic context. This is quite a different thing.

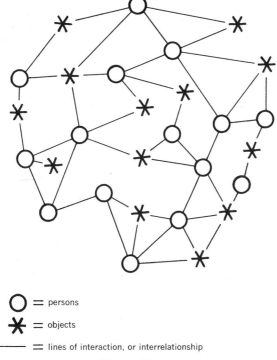

O = persons

✳ = objects

——— = lines of interaction, or interrelationship

Fig. 3. The Locus of Culture

Every cultural element has two aspects: subjective and objective. It might appear that stone axes are "objective," and ideas and attitudes are "subjective." But this is a superficial and inadequate view. An axe has a subjective component; it would be meaningless without a concept and an attitude. On the other hand, a concept or an attitude would be meaningless without overt expression, in behavior or speech (which is a form of behavior). Every cultural element, every culture trait, therefore, has a subjective and an objective aspect. But conceptions, attitudes, and sentiments—phenomena that have their locus within the human organism—may be considered for purposes of scientific interpretation in an extrasomatic context, i.e., in terms of their relation to other symboled things and events rather than in terms of their relationship to the human organism. Thus, we may consider the subjective aspect of the mother-in-law taboo, i.e., the conceptions and attitudes involved, in terms of their relationship, not to the human organism, but to other symbolates such as forms of marriage and the family, place of residence after marriage, and so on. On the other hand, we may consider the axe in terms of its relationship to the human organism—its meaning; the person's conception of it; his attitude toward it—rather than to other symboled things and events such as arrows, hoes, and customs regulating the division of labor in society.

We shall now pass in review a number of conceptions of culture, or conceptions with regard to culture, widely current in ethnological literature, and comment critically upon each one from the standpoint of the conception of culture set forth in this paper.

I.   "*Culture consists of ideas.*" Some anthropologists like to define culture in terms of ideas only. The reason for this, apparently, is the notion that ideas are both basic and primary, that they are prime movers and as such originate behavior which in turn may produce objects such as pottery bowls. "Culture consists of ideas," says Taylor;[30] it "is a mental phenomenon ... not ... material objects or observable behavior. ... For example, there is present in an Indian's mind the idea of a dance. This is the trait of culture. This idea influences his body so that he behaves in a certain way," i.e., he dances.

This conception of sociocultural reality is a naive one. It is based upon a primitive, prescientific, and now obsolete metaphysics and psychology. It was Thought-Woman among the Keresan Pueblo Indians who brought about events by thinking and willing them to happen. Ptah created Egyptian culture by objectifying his thoughts. And God said "Let there be light," and there was light. But we no longer explain the origin and development of culture by simply saying that it has resulted from man's ideas. To be sure, an idea was involved in the invention of firearms, but we have explained nothing when we say that firearms are the fruit of thought, because the ideas themselves have not been accounted for. Why did the idea occur when and where it did rather than at some other time and place? And, actually, ideas—matter of fact, realistic ideas—enter the mind from the outside world. It was working with soils that gave man, or woman, the idea of pottery; the calendar is a by-product of intensive agriculture. Culture does indeed consist in part of ideas; but attitudes, overt acts, and objects are culture, also.

II.   "*Culture consists of abstractions.*" We return now to the presently popular definition: "culture is an abstraction, or consists of abstractions." As we observed earlier, those who define culture in these terms do not tell us what they mean by "abstraction," and there is reason to believe that they are not very clear as to what they do mean by it. They make it emphatically clear, however, that an abstraction is not an observable thing or event. The fact that doubts have been raised as to the "reality" of an abstraction indicates that those who use this term are not sure what "it means," i.e., what they mean by it. We do have some clues, however.

Culture is "basically a form or pattern or way," say Kroeber and Kluckhohn;[31] "even a culture trait is an abstraction. A trait is an 'ideal type'—because no two pots are identical nor are two marriage ceremonies ever held in precisely the same way." The culture trait "pot" therefore appears to be the ideal form of which each particular pot is an exemplification—a sort of Platonic idea, or ideal. Each and every pot, they reason, is real; but the "ideal" is never realized in any particular pot. It is like the "typical American man": $5'8\frac{1}{2}''$ high, weighs 164.378 pounds, is married, has 2.3 children, and so on. This is, we suppose, what they mean by an abstraction. If so, we know it well: it is a conception in the mind of the observer, the scientist.

There is a slightly different way of looking at an "abstraction." No two marriage ceremonies are ever held in precisely the same way. Well, let us tabulate a large sample of marriage ceremonies. We find that 100 percent contain element a (mutual acceptance of spouses). Ninety-nine percent contain element b. Elements c, d, and e

[30] Walter W. Taylor, *A Study of Archaeology*, American Anthropological Association Memoir No. 69, pp. 98–110.

[31] Kroeber and Kluckhohn, 1952, pp. 155, 169.

appear in only 96, 94, and 89 percent, respectively, of the cases. We construct a distribution curve and determine an average or norm about which all particular instances are distributed. This is the typical marriage ceremony. But, like the typical American who has 2.3 children, this ideal is never fully and perfectly realized in any actual instance. It is an "abstraction," that is, a conception, worked out by the scientific observer and which exists in his own mind.

The failure to recognize the fact that abstractions are conceptions has led to confusion both as to their locus and their reality. Recognition of the fact that the so-called abstractions of science (such as a "rigid body" in physical theory; rigid bodies do not exist in actuality) are conceptions in the mind of the scientist clears up both these points: cultural "abstractions" are conceptions ("ideas") in the mind of the anthropologist. And as for their "ontological reality," conceptions are none the less real for being in the minds of men—nothing is more real, for example, than an hallucination.

This point was well made by Bidney in his review of *Culture, A Critical Review etc.*:

> The real crux of the problem centers about what is meant by abstraction and what is its ontological import. Some anthropologists maintain that they are dealing only with logical abstractions and that culture has no reality other than that of an abstraction, but they can hardly expect other social scientists to agree with them, conceding that the objects of their sciences have no ontological, objective reality. *Thus Kroeber and Kluckhohn have confused the concept culture, which is a logical construct, with the actual existential culture* . . . [emphasis ours].[32]

It is interesting to note in this connection that one anthropological theorist, Cornelius Osgood,[33] has defined culture explicitly as consisting of ideas in the minds of anthropologists: "Culture consists of all ideas of the manufactures, behavior, and ideas of the aggregate of human beings which have been directly observed or communicated to one's mind and of which one is conscious." Spiro,[34] also, holds that "culture is a logical construct, abstracted from human behavior, and as such, it exists only in the mind of *the investigator*" (Spiro's emphasis).

III.   "*There is no such thing as 'material' culture.*" Those who define culture in terms of ideas, or as an abstraction, or as behavior, find themselves obliged logically to declare that material objects are not, and cannot be, culture. "Strictly speaking," says Hoebel,[35] "material culture is really not culture at all." Taylor[36] goes farther: ". . . the concept of 'material culture' is fallacious" because "culture is a mental phenomenon." Beals and Hoijer:[37] ". . . culture is an abstraction from behavior and not to be confused with acts of behavior or with material artifacts, such as tools. . . ." This denial of

---

[32] David Bidney, "Review of Culture, A Critical Review, etc.," by Kroeber and Kluckhohn, *American Journal of Sociology*, LIX (1954), 488–489.

[33] Cornelius Osgood, "Culture: Its Empirical and Non-Empirical Character," *Southwestern Journal of Anthropology*, VII (1951), 208.

Cornelius Osgood, *Ingalik Material Culture*. Yale University Publications in Anthropology No. 22, 1940.

[34] Spiro, 1951, p. 24.

[35] E. Adamson Hoebel, "The Nature of Culture" in *Man, Culture and Society*, Harry L. Shapiro, ed. (New York: Oxford University Press, 1956), p. 176.

[36] Taylor, 1948, pp. 98, 102.

[37] Beals and Hoijer, 1953, p. 210.

material culture is rather awkward in view of the long established tradition among ethnographers, archeologists, and museum curators of calling tools, masks, fetiches, and so on, "material culture."[38]

Our definition extricates us from this dilemma. As we have already seen, it would not be absurd to speak of sandals or pottery bowls as behavior; their significant attribute is not mere deer hide or clay, but human labor; they are congelations of human labor. But in our definition, symboling is the common factor in ideas, attitudes, acts, and objects. There are three kinds of symbolates: (1) ideas and attitudes, (2) overt acts, and (3) material objects. All may be considered in an extrasomatic context; all are to be reckoned as culture. This conception brings us back to long established usage in cultural anthropology: "Culture is that which is described in an ethnographic monograph."

 "*Reification of culture.*" There is a kind of conception of culture held by some anthropologists that is much deplored by others who call it "reification." As one who has been especially singled out as a "reifier" of culture,[39] I may say that the term is singularly inappropriate. To reify is to make a thing of that which is not a thing, such as hope, honesty, or freedom. But it is not I who have made culture things. I have merely found real things and events in the external world which are distinguishable as a class by being dependent upon symboling, and which may be treated in an extrasomatic context, and I have called these things and events culture. This is precisely what E. B. Tylor did. It is what Lowie, Wissler, and most early American anthropologists have done. To Durkheim[40] "the proposition which states that social facts [i.e., culture traits] are to be treated as things" lay "at the very basis of our method." It is not we who have reified culture; the elements comprising culture, according to our definition, were things to start with.

To be sure, if culture is defined as consisting of intangible, imponderable, ontologically unreal "abstractions," then to transform these wraiths into real, substantial bodies would indeed be to reify them. But we do not subscribe to such a definition.

V.   "*Culture: a process sui generis.*" "Culture is a thing *sui generis* . . ." said Lowie many years ago.[41] This view has been held also by Kroeber, Durkheim, and others.[42] It has been misunderstood and opposed by many. But what Lowie meant by this statement is made clear in the rest of the passage cited above[43] "Culture is a thing *sui generis* which can be explained only in terms of itself . . . the ethnologist . . . will

[38] It is interesting to note that Durkheim (Emile Durkheim, *Suicide, A Study in Sociology*, George Simpson, ed.; Glencoe, Ill.: The Free Press, 1951) who uses the term "society" when many an American anthropologist would say culture, or socio-cultural system, remarks that "it is not true that society is made up only of individuals; it also includes material things, which play an essential role in the common life." He cites as examples such things as houses, instruments and machines used in industry, etc. "Social life . . . is thus crystallized . . . and fixed on material supports . . . externalized. . . ."

[39] Max Gluckman "reifies structure in precisely the way that White reifies culture . . . ," says Murdock (George P. Murdock, "British Social Anthropology," *American Anthropologist*, LIII (1951), 465–473). Strong (Wm. Duncan Strong, "Historical Approach in Anthropology," in *Anthropology Today*, A. L. Kroeber, ed., Chicago: The University of Chicago Press, 1953, pp. 368–397) feels that "White reifies, and at times almost deifies, culture. . . ." See also C. Judson Herrick, *The Evolution of Human Nature* (Austin: University of Texas Press, 1956).

[40] Emile Durkheim, *The Rules of Sociological Method*, George E. G. Catlin, ed. (Chicago: The University of Chicago Press, 1938).

[41] Robert H. Lowie, *Culture and Ethnology* (New York: Boni and Liveright, 1917), pp. 17, 66.

[42] Leslie A. White, 1949, pp. 89–94 for citation of examples.

[43] Lowie, 1917, p. 66.

account for a given cultural fact by merging it in a group of cultural facts or by demonstrating some other cultural fact out of which it has been developed." For example, the custom of reckoning descent partilineally may be explained in terms of customs of division of labor between the sexes, customs of residence—patrilocal, matrilocal, or neolocal—of a married couple; mode of subsistence; rules of inheritance, and so on. Or, to express it in terms of our definition of culture: "a symbolate in an extrasomatic context (i.e., a culture trait) is to be explained in terms of its relationship to other symbolates in the same context."

This conception of culture, like "reification" with which it is closely related, has been much misunderstood and opposed. In general, it has been regarded as "mystical." How can culture grow and develop by itself? "Culture . . . seems to grow of itself."[44] "It seems hardly necessary," says Boas,[45] "to consider culture a mystic entity that exists outside the society of its individual carriers, and that moves by its own force." Bidney[46] brands this view of culture as a "mystical metaphysics of fate." And it has been opposed by Benedict,[47] Hooton,[48] Spiro,[49] and others.

But no one has ever said that culture is an entity that exists and moves by, and of, itself, quite apart from people. Nor has anyone ever said, as far as we know, that the origin, nature, and functions of culture can be understood without taking the human species into consideration. Obviously, if one is to understand culture in these aspects he must consider the biological nature of man. What has been asserted is that, given culture, its variations in time and place, and its processes of change are to be explained in terms of culture itself. This is precisely what Lowie meant when he said that "culture is a thing [process would have been a better term] *sui generis*," as the above quotation from him makes clear. A consideration of the human organism, individually or collectively, is irrelevant to an explanation of processes of culture change. "This is not mysticism," says Lowie,[50] "but sound scientific method." And, as everyone knows, scholars have been working in accordance with this principle of interpretation for decades. One does not need to take human organisms into account in a scientific explanation of the evolution of currency, writing, or of Gothic art. The steam engine and textile machinery were introduced into Japan during the closing decades of the nineteenth century and certain changes in social structure followed; we add nothing to our explanation of these events by remarking that human beings were involved. Of course they were. And they were not irrelevant to the events which took place, but they are irrelevant to an explanation of these events.

"*It is people, not culture, that does things.*" "Culture does not 'work,' 'move,' 'change,' but is worked, is moved, is changed. It is people who do things," says Lynd.[51] He supports this argument with the bold assertion that "culture does not enamel its fingernails . . . but people do . . ." He might have clinched it by demonstrating that culture has no fingernails.

The view that "it is people, not cultures, that do things" is widely held among

[44] Robert Redfield, *The Folk Culture of Yucatan* (Chicago: The University of Chicago Press, 1941), p. 134.
[45] Frank Boas, *Anthroplolgy and Modern Life* (New York: W. W. Norton & Company, Inc., 1928), p. 235.
[46] David Bidney, "The Concept of Cultural Crisis," *American Anthropologist*, XLVIII (1946), 535.
[47] Ruth Benedict, *Patterns of Culture* (Boston and New York: Houghton Mifflin Co., 1934), p. 231.
[48] Ernest A. Hooton, *Crime and the Man* (Cambridge, Mass.: Harvard University Press, 1939), p. 370.
[49] Spiro, 1951, p. 23.
[50] Lowie, 1917, p. 66.
[51] Robert S. Lynd, *Knowledge for What?* (Princeton, N. J.: Princeton University Press, 1939), p. 39.

anthropologists. Boas[52] tells us that "the forces that bring about the changes are active in the individuals composing the social group, not in the abstract culture." Hallowell[53] remarks that "in a literal sense cultures never have met nor will ever meet. What is meant is that peoples meet and that, as a result of the processes of social interaction, acculturation—modifications in the mode of life of one or both peoples—may take place. Individuals are the dynamic centers of this process of interaction." And Radcliffe-Brown pours fine scorn on the notion that cultures, rather than peoples, interact:

> A few years ago, as a result perhaps of re-defining social anthropology as the study, not of society, but of culture, we were asked to abandon this kind of investigation in favor of what is now called the study of "culture contact." In place of the study of the formation of new composite societies, we are supposed to regard what is happening in Africa as a process in which an entity called African culture comes into contact with an entity called European or Western culture, and a third new entity is produced ... which is to be described as Westernized African culture. To me this seems a fantastic reification of abstractions. European culture is an abstraction and so is the culture of an African tribe. I find it fantastic to imagine these two abstractions coming into contact and by an act of generation producing a third abstraction.[54]

We call this view, that people rather than culture do things, the fallacy of pseudo-realism. Of course culture does not and could not exist independently of people.[55] But, as we have pointed out earlier, cultural processes can be explained without taking human organisms into account; a consideration of human organisms is irrelevant to the solution of certain problems of culture. Whether the practice of mummification in pre-Columbian Peru was indigenous or the result of Egyptian influence is an example of a kind of problem that does not require a consideration of human organisms. To be sure the practice of mummification, its invention in Peru, or its diffusion from Egypt to the Andean highlands, could not have taken place without the action of real, flesh-and-blood human beings. Neither could Einstein have worked out the theory of relativity without breathing, but we do not need to take his respiration into account when we trace the history, or explain the development, of this theory.

Those who argue that it is people, not culture, that do this or that mistake a description of what they see for an explanation of these events. Seated in the Senate gallery they see men making laws; in the shipyards men are building freighters; in the laboratory human beings are isolating enzymes; in the fields they are planting corn, and so on. And, for them, a description of these events, as they observe them, is a simple explanation of them: it is people who pass laws, build freighters, plant corn, and isolate enzymes. This is a simple and naive form of anthropocentrism.   ??

A scientific explanation is more sophisticated. If a person speaks Chinese, or

---

[52] Boas, 1928, p. 236.

[53] A. Irving Hallowell, "Sociopsychological Aspects of Acculturation," in *The Science of Man in the World Crisis*, Ralph Linton, ed. (New York: Columbia University Press, 1945), p. 175.

[54] Radcliffe-Brown, 1940, pp. 10–11.

[55] "To be sure, these cultural events could not have taken place had it not been for human organisms ... the culturologist knows full well that culture traits do not go walking about like disembodied souls interacting with each other ..." (White, *The Science of Culture*, pp. 99–100).

avoids his mother-in-law, loathes milk, observes matrilocal residence, places the bodies of the dead on scaffolds, writes symphonies, or isolates enzymes, it is because he has been born into, or at least reared within, an extrasomatic tradition that we call culture which contains these elements. A people's behavior is a response to, a function of, their culture. The culture is the independent, the behavior the dependent, variable; as the culture varies so will the behavior. This is, of course, a commonplace that is usually expounded and demonstrated during the first two weeks of an introductory course in anthropology. It is indeed people who treat disease with prayers and charms or with vaccines and antibiotics. But the question, "Why does one people use charms while another uses vaccines?" is not explained by saying that "this people does this, that people does that." It is precisely this proposition that needs to be explained: why do they do what they do? The scientific explanation does not take the people into account at all. And as for the question, "Why does one extrasomatic tradition use charms while another uses vaccines?" this also is one to which a consideration of people, of human organisms, is irrelevant; it is answered culturologically: culture, as Lowie has observed, is to be explained in terms of culture.

Culture "cannot be realistically disconnected from those organizations of ideas and feelings which constitute the individual," i.e., culture cannot be realistically disconnected from individuals, says Sapir.[56] He is quite right, of course; in actuality culture is inseparable from human beings. But if culture cannot be realistically (in actuality) disconnected from individuals it most certainly can be disconnected in logical (scientific) analysis, and no one has done a better job of "disconnecting" than Edward Sapir: there is not a single Indian—or even a nerve, muscle, or sense organ— in his monograph, *Southern Paiute, a Shoshonean Language*.[57] Nor are there any people roaming about in his *Time Perspective in Aboriginal American Culture*.[58] "Science must abstract some elements and neglect others," says Morris Cohen[59] "because *not all things that exist together are relevant to each other*" (emphasis ours). Comprehension and appreciation of this fact would be an enormous asset to ethnological theory. "Citizenship cannot be realistically disconnected from eye color," i.e., every citizen has eyes and every eye has a color. But, in the United States at least, color of eyes is not relevant to citizenship: "things that exist together are not always relevant to each other."

And so it is perfectly true, as Hallowell, Radcliffe-Brown, and others say, that "it is *peoples* who meet and interact." But this should not keep us from confining our attention, in the solution of certain problems, to symbolates in an extrasomatic context: to tools, utensils, customs, beliefs, and attitudes; in short, to culture. The meeting and mixing of European culture with African culture and the production thereby of a mixture, Euro-African culture, may seem "a fantastic reification of abstractions" to Radcliffe-Brown and others. But anthropologists have been concerned with problems of this sort for decades and will continue to deal with them. The intermingling of customs, technologies, and ideologies is just as valid a scientific problem as the intermingling of human organisms or genes.

[56] Edward Sapir, 1932, p. 233.

[57] Edward Sapir, "Southern Paiute, A Shoshonean Language," *Proceedings of the American Academy of Arts and Sciences*, LXV, 1–296.

[58] Edward Sapir, "Time Perspective in Aboriginal American Culture," *Canada Department of Mines, Geological Survey Memoir No. 90*, 1916, Ottawa.

[59] Morris R. Cohen, "Fictions," *Encyclopedia of the Social Sciences*, VII (New York: The Macmillan Co., 1931).

We have not asserted, nor do we imply, that anthropologists in general have failed to treat culture as a process *sui generis*, i.e., without taking human organisms into account; many, if not most, cultural anthropologists have in fact done this. But some of them, when they turn to theory, deny the validity of this kind of interpretation. Radcliffe-Brown himself provides us with examples of purely culturological problems and culturological solutions thereof—in "The Social Organization of Australian Tribes,"[60] "The Mother's Brother in South Africa,"[61] etc. But when he dons the philosopher's cap he denies that this procedure is scientifically valid.[62]

However, some anthropologists have recognized, on the theoretical level, that culture can be scientifically studied without taking human organisms into account, that a consideration of human organisms is irrelevant to the solution of problems dealing with extrasomatic traditions. We have cited a number—Tylor, Durkheim, Kroeber, Lowie, et al.—who have done this. But we may add one or two new references here. "The best hope . . . for parsimonious description and 'explanation' of cultural phenomena," say Kroeber and Kluckhohn[63] "seems to rest in the study of cultural forms and processes as such, largely . . . abstracted from individuals and personalities." And Steward remarks that "certain aspects of a modern culture can best be studied quite apart from individual behavior. The structure and function of a system of money, banking, and credit, for example, represents supra-individual aspects of culture." Also, he says: "form of government, legal system, economic institutions, religious organizations, educational systems," and so on, "have aspects which are national . . . in scope and which must be understood apart from the behavior of the individuals connected with them."[64]

There is nothing new about this; anthropologists and other social scientists have been doing this for decades. But it seems to be difficult for some of them to accept this as a matter of theory and principle as well as of actual practice.

VII .   "*It takes two or more to make a culture.*" There is a conception, not uncommon in ethnological theory, that whether a phenomenon is an element of culture or not depends upon whether it is expressed by one, two, or "several" individuals. Thus Linton[65] says that "any item of behavior . . . which is peculiar to a single individual in a society is not to be considered as a part of the society's culture. . . . Thus a new technique for weaving baskets would not be classed as a part of culture as long as it was known only to one person." Wissler,[66] Osgood,[67] Malinowski,[68] Durkheim,[69] have subscribed to this view.

Two objections may be raised against this conception of culture: (1) if plurality of expression of learned behavior be the significant distinction between culture and not-culture, then the chimpanzees described by Wolfgang Köhler in *The Mentality of Apes* (New York, 1925) had culture, for innovations made by a single individual were

[60] A. R. Radcliffe-Brown, "The Social Organization of Australian Tribes," *Oceania*, I, 34–63, 206–246, 322–341, 426–456.

[61] A. R. Radcliffe-Brown, "The Mother's Brother in South Africa," *South African Journal of Science*, XXI (1924), 542–555. Reprinted in *Structure and Function in Primitive Society*.

[62] White, *The Science of Culture*, pp. 96–98, for further discussion of this point.

[63] Kroeber and Kluckhohn, 1952, p. 167.

[64] Julian H. Steward, *Theory of Culture Change* (Urbana, Ill.: University of Illinois Press, 1955), pp. 46, 47.

[65] Ralph Linton, *The Cultural Background of Personality* (New York: D. Appleton-Century Co., 1945) p. 35.

[66] Clark Wissler, *Introduction to Social Anthropology* (New York: Henry Holt and Co., 1929).

[67] Osgood, 1951, pp. 207–208.

[68] Bronislaw Malinowski, "Man's Culture and Man's Behaviour," *Sigma Xi Quarterly*, XXIX, 170–196.

[69] Durkheim, 1938, p. lvi.

often quickly adopted by the whole group. Other subhuman species also would have culture according to this criterion. (2) The second objection is: if expression by one person is not enough to qualify an act as a cultural element, how many persons will be required? Linton[70] says that "as soon as this new thing has been transmitted to and is shared by even one other individual in the society, it must be reckoned as a part of culture." Osgood[71] requires "two or more." Durkheim[72] needs "several individuals, at the very least." Wissler[73] says that an item does not rise to the level of a culture trait until a standardized procedure is established in the group. And Malinowski[74] states that a "cultural fact starts when an individual interest becomes transformed into public, common, and transferable systems of organized endeavor."

Obviously such a conception does not meet the requirements of science. What agreement could one find on the point at which an "individual interest becomes transformed into public, common, and transferable systems of organized endeavor"? Or, suppose an ornithologist said that if there were but one specimen of a kind of bird it could not be a carrier pigeon or a whooping crane, but that if there were an indefinite number then they could be pigeons or cranes. Or, suppose a physicist said that if there were but one atom of a certain element that it could not be copper, but if there were "a lot of such atoms" then it might properly be called copper. One wants a definition that says that item x belongs to class y or it does not, regardless of how many items of x there may be (and a class, in logic, may have only one member, or even none).

Our definition meets the requirements of a scientific definition: an item—a conception or belief, an act, or an object—is to be reckoned an element of culture (1) if it is dependent upon symboling, and (2) when it is considered in an extrasomatic context. To be sure, all cultural elements exist in a social context; but so do such nonhuman (not dependent upon symboling) traits as grooming, suckling, and mating exist in a social matrix. But it is not sociality, duality, or plurality that distinguishes a human, or cultural, phenomenon from a nonhuman or noncultural phenomenon. The distinguishing characteristic is symboling. Secondly, whether a thing or an event can be considered in an extrasomatic context does not depend upon whether there is only one such thing or event, or two, or "several." A thing or event may be properly considered an element of culture even if it is the only member of its class, just as an atom of copper would still be an atom of copper even if it were the only one of its kind in the cosmos.

And, of course, we might have pointed out in the first place that the notion that an act or an idea in human society might be wholly the work of a single individual is an illusion, another one of the sorry pitfalls of anthropocentrism. Every member of human society is of course always subjected to sociocultural stimulation from the members of his group. Whatever a man does as a human being, and much of what he does as a mere animal, is a function of his group as well as of his organism. Any human act, even in its first expression in the person of a single individual, is a group product to begin with.[75]

---

[70] Linton, 1936, p.274.

[71] Osgood, 1951, p. 208.

[72] Durkheim, 1938, p. lvi.

[73] Wissler, 1929, p. 358.

[74] Malinowski, 1941, p. 73.

[75] More than one hundred years ago Karl Marx wrote: "Man is in the most literal sense of the word a *zoon politikon*, not only a social animal, but an animal which can develop into an individual only in society.

VIII.   *Culture as "characteristic" traits.* "Culture may be defined," says Boas,[76] "as the totality of the mental and physical reactions and activities that *characterize* the behavior of the individuals composing a social group . . ." (emphasis ours). Herskovits[77] tells us that "when culture is closely analyzed, we find but a series of patterned reactions that characterize the behavior of the individuals who constitute a given group." (Just what "close analysis" has to do with this conception is not clear.) Sapir[78]: "The mass of typical reactions called culture. . . ." This view has, of course, been held by others.

Two objections may be raised against this conception of culture: (1) how does one determine which traits characterize a group and which traits do not—how does one draw the line between the two classes, culture and not-culture? And, (2) if we call the traits that characterize a group *culture,* what are we to call those traits that do not characterize it?

It seems probable that anthropologists who hold this view are really thinking of *a* culture, or cultures, plural, rather than of culture in general, culture as a particular kind of phenomena. Thus, "French culture" might be distinguished from "English culture" by those traits which characterize each. But if, on the one hand, the French and the English may be distinguished from each other by differences of traits, they will on the other hand be found to be very similar to each other in their possession of like traits. And the traits that resemble each other are just as much a part of the "way of life" of each people as the traits that differ. Why should only one class be called culture?

These difficulties and uncertainties are done away with by our conception of culture: culture consists of all of the ways of life of each people which are dependent upon symboling and which are considered in an extrasomatic context. If one wished to distinguish the English from the French on the basis of their respective culture traits he could easily specify "those traits which characterize" the people in question. But he would not assert that nontypical traits were not culture.

In this connection we may note a very interesting distinction drawn by Sapir[79] between the behavior of individuals and "culture."

It is always the individual that really thinks and acts and dreams and revolts. Those of his thoughts, acts, dreams, and rebellions that somehow contribute in sensible degree to the modification or retention of the mass of typical reactions called culture we term social data; *the rest, though they do not, psychologically considered, in the least differ from these, we term individual and pass by as of no historical or social moment* [i.e., they are not culture]. It is highly important to note that the differentiation of these two types of reaction is essentially arbitrary, resting, as it does, entirely on a principle of selection. The selection depends on the adoption of a scale of values. Needless to say, the threshold of the social (or historical) [i.e., cultural] *versus* the individual

Production by isolated individuals outside of society . . . is as great an absurdity as the idea of the development of language without individuals living together and talking to one another," *A Contribution to the Critique of Political Economy* (Chicago: Charles H. Kerr & Co., 1904), p. 268.

[76] Frank Boas, *The Mind of Primitive Man,* Revised Edition (New York: The Macmillan Co., 1938), p. 159.
[77] Melville J. Herskovits, *Man and His Works* (New York: Alfred A. Knopf, 1948), p. 28.
[78] Edward Sapir, "Do We Need a Superorganic?" in *American Anthropologist,* XIX (1917), 442.
[79] Sapir, 1917, p. 442.

shifts according to the philosophy of the evaluator or interpreter. I find it utterly inconceivable to draw a sharp and eternally valid dividing line between them [emphases ours].

Sapir finds himself confronted by a plurality, or aggregation, of individuals. (He would have preferred this wording rather than "society," we believe, for he speaks of "a theoretical [fictitious?] community of human beings," adding that "the term 'society' itself is a cultural construct.") These individuals do things: dream, think, act, and revolt. And "it is always the individual," not society or culture, who does these things. What Sapir finds then is: individuals and their behavior; nothing more.

Some of the behavior of individuals is culture, says Sapir. But other elements of their behavior are not-culture, although, as he says, psychologically considered they do not differ in the slightest from those elements which he calls culture. The line thus drawn between "culture" and "not-culture" is purely arbitrary, and depends upon the subjective evaluation of the one who is drawing the line.

A conception of culture could hardly be less satisfactory than this one. It says, in effect: "culture is the name that we give to some of the behavior of some individuals, the selection being arbitrary and made in accordance with subjective criteria."

In the essay from which we have been quoting, "Do We Need a Super-organic?" Sapir is opposing the culturological point of view presented by Kroeber in "The Superorganic." He (Sapir) virtually makes culture disappear; it is dissolved into the totality of the reactions of individuals. Culture becomes, as he has else-where called it, a "statistical fiction."[80] If there is no significant reality that one can call culture, then there can be no science of culture. Sapir's argument was skillful and persuasive. But it was also unsound, or at least misleading.

Sapir's argument was persuasive because he bolstered it with authentic, demonstrable fact. It was unsound or misleading because he made it appear that the only significant distinction between the behavior of individuals and culture is the one that he had made.

It is perfectly true that the elements which comprise the human behavior of individuals and the elements which comprise culture are identical classes of things and events. All are symbolates—dependent upon man's unique ability to symbol. It is true, also, that "psychologically considered," they are all alike. But Sapir overlooks, and by his argument effectively obscures, the fact that there are two fundamentally different kinds of contexts in which these "thinkings, actings, dreamings, and revolts" can be considered for purposes of scientific interpretation and explanation: the somatic and the extrasomatic. Considered in a somatic context, i.e., in terms of their relationship to the human organism, these acts dependent upon symboling constitute *human behavior*. Considered in an extrasomatic context, i.e., in terms of their relationships to one another, these acts constitute *culture*. Instead, therefore, of arbitrarily putting some in the category of culture and the rest in the category of human behavior, we put all acts, thoughts, and things dependent upon symboling in either one context or the other, somatic or extrasomatic, depending upon the nature of our problem.

Summary. Among the many significant classes of things and events distinguish-able by science there is one for which science has had no name. This is the class of

---

[80] Sapir, 1932, p. 237.

phenomena dependent upon symboling, a faculty peculiar to the human species. We have proposed that things and events dependent upon symboling be called symbolates. The particular designation of this class is not as important, however, as that it be given a name of some kind in order that its distinction from other classes be made explicit.

Things and events dependent upon symboling comprise ideas, beliefs, attitudes, sentiments, acts, patterns of behavior, customs, codes, institutions, works and forms of art, languages, tools, implements, machines, utensils, ornaments, fetiches, charms, and so on.

Things and events dependent upon symboling may be, and traditionally have been, referred to two fundamentally different contexts for purposes of observation, analysis, and explanation. These two contexts may properly and appropriately be called somatic and extrasomatic. When an act, object, idea or attitude is considered in the somatic context it is the relationship between that thing or event and the human organism that is significant. Things and events dependent upon symboling considered in the somatic context may properly be called human behavior—at least, ideas, attitudes, and acts may; stone axes and pottery bowls are not customarily called behavior, but their significance is derived from the fact that they have been produced by human labor; they are, in fact, congelations of human behavior. When things and events are considered in the extrasomatic context they are regarded in terms of the interrelationships among themselves rather than in terms of their relationship to the human organism, individually or collectively. Culture is the name of things and events dependent upon symboling considered in an extrasomatic context.

Our analysis and distinctions have these advantages. The distinctions made are clear cut and fundamental. Culture is clearly distinguished from human behavior. Culture has been defined as all sciences must define their subject matter, namely, in terms of real things and events, observable directly or indirectly in the actual world that we live in. Our conception rescues anthropology from the incubus of intangible, imperceptible, imponderable "abstractions" that have no ontological reality.

Our definition extricates us, also, from the dilemmas in which many other conceptions place us, such as whether culture consists of ideas and whether these ideas have their locus in the minds of peoples studied or in the minds of anthropologists; whether material objects can or cannot be culture; whether a trait must be shared by two, three, or several people in order to count as culture; whether traits have to characterize a people or not in order to be culture; whether culture is a reification or not, and whether a culture can enamel its fingernails.

Our distinction between human behavior and culture, between psychology and culturology, is precisely like the one that has been in use for decades between speech and language, between the psychology of speech and the science of linguistics. If it is valid for the one it is valid for the other.

Finally, our distinction and definition are in very close accord with anthropological tradition. This is what Tylor meant by culture, as a reading of *Primitive Culture* will make clear. It is the one that has actually been used by almost all nonbiological anthropologists. What is it that scientific field workers among primitive peoples have studied and described in their monographs? Answer: real observable things and events dependent upon symboling. It can hardly be said that they were studying and describing imperceptible, intangible, imponderable, ontologically unreal abstractions. To be sure, the field worker may be interested in things and events in their somatic context, in which case he would be doing psychology (as he would be if he considered words in their somatic context). And anthropology, as this term is actually used, embraces a number of different kinds of studies: anatomical, physiological, genetic, psychological, psychoanalytic, and culturological. But this does not mean that the distinction between psychology and culturology is not fundamental. It is.

The thesis presented in this paper is no novelty. It is not a radical departure from anthropological tradition. On the contrary, it is in a very real sense and to a great extent a return to tradition, the tradition established by Tylor and followed in practice by countless anthropologists since his day. We have merely given it concise and overt verbal expression.

2-3   THE FUNCTIONS OF CULTURE

John Biesanz and Mavis Biesanz

John Biesanz is professor of sociology and anthropology and director of the social science program at Wayne State University. He obtained his Ph.D. in sociology from the University of Iowa, and has served as an exchange professor to Costa Rica, a research associate at Tulane University, a Smith-Mundt Professor to Guatemala, and a Fulbright scholar to Germany. He has written extensively on Latin American countries, on marriage and the family, and on modern society. This description of what culture does was taken from an introductory sociology text written in collaboration with his wife, Mavis Biesanz.

Man's culture serves him in three ways: (1) It adapts man as a biological species to his environment; (2) It provides the individual with ready-made adjustments to his natural environment, his fellows, and his own biological and psychological needs and drives; and (3) It ensures the unity and survival of the social group. . . .

WHAT CULTURE DOES FOR THE INDIVIDUAL

Culture provides the individual with a blueprint for behavior, thought, and feeling in almost any situation. The newborn baby no more analyzes the culture into which he is born than he analyzes the air before he breathes it. The culture is there, and the intimate groups with which the child is associated most closely during his early years—family, play group, school, and church—teach him the ways of the culture as if there were no others. If he questions with a rebellious "Why?" he hears, "Because that's the way it's done."

Culture provides for the satisfaction of the individual's biological needs. He does not have to work out a way to keep warm, to satisfy hunger and thirst, to fulfill his sexual desires, to get his rest. Patterns that regulate and channel these elemental functions are present in the culture and confront the child from infancy on. He is taught how and when and where he may satisfy his needs. He learns the diet pattern of his

---

John Biesanz and Mavis Biesanz, *Modern Society: An Introduction to Social Science*, pp. 59–71. © 1954, by permission of Prentice-Hall, Inc., Englewood Cliffs, N. J.

culture, modesty and hygiene of elimination, proper conduct in sexual affairs, patterns of propriety in dress. Culture heightens man's satisfaction of biological pleasures by building upon them an enormous superstructure of ritual. In our culture, for example, eating is made more pleasurable by concentrating upon the preparation and serving of food; in some cultures feasting and fasting alternate to heighten enjoyment. Sexual restrictions also heighten interest in eventual satisfaction. And nowhere is man satisfied merely to cover his nakedness for the sake of warmth and modesty; style or fashion in dress has been an area of great interest in most cultures.

Culture not only provides patterns for satisfying man's elemental needs, but also *creates* needs. A person's desire for cigarettes or alcohol may be just as compelling as his requirements for food or sleep. His need for success or wealth in a culture where these things are highly valued is often stronger than his sexual drives. The present-day American needs many things that his parents got along without, because many items previously unknown or considered luxuries are now defined in our culture as necessary to the good, full life—a new-model car, a TV set, a one-story house with a picture window, season tickets to the opera or symphony, a college degree, a fur coat.

Culture provides the individual with ready-made explanations of the origin of man, the nature of the universe, and man's role. These may be mystical or superstitious explanations, or they may be in large part scientific. In either case, they answer fundamental questions. Culture determines whether a child asking about a thunderstorm will be told that the god Thor is angry and throwing his hammer across the sky, or that the storm is a natural phenomenon caused by atmospheric pressure and electrical charges. The modern schoolboy may be told the story of Thor as an interesting myth, and may, in spite of his scientific knowledge, also imitate his mother's unreasoning fear of the storm.

Culture defines situations for its participants. It provides them with meanings for things and events. The individual's definitions of what is natural and unnatural, logical and illogical, normal and abnormal, moral and immoral, beautiful and ugly, important and unimportant, interesting and uninteresting, and good and bad, are derived from his culture. In a broader sense, culture gives meaning to life, purpose to existence. It provides the individual with values and goals, hopes and aspirations, "something to live for."

Culture also largely determines a person's fears. In one culture, a strong warrior may quail at the sight of a menstruating woman. His culture defines such an occurrence as dangerous and requires that women be isolated at this time. The early settlers of New England feared witchcraft. A generation ago many Americans feared a penniless old age; today many of us fear that we may not reach old age at all because of such threats as the atomic bomb.

Culture gives men a conscience. This is not an inborn, universally similar trait. It may be a still, small inner voice, but it comes from the group's definitions of right and wrong. It results from the *internalization* of the group's values and standards, their incorporation into the personality. When a person violates these standards, he feels ashamed or guilty, even when there is slight chance of his being found out. Conscience exercises a strong control over his behavior. In our culture, pre-marital sex relations arouse guilt feelings; in some they do not. A Catholic's conscience will prevent his eating meat on Friday, or trouble him if he does so; but a Protestant does not have this standard to live up to. Both, if members of American society, typically find conscience an effective deterrent to rape, murder, or bigamy.

A common culture gives men a sense of belonging or identification. It binds men together into a "we-group" in contrast to those of another culture. Going over to Europe on a freighter some years ago, I felt I had little in common with several other young fellows making the same trip, and they evidently felt the same way about me. After two weeks of the strange ways of Holland and Belgium, we ran into one another on the street, greeted one another like long lost friends, and spent most of the next several days together. We shared a common language and common understandings. For the same reason, immigrants to America cluster into colonies.

Culture adapts a person to his place in society. Every culture provides means of training persons for their role and position in the group. Patterns exist for a good housewife, a good farmer, a good President, a good teacher, a good clergyman, and so forth.

Culture is the nourishing milieu for personality. Just as the available foods affect one's bodily condition and growth, determining whether or not the person will reach the potential limit of his stature and strength and good looks, so the available culture is food for the personality. If a person is born into a society where food is scarce and limited, he will probably be small and stunted and weak; if he is born into a culture that is meager, he will have a meager personality. No matter how intelligent, how innately capable of great achievement, the individual cannot surpass the bounds of the culture with which he comes into contact (though he may build inventions upon its existing elements). As Gray's "Elegy Written in a Country Churchyard" says, "Some mute inglorious Milton here may rest, Some Cromwell guiltless of his country's blood." The limited rural culture of the forgotten dead did not give the scope to their innate abilities that the richer life of London would have offered.

A rich and complex culture presents the individual with challenges and opportunities. Just as one may wisely choose from the food available a nutritious and varied and enjoyable fare, or stick to a habitual but poorly planned diet, so an individual may avail himself of the cultural environment in wise and profitable manner or neglect its potentialities and his own.

All that has been said impresses us with the profound influence of culture on the individual. It should not be assumed, however, that all members of a society are mere rubber stamps produced by cultural patterns. Common sense observation shows that this is by no means the case. Within the limits imposed by our culture, which dictates a certain proper apparel for campus wear, certain general types of hairdos, a common language, and a daily routine and etiquette, your classmates are definitely individual personalities. It is not necessary to go into this subject more deeply here. Our purpose is simply to point out that the individual is not merely a sponge soaking up culture. . . . Because of biological and temperamental differences, unique life experiences, and other factors, one person's version of the culture is different from another's, even if both are members of the same family. Furthermore, the individual is the instrument initiating culture change. Rebellious and unconventional though he may be, the major portion of his personality, nonetheless, reflects the cultural influences already mentioned.

CULTURE AS SOCIAL CONTROL

Culture fulfills its third function, that of ensuring the unity and survival of society, by (1) providing patterns for the behavior of individuals and groups within the society, (2) providing means of teaching individuals to behave according to these patterns, or "rules of the game," and (3) providing means of enforcing correct behavior. (You will notice we have not said, "*Culture* teaches the individual to behave and enforces his correct behavior"; culture is the *pattern*; groups and individuals put the patterns into action.)

All these three very closely related functions of culture are aspects of *social control, the means by which society establishes and maintains order.* Every society has a system of social control. Does this mean that no one living in society is really free? Are not freedom and control contradictory terms?

Since the individual cannot exist without society, and society cannot function without controls, the individual's very existence depends upon social control. A child growing up alone, provided in some fantastic fashion with the biological essentials of life—would he be free? Perhaps he would be, in the sense that an animal is free; but he would not be free to develop his potentialities as a human being. Culture provides that freedom; paradoxically enough, it does so by its very nature as a set of patterns for behavior. The individual masters the routine habits of dressing, eating, walking, getting to and from his place of work, using language in speech and reading and writing, and makes them so habitual that they require little conscious thought and effort. These habits free his mind and energy for more creative thought and action and enjoyment of life. Furthermore, by patterning the behavior of many individuals and groups within a society, culture makes it possible to predict the behavior of others, and thus enables the group to function more or less smoothly. Much wasted effort and conflict are eliminated by the control that culture exercises over the behavior of members of a society.

Obviously the system of social control is different from culture to culture. The patterns vary, the methods of indoctrinating the individual vary, and the methods of enforcing adherence to the patterns vary. In some cultures all the life situations are defined for the individual; in others only crucial ones are defined, and a person is left free to make a number of choices.

The cultural norms, the standards or patterns of behavior expected by a group, may be classified as customs (folkways and mores), laws, and the systems of folkways, mores, and laws called institutions. These group expectations govern a great portion of behavior in every society. There is, however, some margin for undefined acts or *permissive behavior* in which the individual chooses his own way of doing things with no fear of social disapproval or punishment. This margin is relatively greater in urban society than in rural or nonliterate societies. There are also less enduring forms of cultural behavior such as fads, fashions, and crazes.

I.   *Customs.* Customs are group habits. They are usually classified into two main types, differing not in kind, but in degree of importance to the society and degree of compulsion attached to their observance. These two general types of customs are *folkways* and *mores*.

A.   *Folkways.* Folkways are behavior patterns that define the proper, accepted way of doing things. They arose long ago, gradually and by chance; and as they were passed from one generation to another, they developed the authority of tradition. (This much of our description also holds true of the mores.) The folkways govern most of the routine of daily living and ordinary contacts with other people. A person who does not conform to the folkways is regarded as rude, ignorant, uncouth, or just "queer."

Many folkways, like language, money, systems of weights and measures, driving on the right- or left-hand side of the road, and the like, are purely arbitrary conveniences. Others are rituals of behavior, like the method of celebrating a girl's coming of age, the number of meals per day (our "three squares" and a snack), or business hours (nine to five, or in Latin America eight to six with two hours in midday when all stores and offices are closed up tight for a siesta). Folkways define "men's work" and "women's work." They set up ideals for gentlemanly or ladylike conduct. They provide patterns for greeting friends, from the casual "Hi!" we Americans so often use to the elaborate hat-doffing, hand-shaking, shoulder-patting routine, accompanied by inquiries after one's health and that of one's entire family, which are typical of encounters between middle-class Costa Ricans. The folkways govern our general style of housing, dress, recreation, child-rearing, courtship, and so on. Folkways compose the large underlying body of custom that is strongly rooted in tradition and are by no means superficial or transitory.

Nonetheless, folkways change. The authors can remember when their mothers disapproved of lipstick, nail polish, bobbed hair, and women's smoking; so strongly, in fact, that one might say they considered it not only improper, but verging upon the immoral to use them. Three decades later both mothers use lipstick and wear their hair short; one smokes an occasional cigarette and uses nail polish. Another folkway that is changing is the custom of rising for women on the bus or trolley. Today, probably employing the rationalization that women are competing with them in the workaday world and that even the shopping housewives are probably less tired than they are (what with all their labor-saving conveniences!), men rarely offer their seats to women. In fact, those who rise for expectant mothers or those with small children, or for elderly or ill-looking women, are most often matrons who can readily sympathize with others of their own sex. From a rational standpoint, strong young men and women, say of high-school and college age, should be the least in need of seats, but they seem to feel that their classmates would regard them as "sissy" if they made such a polite gesture.

Some behavior patterns are of such recent origin and so closely associated with new technological developments that they can hardly be called folkways. A convenient term for them is *technicways*. These are often skills, such as driving an auto and using modern appliances, or behaviors, such as watching movies or TV.

B. *Mores.* Mores are those customs that are considered vital to the welfare of the group. Mores are not simply proper, like folkways; they are obligatory. They are intimately tied up with the dominant values of the culture, and like values they are often so deeply imbedded in the personalities of individuals, so taken for granted, that they are not verbalized or consciously formulated. The mores define right and wrong, moral and immoral, without having to answer "Why?" Their violation brings strong disapproval, ostracism, or punishment by others, and produces a sense of sin or wrong-doing in the violator. They may be expressed in terms of "must-behavior" or "Thou shalt"; or they may be negative mores, "Thou shalt not," in which case they are *taboos*.

In our culture, the mores include wearing a certain amount of clothing, having only one husband or wife at a time, and being loyal to our country. Bigamy, murder, theft, treason, and incest are among our taboos.

The mores can make anything right. Like folkways, mores vary from culture to culture. In some cultures it is moral to have several wives, to wear only a loincloth, or to be loyal to a leader whom others would regard as a tyrant. In others it is considered right to kill baby girls or helpless old people. Cannibalism has been considered moral in some cultures. In fact, cannibals are shocked at the conduct of modern warfare—to slaughter our enemies and then allow all those bodies to go to waste! Even incest, which is almost universally tabooed, has been moral in some societies under certain situations. The Ptolemies of Egypt were considered too royal to marry anyone but a brother or sister.

The folkways of other cultures are apt to strike us as interesting, amusing, exotic, colorful, and fantastic. The mores are likely, if they differ sharply from our own, to shock and horrify us; we cannot conceive of such behavior; it is wrong, sinful, immoral. Other peoples often feel the same way about our customs, though anthropologists have found that some presumably primitive peoples are much more tolerant of strange ways than we are.

Mores, like folkways, are subject to change, but somewhat more painfully and slowly than the folkways. Some customs pass from the mores into the folkways, but while they are changing it is hard to tell just which they are. The changing attitude toward women's smoking is a case in point. Some groups in our society still consider the practice immoral; in others it has become a folkway; but in general it is "permissive behavior," open to individual choice. The use of contraceptives is another example. The attitude of the Catholic Church and the legal restrictions put on dissemination of information indicate that contraception is still considered a violation of the mores in a substantial portion of our society. Statistics, however, indicate that the use of contraceptives is passing into the realm of permissive behavior. Premarital chastity is still in the mores, still an ideal pattern, but research shows that the real pattern deviates considerably. Slavery was once considered moral; it is now clearly immoral in our culture. But while the change in attitude was taking place, bitter conflict almost tore American society apart permanently.

There are other less compulsive patterns of cultural behavior. Convention and etiquette are special kinds of folkways. People are aware that there is no deep meaning to them, but they are matters of convenience in social relations; they smooth the way and make a person comfortable. Knowing when to wear what clothes, how to invite and reply to invitations, are expectations of certain social groups. A person's standing in the social pyramid is often judged by the ease with which he observes the conventions and rules of etiquette.

II.   Fashions and fads. Fashions and fads are instances of highly transitory patterns of behavior. They, too, are cultural patterns, however, for as Kingsley Davis says, "Curiously, the human animal manages to be a conformist even when he is seeking change."[1] Fashion appears to be most prominent in a complex urban society where the class system is not rigid, where one is judged largely by externals. In our culture, for example, fashions are followed by the majority of women. The wealthy initiate style changes, but in an incredibly short time copies are seen in the windows of low-priced dress shops. Fads are fashions that alternate very quickly, are utterly superficial, and have an irrational and intense fascination, particularly for adolescents. High-school students are especially subject to swiftly changing fads in wearing apparel and dance steps. Crazes are much like fads. Examples are the Pyramid Club of 1949 and the chain letter craze that still pops up occasionally and dies down just as fast. Their fascination for adults is remarkable.

---

[1] Kingsley Davis, *Human Society* (New York: The Macmillan Company, 1949), p. 76.

Sally, your college classmate, wears something to cover herself because the mores (buttressed by law) dictate it. For the sake of modesty she would not dream of coming to class unclothed. The fact that she wears a sweater and skirt instead of an East Indian sari or a Japanese kimono may be traced to the folkways of our culture. Hearkening to convention, she wears her sweater and skirt to class instead of her Saturday costume of blue jeans and her dad's old shirt. Etiquette will dictate that she change to a long dress, evening slippers, and dainty bag, and wear a corsage sent by her escort when she attends a formal dance. The length of her skirt, the lines of her sweater, and the colors she chooses are dictated by fashion. Her wearing Coronation costume jewelry in the spring of 1953, like a large percentage of the other girls in the class, was a fad. She considered it fun, the latest thing, a sign that she was "hep." In high school she may have worn one red sock and one green sock, or dyed a lock of her hair silver or blue, to be "different" and yet "in the swim."

III.   *Laws.* The folkways and mores set the pattern for most behavior in a small and unified society. In more complex societies, where different groups within the society have different folkways and mores, a special organization is necessary to formulate laws to coordinate the behavior of these groups sufficiently so the society can continue to function. Although folkways and mores are usually followed without much conscious reflection, *laws* are deliberately formulated, clearly stated rules of behavior enforced by a special authority. Many laws enforce the mores. Monogamy, responsibility for the welfare of wife and children, and the taboos against murder, theft, and rape are all reinforced by law. But in a dynamic society, new situations constantly arise that are not covered by custom. The invention of railroads, automobiles, radios, airplanes, and television have all necessitated legal regulation. Laws also meet crises in which traditional ways prove ineffectual. During the depression, the old ways of doing business left many people hungry and ill-clothed, and the government had to enact laws to provide for them.

Occasionally laws are enacted that are really contrary to the mores or, if in a moral category, are not backed up by the mores. Their passage comes about through the influence of pressure groups. Drinking was not tabooed by the mores, and as a result many people violated prohibition. Traffic regulations are not a part of the mores; that is why so many people brag about getting away with violations. The most effective laws are firmly grounded in the mores.

Law may, however, be used as an instrument of social reform, especially where the real patterns do not coincide with ideal patterns. Americans like to speak about equality of opportunity. In actual practice we are guilty of discrimination in housing, education, employment, and other fields. Fair Employment Practices Acts and Federal Supreme Court decisions against state-upheld discriminatory practices have operated to bring real behavior more closely in line with the ideal patterns. Often legislation and judicial decisions prove so-called "practical" objections invalid, and thus bring about real social change.

IV.   *Institutions.* Institutions are not distinct from and additional to folkways, mores, and laws. "An *institution* can be defined as a set of interwoven folkways, mores and laws built around one or more functions."[2] "It is essentially a *pattern* of usages which define the roles of the participating group members in such a way that their aims

---

[2] *Ibid.*, p. 71.

may be achieved through the resulting cooperative behavior. . . . Any institution is a pattern that is definite and stable enough to be passed on from one generation to another."[3]
    An obvious example of an institution is the family. Clustering around the functions of mating, reproduction, and child-rearing, which are essential to the perpetuation of society, and of gratification of the individual's sexual drives and his need for security and affection, are numerous folkways and mores and laws. In our culture, dates, engagement rings, honeymoons, bridal showers, and homes apart from the in-laws are among the folkways associated with marriage. Mores include pre-marital chastity, post-marital fidelity, monogamy, and rights and duties of husband and wife to one another and to their children. A legal framework has grown up to support the mores: licenses, legal ceremonies, laws against bigamy and non-support, laws providing for divorce under certain conditions, laws against intermarriage of close relatives, and, in certain states, of members of different racial groups, laws against marriage of children under a certain age without parental consent, and so forth.
    Institutions are of two types. The family is a *crescive* institution; that is, it arose and assumed its present form gradually and without deliberate planning. A college, a museum, or a library is an *enacted* institution, deliberately conceived and organized.
    The concept of institutions is an extremely fruitful one for the study of culture, society, and personality. . . . "The quickest way to envisage the total social order of a society is to understand its major institutions and the relations between these institutions."[4]

    Social control as a supplement to socialization. The folkways and mores, then, buttressed and supplemented when necessary by law and organized around central functions into institutions, are the patterns provided by culture. They are taught to the members of society by a process of *socialization* or enculturation, the most important part of which is accomplished in childhood by the family, the educational system, and the play group. The patterns are taught so early and so thoroughly that they become part of the person's emotional and psychological make-up. He is "good" because he wants to be good, because he has the habit of being good. His ways are the ways of the group. His interests and values are determined without conscious thought on his part.
    Of course this process of socialization is not complete and perfect. In a disorganized society with conflicting values and patterns, it may be far from adequate. Therefore, the mechanisms for enforcing proper behavior, the techniques of social control, must be brought into play. These are largely informal in the family and neighborhood, and in simple societies are effective preventives. "What will people say?" is a strong deterrent to improper or immoral behavior, especially in an integrated culture. Parents and teachers use threats, commands, rewards and punishments, praise, and ridicule. Fear is associated with taboos. The threat of force (tar and feathers, or a "necktie party" in the rough-and-ready society of the Old West) may also keep people in line. Public shame or ridicule is highly effective. Ostracism by a person's family or community or church is resorted to in the case of extremely serious offenses against the mores.

---

[3]Robert L. Sutherland, Julian L. Woodward, and Milton A. Maxwell, *Introductory Sociology*, Fourth Edition (Chicago: J. B. Lippincott Company, 1952), p. 26.
    [4]Davis, *Human Society*, p. 72.

But in a more complex society, public opinion, conscience, and other informal controls are insufficient; and legal authorities must be given the task of detecting and punishing offenses against the mores as enacted into law. In such a society, too, there are many groups with special interests who resort to such deliberate techniques of social control as propaganda. . . .

2-4   ARE BASIC NEEDS ULTIMATE?

Dorothy Lee

Dorothy Lee received her Ph.D. from the University of California at Berkeley. She has conducted field work in the public schools of the United States as well as in Melanesia, and among the Wintu Indians of California. She was formerly professor of anthropology at Vassar College and a consultant in teaching at the Merrill-Palmer School, Detroit. She is the author of *Freedom and Culture* as well as numerous articles on the conceptual and value aspects of culture. She is currently dividing her time between Iowa State University and San Fernando Valley State College.

In this essay Dorothy Lee elaborates on the statement by John and Mavis Biesanz in the previous selection: culture itself creates needs.

The purpose of this paper is to urge a re-examination of the premise which so many of us implicitly hold that culture is a group of patterned means for the satisfaction of a list of human needs. This is, of course, not a new issue either with psychologists or anthropologists. The concept of an inventory of basic needs rose to fill the vacuum created when the behaviorists banished the old list of instincts. Yet, in spite of dissatisfaction with this, many of us continue to think of cultural behavior in terms of some form of the stimulus-response principle. Anthropologists borrowed the principle from psychology, without first testing it against ethnographic material, so that often, when the psychologist uses anthropological material, he gets his own back again in new form, and receives no new insights. There are two assumptions involved here: (1) the premise that action occurs in answer to a need or a lack; and (2) the premise that there is a list. In recent years, anthropologists, influenced by the new psychology, have often substituted *drives* or *impulses* or *adjustive responses* for the old term *needs*, but the concept of the list remains with us. We hold this side by side with the conflicting conception of culture as a totality, of personality as organismic, as well as with adherence to psychosomatic principles. We deplore the presentation of culture as a list of traits, yet we are ready to define culture as an answer to a list of needs.

This definition of culture has proved a strain. When we found that the original list of basic needs or drives was inadequate, we, like the psychologists, tried

From *Freedom and Culture*, by Dorothy Lee, pp. 70–77. Copyright © 1959 by Prentice-Hall, Inc.; reprinted by permission of Prentice-Hall, Inc., the American Psychological Association, and the author.

to solve the difficulty by adding on a list of social and psychic needs; and, from here on, I use the term *need* in a broad sense, to cover the stimulus-response phrasing of behavior. When the list proved faulty, all we had to do was to add to the list. We have now such needs as that for novelty, for escape from reality, for security, for emotional response. We have primary needs, or drives, and secondary needs, and we have secondary needs playing the role of primary needs. The endless process of adding and correcting is not an adequate improvement; neither does the occasional substitution of a "totality of needs" for a "list of needs" get at the root of the trouble. Where so much elaboration and revision is necessary, I suspect that the original unit itself must be at fault; we must have a radical change.

In applying the list of needs to different cultures, we found that modification was necessary. It was apparent that the need for food of a member of American society is far greater that that of the members of most other societies. Curiously enough, we also find that though a laborer on a New Guinea plantation needs a minimum diet of seven pounds of yams, plus a stated amount of meat, an Arapesh in his own hamlet, working in his fields, climbing up and down steep mountain sides, working hard at ceremonials, can live a meaningful life and procreate healthy children on three pounds of yams a day, and almost no meat.

Is further modification necessary here, or is there another factor at work? Faced with data of this sort, we have been tempted to apply a utilitarian calculus. We have said that when the Arapesh gardens inefficiently in company with his brother-in-law, and when he plants his fruit tree on someone else's distant land, he multiplies his exertions and minimizes his subsistence so as to achieve a maximum of social warmth. But is he really filling two distinct needs, slighting one at the expense of the other? When he takes his pig to another hamlet, and asks someone else's wife to feed and bring it up, what need exactly is he satisfying? And is this need greater than the general human need for food? And does its satisfaction supply a substitute for caloric intake? These questions are nonsense, but we do run into them if we carry the premise of a list of needs far enough.

The assumption of a list of needs was put under its greatest strain, I think, during the recent war. We had assumed that "the role of . . . needs in human behavior is that of first causes." Then how could we explain the behavior of certain small nations, who chose freely to lose necessary food, shelter, security, etc., rather than join the Axis? Why did whole nations court physical annihilation rather than subscribe to Axis doctrines? Why did fathers and husbands and daughters expose their beloved families to danger of torture or death by joining the underground? In this country, why did millions of people who had adequate food and shelter and "security" choose to jeopardize their lives? We can say, of course, that they were satisfying their need for emotional response, in this case the approval of others. One anthropologist did express it in this way. But why was it this particular course of action which was sure to bring them the approval of others? And how could these needs have been the cause of behavior whose goal was neither individual nor group survival?

To my mind, this means that either needs are not the cause of all behavior, or that the list of needs provides an inadequate unit for assessing human behavior. I am not saying that there are no needs; rather, that if there are needs, they are derivative, not basic. If, for example, physical survival was held as the ultimate goal in some society, it would probably be found to give rise to those needs which have been stated to be basic to human survival; but I know of no culture where human physical survival has been shown, rather than unquestioningly assumed by social scientists, to be the ultimate goal.

I believe that it is value, not a series of needs, which is at the basis of human behavior. The main difference between the two lies in the conception of the good which underlies them. The premise that man acts so as to satisfy needs presupposes a negative conception of the good as amelioration or the correction of an undesirable state. According to this view, man acts to relieve tension; good is the removal of evil and welfare the correction of ills; satisfaction is the meeting of a need; good functioning comes from adjustment, survival from adaptation; peace is the resolution of conflict; fear, of the supernatural or of adverse public opinion, is the incentive to good conduct; the happy individual is the well-adjusted individual.

Perhaps this view of what constitutes the good is natural and applicable in a culture which also holds that man was born in sin, whether in Biblical or in psycho-analytic terms. But should we, who believe that other cultures should be assessed according to their own categories and premises, impose upon them our own unexamined conception of the good, and thus always see them as striving to remove or avoid ills? It seems to me that, when we do not take this negative view of the good for granted, other cultures often appear to be maintaining "justment" rather than striving to attain adjustment. For example, for the Hopi, the good is present and positive. An individual is "born in hopiness," so to speak, and strives throughout life to maintain and enhance this hopiness. There is no external reward for being good, as this is taken for granted. It is evil which is external and intrusive, making a man kahopi, or unhopi; that is, un-peaceful, un-good.

In my opinion, the motivation underlying Hopi behavior is *value*. To the Hopi, there is value in acting as a Hopi within a Hopi situation; there is satisfaction in the situation itself, not in the solution of it or the resolution of tension. I speak of value, but rather than define it I shall indicate what I mean by presenting value situations. I want to point out that the notion of value is incompatible with that of a list of needs, or adjustive responses, or drives; so that, wherever it is held, the list must go.

Now, if we substitute the notion of value for that of needs, we are no longer troubled with the difficulty of trying to assess a totality in terms of an aggregate, since value is total and is to be found in a total situation. When we listen to a symphony, we get satisfaction from a whole, not from eighteen thousand notes and a series of arrangements. I can give you an inventory of my daughter, her three teeth, her seventeen pounds, her inability to sit up yet, her mixed smell, her bald head; is it this which causes my behavior when I rush joyfully home to her as soon as I leave my office?

Again, we find that the Hopi like to eat corn; would we be justified in assuming that a Hopi would therefore find it good to work for wages so as to earn money to buy corn to satisfy his hunger? To the Hopi, corn is not nutrition; it is a totality, a way of life. Something of this sort is exemplified in the story which Talayesva tells of the Mexican trader who offered to sell salt to the Hopi group who were starting out on a highly ceremonial Salt Expedition. Within its context this offer to relieve the group of the hardships and dangers of the religious journey sounds ridiculous. The Hopi were not just going to get salt to season their dishes. To them, the journey was part of the process of growing corn and of maintaining harmonious interrelations with nature and what we call the divine. It was the Hopi Way, containing Hopi value. Yet even an ethnographer, dealing with Hopi culture in terms of basic needs, views the Salt Expedition as the trader did, and classifies it under *Secondary Economic Activities*.

So also with our earlier example of the Arapesh. Their eating is not a distinct act satisfying a single need. Food to the Arapesh is good; it incorporates intensive social intercourse; it is the medium of intimacy and identification with others, the symbol of human relations which to them are the primary good. It satisfies the total individual. When we analyze the mouthful of yams into so much nutrition plus so much social warmth, that is exactly what we are doing and no more; we do not find these distinctions or elements—we create them. What we find are aspects of a total situation without independent existence. Our impulse is to break up the situation because we are culturally trained to comprehend a totality only after we break it up into familiar phrasings. But in this way we miss the value inherent in it, since it disappears with analysis, and cannot be recreated synthetically afterwards. Having created a series of elements, we then find no difficulty in motivating them according to a series of needs.

If needs are inborn and discrete, we should find them as such in the earliest situations of an individual's life. Yet take the Tikopia or the Kwoma infant, held and suckled without demand in the mother's encircling arms. He knows no food apart from society, has no need for emotional response since his society is emotionally continuous with himself; he certainly feels no need for security. He participates in a total situation. Even in our own culture, the rare happy child has no need for emotional response or approval or security or escape from reality or novelty. If we say that the reason that he has no need for these things is that he does have them already, we would be begging the question. I believe, rather, that these terms or notions are irrelevant when satisfaction is viewed in terms of positive present value, and value itself as inherent in a total situation.

On the other hand, it is possible to see needs as arising out of the basic value of a culture. In our own culture, the value of individualism is axiomatically assumed. How else would it be possible for us to pluck twenty infants, newly severed from complete unity with their mothers, out of all social and emotional context, and classify them as twenty atoms on the basis of a similarity of age? On this assumption of individualism, a mother has need for individual self-expression. She has to have time for and by herself; and since she values individualism, the mother in our culture usually does have this need for a private life.

We also believe that a newborn infant must become individuated, must be taught physical and emotional self-dependence; we assume, in fact, that he has a separate identity which he must be helped to recognize. We believe that he has distinct rights, and sociologists urge us to reconcile the needs of the child to those of the adults in the family, on the assumption, of course, that needs and ends are individual, not social. Now, in maintaining our individual integrity and in passing on our value of individualism to the infant, we create needs for food, for security, for emotional response, phrasing these as distinct and separate. We force the infant to go hungry, and we see suckling as merely a matter of nutrition, so that we can then feel free to substitute a bottle for the breast and a mechanical bottle-holder for the mother's arms; thus we ensure privacy for the mother and teach the child self-dependence. We create needs in the infant by withholding affection and then presenting it as a series of approvals for an inventory of achievements or attributes. On the assumption that there is no emotional continuum, we withdraw ourselves, thus forcing the child to strive for emotional response and security. And thus, through habituation and teaching, the mother reproduces in the child her own needs, in this case the need for privacy which inevitably brings with it related needs.

Now the child grows up needing time to himself, a room of his own, freedom of choice, freedom to plan his own time and his own life. He will brook no interference and no encroachment. He will spend his wealth installing private bathrooms in his house, buying a private car, a private yacht, private woods and a private beach, which he will then people with his privately chosen society. The need for privacy is an imperative one in our society, recognized by official bodies of our government. And it is part of a system which stems from and expresses our basic value.

In other cultures, we find other systems, maintaining other values. The Arapesh, with their value of the social, created a wide gap between ownership and possession, which they could then bridge with a multitude of human relations. They plant their trees in someone else's hamlet, they rear pigs owned by someone else, they eat yams planted by someone else. The Ontong-Javanese, for whom also the good is social, value the sharing of the details of everyday living. They have created a system, very confusing to an American student, whereby a man is a member of at least three ownership groups, determined along different principles, which are engaged cooperatively in productive activities; and of two large households, one determined along matrilineal lines, one along patrilineal lines. Thus, an Ontong-Javanese man spends part of the year with his wife's sisters and their families, sharing with them the intimate details of daily life, and the rest of the year on an outlying island, with his brothers and their families. The poor man is the man who has no share in an outlying island, who must eat and sleep only in a household composed of his immediate family and his mother's kin, when unmarried; and who must spend the whole year with his wife's kin, when married. He has the same amount and kind of food to eat as his wealthy neighbors, but not as many coconuts to give away; he has shelter as adequate as that of the wealthy, but not as much of the shared living which is the Ontong-Javanese good.

In speaking of these other cultures, I have not used the term *need*. I could have said, for example, that the Ontong-Javanese needs a large house, to include many maternally related families. But I think this would have been merely an exercise in analysis. On the other hand, when I spoke of our own culture, I was forced to do it in terms of needs, since I have been trained to categorize my own experience in these terms. But even here, these are not basic needs, but rather part of a system expressing our basic value; and were we able to break away from our substantival or formal basis of categorizing, I think we should find these to be aspects or stresses or functions, without independent existence. Culture is not, I think, "a response to the total needs of a society"; but rather a system which stems from and expresses something had, the basic values of society.

2-5   PARTICIPATION IN CULTURE

Ralph Linton

Ralph Linton (1893–1953) studied at Pennsylvania and Columbia Universities and received his doctorate from Harvard University. He served as an assistant curator of the Chicago Natural History Museum. He taught at the University of Wisconsin, Columbia University, and served as Sterling Professor of Anthropology at Yale. His professional career included editorship of *American Anthropologist* (1939–1945) and presidency of the American Anthropological Association (1946). His extensive field research embraced the island of Madagascar, South Africa, Peru, Brazil, and the Marquesa Islands. Dr. Linton was also a prolific writer; *The Study of Man, The Cultural Background of Personality*, and *The Tree of Culture* served as basic texts in the field of anthropology for many years.

The reader who has come thus far will have a fairly clear idea of the meaning of the term *culture*. It has already been defined in various ways and used in numerous connections. He should also have a clear idea of the nature of society and should realize that culture and society are mutually dependent. Neither can exist as a functioning entity without the other. It is the possession of a common culture which gives a society its *esprit de corps* and makes it possible for its members to live and work together with a minimum of confusion and mutual interference. At the same time, the society gives culture overt expression in its behavior, and hands it on from generation to generation. However, societies are so constituted that they can only express culture through the medium of their component individuals and can only perpetuate it by the training of these individuals. It is with the participation of these individuals in the total culture of their society that we will deal. . . .

No one individual is ever familiar with the total content of the culture of the society to which he belongs. Even in the simplest cultures the content is too rich for any one mind to be able to apprehend the whole of it. The patterns of division of and specialization in activities make it possible for the individual to function successfully as a member of his society without such complete knowledge. He learns and employs certain aspects of the total culture and leaves the knowledge and exercise of other aspects to other individuals. At the same time, every person is usually familiar with elements of his society's culture which he will never be called upon to express in action. Thus a lame man may be thoroughly familiar with the behavior appropriate to men on war parties although he himself can never take part in one. The same situation may hold for whole categories within the society. Thus all men may know the taboos incumbent upon pregnant women, although obviously they will never be called upon to practice them. To come closer home, the conventions governing male and female costume are quite different, yet each sex has a fairly clear idea of what is appropriate for the other.

From *The Study of Man* by Ralph Linton, pp. 271–287. Copyright 1936, D. Appleton-Century Company, Inc. Reprinted by permission of Appleton-Century-Crofts.

A surprising number of women help to buy their husbands' clothes, while husbands not infrequently veto their wives' lipsticks or bathing suits or advise them to imitate the costume worn by Mrs. X.

These factors increase the degree of the individual's participation in culture, but it never reaches completeness. If we observe the culture of any homogeneous society, we will find that the content of this culture can be divided into three categories, these being derived from the extent to which the elements within each category are shared by the society's members. As in all classifications, there may be some difficulty in assigning certain elements to their places in this three-fold division, but the position of most of them will be plain enough.

First, there are those ideas, habits, and conditioned emotional responses which are common to all sane, adult members of the society. We will call these the *Universals*. It must be understood that this terminology applies only to the content of a particular culture. An element classed as a Universal in one culture may be completely lacking in another. To this category belong such elements as the use of a particular language, the tribal patterns of costume and housing, and the ideal patterns for social relationships. This category also includes the associations and values which lie, for the most part, below the level of consciousness but which are, at the same time, an integral part of culture.

Second, we have those elements of culture which are shared by the members of certain socially recognized categories of individuals but which are not shared by the total population. We will call these the *Specialties*. Under this head come the patterns for all those varied but mutually interdependent activities which have been assigned to various sections of the society in the course of its division of labor. In all societies certain things are done by or known to only a designated part of the population, although they contribute to the well-being of the whole. Thus all the women within a tribe will be familiar with certain occupations and techniques, while the men will be familiar with a different series. As a rule, the men will only have a rather vague general knowledge of the things which belong in the women's province and vice versa. Under this head there can also be classed the activities which the society has assigned to special craftsmen or functionaries such as the smith, carpenter, doctor, and priest.

The cultural elements which fall into this class are, for the most part, manual skills and technical knowledge. The greater part of them are concerned with the utilization and control of the natural environment. Although such elements are not shared by the entire society, the benefits arising from them are shared, and all members of the society will have a fairly clear idea as to what the end product of each specialized activity should be. Thus a husband may have only a general idea of the processes involved in making bread, but he will be keenly conscious of whether it has been made properly or not. Again, the average man does not know the techniques of the smith and regards his skill in metal-working with some awe, but he has a clear mental picture of what constitutes a good knife or hoe and will be both resentful of inferior workmanship and suspicious of innovations. The same thing holds for the activities of the doctor or priest. The uninstructed do not know the full details of their procedure, but every one has a general knowledge of how healing or sacrificing should be done and of the results to be expected from it. Any departure from the accustomed procedure or failure to achieve the expected results brings an emotional reaction.

Third, there are in every culture a considerable number of traits which are shared by certain individuals but which are not common to all the members of the society or even to all the members of any one of the socially recognized categories. We will call these _Alternatives_. The elements of culture which may be included in this class have a very wide range, varying from the special and often quite atypical ideas and habits of a particular family to such things as different schools of painting or sculpture. Aside from the nature of the participation in them, all these Alternatives have this in common: they represent different reactions to the same situations or different techniques for achieving the same ends. The cultures of small societies living under primitive conditions usually include only a moderate number of such Alternatives, while in such a culture as our own they are very plentiful. Examples of such Alternatives for ourselves would be such things as the use of horses, bicycles, railroads, automobiles, and airplanes for the single purpose of transportation over land; our variety of teaching techniques; or our wide range of beliefs and attitudes toward the supernatural.

IV.   Beyond the limits of culture there lies still a fourth category of habits, ideas and conditioned emotional responses; that of _Individual Peculiarities_. These include such things as one person's abnormal fear of fire, due perhaps to some accident of his early experience, a craftsman's individual tricks of technique or characteristic muscular habits, or a purely personal doubt regarding some generally accepted article of faith. Every individual has certain peculiarities of this sort whether he is a member of a primitive tribe or a modern urban community, and the sum total of such individual differences within any society is enormous.

Individual Peculiarities cannot be classed as a part of culture, in the sense in which the term is ordinarily used, since they are not shared by any of a society's members. At the same time they are of extreme importance in cultural dynamics since they are the starting point of everything which later becomes incorporated into culture. There is always some one individual in a community who is the first to discover, invent, or adopt a new thing. As soon as this new thing has been transmitted to and is shared by even one other individual in the society, it must be reckoned a part of culture. Individual Peculiarities occupy somewhat the same position with regard to culture that individual mutations occupy with regard to a biological species. Most Individual Peculiarities, like most physical variations, are never transmitted at all or are transmitted to only a few individuals and ultimately disappear. However, if the Peculiarity is of a sort advantageous to its possessor, it may be transmitted to an ever-widening circle of individuals until it is accepted by the whole society.

It is easiest to apply the foregoing classification to elements within cultures of the sort carried by small, closely integrated social units such as the local groups. . . . When we turn to larger units such as tribes, or more especially modern states, we find a vastly more complex situation. While ethnologists have been accustomed to speak of tribes and nationalities as though they were the primary culture-bearing units, the total culture of a society of this type is really an aggregate of sub-cultures. Within tribes or unmechanized civilizations these sub-cultures are normally carried by the various local groups which go to make the total society and are transmitted within these groups. In a few cases there may also be sub-cultures which are characteristic of particular social classes and which are transmitted within them, but this arrangement is much less characteristic than the local one. Every sub-culture always differs in some respects from all the rest, and the total culture consists of the sum of its sub-cultures plus certain additional elements which are a result of their interaction.

If we attempt to apply our three-fold classification to a tribal culture we will find that, in comparison with any of the sub-cultures which compose it, it shows fewer

Universals and a marked increase in Specialties. The peculiarities of the various sub-cultures must be listed as Specialties rather than Alternatives since they are not presented to the individual as traits toward which he can exercise choice. Each individual accepts the patterns of his own sub-culture as proper guides to behavior and rarely attempts to imitate the patterns of other sub-cultures even when he is familiar with them. In fact, the presence of such differences usually makes him cling more tenaciously to the habits of his particular sub-culture, since these become a symbol of his member-ship in his particular social unit.

When we take such a culture as a whole, the number of Alternatives will also show some increase over those within a given sub-culture, since all the Alternatives within all the sub-cultures will be included. However, as long as the contacts between the social units which bear the sub-cultures are not very close or frequent, the total number of these Alternatives will bear little relation to the number of them which are submitted to any given individual for choice.

The sub-cultures within a tribal culture must of necessity be adapted to each other and have a considerable number of elements in common, else it will be impossible to maintain a feeling of tribal unity or for the tribe to function as a unit. However, the degree of adaptation necessary will depend largely upon the amount of contact between the units bearing the sub-cultures and especially upon the degree to which they are interdependent. Thus the various sub-cultures within a Plains Indian tribe could exist and develop with little reference to each other. The bands bearing them were economic-ally self-contained and came together only at fairly long intervals. When, on the other hand, the groups which bear the sub-cultures are in close and frequent contact, or when the products of certain of these groups are necessary to the rest, there will have to be a much greater degree of adjustment. In particular, changes in any one of the sub-cultures will be strongly influenced by the situation existing in the rest.

Even when there is close contact and marked interdependence between the groups which bear sub-cultures, it is still possible for the sub-cultures to maintain their integrity. They become adapted to each other and to the total social structure, each of them performing certain functions with relation to the whole. Once a satisfactory adaptation has been achieved, there is no incentive for the individuals who share a particular sub-culture to give up their distinctive habits. These habits constitute Specialties, from the point of view of the culture as a whole, and are an integral part of it. While they may subject those who share them to jests and good-natured ridicule, as when the peasants of one village laugh at the costume of those in the next, they have the reinforcement of general recognition. As long as the groups which bear the sub- *Blacks* cultures remain conscious of themselves as distinct entities and retain their hold on the individuals who compose them, the sub-cultures will persist.

It is only when the hold of the local group or social class upon its members is broken, as it is beginning to be in our own society, that the sub-cultures tend to merge *Anti-Pluralism* and disappear. The first effect of this merging is that the distinctive features of the sub-cultures cease to be Specialties and become Alternatives, i.e., are thrown open to individual choice. As competing Alternatives, most of them will finally be eliminated, with a consequent loss to the total content of the culture. However, until this elimination has taken place there will be a marked increase in the number of culture elements made available to any individual within the society.

The incomplete participation of all individuals in the culture of their societies is reflected in the presence within all societies of differential lines for the transmission of various culture elements. These lines correspond not only to the membership of the social units which carry particular sub-cultures but also to the various socially established categories of individuals within each of the functional social units. Thus certain elements are transmitted in family lines. The members of one family may be taught to say a particular form of grace at meals, perhaps the Lord's Prayer in German, and this custom may be handed down within it for generations, while other families transmit a grace of a different sort. Similarly, in all cultures the knowledge of the Specialties assigned to women will be transmitted almost entirely in the female line, while knowledge of those assigned to men will be transmitted in the male line.

One of the most interesting aspects of this differentiation of lines of cultural transmission, and one very frequently overlooked, is that the various age categories within a society also correspond to lines of cultural transmission. While the growing individual learns much from his elders, he learns even more from his contemporaries, as many baffled parents can attest. His contacts with his contemporaries are normally closer and less formal, and the heroes whom he strives to imitate are usually not adults, whose interests and activities lie largely beyond his ken, but individuals within his own general age category. In particular he will copy those who are slightly older than himself and more expert in the activities socially ascribed to the particular category. Even in our own culture there are many elements which are transmitted almost exclusively within certain age brackets. For example, adults very rarely teach children to play marbles, this particular item being transmitted from boy to boy. Similarly, the techniques employed by adolescents in their first romantic advances to each other are constantly transmitted from older to younger adolescents without penetrating either the adult level or the child level. Although individuals naturally carry a knowledge of these techniques with them when they pass into the higher age groups, they would never think of employing them, still less of teaching them to their offspring. It seems quite possible that even the antagonism between adolescents and their elders and those questionings of certain values which we call "the revolt of youth" represent simply culture elements which are differentially transmitted in the adolescent line. . . .

The ability of all cultures to incorporate numerous Alternatives without serious interferences with their functioning is of vital importance to the processes of cultural growth and change. . . . In spite of the occasional realization of brand-new needs by a society, with the consequent introduction into the culture of elements with new functions, the bulk of all cultural changes are in the nature of replacements. The newly introduced element takes over the uses or functions of a pre-existing element. Its general acceptance by the members of a society will depend very largely on whether it performs these functions more efficiently. Thus men had cutting tools long before they had metal, and the introduction of the new material was by a process of gradual replacement. Stone knife and metal knife were, for a time, used side by side. Even the forms of the older tools were carried over and copied in the new medium. Again, our own need for transportation was already met by a variety of appliances at the time the automobile was invented. The new appliance was accepted because it was superior in one way or another to each of the pre-existing ones, but it still has not replaced any of them completely.

When a new element is offered to any society, full acceptance is always preceded by a period of trial. During this period both the new trait and the old trait or traits with which it is competing become Alternatives within the total culture complex. They are presented to individuals as different means to the same end. In all cultures the Alternatives serve as a proving ground for innovations. If the new trait meets the need more adequately than the old one and if it can be successfully adapted to the total pattern of the culture, it will be taken over by more and more individuals until it finally achieves general acceptance and wins a place among the Universals or Specialties. Simultaneously, the trait or traits which it is replacing will lose adherents until it finally drops out of the culture. The waning use of the bicycle in our own culture in competition with the automobile is a case in point. If the new trait cannot meet the test, it never reaches the Universals or Specialties. The individuals who have accepted it gradually relinquish it and ultimately it will be forgotten. Bridge and mah jong may serve as an example of this in our own culture. They had the same social and recreational functions and required about the same degree of attention. The old trait, bridge, appeared to be seriously threatened for a time, but it reasserted itself and mah jong dropped out.

In all cultures the Universals and Specialties represent the traits which have been successfully assimilated. The changes necessary to adjust them to each other and to prevent interference in their overt expressions have been made and the situation has temporarily stabilized. Many of the Alternatives, on the other hand, may be in process of assimilation. New traits, especially if they have been borrowed from other cultures, have to be modified to fit the preëxisting patterns, and whether they can be successfully modified is as important to their ultimate acceptance as any factors of immediate utility. While they are Alternatives they lack the stabilizing effects of full group participation and offer a fair field for modifications and improvements. The society's attitude toward them is quite different from its attitude toward the Universals and Specialties. Most of the Alternatives are frankly on trial, with no long-established associations or rationalizations to protect them, and must stand or fall on their own merits.

Although certain traits may remain in the zone of Alternatives indefinitely, neither achieving general acceptance nor dropping out of the culture, the bulk of the elements in this category are always on their way into or out from the solid core of Universals and Specialties. It seems that the only traits which can survive indefinitely as Alternatives are those which have only a superficial influence upon the behavior of the society. Half a dozen ways of playing solitaire, two or three versions of an amusing story, or several conflicting theories as to the nature of the stars may persist side by side for generations. Even two techniques for the manufacture of identical products may persist in this way if they are of approximately the same efficiency. However, if one of them is markedly more efficient, the other will ultimately be forced out. When it comes to socially important ideas and values, the competition is much keener and always results in the elimination of one or the other Alternative. When different groups which do not constitute socially recognized categories of individuals within the society come to hold divergent views with regard to such matters as sexual morality or the private ownership of the group's natural resources, one view must ultimately triumph and drive out the other.

While the Universals and Specialties within any culture normally form a fairly consistent and well-integrated unit, the Alternatives necessarily lack such consistency and integration. Many of them are in opposition to each other, and some of them may even be at variance with elements in the first two categories. Actually, all cultures consist of two parts, a solid, well-integrated, and fairly stable core, consisting of the mutually adapted Universals and Specialities, and a fluid, largely unintegrated, and constantly changing zone of Alternatives which surrounds this core. It is the core which gives a culture its form and basic patterns at each point in its history, while the presence of the fluid zone gives it its capacity for growth and adaptation. If we study any culture continuum we will be able to detect a constant process of give-and-take between these two parts, with traits moving from one to the other. New traits, beginning as Individual Peculiarities, gain adherents, rise to the status of Alternatives, and finally pass into the core as they achieve general recognition. Old ones, as soon as they are brought into competition with new ones, are drawn into the zone of Alternatives and, if they are inferior, finally drop out of the culture. This exit, in turn, takes place by way of the Individual Peculiarities. Some die-hard individual may insist on driving a horse and buggy after all the rest of his society have automobiles, and the trait will not finally disappear until his death.

The proportion which each of these two parts of a culture bears to its total content may vary greatly at different points in its history. In general, the more rapid the contemporary rate of change, the higher the proportion of Alternatives. The proposition is stated in this form simply because most of the stimuli to change, as well as the bulk of the new traits by the acceptance of which it is accomplished, normally originate outside the culture. When a culture is changing very rapidly, as our own is at present, the Alternatives may become so numerous that they quite overshadow the Universals and Specialties. Each new trait, as soon as it is accepted by any part of the society, draws certain traits which were formerly Universals or Specialties out of the core of the culture into the fluid zone. As the content of the core is reduced, the culture increasingly loses pattern and coherence.

Such a fluid, disorganized condition within culture has inevitable repercussions upon the society which bears it. It is the common adherence of a society's members to the elements which form the core of their culture which makes it possible for them to function as a society. Without a wide community of ideas and habits the members of the group will not react to particular stimuli as a unit, nor will they be able to cooperate effectively. Such cooperation really rests upon the predictability of the other individuals' behavior. When there are very few elements of culture in which all the members of a society participate, i.e., when the proportional size of the culture core has been greatly reduced, the group tends to revert to the condition of an aggregate. The society is no longer able to feel or act as a unit. Its members may continue to live together, but many forms of social intercourse will be hampered by the impossibility of predicting the behavior of individuals on any basis other than that of their known personalities. Even economic coöperation will be seriously interfered with, due to the lack of fixed standards of integrity and fair dealing. It is obvious that this condition puts the society at a marked disadvantage, and it is probable that there is a point below which participation cannot fall without a resulting collapse of both the society and the culture.

(1) The difference between folk cultures and modern civilizations, or between genuine and spurious cultures, as Sapir calls them, is primarily a matter of the proportion which the core of Universals and Specialties bears to the fluid zone of Alternatives. Folk cultures are borne by small, closely-integrated social units or by aggregates of such units which have already worked out satisfactory mutual adjustments. In such cultures, new items are not appearing with any great frequency and the society has plenty of time to test them and to assimilate them to its preëxisting patterns. In such cultures the core constitutes almost the whole.

(2) In modern civilizations, on the other hand, the small, closely integrated social units are being broken down, giving place to masses of individuals who are much more

loosely interrelated than the members of the former local groups and classes. The very size of these masses confers a considerable degree of anonymity upon the individual and protects him from the pressure toward cultural conformity which neighbors exert in a small group. Coupled with this there has been an extraordinarily rapid increase in the total content of civilized cultures. Due to the organization of research and invention, new items are appearing with such frequency that our society has had no time to really test them, still less to bring them into readily assimilable form. Many of these new items are of a sort which will necessitate radical changes in other phases of our culture. Thus the mechanization of agriculture or the acceptance of organic evolution as an established fact entails a series of compensating changes in other aspects of our life and thought which it will require years to accomplish. In modern civilizations, therefore, the core of culture is being progressively reduced. Our own civilization, as it presents itself to the individual, is mainly an assortment of Alternatives between which he may or frequently must choose. We are rapidly approaching the point where there will no longer be enough items on which all members of the society agree to provide the culture with form and pattern.

The disruptive trends in our own culture have not yet had time to work themselves out completely. In our rural districts the local groups still retain a good deal of their former function as culture-bearing units. There are often striking differences in the ideas and habits of communities living only a few miles from each other. The older generation in such communities shares a fairly consistent sub-culture, but the younger generation shows the influence of the new conditions. The young people are usually at odds with their elders and critical of the old standards without having any definite new standards to substitute for these. The facts of common residence and economic dependence force the young people to an outward conformity with the community patterns, but they no longer accept these as natural or inevitable. They have ceased to give emotional allegiance to the culture of their parents and are ripe for change, but the wider society with which automobiles, movies, and the press have brought them into contact has, as yet, no coherent pattern of life to offer them.

In cities the results of cultural disintegration are even more marked. Here the local groupings have already almost disappeared, while the now evolving interest and congeniality groups have not yet developed to the point where they can serve as culture-bearers. The individual has to make constant choices from among the wealth of culture Alternatives presented to him, and after he has chosen there is no way for him to establish contacts with other individuals whose choices have been similar. Without the backing of a group of like-minded people, it is impossible for him to feel absolutely sure about anything, and he falls an easy prey to any sort of high-pressure propaganda.

Such a condition is fatal to the effective operation of democratic institutions, since these depend upon a high degree of cultural participation, with the united will and consciousness of social as apart from individual interests which this confers. A low degree of cultural participation makes the rule of organized minorities not only possible but almost a necessity if society is to be maintained as a functioning entity. The members of such minorities do have a number of ideas and values in common, and the knowledge that these are shared by a number of other members reinforces them in every individual. Such minorities are capable of concerted action, while the bulk of the population, lacking common attitudes and values which might serve as rallying points, can do nothing against the minority or for themselves.

The situation which confronts us today is not altogether unique. Something very much like it existed during the later phases of the Roman Empire. Here also the rural local groups were broken down, in this case by economic forces which drove the peasants out of existence. In the cities the old Roman culture, which had served as a unifying core for the empire during its period of growth, passed into solution as it was compelled to compete with new elements drawn from the diverse cultures of a multitude of subject peoples. Although the Roman situation was not complicated by any revolution in technology, the derangement of the economic system was probably as great as that from which we are now suffering. During the empire's growth, Roman culture adapted itself to the conditions created by a constant inflow of loot and tribute and a seemingly inexhaustible supply of slaves. These conditions made it possible for the society to maintain its unemployed on doles. One is reminded of the present European and American systems, with their dependence on selling to societies which have not yet been mechanized. When, under the later empire, the inflow of wealth began to dwindle, the sufferings of the lower classes became acute, but their members did not have enough cultural unity to do anything about it. There were no plebeian movements comparable to those in the early Roman state, and, in spite of half-hearted attempts to right things from above, conditions became increasingly bad until both the society and culture practically collapsed.

Out of the chaos of this collapse there finally emerged a new type of culture and a reintegrated society which were built about the ideas and values which had persisted through the period of confusion among certain sections of the population. The strongest of these was the idea of personal loyalty to a commander, which always survived in the army and had been strong among the barbarian invaders. The ideas held by the Christians, for long an organized minority, served as a second focal point about which culture and society could reintegrate. Together they recrystallized the fluid culture of the period of Roman decline and barbarian invasion into that of medieval Europe with its Feudal System and its Church Triumphant.

That our own culture and society will eventually stabilize and reintegrate can hardly be doubted, but two things will have to happen first. We shall have to develop some sort of social unit which can take the place of the old local groupings as a bearer and transmitter of culture and ensure a similar high degree of individual participation. There must also be some diminution in the flood of new elements which are being poured into our culture from the laboratories of the scientists and technologists. The breakdown of our present economic system would solve both problems. The descendants of those who survived would be forced to return, for the most part, to life as peasants in small communities, while research would cease through lack of the economic surplus and trained personnel which it requires.

None of the problems involved in the present situation are really insoluble, and, if our culture and society collapse, they will not fall from lack of intelligence to meet this situation, but from lack of any united will to put the requisite changes into effect. What the modern world needs far more than improved production methods or even a more equitable distribution of their results is a series of mutually consistent ideas and values in which all its members can participate. Perhaps something of the sort can be developed in time to prevent the collapse which otherwise seems inevitable. If not, another "dark age" is in order, but we can console ourselves with the knowledge that the darkness is never of very long duration. Unless all history is at fault, our descendants of half a thousand years hence will once more have achieved a consistent, patterned culture and an integrated society. However, it is quite impossible to predict what forms these will assume. There is no way of knowing which of our present alternative values will survive the present turmoil, or what new values may be developed to serve as crystallization points for the new culture patterns. The Roman philosophers thought and wrote very little about military loyalty, accepting it as a matter of course, and the ideas of the Christians seemed to them utterly illogical and ridiculous.

2-6 THE ROLE OF CULTURE IN PERSONALITY FORMATION

Ralph Linton

One of Ralph Linton's major contributions to anthropological theory was his theory of the effect of culture on personality formation; its implications for education are obvious.

One of the most important scientific developments of modern times has been the recognition of culture. It has been said that the last thing which a dweller in the deep sea would be likely to discover would be water. He would become conscious of its existence only if some accident brought him to the surface and introduced him to air. Man, throughout most of his history, has been only vaguely conscious of the existence of culture and has owed even this consciousness to contrasts between the customs of his own society and those of some other with which he happened to be brought into contact. The ability to see the culture of one's own society as a whole, to evaluate its patterns and appreciate their implications, calls for a degree of objectivity which is rarely if ever achieved. It is no accident that the modern scientist's understanding of culture has been derived so largely from the study of non-European cultures where observation could be aided by contrast. Those who know no culture other than their own cannot know their own. Until very recent times even psychologists have failed to appreciate that all human beings, themselves included, develop and function in an environment which is, for the most part, culturally determined. As long as they limited their investigations to individuals reared within the frame of a single culture they could not fail to arrive at concepts of human nature which were far from the truth. Even such a master as Freud frequently posited instincts to account for reactions which we now see as directly referable to cultural conditioning. With the store of knowledge of other societies and cultures which is now available, it is possible to approach the study of personality with fewer preconceptions and to reach a closer approximation of the truth.

It must be admitted at once that the observation and recording of data on personality in non-European societies is still fraught with great difficulty. It is hard

From *The Cultural Background of Personality* by Ralph Linton, pp. 125–153. Copyright 1945, D. Appleton-Century Company, Inc. Reprinted by permission of Appleton-Century-Crofts.

enough to get reliable material in our own. The development of accurate, objective techniques for personality study is still in its infancy. Such appliances as the Rorschach tests and Murray's thematic apperception tests have proved their value, but those who have worked with them would be the first to recognize their limitations. In the present state of our knowledge we still have to rely very largely upon informal observations and upon the subjective judgments of the observer. To complicate matters still further, most, although by no means all, of the information which we have on personality in non-European societies has been collected by anthropologists who had only a nodding acquaintance with psychology. Such observers, among whom I include myself at the time that I did most of my ethnological field work, are seriously handicapped by their ignorance of what to look for and what should be recorded. Moreover, there is a lamentable lack of comparative material on the various non-European societies which have been studied. The rapidity with which primitive societies have been acculturated or extinguished during the last hundred years has led to the development of a particular pattern of anthropological investigation. Since there were always far more societies available for study than there were anthropologists to study them and since most of these societies had to be investigated immediately or not at all, each investigator sought a new and unknown group. As a result, most of the information which we have has been collected by one investigator per society. The disadvantages of this are obvious in any case, but especially so in connection with personality studies. In a field where so much depends upon the subjective judgment of the observer and upon the particular members of the society with whom he was able to establish intimate contacts, the personality of the observer becomes a factor in every record. It is to be hoped that with the increasing number of anthropologists and the dwindling number of unstudied societies this pattern of exclusiveness will be broken down and that personality studies will benefit accordingly.

In spite of this frank recognition of difficulties and limitations which only time can remove, certain facts seem to be well established. All anthropologists who have come to know the members of non-European societies intimately are in substantial agreement on certain points. These are: (1) Personality norms differ in different societies. (2) The members of any society will always show considerable individual variation in personality. (3) Much of the same range of variation and much the same personality types are to be found in all societies. Although anthropologists base these conclusions on informal observations, they seem to be substantiated by the results of certain objective tests. Thus Rorschach series from different societies reveal different norms for such series as wholes. They also reveal a wide range of individual variation within each series and much overlapping between series. Even without this evidence, the consensus of opinion on the part of those who should be in a position to know cannot be dismissed lightly. In the absence of more complete and accurate information it seems justifiable to accept these conclusions as facts and to take them as the starting point for our investigation of the rôle of culture in personality formation.

That the norms for personality differ in different societies will scarcely be doubted by anyone who has had experience of societies other than his own. In fact the average individual tends to exaggerate rather than minimize such differences. The only question likely to be raised in this connection is whether a given society should be thought of as having a single personality norm or as having a series of different personality norms each of which is associated with a particular status group within the society. Any difficulty in reconciling these two points of view will disappear when one sees them in proper perspective. The members of any society will always be found to have a long series of personality elements in common. These elements may be of any degree of specificity, ranging from simple overt responses of the sort involved in "table manners" to highly generalized attitudes. Responses of the latter type may underlie a wide range of more specific responses in the individual. Similarly, value-attitude systems which are shared by the members of a society may be reflected in several different forms of status-linked overt behavior. Thus the men and women within a society may share the same attitudes with respect to feminine modesty or masculine courage, although the behavior linked with these attitudes will necessarily be different for each sex. For the women the common modesty attitudes will be expressed in particular patterns of dress or conduct, for the men in more generalized responses of approval or disapproval for particular costumes or conduct. These common personality elements together form a fairly well-integrated configuration which may be called the *Basic Personality Type* for the society as a whole. The existence of this configuration provides the members of the society with common understandings and values and makes possible the unified emotional response of the society's members to situations in which their common values are involved.   *UNIFIED ?*

It will also be found that in every society there are additional configurations of responses which are linked with certain socially delimited groups within the society. Thus, in practically all cases, different response configurations are characteristic for men and for women, for adolescents and for adults, and so on. In a stratified society similar differences may be observed between the responses characteristic of individuals from different social levels, as nobles, commoners and slaves. These status-linked response configurations may be termed *Status Personalities*. They are of the utmost importance to the successful functioning of the society, since they make it possible for its members to interact successfully on the basis of status cues alone. Thus even in dealings between complete strangers, simple recognition of the social positions of the two individuals involved makes it possible for each to predict how the other will respond to most situations.

The status personalities recognized by any society are superimposed upon its basic personality type and are thoroughly integrated with the latter. However, they differ from the basic personality type in being heavily weighted on the side of specific overt responses. The weighting is so pronounced that it might even be questioned whether status personalities can be said to include any value-attitude systems distinct from those included in the basic personality. However, I feel that it is legitimate to distinguish between *knowledge* of a particular value-attitude system and *participation* in such a system. A status personality will rarely include any value-attitude system which is unknown to the members of other status groups, although it might come to do so under conditions of extreme intergroup hostility. On the other hand, it may very well include value-attitude systems in which the members of other status groups do not participate. Thus free men may know and allow for the attitudes of slaves without actually sharing them. In any case, it is the specific, overt responses which give status personalities most of their social significance. As long as the individual develops these responses, he can function successfully in the status whether he shares the associated value-attitude systems or not. Informal observation leads us to believe that such cases are fairly numerous in all societies. The specific response patterns of a status personality are presented to the individual in simple, concrete terms which make it easy to learn them. Social pressure toward their assumption is constant, and adherence to them is socially rewarded and deviation from them punished. Even the internal conflicts which may arise during the assumption of a specific response pattern which is at variance with one of the individual's value-attitude systems are not too disturbing. Although they may be vigorous at first, they tend to diminish and finally disappear as the response becomes automatized and unconscious.

Every society has its own basic personality type and its own series of status personalities differing in some respects from those of any other society. Practically all societies tacitly recognize this fact, and many of them have explanations for it. Our own society has, until very recent times, based its explanation on biological factors. Differences in basic personality type have been regarded as due to some linkage between race and personality. Status personality differences have been referred to sexual factors, in the case of male and female statuses, or to heredity. The latter explanation is not too familiar to Americans, since it is one of our culture patterns to ignore the existence of status personalities other than those which are sex-linked, but it is an integral part of European culture. Folk tales inherited from the days of a rigidly stratified society bristle with incidents in which the child of noble ancestry reared by low-rank foster parents is immediately recognized by his real relatives on the basis of his noble personality. These biological explanations are a good example of . . . culturally transmitted "knowledge." . . . They have been passed on in our society for many generations, and it is only recently that anyone has had the temerity to subject them to the tests of scientific investigation. Such an investigation really has to deal with three distinct problems: (1) In how far is personality determined by physiological factors? (2) In how far are such physiological determinants hereditary? (3) What is the probability of such hereditary determinants becoming so widely diffused in a society as to affect its basic personality type, or, in stratified societies, its status personalities?

Definition   I A.   We have already seen that the personality is primarily a configuration of responses which the individual has developed as a result of his experience. This experience, in turn, derives from his interaction with his environment. The innate qualities of the individual will influence strongly the sort of experience which he derives from this interaction. Thus a particular environmental situation may result in one sort of experience for a strong child and a quite different sort for a weak one. Again, there are many situations which will result in one sort of experience for an intelligent child and another sort for a dull one. However, it is also obvious that two children of equal intelligence or strength may derive quite different experience from different situations. If one of them is the brightest member of his family and the other the dullest member of his, their experience and the resulting response configurations will be quite different. In other words, although the innate qualities of the individual influence personality development, the sort of influence which they exert will be largely conditioned by environmental factors. Everything which we now know of the processes of personality formation indicates that we must substitute for the old formula of nature versus nurture, a new formula of nature plus or minus nurture. There seems to be abundant evidence that neither innate abilities nor environment can be regarded as constantly dominant in personality formation. Moreover, it appears that different combinations of the two may produce closely similar results as far as the developed personality is concerned. Thus any combination of innate and environmental factors which places the individual in a secure and dominant position will result in the development of certain basic attitudes; any combination which exposes him to insecurity and a subordinate position will result in the development of others.

It seems safe to conclude that innate, biologically determined factors cannot be used to account for personality configurations as wholes or for the various response patterns included within such configurations. They operate simply as one among several sets of factors responsible for the formation of these. However, the personality configuration consists of more than response patterns. It includes certain features of all-over organization which are vaguely referred to as the individual's temperament. The current definitions of this term imply that these features are innate and physiologically determined, but it is still uncertain in how far this is really the case. We do not know, for example, whether such a feature as nervous instability is really innate or a result of environmental influences or, as seems most probable, a product of the interaction of innate and environmental factors. Until this question can be answered it seems safest to leave temperament out of the discussion, while recognizing that such an omission must leave our conclusions incomplete.

In addition to response patterns and "temperamental" factors, every personality configuration includes the ability to carry on various psychological processes. It might be safer to speak of abilities, since there is plenty of evidence that a given individual may differ markedly in his facility with respect to different processes. Thus low intelligence may be linked with extraordinary ability in certain forms of learning and memory. That there are also individual differences with respect to particular abilities no one will question, although these differences seem to be a matter of degree rather than of kind. Thus all individuals are capable of some measure of learning and of thought, but they differ widely in their facility with respect to these processes. While facility can be increased by training and practice, the observed differences seem to be too great to be accounted for on this basis alone. Thus it may be questioned whether any amount of training would enable the average individual to memorize the entire Bible or to equal many of the recorded feats of lightning calculators. We are forced to conclude that there are certain innate factors which set upper limits to the possible development of particular psychological abilities and that these factors vary from one individual to another. We may also assume that such factors have some sort of physiological basis, although we still have no clear idea of what this basis may be.

To sum up, it appears that physiological factors cannot be held accountable for the developed response patterns which compose the bulk of the personality but that they may be responsible, in part, for the individual's psychological abilities. This brings us at once to our second problem: "In how far are such physiological determinants hereditary?" Unfortunately we are unable to solve this problem on the basis of our present knowledge or techniques. There is no way in which we can analyse out the psychological abilities of the individual in their "pure" state. We can only judge them by their overt manifestations, and these are always influenced by past experience. The unsatisfactory results obtained when even the best intelligence tests are applied to groups with different culture backgrounds brings this out clearly. This makes it impossible to establish the innate abilities of individuals in the terms required for a real genetic study. We can never tell in how far the apparent intelligence level of any individual is due to heredity or to opportunity. If we grant that psychological abilities have a physiological basis, it seems highly probable that at least some of the physiological factors involved are affected by heredity. At the same time, such evidence as we have on the occurrence of various levels of psychological ability seems to indicate that these are not inherited directly. Their appearance in individuals of known heredity cannot be predicted in the same simple mathematical terms as that of, say, eye color. In view of the almost infinite series of individual gradations in these abilities, it would be surprising if they were inherited directly. The most probable explanation seems to be that the physiological factors which are responsible for a particular level of ability result from certain highly complex combinations of genes and that in heredity these combinations do not move as units.

Even if this explanation is correct, it does not rule out the possibility that the basic personality type for a society may, in certain cases, be influenced by hereditary factors. The members of any society normally tend to intermarry among themselves. If the society is able to maintain its isolation for a long enough period, all its members will come to have much the same heredity. The length of time required to arrive at this condition will depend both upon the size of the original group from which the society's members are descended and on the homogeneity of this group's ancestry. The larger the original group and the more heterogeneous its origins, the longer the time required to establish a homogeneous heredity in its descendants. When the genes required to produce a particular combination are present in the bulk of a society's members, the chances of the combination appearing among their offspring are greatly increased. There is thus an excellent possibility that a small, long-isolated population may come to include a large proportion of individuals who stand at a particular level of psychological ability. Even in closely inbred societies there is always a considerable range of individual variation, so that the stupidest member of an intelligent group might well be duller than the most intelligent member of a stupid one. However, the basic personality type for any society is a matter of averages, and these averages may differ from one society to another as a result of hereditary factors. For the reasons already stated, such hereditary differences in psychological abilities would be especially likely to occur in small "primitive" societies of the sort with which anthropological studies have, for the most part, concerned themselves.

The foregoing discussion of the possibility of hereditary differences in the psychological norms for various societies may seem unnecessarily detailed. However, there is strong disagreement on this point even among anthropologists. One group takes it for granted that there are marked differences in the inherited abilities of most societies, while the other flatly denies the possibility of such differences. Apparently neither group has troubled to examine its position in the light of modern knowledge of genetics. The truth almost certainly lies somewhere between the two extremes. Small, long-isolated societies probably do differ in their inherited psychological potentialities. On the other hand, the members of most large societies, and indeed of all civilized ones, are so heterogeneous in their heredity that any physiological explanation of the observed differences in the personality norms for such societies is quite untenable. The genetic differences between, for example, the French and the Germans are so much smaller than the differences in their personality norms that it is ridiculous to try to account for the latter on a genetic basis. Even the most racialistic Germans have had to introduce the mystic concept of a Nordic soul capable of incarnation in a Mediterranean or Alpine body to bolster their concepts of racial superiority.

American anthropologists, led by the late Dr. Boas, were among the first to recognize the inadequacy of hereditary physiological factors as an explanation of the differing personality norms for various societies. Unfortunately, in their eagerness to combat doctrines of racial inequality and to emphasize the essential unity of our species they overlooked one important point. The processes of scientific advance, aside from the simple gathering of facts, are primarily processes of substitution. When accumulating knowledge renders one explanation of a particular phenomenon untenable, a new and better explanation has to be developed. It is not enough simply to point out that the previously accepted explanation was wrong. It is a readily observable fact that the personality norms for different societies do differ. Instead of accepting this frankly and attempting to account for it, certain anthropologists have contented themselves with trying to minimize the extent and importance of such differences. They have mustered the evidence to show that the differences which they are willing to admit cannot be due to racial factors, but they have done little to develop any better explanation. The belief that the differences in personality norms for various societies are due to innate hereditary factors is deeply rooted in the popular mind. It cannot be eradicated unless science is prepared to offer a better explanation. To believe that all human groups have the same psychological potentialities without trying to account for their very obvious differences in overt behavior and even in value-attitude systems calls for a degree of faith in scientific authority of which few individuals are capable. Even general statements that the observed differences are due to cultural factors remain unconvincing as long as they are not accompanied by explanations of what these factors may be and how they operate.

Our discussion of the possible rôle of hereditary factors in determining the personality norms for various societies should have made it clear that these factors are quite inadequate to account for many of the observable differences. The only alternative is to assume that such differences are referable to the particular environments within which the members of various societies are reared. . . . The environmental factors which appear to be most important in connection with personality formation are people and things. The behavior of the members of any society and the forms of most of the objects which they use are largely stereotyped and can be described in terms of culture patterns. When we say that the developing individual's personality is shaped by culture, what we actually mean is that it is shaped by the experience which he derives from his contact with such stereotypes. That it actually is shaped by such contacts to a very large extent will hardly be doubted by anyone familiar with the evidence; however, the literature on the subject seems to have largely ignored one important aspect of the shaping process.

The influences which culture exerts on the developing personality are of two quite different sorts. On the one hand we have those influences which derive from the culturally patterned behavior of other individuals *toward* the child. These begin to operate from the moment of birth and are of paramount importance during infancy. On the other hand we have those influences which derive from the individual's observation of, or instruction in, the patterns of behavior characteristic of his society. Many of these patterns do not affect him directly, but they provide him with models for the development of his own habitual responses to various situations. These influences are unimportant in early infancy but continue to affect him throughout life. The failure to distinguish between these two types of cultural influence has led to a good deal of confusion.

It must be admitted at once that the two types of influence overlap at certain points. Culturally patterned behavior directed toward the child may serve as a model for the development of some of his own behavior patterns. This factor becomes operative as soon as the child is old enough to observe and remember what other people are doing. When, as an adult, he finds himself confronted by the innumerable problems involved in rearing his own children, he turns to these childhood memories for guidance. Thus in almost any American community we find parents sending their children to Sunday School because they themselves were sent to Sunday School. The fact that, as adults, they greatly prefer golf to church attendance does little to weaken the pattern. However, this aspect of any society's patterns for child-rearing is rather incidental to the influence which such patterns exert upon personality formation. At most it insures that children born into a particular society will be reared in much the same way generation after generation. The real importance of the patterns for early care and child-training lies in their effects upon the deeper levels of the personalities of individuals reared according to them.

It is generally accepted that the first few years of the individual's life are crucial for the establishment of the highly generalized value-attitude systems which form the deeper levels of personality content. The first realization of this fact came from the study of atypical individuals in our own society and the discovery that certain of their peculiarities seemed to be rather consistently linked with certain sorts of atypical childhood experiences. The extension of personality studies to other societies in which both the normal patterns of child-rearing and the normal personality configurations for adults were different from our own only served to emphasize the importance of very early conditioning. Many of the "normal" aspects of European personalities which were accepted at first as due to instinctive factors are now recognized as results of our own particular patterns of child care. Although study of the relations between various societies' techniques for child-rearing and the basic personality types for adults in these societies has barely begun, we have already reached a point where certain correlations seem to be recognizable. Although a listing of all these correlations is impossible in a discussion as brief as the present one, a few examples may serve for illustration.

In societies in which the culture pattern prescribes absolute obedience from the child to the parent as a prerequisite for rewards of any sort, the normal adult will tend to be a submissive individual, dependent and lacking in initiative. Even though he has largely forgotten the childhood experiences which led to the establishment of these attitudes, his first reaction to any new situation will be to look to someone in authority for support and direction. It is worth noting in this connection that there are many societies in which the patterns of child-rearing are so effective in producing adult personalities of this type that special techniques have been developed for training a few selected individuals for leadership. Thus, among the Tanala of Madagascar, eldest sons are given differential treatment from birth, this treatment being designed to develop initiative and willingness to assume responsibility, while other children are systematically disciplined and repressed. Again, individuals who are reared in very small family groups of our own type have a tendency to focus their emotions and their anticipations of reward or punishment on a few other individuals. In this they are harking back unconsciously to a childhood in which all satisfactions and frustrations derived from their own fathers and mothers. In societies where the child is reared in an extended family environment, with numerous adults about, any one of whom may either reward or punish, the normal personality will tend in the opposite direction. In such societies the average individual is incapable of strong or lasting attachments or hatreds toward particular persons. All personal interactions embody an unconscious attitude of: "Oh, well, another will be along presently." It is difficult to conceive of such a society embodying in its culture such patterns as our concepts of romantic love, or of the necessity for finding the one and only partner without whom life will be meaningless.

Such examples could be multiplied indefinitely, but the above will serve to show the sort of correlations which are now emerging from studies of personality and culture. These correlations reflect linkages of a simple and obvious sort, and it is already plain that such one-to-one relationships between cause and effect are in the minority. In most cases we have to deal with complex configurations of child-training patterns which, as a whole, produce complex personality configurations in the adult. Nevertheless, no one who is familiar with the results which have already been obtained can doubt that here lies the key to most of the differences in basic personality type which have hitherto been ascribed to hereditary factors. The "normal" members of different societies owe their varying personality configurations much less to their genes than to their nurseries.

While the culture of any society determines the deeper levels of its members' personalities through the particular techniques of child-rearing to which it subjects them, its influence does not end with this. It goes on to shape the rest of their personalities by providing models for their specific responses as well. This latter process continues throughout life. As the individual matures and then ages, he constantly has to unlearn patterns of response which have ceased to be effective and to learn new ones more appropriate to his current place in the society. At every step in this process, culture serves as a guide. It not only provides him with models for his changing roles but also insures that these roles shall be, on the whole, compatible with his deep-seated value-attitude systems. All the patterns within a single culture tend to show a sort of psychological coherence quite aside from their functional interrelations. With rare exceptions, the "normal" individual who adheres to them will not be required to do anything which is incompatible with the deeper levels of his personality structure. Even when one society borrows patterns of behavior from another, these patterns will usually be modified and reworked until they become congruous with the basic personality type of the borrowers. Culture may compel the atypical individual to adhere to forms of behavior which are repugnant to him, but when such behavior is repugnant to the bulk of a society's members, it is culture which has to give way.

Turning to the other side of the picture, the acquisition of new behavior patterns which are congruous with the individual's generalized value-attitude systems tends to reinforce these systems and to establish them more firmly as time passes. The individual who spends his life in any society with a fairly stable culture finds his personality becoming more firmly integrated as he grows older. His adolescent doubts and questionings with respect to the attitudes implicit in his culture disappear as he reaffirms them in his adherence to the overt behavior which his culture prescribes. In time he emerges as a pillar of society, unable to understand how anyone can entertain such doubts. While this process may not make for progress, it certainly makes for individual contentment. The state of such a person is infinitely happier than that of one who finds himself compelled to adhere to patterns of overt behavior which are not congruous with the value-attitude systems established by his earliest experiences. The result of such incongruities can be seen in many individuals who have had to adapt to rapidly changing culture conditions such as those which obtain in our own society. It is even more evident in the case of those who, having begun life in one culture, are attempting to adjust to another. These are the "marginal men" whose plight is recognized by all who have worked with the phenomenon of acculturation. Lacking the reinforcement derived from constant expression in overt behavior, the early-established value-attitude systems of such individuals are weakened and overlaid. At the same time, it seems that they are rarely if ever eliminated, still less replaced by new systems congruous with the cultural milieu in which the individual has to operate. The acculturated individual can learn to act and even to think in terms of his new society's culture, but he cannot learn to feel in these terms. At each point where decision is required he finds himself adrift with no fixed points of reference.

In summary, the fact that personality norms differ for different societies can be explained on the basis of the different experience which the members of such societies acquire from contact with their cultures. In the case of a few small societies whose members have a homogeneous heredity, the influence of physiological factors in determining the psychological potentialities of the majority of these members cannot be ruled out, but the number of such cases is certainly small. Even when common hereditary factors may be present, they can affect only potentialities for response. They are never enough in themselves to account for the differing content and organization which we find in the basic personality types for different societies.

Early in this chapter I cited three conclusions which anthropologists had arrived at as a result of their studies of personality in a wide range of societies and cultures. That personality norms differ for different societies is only the first of these. It is still necessary to explain why the members of any society always show considerable individual variation in personality and also why much the same range of variation and much the same personality types seem to be present in all societies. The first of these problems presents few difficulties. No two individuals, even identical twins, are exactly alike. The members of any society, no matter how closely inbred it may be, differ in their genetically determined potentialities for growth and development. Moreover the working out of these potentialities is affected by all sorts of environmental factors. From the moment of birth on, individuals will differ in size and vigor, while a little later differences in intelligence and learning ability will become apparent. It has already been said that the process of personality formation seems to be mainly one of the integration of experience. This experience, in turn, derives from the interaction of the individual with his environment. It follows that even identical environments, if such things are conceivable, will provide different individuals with different experiences and result in their developing different personalities.

Actually, the situation is much more complicated than this. Even the best-integrated society and culture provides the individuals who are reared in it with environments which are far from uniform. Culture expresses itself to the individual in terms of the behavior of other people and of his contacts with the objects which members of his society habitually make and use. The latter aspect of the cultural environment may be fairly uniform in some of the simpler societies where a combination of general poverty and patterns of sharing prevents the development of marked differences in living standards, but such societies certainly are in the minority. In most communities the various households vary in their equipment and thus provide the children reared in them with somewhat different physical environments. We do not know in how far differences of this sort are significant in personality formation, but everything indicates that they are of rather secondary importance. People have an infinitely greater effect on the developing individual than do things. In particular, the close and continuous contact which the child has with members of his own family, whether parents or siblings, seems to be crucial in establishing his generalized value-attitude systems. Needless to say, the experience which he may derive from such contacts is as varied as the individuals themselves. Even the most rigid culture patterns allow a certain amount of latitude in individual behavior, while the patterns for family relationships can never be too rigid in practice. Someone has said, "Nothing is as continuous as marriage," and the same would apply to parent-child relations. Repeated personal interactions lead to the development of individual patterns of behavior whose range of variation is limited only by fear of what the neighbors may say. Even while acting within the limits imposed by culture, it is possible for parents in any society to be affectionate or indifferent, strict or permissive, sources of aid and security in the child's dealings with outsiders or additional dangers in a generally hostile world. Individual differences and environmental differences can enter into an almost infinite series of permutations and combinations, and the experience which different individuals may derive from these is equally varied. This fact is quite sufficient to account for the differences in personality content which are to be found among the members of any society.

Why much the same range of variation and much the same personality types seem to be present in all societies presents a more difficult problem. Anthropologists themselves are in much less complete agreement on these points than on the preceding ones. Most anthropologists who have had intimate contacts with a number of different societies believe that such is the case, but any real proof or disproof must await the development of much better techniques for personality diagnosis. It must also be understood that when anthropologists say that much the same personality types seem to be present in all societies, in spite of marked differences in their frequencies, the term *personality* is used in a special sense. Most of the specific responses of individuals always fall within the limits set by culture, and it would be too much to expect to find them duplicated in members of different societies. What the anthropologist means is that when one becomes sufficiently familiar with an alien culture and with the individuals who share it, one finds that these individuals are fundamentally the same as various people whom he has known in his own society. While the specific, culturally patterned responses of the two will differ, their abilities and their basic value-attitude systems will be very much the same. This sort of matching does not require any elaborate typing of personalities in technical terms. What it does require is an intimate and sympathetic knowledge of the individuals and cultures involved. One must become exceedingly familiar with the culture of another group before the differences between individual norms of behavior and cultural norms become sufficiently obvious to serve as a guide in judging the deeper levels of individual personalities.

Similarities in the ability levels of members of different societies are not difficult to explain. All human beings are, after all, members of a single species, and the potential range of variations in this respect must be much the same for all societies. Similarities in the generalized value-attitude systems of individuals reared in different cultural environments are more difficult to account for, but there can be no question that they do occur. In the light of our present knowledge the most probable explanation seems to be that they are primarily a result of similar family situations operating upon individuals with similar levels of ability. It has already been noted that culture patterns for the interactions of family members always permit a considerable range of individual variation. In all societies the personalities involved in family situations tend to arrange themselves in much the same orders of dominance and to develop much the same patterns of private, informal interaction. Thus even in the most strongly patriarchal societies one encounters a surprising number of families in which the wife and mother is the dominant member. She may accord her husband exaggerated respect in public, but neither he nor the children will have any doubts as to where real power lies. Again, there are a whole series of biologically conditioned situations which repeat themselves irrespective of the cultural setting. In every society there will be eldest children and youngest children, only children and those reared as members of a large sibling group, feeble, sickly children and strong, vigorous ones. The same thing holds for various sorts of parent-child relationships. There are favorite children, wanted or unwanted children, good sons and black sheep who are constantly subject to suspicion and discipline. Even while operating within the culturally established limits of parental authority, various parents may be affectionate and permissive or take a sadistic delight in exercising their disciplinary functions to the full. Each of these situations will result in a particular sort of early experience for the individual. When essentially similar individuals in different societies are exposed to similar family situations, the result will be a marked similarity in the deeper levels of their personality configurations.

Although the family situations just discussed operate at what might be termed a subcultural level, the frequency with which a particular situation arises in a particular society will be influenced by cultural factors. Thus it is much more difficult for a wife to establish control in a strongly patriarchal society than in a matriarchal one. In the former case she has to work counter to the accepted rules for the marital relationship and to brave all sorts of social pressures. Only a woman of very strong character, or one with a very weak husband, will be able to establish dominance. In the latter case any woman with ordinary strength of character can dominate her household with the aid of social pressures. In every society the bulk of the families will approximate the culturally established norms in their members' interpersonal relationships. It follows that most of the children reared in a particular society will be exposed to similar family situations and will emerge with many elements of even the deeper levels of their personalities in common. This conclusion seems to be borne out by the study of a wide range of societies. In every case numerous correlations can be established between the culture patterns for family organization and child-rearing and the basic personality type for adult members of the society.

Summary   In summary, culture must be considered the dominant factor in establishing the basic personality types for various societies and also in establishing the series of status personalities which are characteristic for each society. It must be remembered that basic personality types and status personalities, like culture construct patterns, represent the modes within certain ranges of variation. It is doubtful whether the actual personality of any individual will ever agree at all points with either of these abstractions. With respect to the formation of individual personalities, culture operates as one of a series of factors which also includes the physiologically determined potentialities of the individual and his relations with other individuals. There can be little doubt that in certain cases factors other than the cultural ones are primarily responsible for producing a particular personality configuration. However, it seems that in a majority of cases the cultural factors are dominant. We find that in all societies the personalities of the "average," "normal" individuals who keep the society operating in its accustomed ways can be accounted for in cultural terms. At the same time we find that all societies include atypical individuals whose personalities fall outside the normal range of variation for the society. The causes of such aberrant personalities are still imperfectly understood. They unquestionably derive in part from accidents of early environment and experience. In how far still other, genetically determined factors may be involved we are still unable to say.

In bringing this discussion to a close I am keenly conscious of the number of problems which I have indicated without being able to provide solutions. I am also conscious of the extent to which I have had to depend on techniques which will appear unscientific to those who regard science as something inseparably linked with the laboratory and slide rule. Those who are investigating culture, society and the individual and the complex interrelations of these phenomena are pioneers and, like all pioneers, they have to live by rough and ready methods. They are laboring in the lonely outposts which science has set up on the fringes of a new continent. Even their longest expeditions into the unknown have been mere traverses leaving great unexplored areas between. Those who come after them will be able to draw maps in the terms required by exact science and to exploit riches. The pioneers can only press on, sustained by the belief that somewhere in this vast territory there lies hidden the knowledge which will arm man for his greatest victory, the conquest of himself.

CONCLUSION

In this section the term culture has been defined and described by social scientists. On the basis of these selections, the reader now has some workable definitions of culture and an understanding of the distinction between culture and society. An understanding of culture is necessary in order to "use" the concept of culture in interpreting the following essays.

While developing the reader's understanding of social scientists' use of the term "culture," this section has introduced some questions about education. In his essay "Queer Customs," Clyde Kluckhohn indicates that cultural elements must meet the needs of the group in order to survive. In considering his statements, one might ask: how many of those elements of our culture found in the school curriculum are meeting the needs for survival? Is there a portion of school practice or a part of the school curriculum that serves a latent function? Kluckhohn also suggests that a major difference between non-technological and modern societies is the numerous exceptions to any generalizations that can be made about a stratified, technological society. Ralph Linton explains these differences by saying that there are few cultural universals in a modern society; consequently, the enculturation of a child in a modern society is much more difficult because there are few common patterns of behavior and many alternative ways of behaving.

In "The Concept of Culture," Leslie White makes a distinction between psychology and what he calls culturology. If this distinction is correct, one could refer to two types of learning: one based on psychology, the other on culture. Is it possible to provide examples of the two types of learning? Can one really make a discrete distinction between the two types of learning in a classroom? White's description of the nature of symbolic experience is especially significant to the teacher, as it implies that one of the school's major tasks, especially in the early grades, is to teach the child the meaning of events, objects, and ideas present in the extra-somatic world, that is, to symbolize. The current method of teaching reading—in which the child learns to pronounce words and, in this sense, to read without understanding the meanings of the words he "reads"—might be considered to have failed in developing a compatible relationship between practice and theory. Another example of this inability to symbolize properly is the difficulty experienced by the child from a "culturally deprived" neighbor-hood in interpreting the meanings of school events.

John and Mavis Biesanz, at the conclusion of their essay, suggest that the social controls present in primitive societies are inadequate in a modern society. Does this apply to the modern school setting?

Ralph Linton's description of cultural universals, specialties, and alternatives is especially applicable to curriculum construction. An analysis of the cultural universals of our society could provide the basis for a general education program. All students should be familiar with these universal patterns, regardless of their adult vocations. The cultural specialties provide the basis for vocational education, homemaking, auto shop, or college-preparatory courses. Finally, the cultural alternatives provide the basis for determining the elective courses. In such a manner, the school curriculum could be determined by an analysis of American culture rather than by tradition or the influence of pressure groups.

Since culture is not static, some of the cultural alternatives (electives) may eventually become cultural universals (a part of general education). In any event, as our culture possesses few universals, the school curriculum will always contain a variety of courses designed to meet society's needs. This variety should be based on the large numbers of cultural specialties and alternatives in our society and the increase in total content of the society.

In the final essay, Ralph Linton raises some interesting questions. Is there such a configuration as an "American personality"? If not, what factors affect the develop-ment of personality in America? Is there a "school personality" which is sanctioned in our schools but not in adult society? Finally, have the schools properly assumed the responsibility of helping a child unlearn patterns of response which may no longer be appropriate as he grows older, or do schools perpetuate childhood?

It should now be apparent that the science of culture can contribute to a theoretical perspective of the role of education in American society as well as to the practical solution of many problems that face education. To that end, we direct the reader to the specific examples of the role of culture in education, provided in Section 3.

ADDITIONAL READING

Felix Keesing, *Cultural Anthropology* (New York: Rinehart and Company, Inc., 1958). A standard text in the field.

Solon T. Kimball, "Transmission of Culture," *Educational Horizons*, XLIII, No. 4 (Summer 1965), 161–186. Provides an analysis of the distinction between the psychological and anthropological approach to learning theory.

Douglas L. Oliver, *Invitation to Anthropology* (Garden City, N. Y.: The Natural History Press, 1964). A simple, concise statement describing the discipline of anthropology.

Hilda Taba, *Curriculum Development: Theory and Practice* (New York: Harcourt, Brace and World, Inc., 1962). A good statement on culture may be found on pages 48–52.

3

The Science of Culture in Education

INTRODUCTION

An increasing number of social scientists are using the concept of culture to study the process of education in both pre-literate and industrial societies. The selections in this section are designed to provide examples of anthropological approaches. The use of the science of culture to analyze specific school problems will be considered in later sections.

American education is forced to deal with cultural pluralism—the idea that cultural differences that are not in gross conflict with the dominant culture should not only persist, but be encouraged. Cultural pluralism is best reflected in the statement, "It is our differences that make America great!" To carry out this philosophy, educators must become "culturally literate"; they must understand the nature of culture, how it is learned, how it shapes a child, and how the process of education varies in different cultures. They must be able to relate this understanding to decision-making at all levels of instruction so as to provide learning experiences for pupils from varied cultural backgrounds. The "culturally literate" educator is aware of alternatives available to him and can make wise choices among the alternatives.

3-1   EDUCATION AND THE SANCTIONS OF CUSTOM

Melville J. Herskovits

Melville J. Herskovits (1895–1963) was professor of anthropology at Northwestern University and director of its Program of African Studies. He trained under Boas at Columbia University and did field work in Dutch Guiana, Africa, Haiti, Trinidad, and Brazil. Among his many books are *Dahomey, An Ancient West African Kingdom, Man and His Works*, and *The American Negro*. This statement on education is taken from his introductory text in anthropology.

In its widest sense, education is to be thought of as that part of the enculturative experience that, through the learning process, equips an individual to take his place as an adult member of his society. The process, in most nonliterate communities, is carried on until the onset of puberty for girls, and slightly later for boys. In Euroamerican groups, especially at upper socio-economic levels, the period is appreciably lengthened. A much more restricted sense of the word "education" limits its use to those processes of teaching and learning carried on at specific times, in particular places outside the home, for definite periods, by persons especially prepared or trained for the task. This assigns to education the meaning of *schooling*.

Despite the fact that, in the broadest sense, education can be regarded as synonymous with the cycle of early enculturation, it is important for purposes of analysis to differentiate the conceptual significance of enculturation from that we shall assign here to the word education; and equally important to set off both these terms from the designation "schooling." All three are to be regarded as expressions of a single process, whereby an individual masters and manipulates his culture. But, as we have seen, enculturation continues throughout the entire life of an individual. It not only includes the training he receives at the hands of others, but also the assimilation of elements in his culture that he acquires without direction, through his own powers of observation and by imitation. A new dance he learns as an adult is a part of his enculturation, but hardly of his education; so is the manner in which, so to speak, he absorbs the motor and speech habits of his group. Training in etiquette, however, is education, as is instruction in some special technique such as pottery-making or gardening, or the inculcation of moral values by the tales a boy or girl is told for the purpose.

We must, therefore, be as cautious in evaluating definitions of education that are too inclusive, such as that which holds this process to be "the relationship between members of successive generations,"[1] as in accepting definitions that are drawn too narrowly. Just as enculturation is a term of wider applicability than education, so education, in its ethnological sense of directed learning, is of broader reference than schooling, that aspect of education carried on by specialists. Enculturation and education are also broader than schooling in another sense—enculturation and education are universals in culture; schooling is not.

Copyright 1947, 1948 by Melville J. Herskovits. Reprinted by permission of Alfred A. Knopf, Inc., from *Man and His Works* by Melville J. Herskovits, pp. 310–314.
[1] Otto F. Raum, *Chaga Childhood* (London: Oxford University Press, 1940), p. 62.

In any society, what the young may be taught is only limited by the scope of the culture. Even where enculturation is achieved without any formalized direction, a certain amount of guidance will be required. Communication can be achieved after a fashion by the use of baby talk, which in turn is effortlessly transmuted into language. Yet there are always special usages, such as honorific terms, or relationship designations, or even plurals, that must be made explicit to the growing child if he is to use them properly. Or, again, little attention may be paid motor habits, but gesturing or modes of locomotion too far removed from the pattern will call for correction.

In this sense, education may be thought of as the buffer that polishes the rough surface of untutored behavior. It is a process whose function is to bring individual behavior into line with the specific requirements of a culture. In stating this, there is no need for us to take sides in the debate over theories of learning. Controversies as to the role of imitation *versus* conditioning, of reward and punishment *versus* association, have stimulated study and sharpened perceptions of the problems involved. . . Time and experience have so frequently demonstrated that no single explanation can account for any phenomenon of culture that, in principle, judgment must be withheld, with the expectation that the operation of each mechanism in the learning process will eventually be revealed and its function weighted.

Most persons of Euroamerican culture tend to regard education as synonymous with schooling. Few anthropologists who have discussed the training given boys and girls in nonliterate societies, and stressed the care taken by parents to make available to their children the cultural resources of their society, have not subsequently been confronted with statements such as, "The X—tribe has no system of education." What is meant by such a statement is almost always revealed to be something quite different—that the people in question have no *schools*. The significance of the distinction between "schooling" and "education" is to be grasped when it is pointed out that while every people must train their young, the cultures in which any substantial part of this training is carried on outside the household are few indeed.

When we treat of education, we must again consider the important place specialization plays in machine cultures, as against its relative absence in nonliterate societies. What we call "vocational training" affords an excellent example. There is little need for specific training of this sort in nonliterate societies; no need for special buildings stocked with intricate machines that young men and women learn to operate so that they may function the more effectively in the economy of their society. Where the technology of a people is simple, every young person becomes proficient over its whole range. Within the limits of sex lines of division of labor, the child has from his early years been continuously engaged in learning the processes he must later employ in getting his living. He may be more effective in one activity than in another, but his opportunities to learn embrace all the techniques which in later life, as a grown man or woman, he will be called upon to handle.

The effectiveness of these systems has often been commented on, especially the sureness with which children are trained, early in life, to manipulate elements of their material culture that require no little skill. Among river-peoples, boys six and seven years old can be observed paddling canoes quite alone. In their villages even younger children will be seen using long, sharp bush-knives to cut a branch off a dead limb. Little girls will tend a fire and see to it that the food in the cooking pots does not burn. Perhaps one reason for this seeming competence at an early age is that the material culture of nonliterate peoples, which is the aspect wherein it can best be observed, has less content than machine cultures and involves the use of less complicated implements. This permits children to be trained to do useful work at an earlier age. In linguistic proficiency, or in art or in a knowledge of the gods, however, most nonliterate children will be no more proficient, and indeed, no more concerned, than most children in literate societies who will eventually learn how to read and write.

An outstanding contrast between education in nonliterate cultures and in the Euroamerican scene is found in our attitude toward both learning and teaching.

Thus, in Wogeo, New Guinea, Hogbin reports that, "The children are in most cases even more eager to learn than the elders are to teach." He illustrates this with an example: "Sabwakai took up the adze on his own initiative [to help his father make a dugout] and on another occasion asked permission to come along with his father to one of our conferences at my house. 'By listening to what I tell you,' the father explained to me with a smile, 'he thinks he'll find out about the things he'll have to do when he's a man.' "[2]

In nonliterate society, it is far more evident than among ourselves, for example, that all must master the techniques that provide a living. These techniques do not operate at a distance, as in more complex economies, where urban children can be found who have no idea that milk does not originate in a milk-bottling plant or a milk-wagon; or do not realize that a loaf of wrapped bread comes from a cereal called wheat. Where special skills are to be learned, the child in nonliterate societies is, as a rule, eager to acquire what its parent knows. The pride of workmanship and the prestige of the good craftsman carry over to him, and he needs only slight encouragement to seek these for himself.

Even where the esoteric enters, the emphasis is on learning. The priest is not eager to teach the novice; he must be convinced that the boy or girl who desires to serve the god is spiritually endowed for learning how to do this. This emphasis on learning as against teaching is to be correlated with the smallness of nonliterate groups, and the homogeneity of their cultures. Those from outside a society who wish to acquire a technique, a healing formula, a rite, or a knowledge of certain tales, must seek to learn it. Once learned, it is taken home, where it is made available for others either as a free good, with the reward for its transmission expressed in prestige, or for a price. Pressure is rarely laid on even at this point to convince fellow-tribesmen it should be accepted. Except where the new acquisition is sold for a price, those who wish to learn it, may; those who do not wish to, need not.

The urge to learn is basic in all children, and in nonliterate societies, this drive is pointed toward culturally sanctioned ends that are much broader in relation to the cultural resources available than in a highly specialized culture such as our own. Here, where because of intense specialization choices are numerous, training must be along narrower lines—whether in terms of general behavior associated with one class as against another, or for a particular occupation, or even in chosen recreational pursuits. In nonliterate societies there are few square pegs in round holes. These are essentially the product of cultures wherein there are so many alternative possibilities that no individual can range at will over the entire body of traditions of his society, knowing the totality of his culture, being competent in most of it, and attaining special skill in such of its aspects as may appeal to him. To permit a child to explore as he wishes first one,

---

[2] I. A. Hogbin, "A New Guinea Childhood: From Weaning until the Eighth Year in the Wogeo," *Oceania*, XVI (1946–47b), 282.

then another compartment of a machine culture of Europe or America would make of him, in much more than the occupational sense, a "Jack of all trades and master of none."

It must not be supposed that because nonliterate peoples do not ordinarily educate their children in schools, educational devices are lacking. Knowledge must be acquired by learning, and it is not sufficient to lay it before even the most eager learner without organization and direction. Therefore, though schooling is not a factor in the education of the young of nonliterate peoples, there is no lack of educational techniques to encourage, to discipline, to punish. Punishment can be harsh indeed where consistent failure in some important aspect of life is continuous or incompetence is wilful. On the other hand, methods of arousing interest through rewards for the performance of duties laid on a child, or even by dramatizing the right to learn these duties, are frequently reported. Where a culture stresses competition, the play of competitive drives will be utilized to induce learning. Where competition is not important in ordering behavior, other methods of stimulating a child to want to be competent will be found. The process of educating the young, that is, like any other aspect of culture, is patterned and institutionalized.

Childhood is a carefree period of life for most human beings, despite the fact that they are continuously subjected to pressures and disciplines to shape them into functioning members of their society. The techniques of education used by nonliterate peoples vary as widely as any other aspect of their culture. They are expressed in overt training by elders, in emulating older children, in observation at ceremonies where only the mature are active participants, or sitting by while a parent or other elder relative goes about the daily tasks of a man or a woman, and watching what is done. They include the inculcation of moral values and proper conduct by direct instruction, the correction of an infringement of an accepted code by admonition, ridicule, or corporal punishment. Positive as well as negative measures are employed in bringing up a child. In many cultures, praise is lavished on the child who successfully performs an act, and various ways of encouraging him to attempt to do things he may be hesitant to try have been recorded, as where in West Africa bells are attached to the ankles of an infant who is learning to walk, so that he will increase his efforts.

It must be remembered that when we emphasize the primacy of the family in the education of children, we must accept this institution in a given culture in whatever form it may be defined. Within the family, education is principally carried on by the members of a household. Where family units are small, as among ourselves, this means that the father and mother, with perhaps a grandparent or uncle or aunt who is for a time a member of this grouping, discharge this obligation. In unilineal systems, where the classificatory relationship pattern prevails, the immediate contacts of the child will be far different from those of the individual brought up in a household whose members count their collaterals bilineally. Under a classificatory kinship structure, there will be several "fathers" or "mothers" to whom the upbringing of a child is of concern. All of these, by right, can admonish, encourage, punish, or reward in ways that even uncles and aunts in our own culture would rarely presume to do. Thus in a survey of the educational practices of American Indian tribes north of Mexico, Pettitt[3] names forty-three groups where the mother's brother plays a principal part in the education of the child.

---

[3]George A. Pettitt, "Primitive Education in North America," *University of California Publications in American Archaeology and Ethnology*, XLIII (1946), 19–22.

In Zuñi, Li assigns this broad base of supervision an important place in the "working mechanism" of educational discipline the child is submitted to. "All the members of the family besides the parents cooperate to see that the child behaves well. In fact, any member of the community who happens to pass by will say something to correct some misbehavior of a child. Confronted with this united front of adults, so to speak, the child does not have much chance in trying to play one against the other. And if he is not unduly constrained, why should he make it unpleasant both for himself and for others? It is often observed that a very obstreperous child is easily hushed by a slight sound of any adult, in fact, by any facial expression which is seen by the child."[4] Here we have an extension of the function of correction from classificatory relatives to the other adults of the community. This, again, entails no difficulty. The homogeneity of the culture makes for a unity of teaching objectives that reflect unity of cultural aims and methods of inculcating them in the young, and thus leaves little room for conflict between the directives given by different preceptors.

[4]Li An-Che, "Zuñi: Some Observations and Queries," American Anthropologist, XXXIX (1937), 62–76.

3-2   SOCIALIZATION AND ENCULTURATION

Margaret Mead

Margaret Mead is associate curator of ethnology at the American Museum of Natural History. She was educated at Columbia University, where she was a fellow student of Melville Herskovits. Her principal field work has been among the peoples of New Guinea (Manus, Arapesh, Mundugumor, Tchambuli), Samoa, and Bali. She has a wide interest in anthropological topics, from cultural character studies to the application of anthropology to psychiatry, education, mental health, nutrition, and cross-cultural communication. In addition, she has become well known as an interpreter for anthropology to the popular press. This essay was selected from a series of papers written in honor of Melville J. Herskovits.

Steadily and consistently, in all his work, Melville Herskovits has stood for the significance of the historical uniqueness of each culture and each cultural tradition. In the tasks he has set himself, his discussions of the problems inherent in this position have been illuminated by a meticulous attention to detail—the complex technical detail of music and drumming, of divining, of cadence and style in oratory. This attention to intricate, patterned detail has been one of the sources of delight in work which is not otherwise fully accessible to the anthropologist who is not a specialist in Afroamerican cultures. Throughout a period in anthropology in which the importance of the historical uniqueness of each different culture has been overshadowed by an emphasis on universals, his has been one voice which has never faltered.

But there is one field in which Herskovits has not worked with the attention to fine detail which is so characteristic of his research. In 1949, as I listened to the paper, "Some Psychological Implications of Afroamerican Studies," which he was

From Current Anthropology, IV, No. 2 (April 1963), 184–188. Copyright © 1963 by Current Anthropology; reprinted by permission of Current Anthropology and the author.

presenting to the 29th International Congress of Americanists, he made a pronouncement which struck me with amazement. Following a discussion of enculturation and of the need for finely observed and recorded data for analyses of culture change, he turned to a consideration of "research into the relationships between culture and personality." Referring to "what has come to be thought of as the 'national character' approach . . . which lays stress on the patterns of infant training in accounting for differences between personality types which characterize different societies," he said:

> If we consider the conventions of infant care of two West African peoples, the Ashanti and the Dahomeans, we find the resemblances between them in this element of their culture [i.e., the patterns of infant training] are such that, on the face of it, the security constellations held to be of primary importance in determining the adult personality structure would be expected to yield quite similar types. Children are nursed over a long period; [sic] and at their desire, bodily contact between infant and mother is continuous, intimate, and protective; hygienic training is not such as to give rise to traumatic experiences; children are taught to walk and to talk by being praised for success rather than by punishment for failure. Yet no precision instruments are needed to force the recognition of striking personality differences between adult Ashanti and Dahomeans. The latter are characterized by strong and pervasive patterns of competition for prestige and power that give a harshness to interpersonal relations which are merely brought into relief by the institutionalized sentimentalism of such a convention as that of the best friend. Among the Ashanti, however, such emphases are of minor import.[1]

This statement with all that it implies so startled me that I sat bolt upright with surprise. Everything that has been patiently accumulated on the subject of child rearing in different cultures has demonstrated the most minute correspondence between the over-all patterns of a culture and the patterns of child rearing in that culture. In the United States it has even been found that there is a finely graded sequence of differences in the way in which mothers hold their children as one moves from a mountain area in Kentucky to the lowlands and into a nearby large city.[2]

My initial reaction to Herskovits' statement was one of simple annoyance. But I did not give it further thought until, in 1951, a somewhat similar comment by Clyde Kluckhohn recalled the incident to my mind. At the AAAS meeting in Philadelphia when Kluckhohn, as incoming chairman of Section H, and I, as outgoing chairman, sat next to each other at the anthropology dinner, he remarked, "You know, you will just have to stop emphasizing all that swaddling stuff about the Russians, because Russian and Albanian swaddling are identical." When I asked who had made the observations on Albanian swaddling, he told me that the information was based on Carleton Coon's account, and he added, "You know what a good observer Carl is!" I did know. The next day I asked Coon to describe Albanian swaddling. It turned out that there were five important differences between their practices and those of the Russians.

As I thought about these two incidents, I also remembered how often students

---

[1]Melville J. Herskovits, "Some Psychological Implications of Afroamerican Studies," in *Acculturation in the Americas, Vol. II of Proceedings of the 29th International Congress of Americanists*, edited by Sol Tax (Chicago: University of Chicago Press, 1952), pp. 152–160.

[2]Ray L. Birdwhistell, personal communication.

of behavior use the words *socialization* and *enculturation* uncritically and interchangeably. Then I began to see what had happened. In their discussions of child rearing, anthropologists (in these two instances, Herskovits and Kluckhohn) had failed to exercise the kind of vigilance and to make the necessary distinctions between universals and historical particulars which, in general, have so outstandingly characterized the work of Herskovits and have made possible the whole range of his Afroamerican studies.

However, this failure to distinguish clearly between socialization and enculturation—between abstract statements about learning as a universal process and the actual process of learning as it takes place in a specific culture—was not the only difficulty. In addition, we had failed to provide fully effective, specific theoretical safeguards for the generalizations which could be made on the basis of anthropological studies of child rearing practices and of education and which, in various forms, had entered into the conceptual schemes of social psychiatry, and sociology.

Since it was the incongruence between Herskovits' statement on this subject and his customary respect for detail and for the placement of detail in context that alerted me to the problem, I believe that this series, written in his honor, is an appropriate setting in which to spell out what did happen—and what is still happening— and to suggest some steps which can be taken so that this branch of anthropology may measure up to the standards he himself has set in other fields of comparison between cultures.

In the first quarter of this century, American cultural anthropologists were already fully prepared to accept the idea that as culture is learned, it must be learned by each new individual coming into the group. It was also evident to them that this learning has, as have all other parts of culture, both unique and universal aspects. It could be assumed that the universals proceed from a man's human situation, that is, from the need in each generation to teach what is known to the newborn human infants who (in our contemporary phrasing of the point) share species-characteristic capacities. In their field work, anthropological investigators were concerned with the particular ways in which an individual was inducted into his specific culture: with the way he was named, the way he was carried and then was taught to walk and talk, the way he was placed in the kinship system, the way he acquired property, the way he was initiated, married, and buried, and finally, after death, was given attributes of immortality or personal extinction.

In general, anthropologists regarded learning as relatively smooth and easy. It was recognized, of course, that in some cultures the process was punctuated by extremely drastic initiation ceremonies; as marked individual differences within a culture were also recognized. But as it was clear that, generation after generation, the culture was handed on successfully, the individual vicissitudes of cultural learning were little emphasized. Such concepts as those of Tarde[3] about the laws of imitation were regarded as sufficiently explanatory. The theoretical framework, in which the intrinsic integrity of each culture and each language was of crucial importance, made it all the easier for anthropologists to look upon education as one part of the cultural process that could be relied on to work with almost automatic simplicity. In fact, Boas used the word *automatic* in describing those acquired habits which seemed to exist below the level of awareness at which

---

[3]G. Tarde, *The Laws of Imitation*, translated by Elsie Parsons (New York: Holt and Co., 1903).

questioning becomes a possibility.[4] Radcliffe-Brown and Malinowski both dealt with the things which are learned by "the child" and by "the youth" at puberty without systematic reference to particular children or adolescents—though Malinowski was interested in and worked with Trobriand children and referred to individual children anecdotally.[5] In their discussions they made only the most general reference to the biologically-given characteristics of children or of some individual child, in particular. Childhood, youth, maturity, old age—these were, by and large, treated as statuses. Ruth Benedict, in her earlier papers and in *Patterns of Culture*,[6] invoked innate differences between individuals as an explanatory principle in her delineation of differences between cultures, and she allowed for the individual whose innate capacities were at variance with the emphases of the culture in which he had been reared. But not until the 1940's, did she make specific allowance for differences in methods of child rearing in the systematic comparison of cultures.[7]

However, as the importance for Freud's theories about childhood came to be recognized in the second quarter of the century, a new influence was brought to bear on thinking in those parts of anthropology which were concerned with problems of personality and culture as well as on thinking in the new science of child development, in social psychology with its interest in personality, and in sociology as it reached out to encompass more complete studies within single societies. At the very simplest level, the essential theoretical point made by Freud, namely, that human beings carry a burden of instinctual behavior that is fundamentally antagonistic to culture, can be translated into the statement that cultural learning, far from being the relatively automatic and painless process anthropologists had assumed it to be, is hard and painful and, in fact, often miscarries. The very newness of this idea increased its impact. So the painfulness of the process of learning was heavily underscored in the work of those whose thinking reflected a close interaction between anthropological and psychoanalytic theory, for example, in the philosophical and programmatic writing of L. K. Frank[8] and in John Dollard's *Criteria for the Life History*.[9] Even Gesell, who did not accept the Freudian position, heavily emphasized the contrast between the needs and the capacities of the child at different stages of growth and the demands made on the child by the culture, and he began to think in terms of a culture tailored to the needs of the child.[10]

Anthropological studies made in this period traced out in ever greater detail the processes of child rearing and the relationship between an emphasis, in a particular culture, on certain stages or phases of growth and such instinctual processes as the

---

[4]Margaret Mead, "Apprenticeship under Boas," in *The Anthropology of Franz Boas*, edited by Walter Goldschmidt, *Memoirs of the American Anthropologist Association*, LXI, 29–45.

[5]B. Malinowski, "Prenuptial Intercourse between the Sexes," *The Sexual Life of Savages* (London: Routledge, 1929), pp. 44–64.

[6]Ruth Benedict, *Patterns of Culture* (Boston: Houghton Mifflin, 1934).

[7]Ruth Benedict, "Child Rearing in Certain European Countries," *American Journal of Orthopsychiatry*, XIX, 342–350; and "The Study of Cultural Continuities and an Outline for Research on Child Training in Different Cultures," in *Towards World Understanding, VI, The Influence of Home and Community on Children under Thirteen Years of Age* (Paris: UNESCO, 1950), pp. 5–13, 15–25.

[8]L. K. Frank, "Cultural Coercion and Individual Distortion," *Psychiatry*, II (1939), 11–27.

[9]John Dollard, *Criteria for the Life History* (New Haven: Yale University Press, 1935).

[10]Arnold Gesell and Frances Ilg, et al., *Infant and Child in the Culture of Today* (New York: Harper & Brothers, 1943).

need for nurturance or sex. But in spite of the fact that they paid much greater attention to the details of learning, anthropologists—fully caught up in the completeness of cultural learning within a living culture—still tended to see the essential ease of the process. Babies on cradle boards cried for the cradle board. Babies suddenly pulled out of warm fur hoods into sub-zero temperatures remained rosy and chubby. Eskimo children spoke Eskimo; Chinook children spoke Chinook; Pukapuke children spoke Pukapuka. Much of the fascination of tracing out the process of learning in minute detail came from attempts to answer the kind of question that the psychologist, Robert Woodworth, put to me when I returned from Samoa: "When does an Indian become an Indian?" To be anthropologically meaningful, this question had to be made specific to a particular Indian group: When does a Cheyenne become a Cheyenne; a Zuñi, a Zuñi; a Navaho, a Navaho? But Woodworth's question set me thinking, and it led me to recognize that just as a 40-year-old Zuñi is a Zuñi, 40 years old, so also an hour-old Zuñi infant is a Zuñi, an hour old.

In the minds of specialists in other disciplines the idea that culture is not inborn but is learned became firmly associated with questions about reward and punishment, frustration and aggression, security and insecurity, and for those who were willing to face the full implications of psychoanalytic theory, with problems arising from the Oedipus complex and castration fear. As consumers of anthropologists' work, these specialists made extensive use of data from anthropological accounts to broaden the scope of their own discussions of the vicissitudes of learning. In their work the process of learning, in its *universal* form, came to be called *socialization*.

But these specialists treated the socialization process and made use of extracts from accounts of the Samoans or the Zuñi or other primitive peoples much as, in another context, one might treat the problem of man as a tool-using animal, illustrating one's conclusions with a few well chosen examples—hammer stones, Solutrean laurel leaf blades, Bronze Age axes, Medieval cavalry lances, and contemporary bull dozers— selected without regard for time and place from the whole vast repertoire of that tool-using animal, man. In much the same way, the human child, born into a world filled with requirements about eating, sleeping, eliminating, respecting property, conforming to rules, and so on, was described as experiencing *socialization*, and the process was illustrated with assorted samples selected from the world's cultures.

Gradually, a set of "disciplines" was singled out, each of which became a general area of interest. Taken alone and generally out of cultural context, each such discipline—a method of weaning or toilet training or cradling—was something one could focus on and treat as causally related (or prove not to be so related) to the behavior of some group: the upper class, the lower class rural American Negro, or a cluster of individuals who showed some consistency of psychosomatic disorder. In actual fact, the details were descriptive and illustrative, not explanatory.

Although those who used these approaches referred voluminously to the findings on primitive societies, they ignored, and very deeply ignored, the central principle on which work like that of Herskovits is based. For they failed to recognize the implications of the fact that while a type of activity—tool using or music making—is universal, it always occurs in specific contexts and always must be seen in its complete past and present historical context. The tendency to ignore the historical specificity of the particular culture was reinforced by the desire for quantification, however premature it might be. If sections of the culture, such as feeding practices and types of black magic, are lifted from their context and one is treated as a dependent variable and the other as an independent variable (as has been done by Whiting and Child[11]), then operations familiar to other branches of science can be performed.

But the immensely complex web of integration in a culture will not yield to piecemeal correlation studies, and the anthropologist in making a detailed study of cultural learning is not looking for simple "causes" by means of which a culture can be "explained." The detailed attention given to the way in which children with species-characteristic capacities, an immense range of individual differences, and an extraordinary ability to learn under the most markedly different conditions, are reared is relevant *both* to the comprehensive delineation of particular, historically unique cultures and to an understanding of the processes of learning, as such. But two different levels of abstraction are involved in a discussion of enculturation, on the one hand and socialization, on the other. It is the failure to realize this, particularly by those specialists who have primarily illustrated their work with extracts from the work of anthropologists, which has led to confusion. And this confusion between the problems of enculturation and those of socialization was compounded when thinking derived in part from anthropology was reimported into anthropology by some of those who were taking their leads from related disciplines.

This has been especially unfortunate when general statements about childhood have been made by those anthropologists who have stood for detailed cultural work but who have not worked intimately and cross-culturally on child rearing practices and problems of learning. In *Children of the People*, for example, Leighton and Kluckhohn present a beautifully detailed description of the vicissitudes of the feeding and weaning process. But later, in a discussion of adult Navaho personality, there occurs a paragraph which, taken out of context, can be— and has been—misunderstood. Discussing the adult Navaho emphasis on "security" at the expense of "ambition," the authors write:

> Perhaps some readers who are familiar with modern psychological theories are asking: how can the anxiety level be so high among a people where infants are nursed whenever they want to be, where childhood disciplines are so permissive, where there is so much affection for children? It is true that, if the writings of certain psychoanalysts and other child psychiatrists and psychologists were literally true (and were the whole truth), adult Navahos would inevitably have calm and beautifully adjusted personalities. However, this is certainly not the case. In spite of the fact that Navaho infants receive a maximum of protection and gratification, when they grow to be adults they are very moody and worry a great deal.[12]

Here, in this generalization, the nexus between the full detail of cultural practice and the character of the adults who rear the infant—and who themselves were so reared—not only is not noted, but even is temporarily dropped out of the discussion.

What was brought back into anthropology was a debased coinage. Scientific

---

[11]John Whiting and Irvin L. Child, *Child Training and Personality* (New Haven: Yale University Press, 1947).

[12]Dorothea Leighton and Clyde Kluckhohn, *Children of the People* (Cambridge: Harvard University Press, 1947).

work would have been enormously enhanced had comparative studies been based on careful analyses in which, for example, the full range of weaning practices was systematically worked out and sifted until some normative statement could be developed which took into account the pattern of each culture. Instead, we have had tabulations, such as those made by Ford and Beach on sex, from 190 societies, selected in terms of mere availability of data and "scattered around the world from the edge of the Arctic Circle to the southernmost tip of Australia,"[13] in which the details have, moreover, been torn from the context of their descriptive setting and from the context of the culture as well. Or, from time to time, anthropologists have used the generalizations derived from studies of socialization in their discussion of a particular people (as in Leighton's and Kluckhohn's discussion of adult Navaho personality) or in discussions of personality and culture (as in Herskovits' paper) and, recognizing the lack of fit between the generalizations and actual situations, have been critical of the approach to an understanding of personality through studies of the learning process rather than of the piecemeal and inappropriate methods by which generalizations about socialization have been reached.

In general, the pattern of the whole culture was ignored in comparative studies until, in *Social Structure and Personality*, Yehudi Cohen once more demonstrated the feasibility of using whole monographs and other detailed presentations, over and over again, to test out hypotheses, for example, about the relationship between "the ways in which parents bring up their children and the ways in which these practices are affected by social-structural processes outside the family" or "the treatment of aggression in the course of socialization, the fantasies of young children, and the transition from childhood to adolescence."[14] A first attempt to trace relationships between widely occurring practices to specific parts of particular cultural patterns was made in *Cooperation and Competition among Primitive Peoples*.[15] But research workers who are interested in problems of *socialization* have all too rarely been willing to engage in painstaking, detailed analysis, and they have all too seldom had the knowledge or the skills to enable them to differentiate between levels of analysis—between the presentation of data and interpretations of those data—in the materials on which they have drawn.

The problem of interdisciplinary exchange of concepts, findings, and methods is particularly acute in the human sciences. For here several disciplines, whose initial inquiries have had different starting points, have come to overlap in many ways and to share in both methods and results. In this situation, the ability of each discipline to clarify and preserve its central concepts is crucial. The misuse or the misunderstanding of the concepts of one discipline by another discipline leads to scientific waste, as psychologists labor to test hypotheses anthropologists never formulated and anthropologists reimport into their own work, in debased form, concepts once partly theirs.

So it is important to reaffirm the difference between the study of enculturation—the process of learning a culture in all its uniqueness and particularity—and the study of socialization—the set of species-wide requirements and exactions made on

---

[13] Clellan S. Ford and Frank A. Beach, *Patterns of Sexual Behavior* (New York: Harper & Brothers, 1951).

[14] Yehudi A. Cohen, *Social Structure and Personality: A Casebook* (New York: Holt, Rinehart and Winston, 1961).

[15] Margaret Mead, ed., *Cooperation and Competition among Primitive Peoples* (New York: McGraw-Hill, 1937; Boston: Beacon, revised ed., 1961).

human beings by human societies. Unless, in each case, the full details of enculturation are recorded and, later, are examined as meticulously as are techniques of drumming or singing, and are analyzed, in context, in many systematically chosen cultures, the probability of our developing a cross-culturally viable theory of socialization is negligible.

Each time a member of some other discipline arrives at a generalization about socialization based on an indiscriminate use of anthropological materials, each time an anthropologist applies to his own work the treatment of socialization currently in vogue in the behavioral sciences, which has not passed through the refining crucible of comparative study of enculturation, the confusion is further compounded. Controversies arise in which the anthropologist, or someone with a genuine knowledge of enculturation, objects that the particular generalization made by a behavioral scientist does not take culture (by which he means *cultures*) into account; in reply, the behavioral scientist insists that he has taken as a basic premise the idea that man is a cultural animal, that all culture is learned, and so forth. But to the extent that they are talking past each other, the controversy remains unresolved.

It is important that we should develop an interlocking set of conceptual frames. Within the larger whole, it is important that we should develop a conceptual framework for the understanding of human universals. The study of socialization is a field which can provide us with a common ground for the development of viable methods. But in this, as in other fields, the anthropologist's basic position—the position for which Herskovits has always stood—that one cannot talk about Culture until one has systematically studied cultures, that one cannot talk about Language until one has studied languages of many different sorts, is a fundamental one.

The value of such an approach is nowhere better illustrated than in a recent paper by Melville and Frances Herskovits, "Sibling Rivalry, the Oedipus Complex, and Myth."[16] In this paper, the psychoanalytically based, species-characteristic universal—sibling rivalry—is discussed in the light of a known, complete cultural pattern, that of Dahomey, and the groundwork is laid for a more complex statement of the Oedipal situation in the light of a comparison of Euroamerican and West African culture patterns. Here the procedures for which I am pleading are fully exemplified. The universal is not presented divested of the significant relevant detail. Instead the particular culture from which the myths are taken is itself taken fully into account. And in turn, the members of other human sciences who wish to draw on cultural anthropology are provided with material which, instead of being stripped down to the point at which culture vanishes, is set in a context so specific as to be unmistakable, and the generalization, with its theoretical implications, develops out of a full set of complexly organized, specific details.

---

[16]Melville Herskovits and Frances Herskovits, "Sibling Rivalry, the Oedipus Complex, and Myth," *Journal of American Folklore*, LXXI, 1–15.

3-3   GROWING UP IN A CULTURE

Mischa Titiev

Mischa Titiev was born in Russia and educated at Harvard University, where he received his doctorate in 1935. He has written extensively on the Hopi Indians, including *Notes on Hopi Witchcraft* and *Old Oraibi: A Study of the Hopi Indians of Third Mesa*, and has done field research with the Araucanian Indians in Chile and with rural Japanese. He is also the author of an introductory text, *The Science of Man*. He is presently professor of anthropology at the University of Michigan.

Not so long ago it became apparent that something vital was being omitted from traditional studies of culture in terms of models or biocultural configurations. It seemed clear to some ethnologists that scant attention was being paid to the individual men and women who, in all instances, were the sole carriers and transmitters of patterns of culture. It was felt particularly that the impact of culture on the personalities of specific individuals was being neglected. If every human being must learn to adjust his behavior to the sanctioned values of his society, certain anthropologists held, the very process of adjustment could not fail to have a weighty effect on everyone's adult personality.

Today there is increasing reluctance to deal with biocultural configurations as if they existed in a vacuum. More and more attention is being devoted to efforts to understand what happens to the personalities of individuals as they learn to conform to the culture patterns that prevail in their societies. To be truly valuable, these studies require detailed investigation into the lives of many particular persons. Resort to generalities, averages, or types is considered of small worth in this kind of approach. A host of modern anthropologists, including Kluckhohn, Mead, Benedict, DuBois, Hallowell and Linton, whose names are among those best known to the general public, have made important contributions toward an understanding of the ways in which socially sanctioned mores affect the conduct and temperaments of specific persons. Kluckhohn has neatly characterized this aspect of the science of man as being concerned with the "person-in-a-culture."

All researches into personality formation owe much to the hypotheses so convincingly advanced by Sigmund Freud. Even those who most violently disagree with parts of his teachings or methods are likely to take for granted some of his ideas. Over the years many criticisms have been made of Freud's concepts, but a number of his most fundamental tenets have never been proved wrong. This is certainly not the place for a complete review and evaluation of Freudian doctrine, but two of his cardinal points have stimulated a great deal of research on the part of numerous anthropologists. These are the concept of infantile sexuality, which seems to be inborn and which perpetually seeks gratification, not necessarily intercourse and orgasm; and the notion that feelings of love, hate, anger, and frustration that are experienced in early life may

From *The Science of Man*, Revised and Enlarged, by Mischa Titiev, pp. 481–499. Copyright 1954, © 1963 by Holt, Rinehart and Winston, Inc. All rights reserved. Reprinted by permission.

be buried for years before expressing themselves overtly in ways that may not directly reveal their true causes. These features of Freudian doctrine have led investigators to devote much attention to child-rearing customs and, since toilet training and weaning are widely interpreted as inducing frustration or resentment in babies, great stress is laid on studying these practices in varied societies. It is true that a few students of man have read far more meaning into toilet training and swaddling habits than the average cultural anthropologist considers to be justified. Nonetheless, it is generally agreed that the experiences of early childhood are likely to play important parts in the formation of adult personalities.

It is customary to use *projective tests* for determining those grievances, resentments, hatreds, delights, or loves that an individual may never speak about, yet may carry below the level of his conscious thoughts and attitudes. These tests fall into several groups. One type asks a subject to perform tasks, such as drawing a man or a horse, wherein the things that he emphasizes or omits may provide clues to his innermost traits of personality. Another kind confronts a person with a series of vaguely defined pictures, based on inkblots or deliberately ambiguous sketches, which the subject is asked to explain or interpret in any way that he pleases. Other sorts of projective tests require a subject to judge the behavior of people in standardized situations, such as that of a man who beats his wife; or to tell what values or associations a given list of words brings to mind.[1]

Answers obtained from projective tests have been found to reveal about a person many things that lie below the threshold of his consciousness. A number of ethnologists now give projective tests as part of their research programs in the field. Sometimes they turn the results over for analysis and interpretation to third parties, and in a surprising number of cases psychologists unfamiliar with the individuals and cultures concerned have made diagnoses of personality that closely agree with the independently formed judgments of the field workers.

A few psychologists and psychologically oriented anthropologists go so far as to try to explain the nature of culture itself as a reflection of individual personality traits. This reflects a time when the emphasis on war, for instance, which characterizes numerous societies, was attributed to the workings of a "death instinct" in the populace. Most modern scholars are reluctant to make such assumptions, and the origins of cultural emphases are usually left unexplained. Contemporary anthropologists are content to agree that each newly born child is faced with a pre-existent society and culture to which it must learn to adjust its built-in, biogenetically inherited mechanisms. Put another way, it amounts to saying that every baby must learn to conform to its society's sanctioned patterns for group living. What is called *learning theory* is thus involved, and to this vital subject many research workers have turned their attention. A common interest in learning theory is only one of several fruitful mergers between cultural anthropologists and psychologists.

Another area of joint activity concerns the awareness that the psychological potentials of a human being can be realized only if he is given the chance of interacting with other representatives of *Homo sapiens*. Ordinarily, these representatives will be

---

[1] Harold H. and Gladys L. Anderson, *An Introduction to Projective Techniques and Other Devices for Understanding the Dynamics of Human Behavior* (New York: Prentice-Hall, Inc., 1951). Best known of the tests based on indefinite pictures is Murray's Thematic Apperception Test (TAT). Standardized ink blots are used in Rorschach tests. A discussion of this subject may be found in this book.

found to stand in definite relationships to a child and to accept the obligations of attending to his physical needs and of teaching him the systems of values that are essential ingredients of their way of life. Through the combined efforts of all concerned, the sum total of the cultural norms of his social unit is brought home to a neonate, and as he grows older he becomes increasingly aware of the forms of behavior that are expected of him. Anthropologists and psychologists subscribe to the belief that an individual's personality can be understood only if one knows as much as possible about his teachers and about the whole cultural system in which he lives.

THE PROCESS OF ENCULTURATION

Although there are a great many definitions of culture, it is generally agreed that cultural concepts cannot be transmitted through genetic inheritance. Thus each child must start to learn the culture of its group after it has emerged from its mother's body. In any study of neonatal development, therefore, an anthropologist must begin with the assumption that a child is born with a set of complicated biological organisms but without a shred of culture. However, from the first moment of its birth a human baby begins to feel the impact of culture—in the way it is delivered, the mode in which its umbilical cord is cut and tied, the fashion in which it is washed and handled, and the manner in which it is swaddled or clothed.[2] At first it is passive, but somewhat later a newly born infant begins to be actively biocultural, and as it matures, in a country like the United States, it will find itself playing down the purely biological aspects of its conduct and stressing cultural values. It is as though each child began postnatal life as a 100 percent biological mechanism and thereafter tried to reduce its biological conduct to a hypothetical vanishing point. In reality, of course, biological activities can never be totally eliminated from human behavior.

For the process of adjusting individual responses increasingly to a society's patterns of culture, Melville Herskovits has chosen the fitting name *enculturation*. Enculturation or, as it is sometimes called, the *socialization* of a child, may be regarded as the manner in which each society molds the genetically controlled organization of its neonates to a set of pre-existing cultural norms.[3]

If it be granted that a baby's very first activities in postnatal life cannot be other than biological, it follows that many of its earliest experiences with the process of enculturation will be restrictive or frustrating. Tribes differ in responding to the desires of babies, but no matter how eager societies and their cultures may be to satisfy infantile demands, there is no group of human beings that drops everything instantaneously to feed a child at the first sign of hunger, allows it absolutely unlimited freedom of muscular movement, or everlastingly permits it to excrete when and where it will. Sooner or later each child must learn to eat, move, and eliminate in accord with the culturally determined set of rights and wrongs that prevails in its society. No doubt neonates differ in the degree to which they can tolerate restriction, but no human infant can completely avoid developing some feelings of displeasure or hostility as it reacts to

---

[2]H. Thoms and B. Bliven, Jr., "What Is a Baby?" *McCalls*, January 1957, p. 38 *et passim*. An interesting account of neonatal reactions and behavior.

[3]Paul H. Mussen and John J. Conger, *Child Development and Personality* (New York: Harper & Row, 1963, 2nd edition). A fine study of some of the problems involved in this process, analyzed from a psychological point of view, is presented in this text.

enculturation. There is an assumption that a child reared under easygoing conditions that hold in check very few of its activities, cater to its wants, and permit toilet training and weaning to occur without signs of grown-up impatience or distaste, will develop into a well-adjusted adult. Unfortunately, there has been little proof of the truth of this assumption.

Studies of enculturation may throw new light on such traditional Freudian concepts as the important *Oedipus complex*. Hitherto it has been assumed that a male child got so much loving attention from his mother that he grew up to hate his father as a rival whom he hoped to displace in his mother's affections. Now it can be shown that a baby also resents the *enculturators* who impose cultural checks on his actions. In the vast majority of known societies the biological or quasi-biological parents of an infant are its earliest and most important enculturators, but this need not always be the case. Theoretically, at least, a neonate may grow up to hate his enculturators, but may have no resentment at all toward his father.

Most of the requirements of enculturation are patterned similarly for all normal children of comparable age, sex, social background, and place of residence. They are so regularly repeated that they can be predicted without much difficulty by any competent observer who is well acquainted with a particular society and its culture. Thus, we know that all girls among us will be taught not to reveal their breasts when wearing street dress, and we anticipate that boys will show an interest in athletics. Furthermore, these undiscriminating, patterned regularities of conduct may be imposed even on children who have been subjected to unexpected conditions, as when an American youth is injured so severely that he can neither play nor watch sporting events. Such random experiences, in conflict with inflexible behavior patterns, may place a severe strain on the formation of individual personalities, yet the demands of cultural conformity are so relentless that something approximating normal adjustment is expected despite all handicaps.

All in all, the process of enculturation may be envisioned as a continuum marked into a number of stages (Fig. 1). The first stage, labeled "A," shows a neonate beginning to move away from the strictly biological condition in which he was born. Throughout the beginning phases of this stage an infant is the helpless and passive recipient of whatever forms of culture its handlers may choose to impose upon it. At this time, too, a baby cannot be made significantly aware of its sex, socioeconomic status, religious affiliation, or locale. Only gradually does it become conscious of the differences that these and similar factors may cause or imply. Nor, at the outset of postnatal life, can the adult members of a society place too many restrictions on a neonate's behavior. Gesell and others have satisfactorily shown that physical maturation proceeds by degrees in infancy, one step at a time. Accordingly, it would be impossible to toilet train a youngster before his brain was capable of giving the appropriate orders to those mechanisms that control the bladder and sphincter muscles.

Children born into any society must go through a stage "A." What differs from one group to another are the detailed forms of the culture that will be imposed on a neonate, the manner in which they will be applied to him, the severity with which transgressions will be punished and the time when a child is assumed to have entered stage "B." Wherever, figuratively speaking, a social unit may decide to end the first stage, and no matter how unobtrusively or indefinitely a crossline may be placed, it always represents a critical threshold, after crossing which a child is no longer expected to behave as it did in "A." This is what underlies the remark, so often heard in our society, that runs somewhat as follows: "Cut it out, you're not a baby any more!"

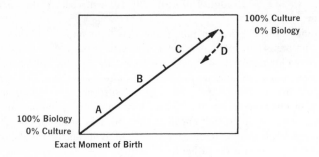

FIG. 1.

The process of enculturation. In every society each neonate must go through the process of enculturation. This is divided into four stages. "A" stands for infancy, "B" for adolescence, "C" for adulthood, and "D" for old age. It should be noted that in each society "A" has the highest percentage of biological behavior and that "D" reverts somewhat toward "A."

Of course, many of the growing-up experiences of a baby may occur at different times. In any society, infants are likely to be weaned at one time, to begin to talk at another, and to complete their toilet training at a third. Nevertheless, all of these things ultimately reach a culminating point, and each society recognizes when a child has moved from "A" to "B." In Greece, for instance, coffeehouses are masculine preserves, yet young girls regularly play in them. Then comes a day when a girl becomes aware of her sex, and from that time on she never enters a coffeehouse. In a similar way, a very young boy among us unhesitatingly accompanies his mother to a ladies' room; but a time always arrives when he becomes self-conscious and insists on going to a men's room. Such examples illustrate what is meant by the critical thresholds that divide into stages the continuous process of enculturation.

Broadly considered, stage "B" of Figure 1 covers the period of adolescence. This is always a difficult stage because a twofold series of changes is taking place simultaneously. Not only is the body undergoing numerous alterations, involving no one knows how many physical strains and stresses, but at the same time an adolescent must conform to a new set of cultural forms. Too often are adults likely to underestimate the cultural trials and tribulations of adjusting to stage "B." No grownup would view without alarm the necessity for changing his manner of speech, as well as his food and clothing habits, methods of movement, and so forth. Yet, we blithely expect every adolescent to talk, eat, dress, and move in a fashion that is recognizably different from that of a baby. Of course, the changes required in "B" are not immediate. Time is generally allowed for these changes to take place, and youngsters are usually forewarned that they will someday have to modify their habits, but even so it is no trivial matter to adjust to so many changing ways of life at the same time that one's body is in a state of turmoil.

There is a danger, too, at the close of this stage, that the end of biological adolescence may not coincide with the termination of cultural adolescence. To be explicit, we assume that a child will become a biological adult several years before our country permits him to vote. Some of these discrepancies may lead to biocultural unconformity.

Stage "C" may be said to represent full maturity and is usually marked by marriage. Once more a degree of variation exists in establishing this threshold, but again every society insists that adult behavior must be clearly different from adolescent conduct, and that everyone must "act his age!" In some ways the transition to "C" is less difficult than the move into "B," but it is not without its problems.

On the assumption that marriage takes place during stage "C," a striking change takes place in every newlywed's way of life. Before marriage an individual ordinarily lived in his family of orientation. Here he found himself forced to establish reciprocal ties of behavior with each of his parents and, if he had a brother and sister, with each of his siblings. Within his family of orientation *Ego* was subordinate to his father and mother, but more or less on a par with his brother and sister. At marriage, and particularly after he has begotten children, all this changes. Now a person finds himself occupying a different status in a *family of procreation*. Not only must he develop and maintain new bonds with his spouse, but he also finds himself dominant over his children.[4] Complications are likely to arise because a person is not expected to cancel all of the old ties in his family of orientation when he assumes different responsibilities in his family of procreation.

What has been said so far about "C" applies universally to all human societies. But in the United States additional strains may arise from our lack of firm standards of values regarding the change-over from one family system to the other (Fig. 2). Suppose, in the case of a son, that his father were elderly and sick. As long as a male *Ego* continued to live in his family of orientation he would be expected, from the

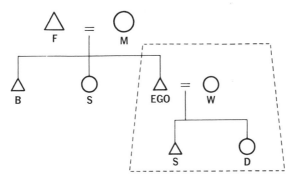

FIG. 2.

Ego in his families of orientation and procreation. While *Ego* is unwed, he resides in his family of orientation (left), where he is equal to his siblings but subordinate to his parents. When, at marriage, he shifts to his family of procreation (right), he becomes dominant over his children.

[4]W. Lloyd Warner, *American Life: Dream and Reality* (Chicago: University of Chicago Press, 1953), pp. 81–83.

time that he was old enough, to help his father. But if the father were still living when *Ego* married, what then? *Ego* is obligated to look after his wife and children, and he may not be in a position to help his father. Most Americans would agree that a man's first duty is toward his wife and children, but they would also insist that it is not right to neglect a sick and aged parent. Not all societies permit conflicts of this kind to arise. In old Japan, a man's obligations to his father were paramount and remained fixed. A filial son would neither feel upset nor would he arouse social criticism merely because he favored a parent over his wife and children. This is not to say that all Japanese cultural values were permanently fixed, but the values in this particular case were.

Last of the stages of the enculturational process is the one marked "D." It is entered in old age, as any society chooses to define senescence. Ordinarily, a person who crosses this point is assumed to have a fairly complete knowledge of his group's culture. Thus, as he approaches a greatly advanced age he is no longer expected to add still more cultural factors to his conduct. On the contrary, a very old person is permitted in all societies to revert somewhat to the biological behavior of a neonate. Our popular sayings about second childhood reflect an awareness of this reversion. If an extremely aged person soils himself or happens to expose his body, not much more is thought about it than if a small baby does the same things. Some of the behavior manifested in "D" may be rationalized or considered unavoidable because it is an outgrowth of physical change, but all cultures make allowances for such changes. Inevitably, death intervenes to halt the complete reversion from "D" to "A."

INTERIORIZING CULTURAL VALUES

As a baby grows up in any society it learns that much of what it was permitted to do as an infant is not allowed at a somewhat later date. Such teachings take the form of negative statements directed to a youngster by older people. "Don't do this," "Don't be naughty," "Don't do that," "You mustn't," is what a child hears repeatedly. Consciously or not, a baby finds itself recurrently in a hostility-fraught situation wherein it will arouse adult displeasure if it persists in following its own dictates; and adult displeasure, it soon learns from experience, leads to punishment in one form or another. Yet, an infant can never become emotionally content if it is constantly prevented from doing what it wishes. The commonest way out of this inescapable dilemma is for a child to bring itself to identify its own views with those of the more powerful grownups, until it gradually acquires the feeling of wanting to do what they think it ought to do. If, and when, such a point is reached the instances of open hostility diminish and the youngster may be said to have *interiorized* the cultural values of his society. Much of the earlier antagonism may persist in the subconscious levels of personality, but on the surface conformity without compulsion seems to prevail. Studies of personality formation, as well as analyses of the interplay between individuals and their cultures, must take into account the process of *value interiorization*. In reality, a child's formation of a *social conscience* may refer to the internalizing of its group's standards of values.

Interiorization is most successful and complete when a person comes to carry out the teachings of his culture without conscious thought. If the welfare of a society depends on promptness, for instance, it would never be enough for each individual to have to remind himself continuously that he must be on time. Only when everyone concerned has so completely interiorized the value of promptness that he no longer has to think about it can promptness be taken for granted by the society as a whole. This type of thoroughgoing interiorization provides the only guarantee that a pattern of culture will function properly.

Because the processes of enculturation and value interiorization go on simultaneously, or nearly so, they are sometimes regarded as one and the same. They are not, however, alike. During the earliest stages of enculturation, a baby has no option, at the outset, but to allow himself to become enwrapped, as it were, in its society's culture. On the other hand, interiorization is a completely active process, and a child has a small degree of choice with respect to the selection of the items it will interiorize as well as to the method, time, and order in which interiorizing will take place. A crude analogy may help to illustrate the essential difference between the two processes. A young child may be likened to a little customer with one cent in a candy store. The cent represents his limited facility for coping with a culture. When the storekeeper, who stands for parents or enculturators in a society, puts out a few bits of penny candy (cultural traits) it is *he* who makes the choice of what to offer. He may even go so far as to push one particular piece forward, which the little purchaser is very likely to choose. When the child makes the selection and actively absorbs the candy by sucking or chewing, it is as though he were interiorizing an item of culture.

To drop the analogy, we seem to have arrived at a pair of universal laws governing the interplay of an individual and his culture. Each society insists that its neonates adjust themselves to the pattern of culture that begins to enfold them as soon as they have been born; and value interiorization is one of the major mechanisms by which every baby makes the compulsory adjustment. Within the limits of even a single segment of a society and its particular subculture, the process of interiorization is complex and multidimensional. It appears to be compounded from at least three sets of variables, which probably differ for each infant. The first variable is biological, for it cannot be assumed that each neonate begins life with exactly the same genes and inborn equipment. This may help to account for the differing degrees of acceptance, or *thresholds of frustration*, that have been observed in babies. Experiments with very young children have proved that they react differently to stimuli that are precisely alike. The second variable is sociological, for every additional child that is born to a family occupies a different place in respect to its siblings and confronts its parents at a different stage of their age and experience. The third variable is cultural, inasmuch as patterns differ from one social unit to another and no design for group living remains static forever. Hence, something a child first learned to regard as wrong may later be considered acceptable. In 1900, for example, it was illegal and daring in New York City for women to smoke in public, but today such behavior is commonplace and perfectly legal.

This discussion may also serve to throw light on why a pattern of culture may, in theory, be treated as something that has an existence independent of the people who are its bearers. For one thing, patterns of culture are transmitted from one generation to another quite apart from the life and death of particular persons. They can also be more or less completely accepted and interiorized in different ways by different people. Moreover, the origins and changes of cultural patterns are not entirely controlled by the wishes or desires of the persons whose conduct they help to regulate. How subtly the forces of a culture can affect individual behavior is strikingly shown in the studies conducted by Gesell. The maturational sequences of an infant's physical development,

which were carefully worked out in his clinic at Yale University[5] and which were
assumed at first to be biologically universal for all of *Homo sapiens*, were later found
to be partly cultural and to have their best application to children born into the
subculture of middle-class parents in New Haven.

. . . A human baby-to-be can exercise no choice over the genetic elements that it
will receive from its parents at the moment of conception. This situation is contrasted
with an infant's postnatal acquisition of culture with respect to which it can exercise
a measure of selection. Theoretically, a growing child can decide to accept, modify, or
reject any trait of culture whatsoever. Why, then, do people so seldom fail to accept and
interiorize the values of their culture, even if many items are personally uncongenial
or distasteful? The answer revolves around a few basic points. In the first place,
enculturation begins at so early an age that a baby must be a passive recipient, without
much capacity for active agreement or disagreement. In the second place, it is impossible
during the early stages of life to reject a culture without repudiating parents, kinfolk,
and other enculturators—members of the society on whom one's welfare depends. In the
third place, how is a baby to know what other ways of life there may be? Finally it takes
a long time and it is not easy for an individual to learn any pattern of culture thoroughly.
We know full well that if we were asked to name an informant who could properly explain
our culture to an outsider we would suggest neither a young child nor an adolescent, but
a mature person 25 years of age or older. This is equivalent to saying implicitly that we
think it takes at least a quarter of a century to learn thoroughly a single manner of
living. Even though, admittedly, a second way of life might be learned more rapidly
than a first, it would still be extremely time-consuming and difficult for an adult who had
been brought up in one fashion to learn flawlessly the requirements of speaking a new
language, to form new motor habits, to adopt new eating habits and preferences, and to
accept a new set of outlooks on life, including new political allegiance and the practice
of a new religion. The sheer hardship of learning another culture pattern thoroughly is
enough to discourage all but a small number of people from voluntarily forsaking the
way of life that they had learned as children. Immigrants, it is true, often make drastic
changes of culture, but it generally takes an exceptionally strong expulsive force to get
them to leave their home societies.

THE INTERACTION OF INDIVIDUAL TEMPERAMENTS AND PATTERNS OF CULTURE

In all investigations of enculturation and value interiorization there is one
question that always stands forth prominently. What does each child bring into the world
with which it must confront its society's culture? No matter what reply is made, one fact
seems indisputable. Owing to the complexities of human reproduction, . . . the likelihood
is slim that any two offspring, excepting identical twins, will have inherited precisely
the same genetic composition. To this extent it may be said that no two neonates face the
world with exactly the same inborn equipment.[6] Even if they found themselves in
absolutely identical societies and cultures, which is impossible in practice, they would
still react in different ways. Yet, in spite of individual variability, each would resemble

---

[5] Arnold L. Gesell, *The Embryology of Behavior* (New York: Harper & Brothers, 1945).

[6] Roger J. Williams, *Biochemical Individuality* (London and New York: John Wiley and Sons, Inc.,
1956). Much new light is being shed on this topic by the investigations of the author who has published
some of his findings in this book. The author does not believe that any two people are exactly alike.

others of its kind in seeking air, food, warmth, dryness, and stability; each would respond to some stimuli by crying and to others by falling asleep; and each would digest food and excrete waste matter in fairly similar ways. In the most minimal and essential aspects of its bodily activities, therefore, every infant somehow reaches an equilibrium between its unique nature and the conformity of behavior that applies to its whole species. As it grows older another kind of balance has to be struck, this time between the child's inherited biological character and the culture pattern to which it must mold itself.[7] By the time it has reached maturity each youngster will have learned to conform reasonably well to the demands of its culture, but it should not be assumed that all children end up exactly alike. It is much more likely that each child will have retained a measure of individuality and that each will have paid a different price in terms of suppressions and repressions. Cultural conformity is a hard taskmaster, and it has also been known to exact high fees in the shape of warped personalities.

Individual personality is the product of an inherited biological character modified by the demands of culture. From this standpoint it becomes clear that variations in people may result either from the effects of a similar pattern of culture imposed on different organisms, or else from the impact of essentially dissimilar ways of life on reasonably similar biological entities. The possibilities inherent in these situations may be illustrated by combining some of William H. Sheldon's notions with some of the late Ruth Benedict's.[8] According to Sheldon, people of mesomorphic type, who are muscular and sturdily built, are somatotonic of temperament, and enjoy physical exercise, show a love of daring and boldness, seem indifferent to pain, and are assertive and aggressive, especially when under the influence of alcohol. These temperamental characteristics agree quite well with Benedict's portrayal of Dionysian patterns of culture, which honor aggression and reckless conduct in men.

Almost exactly opposite are the personality traits of those whom Sheldon calls ectomorphic. They are thin and fragile in anatomical structure and have cerebrotonic dispositions. Their actions are restrained, and they are inhibited in dealing with others. They are hypersensitive to pain, and they resist alcohol and other drugs. On the whole their temperaments are in accord with Benedict's account of Apollonian culture, which rewards self-restraint and sobriety.

If a male of mesomorphic build and somatotonic temperament should happen to be brought up in a Dionysian culture, it seems likely that he would conform easily, without conflict and with little cause for psychological maladjustment. Similarly, there seems to be little reason why an ectomorph who is cerebrotonic could not be expected to adjust smoothly to the requirements of an Apollonian way of life. But youngsters of all kinds are born into every sort of society, which suggests that somatotonics might find it hard to suit themselves to Apollonian patterns and that cerebrotonics would suffer where Dionysian standards prevailed.

The use of Sheldon's and Benedict's terminology does not mean that the author accepts their teachings without any reservation.[9] Some peoples and cultures can

[7] Icie G. Macy and H. J. Kelly, *Chemical Anthropology* (Chicago: University of Chicago Press, 1957). A great deal of information on the biochemistry of child growth may be found in this book.

[8] Ruth Benedict, *Patterns of Culture* (Boston: Houghton Mifflin, 1934); W. H. Sheldon, *Varieties of Human Physique* (New York: Harper & Brothers, 1940). Sheldon is one of the pioneers in constitutional anthropology. He believes that a person's biological inheritance, as expressed by his body build, always conditions his reaction to culture.

[9] The Pueblo Indians are not at all ectomorphic in body build, yet their culture and behavior are largely Apollonian.

be found that conform reasonably well to their descriptions. At the same time, what Sheldon and Benedict have brought out applies best to extreme cases and has less application to the majority of individuals and patterns of culture, which tend to be mixed rather than purely of one type or the other. The extremes have been used here only to bring the main issues into sharp focus. Now we must ask: "What psychological price do individuals physically given to one kind of behavior actually pay when they force themselves to conform to a way of life that is uncongenial to their innate temperaments?" and "How many maladjusted and neurotic individuals in any society result from the unspoken insistence that everyone, regardless of his inborn disposition, must regulate his conduct in agreement with predetermined cultural norms?"

At this point the danger of biocultural unconformity . . . looms large. Suppose an American father whose son was neither physically nor temperamentally suited for athletics insisted that the boy should become a football player. In such a dilemma, what is a poor child to do? If he disobeys his father, he runs the risk of losing his affection and support; but if he obeys, he is in danger of becoming internally upset. So it often is with the requirements of culture. From time to time every individual is placed in a situation where he offends his fellow men if he follows his own personal leanings, but where he must take a chance on personality maladjustment if he makes himself conform to the dictates of his society.

A program ought to be undertaken to discover exactly what happens to a neonate's biological system as a child modifies it in keeping with the requirements of his culture. At the moment it is conventional to say that cultural restrictions induce feelings of frustration in babies, who cry when they are prevented from doing what they would like. Norman R. Maier, a psychologist, suggests a contrasting interpretation. He defines frustration as "behavior without a goal,"[10] and he asks whether infantile crying may not be a "problem-solving technique." Perhaps Maier's theory is right. It is just as likely that infants cry deliberately for the express purpose of being taken out of an unpleasant situation as that they weep only to express resentment and helplessness. Answers to vital questions of this sort will never be found if students of personality and culture start with personality structures that are fully or reasonably well formed and then try to deduce the kind of childhood experience that a subject may have had. Such a deductive method puts students of personality on the level of medical researchers before the causes of most diseases were well known. In those days doctors could not recognize an ailment until it was well advanced, which made cures exceedingly difficult and preventive medicine impossible. Only when investigators begin to examine inductively the mechanisms by which newly born infants adjust their inherited natures to prescribed standards of culture will students of personality reach the scientific goal of knowing how personalities are formed. Then corrective measures could be applied where necessary.[11]

---

[10]Norman R. F. Maier, *Frustration: The Study of Behavior without a Goal* (New York: McGraw-Hill Book Company, 1949).

[11]Claims have recently been put forward for psychological tests that enable investigators of youngsters to detect future alcoholics. Proponents believe that if these tests are given early enough, proper diet can keep susceptible children from becoming chronic alcoholics later on. These claims have not yet been substantiated, but such tests are indicative of a trend toward discovering and correcting defects of personality before they are fully formed.

PERSONALITY FORMATION AND CULTURE CHANGE

There is no reason to believe that very poor, neglected, or abnormal children, unwanted (rejected) offspring, or children from broken homes are the only ones to encounter difficulties in moving from one enculturational stage to another. Normal youngsters, too, find it no trifling matter to grow up properly in any society and culture. Enculturation is a difficult process, and it is high time that we stopped regarding as abnormal every person who stumbles and requires help somewhere along the line. Occasionally, in a perfectly sound home, a boy may come to resent his enculturating father in a way that has little to do with sexual jealousy. A son may regard a very successful parent as an unfair rival who started long ahead of him in the race of life and who has reached a position of prominence that the son feels he can never attain. In such cases a good boy from an unbroken home sometimes "goes to pieces."

Enculturation is harder than ever when socially sanctioned values are indistinct or subject to rapid change. Theoretically, every individual should be prepared to accept different standards of values whenever necessary. But it is not easy to make such shifts, especially if the new values run counter to the old and little time is provided for making the transition. A child who has thoroughly interiorized the belief that a particular way of life is right cannot quickly accept the opposite premise. Not enough attention has heretofore been given to the problems created by pressures to accept new, and sometimes contradictory, standards of values on short notice.

American marriage counselors are all familiar with the phenomenon of *marital frigidity* on the part of numerous wives. Many advisers have long realized that the problem is more often cultural than biological, yet they do not seem to have given enough weight to the difficulties of making quick shifts of culture values. We are naïve if we think that every girl who has been taught to cherish her virginity and has resisted masculine advances for twenty years or so can without uneasiness give herself to her husband one night later, simply because she has been officially married to him earlier that day. No wonder a number of wives find it hard to make such a rapid change-over and no wonder that feelings of shame or guilt regarding sexual relations often arise even in the legally married.

Up to the present it has been customary for psychoanalysts and others who try to correct such difficulties as marital frigidity to seek the causes along the line *AB*, as shown in Figure 3. "Perhaps," it is said or implied, "the patient once experienced an emotional block in her premarital upbringing and has transferred her hostility from the man who caused the block to her husband." Theoretically, it is just as possible that the source of trouble lies along the line *BC* instead of *AB*, and is caused by sociocultural insistence on an overnight reversal of what had previously been considered wrong. The causes of personality maladjustments need not be sought exclusively in one direction or the other.

MODAL PERSONALITIES AND NATIONAL CHARACTER

Despite the feeling that studies of "persons-in-a-culture" should be conducted on specific individuals, some scholars have tried, in a manner of speaking, to combine the results of the investigations of numerous individuals into a kind of average, usually known as a *modal*, or *basic*, *personality type*. In addition to the convenience of grouping

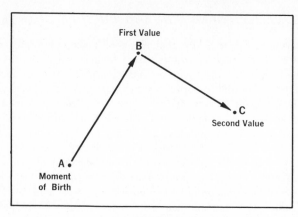

FIG. 3.

Value changes. As a person grows up, he must inevitably change some of his values.
Adjustments become harder in proportion to the length of time that a first value has
been held, in regard to the thoroughness with which a first value has been interiorized,
in relation to the degree of contradiction or opposition between "B" and "C," and in
accord with the preparation and length of time allowed for a change.

a large number of discrete studies under a single head, efforts to establish modal
personality types have some scientific justification. Supporters argue that it is to be
expected that people who are brought up in the same patterns of culture and who are
subjected to the same systems of values will show, at least on the surface, a number of
common personality characteristics. These are what descriptions of modal personality
types attempt to depict.

Following along similar lines, there has recently arisen an interest in what
is often called *national character*. Such studies do not restrict themselves to culturally
homogeneous tribal groups, but undertake to deal with large, literate, heavily industrial-
ized and heterogeneous social units on the scale of the United States or the Soviet
Union. They are based on the assumption that all citizens of a modern nation are
exposed to so many uniform cultural institutions—such as public schools, widely
distributed newspaper features, economic regulations, and dealings with federal government—that they develop similar characteristics of personality and behavior. Efforts
are made to delineate national character in terms of regularities of behavior that can
be predicted.

Proponents of national character studies, led in the United States by Margaret
Mead, are confident that this is a legitimate branch of cultural anthropology. They
recognize that big societies tend to divide into subgroups with distinctive subcultures,
but they claim that it is possible to reconcile the customs of the smaller divisions with
the established ways of life of the larger units. One American, they insist, especially
in the case of conformists, is more like another American than he is like a Balinese,
whether the American is a New England textile worker or a Texas rancher.

As for the use of cultural anthropologists in this type of research, it is felt
that they have much that is valuable to contribute. They are supposed to be able
to make disciplined studies of primitive societies, which may serve as models for
analyzing large nations; their research tools and techniques should prove applicable

to social units of any kind irrespective of location; they are accustomed to integrating the various aspects of culture into one whole structure; they have been schooled to discount their personal biases and prejudices; and they are so intimately acquainted with many diversified ways of life as to make possible valid intercultural comparisons.[12] At the same time it is realized that whereas one observer might be competent to make a singlehanded study of a small community, he might not be able singlehandedly to note and understand all the complexities of a large nation-state. For this reason teams of investigators are recommended, at least one of whom should be thoroughly acquainted with anthropological concepts and methods.

As in the case of all personality and culture studies, it is suggested that a thorough knowledge of culture patterns should be acquired before research on basic personality formation is begun. Child-training practices, especially, the effects of which are thought to be essential to the development of each individual's adult personality, are supposed to be carefully studied, not only for their own sakes and the understanding of personality formation that they may yield, but also because they may be expected to provide clues to a society's system of values. Plots of popular films and novels, autobiographical accounts, and large-scale projective tests may likewise throw much light on national outlooks, values, and emphases. Ultimately, it will probably be found that although all cultures and subcultures appear to be unique when studied one at a time, they are likely to reveal many similarities when examined on a comparative basis. Investigators of national character feel that if we acquire an understanding of the universal elements that exist in all patterns of culture, we shall have in our hands the potential for a better control of the biocultural behavior of all mankind.

[12]For many years a number of scholars have been assembling data from all over the world for the "Human Relations Area File" at Yale University. These data are arranged by topics, tribes, and regions. They are so cross-indexed as to make possible a large number of cross-cultural comparisons.

3-4   CULTURAL INFLUENCES SHAPING THE ROLE OF THE CHILD

Solon T. Kimball

Solon T. Kimball, who has done field work in Newburyport, Massachusetts; County Clare, Ireland; rural Michigan; Talladega, Alabama; and among the Navajo Indians, is professor of education and anthropology, Department of Social and Philosophical Foundations at Teachers College, Columbia University. He was formerly chairman of the Department of Sociology and Anthropology at the University of Alabama, and has published many articles on cultural dimensions in education and books on community studies.

It seems somewhat incredible that anything new or different could or should be said or written about children so soon after the close of the 1960 White House Conference on Children and Youth. The thoroughness with which the experts and the interested

From *The National Elementary School Principal*, XL, No. 1 (September 1960), 18–32. Copyright © 1960 by National Education Association; reprinted by permission of National Education Association and the author.

were solicited to participate reflects credit upon the abilities of the Conference organizers. From these efforts came an outpouring of articles from dozens of contributors covering nearly every conceivable aspect affecting youth. Their authors ranged the gamut of professional, religious, organizational, social, and intellectual segments of American life. Only one group seems to have remained unsolicited in this search for wisdom, namely, youth itself.

This type of oversight is not uncommon in the traditional American procedure of examining institutions and social problems. Those who are most directly affected by the preparation of a program are the ones most likely to be overlooked in the formulation of policy or of its instrumentation through organization. Patients, prisoners, or students are seldom consulted in the operation of hospitals, prisons, or schools. Perhaps this is as it must be, but then, again, perhaps those who suffer or benefit from the effects of the exercise of responsibility by others might also make a contribution, if it could be remembered to ask their participation.

That this remark is not completely gratuitous will become apparent as the analysis of the role of children in our society is developed in the next several pages. Possibly, an understanding of its relevance may well be the most important contribution which can be made to those who are charged with the responsibility of formal education in the early childhood years. But first, it is necessary to establish at least some minimum justification to add one more statement to this recent flood of analyses and opinions by those judged most competent to speak to the subject.

An attempt to rationalize or clarify disagreements and confusion among the experts might serve as a legitimate excuse for further treatment. Actually, differences in interpretation are surprisingly minor. The confusion is more a matter of indigestion, due to the quantity of data, than of methodological deficiencies. For this reason, such justification as is offered must be upon conceptual grounds, that it is possible through reorganization and re-examination from a different set of assumptions and with different objectives in mind to extract more meaning from the available data than has yet been achieved.

The initial step in this process is to shift our focus away from the subject, in this case children, to the environment—physical, psychical, social, and cultural— which surrounds and influences the child in his development. This emphasis does not exclude examination of the subject; it simply recognizes the interdependency between the individual and the systems of which he is a part or representative. Precedence for this procedure has been well developed in the natural sciences. Within anthropology, for example, although culture constitutes the central focus of study, it can be objectified only as individuals are examined. Contrariwise, when we come to study personality, we assume that it reflects a mirror image of the cultural experiences of the individual.

Following these introductory comments, we can now turn to an examination of the role or roles assigned to children in our society.

FORCED ABANDONMENT OF CHILDHOOD

Although it is seldom stated in this way, the major role of the child *qua* child is to submit to and assist in the activities and processes which prepare him for adult status. The extreme dependency of early infancy permits no choice in the selection of the external environment in which the initial learning occurs. Later when, presumably, the child has developed some rational discrimination in his response to demands placed upon him, it is too late for him to make effective protest. He has already internalized the emotional set of a system which requires that he eventually abandon the thought and habit ways of children and substitute those of the adult world.

However rewarding the culture of childhood, that of the grown-up world is continuously and persistently presented as more rewarding and desirable, and childhood is defined as a transitory and to-be-abandoned stage of life. No matter how entrancing, the never-never world of Peter Pan turns out to be just that, a fantasy in which childhood is forever threatened by pirates symbolizing demanding adults who must eventually win in the age-old struggle between old and young. Although James Barrie allows the illusion of a different solution, both child and adult know that his ending is founded in the realm of dreams.

This forced abandonment of childhood in which, if it is successful, the child is a willing participant, represents the first of a sequential series of tragedies which each individual encounters on the road of life. No matter how sentimental or protective adults may be, the gradual and sometimes forcible destruction of the innocence of childhood is a necessary function of the relationship between adult and child. The latter is not the only one who suffers in this nearly abrupt destruction of childhood certainties. The transition also demands its costs of the adult. The mother's mixed emotion of anguish and pride when her "baby" first enters school is repeated later when her child, turned young adult, leaves home for marriage, college, or the world of work. She may also carry a sense of guilt because of the contradictory desire to both hold and eject, and guilt because there can never be assurance that one has done enough or that what one has done has been right. There is solace in believing that one has done the best he could, but doubt may also nag the conscience.

The male response to these crises is different only in degree, and both parents share the knowledge that they have been parties to a failure, concealment, or perhaps even deception in communicating to the growing child what the world is really like. This conspiracy of silence is in part a function of the inability to articulate the realities; in part, it is an attempt to continue the protective role assumed during infancy; and, in part, it is a result of the parents' own unwillingness or incapacity to face the realities of their own lives. The delusion they have perpetuated, the illusion they have lived under and passed on to their children, should not be assessed as deliberate. Not that adults and parents are blameless, for they are not. The offense with which they may be charged is the same one as that which they first permitted and then prohibited, that of innocence.

The adult world is no more free of fantasy and illusion than is that of the child. The Walter Mittys are everywhere among us. Shaw's *Pygmalion* expresses a contemporary version of the Cinderella story. Our devoted adherence to romantic love as a necessary prerequisite to marriage and adult responsibilities of family and parenthood is real enough, but do we not deceive ourselves when we act as if erotic love is the panacea for the tough job of cementing relations between men and women in domestic functions?

These beliefs, and similar ones in other spheres of life, sustain us through bitterness, tragedy, and boredom. They are undoubtedly a necessary aspect in our kind of cultural world and as such should not, even were it possible, be either dispelled or destroyed. Our sin is that we let them delude us, that we insist upon maintaining an innocence of realities. Perhaps there is no simple way to explain why this is so, but probably these tendencies are linked with the generalized guilt which our culture so successfully inculcates during that period of defenseless infancy. If so, then it is all the more apparent why we can understand the child's role only by examining the nature of the world surrounding him. In that quest, we turn to a brief look at the distinctive aspects of the American family in its metropolitan middle class manifestations.

THE AMERICAN FAMILY SYSTEM

We can begin by examining how labels are used to describe and perhaps also obscure. There is some advantage but also danger in using apt phrases or slogans such as "the whole child." There is the tendency to treat such slogans as statements of objectives and to assign to the words themselves some magical quality which through their repeated utterance may produce the condition desired. There is also a failure to understand that, in most instances at least, the slogan—and the movement which it represents—is an after-the-fact situation. That is, that the conditions which permit some approximate realization of stated goals called for in the slogan are, in fact, already existent. An example will illustrate the point.

The now shop-worn label, "the family of togetherness," generated a profusion of slogans which served the special interests of varied groups. Some were self-seekers in their commercialization of this theme. Others were genuinely altruistic in their desire to promote the better life through encouraging praying together, playing together, learning together, and similar activities which, if performed as a family, might somehow enrich and fulfill life. The image of this family type is that of parents and their dependent children. The representation does not include grandparents, other relatives, or neighbors. In technical language, this is the "family of procreation," the biological and nuclear family typical of American culture. Neither slogans nor exhortations created it, and the definition of the roles of its members has been set by conditions which do not include the effects of conscious propaganda. Its natural history and functions differ from and may be contrasted with other types of family systems such as the stem, joint, or extended.

The succinct and penetrating analysis by Arensberg of the small family type— its historical antecedents, gradual modifications and evolution within the specific conditions of American society, and internal structure—permits one to establish a relation between scientific analysis and popular movements and their accompanying slogans. From his evidence, it is possible to demonstrate that what many conceive to be new approaches or discoveries are, in fact, only an emergent awareness by professional practitioners in education, health, and welfare of already prevalent characteristics of family life. Thus those who advocate democratic family life, togetherness, permissiveness, child-centered education, and individuation are less the creators of new progressive movements in family life and education than they are publicizers of an existing state of affairs. Of the American small family type Arensberg writes:

> . . . The imperatives of our family system, basing the small household on the conjugal pair, isolating that pair to free them to command their own destinies and satisfactions and to confer on them nearly complete and untrammeled authority over minor children (except where the state and community limit them), are not easy ones. Nor is the task our educational ideal assumes

a simple one: to prepare each and every man and woman to be in adulthood spouse, parent, householder, and family head all at once. These imperatives of our present small, conjugal type of family, with its minimum of kinship entanglement and support, ideally require each person to find a mate for himself, to love that spouse, to share the upbringing of children with him or her, to maintain a household with him, to find chief emotional identification in the little family growing up around this spouse and partner freely chosen and freely retained.[1]

Anthropologists know of no other family system which places such heavy responsibilities upon so few. In other times and places, the burden of obligations to succor and protect, to share and alleviate the tensions which arise from internal difficulties or external threat are diffused through kin and the institutions of community. In contrast, the American family in both its ideal and actual state stands nearly alone. And if this imperative, rooted in historical continuity and contemporary conditions, applies to the family as a unity, it also applies to the individuals who comprise the unity. They, too, have been taught the necessity of standing alone. Nor does the child in his period of dependency escape the requirement. If, by circumstance, he no longer contributes economically to the whole, as in an earlier agrarian period, his total burden is not thereby lightened in some degree. The responsibility he now shoulders is, if anything, heavier and more difficult than before.

STANDARDS OF ADULTHOOD

The course which begins in infancy inevitably leads through childhood and adolescence into adulthood. This progression can be viewed in part as the result of natural processes, in part as the consequence of training received from parents, peers, and teachers, but in even larger measure as directed, purposeful, and at times aggressive activity of the child himself. If the question were asked, "Is not this the universal process of acquiring adulthood in all cultures?" the answer given could not be an unqualified affirmative. The major difference is found in the early inculcation in the American child of certain standards of self-performance, the full realization of which will be achieved simultaneously with maturity. Later on we shall show that this expectancy proves to be an illusion which is, nonetheless, also transmitted to each succeeding generation.

First, however, the problem of what these standards are and how they become internalized and are maintained should be examined. Simple observation establishes that a parent comforting a hurt child often urges that he behave like a little man and stop his crying. In hundreds of other instances in the life relationship of parent and child, each time the former holds up adult behavior as superior there is implicit in the action a denigration of child behavior and an affirmation of superior adult standards. When boys are told, "Done like a man!" the implications of the praise for the action performed are quite explicit. Has anyone ever intended praise when he exclaimed, "You act like a child!"? And when older people do childish things, we call them senile or foolish.

---

[1] Conrad M. Arensberg, "The Family and Other Cultures," in *The Nation's Children* (New York: Columbia University Press, 1960), pp. 60–61.

Just when and where do we, in our multi-faceted relations with children, ever really judge their behavior except against the measure of progress they exhibit in the acquisition of adult standards? Irrespective of the steps by which the process is initiated, it is not difficult to observe the relentless insistence upon acquiring adult standards. If, by chance or intention, parents and teachers should abandon this aspect of their role, they would then have, to this extent, abandoned their function as adults.

The other part of the problem posed earlier, the question of what should be included under any listing of adult standards, was answered in large measure by Arensberg in his enumeration of the imperatives of our family system. Within this framework, however, there are certain specificities that need to be mentioned and their relevance elaborated if we are to grasp the role of the child.

It is generally accepted that family, school, and church transmit a greater portion of the cultural heritage to the child than do other agencies. What, then, among the many things which adults expect the child to learn, may we count as significant? The broad categories include skills for handling, knowledge for understanding, and feelings for evaluating the things, persons, and ideas which are encountered in the business of living. These requirements are so universal, however, that their generality does not help us much. If we look at some of the requirements imposed upon the individual in the American cultural system and then examine these in their relation to the family and respective roles within it, we shall encounter those specific traits which have been idealized for all members of the society.

Commitment to change. The central and perhaps most crucial commitment of American civilization is to the inevitability and, in most instances, the desirability of change. The activities and events of everyday life are interpreted through such terms as "progress," "advancement," and "development" within the context of the never-constant environment in which we live. If the individual is to be successful in this type of society, and the promise of success is one of the imperatives which move him, he must at least keep up with the times. Even those not motivated by promises of success know that stagnation is penalized. For the individual, this imperative means that he must be continuously poised to take advantage of opportunities for advancement. In fact, he must actively seek and, if possible, modify the environment to insure that situations favorable to him present themselves. Favorable chances and maneuvering avail nothing if there is resistance to working in new surroundings with new people and possibly learning new skills for new activities.

The successful meeting of new demands requires, first of all, readiness to abandon the present whether it be locality, associations, or activity. Under such circumstances, it is unwise to invest too deeply either emotionally, professionally, or financially, for the wrench which change demands may require a sacrifice too great to make. The easy fashion in which Americans establish and abandon new relationships disconcerts Europeans who accuse us of emotional superficiality. Their projection of values hardly explains the situation, nor are they likely to understand the necessity of such behavior as a function of our commitment. And the more deeply imbedded guilt with its corollary of tragedy they utterly fail to comprehend.

Self-fulfillment. These imperatives of mobility, independence, adaptability, and the capacity for continued growth represent, in one sense, subsidiary aspects of a more central requirement, that of self-fulfillment. Implied in the objective of adulthood achieved is the acquisition of competence, wisdom, and maturity. But fulfillment in the context of perpetual change contains a contradiction incapable of resolution. Final achievement is impossible because the objectives themselves are not fixed. They expand, recede, or are modified as the conditions within the system are changed, changes to which the individual in his progression also contributes. There can be no ultimate in the world view of those who adhere to the concept of an ever-expanding system. One might suppose that these circumstances would breed frustration and defeat, but apparently this occurs rarely since one is taught to accept striving as a lifelong necessity.

Perpetual optimism. Finally, the role must be performed in a mood of perpetual hopefulness, a trait which has also been set by the culture. The extent to which this mood has been integrated into the events of daily life may be met in many contexts. The language of salutation reveals the extraordinary extent to which we have carried our insistence upon a positive and optimistic approach to the world. No matter how we really feel, we are obligated to meet the world with a sunny disposition. Our conventional "Good day" has no relation to the actual state of the weather nor do our replies to inquiries about our well-being have relation to the actual situation. The response of "Fine," or one of its many variations, expresses how we ought to be. Any other admission is incorrect. The child learns this ritual language and the accompanying values in his earliest years. He is taught to condemn whining, complaining, crybabies, and pessimists. We should also like to deny that pain, evil, and death exist, and although we are forced to recognize them we assign them only marginal status. We would like to believe that all beings are basically good and should be trusted, a character quality which sometimes causes others to accuse us of being naive. These optimistic and positive traits found expression in the 1920's in the ringing slogan of Coué, "Day by day in every way I am getting better and better!"

Our culture demands that we maintain this euphoric facade in our own perception of the world and our place in it. Furthermore, we demand that our children acquire and exhibit the same psychological posture. Obviously, at times, this optimistic perceptual screen through which we interpret the events of the world must lead to some distortions in our apperception of reality. The truth is that, on occasions, the situation we find ourselves in, individually or collectively, is damned bad. But our "natural" optimism carries us through with the belief that tomorrow or next year will be better, that all things work out for the best, it's always darkest before the dawn, and so on through the dozens of aphorisms which give expression to the same point of view. The fact that events usually do turn toward the better lends credence to the belief.

It is my contention that the configuration of beliefs that we have been examining is a necessary corollary to the central value of self-fulfillment. To deny, in any degree, that societal conditions are not improving (through change) or that individual incapacitation prevents further growth is to admit that this keystone (self-fulfillment) upon which the structural unity of purpose in life has been erected is faulty—denies, then, the very basis of the American's conception of himself in his life role.

It should be apparent now why it has been necessary to examine these interconnections before we could turn to the direct study of the role of the child. The American small family, relatively isolated in its activities from other communal institutions, with the insistence upon the capacity for independence and mobility of its members, building and maintaining in each person the psychological posture of perpetual optimism with its corollary of self-fulfillment, taken as a whole and as functionally interdependent with other cultural systems, provides the conditions within which the role of the individual is defined.

Under such circumstances, the role of the child is as much central to the continued functioning of the whole as is the role of any other family member. A mutual dependence exists between children and their parents since the latter seek some portion of their own fulfillment through their children. In part, they fulfill themselves by providing a sheltering environment which expresses and enforces a temporary dependence. The dependency relationship, however, contains both contradiction and conflict for eventually, as both child and parent know, the independent and mobile condition must be claimed by or forced upon the child since adulthood is a necessary step for continued growth. This brings us to the point where we can more adequately conceptualize the child's role.

PROGRESSION INTO ADULTHOOD

Those who propose two alternative ways of viewing the child, namely, either as a miniature adult or as an undeveloped person but possessing the capacities for achieving maturity, may come to conclusions that distort reality. There is no intention to pose a conundrum by saying that the child is neither and both. For example, most children by the time they have reached the age of three or four have already learned a number of important adult skills. They walk, talk, control the elimination of bodily wastes in socially acceptable ways, and have developed habits, points of view, and skills around sleeping, eating, and their relations to a limited number of other persons. Childish ways may still adhere to some of their activities, but any realistic appraisal of the contrast between behavior in the first year of life with that of the fourth must grant that in some directions adult standards have been successfully transmitted. By six or seven, some children are judged precociously mature. For most children, however, the period of development coincides with physical growth, except that in our society the dependence is maintained for a much longer period because of the requirement for formal training through post-adolescent years.

Thus, at a very early age the child acquires some of the requisite skills of an independent individual. To this extent, he has cleared some hurdles which test for adult competency. In other areas, he remains dependent, undeveloped, and not yet capable of unguided mobility. We again restate the point made earlier that the fundamental role of the child is to become an adult. All his activities are either contributory or incidental to this end. The progression is partly a function of physical and neural growth, partly a function of the social and cultural environment within which the child learns, but it is continuous although uneven.

PRESSURES ON CHILDREN TO BE ADULT

The responsibility parents feel for converting their children into adults is so great that they impose a rigorous regime upon them during their dependent years. The intensity of parental concern reaches into every aspect of child behavior. It is expressed by an overconcern and overdirection of the child's activities. All types of special "opportunities" for developing skills are sought out. One manifestation has been the downward extension of formal schooling to pre-kindergarten classes.

The reality eventually became sloganized in the phrase "child-centered." Whatever excesses have been committed in home or school by adults who abdicated responsibility because of this doctrine, their behavior never violated the fundamental principle that children must be turned into adults. The freedoms given the child in activity or temperament were never justified on the grounds that these would permit him to remain a child; it was because this freedom ensured a healthier, better-adjusted adult. In effect, child-centered dogma was an unwitting device for putting ever-greater pressures upon the child. In its rationale, the adults deluded both themselves and the children they tended because it was never explained that this was a long-term transaction with an expected profitable pay-off at the end.

Perhaps we should be more explicit about the pressures to which the child is subject. The cultural context within which these appear is, of course, that children cannot just be allowed to grow up; they must be wisely directed. The justification is based upon the great latent "potential" in the unformed young which is waiting to be realized. Only as the potential is realized can the child fulfill himself, and fulfillment is a function of adulthood, not childhood. What is not made explicit to the child and is probably perceived by only a few parents and teachers is that their own role is dependent upon child accomplishments. Under these conditions, the child carries a heavier burden of responsibility in the proper performance of his role than that placed upon the young in any other society.

The child is expected to grow not only into an adult but into a successful one. The definition of the latter is, of course, adult determined. Success must be found in career, in marriage, in family, in community, and in one's personal life The adult believes and the child comes to accept early that the route to these objectives can be reached through training. The apparatus through which much of this training is transmitted is the formal educational system. It is here that performance is judged by agreed-upon standards and a preliminary preview of the future seen. Hence, the parental pressures on the child for academic striving.

BARRIERS TO ADULTHOOD

Unfortunately, there are several conditions which inhibit and limit the child's efforts in acquiring that experience necessary for adulthood. The culturally isolating centripetence of metropolitan life reduces enormously the opportunities for significant cross-group experience. The capacity to make social adaptations cannot be learned in the severely limited urban enclave or homogeneous suburb. Emphasis upon personal adjustment is probably related to the narrow range of inter-personal experiences and the ultimate necessity to rely upon oneself. The poverty of cultural variation must have a serious distorting effect on capacities for comparative perception. Vicarious experiences provided by fantasy or documentary in television, cinema, drama, or literature are no substitute and cannot be truly comprehended unless there is a substantial comparative understanding from which these can be interpreted. Situations portraying romantic love, the vicissitudes of family life, or the struggle for power may be dramatized in African, Asian, or American settings but the meaning is reduced to horizons found in Scarsdale, Plainville, or Little Rock.

In spite of our insistence upon cultural pluralism and the tolerance of deviancy, the danger of cultural diversity remains a powerful threat. Is it possible that the social isolation of the American small family intensifies the internalization of its values, manners, and behavior to the exclusion of differing standards? Forced to depend largely upon its own resources, as it is, this may be an expected consequence. In any event, family restrictions present another hazard in the child's struggle to grow up. These are found in the nature of the relationships between old and young and the sexes and exhibit emotional correlates. Informed observers agree that not all is well in our family system, and yet what degree of credence should we give to those who see our children as guilt-ridden and hostile?[2] Does the American mother exhibit the black widow spider tendencies as described by Philip Wylie? To what extent have males abdicated their role in the squeeze of demands between wife and job and to what extent are they delinquent in claiming their sons for manhood?

Perhaps these questions really have no answers. Yet they have been repeatedly asked and answered by those with ready replies. The concern should be evidence enough that the child finds himself in a confused and hence difficult position. There seems little doubt, however, that there has been both an increase in pressure upon the child from home and school and at the same time a diminution in his opportunities and hence his ability to act independently. This combination is bound to produce serious trouble.

POSTSCRIPT

Parents and teachers are particularly susceptible to exhortations by "experts" on child rearing and child life. Their position requires that the specialist appear authoritative. And we should be tolerant of their necessity to change emphasis and direction from time to time. But parents and teachers cannot forgive themselves nor can they be forgiven by their children for the consequences of following ill-advised fads of the moment. Our attitude toward the expert should be one of hesitant caution— once bitten, twice shy. The doctrine of the 1950's which extolled the virtues of the democratic family with its security through love, its togetherness, its permissiveness, and its equalitarianism is now being modified. Although the new doctrine of the 1960's has not yet been fully formulated, we may anticipate some of the line. The avant-garde has already abandoned the term "democratic" in its application to family life. Only those who lack sensitivity to the outmoded continue to champion what is dying, not family life but a style of exhortation about it.

Perhaps Bronfenbrenner is right when he suggests that he detects a cyclical trend toward "explicit discipline techniques of an earlier era" but adds that the most important forces redirecting "both the aims and methods of child training in America emanate from behind the Iron Curtain." Achievement has begun "to replace adjustment as the highest goal of the American way of life." He foresees that guidance counselors, parents, and even youth itself will do their part to prepare "youngsters for survival in the new competitive world of applications and achievement tests."[3]

---

[2] William Line and Margery R. King, "Cross Cultural Research," from *The Journal of Educational Sociology*, XXIX (March 1956).

[3] Urie Bronfenbrenner, "The Changing American Child," *Reference Papers on Children and Youth, Golden Anniversary White House Conference on Children and Youth, Inc.*, the National Committee for Children and Youth, 1960.

Sputnik may have provided the dramatic incident which focused our attention upon competitive achievement in education but the seeds had been sown long before. Parental pressure upon their children in high school to compete through college entrance examinations for the scarce commodity of quality higher education is no new phenomenon. The band wagon for this new party line of achievement is gaining momentum. Those who disputed adjustment as the central goal of child training were labelled "anti-democratic." Those who question achievement may be considered "anti-American." Such are the caprices of the spin of the wheels of fortune.

The serious question which should concern us all is that of the consequences of the compulsive pressures which are now force-feeding the process of turning children into adults but at the same time extending the period of dependency.

3-5   THE IMAGE OF THE CHILD IN CONTEMPORARY FILMS

Martha Wolfenstein

Martha Wolfenstein is visiting professor of psychology at the Graduate School of The City College of New York and guest lecturer in the New York Psychoanalytic Institute School of Applied Psychoanalysis. Child psychology is her main area of interest, and she is the author of *Children's Humor*. In this essay she uses the cross-cultural approach to portray the image of the American child.

Children as they appear in art, literature, drama, or films embody a complex mixture of fantasy and reality. They represent memories and dreams of adults about their own lost childhood, as well as feelings about those mysterious beings, their own children. These feelings and fantasies often undergo elaborate transformations. Mythologies abound in figures of divine children.[1] In ancient legend, there was Eros, the son and constant companion of Aphrodite, the capricious boy who brought confusion into the lives of mortals by his well-aimed arrows, inspiring unassuageable passion. The divine child of Christianity was a god of love of a less earthly kind and the son of a virgin mother. In the art of different countries and times he has assumed a variety of appearances. In Italian Renaissance painting, for instance, we find the plump and beatific infant, with his hand on the rich maternal breast, the first and adored son of a young mother. Flemish painters, in contrast to this, portrayed a thin, anxious-looking infant, already devoted to an ascetic ideal.

Earthly children similarly assume a variety of guises as they appear in literature and art. The ways in which they are portrayed express a complex of feelings about children prevailing in a given culture at a given time: the legend of the childhood one

Reprinted from *Childhood in Contemporary Cultures*, by Margaret Mead and Martha Wolfenstein, eds., pp. 272–292, by permission of the University of Chicago Press. Copyright © 1955 by The University of Chicago Press.

[1] C. J. Jung and C. Kerenyi, *Essays on a Science of Mythology: The Myth of the Divine Child and the Mysteries of Eleusis* (New York: Pantheon Books, 1949).

had or should have had, the image of the ideal child or of the demonic child, models and hazards for relations between adults and children. The story of Tom Sawyer and Huckleberry Finn expresses certain characteristic American attitudes about children. These boys are resourceful and independent and repeatedly prove that adults' alarms and anxieties about them are unfounded. The adults, whether Huck's drunken father or Tom's good, fussy Aunt Polly, are superfluous. The boys pursue their own adventurous existence and, despite appearances of waywardness, are fine, noble-hearted fellows. This legend of the good, strong, self-sufficient child expresses an American ideal: that the child should from an early age sally forth and join his peers and be able to hold his own. Dependence and weakness in the child tend to be played down or disparaged.

The image of the child in Dickens' novels is a very different one. While children appear as exceedingly noble, they are vulnerable and weak and need the protection of kindly adults. Without it they become helpless, suffering victims of wicked and cruel characters. A major theme in British culture is the danger of cruelty to the weak; a major corresponding character trait is a defense against this temptation, the cultivation of gentleness. The weak, who represent a temptation to cruelty and who must be protected from it, include women, children, and animals. In Dickens' novels there is a rich evocation of the sufferings of the weak and good, particularly children, and an appeal to adult pity and protectiveness. This contrast between British and American attitudes is epitomized in the endings of *Oliver Twist* and *Huckleberry Finn*.[2] Oliver, after having undergone many gruesome experiences as a helpless, unprotected child, finally enters into the haven of a good home into which he is adopted. Huck, faced with a similar prospect of adoption, decides to light out for the open road.

In the films of contemporary cultures we find a series of contrasting images of children. I shall deal with those that appear in recent Italian, French, British, and American films. This account is not intended to be exhaustive. Rather I shall concentrate on certain distinctive themes which recur in the presentation of the child in the films of each of these cultures. In Italian films there is an image of the child as a saviour; in the French, an evocation of the disappointments of childhood; in the British, the issue whether the adults are worthy of the child's trust; in the American, a quest of the child for an ideal man. These themes relating to children are connected in a variety of ways with other major and distinctive themes in the films of each of these cultures. I shall try to indicate some of these connections. Finally, I should like to bring out a quality of the child, namely, his nobility and his function as a touchstone of virtue, which is common to the child protagonists of all four groups.

ITALIAN FILMS: THE INFANT SAVIOUR

The image of the infant saviour continues to shine forth from the walls of Italian cathedrals and churches. Other pictures, close by, evoke the fated role of the beautiful and beloved child as he becomes the bearer of the cross, the crucified one, and the judge of mankind.

Child heroes in Italian films are likely to retain something of this aura. The

---

[2] W. H. Auden, "Huck and Oliver," British Broadcasting Company Third Programme Broadcast, October 1953.

burden of saving the erring people around them falls upon their slight shoulders, and they may die to save or die because the task is too great for them. They recall corrupt adults from their misguided ways. The adult feels himself judged when the sad gaze of a noble child falls upon him like an accusation, and the adult becomes aware of his weakness and sinfulness.

In *The White Line,* the Christlike role of the boy hero is most explicit. The scene is laid in a town on the Italian-Trieste border. Following the war, a boundary line (the white line of the title) is drawn through the town, dividing it in two. Animosities arise among the townspeople as some cross back from the Trieste side to remain Italian, while others renounce their Italian allegiance. There are disputes about property as farms have been cut in two; a farmer can see his ancestral property being expropriated by a turncoat on the other side of the line, and so on.

The hill down which the boys used gaily to coast in their wagons has also been cut in two by the line. Having become involved in the hostilities of their elders, the boys gather in two gangs on either side of their old coasting hill and exchange insults. Someone throws a stone, and the hero is hit on the forehead. The boy who hit him, suddenly overwhelmed with what he has done, bursts into tears. The hero, with his head bleeding, walks slowly across the line to comfort his old friend. With this the boys all become friends again. In a gesture of revolt against the boundary, they uproot a boundary post and throw it down a ravine.

The townspeople now react strongly to the disappearance of the boundary post. There are accusations of each side against the other as to who has removed it. The boys become alarmed and hold a secret meeting. They decide that some one of them must confess. The question is raised: Whose father will not beat him for it? The boys agree that the hero's father will not beat him. Thus the beloved of his father must take the common sin upon himself and become the sacrifice.

The hero, disconsolate, wanders around the town that evening. He sees through lighted windows how men are getting out their guns, to guard the boundary against further depredations. Then he decides to restore the boundary marker rather than confess. He descends the slope and takes up the burden of the heavy, cross-shaped marker, and struggles up the hill with it. One of the night watchers spies him and shoots. The boy falls, fatally wounded. Later he is found and carried home. The townspeople are sad and sobered, ashamed of their senseless quarrels. The boys come, across the line, to visit their dying comrade. Shortly after this farewell visit, he dies.

The boy hero of this film embodies the essentials of the Christ-legend. He forgives his enemies, he bears the cross, he dies for the sins of others; by his example he teaches his fellow-men that they should love instead of hate one another.

In the somber and tragic *Germany, Year Zero* (made by Rossellini in Berlin), the boy hero is also called upon to save, but the task exceeds his powers; he fails and is crushed by it. The boy has to support his aging, invalid father and his elder brother, who is in hiding from the authorities because of his Nazi past. He is also the sole protector of the virtue of his older sister. In his struggles to find a livelihood, the boy appears as the only noble character in a totally corrupt city. When he seeks help from a former schoolmaster, the teacher tries to seduce him into homosexuality. His family is close to starvation, and the boy assumes the terrible task of deciding who shall be saved; there is not enough for all. He decides to kill his sick and helpless father so that his brother may live. Having given poison to the father, the boy climbs to the top of a ruined building and jumps down. He has tried to save; he has taken the terrible role of judging and of meting out life and death. In his inability to save, he has become a destroyer. And he dies self-condemned for his crime. His fate is a testimony to the wickedness of a world that corrupts the goodness and subverts the noble impulses of a child. The boy has been prevented from fulfilling his destiny as a saviour by a world that appears beyond redemption.

In a more hopeful vein, *His Last Twelve Hours* shows a child, this time a girl, who succeeds in saving. The girl's father, unknown to the other characters in the film, has been run over and killed. Having been called up to a higher sphere, he is informed by a woman judge that he is damned. But she yields to his pleading to grant him twelve hours in which to redeem his bad life. Returning to earth and in haste to seek virtue, he is surrounded by cold and selfish people who do not understand his sudden impulses of generosity and think he has gone mad. Only his little daughter, a beautiful, serious-looking child, feels that something fateful is happening to her beloved father. And it is she who leads him to find salvation. The father has been directed by the otherworldly judge to concentrate his efforts on a poor man whom he has unknowingly wronged. The father makes this poor man rich, sets him up in the mansion of his dreams, and strives to satisfy all his whims. The man then begins to put on airs, tries to break up the engagement of his niece to a poor workman, and demands an aristocratic husband for her. The father in desperate haste arranges this, with the result that the niece and her lover are miserable and the household into which he was to bring happiness is torn by dissension. When the little daughter enters the scene, she sees at once what should be done. She is moved by the plight of the young lovers and urges her father to help them. The father, exasperated with the demanding old man who has given him so much trouble to no avail, makes an impulsive, generous gesture and gives the mansion to the young couple. He is sure that thereby he has lost his chance of heaven. But when his time is up and he again faces his judge, he learns that this last act, to which his child prompted him, has achieved his salvation.

In other Italian films, the saving role of the child may be less fully elaborated. But repeatedly it is a hurt look on the face of an innocent child which recalls an adult from the wrong path, or makes him aware of the depth of his fall from grace. So the ignominy of the father in *The Bicycle Thief*, who is reduced to becoming a thief himself, is underscored by the fact that his devoted little son is the witness of his shameful act. In *Father's Dilemma*, an egotistical, overbearing man is meanly belaboring a poor dressmaker for an unfinished task. Suddenly he notices the dressmaker's little girl, who is looking at him silently with big, sad eyes. The man is at once conscience-stricken and attempts to be placating toward the child and to win her forgiveness. In the same film, the tears of an innocent child save her parents from committing a degrading act. The egotistical man, who is very rich, is desperate to obtain a first communion dress for his little girl (as he has lost in the meanwhile the dress he got from the tardy dressmaker). He attempts to bribe a poor neighbor to give up the communion dress of his daughter. The poor man and his wife are about to yield, but they cannot withstand the tears of their little girl. They are later seen beaming with happy pride as their child kneels angelically at the communion rail.

I can indicate only briefly some connections between this presentation of the child and other themes in Italian films. Saving and, more often, sacrificial and unsuccessful attempts to save constitute major motifs in these films. The would-be saviour, the one he attempts to save, or both, may perish in the attempt. In *Il Bandito*, the hero is about to rescue his sister from a house of prostitution, into which she has fallen while he was away at the war. Their path is barred by her procurer, who draws a gun. The hero struggles with the other man, the gun goes off, and the sister is killed.[3] The mother of a young man, in *Under the Sun of Rome*, runs out into the street when she hears her son is in danger and suffers a fatal heart attack. In the same film the young man's father learns that the son is about to participate in a robbery. He rushes to the place where the planned robbery is to occur, in the hope of dissuading his son, and is shot in the cross-fire between the robbers and the police. In *Without Pity*, a Negro GI attempts to rescue a girl who has been forced to become a prostitute. In their flight, she is shot, and he also perishes. Rescue in these plots involving adult characters seems often to stand in place of a love act for persons who are forbidden to each other. In the fatality precipitated by the rescue attempt there may be a final embrace in death. The hero of *Il Bandito* clasps his dead sister in his arms. The last shot of *Without Pity* shows the joined hands of the dead Negro soldier and the white girl he loved.

Forbidden wishes and their noble counterpart, the wish to save, combine in a single protagonist where the plot deals with adult characters. Where the innocent child appears, he may embody purely the motive to save as over against the sinfulness of the adults. However, the purity of the saving motive in the child is not without exception. Its evil counterpart breaks through when the little boy who cannot save, in *Germany, Year Zero,* murders his father.

Another distinctive feature of Italian films is their idealization of the pure young girl, the virgin. It is she alone whom men love, toward whom they turn adoringly, and in favor of whom they scorn and repudiate alluring but bad or tarnished women. This is in contrast to American, French, and British films, in all of which a bad woman, or at least one who looks bad, is likely to triumph over a girl who is simply and sweetly good.[4] In Italian films it is regularly the good girl who wins out over her more experienced and seductive rival. The bad woman who despairs because no man can really love her is filled with hopeless yearning at the sight of the virgin bride.[5] An older ideal of womanly purity and virtue, which seems to have lost its hold on other Western cultures, remains in the ascendant in Italy. The blessed and beloved virgin retains her place beside the infant saviour.

FRENCH FILMS: DISAPPOINTMENTS OF CHILDHOOD

Of the cultures under consideration here, the French are least concerned in their films with issues of good and evil. Rather they are preoccupied with the ironical or tragic discrepancy between human wishes and the way the world goes. A lover is taken away by the police just as he is about to join his beloved. When he gets out of jail, he finds she has become the sweetheart of another man (*Sous les toits de Paris*). A moment after an innocent man dies, the police discover the evidence that would have cleared him (*Panique*). Things do not turn out the way men would wish, and their dreams of justice are as unrealistic as their dreams of happiness. This is the recurrent burden

[3] Margaret Mead and Rhoda Métraux, eds., "Themes in Italian Culture: A First Discussion," in *The Study of Culture at a Distance* (Chicago: University of Chicago Press, 1953), pp. 131–140.

[4] Martha Wolfenstein and Nathan Leites, *Movies: A Psychological Study* (Glencoe, Ill.: Free Press, 1950).

[5] Martha Wolfenstein, "Notes on an Italian Film, *The Tragic Hunt*," in *The Study of Culture at a Distance* (Chicago: University of Chicago Press, 1953), pp. 282–289.

of French films. Their aim appears to be that of mastering past disappointments and of inuring one to those of the present.[6]

   If one wants to re-evoke disappointments rather than deny them, it is not difficult to find a wealth of material in childhood. It is the time in life when the most impossible wishes are cherished, when one has yet to learn how unsatisfactory the world is, and when one is therefore most vulnerable. Children in French films are not innocent in the sense of being free of amorous or destructive impulses. They are replete with human longings. And they are exemplars of human disappointment.

   In the episode entitled "Lust" in *The Seven Deadly Sins*, a girl of thirteen, a prim and serious child in pigtails, thinks she is pregnant. When her mother, a handsome widow, demands to know who the man is, she names an attractive artist who is staying at the inn which the mother runs. There follows a confrontation of the mother and daughter with the man. In amazement, he denies what the girl says. She then tells the mother he was really not to blame; he did not even know it happened. As the adults, with growing skepticism, question her further, she admits that she had sat in the man's armchair just after he had left it, while it was still warm from his body—that is how she became pregnant. The mother and the man laugh with relief, assuring her that she will not have a baby. The girl angrily demands that they leave her alone and, when they have left, throws herself on her bed in a storm of tears.

   To complete the little girl's frustration, her mother succeeds where she has failed. The child's fantasy stimulates the mother and the man, who have already been flirting with each other, and serves to precipitate an affair between them. The mother goes that night to the artist's room. She seats herself in his armchair and they joke about how risky this is. As he sits on the arm of the chair and caresses her, she recalls her own girlhood, how she had believed you could get a baby from being kissed, and how at twelve she had a hopeless love for a man of forty who had not even known she existed. The artist persuades her to spend the night with him. The girl, in her high-necked nightgown in the room above, looks down from her window to see them closing the shutters. The lovers turn on the phonograph so as not to be overheard. The needle gets stuck in a groove and the same phrase plays over and over intolerably as the girl listens. The servants of the inn gather in the hall, wondering whether the phonograph has been left on and there is no one there; perhaps they should go to turn it off. The girl rushes downstairs to warn her mother and save her from being found by the servants. Restless and despairing, the girl then wanders through the dark and vacant inn parlor and out alone onto the country road.

   The girl in this film is moved by deep longings which the adults do not take seriously.[7] This is the recurrent fate of children. The mother recalls a similar hopeless love of her own childhood. Stimulated by her daughter's dreams, the mother is impelled to have the affair with the older man which the daughter cannot have and which she herself had been unable to have when she was twelve. But it is not the dream of magic love that transforms the adoring beloved with a touch which she now achieves. It is a light and easy affair. By the time one can gratify the wishes of childhood, they no longer mean what they had meant. There is here an implicit complaint about how badly

---

   [6] Wolfenstein and Leites, 1950; and Martha Wolfenstein and Nathan Leites, "Plot and Character in Selected French Films: An Analysis of Fantasy," in *Themes in French Culture: A Preface to a Study of French Community*, by Rhoda Metraux and Margaret Mead, Hoover Institute Studies (Stanford, California: Stanford University Press, 1953), pp. 89–108.

   [7] *Ibid.*, p. 99, "French Parents Take their Children to the Park."

things are timed, which constitutes a recurrent theme of French films. The situation in which the one who is most filled with longings is the excluded onlooker at the pleasures of others, as in the case of the girl in this film, is also many times repeated in French movies.[8]

The Male Brute relates a similar story of a child's intense and disappointed love. The hero is an eleven-year-old boy whose mother is a prostitute. She has had him reared in the country, but now she brings him to live with her in Marseilles. There is at first an idyllic interlude, as the adoring little boy happily brings his mother her morning coffee and they have breakfast together. But he soon feels how much he is excluded. From the door of his room, on the floor below hers, he sees men entering her room, and, looking out the window, he sees her closing her shutters. He becomes increasingly pushed aside as his mother forms an attachment to a small-time crook with whom she falls hopelessly in love. The abandoned and jealous little boy sees his mother constantly with this man, whom he detests. The man is very impatient about having the boy around, and the mother defers to his wishes. The boy overhears how his mother plans to send him away to school and to redecorate his room for her beloved man. The man cynically takes money from the mother, is unfaithful to her, and, when enraged, smashes her belongings and beats her. The boy, overhearing the fight from his room, rushes to the mother's defense, attacking the man with a knife. Later, when the man tries to beat the boy, the boy threatens to expose him for passing counterfeit money, which the boy has found out about by chance. The man becomes placating and tries to find out what he can do to please the boy. The boy then says that he wants to have dinner with his mother alone. This long-postponed dream is realized, but the wonderful evening is spoiled in the end as the mother shows her incessant preoccupation with the man and tries to persuade the boy to give up the counterfeit bill which he is holding as evidence. The boy becomes obsessed with getting rid of the man and makes an unsuccessful attempt to shoot him. The man, meanwhile, alarmed at the danger of exposure of his connection with the counterfeiters, goes to the police and buys his immunity by giving information about the gang. This is discovered by the gang, and they shoot their betrayer.

Earlier in the film, when the boy had been in despair at his mother's desertion, he had tried to drown himself and had been rescued and befriended by a kindly ship's captain, who offered to take him on as cabin boy. After his unsuccessful attempt on the life of his mother's lover, the boy takes refuge on the ship. The mother learns he is there and speaks with the captain just before the ship is about to sail. The captain explains that the boy loves her. She says she loves him, too (and indeed she has been shown as always charming to the boy when she was not preoccupied with more important things). The captain says: "But he loves only you. That is what love is like at the age of eleven." At the end of the film the mother, not knowing that her lover is dead or that, if he had lived, he was about to go off with another woman, is patiently waiting for him. The boy, as the ship sails out to sea, stands at the prow with a fresh, elated face.

That is what love is like at the age of eleven: exclusive, uncompromising, gallant, violent—and doomed to disappointment. The little boy would like to be the only man in his mother's life, and this is impossible. It is a major theme of French films that intense longings arise under circumstances, or at a time in life, when it is impossible to satisfy them. The predicament of the child is one instance of this. Another which frequently

---

[8] Martha Wolfenstein, "Movie Analysis in the Study of Culture," in *The Study of Culture at a Distance* (Chicago: University of Chicago Press, 1953), pp. 267–280.

recurs deals with the other end of the life-cycle—the comedy or tragedy of the aging man who is overwhelmed with love for a woman young enough to be his daughter. This theme of French films has been dealt with at length elsewhere.[9] *Symphonie pastorale* and *Le Silence est d'or* are among the many illustrations of it. In French films the bad timing of events in relation to human wishes appears repeatedly. This bad timing may be a matter of accidental circumstances. But the basic instances of it, those of the aging man and of the child, express the belief that it is rooted in the nature of life itself. Desires are not synchronized with the capacity to satisfy them: they arise both too early and too late.

BRITISH FILMS: ARE THE ADULTS WORTHY OF THE CHILD'S TRUST?

Turning to British films, we enter an atmosphere where moral issues are again in the ascendant. Here it is not a question of whether life is disappointing but of whether one is measuring up to the proper standards. British films alone, among those of the cultures considered here, contain an image of a perfect father. This is a father who has complete control over his impulses and presents a model of such control to his son. Conversely, there are fathers who fail to control bad impulses and who therefore do not provide an adequate model. A heavy reproach is leveled against them.[10] A murderer bitterly blames his father, who was a public hangman and who took a perverse delight in his work; the father has made the son what he is (*Wanted for Murder*). The impulses which must be controlled are particularly those of cruelty toward the weak, toward women and children. As the child is particularly vulnerable, he represents a test of the adult's virtue: the ideal adult will treat him gently, as the wicked one treats him cruelly. The child thus makes a double demand on the adult: to provide a worthy model and to treat him with gentleness.

The children are likely to look up to adults with worshiping eyes. The danger that the adult will fall short of the child's expectations is summed up in the title of *The Fallen Idol.* In this film a little boy is intensely attached to his parents' butler, whom he takes as his ideal. The parents are away throughout the action of the film, so that the butler and his wife stand in the place of parents to the child. In contrast to the kindly butler, his wife is the epitome of everything the adult should not be to the child. In a fit of wicked rage she seizes the little boy's pet snake and burns it up in the stove. Relations between the butler and his wife are strained, as the butler has fallen in love with the beautiful secretary of his employer. There is a violent quarrel between the butler and his wife, following which the wife, trying to spy on the husband and the secretary, climbs onto a high window ledge, loses her balance, falls, and breaks her neck. The frightened little boy has glimpsed part of these events and mistakenly pieces them together, imagining that the butler has pushed his wife down the stairs. The idolized man thus appears to have failed to control his destructive impulses toward women. The boy strives, nevertheless, to remain loyal to him. When the police come to investigate, the boy lies in a way which he thinks will protect the butler but which in effect tends to implicate him. So, unwittingly, the boy's suspicions and reproach break through. The man's fate appears to depend on the boy's faith in him. As this faith wavers, the man's very life is at stake. In the end, of course, the butler is exculpated (Scotland

---

[9] Wolfenstein and Leites, 1950, 1953.

[10] Wolfenstein and Leites, 1950; and Wolfenstein and Leites, "Movie Psychiatrists," *Complex*, No. 4 (1951), 19–27.

Yard, another embodiment of ideal authority, is always just). The little boy's parents return, and he escapes from the nightmare in which the idolized man seemed to turn into a destroyer of women.

In *The Browning Version*, a man's faith in himself depends on the genuineness of a boy's belief in him. The man is an unsuccessful schoolmaster. While he is devoted to classical learning, his teaching of it remains dull. Excessively reserved, unable to express positive feelings, he cannot compete with the more hearty and jovial masters for the boys' affections. Among the boys, who generally dislike or are indifferent to him, there is, however, one, more scholarly and sensitive than the others, who feels an affectionate admiration for him. He is not put off by the teacher's aloofness, and his responsiveness and interest are of great value to the teacher. At the end of the term, this boy comes to the teacher's house to give him a fine edition of a book which they had discussed together. The teacher is moved to tears and has difficulty concealing his emotion. Subsequently the teacher's wife, who is contemptuous of him and unfaithful to him, disillusions him with the boy's motives in giving the present, suggesting it was given for some self-seeking purpose. The teacher is then deprived of the one thing in his life, this boy's admiring devotion, which made him feel not quite a failure. Eventually, the teacher finds the courage to break with his wife. And he gains the happy realization that the boy's attachment to him was genuine. With this he is able to resume a piece of work that he had long abandoned and which the boy's interest encourages him now to complete.

The Stranger in Between shows how a man is moved to self-sacrifice in response to a child's devotion to him. The man has committed a murder and is running away. By chance he encounters a little boy who is also running away. The boy has accidentally set fire to the curtains in his foster-parents' home and fears a terrible beating. The boy attaches himself to the man, who at first finds him a nuisance, then decides it will be a form of disguise if he travels with a child. In the course of a long and desperate flight, these two become close companions. The man grows increasingly fond of the boy, who responds with intense love to this, the first person who has been kind to him. They finally reach their goal, a small boat on the coast in which they can make their escape. They put out to sea, but by this time the boy, from sleeping in fields and having little to eat, has become sick. As the man sees him feverish and weak, he is torn between the urge to escape and the need to get the requisite care for the child. He turns back. We see him at the end, walking up the quai, carrying the sick child in his arms, to save the boy and to forfeit his own life.

In *The Man Between*, a boy is intensely attached to a man of dubious character. The man is involved in shady machinations in postwar Berlin, while the boy, dashing about on a bicycle which the man has procured him, is his messenger, his spy, his aide, and his vassal. When the man finally decides to abandon his operations, he dismisses the boy from his service, telling him to go back to school. The boy is terribly sad, and the man tries to tell him kindly that he is not really worthy of such devotion. Yet in the end he proves himself worthy—he dies gallantly to save the woman he loves.

In these plots the crucial relation seems regularly to be between a man and a boy. The man is called upon to justify the boy's idealizing devotion. A girl does not seem to require the same nobility: it is possible for her to love a man who treats her cruelly (*The Seventh Veil*). Reversing the situation, women in relation to children are often cruel, like the butler's wife in *The Fallen Idol*. This image of the wickedness of women gives a clue to the destructive impulses of men toward them, impulses which the ideal man holds firmly in check while he substitutes the picture of the weak woman for that of the cruel one. In *The Stranger in Between*, it is his wife whom the man has murdered, a vicious woman who has wrecked his life. But the fact that he is capable of great kindness is subsequently demonstrated toward the little boy. The child provides the possibility for the man to prove that his gentleness is stronger than his violence.

In British films the issue of whether a protagonist measures up to his own ideal standards is of major importance. The child is an external embodiment and also an activator of these internal moral demands. In his idealizing faith he calls upon the adult man to be worthy of it. In his vulnerability he makes an appeal and provides an opportunity for the demonstration of the crucial virtue of gentleness.

AMERICAN FILMS: SEARCH FOR AN IDEAL MAN[11]

Where the child in British films easily finds among the adults around him someone to idolize and it then behooves the adult to deserve this trust, the child in American films longs for an ideal man to appear from afar. Father is not a hero, though great-grandfather may have been. The child's capacities for hero worship lack an object. A stranger must come from afar, the child must journey away from home, or visions of a remote past must be conjured up to provide the missing hero.

In *Shane*, a boy lives with his parents on a lonely frontier farm. The father is a good, hardworking man, who lacks any aura of grandeur. The boy longs to be endowed with masculine powers, to learn to shoot a gun, but the father is always too busy with his farmwork to teach him. Then appears the mysterious stranger, Shane, dressed in buckskin, with a gleaming gun hanging from his belt. The boy is immediately fascinated with him, wonders whether Shane could beat his father in a fight, secretly and in awe handles Shane's gun, and confesses to his mother that he loves Shane almost as much as his father. Shane stays on the farm as a hired man. A conflict is brewing between the group of homesteaders to which the boy's parents belong, and the cattle ranchers, who want to dispossess them. While Shane is at first quiet and in the background, slow to react to minor provocations, it is evident that he is to be the protector of the homesteaders against the powerful ranchers. In the meantime Shane satisfies the boy's long-standing wish to be taught how to shoot and demonstrates his extraordinary quickness with a gun.

As the conflict between the two factions becomes increasingly aggravated, the leader of the ranchers invites the boy's father to a parley. When his wife pleads with him not to go, the father indicates that if anything happens to him she will have a better man to take care of her. He has understood that she, like the boy, cannot help preferring the heroic Shane to him. Shane has been warned that the parley is really a trap and means to go in the father's place, as he knows that he alone would be able to handle it. The father is obstinately intent on going to the dangerous encounter, and Shane can only dissuade him by knocking him out. In the fight, Shane fights unfairly, clubbing the father over the head. The boy becomes for the moment disillusioned with Shane and

---

[11] For studies of American culture relevant to the following discussion see:
Margaret Mead, *And Keep Your Powder Dry* (New York: William Morrow & Co., 1942).
Margaret Mead, *Male and Female* (New York: William Morrow & Co., 1949).
Erik H. Erikson, *Childhood and Society* (New York: W. W. Norton & Company, 1950).
Geoffrey Gorer, *The American People* (New York: W. W. Norton & Company, 1948).

calls after him that he hates him. The mother then explains to the boy that Shane had to do this to save the father. The repentant boy runs after Shane to say he is sorry and follows him to the saloon, where the showdown is to take place. The ranchers have hired a notorious gunfighter, but Shane is, of course, quicker on the draw, shoots him and the leader of the ranchers too. As another, concealed enemy is about to shoot Shane, the watching boy cries a warning, and Shane also eliminates him. His work done, Shane will go away. He gives the boy a message for his mother. The mother had been against guns and fighting. Shane, the great fighter, wants her to know that now there will be no more guns in the valley; he has silenced them. The boy weepingly pleads with Shane to stay, but Shane has to travel on. He does not belong to this good, tame world of the home-steaders, but to a world of the past. He is a bad gunfighter turned good, who has put himself briefly into the service of the new workaday life in which he cannot share.

It is significant that when the boy is disillusioned with Shane for fighting unfairly, this is a misunderstanding. There does not have to be a transformation of the man's character to make him worthy of the boy's trust, only an explanation which clears up the misunderstanding. This is a general rule in American films. Instead of inner changes of character, from sin to redemption (as in the British *The Stranger in Between*), there are temporary false appearances, which may make a hero look bad when he is good all along and in the end succeeds in proving it.

The boy in *The Little Fugitive* has no father. On an adventurous journey away from home, when the seven-year-old boy goes all alone to Coney Island, he finds an ideal man, a "cowboy" in charge of the pony concession. This man is for the boy replete with the skills and accouterments of longed-for masculinity, with his aura of the Far West and his knowledge of horses. There is a brief interlude when the boy thinks it will be possible for him to work for the "cowboy," to learn how to handle horses, and to gain all the admired powers of the man. However, this plan proves unfeasible, and in the end he has to go back to the flat in Brooklyn and the shadowy cowboys of television.

This film exemplifies a number of major American themes. The little boy's flight to Coney Island is precipitated by his older brother's friends playing a trick on him. They are tired of having this kid brother always tagging along and trying to get into games which he is not yet up to.[12] To scare him off, the older boys offer him the privilege of shooting a rifle, then fool him into thinking he has killed his brother. The boy then runs away. Like the heroes of many American movie melodramas, he has been framed, appears guilty, is really innocent. At Coney Island, after he has used up all his money, he wanders disconsolately on the beach. There he finds another boy picking up bottles and turning them in for refunds—five cents a bottle. The boy immediately goes into the bottle business, makes enough for repeated rides on the ponies, and so attracts the interest of the "cowboy." With his successful bottle enterprise the boy could apparently have maintained himself until the end of the season.

This is the American legend of the self-sufficient child. However, this dream of getting along on his own is shown to be in part the little boy's illusion. When the "cowboy" offers him a job, he is only fooling. It is a ruse to get the boy's name and address so that he can see that the boy gets back home; the man gets the information

---

[12]Margaret Mead, "A Case History in Cross-National Communications," in *The Communication of Ideas*, Lyman Bryson, ed. (New York: Harper & Bros., 1948), pp. 209–229. Margaret Mead has pointed out this characteristic American relationship between older and younger brothers.

by saying he needs it for the boy's social security card. The man then phones the boy's older brother to come and get him. The boy, however, runs away again when he sees the "cowboy" exchanging a casual remark with a policeman; the boy thinks, of course, that he will be turned over to the police for his supposed crime. When the brother comes to find the boy, there is a long search through Coney Island, but the brother succeeds in finding the boy without having recourse to the police. He is like the private investigators in the melodramas. While the boys have been having all these adventures, their mother has been away. They succeed in getting back just before her return, and when she supposes they have been watching television the whole time she was away, they exchange a knowing wink and do not disabuse her. The grownups do not know and do not need to know about the enterprises and hazards of their children's lives which the children can handle quite well on their own.

Returning to the search for the ideal man, *When I Grow Up* presents a vision of such a man in a flashback to the days when grandfather was a boy. The father in the contemporary scene is an ineffectual bank clerk, uninspiring and unable to handle or to understand his son. But grandfather's father—there was a man. He was strong and awe-inspiring, and he whipped his son in the woodshed. But he could be tender and understanding and evoke great love. When his son is sick with typhoid fever, he nurses him, exchanges confidences and jokes, and a real intimacy blossoms between them. In the crisis of the son's illness the father drives out in his buggy in a terrible rainstorm to bring the doctor to save the boy's life. And as a result of the strain and exposure of the night drive, the father becomes ill and dies.[13] Just before the boy learns of his father's death, as he himself begins to recover, he has two dreams about his father. In one of these dreams, father and son are engaged in an amorous, laughing tussle in the hay, in the course of which each playfully spanks the other. In the second dream, father and son lie side by side next to a pond, with their fishing rods hanging out over the water. The boy turns affectionately to the father to clasp his hand. The image of a strong and tender father who can be loved like this appears in a dream within a flashback about great-grandfather.

In an interlude in this film when the boy of the past turns against his father for having whipped him unfairly, the boy and his ragamuffin pal go off to join a circus. There the boy finds one of the away-from-home heroes who can teach a boy such marvelous tricks, the star clown who becomes his friend.

One of the reviews of Geoffrey Gorer's book, *The American People* (1948), bore the title "Sometimes I Feel Like a Fatherless Child."[14] In American culture, fathers who are strong, admirable, and lovable do not seem to be the rule. Rather there are two alternate father-types: the strong, severe father (rather old-fashioned), who is feared, not loved, and the nice likable father who is a pal and falls short of the masculine ideal.[15] These two images of the father as they appear in American films have been discussed elsewhere.[16] In American life, children are expected to surpass their parents. The father

---

[13]This mortality of fathers is a recurrent theme in American films. In *So Big*, there is a very similar episode, in which a big strapping father falls down and dies after a long wagon ride on a stormy night. Children in American films appear to be much tougher and more viable than fathers. There would seem to be a contrast here to cultures like the Eastern European Jewish and the pre-Soviet Russian, where anxiety about probable death from being out in the rain and similar common hazards was concentrated in children.

[14]Alfred Kazan, "Review of Geoffrey Gorer's *The American People*," *New Yorker*, May 20, 1948, pp. 108–110.

[15]Else Frenkel-Brunswik, "Interaction of Psychological and Sociological Factors in Political Behavior," *The American Political Science Review*, XLVI, No. 1 (1952), 44–65.

[16]Wolfenstein and Leites, 1950.

is not the model that the son will follow when he grows up. But the boy longs for a man who can induct him into the mysteries and powers of masculinity, who has the strength and skill to which the boy aspires, and who can show him how.[17] Thus we have seen how the boy heroes of these American films are drawn to men other than their fathers to whom they can look with admiration, men who are masters of wonderful skills—the gun fighter, the cowboy, the acrobatic clown—who might impart to the boy the masculine prowess which he longs to attain. And we have also seen the dream of a father who could be both strong and tender projected into the past—great-grandfather—not the father of today.

The children in films that I have been discussing are heroes or heroines. Malign children sometimes appear in films, but they are rare.[18] When wicked impulses are dramatized, it is much more likely to be through adult protagonists. Children in the films of the four cultures considered here all have something in common. They are noble characters, usually nobler than the adults around them. They are not the embodiment of impulses which, by adult tutelage, must be brought under control. Rather, in one way or another, they represent moral demands and ideals. This is the adults' image of the child, to which two major factors would seem to contribute. First, there is the infantile amnesia of which Freud speaks, in accordance with which adults forget the intense impulsive desires of their own childhood.[19] Second, there is the appeal which the child makes to adult goodness, to be an ideal model and to exercise kindness and protective love. This adult goodness, which the child evokes, is then projected onto the child; it is he who appears as the exemplar of virtue.

There are different nuances to the nobility which the child manifests in the films of these different cultures. In Italian films, the child appears as a saviour. By his suffering and sacrifice, or it may be simply by the unerring reactions of his pure soul, he recalls men from wickedness to redemption. The child's virtue in French films is rather a counterpart to his immaturity. It is a virtue of necessity; he is not yet capable of fulfilling his desires. The sad and yearning child, whose dreams of love are bound to be disappointed, appears to the audience as a touching contrast to the adult characters, but he does not affect them; he cannot divert them from their impulsive pursuits. In contrast to this again, the child in British films appeals to the adult to whom he gives his trust and worship to be worthy of it. The adult is sensitively responsive to this demand, which echoes or strengthens that of his own conscience, and may sacrifice himself in order not to betray the child's trust. In American films the child is the bearer of the hero image. In a prosaic world, he dreams of a man surpassing his father, who would combine masculine strength and tenderness. And, happily, the film may provide an appearance of this hero, who illuminates at least for a time the life of the child.

[17]Grete L. Bibring, "On the 'Passing of the Oedipus Complex' in a Matriarchal Family Setting," in *Drives, Affects, Behavior*, Rudolph M. Loewenstein, ed. (New York: International Universities Press, 1953), pp. 278–284.

[18]The following are among the relatively exceptional bad children in films. In the Italian *Germany, Year Zero* and *Sciusca*, vicious children appeared as products of an impoverished and callous society. In French films a child may be evil or a bringer of evil for various reasons. The tragic little girl in *Forbidden Games* is an instance of the dangerous intruder in a family circle. The malign twelve-year-old girl in *Le Corbeau* is a bad counterpart to the girl in *The Seven Deadly Sins*; being a frustrated onlooker at adults' pleasure impels her to vindictive acts. In *Ballerina*, a little girl injured a dancer who had replaced in the troupe the one she adored. In British films, children are sometimes whimsically naughty, as in *Tony Draws a Horse*. In American films, where children are usually uninterested and unenvious in relation to adults' affairs, an exceptional bad child appeared in *The Children's Hour*, the little girl who spread malicious gossip about her teachers. A wicked, though eventually redeemed boy figured in *Tomorrow the World*, a child of Nazi upbringing.

[19]Sigmund Freud, "Three Contributions to the Theory of Sex," in *The Basic Writings of Sigmund Freud* (New York: Modern Library, 1938), pp. 553–604.

3-6   CROSS-CULTURAL IMPLICATIONS FOR TEACHERS

Norman C. Greenberg

Norman C. Greenberg is a co-editor of this book and professor of anthropology and education at George Peabody College, where he is assisting many Southeastern school systems in their socio-cultural problems. He has taught on the Navaho Indian reservation and he draws upon more than a decade of study and work with the Southwestern ethnic groups that are described in this discussion of the cross-cultural approach to education.

The anthropological and sociological literature of today is replete with emphasis on man as a product of his culture. There appears to be unanimous acceptance of the belief that individual differences among men are dramatically reduced through their willing subjection to the subtle controls of cultural expectations.

As we examine human behavior we find that all persons not only live in social systems, which is to say they are drawn together, but all people also act in such ways as to attain the approval of their fellow man. In this search for approval, they willingly and often eagerly undergo physical torture, mental harassment, or death—and even hard work. Culture, as a learned pattern of actions, beliefs, and feelings shared by a community and society as a system of interactions and organized relations among its members, probably has its base in the animal attributes of man.[1]

The title of this article indicates the widespread concern in America for the many students in our "typical, average" classrooms, who possess neither the value-structure, experience, nor attitudes that educators generally assume necessary for successful participation in the school subculture. Increased study and observation by behavioral and social scientists substantiate the conviction that the first school experiences of children may, in a profound way, determine the entire course of their lives. The following stories and analogies demonstrate this hypothesis.

The Indians on the plains often taught their sons that the highest honor a man could claim was to steal an enemy's horse. Seldom were they concerned with killing a man. Many more honors were attained by removing the man alive from his mode of transportation and riding away with his horse. Soon, however, the white man came; and if you are blessed with one of those television sets, you have long since discovered what the white man thought of a horse thief. The white man hung the horse thief immediately upon capture. So in one culture the fathers were teaching their sons that stealing a horse was

---

[1] Walter Goldschmidt, *Man's Way* (Cleveland and New York: The World Publishing Co., 1959), pp. 28–29.

far better than killing a man; and in another culture—ironically, the more civilized one—fathers were teaching their sons that it was better to kill a man than to steal a horse.[2]

Ethel Alpenfels, the noted socio-anthropologist from New York University, tells the story of the time she became homesick while teaching in Austria. At a dinner meeting she asked the chairman how many Americans he thought were present. He said to her, "I cannot tell you now, but if you will wait until tomorrow at the banquet, and come with me to the balcony overlooking the main dining room, we will be able to determine the number of Americans." And so, in Alpenfels' words:

... just before dessert, he took me up to a balcony that encircled the vast dining room. As we stood looking down, I suddenly realized that he had arranged with the waitresses to place the slice of pie which was going to be for dessert so that the point was pointing either toward the centre of the table or to one side. And as I stood looking down, I saw every young man and woman who had come from Europe, from Asia, from Africa, even from the islands of the South Pacific, start eating that slice of pie exactly the way the waitress had placed it, but all who came from the U.S.—I could just count them—turned the point towards them before they started to eat. That's culture. And I spent the rest of my time in Austria trying to convince that young man that this was the only intelligent, and really the only possible way to eat a slice of pie.[3]

What is basically indicated, of course, is that all of us are, to some degree, products of ethnocentrism. Marjorie Parker says of ethnocentrism:

Each says of himself and of his family, consciously or unconsciously, we are normal, we are the standards, others are deviations, other individuals are good or bad, fortunate or unfortunate.... Sometimes a person who is described as dark or fair, cultured or crude, pleasant or obnoxious, would not even be recognized from his description unless the listener knows the describer and understands that the descriptive judgment, like beauty, is "in the eyes of the beholder."[4]

Robert Klinger in "Moral Values Across Cultures"[5] analyzes exchange students from various national cultures and, from the viewpoint of American values, compares their actions and responses in America. To those of us who really want to understand the effect of national norms, religious attitudes, and other subtle social forces, often unknown, on peoples' concepts of sexual behavior, academic honesty, social practices, religious proselyting and other factors Klinger's results are extremely interesting:

---

[2]Ethel Alpenfels, "Implications of the Development of Science and Technology for Education," *Educational Horizons*, XL, No. 1 (Fall 1961).

[3]*Ibid*.

[4]Marjorie H. Parker, "Developing Values for a New Era," *Educational Horizons*, XL, No. 1 (Fall 1961), 1–9.

[5]Robert Klinger, "Moral Values Across Cultures," *American Personnel and Guidance Journal*, October 1962, 139–144.

The United States Graduate Protestants. When compared to the foreign students, the majority of the United States Graduate Protestants tend to be less severe in judging actions as "bad" or other actions as "best." They differ most from the Indians and least from the Chinese. The majority tend to be less strict than all foreign groups on school and classroom rules, room cleanliness, and nakedness. They show racial bias in tending to consider it bad to marry a person from another race.

The Arab Moslems. The majority of the Arab Moslem group is the most severe of all in its judgment of what is very right or very wrong. The majority tends to consider it more wrong to disobey minor rules, to be naked, not to be clean in one's room, and to be prejudiced. Only on two items are they less strict than the United States Graduate Protestants: helping others even though inconvenient and marrying a person from another race.

The Chinese Non-Christians. The majority of the Chinese students tend to differ from the United States Graduate Protestants in expressing themselves as being more strict on school rules, cleanliness, vandalism, overriding ambition, and tardiness; they seem to be more lenient on religious items.

The Indian Hindus. The Indians are most different from other groups, as regards both mean and standard deviations; this difference may lead to proportionately more misunderstandings. The majority of the Indians tend to differ from the United States Graduate Protestants in expressing themselves as more strict on driving, family, job, and school rules; loyalty; cleanliness; nakedness; and tardiness; they tend to be more lenient on religion and habit-forming drugs.

The South American Roman Catholics. With the majority of Turks, the majority of the South Americans are more lenient in general than are the other foreign student groups. They tend to express themselves as more strict on job rules . . . less strict and consider having premarital sex relations as good.

The Turkish Moslems. The majority of Turks are, with the majority of South Americans, one of the most lenient groups in their expressed values. They do not appear to have much in common as to the strictness or leniency with the other Moslem groups, the Arabs, except for agreeing on modesty— that all forms of nakedness with either sex are bad. The majority of Turks tend to express themselves as more strict than the United States Graduate Protestants on tardiness and nakedness. They tend to be somewhat less strict but still judge as bad the use of habit-forming drugs. They tend to be more lenient on considering premarital sexual behavior as a good thing. They are also more lenient on religion.

United States Pre-Freshmen Protestants. The majority of United States Pre-Freshmen Protestants, the youngest of all and presumably, therefore, least mature, are the most lenient of all. They tend to be more lenient than the foreign groups on nakedness, obeying job rules, slander, stealing, and vandalism. As with the graduates, they are more strict than the foreign students on racial bias in considering it wrong to marry a person from another race.

Several studies have shown the need for developing teacher awareness of the relationship between school procedures and cross-cultural influences. One of the most recent and notable, entitled "Teacher Awareness of Socio-Cultural Differences in a Multi-Cultural Classroom,"[6] was made by Horacio Ulibarri at the University of New Mexico in 1960. Ulibarri found that most teachers in schools with predominantly Indian and Spanish-American enrollments and few Anglo students lacked sensitivity to differences in socio-cultural conditions and orientations among the three ethnic groups. The teachers were unaware of the children's varying abilities in the use of the textbooks prepared for their grade level, although they were strongly aware of differences in English proficiency. They clearly recognized differences in general home environment of the three groups, but failed to differentiate specifics in life space and their implications for education. The teachers lacked sensitivity to motivational patterns of and motivational structures applicable to Indian and Spanish-American children. They showed little comprehension of differences among the groups in relating school-taught concepts of citizenship to out-of-school life, and thought that all groups were interacting quite well. Finally, the teachers did not know how to meet the psychological needs of children from different cultural backgrounds.

Several years ago I conducted an extensive study of administrative problems in the integration of Navajo Indians into public schools[7] that substantiates Ulibarri's findings. Administrators and teachers were genuinely concerned about their students' problems but could not project themselves into the frame of reference of children from other cultures or socio-economic levels. They realized the importance of individual differences and inter-group problems, but they did not recognize inter-group differences or their possible effect on inter-group relations.

Let us examine some ideas from Zintz's Research Study of 1957–1961 in order to gain further insight into cross-cultural perspectives. Zintz examines basic Anglo-culture values in comparison to the values held by the Indian and Spanish-speaking child. (See table, pages 150–151.)

We constantly hear that we are a culturally pluralistic society, but cultural pluralism as a way of life in America seems to be a verbalized ideal rather than an achievable reality. Today all the peoples of the world who are calling for recognition express their desire to participate in the over-all economy; this is especially evident in Africa, but it also occurs in smaller areas such as the Navajo reservation. World economy is a Western culture concept that involves production (heavy industry), imports, and exports. Participation in this economy requires acceptance of Western cultural patterns that impinge upon the traditional, uninformed, and primitive patterns of the past. Each younger generation absorbs more of the Western culture pattern in its cultural tradition.

---

[6]Horacio Ulibarri, "Teacher Awareness of Socio-Cultural Differences in Multi-Cultural Classrooms" (Unpublished doctor's dissertation, University of New Mexico, Albuquerque, 1960).

[7]Norman C. Greenberg, "Administrative Problems Related to Integration of Navajo Indians in Public Education" (Unpublished doctor's dissertation, University of Colorado, Boulder, 1962).

CONFLICTS IN CULTURAL VALUES[8]

American school teachers are sure to place great value on these practices:	Children from traditional Indian families may be said to have accepted general pattern as described below:	Children from traditional Spanish-American families may be said to have accepted these general patterns:
Mastery over Nature. Man must harness and cause the forces of nature to work for him.	*Harmony with Nature.* Nature will provide for man if he will behave as he should and obey nature's laws.	*Subjection to Nature.* An often observed reaction in the traditional Spanish-American was, "If it's God's will."
Future time orientation. All living in our society are future-oriented.	*Present time orientation.* Life is concerned with the here and now. Accept nature in its seasons, we will get through the years, one at a time. "If the things I am doing now are good, to be doing these things all my life will be good."	*Present time orientation.* For the traditional Spanish-American family the only important goal of life was going to heaven after death. One only passed through his temporal life to receive his "reward" in the next.
Level of aspiration. Climb the ladder of success. Success is measured by a wide range of superlatives: *first, the most, the best,* etc.	*Level of aspiration.* Follow in the ways of the old people. Young people keep quiet because they lack maturity and experience. This de-emphasized experiment, innovation, and change.	*Level of aspiration.* "To work a little, rest a little." Follow in one's father's footsteps. Be satisfied with the present.
Work. Success will be achieved by hard work.	*Work.* One should work to satisfy present needs. Accumulating more than one needs could be construed as selfish, stingy, or bigoted.	*Work.* Work to satisfy present need. The Spanish-American was particularistic in nature. He operated on emotional response rather than subordinating the individual to the society' institution. A businessman looks first at himself as a brother to the man who is asking for credit, and secondly as a businessman who is dealing with a customer.

[8] Miles V. Zintz, Director, *The Indian Research Study: Final Report, Section I* (Albuquerque: College of Education, University of New Mexico, 1960), pp. 57–58.

Saving. Everybody should save for the future. "A penny saved is a penny earned." "Put something away for a rainy day."

Sharing. One shares freely what he has. One of the traditional purposes of Shalako was that a man could provide a ceremonial feast for the village if he were able to do so.

Sharing. Traditional pattern included sharing within the extended family group. Those established in the dominant culture accepted Anglo values in sharing.

Adherence to time schedules. "Take care of the minutes and the hours will take care of themselves." In practice, we might be termed "clock watchers."

Adherence to time schedules. Time is always with us. The unhurried inexactness of the Indian with appointments has led to the expression, "He operates on Indian time."

Adherence to time schedules. The expression for "the clock runs" translated from the Spanish is "the clock walks." It has been said that this explains the "mañana attitude" which Anglos have observed in Spanish-Americans.

Acceptance of Change. Change, in and of itself, is accepted as modal behavior.

Reaction to Change. We may follow in the old ways with confidence.

Reaction to Change. We may follow the old ways with confidence. The reason may not be at all the same as the Indian's, however. This life on earth is endured only to win eternal life in Heaven.

Scientific explanation for all behavior. Nothing happens contrary to natural law. There is a scientific explanation for everything.

Non-scientific explanation for natural phenomena. Mythology, fear of the supernatural, witches, and sorcery may be used to explain behavior.

Non-scientific explanation for natural phenomena. Witches, fears, and non-scientific medical practices were used to explain behavior.

Competition. Aggression. One competes to win. Winning first prize all the time is a coveted goal.

Cooperation. Remaining submerged within the group. Traditionally a man did not seek offices or leadership or attempt to dominate his people. In sports if one won once, he was now ready to let others win.

Humility. Acceptance of his status quo. Submission might categorize behavior.

Individuality. Each one shapes his own destiny. Self-realization for each person not limited.

Anonymity. Accepting group sanctions, and keeping life rigidly routinized.

Obedience. The Catholic Church kept life routinized, placed emphasis on obedience to will of God.

In the United States all subcultural and ethnic groups, with the exception of a few Indian, religious, and iconoclastic individuals, demand to be included in the larger economic picture. Even those who maintain that they are independent of it would falter in an economic crisis. The norms, ideas, and goals of the engulfing larger society become identified with those of the culturally diverse group. Therefore, the clamor from those within and without the group for an adherence to patterns of the past appears to be impractical and detrimental as long as it inhibits incorporation into the larger national community. In the final analysis it will be the obligation and prerogative of every individual, regardless of cultural adherence, to determine his degree of participation in the society as a whole.

The United States is a living laboratory for the educator who recognizes the diverse cultural wealth present in his constituency. In the past few years a perceptible concern has arisen for the student whose cultural background deprives him of the preliminary experiences necessary for success in the American school. An educator may face the grim realization that he must surmount his own ethnocentric and social class orientation in order to make sound decisions about the education of the student with different values and goals.

In some parts of the nation, programs have been developed with the major aim of "upgrading" the disadvantaged youngster and the potential dropout; these two areas of concern seem to be inextricably interwoven. Administrators and teachers are beginning to realize that consideration of the sociological, anthropological, and economic factors influencing a child's behavior is essential to successful education.

Such depth of study, with its anticipated improvement in student-teacher-administrator relationships, is desirable because of the absence of sufficient funds to provide a smaller student-teacher ratio, additional trained guidance personnel for student and parent, travel and aesthetic experiences, tutorial services, or additional pay for faculty members who devote many extra hours to enriching the lives of students with limited experiential backgrounds. Recent federal support for various compensatory programs has somewhat improved this situation. However, the one-to-one relationship between teacher and student must be strengthened. A teacher's empathy for students of all groups and awareness of cross-cultural problems, intellectually as well as emotionally, cost little. Students can accurately evaluate a teacher's sincerity and ability, and both are prerequisites for successful education.

To a great degree, individuals maintain the values determined and established by the society into which they are born. As long as the environment that has nurtured these values remains unchanged, we can only hope that some form of direct or indirect education will encourage the change necessary for a society's survival in a constantly fluctuating world. Since a society is the sum total of its component parts—and its component parts are individuals, education must be regarded more as the means for societal survival and adjustment than the mere transmitter of cultural heritage. We might think of education as the development of the individual's ability to absorb the cultural heritage as he securely readjusts his value and evaluative structure in a manner that permits subtle and significantly lasting cultural realignments and readjustments to a constantly dynamic world.

3-7   THE CONTRIBUTIONS OF ANTHROPOLOGY TO THE EDUCATION OF THE TEACHER

Robert Redfield

When Robert Redfield died in 1958, American anthropology lost one of its most distinguished scholars. An astute field worker and prolific writer, Dr. Redfield received his Ph.D. from the University of Chicago in 1928. He served as an instructor in sociology at the University of Colorado and then returned to the University of Chicago, where he eventually became chairman of the department and Robert Hutchins' Distinguished Service Professor. He served as President of the American Anthropology Association in 1944 and was elected a Fellow of the Social Science Research Council. Among his many publications are *Tepoztlan, A Mexican Village; Chon Kom, A Mayan Village; A Village That Chose Progress; The Primitive World and Its Transformation; and The Little Community.* In the concluding essay of this section, Dr. Redfield indicates the role of the school and of the teacher in formal education.

This is far from the first time that an anthropologist has spoken as such about education and teaching. Two other such occasions have fallen within my own direct experience in recent years, and I have consulted the records of these occasions to learn what I should say on this present occasion. The first occasion was a symposium on "Education and the Cultural Process" held at Fisk University in March, 1941, and the other was a symposium on "Environment and Education" held at the University of Chicago in September of that same year. Altogether nine anthropologists contributed ten papers[1] to these two symposiums—all on some aspect of education or teaching as

Reprinted from *The Papers of Robert Redfield, the Social Uses of Social Science*, Margaret Park Redfield, ed., II, 93–102, by permission of The University of Chicago Press. Copyright © 1963 by The University of Chicago Press.

[1] *Education and the Cultural Process*, papers presented at a symposium commemorating the 75th anniversary of the founding of Fisk University, April 29-May 4, 1941. Edited by Charles S. Johnson. Reprinted from the *American Journal of Sociology*, XLVIII, (May 1943). Individual papers of special interest to educators are:

Margaret Mead, "Our Educational Emphases in Primitive Perspective," pp. 5–11.

Robert Redfield, "Culture and Education in the Midwestern Highlands of Guatemala," pp. 12–20.

Mark Hanna Watkins, "The West African 'Bush' School," pp. 38–47.

Scudder Mekeel, "Education, Child-training, and Culture," pp. 48–53.

Ruth Benedict, "Transmitting Our Democratic Heritage in the Schools," pp. 94–99.

Melville J. Herskovits, "Education and Cultural Dynamics," pp. 109–121.

Hortense Powdermaker, "The Channeling of Negro Aggression by the Cultural Process," pp. 122–130.

Environment and Education, A symposium held in connection with the fiftieth anniversary celebration at the University of Chicago. *Supplementary Educational Monographs*, No. 54, Chicago, 1942. Papers presented at the symposium are:

Ernest W. Burgess, "Educative Effects of Urban Environment," pp. 1–15.

W. Lloyd Warner, "Educative Effects of Social Status," pp. 16–28.

Franz Alexander, "Educative Influence of Personality Factors in the Environment," pp. 29–47.

Margaret Mead, "Educative Effects of Social Environment as Disclosed by Studies of Primitive Societies," pp. 48–61.

Franz Alexander, "Additional Remarks," pp. 62–66.

looked upon by an anthropologist. On reading over these papers, I receive a strong impression that, in spite of their apparent diversity, all these anthropologists are, at bottom, saying the same thing. Consequently, I am led to entertain the idea that this is perhaps the only thing that anthropologists have to say, or perhaps that it is the most important thing, and that in either case it is what I had better try once more to say.

BASIC IDEA OF "A CULTURE"

This basic anthropological idea is that every individual lives within something called "a culture"—a body of customs and beliefs which provide satisfaction to his human needs and adjustment to his environment. This culture is thought of as something special to each of the many societies in which mankind lives, and it is the many special cultures, separable and comparable, which these anthropologists are usually thinking about when they talk about education. The people of the Trobriand Islands live within or in terms of a culture which is notably different in content from the culture of the Dakota Indians, and yet it is reported or assumed by these anthropologists that the Trobriand culture does the same thing for the people who happen to live as Trobrianders as that which is done by Dakota culture for the people who happen to be Dakota Indians.

A reading of these ten papers makes it evident that all the contributing anthropologists regard each of these cultures as having a necessary and important character: integration, or wholeness. In words used by Malinowski in his paper, each culture is "an organic unit." The customs and beliefs which are the parts of the whole are consistent with one another and depend on one another. Mekeel refers to such a culture as "an operational totality" and declares that every culture has "a matrix, a configuration, into which the pieces fit." He denies that a culture "is an index of easily movable items" and tells us that "it must be viewed as a meaningful whole." The Dakota Indians serve chicken and dog meat at a wedding feast, not simply because the two are palatable and available, but because chicken symbolizes the American way of life and dog meat the Indian way; in their situation, marginal to two cultures, both configurations are represented by meaningful symbols in the form of food. Mekeel goes on to tell us that even the ways in which very young children are trained in their excretory habits are consistent with the type of character which is adaptive to, or consistent with, their adult life and that, therefore, these ways of infant training are also parts of the culture, the integrated whole.

Plainly these anthropologists regard integrated culture with favor. They are not indifferent to it; they think it good that there be consistency and wholeness in the culture in terms of which the individual lives his life. The thing which it is thought that a culture does for an individual is a good thing. It is thought that the culture provides the individual with goals, with purpose and significance for his actions, and with the sense that all the activities he carries on are contributory toward realization of these goals. In such a culture the individual knows what he ought to do and finds himself doing it. Conversely, these anthropologists view with alarm attempts to educate without due reference to effects of the education in making the culture less integrated, less whole. Malinowski writes that "the anthropologist recognizes more and more fully how dangerous it is to tamper with any part or aspect of culture, lest unforeseeable consequences occur." As an example he chooses sorcery among African natives, advises caution to anyone trying to educate the natives out of a belief in sorcery, and tells us that, examined in its cultural setting, African sorcery turns out to be a crude but often effective way of managing misfortune, disease, and death and that the natives would be worse off without the sorcery than they are with it. He advises the teacher in Africa to abstain from trying to teach natives not to believe in sorcery, but rather to leave it alone until, by gradual introduction of hygiene and other security-giving modifications, the culture no longer has any place for sorcery, which will of itself disappear. Thus the picture we get of a culture is that of a complex structure in which all the parts are fitted together. The anthropologist tells us not to try to pull out a few pieces that we do not like lest the whole come tumbling down; he wants us to understand the relations of the parts to the whole and, guided by this knowledge, to accomplish a change in manner of life through gradual substitutions.

This conception of "a culture" is, it seems, a peculiar contribution of anthropology to the understanding of human behavior. It is a conception certainly related to, but not the same as, the conception of "human culture"—that aggregate of invention and institution which began when the first stick or stone was kept and its use was explained by one ancient primate to another. Culture in the general and singular serves to set off all mankind as against all animals. Culture in the particular and the plural serves to set one society off as against another. The idea of separate and comparable cultures, one to a local community, is an outgrowth of intimate study of tribal and peasant life in the past two or three generations. You do not find the conception in the pages of Edward Burnett Tylor or in those of Sumner's *Folkways*.[2] It appears in the detailed accounts of special primitive groups, finds its most eloquent and persuasive statement in the works of Malinowski, and is expressed also simply and compellingly in Ruth Benedict's *Patterns of Culture*.[3] As it is an idea that would naturally develop out of the study of the various primitive societies, it has been anthropologists who have developed it.

SIGNIFICANCE TO EDUCATION OF IDEA OF INTEGRATED CULTURE

If this is *the* important, or at least *an* important, contribution of anthropology to the understanding of human living, my assignment is to provide an answer to the question: What is the significance of the conception of integrated cultures to the training of teachers? Fortunately there is guidance in the papers of the symposiums to which I have referred. I will, however, state the matter as I see it and use the suggestions of these other anthropologists without making them responsible for the formulations that I reach.

In the first place, I assert that, merely because each of us, with few exceptions, grows up in one of these cultures and by this fact is limited in his understanding of his own conduct and that of other people, the coming to know another culture than our own should be a great liberalizing experience. I think, therefore, that the giving of this experience is a task of those who shape the programs of general education. The point I here make is thus a point for teachers in so far as teachers, like everybody else, should have a general education of which this element should be a part, and also for teachers in so far as teachers make the programs of general education for other people.

---

[2] William Graham Sumner, *Folkways: A Study of the Sociological Importance of Usages, Manners, Customs, Mores, and Morals* (Boston: Ginn and Company, 1907).

[3] Ruth Benedict, *Patterns of Culture* (Boston: Houghton Mifflin, 1934).

The end in view here is to bring the young person to understand that every normal human being is reared in a society with ways of life characteristic of that society; that these ways "make sense" as one way is seen to be related to the next, consistent with it and supporting it; that the motives which people have and the values which they embrace are derived, generally speaking, from this traditional culture. The further objective is to lead the young person to look back upon his own culture from the vantage point secured in the understanding gained of other cultures and thus achieve that objectivity and capacity to consider thoughtfully his own conduct and the institutions of his own society which are, in part, a result of thinking as if within another culture. On the one hand, the end is to cause the individual to see that there are ways other than his own which are compatible with human needs and with the dignity of the individual; on the other hand, the end is, through comprehension of another way of life, to develop the power to think well about one's own way of life so that that way may be improved. To some degree the study of anthropology provides this liberalizing experience through the acquaintance it gives with cultures other than our own, and much of the appeal which anthropology has for young people in schools and colleges comes from the fact that it provides such experience. I think this contribution primarily belongs, however, not in the training of anthropologists but in the general education of everybody. How to get it there is something that is yet to be determined.

Because we cannot move a tenth-grade class every afternoon to China or Central Africa, we shall have to teach about these countries chiefly through books and pictures. A principal requirement is time: vicarious acquaintance with, say, Chinese village culture might be sufficiently achieved in one or two years of persisting attention to the subject. I am sure that almost nothing is accomplished toward the end I have in view by the current practice in primary and secondary schools of dividing a year of social studies into short periods in each of which a new subject is taken up, at fortnightly intervals, from Russia to money or minority groups—and, indeed, I doubt that anything very important is accomplished toward any good end. In place of this succession of bowing acquaintances with miscellaneous subjects which are connected, I suppose, in one way or another with the modern world, I suggest the possibility of substituting a persisting and penetrating consideration of some society and culture notably different from our own and well provided with documentation. This might be a principal part of the social-studies curriculum at some place between the ninth and twelfth school years.

SIGNIFICANCE TO TEACHERS OF IDEA OF INTEGRATED CULTURE

This suggestion is an application of the conception of integrated cultures to the making of a curriculum in general education. I turn now to other ways in which the conception may be relevant to teaching. An application may be made of the conception of an integrated culture to the teaching activity itself. If cultures consist of an integration of customs and institutions, then teaching itself may be looked at as one such element more or less integrated in the culture of the community in which the teaching is carried out. This point is, indeed, made in several of the anthropological papers contributed to the two symposiums that I mentioned at the beginning of my remarks. Seeing formal education in its relation to other aspects of culture, these anthropologists are struck by its relative unimportance. They remind us at the beginning of their discussion that schooling is only a small part of education in the broad sense, "the process of cultural transmission and renewal." By the time the child comes to the teacher, he has already passed his most formative years, and the informal instruments of education have already largely shaped his world. What the school can do after that is correspondingly limited. Furthermore, what the school can do continues to be limited by the more powerful influences of the home, the play group, and the neighborhood. Do not expect to accomplish more than is possible, say these anthropologists to the teacher, and you may successfully teach that which finds some support, some basis of consistency, with the culture as it is transmitted in informal communication outside the schoolroom. So Mekeel is not surprised that Indian children, after many years of residence in government schools, in which attempts are made to teach the ways of white men, so often return to Indian life. So Malinowski warns the teacher in Africa not to separate, by his teaching, the child from the native community where he enjoys the warmth and security of life in an integrated culture. The lesson for the teacher from such observations is that teaching is not to be regarded as a technique of inculcation or of stimulation learned from books or from other teachers and thence applicable to a classroom, as medicine may be administered to a sick man, or fertilizer to a farmer's field. The suggested application is that teaching is effective in so far as it tends toward the development in the young person of a coherent body of attitudes and values adequate to the life-needs in his particular community. The classroom is important only as it is understood in its relation to the society and culture of the children who occupy it, and teaching will be effective only as it is related to society and culture.

Being established in the viewpoint of culture as an organic unity, anthropologists seem to be calling upon the teacher to understand, not so much teaching methods, as the community in which the teaching takes place. The real nature of effective teaching, these anthropologists are in effect declaring, lies not in ways of preparing instruction units nor in devices for testing reading comprehension, but rather in the part played by the school and by what goes on in the school in the cultural life of the children's community. I suspect that in this the anthropologists are telling the teachers to look to matters which teachers in fact do constantly look to because they cannot help it, even though these are not matters that bulk large in the formal training of teachers. In one of the symposium papers Warner looks at the school in the community as he would look at initiation rites in a primitive society, as from the outside. He finds that the high school in the American towns that he has studied is one of many institutions which express and maintain, among other things, the system of ranking according to social status which characterizes the society. The lower-class pupils study commercial and technical courses. The upper-class children take courses that prepare them for college. The children of each class are taught what will fit them for the station in life which it is expected they will assume. Moreover, he finds a marked tendency to classify children in supposed intelligence groups according to the social positions of their parents, so that a child from the upper class is not put in the lowest intelligence group even if his individual performance might put him there. Still further, he finds that what teachers do to warp theoretically impartial educational procedures to fit the local cultures is done largely because the same result is accomplished anyway by the informal groupings of children in and out of the school. The children's cliques bring about an assorting of children according to their parents' social positions, and the school, in effect, is conforming to these other less visible institutions. Warner is thus applying the conception of an integrated culture to the school and its community. "Understand these," he seems to say to the teacher, "if you would understand what your teaching does, can do, and cannot do."

SIGNIFICANCE OF IDEA OF CULTURE
IN MODERN SCHOOLS

The possibility that teaching will not be integrated with the rest of the cultural life of the child is, obviously, increased to the degree that the teacher represents a way of life different from that of the child. The possibility will be very great when an outsider comes to teach in a native community, whether the community be one of Africans or Indians or Kentucky mountaineers. Missionary teaching is often ineffective or disintegrating because it is not related or is unwisely related to the local culture. But the same danger exists, in compound form, in urban schools where the children represent not one integrated culture but many disintegrated cultures, and the teacher not only does not, but could not, teach to develop a single coherent integration if he wanted to. What, then, is the significance of the conception of the individual in one integrated culture in connection with teaching in a society where there is no integrated culture? What is the value of this anthropological conception, developed in primitive society, in modern urban society? It is all very well for the anthropologist to advise the teacher what he may do or even should do in teaching Indians or native Africans, but what can the anthropologist helpfully tell the modern teacher in a modern school?

Half of the answer depends on the extent to which the modern city community is like an Indian tribe or an African village, and part of this half of the answer is given by Warner when he, in effect, urges the student of teaching to study the school in its community. If the student does so, he will find the extent to which the school is integrated with other institutions and helps to perpetuate a local culture. Part of this same half of the answer is expressed in Mead's paper read at the Fisk University symposium. This anthropologist considers the function, not of the school in the community, but of the whole institution of education in modern society, as if she were studying warfare in New Guinea. She finds that its function is different from the function of education in primitive societies. In primitive societies education depends, she says, on the will to learn something that everybody assumes one would want to learn. In modern society it depends on the will to teach something that somebody thinks ought to be taught, even though not everybody wants to learn it. This different nature of education in modern society leads, she goes on to tell us, to a conception of education as something that may not so much perpetuate an old society as make a new one. The society it may make is so new that none of us living now is able to say what it will be, and yet it is supposed that these children whom you and I educate, or their children, will make that society and that the kind of education we give them will somehow fit them for doing so. This is indeed a far cry from the way in which a tribal Indian or isolated African native would look at the educational institutions of his own society. He thinks of education, so far as he thinks of it at all, as something that will perpetuate the kind of life which he has always known. Mead is telling us that, just as modern society is different, in kind, from all primitive societies, taken as another kind, so education is and must be different.

What is this difference in the two kinds of societies or cultures? In the paper that she contributed to the Chicago symposium, Mead enumerates three differences: (1) Primitive cultures are homogeneous, while ours is heterogeneous. (2) Primitive cultures change very slowly, while ours changes rapidly and constantly. (3) The population stocks of primitive societies are relatively less diversified than are ours. Mead thereby recognizes that modern urban culture is different in kind from all primitive societies. As the culture is changing rapidly and constantly, there cannot be one well-integrated culture. What children do is different from what adults do, and indeed adults come to think—some of them—that it is right that children do something different. Moreover, the changes come so rapidly that during the school years of one individual he may be taught completely inconsistent ideas. Benedict, in her paper, makes this point. There are periods when we tell children to be saving of money; there are others when it is a public duty to spend. There have been recent periods when war was unexceptionally evil and "the earth was unanimous for peace," and there have been more recent periods when, as she says, you might go to jail for saying so. As our culture is always changing and is never integrated, Benedict concludes that "education in our world today must prepare our children to adapt themselves to unforeseeable conditions."

At this point it is apparent that the conception of an integrated culture has undergone some significant alteration. The anthropologists to whom we have looked for guidance began by telling us that every individual lives in a well-integrated culture. Now some of them seem to be confirming our suspicions that, in the case of our own society, no individual does. The question may then be repeated: What is the significance of the conception of the individual in one integrated culture in connection with teaching in a society where there is no one integrated culture? Again, the first half of the answer may be repeated: In some degree, as in Warner's studies of the place of the school in the status system, there is integration in modern society, and the school is part of that integration. But the other half of the answer may be given also. The value of the conception of the individual in a well-integrated culture lies, in part, in the suggestive contrast between our own case and the case of the stable primitive societies. We should not so well see the peculiar problems and responsibilities of modern education if we did not see modern education as a special and variant case of education in all societies. That it is special and variant is expressly stated by Mead. In stable societies with well-integrated cultures, all educative influences, she says, operate simultaneously and consistently upon the individual, and she has illustrated this fact vividly in her series of photographs showing the treatment accorded babies in Bali. But in our heterogeneous and changing society there is a qualitative difference, she says; what the radio says may be quite unrelated to what mother says to baby, and what mother-in-law over in the corner manages to convey by a gesture is emphatically in contradiction. It is the inconsistencies, the lack of integration, that make our society different from stable primitive societies. In a sort of definition by indefinition, it is this lack of integration which gives our society its character. Interestingly enough, of all the contributors to these two symposiums, it is not an anthropologist but a psychiatrist, Franz Alexander, who says this most plainly. "Paradoxically stated," he says, "the pattern of our world is that it has no fixed pattern." For the psychiatrist the significance of this conclusion lies in the need to study individual careers in terms of individual life-histories. For the teacher the significance lies in the need to develop the capacities of the individual to deal with circumstances which the teacher cannot foresee.

THE TEACHER'S TASK

The conception of one integrated culture leads, therefore, to a view of the task of the teacher which sees it as double. The conception is helpful to the teacher, in part because it is directly applicable to the child in "this" school in "this" community. The conception is helpful, in part because it is not directly applicable. The apparent contradiction is resolved by distinguishing the short run in time and the local setting from the long run in time and the wider setting. So far as the short span of years is concerned, and in the local neighborhood (especially if that neighborhood be in one of the more stable towns and not in a community of rapidly changing population), the school will be found reasonably well integrated with the rest of the cultural life, and what can be accomplished by the teacher will be limited by these relationships which it is, therefore, necessary for him to understand. On the other hand, the school is an instrument for social change and is accepted as such, both by laymen and by educational leaders. For example, while it is true, as Warner says, that the high school perpetuates the status system of the community, it is also true, as Mead says in her paper read at Fisk University, that education is a recognized means by which the individual may leave his social rank and move to another. For the more remote future, education, to us, exists to develop powers to deal with contingencies beyond our powers of prediction. Children are to be educated so as to find what personal and cultural security they can find in the communities that now exist, and they are also to be educated to make, by effort and understanding, new integrations out of whatever pieces of living the future may bring them. The teacher today is both a perpetuator of an old integration and a builder of the power to meet disintegration. If a paradox remains, it is not one that I have invented; it exists in the nature of modern life.

CONCLUSION

After reading these selections, the reader is immediately aware of the increasing complexity of education in industrial societies. As the culture increases in content, a number of shifts take place in education that present difficulties for the transmitters of the culture.

One such shift is the removal of much of the adult culture from the immediate experience of children. In a primitive society the children see, hear, and live in close physical contact with adults; they participate to an ever-increasing degree in culture. The children are provided a concise picture of what their future role will be. A girl observes and often emulates her mother grinding corn at the same time she listens to the conversation of the women. Her ascent into adult life is relatively easy and gradual.

In an industrial society the child tends to be isolated in his own world of peers; he may experience adult life only through television programs. Most of the technical skills that he must learn exist at a distance. The school may attempt to compensate for this with field trips to the "world of work," literature, and films, but these are not the direct experiences found in primitive societies. Consequently, the teacher must be cautious lest the children misconstrue these experiences.

Another problem in the transmission of industrial culture is the diversity of society's cultural expectations—a diversity lacking in a primitive society. The different preceptors present in the industrial society can easily provide conflicting views of the adult world. To avoid this conflict, children must be made aware of the available alternatives and learn how to choose wisely from among them. One of the major functions of the school, therefore, as Redfield states, is to determine what elements of the culture are to be transmitted and how they are best transmitted so as to promote "self-activating" children, yet at the same time to provide mechanisms whereby children gradually assume responsibility for their own conduct.

As the content of a culture increases through improved storage of knowledge and purposeful expansion of this knowledge, there is a similar increase in the inventory of techniques for transmitting the cultural content. Some social scientists feel that the primitive society's techniques of transmission are inappropriate and insufficient for an industrial society; others argue that the techniques differ in degree rather than kind. Perhaps, because of this argument, educators have ignored the cultural lag that exists between the increased knowledge and the techniques designed to disseminate this knowledge.

On an individual level, studies of the process of education indicate that the cultural conditioning of a child during his early years makes it very difficult for him to forsake his childhood culture for another way of life or to assimilate thoroughly another culture. This has considerable significance for the schools in their attempts to acculturate children from the "ethnic" sub-cultures in America. But perhaps a more important consideration here is that this cultural conditioning makes it difficult for the *adult* to adjust to new cultural norms brought about by rapid shifts in technology, social organization, and value systems. Thus, "culturally literate" educators, using the science of culture in education, can determine the culturally defined limits within which they can most effectively transmit the culture.

ADDITIONAL READING

Norman C. Greenberg and Gilda M. Greenberg, "Learning with the Navajos at Bah-ha-li," *Education of the American Indian in Today's World* (Dubuque: William C. Brown Book Company, 1964), pp. 35–42. Discarding ethnocentric tendencies in order that learning across cultures may be accelerated through humane understanding.

Jules Henry, "A Cross-Cultural Outline for the Study of Education," *Current Anthropology*, I, No. 4 (July 1960), 267–305. An excellent start in structuring the educational process in both non-literate and industrial societies. His comments provide numerous differences in education between non-literate and industrial societies.

George F. Kneller, *Educational Anthropology* (New York: John Wiley and Sons, Inc., 1965), pp. 11–16. An excellent summary of the relationship between anthropology and education.

George D. Spindler, ed., "Anthropology as a Resource in the Analysis of Educational Process," *Education and Culture* (New York: Holt, Rinehart and Winston, 1963), pp. 57–62. Some suggestions on how anthropology can shed light on human behavior in educational situations.

Miles V. Zintz, *Education Across Cultures* (Dubuque: William C. Brown Book Company, 1963). A compilation of some of the research and methods employed by those interested in education among cultures in the American Southwest.

4

American Society and Values

INTRODUCTION

One salient characteristic of American society is its heterogeneity. Peopled by representatives of many and diverse cultures, the United States is often described as a loose collection of cultural elements held together by an ideology that is vaguely described as "the American way of life." Many have attempted to define "the American way of life," but as population increases and subsequent shifts take place in social, political, and religious institutions, the old sentiments that once held the heterogeneous mass together are being challenged and, in some cases, altered.

In America, education itself is a value; it is to education that the citizen often turns as he seeks satisfaction and meaning for his life. The degree to which the school meets these cultural expectations is also being challenged. Since values tend to codify a society's committed way of life, they provide meaning, identification, and focus. An understanding of the values of a social group is, therefore, essential before any meaningful curriculum can be initiated. This section seeks to define the "core" (traditional) and "emergent" (in transition) values of the dominant American culture in an effort to provide a better understanding of the school's dilemma in transmitting these values.

It is also important to realize that the "core" values reflect the middle-class Puritan ethic and that, because of the heterogeneity of our society, there are many Americans whose first contact with this value orientation occurs in the public school. For those to whom these values are new, the task of education is acculturative, and the discontinuity between the school and other socializing agents in the community may have far-reaching effects on the behavior and participation level of these individuals as adults.

It should be clear that values are accumulative and that America, like other modern nations, "stands on the shoulders of giants," looking out from a value orientation that is an idealized synthesis of "the good life" to which society is deeply committed. But to merely know the values is not enough; this knowledge must be translated into the process of cultural transmission and curriculum decision-making. The curriculum tends to be programmed around the values of the society supporting the educational institutions. It is important, then, for the teacher to be aware of the values available and to develop with the student a set of criteria for value selection.

4-1   TRADITIONAL VALUES AND THE SHAPING OF AMERICAN EDUCATION

Merle L. Borrowman

Merle L. Borrowman, formerly assistant professor of education at the University of Wisconsin, is the author of several books and articles, including *The Liberal and Technical in Teacher Education: A Historical Survey of American Thought*, and co-author with Lawrence A. Cremin of *Public Schools in Our Democracy*. At the time the following article was written, he was a member of the Committee on Social Forces Influencing American Education, which was formed by the National Society for the Study of Education.

The history of any group of people tends to shape its cultural traditions and corresponding values. In turn, these reinforced values motivate or deter individuals and groups in their decision-making processes, thereby influencing and shaping further historical development. In his essay, Merle Borrowman uses historical data to demonstrate that traditional values continue to influence our modern concept of education.

Discussion of educational values is usually derived from the commitments of formal religion, the folklore of democracy and capitalism, widely accepted ethical canons, and such specific educational traditions as humanism, scholasticism, and pragmatism. These are important reservoirs of moral capital. To explore their depths and appraise their content is important. Nevertheless, such appraisal and exploration, if carried on with traditional terminology, tends to degenerate into a battle of quickly recognized clichés around which patrons and educators rally. When time-honored guidons fly, it is not difficult to anticipate which armies will take the field.

In recent years, however, much educational debate has cut across conventional groups. The policies and practices which the public has been inclined to support or to resist indicate the operation of values that have not been clearly enough defined in normative (value) discussions to date. It would seem that certain inadequately recognized concepts have acquired sufficient emotional power to enter significantly into educational judgments. What follows is an attempt to supplement existing literature on educational values by making explicit a few of these concepts. Since, in a single essay, one cannot cover the entire range of such concepts, even if he adequately understands them all, this essay is intended merely to be suggestive. The concepts with which we shall be concerned here are of community, work and play, authority, and human nature.

In one sense, of course, such concepts are not values at all; they are descriptive rather than normative terms. They enter the domain of values only when human emotion and preference become strongly attached to them; that is, when people feel that a

From *Social Forces Influencing American Education*, 60th Yearbook, II, National Society for the Study of Education, 144–170. Copyright © 1961 by Herman G. Richey, Secretary. Reprinted by permission of National Society for the Study of Education.

community "ought" to have certain characteristics, that one set of relations between inferiors and superiors possesses moral superiority over another, that human nature "must" be viewed in a particular manner to avoid the risk of eternal or temporal damnation, and that "good" people have one attitude toward work and play while "bad" people have another.

The processes by which strong emotional support is brought to such concepts are several. It may be, as Erich Fromm implies in his books, e.g., *The Sane Society*, that the human animal is of such nature that some social conditions simply are satisfying while others are intolerably frustrating; and surely contemporary rhetoric moves some people emotionally to prefer particular alternatives. The process with which the historian is concerned, however, is that in which social re-enforcement over a long period of years conditions members of a particular human group to certain preferences. Only in a group which is somewhat isolated from alien influences, and in which considerable ideological homogeneity prevails, do the strongest of such preferences occur. When, as most Americans have done, an individual leaves a close-knit ideological group and encounters opposing views, it is difficult to predict his action.

The historian cannot, therefore, say that a particular value will actually enter the decision-making activity of a specific individual. Such is the province of other social scientists. As the geneticist can only say that among those who receive a specified biological inheritance one can anticipate the possible emergence of a particular trait, so the historian can only say that, since certain historical groups have held certain concepts long enough for them to have acquired normative significance, one can expect them to show up sooner or later in some form. This essay deals with a kind of heredity—that which one inherits from the culture into which he is born.

CONCEPTS OF COMMUNITY

The Puritan View

The kind of communal life which the Puritans sought to build and maintain in New England cradled our system of higher education and nurtured our common schools. Many Americans turn in nostalgia to certain of its characteristics, as did Louis Mumford in writing the text for the great documentary film, *The City*. To others, however, the term "Puritan" has become representative of community efforts to interfere in a most repressive and bigoted manner in the life of an individual. A study of the Puritan attitude toward community might, then, permit us to identify continuing normative issues.

The New England Puritan believed that ideological unity was essential, that a considerable degree of co-ordination and control of economic activities was necessary, and that political authority should seek to maintain both ideological conformity and economic efficiency. The economically unproductive citizen, the "squatter" who preempted land and was careless about the law, and the Quaker or Catholic who held unorthodox religious views were equally dangerous.

The Puritan did not believe that these functions should be sharply differentiated. To be sure, one could discriminate among the roles of the merchant, the elder, and the member of the General Court or town meeting. But so long as all were controlled by the oligarchy, the "elect" to use their term, no sharp conflict was conceivable.

The elect were divided between congregationalism and presbyterianism as forms of church government, and between town and colony as foci of political and economic power. In New England they formally adopted congregationalism, a system in which religious authority was vested in the local communion, but they hedged against the possibility of local congregations becoming heretical by adopting the principle of "consociation," a principle under which, as in presbyterianism, colony-wide meetings of elders and ministers met annually to adjudicate theological controversy. Though much political and economic responsibility was delegated to the town meeting, the General Court held the reins. As the colony spread geographically, the congregation and the town tended to gain power at the expense of synod and colony.

The New England Puritan lived with deep anxiety. Save for a brief period during Cromwell's regime in England, there was an ever-present threat that the Crown would so revise the Charter that the oligarchy would lose its power. For many years the economy operated so closely to the subsistence level that potential starvation was faced. Even though covenant theology gave the elect some assurance of salvation, which was denied them under a rigorous predestinarian theory, the Puritan was left in constant concern about the destiny of his immortal soul. These constant threats gave emotional support to the Puritan's feelings that a community "ought" to be characterized by ideological uniformity, regulated economic interdependence, and political authority exercised by an oligarchy in the interest of perpetuating a stable ideological and economic system.

Early Massachusetts school legislation was consistent with this view of the community. The laws of 1642 and 1647 explicitly affirm economic and political objectives as well as the more frequently cited religious ones. Characteristically, responsibility was delegated, so far as possible, to the local community where face-to-face relationships were easily maintained. Curricula were designed to insure conformity with the dominant ethos.

Separatist Religious Groups

Although the Puritans were, perhaps, the most influential immigrant group, their view of community was not totally unique. Other Protestant groups, particularly such pietistic sects as the Mennonites of Pennsylvania, Delaware, and New Jersey, had similar views. Because they did not have political control of any colony and because they had in most cases been persecuted minorities in their homeland, these groups became in some respects even more parochial than the Puritans.

Like the Pilgrims of Plymouth, these groups were separatists, committed to a congregational church polity and anxious to isolate themselves as much as possible from other social groups who might tempt their own members into error and sin. They came quickly to favor minimal government on the colonial level, preferring, instead, to keep controls within local, religiously homogeneous centers. It is small wonder, then, that such groups as the Mennonites resisted Penn's efforts to set up a colony-wide educational program in Pennsylvania. While such groups differed widely concerning the amount and kind of education they considered desirable, they were alike in viewing the local, usually parochial, school as a community center, designed, among other ends, to perpetuate ideological conformity and local community loyalty.

When in the nineteenth century the tradition of local control of public schools had become strongly entrenched, some separatist religious-ethnic groups came to the support of public schools, partly because they could completely dominate local school boards. Thus, for example, when the public school-parochial school controversy was raging among new Lutheran groups in the Old Northwest, some fascinating arguments were heard. At an 1869 conference in Wisconsin, ministers and laymen from the Lutheran state church insisted on parochial schools. Leaders of the pietistic groups, on the other hand, having been repelled by developments in the Lutheran states and in "high-church" Lutheranism, argued for public schools, noting that the public school could be controlled in the interest of the local community while parochial schools may be subordinated to the state and to state-church ministers. Particularly in the Midwest, and in Pennsylvania, school consolidation has met with especially virulent opposition in small communities where religious-ethnic homogeneity persists.

The Views of the Southern Gentry

Provincialism, a tendency to define values in terms of the interests and beliefs of the local oligarchy, was as marked in the southern tidewater communities as it was in New England. Here, too, a local aristocracy, which thought of itself as called to lead, quickly emerged. The same threat of English interference and exploitation, the same possibility of economic disaster, and the same fear that the influences of the frontier and the irresponsible classes would lead to barbarianism that plagued the Puritan were sharply felt by his southern counterpart. Here, too, they re-enforced the inclination of the gentry to concentrate power on the local level and to guard the seats of power from encroachment by undesirable elements. The southerner derived an ideal from an image of the English landed gentry, who in the spirit of *noblesse oblige* assumed the gentlemen's responsibility for the maintenance of high culture, the economic well-being of the community, and political stability.

But in the plantation areas there were no congregations of saints; the individual squire was likely to stand alone. To be sure, he met with his peers in Williamsburg or elsewhere to discuss common problems and colonial policies. As if father to the whole group of small farmers, artisans, indentured servants and slaves who lived nearby, however, he ministered to their economic needs, advised them on political matters, provided such education as many of them received, and tried to set a pattern of civilized life that would inspire them. That he tried very hard is attested by such volumes as the *Secret Diary of William Byrd II*.

In contrast to members of the New England oligarchy, the southern squires developed a way of life less dominated by theological considerations. Because of the episcopalian pattern of church government and the system of priestly ordination which prevailed in the southern, Anglican colonies, religious authority remained largely in England. Frequently the ministers were conceived almost as aliens. Since the layman did not participate in church government as fully as was the case in other colonies, he tended to define community mores in secular terms. Though he was not irreligious, the "southern gentleman" rather than the Puritan "saint" was his ideal.

Anticommunitarian Elements

It is interesting to note that colonial leaders in both Massachusetts and Virginia thought they saw in neighboring colonies examples of communities destroyed by rampant individualism and community irresponsibility. As early as 1729 William Byrd II, of Virginia, described the inhabitants of North Carolina as largely criminals, debtors, and run-away servants and slaves addicted to sloth and lapsing rapidly into savagery. Two centuries later Samuel Eliot Morison, distinguished, scholarly heir and defender of the Puritan tradition, scarcely concealed his delight in reporting that for many generations libertarian Rhode Island failed to create effective schools and other social institutions. To Morison's ancestors, Roger Williams and his kind had created a colony which epitomized anarchy and social degeneracy.

Every human community has its rebels, those who perceive the demands of organized society as designed to preserve special privilege and to destroy the legitimate aspirations of the less privileged or to stamp out personal idiosyncrasies. Among those who moved into frontier areas were many of these rebels. Folklore concerning such men as Daniel Boone, Davy Crockett, and John Sevier attests to their generally incorrigible tendencies and their desire to hold organized society at a distance. Probably the necessity for reliance on one's self and family, supported only by occasional short-term co-operative projects among the settlers of a given region, sharpened the anticommunitarian proclivities of the frontier's natural rebels.

As Louis Booker Wright points out in his *Culture on the Moving Frontier*, there were always on the edge of expansion those dedicated to building a community with the high culture and social organization of the older cities. But the ratio of such people to those who protested against, or were merely careless toward, community sentiment and organization was no doubt smallest in the frontier communities. It was against the frontier towns that the Massachusetts General Court most frequently brought action for carelessness in observing educational legislation; it was to the new Middle West and the Pacific coast that the missionary societies sent young men from Yale and Princeton carrying higher education.

However, most of the extreme individualists were silent men so far as the historical record is concerned. Unbounded by geography, religious background, or ethnic origins, they arose in every group, but were of none. The lonely trapper, the isolated farmer, the noncommunicative tradesman, the wealthy recluse remained anonymous. They were, however, temperamentally related to certain literary figures who, either because they had to write to know themselves or because basically they yearned for communion with others who would understand, wrote of their convictions.

Two spokesmen of extreme individualism who, although somewhat ignored in their own day, have since appealed to a considerable number of Americans were Henry Thoreau and Herman Melville. Neither was pleased with the direction in which American culture moved under the banners of co-operation and progress; each withdrew into himself. Thoreau was appalled at the growing power of the community over the individual, and he saw in the developing technology and the growing preoccupation with material goods a dire threat to the good life and to human dignity. But he remained in a sense optimistic, ever believing in human virtue and the eventual triumph of the good.

Melville, on the other hand, remained to the end deeply pessimistic. To him God was silent, evil was and would ever be present, and individual men were eternally doomed to fight in darkness and without hope for victory against it. The pride which men took in their social systems was purchased at the price of ignoring evil and thus, ultimately, of abandoning their destiny. Only the recluse, the lonely prophet and warrior, could be true to himself. Melville's pessimism was even more profound than that of the sin-obsessed Puritan who at least believed that God spoke clearly and who accepted the support and re-enforcement of the congregation of the elect.

In the older cities, some groups in opposition to the dominant community mores developed in such numbers that they could maintain themselves as islands of resistance. Within these islands they created as strong a sense of ideological unity and economic co-operation as was achieved by the dominant majority; but they lived in, and were not of, the larger community. When the number and strength of such groups were sufficient, they at times formed through temporary alliances concurrent majorities which could exert economic and political power. Illustrative of such an alliance was that of the Irish, the Jews, and the Italians in New York City. Such alliances as these were not opposed to community action as such, but, precisely because they were alliances, they were likely to combine for rather specific ends and to treasure a social system which allowed for maximum diversity in ways of living.

The Community and the Common School

Perhaps more thoroughly than that of any other person, Horace Mann's attitude toward community is imbedded in the traditions of the American common school. Mann's concept was a modification of the Puritan attitude; some of the same elements, with further modification, are found in the views of John Dewey and James B. Conant. As had his ancestors, Mann believed in the absolute necessity of ideological unity in a society. Like them, he conceived property and labor as being in a sense public; the property-holder was a steward, managing God's earth in trust for the well-being of the entire human race, and the laborer was "called" to serve in God's kingdom to the interest of all. Ideology, economics, and politics were, he thought, inseparable. The school, he argued, was the greatest instrument ever created to build a good society, and its central purpose was to create among all a common faith, a sharp sense of common interest, and love for a political order which served this faith and these interests.

But New England was no longer a community in the Puritan sense. What had been basic dogma in theology, economics, and politics was now at issue. A common ideology could be created only by emphasizing the beliefs shared by all Christian groups and all political-economic groups. The "common elements of Christianity" and the "common elements of republicanism" were, by implication, to become the important elements so far as the community and school were concerned. Issues on which fundamental disagreement existed were, as far as possible, to be kept out of the school. To restore a community of conviction, Mann thus excluded discussion of problems deeply concerning the public.

Mann reduced the ideological content of the public school faith to a minimum, and as non-Christian groups grew in power, and differences among Christian groups became more clear, even his "common elements" were subject to dispute. Yet, in Mann's approach to community-building through the schools were certain ideas to be emphasized by John Dewey. The first was to call into participation a wider range of communities—Dewey's term was "publics"; the second was to focus attention on the process of shared decision-making through political discussion and persuasion.

The Puritan community of belief in a detailed set of specific principles had become, with Dewey, a community bound only by a common commitment to the scientific processes of inquiry and the political processes of persuasion and legislation in which all interest groups participate. Where the Puritans had sought to prevent the development of ideological differences, and Mann had banned the discussion of such issues from the schools, Dewey found it essential that they be openly debated in the schools so that students might learn the processes on which his kind of ideal community depended. Confronted with Puritan-like community attitudes, the descendants of Dewey were to call in other groups as countervailing forces.

Neither Mann nor Dewey abandoned, however, the Puritan conviction that only through close and active association on a face-to-face basis could a sense of community be built. In this they were to be joined by James B. Conant, who, while advocating ability grouping for the study of most subjects, still insisted that representatives of all groups and intellectual levels be periodically brought together for a discussion of basic social issues.

Yet, in the sixth decade of this century there were many who, like Roger Williams, Thoreau, and Melville before, found the community and its common schools oppressive. In the South, those who resented the intrusion of outsiders were in protest; in rural areas, groups sharing particular religious-ethnic backgrounds held out for small, easily controlled school districts; and, throughout the nation, powerful churches sought to expand schools in which loyalty to their religious community was a fundamental aim.

WORK AND PLAY

In discussing how emotion-laden attitudes toward work and play influence men's judgments of educational practices, it may be useful to note two ideal types, both extreme abstractions never found in their pure form among actual groups of people. Let us call these two stereotypes the "Hebraic-Puritan" and the "Hellenic-Romantic," since certain elements of the ideal types were in fact found among the groups whom these titles fit. But one need not literally have descended from the designated groups to have developed the attitudes to be described. The Western tradition has exposed all the well-educated to both views.

The Hebraic-Puritan Attitude

The Hebraic-Puritan attitude derives from the biblical tale of the fall of Adam and his expulsion from the Garden of Eden. It grants that the child's world of irresponsible play and naïveté is idyllic, that to which the natural man will aspire. The Garden is a child-centered world; the Father provides all that is required for a life of joy and comfort and spontaneity. Yet this world of play is one in which the tempter runs free, and man's natural hankering for pleasure ever makes him subject to sin. Because Adam fell from grace, as inevitably would all his descendants, God justly condemned them to live in a vale of tears where they were to subsist by the sweat of their brow until redeemed. Henceforth, one who made of play a virtue and a goal was doubly sinful. He not only ignored a specific commandment of God but he continued to subject himself to the tempter.

The American Puritan never doubted that this life had justly been made one of suffering and hard work. Duty and obligation were his watchwords, and, next to pride, irresponsibility and frivolous consumption were the greatest sins. But he did not rely solely on the negative commandment that "thou shalt not play too freely"; he added positive sanctions for work and success. So long as it was the result of honest, frugal, and untiring effort, material success was viewed as evidence that one was of the elect. It seemed reasonable that God would inspire his chosen followers to behave in this manner and that prosperity would be the inevitable consequence of such behavior just as poverty inescapably followed from slothfulness. The able-bodied poor must obviously have yielded to the desires of the natural man, as all from whom God withheld the gift of grace would do. The prosperous could find great spiritual comfort in their work. Were they to forget, however, that success was ultimately due to God and attempt to use wealth for the gratification of physical appetites instead of in the interests of God and the human community, they would be guilty of the cardinal sin of pride.

This attitude did not begin with the New England Puritans, nor was it peculiar to them. It was rooted in the Hebraic tradition to which all Christianity was heir. In the nineteenth century it was secularized, as were many attitudes formerly based on theological premises. The most commonly cited secular sanction was the "survival of the fittest," as interpreted by the social Darwinists. Its influence ebbs and flows throughout our history. One suspects (a hypothesis worth testing through more extensive research) that, in times perceived as "times of trouble," a sense of guilt for having done something wrong pervades American thought and re-enforces the Hebraic-Puritan tendency. Certainly in recent years the critics of American education have emphasized the desirability of hard, even unpleasant, work and have stressed the student's duty to serve his society.

The Hellenic Attitude

The image of the classical Greek, with his games, his festivals, his gymnasiums, his poetry, and his sculpture is one of a people at play. Even when he spoke of his most serious business, politics, religion, and the pursuit of understanding, the literate Hellenist tended to stress leisure. His Gods were incessantly at play, and his most profound conversations often occurred over the banquet table. The vocations, the callings, worthy of a true man were thought of as liberal, that is, best carried out when one had leisure to play with ideas.

Though Plato, one among the most influential Greeks, is often described as condemning the masses to an unsatisfying life of drudgery and servitude, it seems reasonable to argue that this charge is unjust. His big "lie" is the literal story that some men are born of brass, others of silver, and others of gold. Behind this lie is what he considered the truth—that men find realization in different types of callings. What one who knows himself best would choose to do, the activity in which he does in fact find greatest satisfaction, is that to which Plato suggests he be assigned. That Plato denied the ability of all men to judge for themselves is true and warrants the charge that he was antidemocratic. It does not justify the claim that he believed men should be compelled to work at tasks which they found to be unsatisfying. Even the artisan was to engage in activities that followed his natural bent and were, therefore, playful in a sense. Plato remained a true Hellene.

Perhaps it was this element of Plato's which led Rousseau, the great eighteenth-century romanticist, to describe *The Republic* as the greatest pedagogical treatise ever written. Ever the exponent of following the unspoiled impulses of the natural child, Rousseau reversed the Hebraic-Puritan picture of play and work. Provided always that the man had not been corrupted by society, Rousseau believed that those activities in which the individual freely chose to engage out of his own self-interest, and which were therefore characterized by spontaneity, joy, and immediate satisfaction, were not only the more virtuous but also the more productive. Distaste for that which is usually called "work" was to him a function of the fact that it was imposed from without and entailed exploitation of the individual by others. In Rousseau's Garden of Eden, productive effort abounded and sin was absent.

In America the transcendentalists, the members of those religious groups which place great emphasis on "love" rather than sin and which have great confidence in human nature, the aristocracy of wealth not controlled by the Hebraic-Puritan ethos, a number of educational leaders in the romantic and pragmatic traditions, and certain industrial and labor leaders have, in greater or lesser degree, held a Hellenic-romantic attitude toward work. The influence of a philosophic tradition can be clearly seen in some instances. In other cases, people have acted as if adhering to this tradition although no literal influence can be established.

Thus, for example, the influence of Plato and Rousseau on Emerson and other transcendentalists was clear. Emerson's essay on *Education*, like Rousseau's *Emile*, was a plea that the child's natural genius, his native bent, be followed to the fullest. Were this done, Emerson argued, a vocation which was a true calling would emerge. This vocation would in time lead one to all truth, to an understanding of one's ideal relationship with both animate and inanimate nature, and, above all, to a knowledge and full realization of self.

Dewey and his followers parted company with Plato, Rousseau, and Emerson by rejecting the concept of the "enfolded," "natural" self. Their alternative was the social self of George Herbert Mead. But they continued to propose that one should start with those activities in which a presently lively interest existed, that he should work in terms of pleasurable activities, and that, as the student's interest took on the characteristics of a vocation, other necessary learnings could be provided as extensions in the social significance of the chosen calling. As had Plato, Rousseau, and Emerson, Dewey insisted that one's total life be integrated in terms of a calling, a vocation, viewed as a way of life sanctioned by the inter-relationships of an entire social system.

Partly under the leadership of such social psychologists as Elton Mayo, American industry has moved in a direction paralleling that proposed by Dewey. Just as the "whole child," learning through the study of economic and other social callings, was the concern of the Dewey school, the "whole worker" came to be of concern to management. Industry came increasingly to care for the morale of face-to-face working groups, to establish health and welfare plans, to sponsor company recreational activities, and even to be concerned with such matters as family counseling. Organized labor augmented this trend. In so far as workers could be led to organize their recreational, political, and welfare interests around their vocational roles, the significance of the union in their lives could be enhanced. Quite obviously, neither the pragmatists nor industrial and labor leaders came to this position solely and directly by way of the Hellenic tradition. Social scientific research gave new support, and sometimes a new rationale, to an older attitude.

Similarly, the "gentleman" class reached a position like that of the Hellenes through a devious route in which current social and economic conditions played a major part. Yet, the tradition of the landed gentry was partly shaped by the Renaissance view of the good life, a view rather directly derived from the literature of the classical era. The humanistic secondary school, like one of its descendants, the finishing school, was originally designed for a new leisure class. As had been the case in ancient society, this class had a vocation, that of governing, conducting military operations, and managing the economic system. Policy-making and negotiation, not immediate production of economic goods, were its major responsibilities.

The forum and symposium of classical times, the court and castle of the Renaissance, the salon of the enlightenment, and, perhaps, the country club of the twentieth century were the places in which this group conducted many of its vocational tasks. Pleasant, tactful conversation, shared recreational activities, inter-group loyalty, and leisure facilitated the performance of these tasks. Being a gentleman was a way of life, and, though the activities in which this group participated bore little resemblance to those of the proletariat, one ought not be blind to the vocational elements involved. For one to be accepted among those with whom he shared responsibilities, and therefore effective in his vocation, the ancient Greek had to be a skilled wrestler, the Italian courtier a talented fencer, and the twentieth-century manager a reasonably competent golfer. Just as Dewey's school child and Mayo's industrial worker were to find work pleasurable because of its integration into a way of life, those aristocrats not tormented by a Hebraic-Puritan conscience found tremendous satisfaction in their vocation.

There has, however, been an interesting paradox in the classical tradition. During Athens' "time of troubles," and increasingly through the Hellenistic period, philosophies of renunciation and restraint developed. One of the most important of these, Stoicism, flourished in ancient Rome. The Stoics who, it was alleged, "made their heart a desert and called it peace" profoundly influenced the classical tradition, particularly through Cicero and Seneca. There have always been what Crane Brinton called the "spare humanists," those who emphasized the doctrine of restraint. These were easily accepted within the Hebraic-Puritan tradition, a fact which explains why the New England Puritans remained avid students of the classics.

Attitudes Outside the Hebraic-Puritan and the Hellenic-Romantic Traditions

Two further attitudes toward work and play should be noted. One, based on what Veblen called "instinct for workmanship," was similar to the Hellenic-romantic notion in that it made of work an inherently, almost instinctively, rewarding activity. Veblen and others viewed the skilled artisan, who worked largely with hand tools and converted raw materials by his own imagination and skill into finished products, as finding sufficient satisfaction in the work itself. Neither profit, nor duty, nor an elaborate scheme of planned social and welfare activity were primary motives to this kind of worker. As in the Hellenic-romantic tradition, work was viewed as a process of creative self-realization. Unfortunately, from the point of view of those holding this attitude toward work, the rise of the entrepreneur, the system of mass production, and the ethic of consumption led to such specialization of function that the inherent pleasure of a job well done was denied a large segment of the population. Indeed, as Veblen saw it, the instinct for skilful work was increasingly degenerating into a passion for consumption.

David Reisman, C. Wright Mills, and others, accepting as inevitable the trend which Veblen has observed, have suggested an attitude toward work which may well have dominated the thinking of most Americans throughout our history. This attitude views work as simple necessity, neither good nor bad, or rather both good and bad. One engages in it as a means of sustenance and seeks self-realization in his avocational pursuits: in religion, family activities, politics, art, and recreation. Work cannot, save for the fortunate few, be an end in itself.

Attitudes Toward Work and Attitudes Toward Education

At the price of over-simplification, it might be useful to suggest how the above-sketched attitudes toward work and play might affect people's judgment of educational practices. That of the Hellenic-romantic would seem clear; unless students are "playing" at school tasks—that is to say, approaching them with joy, spontaneity, self-direction, and enthusiasm—the Hellenist would suspect that the student is being exploited in terms of someone else's interests. If, on the other hand, the student is obviously "having fun," the Hebraic-Puritan would be suspicious, if not actually offended. The recent *Life* series on the "Crisis in Education" beautifully illustrates this conflict by contrasting the relaxed good humor of American students and schools with the austere severity of Soviet schools and students. The representative of American students, Stephen Lapekas, is characteristically pictured with a broad grin; his Soviet counterpart, Alexei Kutzkov, is never shown as smiling. *Life's* sympathies seem clearly to be with the Puritan atmosphere of the Soviet school, where duty is stressed, rather than with the "country-club" aura of the American school.

One would expect the Hellenist of the Deweyan variety to seek an integration of class activities with extracurricular projects. He might expect those of the Reisman persuasion, as loosely described here, to favor extracurricular activities but to expect students in class to get down to business and get the work done.

Since none of these attitudes has completely dominated a distinct historical group, one is likely to find many Americans who vacillate from one to another, or who accept one attitude toward their own work and play activities while advocating another for their children. There are duty-driven parents who want their youngsters to enjoy youth, just as there are adults who rationalize their play as "good business," or good for shop morale, while demanding long hours of homework for students.

AUTHORITY AND SUBMISSION

The problem to be examined here concerns feelings about the pattern of relationships that should characterize adult-child interactions. Anthropological and social psychological research has amply demonstrated a tremendous range of attitudes concerning the pattern and amount of deference the young are expected to show their elders, or the elders the young. Historical research, on the other hand, has not yet yielded enough evidence on this problem that trends can be clearly established. One suspects that further research will reveal in this case, and in the cases of values described above, that a simple scale of "traditional" and "emergent" attitudes used by such researchers as Spindler and Getzels will prove to be inaccurate. No one attitude appears to have been completely dominant in any era, and the pendulum stroke from one attitude to another appears too short to warrant the assumption of a long-term trend. It might be wiser to anticipate the entire range of attitudes in the school's public at any time and to calculate the relative strength of each set of values at the moment a controversial issue arises.

Let us consider, for example, the colonial and early national periods. Among the most popular of writers with early Americans was John Locke, who expressed in his

Thoughts concerning Education perhaps the dominant attitude so far as formal expressions of it are concerned. The first and most important habit which the child should develop, Locke believed, was that of unquestioned obedience to legitimate adult authority. The child was to be "seen and not heard," "silent unless spoken to." Only after he had thoroughly accepted the iron law of obedience could he be gradually admitted to a status of near equality to his elders.

American writers differed on how obedience was to be taught. The Puritans, for example, insisted that the child's "pride," his aspirations for complete independence, should be broken through a rather harsh discipline. As Cotton Mather argued in *A Family Well Ordered*, only one who had first learned to accept his dependence on, and the obligation to submit to, the authority of parents and other adults would easily accept his life-long, complete dependence on God. The same sinful nature which impelled an adult to rebel against God was thought to be at work in the child who resisted his elders.

The Puritan was not lacking in affection for children, as is widely believed, nor did he fail to reveal this affection. Love for their children was, in fact, a powerful motive to which Mather appealed in his advice to parents. Yet, the contrast between the method of the Puritans, for example, and that of the Moravian Christopher Dock is clear. Dock's appeal, like that of the Quakers and other pietistic groups, was to love, to the child's "better nature." Nevertheless, the ultimate necessity of obedience and submission to adult authority was accepted as completely by Dock as it was by Mather.

Children's textbooks, from the *New England Primer* through Webster's "Blue-back Speller" to the McGuffey readers, echoed the themes of obedience and respect for elders. If one judges by these formal statements, it seems clear that the traditional American had no desire to live in a child-centered world.

Yet, paradoxically enough, foreign visitors to the American scene during the early centuries almost invariably commented on the liberties granted by American parents to their children. To the visitors, American children were bad mannered; to at least one American host, they were "sturdy young republicans." While Emerson had little tolerance for foolishness and horseplay, he noted with approval that in America boys were freely admitted and treated with affection everywhere.

Morison reminds us that among the reasons given by the Reverend Solomon Stoddard for the need of a new college in 1703 was the charge that indulgent, "fond and proud" parents had encouraged their sons to introduce frivolous and evil customs into Harvard life. And these were largely New England parents. A century later the parentally encouraged indulgences of southern students were the despair of college educators North and South. The formal emphasis on obedience and submission was evidently considerably softened by indulgence in practice.

The dominant tradition might, then, be characterized as one of continuous tension between an explicit ideal of child submissiveness and implicit delight in the child's assertions of independence from adult authority. Those who have grown up in this tradition will have a certain ambivalence. Perhaps, again, in times when the adult feels that the world, or his own personal life, is "getting out of control," we might expect him to be emotionally offended at the sight of a classroom in which the mantle of authority is lightly worn by adults. Those who feel more secure in their own lives may be expected to be more comfortable in the presence of educational practices which emphasize the initiative and freedom of the child.

An interesting variant of this tension in the dominant group can be found in the attitudes of certain more recent immigrant groups. Oscar Handlin, in *The Uprooted*, described conditions which could well have created ambivalence on the part of both adults and children in such families. The central tendency among societies from which these groups came was that of an authoritarian family, usually of the patriarchal sort. Yet, when the immigrant adult was placed in a strange culture late in life, confronted with incredible difficulties in making an adequate living, and denied educational opportunities which would have eased the transition, he often found himself dependent on the child as a mediator of the new culture. The child was, on the one hand, expected to give unquestioned obedience and deference to his elders. On the other hand, he was painfully aware of the parent's ineptness with American ways, of the ridicule to which the unacculturated immigrant was subject, and of his elder's dependence on him for help and advice. Since neither immigrant adult nor child lived according to a clearly defined and consistently operating concept of the proper relationships between adult and child, tension and vacillation could be expected. Anxiety about teacher-child relationships was perhaps the inevitable consequence.

HUMAN NATURE

Underlying all the concepts described above were concepts of human nature. The problem "what is man?" has concerned our greatest thinkers, and every judgment about whether to approve or resist a given educational practice involves one's sense of what is appropriate treatment for the kind of creature man is thought to be. Yet, of all the concepts here treated, this is the most complex; with all the speculation that has occurred we remain, perhaps, farthest from consensus on this issue.

The mere cataloguing of questions which those holding differing concepts of human nature will answer differently suggests the complexity of this particular problem: Ought man to regulate his life with reference to the achievement of certain temporal conditions or with reference to his individual eternal salvation? What are the relative effects of "grace," "will," genetic heredity, geographical conditions, social institutions, and historical accident on the behavior of an individual? Would the "natural" man tend toward love and altruism in his treatment of others, or would he be dominated by greed and brutality? Is reason capable of dominating the behavior of man or merely a tool which he uses to mediate between the demands of an insatiable *id* and an uncompromising *super-ego*? Does human nature never change, or is it, as Hocking suggests, "human nature to change itself"? Can virtue be taught? What are the limits of educability?

In *The Image of Man in America*, Don M. Wolfe discussed these and other questions as they have been implicitly or explicitly answered in the writings of such men as Jefferson, Holmes, Whitman, Mark Twain, Dreiser, Lincoln, and John Dewey. He concluded with a brief summation of recent anthropological, psychological, and biological research bearing on the nature of man and described this research as constituting barely a start toward a "science of man." He noted that even such tentative findings as those which suggest the tremendous plasticity of human nature and the determining effects of biochemistry and enculturation have not yet penetrated into the awareness of the average citizen. Education's public, therefore, remains under the control of traditional views, of which there are many. Let us sample them, utilizing, in several cases, portraits painted by Wolfe.

The Depravity of Man

At the head of a long stream of American writers who have been convinced that man is dominated by a sinful nature stood the founding fathers of New England. As one of them, John Winthrop, stated the case in his *Journal*, natural liberty, which man shares with the beasts, "makes men grow more evil, and in time to be worse than brute beasts. . . . [It] is that great enemy of truth and peace, that wild beast, which all the ordinances of God are bent against, to restrain and subdue it." Only the grace of God, supported by the well-organized society of saints, could enable a man to overcome this beastly nature.

Some generations removed from Winthrop and his own early New England ancestors, John Adams still described man as dominated by ambition, jealousy, envy, and vanity. Altruistic tendencies, the existence of which was granted, could, he argued, be expected to dominate only in the rarest of cases. Evil, he assumed, was ineradicably rooted in man's nature, and such social institutions as schools and governments were established primarily to control human passions. Though, through schooling, the passions might be harnessed by social control, their basic tendency could not be fundamentally altered.

At the end of the nineteenth century, one of John Adams's progeny, Brooks Adams, still held this view: "As I perceived that the strongest of human passions are fear and greed, I inferred that so much and no more might be expected . . . from any automation so actuated." The reform of social institutions might create the illusion of progress; for example, the growth of democracy yielded a small advance in altruism, but in the long run even democracy, according to Adams, promised only the triumph of greed and the surrender to passion.

For a time Mark Twain had been even more depressed over the depravity of human nature than Adams was. Among the most stinging denunciations of the human race and the God who created it was Twain's *The Mysterious Stranger*. Here, too, depravity was assumed to be innate. Later in his life, however, Twain mellowed somewhat. His *What Is Man?* suggests that so far as inheritance is concerned, man is morally neutral. What he becomes is a function of environment; one inherits possibilities, and the environment determines which of them will be realized. Twain thus came, in time, to a position similar to that later held by Clarence Darrow and Theodore Dreiser.

Few Americans studied the criminal mind more carefully than Darrow; few described men's surrender to evil more clearly than Dreiser. Both, however, maintained a high level of compassion based on the conviction that individual men were inescapably the products of environmental factors beyond personal control. Neither had great hope for the reform of social institutions to the point where the good would, in most cases, triumph. We must turn to the writings of Jefferson, Horace Mann, and John Dewey for a more optimistic view.

Meliorism and the Plasticity of Human Nature

Jefferson was no naïve optimist. He seldom used the popular enlightenment phrase, "the *infinite* perfectability of man." Though he considered great progress possible, he expected it to come much more slowly than did the more exuberant sons of the enlightenment. He did, however, maintain that man's behavior was the result of purely natural causes, of biological inheritance and of experience in the physical and social environment. Through the use of intelligence in the control and manipulation of these environmental factors, he believed that the natural man could be greatly improved.

This conviction, which Jefferson shared with other reformers, provided a major argument in the French and American campaigns for universal education. Education, it was claimed, would expand the use of intelligence in social affairs. As social institutions were reformed in light of new knowledge, the mind and character of man would be raised to new heights. The new man would then be capable of further institutional reform and the more effective utilization of natural forces and resources. Thus was the wheel of progress ever to turn.

Jefferson's belief in the existence of a natural aristocracy and his suggestion that the educational system be used to "rake from the rubbish" those capable of leadership are often cited as evidence that he was no egalitarian. The charge is valid if, by egalitarianism, one refers to a belief that all men are capable of the same kind and same order of behavior. Jefferson recognized that the biological inheritance of individuals differed, and he granted that such inheritance defined the bounds, however broad, within which subsequent development must occur. He was even inclined to believe that there existed racial differences in intellectual potentiality, although he was still suspending final judgment and seeking new evidence on this point to the end of his life.

Yet, in a way these differences were relatively insignificant for Jefferson. All men, he thought, were rational, all educable, and all possessed of sufficient basic talent to participate in the making of fundamental social decisions. There was none whose intelligence was so unmalleable that his capacity for more effective living could not be increased by education.

Jefferson did, however, remain convinced that man had an innate moral sense. The social instinct, the disposition to love and serve, exists, he thought, in every man. On this point Jefferson agreed with the romantics and the transcendentalists. Here, too, he anticipated the views of Horace Mann.

Few have had such confidence in the educability of mankind as did Mann. Human tendencies, even the innate moral sense, were, he was convinced, so easily shaped by experience that the nature of social institutions largely determined whether a specific individual would be noble or mean. Given proper institutions, and especially adequate schools, Mann expected poverty, crime, bigotry, and selfishness to disappear. If educational opportunities were widely enough distributed, Mann believed that highly significant differences in virtue and talent would no longer exist.

John Dewey, heir to both Jefferson and Mann, was more of an environmentalist than either. Though he, too, began his philosophical journey with a belief in man's innate moral sense, he came to believe that human nature was completely amoral at base. Indeed, he thought those characteristics considered most distinctively human, moral commitment and the capacity of rational thought, were the result of experience and learning. Though he ultimately parted company with the systematic behaviorists in psychology, he continued to assume that an infant could be made into almost any kind of a person desired by those who controlled his environment. He was always fearful of the mental-testing movement, since the limits revealed by testing under a specific set of conditions, and based on a particular kind of educative experience, were too easily taken as measures of innate potential. To Dewey, as to Jefferson and Mann, failure to have developed needed intelligence and skill pointed to the necessity of reconstructing the environment to which the young were exposed.

Neither Jefferson nor Dewey had quite the exalted faith in the power of the formal school that Horace Mann had possessed. Both agreed with him, however, that it was among the more effective forces for the improvement of human nature.

The belief that human nature is highly plastic and subject to being molded by culture into an almost infinite number of shapes has, of course, been shared by a great many social scientists and, particularly, by American anthropologists. This view has been shocking and frightening to many Americans, particularly when they perceive that the Communist world has, through "brain washing," used scientific knowledge to undermine values which Americans had thought to inhere in the soul and conscience of men. Whether belief in the plasticity of human nature has been rationalized as untrue because it is frightening to admit that beliefs held dear have no supernatural supports, or because adequate evidence concerning an innate and ineradicable moral sense is thought in fact to exist, cannot be determined as a generalization. One suspects, however, that a belief in the innate goodness of man is, in most cases, a psychological rather than a logical or scientific necessity. Nevertheless, there is a long tradition to support this belief.

The Natural Man as Virtuous

Among American Christian sects have been a number which assumed, as did Jefferson and Mann with qualifications, that the natural man was a man of virtue. The debate between these groups and those obsessed with man's depravity concerns, in religious terms, the relative strength of the spirit of God dwelling within and the sinful nature also believed to be present. The Quakers and the early Unitarians, for example, were willing to grant to their Calvinist compatriots that man was subject to acute temptation arising from his physical passions and social conditions. Nevertheless, they argued, the spirit of love, the God within the natural man, was sufficiently strong to lead most men on the path to righteousness.

In secular terms, Emerson nicely illustrates the popular faith in the natural goodness of man. To Emerson each individual was essentially a part of the great oversoul and his unspoiled inclination was to seek and maintain contact with the sublime. To be sure, he could be made a monster if others sought to constrain him to a life pattern not his own. Emerson believed, as had Rousseau, that all things, all men, came from nature essentially good. They were spoiled by the meddling of men. Though Emerson did from time to time praise the public school system, he was ever fearful that formal social institutions, even schools, would be destructive of the individual's natural genius, that which impelled him to live the good life. Attempts to mold the individual, as if he were clay, were, Emerson believed, offenses against nature. No good could come of them. Meliorism, the attempt to improve human nature through social reform, he considered a delusion.

Rational and Irrational Man

Cutting across the arguments concerning the virtue or evil of natural man, and the degree to which he can be molded by environmental factors, has been the question of his essential rationality. Tension between the mystic and the intellectual has been ever present throughout the Christian tradition. There have always been those who "felt" their way to truth as well as those for whom rational analysis was considered essential to understanding. The early argument between the rationally oriented Puritans and those who would exploit religious "enthusiasm" was but one of many conflicts on this issue. So, too, was the nineteenth-century frontier struggle between those churches that insisted upon a "learned ministry" and those stressing the simple faith of the relatively unlettered.

On the political front a related issue was spelled out by Justice Stone in his dissent on the Barnette (flag saluting) case. Justice Stone granted that a society was legitimately concerned with insuring reasonable loyalty among its members. He noted, however, that a choice of methods was available. One was the method of securing loyalty through emotionally charged rituals, making little direct appeal to reasoned judgment. The other was the slower, but he believed more just, method of disseminating information concerning the society's tradition and usages in the hope that a reasoned commitment would ensue.

With the growing acceptance of psychoanalytic theory in the 1920's, the old argument of the rational versus the nonrational took new form in its effects on attitudes toward education. Nowhere was the argument sharper than between two leaders of the progressive-education movement, John Dewey and Margaret Naumberg, the founder of Walden School. Their differences were partially concerned with the relative emphasis given to group activities and group loyalties. Behind this issue, however, was Miss Naumberg's conviction that the school should be primarily concerned with the child's emotional development. Under the influence of psychoanalytical theory, she apparently believed that learning and the development of rational powers would be a relatively simple matter if the child's emotional life were in order. Dewey, on the other hand, though not unconcerned with emotion, was never comfortable with the Freudian and neo-Freudian movements. He was far too much a rationalist.

Views on Human Nature and Attitudes Toward Education

The historian always finds it difficult to compare published views of intellectuals with those of people whose views are not published. Dependent on documentary evidence, he is compelled to base his conclusions on the study of an atypical population. In the present case many of the people whose points of view have been described were of groups which may have held consistently the positions set forth. It seems reasonable to assume that the Adamses, Mann, and Emerson represented significant portions of the old New England Congregationalist and Unitarian families. The religious traditions that have emphasized man's sinful nature, as well as those which have stressed man's natural virtue, can be identified. One can roughly describe the communities in which Jefferson, Dewey, and Naumberg were most popular. It remains true, however, that historical research has done very little to correlate attitudes toward human nature with identifiable social groups.

Moreover, one can only speculate on the way a given attitude toward human nature will enter as a value in educational judgments. It does seem reasonable to assume that one who has great faith in the plasticity of human nature will be uncomfortable in the presence of efforts to restrict educational opportunities; that one who considers students naturally evil, or at least rebellious, will favor a rather tightly organized classroom situation; that a Jeffersonian or Deweyan will be greatly concerned with group morale and will desire a curriculum organized around those disciplines which promise to extend control over the physical and social environment; that an Emersonian will favor a child-centered school, though not one of the Deweyan or Freudian sort; that the mystics and those who follow Mark Twain will have little confidence in the power of the formal school while a disciple of Horace Mann may expect the school to solve most acute social problems; and that a follower of Darrow will have great tolerance and compassion for the deviant student.

When educational conflict arises, the educational practitioner must determine on the spot what values actually enter in. A historical discussion of concepts of community, work and play, authority, and human nature can only alert him to certain factors which might be present.

4-2   COMMUNICATION AND AMERICAN VALUES: A PSYCHOLOGICAL APPROACH

Jurgen Ruesch

Jurgen Ruesch is associate professor of psychiatry at the University of California School of Medicine and research psychiatrist at the Langley Porter Clinic. He is well known for his efforts to introduce social science methodology into psychiatry. In the following essay, written with Gregory Bateson, he provides an excellent description of the "core" and "emergent" values of the dominant American culture.

. . . The verbal and non-verbal procedures of psychiatrists are designed to improve the processes of communication of their patients. The systems of communication of both psychiatrists and patients are in turn derived from the wider social matrix in which doctor and patient operate. While the conventional relationships are clearly defined in terms of the culture in which they occur, the more deviant relationships and methods of communication encountered in psychiatry are likewise embedded in the superpersonal networks of group and culture. The [following,] . . . therefore, are . . . a discussion and illustration of the more specifically American features of the social matrix and their relationship to present-day therapeutic practices.

A great many schemes[1] have been suggested for understanding the psychology of the American people, and depending upon the purpose for which an approach was designed, they have had their advantages, disadvantages, and distortions. The method which we are going to present in this chapter is characterized by the fact that we have attempted to understand some basic characteristics of human communication in America. Though the Anglo-Saxon countries have many similarities in their systems of com-

---

From *Communication, The Social Matrix of Psychiatry* by Jurgen Ruesch, M.D., and Gregory Bateson, pp. 94–124. By permission of W. W. Norton & Company, Inc. Copyright 1951 by W. W. Norton & Company, Inc.

[1] F. L. Allen, *Only Yesterday* (New York: Harper & Bros., 1932); S. Anderson, *Winesburg, Ohio* (New York: Viking, 1919); C. A. Beard and M. R. Beard, *The Rise of American Civilization*, 2 volumes (New York: Macmillan, 1937); D. W. Brogan, *The American Character* (New York: Knopf, 1944); A. de Tocqueville, *Democracy in America*, 2 volumes (New York: Knopf, 1946); J. Dos Passos, *U. S. A.* (New York: Modern Library, 1939).

munication, it would be a mistake to assume that the systems of evaluation are identical or even similar in all the countries where English is spoken. For example, the general rules which pertain to the interpretation of messages in the United States are not only based upon the symbols, words, and gestures used, but include such subtle things as timing and spacing of messages, the evaluation of figure-ground phenomena, the interpretation of authority, child-raising practices, and many others features.

In the scheme which we have followed, the American psychology has been described as being governed by the premises of equality, sociality, success, and change, which are thought to be interconnected by the multiple premises of puritan and pioneer morality. These four values, together with the core of moral principles, can be conceived, on the one hand, as pivotal points around which American life revolves, and on the other, as cornerstones upon which communication is based. Each of these values either may refer to goal-directed behavior or may express an intermediate implementation, instrumental to a more remote goal. Accordingly, messages exchanged regarding these activities or purposes must be interpreted in the same light. Therefore, when we as scientists make statements about value premises which prevail in the American culture, we refer on the one hand to the written or verbal comments about activities, and on the other hand to the experiences which are the result of participant action. It follows that these premises are a code for the interpretation of statements about actions and of actions themselves.

In reading the analysis of American values to be presented here, the reader will feel that the authors are biased in one way or another. Far be it from us, the authors, to deny the correctness of such a feeling. Rather, we would remind the reader that it is the essence of epistemology to view one system in the light of another. Depending upon the choice of the second system, this or that feature will by contrast appear to be exaggerated or perhaps even distorted. . . . We have chosen to look at America from a western European perspective; if we were more familiar with other cultures, we might have chosen a South American or Chinese standard of comparison.

Furthermore, in discussing cultural premises and in developing generalizations about the behavior of people, everybody is able to cite, for practical purposes, examples of an antithesis which would contradict the thesis presented by the authors. However, such contradictions are to be expected. In part they are due to the fact that the data used for deriving generalizations belong to the historical past, and that in the meantime the situation has already changed; in part, they may be based on selective experiences of both author and reader; and in part they may be due to the levels of abstraction at which statements are interpreted. As a general rule, it may be stated that contradictions can usually be resolved either by interpreting a statement at a higher level of abstraction or by breaking a statement down into its more concrete components. Be that as it may, such difficulties are unavoidable, but to us as authors, it seems as if the gain of such an analysis is greater than the loss associated with a lack of understanding of such superpersonal systems. With this in mind, the following paragraphs were written.

PURITAN AND PIONEER MORALITY

The wave of Protestantism which is associated with the names of Luther, Calvin, Huss, Zwingli, and others found its way to England, where it was identified first with the Reformation and later with the Puritanism of Cromwell. The core of Puritan morality was pietism, the deprecation of carnal passion, the high valuation of self-control and will power, and the assumption of personal responsibility vis-à-vis God. The Puritan valued plain living, industriousness, thrift, cleanliness, consistency, honesty, and favored simplicity of worship and cooperation with other members of the Puritan community. All these values derived from an oppositional tendency of British Puritans, a protest—both political and religious—against the existing conditions in Europe. Broadly, the Puritans strove for simplicity and coherence; and the confusion against which they strove may well have been due to cultural heterogeneity. The ideas of the Renaissance gradually seeped through the mass of the population, creating contradictions of value and belief and abuses of action which many may have found intolerable. To escape from the anxieties of multiple choice and lack of direction, the Puritans originated certain rigidities of behavior in order to obtain a long-lost security. The systems they set up met opposition, and they left the scene in protest.[2]

They arrived in America on a new continent inhabited by hostile Indians and with a rigorous climate of rugged winters and hot summers. They had to cope with hardship, and under these totally different living conditions in the Puritans developed what we here call the pioneer morality. Because they were few in number, their lives were valued; in order to survive, they needed rugged individuals who were well versed in the techniques of fighting nature and Indians, able to grow their own food and to clear and cultivate the earth. Adaptability to changing situations and suddenly arising emergencies was valued. There was little time for pleasure if a man wanted to survive, and hard work was his lot. The initial shortage of women, especially in frontier outposts, reinforced the rigid rules regarding behavior toward the opposite sex which the Puritans brought with them. The first settlers were likewise faced with the necessity of setting up social relations which would favor a closely knit group because the odds against them were great and could only be overcome by superior organization. The fusion of the needs of the pioneers with those of the Puritan constituted the root of the American value system.[3]

Subsequently this system was modified by the shift from an agrarian to an industrial-metropolitan economy, by the influx of non-Puritan settlers, and by all those changes which were brought about by the rise of a modern technical civilization.

Pioneer and puritan morality is the core of the American value system. The actual history is, however, not immediately relevant. For the present inquiry it is more important to note that currently, today, there exists a pride in this core of the culture. American youngsters meet a whole literature of truth and fiction romanticizing the frontier and extolling the values which it supposedly fostered. While he is absorbing these notions about the past, the young American is also receiving a barrage of other value-forming impacts from comic magazines and gangster serials, and he is being initiated by other publications into the excitements of engineering and mechanics. These other value-forming sources might seem to contradict the messages of the puritan and the pioneer, but actually the contradiction is only superficial. The virtues extolled are still the same: toughness, resourcefulness, purpose, and even purity.

Also in accord with the traditional pattern, the arbiter and censor of American

---

[2] M. Weber, *The Protestant Ethic and the Spirit of Capitalism* (London: Allen and Unwin, 1930).

[3] C. A. Beard and M. R. Beard, 1937; V. L. Parrington, *Main Currents in American Thought*, 3 volumes (New York: Harcourt and Brace, 1927).

morals is no single individual; instead, authority is vested in the group. Where the European child defers to his parents and a European adult defers to identifiable persons with real and sympathetic authority, the adult American defers to the collective opinion of his peers. This social organization and its reinforcement of morality is characteristic of a society of equals. Actions which violate other American value premises become acceptable when the principle of moral purpose is not violated. These tendencies are clearly reflected in the procedures which exonerate sharp practices, if they were undertaken in the name of free enterprise and rugged individualism. In the American judicial system, the municipal judges have a freedom to rule unparalleled in other countries; they really interpret the meaning of morality, and as long as the rulings do not conflict with the major premises of the American value system, their decisions will usually be upheld in higher courts.

This peculiar role which morality occupies in American life explains in part the many contradictory trends which puzzle the foreign observer.[4] A foreign traveler is made aware of moral principles in situations where impulse gratifications have to be justified. He will recognize that pleasure cannot be indulged in for its own sake; this fact is epitomized by the saying that a puritan can have anything he wants as long as he doesn't enjoy it. Gratifying a personal need is permissible when justified by a socially acceptable motive. For example, recreational pleasures, vacations, sexual intercourse, eating, and all other pleasures become acceptable as long as these activities are undertaken for the purpose of promoting one's own or other people's health.

Another socially acceptable motive is the welfare of the community. In the American system, the stronger person assumes responsibility for the weaker one as long as the weakness is the result of age or circumstance. Weakness owing to lack of will power or to laziness or carnal passion is not tolerated, and the saying goes: "Never give a sucker an even break." A series of institutions take care of the less fortunate people, and everyone tries to help those who through no fault of their own become ill or lose their homes. Such help is rarely outright charity; by and large it is offered in terms of loans or other temporary relief measures. Actions which improve the social welfare or which contribute toward the general raising of standards of living are acceptable for justifying impulse gratifications. Making money, for example, even if it involves ruthless exploitation of others, can be rationalized as being necessary for supporting the family or sending the kids to school, or for some other moral purpose such as providing for the future or starting a business to create employment for others.

The regulation of impulse gratifications has found its repercussion in the American Constitution. The 18th Amendment, for example, introduced prohibition to Americans. Likewise the Mann Act was designed to curb prostitution. A similar purpose is accomplished by the Johnston Office, which, established by the movie industry, acts as a censoring or self-censoring body controlling the "morals" of the movies. It is of interest to note that American motion-picture producers, the church, and the public consider murder, violence, and brutality a perfectly moral subject for presentation in movie houses, where youngsters of all ages are admitted. In contrast, pictures which refer to sexual intercourse or which unduly expose the body are banned. Brutality and toughness are considered necessary for survival, while sensual pleasure is believed to soften the individual. A similar ideology is found in the rules governing the transportation of immoral material in the United States mails.

---

[4] H. J. Laski, *The American Democracy* (New York: Viking, 1948).

Inasmuch as the individual is quite aware of his impulses, Americans develop their own methods for gratifying their instinctual needs. Gratification can be indulged in, if the group behaves similarly. For example, a "regular guy" is he who as a member of a group indulges in all the vices without going overboard. Behavior that is considered immoral when committed by a single person individually is acceptable and free of external sanction when committed in the presence of others. Promiscuity, gambling, and fighting belong in this category. A similar situation is encountered in the peculiar mixture of freedom, restraint, and competition practiced by adolescents in their dating and petting activities in which there is a combination of sex play, popularity contests, and group meetings. It is beyond the scope of this volume to cite the adolescent sex practices of American teen-agers; it may, however, suffice to point out that they are characterized by incomplete unions and by perversions, which at that age are accepted as normal.[5]

These presexual games are commonly engaged in in the presence of other couples, while privacy would really act as a deterrent. The European traveler is struck by the general exhibition of familiarity prevailing at parties and in such places as "lover's lanes," where there may be hundreds of automobiles parked with young couples engaged in exploring each other. Similarly the occasion of the annual convention of the American Legion, class reunion, or a shore leave from a ship permits its members to indulge collectively in pranks, drinking, and fighting, in a manner which would not be permitted in isolated cases.

Situational conformity is considered by Americans to be a form of group service, and submission to group opinion constitutes a moral motive. Meetings are organized so that people can obtain moral approval of their actions through active participation.[6] Thousands of organizations ranging from the Parent-Teacher Association, the Y.M.C.A., and the Boy Scouts to the lodge and fraternal organizations meet with the purpose of sharing a goal which in itself becomes a moral act. The church, for example, is in America a meeting house in which people engage in group conformity rather than in an individualized religious experience. Therefore, the person who dares to go his own way and does not conform either in celebrating, in everyday behavior, or in intellectual or artistic pursuits is frowned upon; if, however, he finally comes through and makes good, obtaining the public's approval, he is admired by the group and past sins are forgiven. This process is shown in countless American films of the bad man who is finally converted and joins the good cause.

Within the family and in small groups the woman is the keeper of the morals for man, woman, and child. In the presence of women, men will dress up and behave. As a matter of fact, they strain themselves to live up to the expectations of the female sex. Men among themselves are more likely to misbehave and to let things ride, a fact which vividly contrasts with the customs prevalent in western Europe, where men are considered the carriers of morals and traditions.

In American daily life, honesty is taken for granted when it concerns such small items as paying a nickel for a newspaper, or leaving the milk and the mail at

---

[5] K. Goldstein, *The Organism, A Holistic Approach to Biology* (New York: American Book Company, 1939); A. C. Kinsey, W. B. Pomeroy, and C. E. Martin, *Sex Behavior in the Human Male* (Philadelphia: Saunders, 1948).

[6] R. Lipitt, "An Experimental Study of the Effect of Democratic and Authoritarian Group Atmospheres," *University of Iowa Study of Child Welfare*. XVI (1940). 43–195.

the door of private homes. However, honesty is doubted when issues of power are involved. Stealing a few cents' worth of merchandise would be such a small crime that it is not
considered worthwhile to risk being caught by irate citizens or to expose oneself to
the feeling of guilt. Furthermore, some of these daily practices involve participation
as citizens in the community in terms of a common convenience for the greatest number
of people. Upsetting this system would mean elimination of milk distribution or newspapers or mail. If, however, a man is aspiring to a position of power, as for example in
politics, it is expected that he will use his power for selfish purposes as far and as long as
he can get away with it. A man who can misuse his power and get away with it is admired
to the extent that for a long time gangsters and racketeers became idols for youngsters,
and the law-enforcing agents that could not catch them were ridiculed. The use of
aggressive and ruthless methods in the pursuit of power is approved, but the group is
expected to control any form of corruption if it goes to excess. The control is exerted
by the press, which acts as a morality-enforcing agency. The public suspects any man
in public office; if a man were entirely honest and interested only in the promotion of
the welfare of others he would be considered a sucker; and to be a sucker is the worst
reputation a person can acquire. Thus, in America no time and effort are spared to set
up administrative procedures to prevent fraud and other misuse of power on a large
scale. The number of forms ordinary citizens have to fill out in multiple copies, the
complicated design of tax forms, and the number of things people have to swear to are
unheard of in other countries. In these matters bureaucracy really flourishes.

After a man has gotten away with acquiring and using his power to the limit
without being tripped, he is expected to return the yields of his success to the
community. The group really engages the power-thirsty individual in a game; if people
yield power to a man, they want him to be selfish; only a selfish man is believed to
have moral character. If he doesn't make use of his power, he must be suspected of being a
weakling or a fool. The group is willing to offer him an opportunity to develop his
bid for power. But once his term is over, the group repossesses power and wealth that
were lent to the man so that it may be reinvested in another individual. Therefore,
political officials are seldom elected for longer than three terms, rarely are fortunes
amassed without a large amount being returned to the state in the form of either taxes
or donations, and very seldom is a racketeer allowed to "do business" for more than
a few years.

EQUALITY

"Fourscore and seven years ago our fathers brought forth on this continent a
new nation, conceived in liberty, and dedicated to the proposition that all men are created equal." That these words have become famous demonstrates the importance of this
principle in the American culture. Based upon the principle of equality, America
became a melting pot of differing nationalities. Equality as practiced in daily life
derived on the one hand from puritan morality and on the other from frustrating
experiences of the early settlers and pioneers. Most immigrants left behind in the old
country what they regarded as either an oppressive social system or an oppressive family
and once they had arrived in America they laid the foundations to prevent oppressive
authority from ever arising again. By vesting functional authority in a tribunal of
equals, the principle of equality was born; its specific American management thus
became a solution for the immigrant's authority problem.

Today the value of equality is expressed in all those processes which result in eradication of extreme deviations and therefore promote a "regression toward the mean." Soon, however, the foreign traveler is struck by many strange contradictions: on the one hand he reads and hears about the notion of equality, while on the other hand he can observe the greatest inequality in terms of wealth, position, and power. An insider will then explain to him that in America the value of equality is interpreted as the assumption of equal opportunities rather than the product of final achievement. Once a person has become successful by exploiting the equal opportunities, he has in fact become superior and unequal; though he may silently dwell upon his achieved status, he will be challenged by the popular remark "Who do you think you are?" to remind him of his background. We thus arrive at the notion that those who achieve status, power, and wealth are presumed to have been skillful in utilizing the circumstances of equal opportunity. Once success has established a difference in prestige, those in power resent being treated as equals, while at the same time they fear their own inequality. To prevent such painful encounters, very elaborate administrative setups have been organized to prevent a meeting of unequals: secretaries guard the doors of their executive bosses like watchdogs; prestige carriers isolate themselves in exclusive clubs, neighborhoods, and social gatherings; while, last but not least, the awe felt by the less successful man establishes a natural barrier to the unprepared encounters of unequals. However, if for some reason or other a meeting of unequals should occur, the external characteristics of equality are adopted by both superior and inferior. For example, during the campaign periods preceding the general elections there will appear numerous pictures showing the candidates in shirtsleeves, "hobnobbing" with farmers and industrial workers. They will call each other by their first names and behave as if they were brothers. It is as if, at the meeting of unequals, a silent conversation took place during which the superior might say, "Look here, bud, I was successful, and if you make an effort you can join our ranks" while the inferior may counter with, "I admire your success—but between you and me, we are two of a kind." And when the persons feel that some such understanding is present, they might both break into laughter to cover their uneasiness.

Americans become anxious when they meet signs of inequality. Comments made by Americans about foreign cultures indicate their disapproval of caste and openly acknowledged class systems. Whenever Americans meet people who do not readily react to group pressure, they betray uneasiness; such people appear as dangerous because they cannot be checked by the usual methods. This applies particularly when the average American meets another person, American or foreign, with an outstanding record in the field of intellectual or artistic achievement. Musicians or singers are tolerated because they contribute toward entertainment and participate in group meetings, but philosophers, writers, painters, and theoreticians in the field of social or natural sciences are met with the greatest suspicion. Thinking as well as artistic expression is only tolerated along conventional lines. Original and new contributions are either flouted or totally ignored. Raids on bookstores and art shops in Boston and San Francisco regularly unearth such "shameful pornography" as reproductions of Michelangelo's frescoes in the Sistine Chapel or perhaps editions of Boccaccio's *Decameron*.

The same tendency is revealed in the political arena, where outstanding scientists, especially theoreticians, are smeared with accusations of being subversive in one or another way. Idiosyncratic thinking and feeling are in America suspect. They are resented essentially because they elude regimentation from without; and rather than acknowledge the limits of external control, the persons in power attempt to stultify individuals with special talents.

It is important to stress that in America the attempt to minimize originality and idiosyncrasy is something very different in its psychological roots from the persecution of scientists and other thinkers which has occurred in Russia and Germany. In America, it is not a matter of stamping out ideas which are subversive because they conflict with the ideology of a rigid governmental policy, but rather a matter of the personal anxiety which the mere existence of the creator may provoke in some politicians or in university administrators. The thinker of new thoughts in America may be labeled as crank or crackpot, but this is probably only a convenient handle. "Any stick can be used to beat a dog"—and it is perhaps not the new ideas that Americans are afraid of so much as the fact of human differences and unpredictability which is made uncomfortably evident whenever a new idea is presented.

As long as proficiency is based upon acquired skill and training, it is acceptable. But as soon as one might have to explain achievement, rightly or wrongly, by recognizing an unusual "talent," it becomes unacceptable. These facts are clearly borne out by the behavior of American artists of the nineteen-twenties who sought refuge in Paris in order to live in an atmosphere of permissiveness, or by the conditions prevailing in the field of science today.[7] American men of science probably have among their members the largest number of highly creative engineers. However, there is a lack of scientific theoreticians, and those scientific thinkers who are American citizens are, by and large, of foreign birth. The pressure to conform does not produce original personalities, and therefore this field has been left almost entirely to Europeans. Strange as it seems, if Europeans in America think or write about a new idea, it is all right; since everybody knows that they are of a different background, deviation can be tolerated. But if American science is to survive, a greater degree of freedom is needed. Inasmuch as permissiveness and tolerance of differences can be learned, a concerted effort of all those who are in responsible positions is needed if the apparent trend towards control of thought is to be reversed.

The faith that freedom and tolerance create sociable and responsible people, and the belief in the individual himself, are at stake. And soon we shall know whether the individual or the collective man, whether Western or Eastern civilization, is going to predominate.

Perception of equality sets an American at ease; knowledge of inequality creates anxiety in him. Therefore, the establishment of equality for the sexes, politically, economically, and socially, has become a common and popular goal. However, in pursuing this ideal several difficulties are encountered. The first hurdle to be jumped is the reciprocal relationship between liberty and equality. In order to make people equal, their liberties have to be cut. Since they are born as unequals in terms of biological or social endowment, the forces of social cohesion must be used to make them look alike. The premise of equality impedes differentiation, and individuals cannot seek that development which, for their individual circumstances, might be best for them. They always have to look and to be like others. The American white child who at home has been implicitly taught that everybody is equal and alike is scared when he meets a Negro child for the first time, primarily because his parent is ill at ease. The premise of equality is upset, and therefore a number of precautions have to be

---

[7] H. J. Laski, 1948.

taken to rationalize the difference; prejudice and discrimination are the end result.

In this respect America differs radically from countries such as Switzerland, for example. Both are republics; both have no caste system; both believe in liberty and equality. But Switzerland puts a higher value on liberty, which includes the notion that people are different, that they develop along idiosyncratic lines, and that such differentiation is likely to result in the greatest benefit for the individual. Switzerland thus became a country in which the greatest differences in terms of beliefs, religion, and language have been synthesized and tolerated. In America, on the other hand, equality is set before liberty.[8]

This is achieved by a variety of methods. First and above all, schools and state universities assure education for all. The cult of "the average man" in newspapers, radio, and movies implicitly scorns all idiosyncratic developments. If an agency wants to elicit contributions for welfare purposes, the preservation of "the typically American home" is used as bait. Thus one invokes John and Jane Doe's "average behavior" as an example, rather than referring to the top-flight men of the nation. The same method is applied in the advertisements for home furnishings, cars, and the like. Furthermore, the "men of distinction" whose images are used in advertising are not different from other men; they are only more successful and "de luxe editions" of the average man. Care is taken to make the outward appearance of all Americans equal. The reader may be reminded of a proposed amendment to the Constitution in 1810 which sought to abolish titles of nobility or, in a totally different sphere, of the way Americans are dressed: outwardly it is almost impossible to tell from his clothes to what class an American belongs. The immigration laws are a further example of this same tendency. Legal provisions have been made for the gradual acculturation of immigrants which provide for a five-year waiting period before full status as a citizen can be applied for; then an examination must be taken before an individual is admitted to citizenship. Such an examination provides a screening of those who cannot read, write, or understand American ideals; in other words, a check is made upon whether or not the candidates could be accepted as equals.

The premise of equality is in some way related to the management of functional authority in America. Authority resides in committees or other steering groups, and these bodies settle matters of policy. Minorities are usually represented in these leadership groups, and though they have a voice in policy-making, they will never obtain the majority vote. These committees, because of their heterogeneity, obtain public respect, and the individual citizen will defer to their opinions. Whenever an American comes in contact with a personalized authority such as a police officer or other law-enforcing agent, the attitudes which are exhibited are difficult for Europeans to comprehend. Briefly, the policeman is simultaneously a social authority and a human equal. The common denominator of these two apparently conflicting ideas is the notion of the policeman as another guy who is doing a job. Within the limits of this premise a certain amount of humor can enter, and even sharp dissension can be expressed. A similar situation is encountered in offices, where the procedure labeled "sassing the boss" expresses the benevolent and friendly teasing of the man in charge because of his function as authority. As soon as a man is labeled an authority he becomes unequal, and every effort must be made to bring him back to the fold of the group and make him an equal again.

---

[8] A. de Tocqueville, 1946.

SOCIALITY

Sociality, or the tendency to form social groups, has its roots in the herd instinct of the individual. In America foremost recognition is given to this group need; as a matter of fact, it has resulted in a culture of living which vividly contrasts with certain foreign civilizations which cater to the development of object systems. At first this statement sounds paradoxical, inasmuch as America is known for its technical genius and the use of machinery in every walk of life. On second thought, however, one can understand this contradiction. Consider, for example, the way machinery is treated in America: a car is unsparingly used until it has to be replaced; typewriters, horses, and cars are lent to neighbors and friends, and no property feelings are attached to any object. In America the object is truly subservient to life. Europeans, in contrast, have less respect for an individual's need for action and expansion, but great interest in protecting inanimate objects; the guarding of works of art, furniture, books, houses, and churches is really put ahead of the needs of the individual. These facts are clearly brought out when American families with children visit their European relatives. The American youngster, when introduced into a European home, is considered ill-mannered when he subjects the home furnishings to wear and tear and, while doing so, exhibits the boastful exuberance of youth, which is accepted with tolerance on this side of the Atlantic.

In America the process of living and of interacting with others is sought as a goal in itself. Americans treat others always as people, while Europeans in many situations will treat other people like objects or as if they did not exist. Regardless of occupation or of the job performed by an individual in America, his superiors or inferiors will always treat him as an individual. Such attitudes indicate that in the minds of the people there exists an awareness that persons have families, want to live, and need a certain environment in order to survive. In brief, in America people are always people; they never become machines or animals. The fact that life is cherished is further borne out by the many excellent provisions for saving lives in emergencies; members of the police and fire departments, lifeguards on public beaches, rangers, members of the Coast Guard and the armed forces are trained to respect and to save lives. During World War II, the medical services of the United States Army were vastly superior to those of any other nation in terms of saving lives of wounded soldiers and rehabilitating them in civilian life. No expense is ever spared if a person is in need of rescue. In addition to these emergency measures there are in the United States all those educational institutions, public health campaigns, insurance companies and the school health services of the medical and dental profession who do everything in their power to preserve health and promote longevity.

The treatment of persons as individuals seems to be an expression of the fact that every person is a representative and member of a group, and the group assumes the responsibility for the individual. Offense against a person is an insult against a group. The American abides by decisions of the group and recognizes it as the ultimate authority. While in the patriarchal system it is quite sufficient to abide by the rules of the chief in order to be a member of the group, in a system of equals it is necessary to please many. This is the meaning of conformance.

Conformance is encountered as a consideration in practically everyone's mind. One "can't do that," "it isn't done," and "he is impossible" are examples of comments which denote the preoccupation with conformance. "Keeping up with the Joneses" is an activity of conformance which permeates social life, the purchasing of homes, automobiles, and household appliances and induces people to join clubs, to contribute to welfare organizations, and to donate their time for worthwhile causes. However, adjusting one's own actions to conform to those of others always has a competitive undertone. While the American conforms to the actions of others, he is at the same time concerned with doing things "bigger and better." Hence, in America, conformance, competition, and group membership are always found together.

In order to sustain group membership the American has to be gregarious. The value of gregariousness has its roots to some extent in the circumstances of the first settlers and pioneers, who were forced to share in order to protect themselves against a hostile environment; hence, getting along in a group was essential for survival. Furthermore, gregariousness is in some ways a substitute for the extended family, which frequently is not available to the American. Either family members live far apart and spread over the continent, or part of the family has remained in Europe. In the course of time, therefore, sociability became a national feature. Today it is associated essentially with middle-class behavior, which is closely identified with the national characteristics of Americans. The value which is placed upon smooth functioning and a friendly front, low intensity and avoidance of deep involvement, as well as readiness to disengage from the existing relations and to enter new human relationships, may be termed sociability. In America this personality feature is frequently taken as one of the most important criteria in assessing adjustment.

The American becomes uneasy when he finds himself alone. To be left alone is a situation to be carefully avoided; girls accompany each other to the rest rooms or for coffee in the afternoon, and boys and girls have roommates, rarely live alone, and practice double-dating. Not only do bathroom, eating, and social habits of Americans portray this fact, but it can also be observed in the arrangement of houses or the structure of resort places. In America houses are built close together even if the owners could well afford much larger lots; in public parks and on the beaches picnickers join one another and one group attracts the other, all avoiding isolation. The foreign traveler who with an open eye inspects the American scene is amazed at the public facilities which have been created for fostering and accommodating gregarious people. From the national parks and picnic grounds to the playgrounds in smaller communities, from the commons is New England towns to the squares of western cities, there are always facilities which enable people to meet. Grange halls and lodge buildings provide meeting places for specific groups which are set aside for social gatherings. Likewise do state and federal government provide for calendar festivals such as Thanksgiving, Fourth of July, Labor Day, Memorial Day, and the like, which provide an opportunity for family gatherings or larger group reunions. In brief, Americans always travel in a group. Lacking associates is a sign of not knowing how to win friends, of not being sociable. In America one associates with others to give the impression of popularity, and if one is popular, one makes more friends. These, of course, disperse when the barometer of popularity declines. This American concept of popularity contrasts with the concept of friendship in Europe; there the test of real friendship comes when hardships and difficult situations make associations survive.

The American form of sociability, which we have termed sociality, finds its climax in the cocktail party. Any foreign traveler is puzzled when he attends this peculiar metropolitan institution for the first time in his life. The first impression he receives is that all or most of the participants are slightly intoxicated. He then will learn that alcohol permits the American to promote his patterns of sociability. In a social situation actions which would otherwise be frowned upon become acceptable when committed under the influence of alcohol. Such behavior is characterized by patterns of increased familiarity, regardless of whether it consists of making a pass at a member of the opposite sex, or whether it is expressed in increased chumminess with a member of the same sex. To have been drunk together is a seal of friendship and insures greater popularity. Hence, at the cocktail party there is a large crowd of people, all attempting to be popular, speaking a few sentences with one person and then going on to the next. Many people loathe cocktail parties, but most people eagerly attend them. It is a place where information is exchanged, popularity ratings are established, new acquaintances are made, and the general status of in-group membership is verified.

The host who gives the party usually makes a "social effort" to improve his position by breaking into new circles and by collecting more interesting people. Social effort, which is greatly appreciated in America, denotes the attempt of the individual or group of individuals to obtain votes through some sort of campaigning. This social effort not only permeates the life of society, but is also found in business and politics. The political candidate combines wisdom with sociability, and the salesman shows a combination of friendly coercion with a need to remain popular. The value of such social effort is unofficially stressed and communicated in the schools and recreational system of America by all the pamphlets and books and friendly advice on how to join an association, how to become a member of a club, how to join an exclusive social clique, and how "to win friends and influence people."[9] Social effort can be tested and proved by winning the popularity rating in dating and dancing in high school, by obtaining a high Hooper rating, by being proclaimed the best-dressed woman of the year, or just by "making the papers."

In this perpetual atmosphere of campaigning in all walks of life, the foreigner is likely to misunderstand the cues of familiarity and intimacy. Superficial and stylized cues of sociability are interpreted by foreigners as deeper, personal interest. In fact, such cues are meant only as an encouragement to the stranger to participate freely at gatherings and thereby to add to the popularity of his American host. On the other hand, the foreigner's habit of not giving superficial cues of sociability is interpreted by Americans as arrogance or hostility. The American, who is extremely conscious of action cues, forgets that the European is less conscious of action; however, the European compensates for this unawareness by including in his own consideration all the style cues derived from objects, belongings, dress, and other personal expressions inherent in a situation, of which the American is usually less aware. The social meeting of European and American is on the whole a beautiful example of how the same events are interpreted in different ways because the two persons do not possess the same system of communications.

The group-oriented American is very conscious of his own status within his group, and he is much less aware of the status of his group as a whole among other groups. The reverse is true of the European. An American is usually conscious of whether his fellow-citizens look up to him or down on him, and to him it is more important to be liked than to like. This sensitive response to status appreciation is in part the result of the American system which enables a person to change his group if he wishes

[9] D. C. Carnegie, *How to Win Friends and Influence People* (New York: Simon and Schuster, 1936).

to do so. Such change may be termed "social mobility."[10] A person who has reached the top of his own group may join the group which is next higher in the hierarchy of prestige, and in the opposite direction, a person is also permitted to decline by lowering his standards of living. The individual who is "on the make" for a higher degree of prestige achieves his goal by joining a different set of associations, clubs, or lodges; he may move to a better neighborhood, buy himself a bigger car, or try to crash some rather exclusive social clique. Social mobility is an accepted phenomenon, and whoever succeeds in entering a new group is admired because of his social success. This fact is clearly borne out in the reports concerning assessment of candidates for office, schools, and clubs. Decisions are not only weighted in favor of the ability to get ahead. By and large it is safe to state that the social climbers possess a greater skill in social techniques and above all are well versed in the use and application of sociability.[11]

The American's basic need to move in a group and his concern with sociability have led to a far-reaching organization and differentiation within the group. From earliest childhood, the child is trained to become a member of a team; baseball, football, and basketball are training grounds for later industrial research and military teams, while fraternities and lodges in the recreational sphere, or town meetings and other organizations in the political sphere, provide the necessary training for teamwork. Every American knows how to behave and how to fit into the organization of a group. Adjusting to the group and engaging in teamwork bring marked advantages to the individual. The group protects its members when they get into trouble with members of other groups, or when disease or disaster strikes. The sort of reliance that an Englishman would derive from the knowledge that the judicial system and the police look out for law and order, the American citizen derives from the knowledge that the group will support him and if necessary exert pressure to protect him. Therefore, no American will shy away from expense or effort to join a team and to subordinate himself to its over-all purpose, and in return, to expect some security from the team for having "played ball."

SUCCESS

In America success is a yardstick with which the value of an individual is measured; it is the result of effort, initiative, and luck.[12] We use the word "yardstick" because, in practice, the success of any individual can be gauged only by comparing it with the success of others; for this purpose external, quantifiable measures are needed. Finally, if an individual is labeled as successful by his peers, it means that "everything is going his way."

In America the prevalent motivation for seeking success is found in the attempt of the individual to secure his own future against the imputed skepticism of others. At a deeper psychological level it is related to a need for approval from peers and equals and to an urge for elbowroom. Needless to say, the historical root of this national

---

[10] W. L. Warner, M. Meaker, and K. Eells, *Social Class in America* (Chicago: Science Research Association, 1949).

[11] J. Ruesch, "Social Technique, Social Status and Social Change in Illness" in *Personality in Nature, Society and Culture* (New York: Knopf, 1948), pp. 117–130; J. Ruesch, "Individual Social Techniques," *Journal of Social Psychology*, XXIX (1949), 3–28.

[12] C. Kluckhohn and F. R. Kluckhohn, "American Culture: Generalized Orientations and Class Patterns," in *Conflicts of Power in Modern Culture* (New York: Harper & Brothers, 1947), pp. 106–128.

ideal of Americans is found in conditions such as the open frontiers, the unlimited possibilities, and the Industrial Revolution. In a fluid frontier society, success was the only measure by which contemporaries could gauge a man's position within his group. Therefore, success in whatever was started became the basis upon which respect and confidence from others could be secured. At the same time the notion of having been successful strengthened the self-respect of an individual, while some degree of self-confidence was necessary to initiate success. This vicious circle is best expressed by the saying, "Nothing succeeds like success."

The mushrooming growth of success has a fatally attractive and infectious effect upon others; "For unto everyone that hath shall be given, and he shall have abundance; but from him that hath not shall be taken away even that which he hath" (Matthew xxv:29). The American will gamble for the sake of success; he will play the horses and the stock market, he will participate in gold and uranium rushes, and he will invest in ventures of all sorts even at the risk of being one of many who will perish. However, if he wins, he is going to be the man who made good, demonstrating to his peers that he has left behind suppression and exploitation, that he is worthy of the attention and admiration of his contemporaries, and that he can be trusted to carry things to a successful conclusion.

The tendency to evaluate actions and things in quantitative terms is a tendency so strong among Americans that they themselves laugh about it. One might speculate that the root of quantification was found in the situation of the pioneer: not having any information about the character or personality of a settler, none the less one urgently needed his help. Because statements out of the mouth of a stranger could not be trusted and because the various pioneers frequently came from different backgrounds, the scales necessary to evaluate a person were not uniform. To prevent misunderstanding, objective and quantifiable terms had to be used, and thus a man's position was determined by his measurable success rather than by convention and tradition. The tendency toward quantification was further promoted by the whole economic trend of the Occidental culture, the rise of commerce, and the Industrial Revolution with its emphasis upon a monetary economy. The presence of a large immigrant population and the constant change in social attitudes resulting from acculturation and social mobility produced a society in which many individuals lived in a social setting in which the major premises were fundamentally different from those of the society in which they had grown up. This diversity of premises and means of communication has the effect of guiding the individual toward the simplest possible statement, the statement in terms of quantities.

Once the tendency toward quantification was established, this tendency became self-promoting. No longer were there persons unable to find a common ground for value agreement, but instead any stranger facing another stranger could rely upon the tacit understanding that action and achievement were to be evaluated in quantitative terms. This shared premise gradually became culturally standardized, and in its most abstract form it became a system of interpretation and evaluation in the realm of communication. Needless to say, the quantitative attitude of the American acts in social intercourse as a pressure which further tends to maximize the quantifiable aspects.

There is no reason to believe that the human organism has an instinctual trend toward quantification. Indeed, what we know of mammalian background would indicate that mammals seek optima rather than maxima of the various conditions which they require. These optima are elements which are so complex that their achievement could only be measured in parameters much more abstract than any normally used in daily life. Therefore, when human beings started to exert pressure upon individuals to act in certain ways in neglect of their own instinctual needs, the possibility of the maximization of variables appeared.

The maximization of quantifiable variables makes its appearance early in childhood. American parents implicitly demand of their small children that they be heavier, bigger, stronger, and smarter than other babies. Love is given conditionally, and only if the baby talks and walks earlier and is "cuter" than other babies will he obtain more love than those who are second or last in the quest for success. The American child has the problem of stating achievement in terms which shall be so demonstrable and so convincing that parents must assent to his demands. The obvious and natural solution to this problem is for the child to take over quantitative cues from the parents. As he grows older, he will boast of his marks at school and of how little effort he has put into achieving them, of how many times he has swum the length of the pool, and of how much money he has earned from selling newspapers.

The parent or leader faces a similar problem, inasmuch as he has to find value propositions which will evoke agreement in a number of persons whose value systems he presumes to be different from his own. If, for example, a public speaker desires a certain policy to be accepted, he has the task of making others desire this policy also, though their reasons may be different ones. In such a situation the bare agreement on policy has to be shared, and all the ideas which might obscure the issue must be shorn off. This means that the suggested policy must be torn away from the complex matrix of each individual's idiosyncratic beliefs and expectations. The result may be a slogan, or it may be a list of separate objectives, or it may be a simple quantitative statement to which all can agree. Thus out of the process of reducing a spectrum of opinions to a single statement emerges the tendency to quantify actions, which affects the whole of American life.

One of the universal indexes of an individual's success is his income, property, or other manifestations of wealth. Thus Americans talk about a "fifteen-hundred-dollar fur coat" or "a forty-thousand-dollar home" rather than describe what sort of fur coat or home they are talking about. Likewise the prestige of a person increases with salary, and Americans talk about "a twenty-thousand-dollar-a-year job." If an individual achieves success in administration or engineering, and his responsibilities are rewarded by a good, but not a top, salary, it is common to translate the prestige gained into monetary terms by imagining the sort of financial position which he could claim. He is, however, given credit for not claiming this position if he so chooses. A Secretary of State, for example, is respected not so much because he is a Secretary of State but because, if he should resign his job, he could claim the chairmanship of a board or the position of the president of an industrial or trust company at many times the salary he receives in government service.

The actual achievement is not the only aspect of success which Americans value. As long as anyone strives for success, as long as he makes an effort, he is a regular guy. This striving has to be smooth, casual, and shrewd, and the effort must not show. The intention to seek success is a socially acceptable motivation, while instinct gratification as such is rejected. It is perfectly permissible, for example, for an American to say that he has joined a lodge system, such as the Rotary, Lions, Masons, Moose, or Elks, or a church group, for the sake of insuring future success. Likewise a boy is sent to college not so much for the sake of learning as for an opportunity to make contacts with other boys of more prominent families, contacts which are considered a stepping-stone to success. While a man who is successful becomes the object of competition and envy, the man who is starting out and who tries hard is the person to whom the already successful persons give a chance and lend a hand. "There's no harm in trying" is a slogan which denotes the appreciation of effort in America.

Making good is a relative achievement; and, as the saying goes, one should not "play ball in the wrong league." This definition of success clearly implies that success is to be judged by a person's position vis-à-vis his peers, and not vis-à-vis those people who belong to another group or social class. As soon as success has made a person distinctly different from his peers, he has to join another league in order to continue competition with equals. This traditional rule is clearly exemplified in the management of baseball leagues, the type of neighborhood people choose to reside in, or the type of clubs they join. It is obvious that success is infectious, and that when it makes its appearance everyone is ready to climb on the bandwagon. This effect seems to be a human characteristic, however, rather than a uniquely American trait.

The end justifies the means, and success exonerates ruthless and sharp practices. If an opportunity looms, a challenge is automatically felt, even though responding to this challenge might bring one into conflict with the law; but if a person is caught cutting corners, he is considered a failure. The emphasis, therefore, is not upon what he does but on whether others permit him to get away with it. Rarely is an American racketeer charged with the crime he has committed. Usually he is caught not for running brothels or for smuggling narcotics or liquor, but for income tax evasion: he is arrested for cutting a corner but not necessarily for his major crime.

The fact that success is a goal in itself and that achievement is more important than the methods used to obtain it is made possible through a class society which permits vertical mobility,[13] where mastery is frequently only incidental to success. In contrast, a caste society with its limitations of success and social mobility promotes mastery and virtuosity as an end in itself.[14] The result of this tendency can be substantiated by the fact that almost all artisans and skilled workers in America are of immediate European descent and that American trained workers will strive for mastery only to the point where success is secured. American houses, for example, are built to last only a generation, and the building of houses, both in structure and in aesthetic appearance, is determined by the needs of the moment. To build a house which would last for hundreds of years would in America be considered a folly. In Europe a high degree of perfection in philosophy, art, and handicrafts is found because the rigid class structure does not permit social mobility; instead mastery of a skill is one of the achievements from which the individual gains satisfaction. In America the acquisition of a skill is a means of securing success, and success is thought to be of the essence in the pursuit of happiness.

The American people have a rich mythology about people who have made good; the myths of Ford, Rockefeller, and Carnegie idealize free enterprise and the poor man's chance to grow rich and powerful. However, this admiration of success is combined with a condemnation of the sharp practices of the robber barons. The public, however, is

---

[13] Warner, *et al.*, 1949.

[14] O. Spengler, *Der Untergang des Abendlandes*, 2 volumes, (Munich: Beck, 1923); A. J. Toynbee, *A Study of History* (New York: Oxford University Press, 1947).

willing to close an eye to questionable procedures if the behavior of a successful man is later mitigated by good works, charitable contributions, establishment of foundations and other public institutions. In contrast to the admiration shown for these business personalities, the respect for a Washington, a Jefferson, or a Lincoln shows unrestricted admiration for their success and their restraint in the use of power. This is not the adoration of free enterprise or of the go-getter, but is rather an expression of admiration for rugged individualism. A similar attitude is exemplified in the slogan "from log cabin to White House," and it is supposed that those persons who gain fame and prestige through political and administrative skills earn their reputation by a wise use of power. Not only the acquisition of power, but also its wise administration, is a factor in earning the label of success in America. Finally we may mention the heroes like Lee, "Stonewall" Jackson, Teddy Roosevelt, and Patton, whose success was due to their ruggedness in military campaigns.

Business executives, governors of states, and presidents are entrusted with great responsibilities, and unusual powers are delegated to them. Success means the achievement of positions of responsibility and the use of power. Power need not be used exclusively for the good of the people. A governor who may be a good and efficient administrator may still be considered a sucker if he does not know how to obtain votes from various political machines or how to make compromises in order to keep himself in office. Since personal acquisition of wealth and power is a publicly acknowledged motive for men in high positions, a great many safety factors have had to be devised to curb those who would go too far on the road of self-glorification and self-interest. Provisions for limiting the power of the corporation president, the government executive, or the legislator indicate that a successful man is compared by the American public to a circus juggler who simultaneously keeps several objects in the air without failing. The achievement of success thus means that a man has not only tasted but also exposed himself to danger, and has learned how to cope with it.

American public life provides individuals with the symbols and props of success. These can be used to exhibit success in order to make an impression, which technique may eventually assure further success; or then may be used to simulate a not yet existing success and thus provide a foundation for later success. It is customary, for example, to establish big offices, to drive large automobiles, to throw large parties, to act and talk as though one were wealthy, in order to impress others, even if money has to be borrowed to achieve this effect. People who engage in such actions hope that other persons will climb on the bandwagon because they are lured by the props of success; for if they do so, real success is likely to be around the corner.

CHANGE

The value of change is identified with social and material progress. Change is always for the better, and in the mind of Americans the good which has been achieved is thought to be almost irreversible. In contrast, the change which Europeans expect is always for the worse; but paradoxical as it sounds, the European notion of change, if it is accepted, has the equality of reversibility. In America one never retraces one's steps, and change, therefore, has the quality of being irreversible.

Life in America is not viewed as being static but is conceived as being in the process of continuous change. Nothing is ever settled, and change is a matter of course. In Europe that which may be viewed as inconsistency or lack of stability may in America be interpreted as adaptability and strength of character. One frequently finds people boasting about the number of occupations and jobs they have held in various fields to emphasize their adaptability to change and their eagerness to encompass the new. Likewise the ups and downs in business success may be romanticized to demonstrate the resiliency to change. A man, for example, may openly acknowledge the fact that he, at one time, went bankrupt, if in later years he can demonstrate that he again achieved success.

In America the readiness to accept and to promote change is revealed in many business procedures. The planning of organizations, construction, and development are undertaken with pleasure; previously erected structures are scrapped without regret, and consideration is given to the need for periodical renewal, inasmuch as obsolescence is feared. The preference for something new, rather than mending the old, is exemplified in the popular practice of trading in a one- or two-year-old car as soon as a more recent model is available; on a governmental scale the sale of war surplus materials documents the same trend.

The tendency to start new ventures rather than to stick to old ones requires special techniques, and the methods which are used to get a new venture going have been compared to pump priming. In order to get things going the American will not shy away from initial expenditure of money and effort, even if lack of success should mean temporary financial ruin. The basic idea which underlies these initial efforts is to increase the circulation and the turnover of money and merchandise. Once the wheel has started to turn and the inertia has been overcome, the American expects that all is going to turn out for the best. The use of money to initiate enterprises has been termed "venture capital," and much has been written to the effect that the pioneer spirit among businessmen is disappearing because legislation and high taxes have curbed all initiative.

The economic manipulation of American markets is quite different from procedures customary in Europe; first, products are advertised so that the public is prepared and alerted to receive the forthcoming products; thus a market is created by creating a shift in fashion trends, and the public's readiness to accept this change is generally great enough so that the goods are successfully sold. Advertisements such as "A change of laxative would be good for you" count on the public's readiness to accept change, and frequently enough this expectation is justified.

Social progress is, in American eyes, at least as important as material change. First of all there is a belief in the ability to change people; this attitude resulted in a rapid development of social science, social welfare, and other programs which are devoted to the study of social engineering. *How to Make Good* and *How to Win Friends and Influence People*[15] are titles of books which document this belief in social engineering, while associationism and social mobility are practices subservient to the notion of social change. Social mobility and acculturation are ways of behavior which are highly rewarded; social success is proof of the adaptability of people who undertake the burden of improving themselves, and therefore they become a living monument of "the American way of life": "from rags to riches."

To this concept of change and adaptation, psychiatry owes its present popularity. The fact that people can be changed, that the techniques to achieve such an end can be learned, fascinates American thinking. And much that was proclaimed in the

---

[15] D. C. Carnegie, 1936.

past to be unalterable behavior, determined by heredity and constitution, now becomes accessible to change because of this refreshing attitude of American psychiatrists. While the belief in education and rehabilitation opens a new vista for many unfortunate and sick people, the notion of change creates at the same time insurmountable problems. There exists, for example, the American tradition that children should emphasize the difference between themselves and their parents, rather than adhere to the similarities. In compliance with this premise they tend to break away from home early, to ridicule the traditions of the elders, and to adhere to patterns which contrast with those of the parents. As a result, young people become isolated from their families at a time when maturation has not progressed to the stage where acceptance of great responsibilities becomes a matter of course.[16]

Assumption of responsibilities at an early age deprives the young adult of the leisurely atmosphere which is necessary for successful social learning. From early childhood the American youngster is trained to push, to exert himself, and to work to the limit of his resources. He is expected to explore new grounds, to seize opportunities, and therefore to abandon the old for the new. In such an atmosphere of constant change, mastery of skills and techniques, the acquisition of information, and the clarification of the position of the self vis-à-vis the world become extremely difficult. The problems and personality disturbances which result from such hasty development are dumped into the lap of the psychiatrist, who in the course of his professional activities is constantly in contact with borderline people who do not know where they belong.

The American citizen views the present as better than the past and therefore believes that any future will be better than the present. The unknown element which is associated with the future invokes anxiety. Though this uneasiness is handled by effort and optimism, the belief in the future is vulnerable in periods of depression. Economic cycles seem to be accompanied by psychological cycles; in periods of prosperity the American believes in the future and in the betterment of mankind, and in times of depression he is shaken in his foundations and believes that the misery is going to last forever; both attitudes in turn have their repercussion in the economic sphere. Practices such as taking out life insurance and retirement programs, which emphasize the possibility of change in the future, or, in another sphere, the care for children by schools, agencies, and the private citizen, express great concern with the future. Almost every American, for example, feels concerned with the welfare of the future generation. The belief in the future, which characterizes all walks of American life, therefore results in the structuring of the parent-child relationship, which puts children first and parents second.

Americans are engineers, and therefore they have respect for science and rational procedures which permit them to develop their material culture.[17] An engineer is in general interested in the question of "how," as it applies to the manipulation and alteration of the human environment. Such an attitude is clearly revealed by the development of American applied science, as seen in medicine and in mechanical, electrical, and chemical engineering. Investigation of nature as it is has much less fascination for the American than the exploration of what can be changed in nature. There-

[16] T. Parsons, *Essays in Sociological Theory, Pure and Applied* (Glencoe, Illinois: Free Press, 1949).
[17] D. W. Brogan, 1944.

fore, applied science triumphs over basic science[18] and the arts, and action predominates over thought and feeling.[19] The notion of engineering is carried into the field of human problems, and the American has the strange belief that social issues can be solved by the progress of material culture. Remarks about "new additions" to family or staff denote the materialistic treatment of social action and interpersonal relations. Inasmuch as inner experience is a less fruitful field for manipulation and engineering than the environment, Americans tend to externalize their inner experience. Externalism or the quantification of internal events by projecting these upon external objects or events characterizes the American personality. The American is geared to cope with change, to revere the gadget, to quantify, and to use action as the principal means of expression. The philosophy of behaviorism was thus a characteristic expression of American culture.[20]

[18]H. J. Laski, 1948.
[19]S. de Madariaga, *Englishmen, Frenchmen, Spaniards* (London: Oxford University Press, 1928).
[20]J. B. Watson, *Behaviorism* (New York: W. W. Norton & Company, 1930; revised edition).

4-3   IMPLICIT AND EXPLICIT VALUES IN EDUCATION AND TEACHING AS RELATED TO GROWTH AND DEVELOPMENT

Rhoda Metraux

Rhoda Metraux had done field work in Haiti, Mexico, Argentina, and Montserrat, British West Indies. She is currently associate director, studies in allopsychic orientation, American Museum of Natural History, and lecturer on cultural aspects of psychotherapy at the Postgraduate Center for Psychotherapy. She completed her graduate work in anthropology at Columbia University, where she was formerly on the research staff in studies in contemporary cultures.

In the following selection, Dr. Metraux considers the influence of human growth and development on values in different cultures and the implications for American education.

In this preface to our discussion, I shall do no more than to suggest certain values which are inherent in our attitudes towards education and, because it would seem to fit in best with our intentions, I shall refer mainly to American attitudes. Nevertheless, because much of what I shall say is so familiar as to be nearly invisible, I shall begin with an illustration from another culture, which may sharpen, through contrast, our view of ourselves.

The values of a culture are reflected in all its aspects, and each detail can be seen in its relationship to the larger whole. In traditional Chinese culture, for instance, calligraphy is much more than a means of setting down ideas—of writing

From *Merrill-Palmer Quarterly*, II (Fall 1955), 27–34. Copyright © 1955 by the Merrill-Palmer School Corporation; reprinted by permission of The Merrill-Palmer Institute and the author.

history or making out a household marketing list or teaching the good life—it is also an art form, and some of the great classical scholars have also been poet-painter-writers. The training was a very long one. A little boy, whose family might hope that one day he would be a scholar—a learned man, an artist, and perhaps the governor of a province—began to learn calligraphy when he was five or six years old. Even younger he might have learned to recognize a few characters, made for him with bold brush strokes on bright red cards by his grandfather. Then he was taught to sit at a table, very straight—his body, his feet, his head, his left hand exactly placed, the brush poised in his right hand; and every day he copied models, the meaning of which no one explained to him, which he did not "understand" perhaps for many years. This teaching was more than a skill; it was also a way of forming his moral character. If he continued to practice for ten years, twenty years, thirty years, and mastered the styles of the great calligraphers, he might one day produce something of his own, original because of its strength and vigor. In traditional Chinese culture, not spontaneity but maturity was valued. And this was reflected in the belief that learning and artistry took long years to come to flower, and in the linking of creativeness to mature strength and vigor. Moreover, the training of the classical writer was such that was reflected in body movement; today, as one watches a Chinese man sitting and speaking, one can tell what kind of education he has had. The man who in his youth had a classical education, and who still values it, sits upright and easily poised, his hand gestures moving out from the center of his body. The rebel against classical education leans away from this central poise, his movements often out of balance. The young man who has attended only modern schools lounges like any other undergraduate. In these postural alterations we can see more than individual learning experience. We are given clues also to the effects of culture change, of changing values in education, upon the life of the individual.[1]

      With this in mind, let us turn to an American situation. For the past several months I have attended a teaching clinic in a hospital in New York City. This has been part not of my research but of my own learning experience of work in a hospital setting. We meet once a week, a small group around a long table, and at each of the sessions one of the participants—it may be an internist, or a psychiatrist, or a medical student, presents a case. The patient comes in and is interviewed, so we can see for ourselves what manner of person this is who has been described to us. Later any of us, participants or visitors, may ask questions or make suggestions to the physician who has the final responsibility. This clinic is part of a pioneering effort in the teaching of psychosomatic medicine, and the explicit emphasis is upon the wholeness of the individual. With great pride I was told that here the doctors are concerned not with isolated symptoms located somewhere in the body of a "36-year-old white female," but with a person, a young woman with parents and brothers, a husband and children, and a unique life history including stressful experiences that have affected adversely her physical, mental, and emotional well-being. Here, in the presence of a group of specialists, the patient—by the shared knowledge of

---

[1] For background material on Chinese child training and education, cf. Ruth Bunzell, *Explorations in Chinese Culture* (New York: Columbia University Research in Contemporary Cultures, 1950, dittoed). For an autobiographical description of classic education, cf. Chiang Yee, *A Chinese Childhood* (New York: John Day, 1952). The material on posture is taken from unpublished research in the Study Program on Human Health and the Ecology of Man in China; Cornell Medical College, New York Hospital.

a life history, known and understood—is reconstituted as a whole living person. This is the expressed intention of the teaching. Implicit in it is our American valuation of the uniqueness of the individual and our sense that the total personality—capabilities and experiences, strengths and weaknesses—must be taken into account if we are to understand who someone is.

But listening and watching in that clinic I, who was a novice in a hospital, learned something quite different that also was implicit in the situation: namely, that such teaching can lead to the development of a multiple conscience in each of the participants. For there sat the students and with them around the table perhaps a dozen specialists, *simultaneously* focusing their trained attention upon the complicated problems of one sick person. So the medical student (as perhaps each of us for our work also) is learning for his future practise to hear not one voice of one teacher nor successively the voices of different teachers, but voices arranged in a kind of polyphony. Explicitly, this method of teaching gives back to the student understanding of the wholeness of the person he is observing. Implicitly it gives him also a sense of the wholeness of the approach. Ideally, it gives him a way of thinking, a way of placing his particular aptitudes and knowledge and experience in an inclusive context. And this too is one of the things we value in our kind of education. So, for instance, no matter how lost we may get in the maze of departmental specializations, we continue to trust, at the undergraduate level, the liberal arts type of education. Or at a much younger age level, with our first graders who are just learning to learn formal knowledge, we try to make this not a fragmented but a total experience in which counting and reading and writing and self-expression and social relationships and play and work are all interwoven. Or, in another context, anyone who has worked on an interdisciplinary research project and who has taken part in the struggle really to share materials, to fit all the bits into a meaningful whole, will understand—however different the superficial aspects—the patterning of teaching and learning in the clinic I have so briefly described.

Now I have given this illustration, taken from a rather unfamiliar setting, for two reasons. First, because this attempt to do a new kind of teaching in a medical school—to modify the relationship between teacher and student, to incorporate new knowledge into a method of work, to overcome difficulties that grew out of previous new knowledge, that is, the difficulties resulting from intense specialization—is shaped by ideas and beliefs inherent in our most general thinking about education. This sense of the uniqueness of the individual and of the need for integration is something we may temporarily lose in our attempts to solve other problems, and then we struggle to find it again.

Secondly, I have used this illustration because it places me as a kind of person thinking about and discussing values in education. One thing the anthropologist has learned is to place himself—for himself and others—inside the observations made. And, of course, I speak here as a cultural anthropologist, not as an educator. For, aside from my own training, my main connection with education has been as an indirect participant in the education of my children and some younger colleagues and as an observer, sometimes in American life, sometimes doing field work abroad, sometimes working with informants on a distant culture. So what I can do here is to point out what seem to be certain regularities in our thinking about education and to suggest how these are linked up to our thinking about human growth and development.

It should be said, however, that it is highly artificial to separate our ideas about education and about growth and development. For one of the most remarkable achievements in our thinking about human beings in the last 50 years or so has been a recognition of the systematic circularity of the learning and teaching processes and of the processes of growth and development. What is new is not the understanding that personality or character is shaped by learning—we have only to turn to any of the old utopias to see that—but that learning and growth are related aspects of man's biological nature. Our new knowledge of maturation and our new understanding of character formation—whether based on our own culture or more broadly on comparisons of cultural materials—have transformed the questions asked and the answers given about learning and teaching; and re-interpretations of educational problems have led us to refine our knowledge of growth. So we have one kind of circularity imposed on another. No less remarkable has been the speed with which we have incorporated this new knowledge into our educational thinking, though often superficially and unevenly into educational practice. Some years ago we could feel as an intensely dramatic climax in a biography the moment when Helen Keller's teacher managed to establish communication with her. Now a large movie audience can feel the dramatic excitement of the moment when, in the movie version of *The Blackboard Jungle*, the young teacher catches the imagination of a classroom group of young hoodlums.[2] Some awareness of the relationship between growth and learning is essential to our recognition of both of these situations as dramatic climaxes.

One thing which this linking up of teaching and learning and growth and development has meant for us is a new sense of the continuity of experience throughout life. In the cultures from which our own traditions have derived, it has been usual to break up education into two main aspects that can be called "up-bringing" and "schooling." In German the terms are *Erziehung* and *Unterricht*; in French they are *formation* and *instruction*.[3] Though in fact they overlap, both aspects of education, so viewed, are highly compartmentalized. There is little need, for example, for French or German parents and teachers to have contact or communication with one another. And both aspects of education are essentially time-limited, although the time span may be different for the two. But in American culture—despite struggles at different times to separate or to bring together home and school—the lines between upbringing at home and education in school have long been blurred. And now, thinking in terms of growth and development—when we have to include pre-natal influences at least on the child's constitution, when we move from the newborn infant's response to the ways it is wrapped and held and fed to the six-year-old's response to the school environment, to the student's learning of skills, to the young mother's and father's responses to their own six-year-old's learning in school. . .—formal education is even more fully incorporated into the whole experience of growing and learning. And, although we have very strong peer group feelings about education—so that we tend to feel that the proper place for a ten-year-old is in the fifth grade with other ten-year-

---

[2] Evan Hunter, *The Blackboard Jungle* (New York: Pocket Books, 1955); screen version, Metro-Goldwyn-Mayer, 1955. The screen version has picked up and amplified this theme, altering the whole emphasis of the story.

[3] On German attitudes towards upbringing and education, cf. three articles by Rhoda Metraux in Margaret Mead and Martha Wolfenstein, *Child Rearing in Contemporary Cultures* (Chicago: University of Chicago Press, 1955). For France, cf. Rhoda Metraux and Margaret Mead, "Themes in French Culture," *A Preface to a Study of French Community* (Stanford: Stanford University Press, 1954).

olds—we also in American culture do not think of formal education as age-limited. So, in New York City, we have special adult education classes for foreigners who are barely literate, and we have places in our grade room classes for them; and we also have certificates of equivalence for adults who have not completed a stage of formal education, so that a mother can, so to speak, graduate from high school together with her eighteen-year-old daughter. What this means is that we do have a notion that "education" is something a person can get at any time of life. Furthermore, with the development of our understanding of growth and maturation, with its emphasis upon the child, upon things beginning, we have also begun to consider the possibilities of special kinds of learning for the aged, for those who have already retired. And therefore, however we approach the problem, it is difficult to visualize "education" as a separate entity.

But from another point of view, education, as we see it, is not at all circular but linear: education is progress; it takes us where we have never been before. Describing what we think higher education has done for us or should do for our children, we are likely to use such images as "new ways" and "open doors" and to picture the liberal arts college as a house with many doors *all* opening out onto the world; or we speak of "broad paths" or "new vistas" or "wider horizons."[4] Considering such images, we can recognize two things. Education is movement— movement forward and outward. And all these images express openness. We are no more willing to shut ourselves up in an ivory tower of learning than, in other circumstances, we are willing to be fenced in. Our conception of education is open-ended. We do not value learning or skills for their own sake, nor the scholar for the sake of his scholarship. We value education for the opportunities learning opens up, for the multiplicity of new directions. So, for example, the studies of American servicemen in World War II written up in *The American Soldier*[5] indicate that while educational status was a factor in a man's promotion, the servicemen themselves did not regard education in itself as an important means to advancement in the services. We think of education as open-ended because it gives the individual tools and skills and trained capacities and a reservoir of knowledge—and perhaps a little "know-how"; we think of the *lack* of education as a real limitation upon what a man can be, but we do not think education determines who a man can be. This open-endedness provides us with a kind of optimism about man's possibilities for development, both the individual and mankind. It fits together with our belief that we should work with an individual's particular strengths in his education and that we can, given special means, overcome at least in part the difficulties of the poorly endowed, the slow, the incapacitated.

When we think of education in American terms, teaching and learning are bound up in our minds not only with values and performance and dreams, with enriching our heritage, with developing skills that will shape a future as yet unknown, but also, continuously, with the making of new Americans. For we have believed that any individual, by wanting to do so, could become an American and, to a greater or lesser degree, could learn a whole new cultural orientation in a lifetime—a highly unusual belief.

---

[4] Patricia W. Cautley, *AAUW Members Look at College Education, An Interim Report* (Washington, D. C.: American Association of University Women, 1949).

[5] S. A. Stouffer, *et al.*, *Studies in Social Psychology in World War II*, 4 volumes (Princeton: Princeton University Press, 1949–50).

Implicit in this is our faith in—for we "believe in"—education and in the human being's continuing powers of adaptation that enable him, if he will, to learn and re-learn, to change from his past to a new present in which he continues as an individual. Partly for this reason, we have been extraordinarily self-conscious about our educational successes and failures and, on the whole, more articulate about more aspects of education than any other people I know about.

And just as we have felt that the individual could learn and re-learn without a break in continuity, without necessarily ever losing a sense of his personal identity (though we recognize as possibilities for those who get caught between two worlds—second generation Americans who do not know where they stand—either loss of identity or some kind of over-rigid identification that is not complete),[6] so too we have kept a kind of flexibility in thinking about education, a willingness to change content and method often and rapidly without fearing that those who have learned one kind of thing one way will necessarily be out of communication with those who have learned another kind of thing another way. We are ready and even eager to look around the world and select, whatever their original context, ways of learning that might add to the enjoyment of our children. We do not expect children to learn as their elders did, or even younger siblings as their elder ones. Instead, we expect elders to make new adaptations and we expect a great deal of learning to take place within the peer group. This has had several consequences for education and for our interpretations of growth and development. For one thing, it means that our present has very shallow roots in the past. In fact, we are even losing the ability to think and feel with the imagery of natural growth that is appropriate to a sense of organic continuity. We are unlikely to think of a new flowering, a new harvest from an old tree. Change is more easily thought of in terms of a new version—a ... [new] model car ... parent ... child, a phrasing which is more congenial to our whole preference for motor imagery.

It also means that we are, in a very real way, perpetual amateurs trying out new things because they are new to us in our own generation as well as because they are genuinely new, and exceedingly dependent on the experiments of our peers in making judgments about success. It is in this light that we must see our tremendous valuation of professionalized skills and of professionalized standards as guides. The importance of standards of excellence may not be so apparent when we think only about ourselves or compare ourselves to a people like the French with their high valuation of individual craftsmanship. But it becomes very clear when we look at some other people whose amateurism—if one may call it that—is not combined with an over-all conception of skill. So for instance, one could consider the culture of Montserrat, a small island in the Leeward Islands Colony of the British West Indies. The peasants of Montserrat have attempted, rather haphazardly, to jettison their whole past, to get rid of their folk tradition and to move into the modern world, at whose outer edge they feel they live. But there, in a sense, each man has been his own innovator and each attempts to interpret and place bits and pieces, to argue with all others about the reality of fragments seen this way or that. There is much emphasis upon "trying it out" and upon "doing your best," but as there is little sense of style in performance

---

[6] This is always a factor to be considered in understanding the American material on prejudice and on "the authoritarian personality" as described, e.g., in several volumes of *Studies in Prejudice*, edited by Max Horkheimer and Samuel H. Flowerman (New York: Harper, 1949–50).

or of excellence, these people have come to accept fragmentation, uncertainty and amateurism as themselves making up a style of living which they cannot—and about this they are quite articulate—alter without going away from their island.[7]

There is also another consequence of our valuation of change and of flexibility in teaching and learning, and that is that we have a very continuous need for information, for facts about a new situation or a new idea or a new ethic. We can only act and act responsibly when our understanding is shaped by facts which we share with one another. This has deeply affected our ideas about the dissemination of news. It has influenced our programs of "learning by doing" in progressive education. It is important in any new national situation—such as we faced when rationing became necessary in World War II—when, in the beginning, people see the new in terms of an enormous variety of images; then it is possible to get responsible acceptance only when people are carefully briefed—are not merely told, "Be good, be good" or "Do this, do that," but are given facts on the basis of which they can make a choice and a commitment.[8] This insistence upon the importance of facts is basic in our particular valuation of reality testing, whether we are meeting a crisis, working out a research problem, or encouraging a toddler to move, to reach out, to taste and smell and touch the objects that make up his world.

In this brief paper I have attempted to indicate what some American values are in education. Looking at education not as an educator but as a cultural anthropologist, I have thought of these different things—our valuation of the uniqueness of the individual, our sense of the whole, our sense of continuity which does not necessarily imply continuity of content, our sense of the open-endedness of learning, our belief in the possibility of change and in its beneficence—as important themes in American culture which are expressed in various ways in education as in other aspects of living. I have not attempted to differentiate between what is made explicit and what remains implicit because in different contexts the same value may be expressed in one or the other way. Rather what I have tried to do is to suggest to you certain themes, certain values which we share as Americans and which are relevant to our thought and feeling and action whether we are concerned specifically with problems of education and teaching or with problems of growth and development or with the relationships of growth and education to our whole style of life.

---

[7] Based on unpublished field work in Montserrat, B.W.I., 1953–54, by Rhoda Metraux and Theodora M. Abel.

[8] Based on qualitative attitude analyses made for the Committee on Food Habits, National Research Council, 1942–43.

4-4   U.S. IDEALS CANCEL OUT EACH OTHER

Sydney J. Harris

Sydney J. Harris was born in London. He has been an essayist, drama critic, lecturer, magazine publisher, and social researcher for the City of Chicago Law Department, but he is best known for his syndicated newspaper column "Strictly Personal."
    Values are sometimes inconsistent, especially if the society is undergoing rapid change. The following brief essay aptly demonstrates the inconsistency in American values. Such a dichotomy presents a dilemma for the educator seeking a "core" of values to transmit.

Want to know what America believes?
    It believes that all people are basically the same everywhere—but that you can't really trust foreigners.
    It believes that private enterprise is a fine idea—but that your own special interest should try to get as much from the government as it can.
    It believes that the Latin people know how to relax and enjoy life better than we do—but that they're lazy and will never get anywhere.
    It believes that everybody should have as much education as possible—but that people who talk and act if they were educated are untrustworthy intellectuals.
    It believes that Russia is a Godless, materialistic state—but that it's good for us to acquire as many material possessions as we can get our hands on.
    It believes that environment creates most criminals—but it spends billions to lock up criminals, and virtually nothing to change their environment.
    It believes that every man is entitled to his opinion—but that it doesn't take any effort or knowledge or careful reasoning to distinguish an opinion from a mere prejudice.
    It believes that children should get pretty nearly everything they ask for—but that parents are to blame if their children become spoiled and willful from this indulgence.
    It believes that the caste system has no place in a democratic society—but that the size and price of the car you drive is a mark of your relative social position.
    It believes that you can't fool all the people all the time—but that you have to respect the politicians and promoters who manage to do so most of the time.
    It believes that Jesus' advice to turn the other cheek is the only Christian way to behave—but that we have to build up our military strength so that we will be in no danger of losing the next war.
    It believes, in short, a mass of contradictory statements, half of which cancel out the other half, and all of which add up to the most confused set of ideals that any mighty nation has fallen heir to in the history of the world.

From *Majority of One* by Sydney J. Harris, pp. 84–85. Copyright © 1957 by Houghton Mifflin Company; reprinted by permission of Houghton Mifflin Company.

4-5 THE HIGHER IMMORALITY

C. Wright Mills

The late C. Wright Mills, formerly professor of sociology at Columbia University was a leading critic of modern American civilization. He was the author of numerous books including *The Sociological Imagination White Collar: The American Middle Classes*, and the co-author of *The Puerto Rican Journey: New York's Newest Migrants*. The following excerpt from his book *The Power Elite* provides many thoughts relating to American values as they affect the responsibility for decision-making. At the same time the author indicates the threats to American society and its values from our power structure which is influential enough to manipulate the direction of American culture.

The higher immorality can neither be narrowed to the political sphere nor understood as primarily a matter of corrupt men in fundamentally sound institutions. Political corruption is one aspect of a more general immorality; the level of moral sensibility that now prevails is not merely a matter of corrupt men.[1] The higher immorality is a systematic feature of the American elite; its general acceptance is an essential feature of the mass society.

Of course, there may be corrupt men in sound institutions; but when institutions are corrupting, many of the men who live and work in them are necessarily corrupted. In the corporate era, economic relations become impersonal—and the executive feels less personal responsibility. Within the corporate worlds of business, war-making, and politics, the private conscience is attenuated—and the higher immorality is institutionalized. It is not merely a question of a corrupt administration in corporation, army, or state; it is a feature of the corporate rich, as a capitalist stratum, deeply intertwined with the politics of the military state.

From this point of view, the most important question, for instance, about the campaign funds of ambitious young politicians is not whether the politicians are morally insensitive, but whether or not any young man in American politics, who has come so far and so fast, could very well have done so today without possessing or acquiring a somewhat blunted moral sensibility. Many of the problems of "whitecollar crime" and of relaxed public morality, of high-priced vice and of fading personal integrity, are problems of *structural* immorality. They are not merely the problem of the small character twisted by the bad milieu. And many people are at least vaguely aware that this is so. As news of higher immoralities breaks, they often say, "Well, another one got caught today," thereby implying that the cases disclosed are not odd events involving occasional characters but symptoms of a widespread condition. There is good probative evidence that they are right. But what is the underlying condition of which all these instances are symptoms?

From *The Power Elite*, by C. Wright Mills, pp. 343–361. Copyright © 1956 Oxford University Press; reprinted by permission of Oxford University Press.

[1] C. Wright Mills, "A Diagnosis of Our Moral Uneasiness," *The New York Times Magazine*, November 23, 1952.

The moral uneasiness of our time results from the fact that older values and codes of uprightness no longer grip the men and women of the corporate era, nor have they been replaced by new values and codes which would lend moral meaning and sanction to the corporate routines they must now follow. It is not that the mass public has explicitly rejected received codes; it is rather that to many of the members these codes have become hollow. No moral terms of acceptance are available, but neither are any moral terms of rejection. As individuals they are morally defenseless; as groups, they are politically indifferent. It is this generalized lack of commitment that is meant when it is said that "the public" is morally confused.

But, of course, not only "the public" is morally confused in this way. "The tragedy of official Washington," James Reston has commented, "is that it is confounded at every turn by the hangover of old political habits and outworn institutions but is no longer nourished by the ancient faith on which it was founded. It clings to the bad things and casts away the permanent. It professes belief but does not believe. It knows the old words but has forgotten the melody. It is engaged in an ideological war without being able to define its own ideology. It condemns the materialism of an atheistic enemy but glorifies its own materialism."[2]

In economic and political institutions the corporate rich now wield enormous power, but they have never had to win the moral consent of those over whom they hold this power. Every such naked interest, every new, unsanctioned power of corporation, farm bloc, labor union, and governmental agency that has risen in the past two generations has been clothed with morally loaded slogans. For what is *not* done in the name of the public interest? As these slogans wear out, new ones are industriously made up, also to be banalized in due course. And all the while, recurrent economic and military crises spread fears, hesitations, and anxieties which give new urgency to the busy search for moral justifications and decorous excuses.

"Crisis" is a bankrupted term, because so many men in high places have evoked it in order to cover up their extraordinary policies and deeds; as a matter of fact, it is precisely the absence of crises that is a cardinal feature of the higher immorality. For genuine crises involve situations in which men at large are presented with genuine alternatives, the moral meanings of which are clearly opened to public debate. The higher immorality, the general weakening of older values, and the organization of irresponsibility have not involved any public crises; on the contrary, they have been matters of a creeping indifference and a silent hollowing out.

The images that generally prevail of the higher circles are the images of the elite seen as celebrities. In discussing the professional celebrities, I noted that the instituted elites of power do not monopolize the bright focus of national acclaim. They share it nationally with the frivolous or the sultry creatures of the world of celebrity, which thus serves as a dazzling blind of their true power. In the sense that the volume of publicity and acclaim is mainly and continuously upon those professional celebrities, it is not upon the power elite. So the social visibility of that elite is lowered by the status distraction, or rather public vision of them is through the celebrity who amuses and entertains—or disgusts, as the case may be.

The absence of any firm moral order of belief makes men in the mass all the more open to the manipulation and distraction of the world of the celebrities. In due course, such a "turnover" of appeals and codes and values as they are subjected to

---

[2] James Reston, *The New York Times*, April 10, 1955, p. 10E.

leads them to distrust and cynicism, to a sort of Machiavellianism-for-the-little-man. Thus they vicariously enjoy the prerogatives of the corporate rich, the nocturnal antics of the celebrity, and the sad-happy life of the very rich.

But with all this, there is still one old American value that has not markedly declined: the value of money and of the things money can buy—these, even in inflated times, seem as solid and enduring as stainless steel. "I've been rich and I've been poor," Sophie Tucker has said, "and believe me, rich is best."[3] As many other values are weakened, the question for Americans becomes not "Is there anything that money, used with intelligence, will not buy?" but, "How many of the things that money will *not* buy are valued and desired more than what money *will* buy?" Money is the one unambiguous criterion of success, and such success is still the sovereign American value.

Whenever the standards of the moneyed life prevail, the man with money, no matter how he got it, will eventually be respected. A million dollars, it is said, covers a multitude of sins. It is not only that men want money; it is that their very standards are pecuniary. In a society in which the money-maker has had no serious rival for repute and honor, the word "practical" comes to mean useful for private gain, and "common sense," the sense to get ahead financially. The pursuit of the moneyed life is the commanding value, in relation to which the influence of other values has declined, so men easily become morally ruthless in the pursuit of easy money and fast estate-building.

A great deal of American corruption—although not all of it—is simply a part of the old effort to get rich and then to become richer. But today the context in which the old drive must operate has changed. When both economic and political institutions were small and scattered—as in the simpler models of classical economics and Jeffersonian democracy—no man had it in his power to bestow or to receive great favors. But when political institutions and economic opportunities are at once concentrated and linked, then public office can be used for private gain.

Governmental agencies contain no more of the higher immorality than do business corporations. Political men can grant financial favors only when there are economic men ready and willing to take them. And economic men can seek political favors only when there are political agents who can bestow such favors. The publicity spotlight, of course, shines brighter upon the transactions of the men in government, for which there is good reason. Expectations being higher, publics are more easily disappointed by public officials. Businessmen are supposed to be out for themselves, and if they successfully skate on legally thin ice, Americans generally honor them for having gotten away with it. But in a civilization so thoroughly business-penetrated as America, the rules of business are carried over into government—especially when so many businessmen have gone into government. How many executives would really fight for a law requiring a careful and public accounting of all executive contracts and "expense accounts"? High income taxes have resulted in a network of collusion between big firm and higher employee. There are many ingenious ways to cheat the spirit of the tax laws, as we have seen, and the standards of consumption of many high-priced men are determined more by complicated expense accounts than by simple take-home pay. Like prohibition, the laws of income taxes and the regulations of wartime exist without the support of firm business convention. It is merely illegal to cheat them, but it is smart to get away with it. Laws without supporting moral conventions invite

---

[3] Sophie Tucker as quoted in *Time*, November 16, 1953.

crime, but much more importantly, they spur the growth of an expedient, amoral attitude.

A society that is in its higher circles and on its middle levels widely believed to be a network of smart rackets does not produce men with an inner moral sense; a society that is merely expedient does not produce men of conscience. A society that narrows the meaning of "success" to the big money and in its terms condemns failure as the chief vice, raising money to the plane of absolute value, will produce the sharp operator and the shady deal. Blessed are the cynical, for only they have what it takes.

In the corporate world, in the political directorate, and increasingly in the ascendant military, the heads of the big hierarchies and power machines are seen not only as men who have succeeded, but as wielders of the patronage of success. They interpret and they apply to individuals the criteria of success. Those immediately below them are usually members of their clique, of their clientele, sound men as they themselves are sound. But the hierarchies are intricately related to one another, and inside each clique are some whose loyalties are to other cliques. There are personal loyalties as well as official ones, personal as well as impersonal criteria for advancement. As we trace the career of the individual member of various higher circles, we are also tracing the history of his loyalties, for the first and overshadowing fact about the higher circles, from the standpoint of what it takes to succeed within them, is that they are based upon self-co-optation. The second fact about these hierarchies of success is that they do not form one monolithic structure; they are a complex set of variously related and often antagonistic cliques. The third fact we must recognize is that, in any such world, younger men who would succeed attempt to relate themselves to those in charge of their selection as successes.

Accordingly, the American literature of practical aspiration—which carries the great fetish of success—has undergone a significant shift in its advice about "what it takes to succeed." The sober, personal virtues of willpower and honesty, of high-mindedness and the constitutional inability to say "yes" to The Easy Road of women, tobacco, and wine—this later nineteenth-century image has given way to "the most important single factor, the effective personality," which "commands attention by charm" and "radiates self-confidence." In this "new way of life," one must smile often and be a good listener, talk in terms of the other man's interests and make the other feel important—and one must do all this sincerely. Personal relations, in short, have become part of "public relations," a sacrifice of selfhood on a personality market, to the sole end of individual success in the corporate way of life.[4] Being justified by superior merit and hard work, but being founded on co-optation by a clique, often on quite other grounds, the elite careerist must continually persuade others and himself as well that he is the opposite of what he actually is.

It is the proud claim of the higher circles in America that their members are entirely self-made. That is their self-image and their well-publicized myth. Popular proof of this is based on anecdotes; its scholarly proof is supposed to rest upon statistical rituals whereby it is shown that varying proportions of the men at the top are sons of men of lower rank. We have already seen the proportions of given elite circles composed of the men who have risen. But what is more important than the proportions

---

[4] C. Wright Mills, *White Collar* (New York: Oxford University Press, 1951), pp. 259 ff.

of the sons of wage workers among these higher circles is the criteria of admission to them, and the question of who applies these criteria. We cannot from upward mobility infer higher merit. Even if the rough figures that now generally hold were reversed, and 90 percent of the elite were sons of wage workers—but the criteria of co-optation by the elite remained what they now are—we could not from that mobility necessarily infer merit. Only if the criteria of the top positions were meritorious, and only if they were self-applied, as in a purely entrepreneurial manner, could we smuggle merit into such statistics—from any statistics—of mobility. The idea that the self-made man is somehow "good" and that the family-made man is not good makes moral sense only when the career is independent, when one is on one's own as an entrepreneur. It would also make sense in a strict bureaucracy where examinations control advancement. It makes little sense in the system of corporate co-optation.

There is, in psychological fact, no such thing as a self-made man. No man makes himself, least of all the members of the American elite. In a world of corporate hierarchies, men are selected by those above them in the hierarchy in accordance with whatever criteria they use. In connection with the corporations of America, we have seen the current criteria. Men shape themselves to fit them, and are thus made by the criteria, the social premiums that prevail. If there is no such thing as a self-made man, there is such a thing as a self-used man, and there are many such men among the American elite.

Under such conditions of success, there is no virtue in starting out poor and becoming rich. Only where the ways of becoming rich are such as to require virtue or to lead to virtue does personal enrichment imply virtue. In a system of co-optation from above, whether you began rich or poor seems less relevant in revealing what kind of man you are when you have arrived than in revealing the principles of those in charge of selecting the ones who succeed.

All this is sensed by enough people below the higher circles to lead to cynical views of the lack of connection between merit and mobility, between virtue and success. It is a sense of the immorality of accomplishment, and it is revealed in the prevalence of such views as: "it's all just another racket," and "it's not what you know but who you know." Considerable numbers of people now accept the immorality of accomplishment as a going fact.

Some observers are led by their sense of the immorality of accomplishment to the ideology, obliquely set forth by academic social science, of human relations in industry;[5] still others to the solace of mind provided by the newer literature of resignation, of peace of mind, which in some quietened circles replaces the old literature of frenzied aspiration, of how to get ahead. But, regardless of the particular style of reaction, the sense of the immorality of accomplishment often feeds into that level of public sensibility which we have called the higher immorality. The old self-made man's is a tarnished image, and no other image of success has taken its once bright place. Success itself, as the American model of excellence, declines as it becomes one more feature of the higher immorality.

Moral distrust of the American elite—as well as the fact of organized irresponsibility—rests upon the higher immorality, but also upon vague feelings about

---

[5] C. Wright Mills, "The Contributions of Sociology to Industrial Relations," Proceedings of the First Annual Conference of the Industrial Relations Research Association, December 1948.

the higher ignorance. Once upon a time in the United States, men of affairs were also men of sensibility: to a considerable extent the elite of power and the elite of culture coincided, and where they did not coincide they often overlapped as circles. Within the compass of a knowledgeable and effective public, knowledge and power were in effective touch; and more than that, this public decided much that was decided.

"Nothing is more revealing," James Reston has written, "than to read the debate in the House of Representatives in the Eighteen Thirties on Greece's fight with Turkey for independence and the Greek-Turkish debate in the Congress in 1947. The first is dignified and eloquent, the argument marching from principle through illustration to conclusion; the second is a dreary garble of debating points, full of irrelevancies and bad history."[6] George Washington in 1783 relaxed with Voltaire's "letters" and Locke's "On Human Understanding"; Eisenhower read cowboy tales and detective stories.[7] For such men as now typically arrive in the higher political, economic, and military circles, the briefing and the memorandum seem to have pretty well replaced not only the serious book, but the newspaper as well. Given the immorality of accomplishment, this is perhaps as it must be, but what is somewhat disconcerting about it is that they are below the level on which they might feel a little bit ashamed of the uncultivated style of their relaxation and of their mental fare, and that no self-cultivated public is in a position by its reactions to educate them to such uneasiness.

By the middle of the twentieth century, the American elite have become an entirely different breed of men from those who could on any reasonable grounds be considered a cultural elite, or even for that matter cultivated men of sensibility. Knowledge and power are not truly united inside the ruling circles; and when men of knowledge do come to a point of contact with the circles of powerful men, they come not as peers but as hired men. The elite of power, wealth, and celebrity do not have even a passing acquaintance with the elite of culture, knowledge, and sensibility; they are not in touch with them—although the ostentatious fringes of the two worlds sometimes overlap in the world of the celebrity.

Most men are encouraged to assume that, in general, the most powerful and the wealthiest are also the most knowledgeable or, as they might say, "the smartest." Such ideas are propped up by many little slogans about those who "teach because they can't do," and about "if you're so smart, why aren't you rich?"[8] But all that such wisecracks mean is that those who use them assume that power and wealth are sovereign values for all men and especially for men "who are smart." They assume also that knowledge always pays off in such ways, or surely ought to, and that the test of genuine knowledge is just such pay-offs. The powerful and the wealthy *must* be the men of most knowledge, otherwise how could they be where they are? But to say that those who succeed to power must be "smart" is to say that power *is* knowledge. To say that those who succeed to wealth must be smart is to say that wealth *is* knowledge.

---

[6] James Reston, *The New York Times*, January 31, 1954, Section 4, p. 8.

[7] *The New York Times Book Review*, August 23, 1953. See also *Time*, February 28, 1955, pp. 12 ff.

[8] Bernard Baruch, an adviser to Presidents, has recently remarked, "I think economists as a rule . . . take for granted they know a lot of things. If they really knew so much, they would have all the money and we would have none." And again he reasons: "These men (economists) can take facts and figures and bring them together, but their predictions are not worth any more than ours. If they were, they would have all the money and we would not have anything." Hearings before the Committee on Banking and Currency, United States Senate, Eighty-Fourth Congress, First Session (U.S. Government Printing Office, Washington, D.C., 1955), p. 1001.

The prevalence of such assumptions does reveal something that is true: that ordinary men, even today, are prone to explain and to justify power and wealth in terms of knowledge or ability. Such assumptions also reveal something of what has happened to the kind of experience that knowledge has come to be. Knowledge is no longer widely felt as an ideal; it is seen as an instrument. In a society of power and wealth, knowledge is valued as an instrument of power and wealth, and also, of course, as an ornament in conversation.

What knowledge does to a man (in clarifying what he is, and setting him free)— that is the personal ideal of knowledge. What knowledge does to a civilization (in revealing its human meaning, and setting it free)—that is the social ideal of knowledge. But today, the personal *and* the social ideals of knowledge have coincided in what knowledge does *for* the smart guy—it gets him ahead; and for the wise nation—it lends cultural prestige, sanctifying power with authority.

Knowledge seldom lends power to the man of knowledge. But the supposed, and secret, knowledge of some men-on-the-make, and their very free use thereof, has consequence for other men who have not the power of defense. Knowledge, of course, is neither good nor bad, nor is its use good or bad. "Bad men increase in knowledge as fast as good men," John Adams wrote, "and science, arts, taste, sense and letters, are employed for the purpose of injustice as well as for virtue."[9] That was in 1790; today we have good reason to know that it is so.

The problem of knowledge and power is, and always has been, the problem of the relations of men of knowledge with men of power. Suppose we were to select the one hundred most powerful men, from all fields of power, in America today and line them up. And then, suppose we selected the one hundred most knowledgeable men, from all fields of social knowledge, and lined them up. How many men would be in *both* our line-ups? Of course our selection would depend upon what we mean by power and what we mean by knowledge—especially what we mean by knowledge. But, if we mean what the words seem to mean, surely we would find few if any men in America today who were in both groups, and surely we could find many more at the time the nation was founded than we could find today. For, in the eighteenth century, even in this colonial outpost, men of power pursued learning, and men of learning were often in positions of power. In these respects we have, I believe, suffered grievous decline.[10]

There is little union in the same persons of knowledge and power; but persons of power do surround themselves with men of some knowledge, or at least with men who are experienced in shrewd dealings. The man of knowledge has not become a philosopher king; but he has often become a consultant, and moreover a consultant to a man who is neither king-like nor philosophical. It is, of course, true that the chairman of the pulp writers section of the Authors' League helped a leading senator "polish up the speeches he delivered in the 1952 senatorial campaign."[11] But it is not natural in the course of their careers for men of knowledge to meet with those of power. The links

---

[9] John Adams, *Discourses on Davila*, (Boston: Russell and Cutler, 1805).

[10] In *Perspectives, U.S.A.* No. 3, Mr. Lionel Trilling has written optimistically of "new intellectual classes." For an informed account of the new cultural strata by a brilliantly self-conscious insider, see also Louis Kronenberger, *Company Manners* (Indianapolis: Bobbs-Merrill, 1954).

[11] Leo Egan, "Political 'Ghosts' Playing Usual Quiet Role as Experts," *The New York Times*, October 14, 1954, p. 20.

between university and government are weak, and when they do occur, the man of knowledge appears as an "expert" which usually means as a hired technician. Like most others in this society, the man of knowledge is himself dependent for his livelihood upon the job, which nowadays is a prime sanction of thought control. Where getting ahead requires the good opinions of more powerful others, their judgments become prime objects of concern. Accordingly, in so far as intellectuals serve power directly— in a job hierarchy—they often do so unfreely.

The democratic man assumes the existence of a public, and in his rhetoric asserts that this public is the very seat of sovereignty. Two things are needed in a democracy: articulate and knowledgeable publics, and political leaders who if not men of reason are at least reasonably responsible to such knowledgeable publics as exist. Only where publics and leaders are responsive and responsible are human affairs in democratic order, and only when knowledge has public relevance is this order possible. Only when mind has an autonomous basis, independent of power, but powerfully related to it, can mind exert its force in the shaping of human affairs. This is democratically possible only when there exists a free and knowledgeable public, to which men of knowledge may address themselves, and to which men of power are truly responsible. Such a public and such men—either of power or of knowledge—do not now prevail, and accordingly, knowledge does not now have democratic relevance in America.

The characteristic member of the higher circles today is an intellectual mediocrity, sometimes a conscientious one, but still a mediocrity. His intelligence is revealed only by his occasional realization that he is not up to the decisions he sometimes feels called upon to confront. But usually he keeps such feelings private, his public utterances being pious and sentimental, grim and brave, cheerful and empty in their universal generality. He is open only to abbreviated and vulgarized, predigested and slanted ideas. He is a commander of the age of the phone call, the memo, and the briefing.

By the mindlessness and mediocrity of men of affairs, I do not, of course, mean that these men are not sometimes intelligent—although that is by no means automatically the case. It is not, however, primarily a matter of the distribution of "intelligence"—as if intelligence were a homogeneous something of which there may be more or less. It is rather a matter of the type of intelligence, of the quality of mind that is selected and formed. It is a matter of the evaluation of substantive rationality as the chief value in a man's life and character and conduct. That evaluation is what is lacking in the American power elite. In its place there are "weight" and "judgment" which count for much more in their celebrated success than any subtlety of mind or force of intellect.

All around and just below the weighty man of affairs are his technical lieutenants of power who have been assigned the role of knowledge and even of speech: his public relations men, his ghost, his administrative assistants, his secretaries. And do not forget The Committees. With the increased means of decision, there is a crisis of understanding among the political directorate of the United States, and accordingly, there is often a commanding indecision.

The lack of knowledge as an experience among the elite ties in with the malign ascendancy of the expert, not only as fact but as legitimation. When questioned recently about a criticism of defense policies made by the leader of the opposition party, the Secretary of Defense replied, "Do you think he is an expert in the matter?" When pressed further by reporters he asserted that the "military chiefs think it is sound, and I think it is sound," and later, when asked about specific cases, added: "In some cases, all you can do is ask the Lord."[12] With such a large role so arrogantly given to God and to experts, what room is there for political leadership? Much less for public debate of what is after all every bit as much a political and a moral as a military issue. But then, from before Pearl Harbor, the trend has been the abdication of debate and the collapse of opposition under the easy slogan of bi-partisanship.

Beyond the lack of intellectual cultivation by political personnel and advisory circle, the absence of publicly relevant mind has come to mean that powerful decisions and important policies are not made in such a way as to be justified or attacked; in short, debated in any intellectual form. Moreover, the attempt to so justify them is often not even made. Public relations displace reasoned argument; manipulation and undebated decisions of power replace democratic authority. More and more, since the nineteenth century, as administration has replaced politics, the decisions of importance do not carry even the panoply of reasonable discussion, but are made by God, by experts, and by men like Mr. Wilson.

More and more the area of the official secret expands, as well as the area of the secret listening in on those who might divulge in public what the public, not being composed of experts with Q clearance, is not to know. The entire sequence of decisions concerning the production and the use of atomic weaponry has been made without any genuine public debate, and the facts needed to engage in that debate intelligently have been officially hidden, distorted, and even lied about. As the decisions become more fateful, not only for Americans but literally for mankind, the sources of information are closed up, and the relevant facts needed for decision (even the decisions made!) are, as politically convenient "official secrets," withheld from the heavily laden channels of information.

In those channels, meanwhile, political rhetoric seems to slide lower and lower down the scale of cultivation and sensibility. The height of such mindless communications to masses, or what are thought to be masses, is probably the demagogic assumption that suspicion and accusation, if repeated often enough, somehow equal proof of guilt—just as repeated claims about toothpaste or brands of cigarettes are assumed to equal facts. The greatest kind of propaganda with which America is beset, the greatest at least in terms of volume and loudness, is commercial propaganda for soap and cigarettes and automobiles; it is to such things, or rather to Their Names, that this society most frequently sings its loudest praises. What is important about this is that by implication and omission, by emphasis and sometimes by flat statement, this astounding volume of propaganda for commodities is often untruthful and misleading and is addressed more often to the belly or to the groin than to the head or to the heart. Public communications from those who make powerful decisions, or who would have us vote them into such decision-making places, more and more take on those qualities of mindlessness and myth which commercial propaganda and advertising have come to exemplify.

In America today, men of affairs are not so much dogmatic as they are mindless. Dogma has usually meant some more or less elaborated justification of ideas and values, and thus has had some features (however inflexible and closed) of mind, of intellect, of reason. Nowadays what we are up against is precisely the absence of mind of any sort as

---

[12] Charles E. Wilson, quoted in *The New York Times*, March 10, 1954, p. 1.

a public force; what we are up against is a disinterest in and a fear of knowledge that might have liberating public relevance. What this makes possible are decisions having no rational justifications which the intellect could confront and engage in debate.

It is not the barbarous irrationality of dour political primitives that is the American danger; it is the respected judgments of Secretaries of State, the earnest platitudes of Presidents, the fearful self-righteousness of sincere young American politicians from sunny California. These men have replaced mind with platitude, and the dogmas by which they are legitimated are so widely accepted that no counter-balance of mind prevails against them. Such men as these are crackpot realists: in the name of realism they have constructed a paranoid reality all their own; in the name of practicality they have projected a utopian image of capitalism. They have replaced the responsible interpretation of events with the disguise of events by a maze of public relations; respect for public debate with unshrewd notions of psychological warfare; intellectual ability with agility of the sound, mediocre judgment; the capacity to elaborate alternatives and gauge their consequences with the executive stance.

Despite—perhaps because of—the ostracism of mind from public affairs, the immorality of accomplishment, and the general prevalence of organized irresponsibility, the men of the higher circles benefit from the total power of the institutional domains over which they rule. For the power of these institutions, actual or potential, is ascribed to them as the ostensible decision-makers. Their positions and their activities, and even their persons, are hallowed by these ascriptions; and, around all the high places of power, there is a penumbra of prestige in which the political directorate, the corporate rich, the admirals and generals are bathed. The elite of a society, however modest its individual member, embodies the prestige of the society's power.[13] Moreover, few individuals in positions of such authority can long resist the temptation to base their self-images, at least in part, upon the sounding board of the collectivity which they head. Acting as the representative of his nation, his corporation, his army, in due course, he comes to consider himself and what he says and believes as expressive of the historically accumulated glory of the great institutions with which he comes to identify himself. When he speaks in the name of his country or its cause, its past glory also echoes in his ears.

Status, no longer rooted primarily in local communities, follows the big hierarchies, which are on a national scale. Status follows the big money, even if it has a touch of the gangster about it. Status follows power, even if it be without background. Below, in the mass society, old moral and traditional barriers to status break down and Americans look for standards of excellence among the circles above them, in terms of which to model themselves and judge their self-esteem. Yet nowadays, it seems easier for Americans to recognize such representative men in the past than

---

[13]John Adams wrote in the late eighteenth century: "When you rise to the first ranks, and consider the first men; a nobility who are known and respected at least, perhaps habitually esteemed and beloved by a nation; Princes and Kings, on whom the eyes of all men are fixed, and whose every motion is regarded, the consequences of wounding their feelings are dreadful, because the feelings of a whole nation, and sometimes of many nations, are wounded at the same time. If the smallest variation is made in their situation, relatively to each other; if one who was inferior is raised to be superior, unless it be by fixed laws, whose evident policy and necessity may take away disgrace, nothing but war, carnage and vengeance has ever been the usual consequence of it . . ." John Adams, 1805, pp. 57–58.

in the present. Whether this is due to a real historical difference or merely to the
political ease and expediency of hindsight is very difficult to tell.[14] At any rate it is
a fact that in the political assignments of prestige there is little disparagement of
Washington, Jefferson, and Lincoln, but much disagreement about current figures.
Representative men seem more easily recognizable after they have died; contemporary
political leaders are merely politicians; they may be big or little, but they are not
great, and increasingly they are seen in terms of the higher immorality.

Now again status follows power, and older types of exemplary figures have been
replaced by the fraternity of the successful—the professional executives who have
become the political elite, and who are now the *official* representative men. It remains
to be seen whether they will become representative men in the images and aspirations of
the mass public, or whether they will endure any longer than the displaced liberals
of the 'thirties. Their images are controversial, deeply involved in the immorality
of accomplishment and the higher immorality in general. Increasingly, literate
Americans feel that there is something synthetic about them. Their style and the
conditions under which they become "big" lend themselves too readily to the suspicion
of the build-up; the shadows of the ghost writer and the make-up man loom too large;
the slickness of the fabrication is too apparent.

We should, of course, bear in mind that men of the higher circles may or may
not seek to impose themselves as representative upon the underlying population, and
that relevant public sectors of the population may or may not accept their images.
An elite may try to impose its claims upon the mass public, but this public may not cash
them in. On the contrary, it may be indifferent or even debunk their values, caricature
their image, laugh at their claim to be representative men.

In his discussion of models of national character, Walter Bagehot does not go
into such possibilities;[15] but it is clear that for our contemporaries we must consider
them, since precisely this reaction has led to a sometimes frenzied and always expensive
practice of what is known as "public relations." Those who have both power and status
are perhaps best off when they do not actively have to seek acclaim. The truly proud
old families will not seek it; the professional celebrities are specialists in seeking

---

[14]In every intellectual period, some one discipline or school of thought becomes a sort of common denominator. The common denominator of the conservative mood in America today is American history. This is
the time of the American historian. All nationalist celebration tends, of course, to be put in historical
terms, but the celebrators do not wish to be relevant merely to the understanding of history as past event.
Their purpose is the celebration of the present. (1) One reason why the American ideology is so historically
oriented is that of all the scholarly community it is the historians who are most likely to create such public
assumptions. For, of all the scholarly writers, the historians have been the ones with the literate tradition.
Other "social scientists" are more likely to be unacquainted with English usage and moreover, they do not
write about large topics of public concern. (2) The "good" historians, in fulfilling the public role of the
higher journalists, the historians with the public attention and the Sunday acclaim, are the historians who
are the quickest to re-interpret the American past with relevance to the current mood, and in turn, the
cleverest at picking out of the past, just now, those characters and events that most easily make for optimism
and lyric upsurge. (3) In truth, and without nostalgia, we ought to realize that the American past is a
wonderful source for myths about the American present. That past, at times, did indeed embody quite a way
of life; the United States has been extraordinarily fortunate in its time of origin and early development;
the present is complicated, and, especially to a trained historian, quite undocumented. The general
American ideology accordingly tends to be of history and by historians. William Harlan Hale, "The Boom in
American History," *The Reporter*, February 24, 1955, pp. 42 ff.

[15]See Walter Bagehot, *Physics and Politics* (New York: D. Appleton, 1912), pp. 36, 146–147, 205–206.

it actively. Increasingly, the political, economic, and military elite—as we have seen—compete with the celebrities and seek to borrow their status. Perhaps those who have unprecedented power without the aura of status will always seek it, even if uneasily, among those who have publicity without power.

For the mass public, there is the status distraction of the celebrity, as well as the economic distraction of war prosperity; for the liberal intellectual, who does look to the political arena, there is the political distraction of the sovereign localities and of the middle levels of power, which sustain the illusion that America is still a self-balancing society. If the mass media focus on the professional celebrities, the liberal intellectuals, especially the academic social scientists among them, focus upon the noisy middle levels. Professional celebrities and middle-level politicians are the most visible figures of the system; in fact, together they tend to monopolize the communicated or public scene that is visible to the members of the mass society, and thus to obscure and to distract attention from the power elite.

The higher circles in America today contain, on the one hand, the laughing, erotic, dazzling glamour of the professional celebrity, and, on the other, the prestige aura of power, of authority, of might and wealth. These two pinnacles are not unrelated. The power elite is not so noticeable as the celebrities, and often does not want to be; the "power" of the professional celebrity is the power of distraction. America as a national public is indeed possessed of a strange set of idols. The professionals, in the main, are either glossy little animals or frivolous clowns; the men of power, in the main, rarely seem to be models of representative men.

Such moral uneasiness as prevails among the American elite themselves is accordingly quite understandable. Its existence is amply confirmed by the more serious among those who have come to feel that they represent America abroad. There, the double-faced character of the American celebrity is reflected both by the types of Americans who travel to play or to work, and in the images many literate and articulate Europeans hold of "Americans." Public honor in America tends now to be either frivolous or grim; either altogether trivial or portentous of a greatly tightened-up system of prestige.

The American elite is not composed of representative men whose conduct and character constitute models for American imitation and aspiration. There is no set of men with whom members of the mass public can rightfully and gladly identify. In this fundamental sense, America is indeed without leader. Yet such is the nature of the mass public's morally cynical and politically unspecified distrust that it is readily drained off without real political effect. That this is so, after the men and events of the last thirty years, is further proof of the extreme difficulty of finding and of using in America today the political means of sanity for morally sane objectives.

America—a conservative country without any conservative ideology—appears now before the world a naked and arbitrary power, as, in the name of realism, its men of decision enforce their often crackpot definitions upon world reality. The second-rate mind is in command of the ponderously spoken platitude. In the liberal rhetoric, vagueness, and in the conservative mood, irrationality, are raised to principle. Public relations and the official secret, the trivializing campaign and the terrible fact clumsily accomplished, are replacing the reasoned debate of political ideas in the privately incorporated economy, the military ascendancy, and the political vacuum of modern America.

The men of the higher circles are not representative men; their high position is not a result of moral virtue; their fabulous success is not firmly connected with meritorious ability. Those who sit in the seats of the high and the mighty are selected and formed by the means of power, the sources of wealth, the mechanics of celebrity, which prevail in their society. They are not men selected and formed by a civil service that is linked with the world of knowledge and sensibility. They are not men shaped by nationally responsible parties that debate openly and clearly the issues this nation now so unintelligently confronts. They are not men held in responsible check by a plurality of voluntary associations which connect debating publics with the pinnacles of decision. Commanders of power unequaled in human history, they have succeeded within the American system of organized irresponsibility.

4-6   ONE HUNDRED PERCENT AMERICAN

Ralph Linton

In this closing essay, Ralph Linton, who has already made two contributions to this book, questions the notion of a purely American culture. With deft insight into the process of diffusion of knowledge, he presents evidence of much borrowing and reliance on other cultures. It is appropriate for United States citizens to become aware that their society, like all others, is the outgrowth of the combined efforts of earlier men and that the values of the material and non-material culture have had a historical development that will continue for many years to come.

There can be no queston about the average American's Americanism or his desire to preserve this precious heritage at all costs. Nevertheless, some insidious foreign ideas have already wormed their way into his civilization without his realizing what was going on. Thus dawn finds the unsuspecting patriot garbed in pajamas, a garment of East Indian origin; and lying in a bed built on a pattern which originated in either Persia or Asia Minor. He is muffled to the ears in un-American materials: cotton, first domesticated in India; linen, domesticated in the Near East; wool from an animal native to Asia Minor; or silk whose uses were first discovered by the Chinese. All these substances have been transformed into cloth by methods invented in Southwestern Asia. If the weather is cold enough, he may even be sleeping under an eiderdown quilt invented in Scandinavia.

On awakening he glances at the clock, a medieval European invention, uses one potent Latin word in abbreviated form, rises in haste, and goes to the bathroom. Here, if he stops to think about it, he must feel himself in the presence of a great American institution: he will have heard stories of both the quality and frequency of foreign plumbing and will know that in no other country does the average man perform his ablutions in the midst of such splendor. But the insidious foreign influence pursues him even here. Glass was invented by the ancient Egyptians, the use of glazed

From *American Mercury*, XL (1937), pp. 427–429. Copyright 1937 by *American Mercury*; reprinted by permission of *American Mercury*.

tiles for floors and walls in the Near East, porcelain in China, and the art of enameling on metal by Mediterranean artisans of the Bronze Age. Even his bathtub and toilet are but slightly modified copies of Roman originals. The only purely American contribution to the ensemble is the steam radiator, against which our patriot very briefly and unintentionally places his posterior.

In this bathroom the American washes with soap invented by the ancient Gauls. Next he cleans his teeth, a subversive European practice which did not invade America until the latter part of the eighteenth century. He then shaves, a masochistic rite first developed by the heathen priests of ancient Egypt and Sumer. The process is made less of a penance by the fact that his razor is of steel, an iron-carbon alloy discovered in either India or Turkestan. Lastly, he dries himself on a Turkish towel.

Returning to the bedroom, the unconscious victim of un-American practices removes his clothes from a chair, invented in the Near East, and proceeds to dress. He puts on close-fitting tailored garments whose form derives from the skin clothing of the ancient nomads of the Asiatic steppes and fastens them with buttons whose prototypes appeared in Europe at the close of the Stone Age. This costume is appropriate enough for outdoor exercise in a cold climate but is quite unsuited to American summers, steam-heated houses, and Pullmans. Nevertheless, foreign ideas and habits hold the unfortunate man in thrall even when common sense tells him that the authentically American costume of gee string and moccasins would be far more comfortable. He puts on his feet stiff coverings made from hide prepared by a process invented in ancient Egypt and cut to a pattern which can be traced back to ancient Greece, and makes sure they are properly polished, also a Greek idea. Lastly, he ties about his neck a strip of bright-colored cloth which is a vestigial survival of the shoulder shawls worn by seventeenth-century Croats. He gives himself a final appraisal in the mirror, an old Mediterranean invention, and goes downstairs to breakfast.

Here a whole new series of foreign things confronts him. His food and drink are placed before him in pottery vessels, the popular name of which—china—is sufficient evidence of their origin. His fork is a medieval Italian invention and his spoon a copy of a Roman original. He will usually begin the meal with coffee, an Abyssinian plant first discovered by the Arabs. The American is quite likely to need it to dispel the morning-after effects of over-indulgence in fermented drinks, invented in the Near East; or distilled ones, invented by the alchemists of medieval Europe. Whereas the Arabs took their coffee straight, he will probably sweeten it with sugar, discovered in India; and dilute it with cream, both the domestication of cattle and the technique of milking having originated in Asia Minor.

If our patriot is old-fashioned enough to adhere to the so-called American breakfast, his coffee will be accompanied by an orange, domesticated in the Mediterranean region, a cantaloupe domesticated in Persia, or grapes domesticated in Asia Minor. He will follow this with a bowl of cereal made from grain domesticated in the Near East and prepared by methods also invented there. From this he will go on to waffles, a Scandinavian invention, with plenty of butter, originally a Near-Eastern cosmetic. As a side dish he may have the egg of a bird domesticated in Southeastern Asia or strips of the flesh of an animal domesticated in the same region, which have been salted and smoked by a process invented in Northern Europe.

Breakfast over, he places upon his head a molded piece of felt, invented by the nomads of Eastern Asia, and, if it looks like rain, puts on outer shoes of rubber, discovered by the ancient Mexicans, and takes an umbrella, invented in India. He then sprints for his train—the train, not the sprinting, being an English invention. At the station he pauses for a moment to buy a newspaper, paying for it with coins invented in ancient Lydia. Once on board he settles back to inhale the fumes of a cigarette invented in Mexico, or a cigar invented in Brazil. Meanwhile, he reads the news of the day, imprinted in characters invented by the ancient Semites by a process invented in Germany upon a material invented in China. As he scans the latest editorial pointing out the dire results to our institutions of accepting foreign ideas, he will not fail to thank a Hebrew God in an Indo-European language that he is a one hundred percent (decimal system invented by the Greeks) American (from Americus Vespucci, Italian geographer).

CONCLUSION

There is nothing more crucial for an educator, nor more vital to the successful transmission of culture, than an understanding of the value structure of the culture and society.

The overview of the American values presented in this section is merely a point of reference from which a teacher can develop insight into the complex nature of that which motivates, identifies, and gives continuity to a culture and its social relationships. Each subcultural group has fairly distinct values that tend to separate it from other groups. Yet there can be noted an overarching value orientation that identifies an American and gives America a "national character."

In a very real sense, each school and its community have a "character" that reflects a value structure possibly distinctive and unique. The educator newly assigned to a school has an obligation to learn the culture of his school and its community in order to ascertain the existence of any discontinuity between the values of the community's dominant culture and those of the subculture represented in the school. Should a marked discrepancy exist, the functioning of the school as an institution within the community will be seriously jeopardized.

It is not the intent of this section to suggest which values should be taught—if, indeed, they *can* be taught—but rather to promote an awareness of the importance of values in determining the goals of the school in order to insure a "cultural fit" with the goals of the community.

ADDITIONAL READING

American Association of School Administrators, Association for Supervision and Curriculum Development, National Association of Secondary School Principals, and National Education Association Department of Rural Education, *A Climate for Individuality*, Statement of the Joint Project on the Individual and the School (Washington, D. C.: National Education Association, 1965). An excellent statement on the importance of values and decisions related to the individual and society.

Theodore Brameld, and Stanley Elam, editors, *Values in American Education*, a report of a symposium sponsored jointly by Phi Delta Kappa International and Alpha Lambda Campus Chapter of Phi Delta Kappa, Boston University (Bloomington, Indiana: Phi Delta Kappa, Inc., 1964). A collection of papers related to values and education, presented at the symposium.

H. Otto Dahlke, *Values in Culture and Classroom* (New York: Harper Bros., 1958), pp. 41–66. An adequate discussion of values and their implication for school and classroom.

Cora Du Bois, "The Dominant Value Profile of American Culture," *American Anthropologist*, LVII (December 1955), pp. 1232–1239. An excellent, concise statement on American "core" values.

Florence R. Kluckhohn, and Fred L. Strodtbeck, *Variations in Value Orientations* (Evanston, Illinois: Row, Peterson and Co., 1961). Concerned with a theory of variation in value orientation and a method devised for cross-cultural testing of this theory.

5

Social Structure and Power: Education as an Institution in American Society

INTRODUCTION

All societies have specific integrative mechanisms that serve to maintain continuity and consistent patterns. Societies also possess status systems whereby all persons hold various positions dependent upon such criteria as age, sex, familial relationship, and group membership. A particular status may be ranked high in one society and low in another. An individual must learn to play the role that he and his neighbors consider appropriate to a specific status. Finally, all societies possess one or more groups arranged in a hierarchical configuration. Any discussion of social organization, social structure, and social institutions must consider the relationship of these three dimensions of society.

The term *social structure* refers to the various elements within a society and to the position of each element in the society as a whole. The term *social organization* is more vague, since it refers to the total cultural configuration and thereby includes the social structure and its corresponding status-role system. *Social institutions* are organized, established ways of manipulating societal action so that the needs of the individual and the group are met simultaneously. Just as a society has structure, so it has one or more social institutions.

As a society becomes more complex, there is a corresponding change and increase in the number of statuses within it. Specialization, complicated division of labor, compartmentalization, differentiation, and many other intricate factors eventually bring about a heterogeneous social organization in which each individual must fill multiple roles. Formal education in such a society is no longer a family responsibility, but an institutional obligation of the entire society. Thus, formal educational institutions that fulfill this function are recent innovations of modern industrial societies.

Educational institutions are concerned with training the young in such a way that societal stability is preserved. Through education individuals achieve status. As they do so, the problems of formal education become compounded. As individuals become oriented and educated into the existing order, they begin to believe that maintenance of the status quo and its corresponding group power structure is essential. Education in a formal sense, therefore, creates the paradox whereby human beings are trained on the one hand to perpetuate the existing order in a way that creates cultural continuity and, at the same time, are expected to develop minds capable of reconstructing society in order that it may adapt to present and future needs. This section of readings focuses on the role that education plays in the social organization of our society and on the structure of educational institutions.

5-1   EDUCATION AND AMERICAN CHARACTER
D. W. Brogan

D. W. Brogan, an Irishman born in Glasgow, has spent much time in the United States and has written extensively about American life. He was educated at the Universities of Glasgow, Oxford, and Harvard and is now professor of political science at Cambridge University.

Social institutions do not exist in a vacuum but influence, and in turn are influenced by, the society of which they are a part. They reflect the cultural patterns established by groups of people as they perceive life's values and goals. Social institutions are an outgrowth of a culture, and each culture reflects its own historical development. The following article outlines the historical forces that have influenced the development of education as an American social institution.

From the beginning the school in America has been a democratic force. I am aware of the social distinctions imported from England (and from other European countries) in the seventeenth and eighteenth centuries. I am aware of class distinctions at Harvard and of private tutors in Virginia. But the American school (using the term in its widest sense) has collaborated with other forces in American life in making for . . . equality. The school has not set itself against the general trend of egalitarianism in American life; for some generations past it has—in its public version, at any rate— been a consciously democratizing force. This marks the American public school system off from some other systems giving almost as universal an introduction to elementary schooling. It is not the aim of the Prussian school system to produce or to aid democracy; its aim was to produce good subjects, good soldiers. It was the effect rather than the aim of the Scottish school system to promote political democracy. In France, after the Revolution, it was impossible—perhaps it still is impossible—to get a consensus as to what kind of society the public school system has aimed at promoting. At any rate, it has been impossible to get agreement on the kind of society it *should* aim at promoting.

The American school system has never, that is to say, tried to thwart the natural development of American society toward a system of minimal hereditary privilege and a system of maximum opportunity. To make possible the "career open to the talents," to foster the talents, to increase the opportunities of the average boy and girl, to give them the tools necessary for the full development and exploitation of their talents—these were and are the objectives of the American school system. They have been imitated as to aims and copied as to methods in many other countries (for example, in modern England) but America has been the pioneer.

But the American school has been, in the past century and in this one, called on to do more. It has not only been called on to make competent boys and girls; it has also been called on to make good American boys and girls. As I have already indicated, the early New England schools inculcated and supported the New England way . . . and that meant more than a church system. From the beginnings of the United States the

From *America in the Modern World* by D. W. Brogan, pp. 67–75. Copyright © 1960 by Rutgers University Press; reprinted by permission of Rutgers University Press.

schools were expected to make good Americans by precept and parable. Parson Weems and the great McGuffey were important makers of the American way of life. All societies live in great part by what it is not offensive to call myths. For much more than a century the American teacher and the American textbook have been creating and fostering helpful myths and thus helping to create and support "a more perfect union." Here, although the detailed aim was different, the American public schools, like the Prussian public schools, were part of the established political order. The orders differed; so did the aims and methods. But this function of the school was common to both systems.

There is no close historical parallel for another function of the American school system—one so important, so dominating, that it is natural that to it much should have been sacrificed and much should continue to be sacrificed even when, as now, the necessity is not so great. That function has been the making of Americans, the induction into the American way of life of the millions of the children of the immigrants who had come to the golden shore with, inevitably, inadequate preparation for a way of life very different from what they had known in Europe.

. . . The great folk movement that poured tens of millions of immigrants into the United States in the nineteenth and twentieth centuries . . . was one of the sources of American wealth and power, one of the proofs of American success, but it was also one of America's problems. Since the United States was based on a dogma laid down by the Founding Fathers in universal terms, it was easy enough to demand adherence to the principles of the American political system. Few doubted the premises or the promises of the Declaration of Independence or were unwilling to subscribe to them in good faith. But the formal adherence was not enough. How could the children of the immigrants in, for example, New England be made to feel the validity for *them* of the appeal to the New England past? Was the God of the early New Englanders their God, Plymouth Rock and Faneuil Hall their inheritance?

How could they be given the loyalty, the emotional attachment to the past that comes naturally to old societies where all share in the ancestral tradition of good and evil fortune? A defeat in common may be as unifying a memory as a victory in common (look at Ireland, look at the South), but the word to stress is *common*. In a deeper sense than probably was meant, the old name for the public school system, the common school system, suggested a great national necessity. The children of the newcomers must be taken into the national tradition and it must be made real for them, part of their inheritance by training, by conditioning if not by blood. Of course, the problem was not uniquely American. In all the industrial countries of Europe, with populations drawn from the traditional life of the land, the schools were called on to make possible the adjustment to the modern, literate, mechanized life. Sherlock Holmes saw the London board schools as so many lighthouses, and some of the successes and failures of the American system can be paralleled in Europe.

Nor was the indoctrination of the young into a common political belief and a common habit of political loyalty peculiar to America. It was one of the objects of the educational policy of the first French Republic with its insistence on a uniform language of instruction and the teaching of loyalty to the republic "one and indivisible." That France is now in her fifth republic suggests that this experiment in political education was not an unqualified success. In other European countries the school system was called on to create loyalties that did not come naturally, to make good Prussians out of Poles, good Germans out of Alsatians. In Ireland, so it is credibly reported, the so-called national schools taught the children to sing "I am a happy English child," but there is reason to believe that the political indoctrination of the Irish children was not complete.

In America it was. The patriotism of the children of the immigrants was not in any way inferior to the patriotism of the children of older stocks and the assimilation, through the school system, of the American patriotic tradition was complete. This is a success story and should be noted as such.

An even greater success story was the creation of a tradition in the new states of the Middle and Far West where all were immigrants, immigrants from Europe, immigrants from the East and from the South. The task was great, the need was great, the success was great. These pioneers, from Massachusetts and from Sweden, moving into the great, lone land had to be given emotionally potent links with the usable American past in the East and had to be given a usable American present. They had to be given a just pride in what they were doing and a just pride in what the ancestors of some of them had done—and that second pride had to be common to all. The common school had as its first purpose, or perhaps just after the mere conquest of illiteracy, the making of Americans and the creating of a common tradition. We all know the story of the college where a notice was put up: "This tradition goes into effect next Monday." We all laugh; we should laugh. But something like that was done by the school system in the new states. It was done with success and it was worth doing.

Yet if this was the primary purpose of the school system, it was obvious that certain alterations would have to be made in the means, since there was this alteration in the end. In the old traditional school system, largely exported and largely preserved in the East, especially in New England, there was a known, if expanding, body of knowledge that was to be imparted. Once primary school was passed, it was assumed that not all boys and girls would be up to the assimilation of this body of knowledge or would find any use for it if they did assimilate it. That everybody, barring the incurably moronic, should learn the "three R's" was one thing; that everybody should be offered whatever it was that "high school" connotated was another.

Much can be said against some of the innocent but not necessarily harmless illusions involved in the twentieth-century doctrine that no one should be refused as much higher education as he or she was willing to be exposed to. But socially, politically, there was and is a great deal to be said for the ideal if its real justification is allowed for; that justification, as I have suggested, is political, social rather than narrowly "educational." To keep boys and girls at school until eighteen so that they may become sharers in a common, although in some degree artificial, American tradition is a political good and an unmixed good if we do not deceive ourselves as to what we are doing. For remember that a generation ago many of those children, those adolescents who are "wasting their time," would have been on the coal breakers, down the mines, in backbreaking and not necessarily character-building labor on remote and miserable farms. The European observer contemplating an American high school ought to say, if he has any social and historical imagination, that here is a great and humane effort to make citizens and to save children from too-early contact with the necessary brutalities of life.

I shall even do what I have done elsewhere, defend the amount of time spent on games, on playing them, on watching them, on thinking about them. It is a lot of time. I lived for some months opposite a high school in an American city. I was, I must confess, a little astonished by the amount of time that seemed to be spent in standing around waiting for a bus to take teams and cheering squads off to some game or other. I did not, I must confess, think that all this standing and waiting was quite necessary or quite admirable. Yet some of the stress on sport is necessary and is admirable. Not because it builds up the bodies of the boys and girls—I am not sure that it does. At any rate, it does not train them in what is one of the oldest of human skills and is still a very useful one, the art of walking. But sport does unite in a common, deeply felt, and on the whole innocuous loyalty boys and girls (and parents) divided by a lot of barriers. Of course, the success of this unity by sport varies from place to place. It may not work very well on Manhattan Island or in other homes of the blackboard jungle.

Sport is the activity in which American race prejudice, still a national weakness, plays the smallest part. Sport is the easiest means of promotion. Outside the South, what basketball manager will turn down a seven-foot star because he is a Negro? What Harvard man would rather lose to Yale with a team of Lowells and Saltonstalls than win with a team of O'Briens and Konskis? This can be pushed too far. I think it is going too far to die for a college, and I think that even star athletes should be required to learn to read and write.

Before I turn to the critical side, I should like to reaffirm my belief in the unifying force of the common high school. Here is the parallel to the Greek city festivals. Who that has seen the return of a victorious basketball team to a middle western town can fail to see the parallel?

> What little town by river or sea-shore
> . . . Is emptied of its folk, this pious morn?

The answer is scores, hundreds; they're off at the game. And if there is no

> . . . heifer lowing at the skies,
> And all her silken flanks with garlands drest . . .

there is the modern equivalent, the drum majorette.

But the Greeks to whom I have appealed not only preached and practiced what they called "gymnastic"; they practiced what they called "music." They prized and rewarded intellectual achievement as they did physical achievement; they even prized it more. And it is the view of the current critics of the American school system that the American school system at all levels, from the primary school right through college, overdoes gymnastic and plays down music. I think the critics are right. I think that the social function of the school is overstressed and that the United States is now rich enough, unified enough, self-critical enough to ask more of the schools than that they should create a national ethos. It is mature enough, or ought to be mature enough, to be ready to ask the schools to lay less stress on making good, loyal Americans and more on making critical, technically competent citizens of a country that can no longer live to itself or be content with meeting its own self-created, historically justified but possibly obsolescent and dangerous standards. Again to harp on my implicit theme, the United States is living in a new, dangerous, unpleasant world, and its educational system is in competition, as are all other sections of the American way of life. No one, I think, since Sputnik went into orbit doubts that.

All that I have described was useful, natural, defensible; it still is. The social functions of the school, especially of the high school, are not at an end. But one result of the concentration on that social function was not so much the lowering as the abandonment of standards. What was thought to be "education" in a European secondary school or old New England academy was too narrow for the new world. It was too narrow because it did neglect some useful and new and necessary techniques of the new world. But it was too narrow also because, if the old standards had been insisted on, many, many pupils whom it would have been necessary to exclude from the formal instruction would also have been excluded, to the national loss, from the social molding. So studies had to be found that these pupils could master and possibly use later, which was all right. But these were deemed to be equal with studies that a smaller group could master and use. Typing was as good as trig. This was a practical and tolerable solution a generation ago, a necessary acceptance of facts about American life. But the American school system is no longer concerned with American life, but just with life . . . and death.

That the shock given to American complacency by the Russian triumph was healthy I suppose no one doubts. It was not only an awakening to a serious military danger; it was a firm suggestion to the American people to look at their educational system and to ponder both its defects and what can be done about them. It may be that by waking the American public from its undogmatic slumbers (in most cases it was plain slumber), Sputnik will rank with the shots at Lexington or Fort Sumter. It was certainly seen if not heard around the world.

What are the defects now being brought to the attention of the American parent? They are to some degree the reverse of the attractive medal to which I have called attention. If the main object of the school system is social and political, why should these aims be sacrificed to the mere pursuit of intellectual eminence? One answer is that among the urgent social and political aims of the United States at the present moment is survival in a highly competitive world, and that world cares little for the achievement of internal harmony in the United States and much for the distribution of mere material power. If the present school system is not producing an adequate supply of first-rate scientists and technicians, it is condemned for not doing a job that may be new but is one that must be tackled if the United States is to survive.

On the detailed criticism of the curriculum, of the teachers, of the standards demanded and attained, I have nothing that is new and probably nothing that is valuable to say. Nevertheless, I shall say my piece. First of all, only a very rich country can afford a school system that takes so long to produce the finished product. In nearly all professions, possibly in all, the American finishes his professional training some years later than does his European opposite number. He may afford it in terms of money and the economy may afford it in terms of money, but can society afford it in terms of time? I wonder and I doubt. For the handful of absolutely top-flight and indispensable specialists perhaps the time is not too long. For the rest it is serious that entry into the productive field, whatever that field may be, should come so late. And it is so late because the boy and girl at the high school stage are not stretched enough.

5-2   RESOLUTION 189

Fifth Constitutional Convention, AFL-CIO

In today's nation, organized labor has become influential in the power structure. The following statement demonstrates the importance attached to formal education by this highly organized group. The AFL-CIO stresses the effect our educational institutions have on modern society as perceived by delegates to the Fifth Constitutional Convention.

The crucial importance of public education has never been so well understood as it is today. Organized labor, since its earliest beginnings, has ardently believed in the rightness of universal free public education. Labor supported public schools because it believed that educated citizens are necessary to the success of political democracy. Labor also supported public schools because it was convinced that the education of poor children and rich children in the same school was the only system of education consistent with democratic beliefs. More than a century before the United States Supreme Court held that segregated schools were essentially unequal schools, organized labor sensed the same principle and held that no equality of educational opportunity was possible so long as the children from different economic backgrounds were educated in separate school systems. They therefore demanded universal free public education in which the children of the rich and the children of the poor would attend classes "under the same roof."

Organized labor also sensed very early that there was a relationship between education and economic opportunity. Workers believed that if their children were to enjoy a better life than they had known, the children would have to receive the fullest possible education. They believed that education was necessary for both individual growth and the growth of the whole community.

Today there is an enormous accumulation of evidence to substantiate their views. We do not assume; we know that there is a close relationship between education and economic growth, and we also know that the relationship is becoming a tighter one as new technological changes take place in industry.

Nations in the world today which are rich in natural resources but low in educational attainment are poor nations. On the other hand, nations such as Switzerland and Sweden, which are relatively low in the amount of their natural resources but high in their educational attainment, enjoy relatively high standards of living. A dramatic illustration is that of Israel and its neighbors. Israel, arid and poor in resources, but with less than 5% illiteracy, has an annual gross national product of $1,070 per capita. Many of its neighbors are much more richly endowed with resources, but Egypt, with 70% illiteracy, has a per capita gross national product of only $139; Jordan,

From *Proceedings of the 5th Constitutional Convention of the AFL-CIO*, pp. 3–15. Copyright © 1963 by the American Federation of Labor and the Congress of Industrial Organizations; reprinted by permission of the American Federation of Labor and the Congress of Industrial Organizations.

70% illiterate, $118; Saudi Arabia, 85% illiterate, $167; and Syria, 40% illiterate, $158. Lebanon, better off than most of its neighbors, produces $391 per capita and has an illiteracy rate of only 25%. There is, of course, no one single factor which accounts for economic growth, but the conclusion is inescapable that Israel and Lebanon are more prosperous than their neighbors in considerable part because their populations are better educated.

What is true among nations is equally true among geographical areas of the United States. Those states in which the population has the highest educational attainment are also the states in which per capita income is highest. Of the ten states which rank lowest in educational attainment, all of them are also lowest in average family income among the states. Of the ten states highest in educational attainment, all but one have a family income higher than the national average. Just as nations low in educational attainment have low income, so it is true of states.

What is true of nations and states is true even of neighborhoods. The Bureau of the Census has recently published detailed neighborhood studies of 36 leading American cities. Those studies show the identical facts in every city. Those neighborhoods which have the lowest level of educational attainment also have the lowest family income and the highest rate of unemployment. The study also shows that low levels of education are self-perpetuating since those neighborhoods which have the lowest level of educational attainment also have the highest percentage of school dropouts. A new generation of under-educated thus grows up in the neighborhoods of low educational attainment, and the new generation in turn is characterized by low income and high unemployment.

There is simply no question that money spent for education is not a social cost but an essential form of investment in economic growth.

Yet for all the evidence establishing the economic importance of education, America's schools are in a state of crisis, the magnitude of which is little understood.

SCHOOL NEEDS

Concerted state and local action has failed to solve our school problems. Per-pupil state and local expenditures for elementary and secondary education have more than doubled since 1950. Teachers' salaries have also approximately doubled in this same period of time. Classroom construction has proceeded at an unprecedented rate, with an annual average of nearly 70,000 new classrooms being built in recent years. The record of achievement has on the whole been impressive. Despite the common notion that it is difficult to get community support for schools, the fact remains that 72.2% of the par value of all school bonds submitted to voters during the past five years was approved.

Yet all of this effort has not been enough to meet the real need. School construction has not kept up with the growing school-age population. A recent study prepared for the Office of Civilian Defense showed that nearly 11 million pupils are in classes with 30 or more students to a room. We would need 66,000 new classrooms, just to reduce the classroom load to a maximum of 30 students to a class. To reduce the ratio to 25 elementary pupils or 20 secondary pupils to a classroom, a standard widely accepted by educators, we would need 271,000 classrooms. The survey also revealed that 235,500 classrooms now in use were built before 1920 and that 154,000 existing classrooms are combustible. In addition to the classrooms which are needed to replace these which are obsolete and to relieve over-crowding, there is a need for additional classrooms to take care of the 15% increase in school-age population which will occur between 1963 and 1970. This means approximately another 200,000 new classrooms in the very near future. We should not deceive ourselves into believing that this will be easy or that it can be done by a little bit more local effort.

If we set out now to construct only the 66,000 classrooms needed to bring class size down to a maximum of 30, still far from ideal, and if we decided to replace only the 51,400 classrooms now in use which are both combustible and built before 1920, the cost of even so modest a goal would be far beyond present expenditures. If we assume an average cost of $35,000 per classroom—and this is less than the present average cost of school construction—the cost of the modest classroom goal would come to over $4,000,000,000. To build all 860,000 of the classrooms that we really need would cost more than $30 billion.

Teachers' salaries have improved during recent years, yet for all this, teachers are still among the lowest-paid professional workers. A recent study by the National Science Foundation indicates that 38.8% of our college graduates earn at least $5,000 a year within two years of graduation, but among education majors, only 17.4% reach this income level within two years. The $5,000 or more a year level is reached by 80% of the engineering majors, 39.3% of the agriculture majors, 56% of the economics majors, 46% of the journalism majors, and 56% of the architecture majors. The teachers lag far behind them all. More than one-fifth of the classroom teachers in the United States earn less than $4,500 a year. It is little wonder that one teacher in every seven leaves his or her job at the end of each year, with three-fifths of those leaving the teaching profession altogether.

As is true of classroom construction, meeting the serious problem of teachers' salaries will require an enormous effort. To raise teachers up to an average salary of $8,000 a year would require an additional expenditure of approximately $3,000,000,000 a year.

TEACHER ORGANIZATION

Schools should themselves be democratic institutions. The personal and professional security of teachers necessitates the development of a strong teachers' union and the right of teachers to engage in collective bargaining. The most dramatic accomplishment in this regard has been the recognition of the AFL-CIO affiliated American Federation of Teachers as the collective bargaining agent for New York City teachers. Collective bargaining is not simply a way in which teachers can win higher salaries and greater financial security. It makes it possible for teachers to work with the school system rather than for it. Unmanageable classroom size, inadequate school housing, and increasing clerical duties for teachers are a few of the problems which can be better solved through collective bargaining. The entire school system benefits when teachers have the right to be heard. In most school systems, collective bargaining for teachers remains an urgent need, not simply for the benefit of the teachers but for the benefit of the schools as well. Every state should remove any possible doubt as to the right of teachers to engage in collective bargaining by enacting legislation specifically guaranteeing this right to teachers and other public employees and setting up workable procedures for exercising the right.

It is, of course, the young people who suffer the most as a result of our failure to solve the school crisis. Crowded into classrooms, taught by overburdened, underpaid teachers, it is little wonder that so many students look forward eagerly to the day when they will reach the age at which they can legally drop out of school. Approximately 30% of our young people drop out of school without graduating, but in many areas the figure is much higher. In many of the large cities dropout figures run as high as 50%. Unemployment among high school dropouts has reached frightening proportions. United States Department of Labor studies indicate that more than half of the high school dropouts are either not working at all or at best working only part-time. In many urban centers, such as New York, Philadelphia and Cleveland, 50% of the 16–21 age group that is out of school is also out of work, and in neighborhoods which are largely Negro the figure runs as high as 70%. The dropouts carry a heavy handicap when they look for jobs in an economy which offers fewer and fewer opportunities for the uneducated, the untrained, and the unskilled.

A determined national effort to convince young people that they should remain in school until they have graduated has sometimes had an unfortunate effect. Thousands of young people, heeding the insistent advice that they finish their education, have returned to school only to find themselves herded into unbelievably crowded classrooms taught by teachers far too harassed to give them the guidance which they need in order to make their return to school meaningful. In all but a few cities they return to schools that have not thought out their needs. They must inevitably wonder if the program was worth going back to.

Hardest hit of all by the present school crisis have been the big cities. Movement of the population to the suburbs in recent years has on the one hand had the effect of reducing tax sources for urban schools, and on the other hand it has created an additional burden on the schools in the form of a larger percentage of students from culturally disadvantaged backgrounds. Such studies as Patricia Sexton's *Education and Income*, Frank Reisman's *The Culturally Deprived Child*, and James B. Conant's *Slums and Suburbs* demonstrate that the large city schools completely fail to meet the educational needs of most of the children whom they serve. Few cities have made any substantial progress in the direction of identifying and encouraging able children from deprived backgrounds. There is consequently a huge waste of potential talent which we can ill afford. The tools and methods for meeting the situation are available if the schools only have the money to work with. Guidance and counseling are most needed by the underprivileged children who make up the largest group of potential dropouts. These children need individual attention, remedial work in such tool subjects as reading and arithmetic, and well-planned library facilities. But these urgent needs are usually least available in schools serving low income families and minority groups. They are most available in schools serving middle and upper income groups whose children need these services least. It is one of the greatest educational tragedies of our time that the schools are least equipped to help the very students who need help the most. These special programs cost money, but it is money we cannot afford not to spend.

In virtually every state, large city schools are the victims of rural-dominated legislatures. The cities are the main sources of taxation in the states, and they receive too little back from the states under the state equalization program. Philadelphia schools receive back from the state only thirty cents out of every educational tax dollar raised by the state in the city. Cleveland receives back only 50%. Such problems plague nearly every large city school system. Legislative reapportionment is clearly a necessary element for any program for the improvement of education.

A special problem which is particularly common to schools in Northern cities is that of *de facto* segregation; that is, school segregation which arises not from laws but from neighborhood housing patterns, the location of schools, and the drawing of school zone lines. *De facto* segregation is no more morally defensible than segregation arising out of the law. All elements in the community, including school officials, urban planners, and unions, need to make positive efforts to ensure that the schools will be meetingplaces for children of different races, different nationality backgrounds, and different levels of family income.

Equal educational opportunity is a goal rather than a reality in large city school systems. It is no more a reality as between the states. In some states per capita personal income is more than $3,000. In other states it is less than half that amount. As a result, some states could easily provide a school system which would be financially impossible in states having more limited resources.

If the state of Massachusetts were to spend 4 percent of its income for public elementary and secondary education, just exactly what the average state now spends, Massachusetts would have enough money to pay its teachers an average salary of $8,000 and to match New York State's average in other school expenditures. To meet this same standard, the state of North Dakota would need to spend more than 10% of its personal income on its schools. Utah would need to spend 11%, and Mississippi would need to spend more than 13%. Equality of educational opportunity clearly cannot be achieved by the states and localities alone. Only action by the federal government can really insure a high standard of educational opportunity throughout the nation.

VOCATIONAL EDUCATION

A conspicuous case of our nation's schools failing to measure up to the needs of the times is vocational education. Our rapidly changing technology has created an increasing demand for a trained labor force. The need for unskilled workers is rapidly shrinking, and the job opportunities of the future will be in occupations which require more education and better training. In addition, old skills often become obsolete and new skills must be acquired to keep a job. Many workers must undergo constant training and retraining during their whole working life.

A growing sense of the failure of vocational education to relate to these realities of the existing and future job market led the AFL-CIO, at its 1959 convention, to call for the formation of a national advisory committee and to investigate the situation. This demand was more than justified by the 1962 report of the Panel of Consultants on Vocational Education. The Panel discovered that vocational education has changed but little since the beginning of the century. Inadequately financed and too rigidly structured, vocational courses were training young people for non-existing jobs, doing little to develop the skills needed in modern industry. Too few teachers have been adequately acquainted with new materials, new production techniques and new job requirements, and few of them have the tools and equipment which they need to do their job properly. Poor vocational guidance and counseling often fail to direct our young people into occupations for which they are best equipped and for which workers are in demand. Altogether expenditures for vocational education have amounted in recent years to only 1.5% of the nation's total school bill.

As a result of the report from the Panel of Consultants there is a new and welcome awareness in the administration and in both Houses of Congress of the need for expansion and modernization of vocational education. Anticipated action by Congress in 1963 can provide the funds and the flexibility that can make vocational education a meaningful part of our public school system.

The labor movement is in full accord with the administration that all young people, regardless of race, must have equal access to job training under vocational education and under the apprenticeship programs and that they must also have equal access to the job market. If adopted, the Vocational Education Act of 1963 will provide a long needed mandate for the development of equal opportunity in skill training and improve the opportunity for providing related training for apprentices under our vocation programs in the public school systems.

Apprenticeship training is a problem closely related to vocational education. Present apprenticeship programs are seeking to provide the number of skilled workers who will be needed in the future. New apprenticeship programs should be introduced in those industries in which employers have long made a practice of recruiting skilled workers by pirating those who were trained in the apprenticeship programs conducted by others. Organized labor has been working energetically to increase the number of apprentices, but the schools must be equipped better than in the past to do their share.

HIGHER EDUCATION

Higher education, like elementary and secondary education, faces a crisis which can be potentially disastrous. Two factors have merged to swell the demand for higher education far beyond the capacities of colleges and universities. One of them is the growing number of young people who continue their education through the college level. Between 1939 and 1961 there was an increase of less than 7% in the 18–21-year-old population group. But in this same period college enrollment increased by more than 180%.

A second problem, just beginning to hit the college campus, is the fact that beginning in the 1940's there was a dramatic increase in the birth rate. This is the generation of post-war babies that has been straining the capacity of our public schools. Now they are just beginning to appear at the colleges and universities. More of them will be arriving within the years to come.

This growing army of college-bound young people presents us with one of our greatest educational opportunities, but if we are to meet the opportunity, we must move positively and swiftly. Colleges and universities have been financing part of the construction and mounting faculty costs by raising student tuition and fees. Unless something is done soon, our impressive gains in more widely diffused higher education will be lost as millions of Americans discover that higher education has become a luxury they can ill afford for their children.

In an attempt to hold enrollment down to their educational capacity, many institutions of higher learning have drastically raised their entrance requirements. Organized labor cannot accept the view that higher education should be the right of only the very rich and the very bright.

To the contrary, the time has come when education beyond the 12th grade should be the right of every young person. More than a century has passed since twelve years was set as the standard for free public education. Since that time there has been a vast multiplication of knowledge and a greatly increased demand for higher levels of education. The twelfth grade can no longer be accepted as the standard for a completed education. Free public education should be extended at least through the fourteenth year. The best way in which to accomplish this is through the expansion of the junior colleges. By making access to higher education available in the communities where the students live, junior colleges make it possible for low income young people to continue their education without entailing the large expenses of room and board at college away from their homes. The junior college also makes possible a kind of flexible program which is well suited to our needs. In saying that at least fourteen years of education should be the normal expectation of every American young person, we do not necessarily mean that all young people should embark on what might be called the traditional college program. For those who do, the junior college offers a sound beginning. For other young people, the junior college provides an opportunity for semi-professional training, for job training in non-apprenticeable occupations, and for better understanding the world in which we live. For some young people, junior college offers terminal education beyond high school; for others it can serve as a preparation for further work in universities. Ability should be the only ceiling on educational attainment, but certainly education through the junior college level should be the normal expectation of every intellectually capable young person.

Higher education, even if tuition is kept low, involves a serious financial burden to young people from low-income families. Existing scholarship programs, including those sponsored by organized labor, have helped thousands of deserving young people to obtain a higher education, but private scholarship programs cannot possibly help all of those who need and deserve help. There is need for a comprehensive program of federal scholarships to ensure that no able young person will be deprived of a higher education simply because he cannot afford it.

Closely related to the problem of increasing the number of years of free public schooling available is the problem of increasing the number of years of schooling actually required. An active campaign has been waged by federal, state and local authorities as well as by private organizations to keep young people from dropping out of school. This campaign is in effect tacit recognition of the fact that sixteen years is too low a figure for compulsory school attendance. Sixteen years of age became the top figure for compulsory school attendance before automation and other technological advances required a better educated work force. Sixteen is no longer a realistic age at which to permit young people to terminate their education. We urge the various states to raise the compulsory school attendance law to eighteen years of age, with free public education provided through the fourteenth grade or two years of junior college.

In view of the need for a better educated youth, it is particularly regrettable that some states in the South have reacted to the Supreme Court's 1954 school desegregation decision by repealing their compulsory school attendance laws. These states will inevitably reap a harvest of economic deprivation in future years, and we urge them to return to the principle of compulsory school attendance.

PROVIDING FINANCIAL SUPPORT

Meeting America's educational crisis at every level requires the best joint efforts of localities, states, and the federal government. Many communities and many states have made great efforts to support their educational systems. Others could do far more than they have done. But above all it is clear that equality of educational opportunity on a standard compatible with the needs of modern democracy requires action by the federal government. States and localities in many instances simply lack the resources needed to finance a modern school system. Even those states which do have the necessary resources often cannot utilize them because of the archaic tax structure through which state and local finances are raised. The sales tax, which is the principal source of state revenues, and the property tax, which is the principal source of local revenues, are both regressive, falling with greatest impact upon those who are least able to pay and missing much of the potential revenue which might support the schools. The federal income tax, much as it needs to be improved, is still far more progressive than most state and local taxes. Much of the opposition to federal aid to education comes from those who want schools financed by the poor through property and sales taxes rather than more fairly and adequately through the income tax on individuals and on corporate profits.

Meeting America's school problems will cost money—a great deal of money. Building the necessary classrooms, raising teachers' salaries to reasonable professional levels, providing the needed extra services and attention for educationally deprived children, developing a meaningful program of vocational education, extending the number of years of free schooling available to our young people—all of these things cost money. But it is a cost which we can afford. We can afford these things because they are investments in our nation's economic growth, investments in the future earning power of our citizens. Our level of income is high enough to support this kind of an investment. It is not an investment which we need to make on a pay-as-you-go basis. Industrialists who build new plants amortize the cost over a period of years. Families who buy homes finance the purchase over the years through long-term mortgages. The same policy makes sense in terms of our school needs. The $30 billion that we need for school construction is a large amount of money, but amortized over the years, it is a cost which the economy can well afford.

Session after session of Congress has debated federal aid to education. There have been bills to aid elementary and secondary schools, bills to aid higher education, and bills to stimulate adult education. Little of the debate has been resolved in action. There has been widespread agreement that the federal government should do something, but two major problems stand in the way, and as yet little progress has been made in the direction of solving them.

One is the problem of school integration. Since the United States Supreme Court in 1954 declared that school segregation is unconstitutional, desegregation has proceeded slowly. The federal government, under the National Defense Education Act, the Impacted Area program, and the Vocational Education program, has actually continued to help pay the operating costs of defiantly segregated school systems. Federal funds should be withheld from any communities which take action in defiance of the decision of the Supreme Court. The federal government should further take the initiative in instituting legislation for school desegregation, rather than leaving the matter up to the parents in the district as has been done up until now.

Proposals for federal aid to education have also become bogged down in the church-state controversy. No American, whatever his religious beliefs, can fail to recognize that non-public schools carry a large share of the burden of educating the young. These non-public schools face the same problems of mounting costs and increased enrollments as do the public schools. The non-public elementary and secondary schools should receive as much assistance as is constitutionally possible. The National Defense Education Act has provided a mechanism by which this may be done; that is, through loans to non-public schools to improve the teaching of science, mathematics, and foreign languages. Enlarging the scope of aid available to non-public schools under the NDEA might go far toward resolving the bitter controversy that has so far balked efforts to enact substantial federal aid for education.

The field of adult education needs to be better supported than it has been in the past. Today, more than ever before, it is true that education is not only for the young. Adults must re-learn their skills, and they must re-learn the responsibilities of citizenship in a democracy. University extension programs have played an important part in adult education. Union members have benefited from the labor extension programs conducted by many of the state universities. Most state universities, however, have not yet established labor education programs, and a national policy aiding those which already exist and stimulating new ones to begin would be in keeping with the spirit of the original Land-Grant Act which held that higher education belongs to working people as much as to scholars.

The surprisingly large amount of illiteracy and semi-literacy in America is an increasing burden to our entire economy. These Americans, lacking necessary basic education, constitute a disproportionate part of our unemployed, and they are seriously handicapped in retraining programs which might otherwise prepare them for new jobs. A concerted national effort to provide basic education for those adults who need it would open the door of economic opportunity for thousands to whom it is now closed.

America's libraries are in a deplorable state. Library construction has come to a near halt and the shortage of professional librarians is proportionally greater than the shortage of qualified school teachers. Libraries are an important part of our educational system, and improving them should be an essential part of any program for better education.

A PROGRAM FOR THE SCHOOLS

The AFL-CIO is committed to the need for quality education for all American young people, wherever their homes may be, however rich or poor their parents, whatever their race or nationality background. To make that kind of education universally available to every child and young person in the nation will require the best efforts of communities, states, and the federal government. It will require a much larger financial commitment to education than we have yet made, but it is a commitment which the nation can and must afford.

There are many elements which the AFL-CIO believes must go to make up quality education:

Every child should attend classes in good classrooms, well lighted and ventilated, equipped with adequate teaching materials. Classes must be kept to teachable size, with the maximum size ordinarily being no more than 25 elementary pupils or 20 secondary pupils to a classroom.

Each class should be taught by a professionally qualified teacher, skilled in the use of new methods of teaching, competently trained in the subject matter of his classes, and paid a salary which will afford a family standard of living comparable to that enjoyed by other professional people in the community.

Special attention must be available to develop to the fullest the potential of every child, particularly those who have until now been educationally deprived, such as the children of low-income and minority families, children in the large cities, and the children of migratory workers.

The school must be a model democratic institution. Teachers must have the right to join organizations of their own choice and to engage in collective bargaining. The school administration must function in a democratic way, and school boards should be responsive to the needs of the total community, with far more union members serving on the boards than is presently true. Democratically operated schools are in the best interests of the teachers, the community, and, above all, the children.

The classroom should be a meetingplace for children of different races, different cultural backgrounds, and different levels of family income. Such variety in the background and experiences of pupils is a democratic virtue which school administrators should not merely accept but should actively seek to achieve.

Schools must be sufficiently flexible institutions to prepare a variety of students with a variety of needs and interests for their future role in society. Young people looking forward to higher education must be able to study those subjects which will prepare them adequately for their future work in the colleges and universities. Those young people who do not look forward to higher education must be able to learn in their schools vocational skills which are realistically related to the needs of modern industry. Schools must treat skilled workmanship as something as worthy of our best young people as is pre-professional training. During their school years all students should explore the meaning of citizenship in a democratic society.

Because of the multiplication of knowledge and the increasing educational demands which modern society places upon the individual, every young person should be required to continue his education until he is eighteen years old, and he should have the opportunity to continue his education, free of tuition, through junior college, either as terminal education or as preparation for further work in college.

There must be available to every qualified young person an opportunity to continue his education through college and through graduate school. The costs of higher education must be low enough to be within reach of all young people. Low-cost higher education requires much greater public support—including federal aid—than has been available so far. In addition to direct aid to the institutions, there is need for a federal scholarship program to insure the availability of higher education to all qualified young people.

Education is never completed, and every adult should have the opportunity to continue his education, whether he be seeking to learn new job skills, to acquire a basic education which he missed when young, to discover more about the problems of the world he lives in, or simply to find more constructive uses for his leisure time. Our public school adult education programs, our library services, and our university extension programs must be available to all Americans who seek to use them.

5-3   EDUCATION AND GOVERNMENT

S. M. Brownell

S. M. Brownell is superintendent of schools in Detroit. He obtained his A.B. at the University of Nebraska, his M.A. and Ph.D. at Yale University. Dr. Brownell has taught at New York State College for Teachers and Yale Graduate School; he has served as president of New Haven State Teachers College and as United States Commissioner of Education from 1953 to 1956. He traveled extensively with UNESCO and was chairman of the United States delegation to the International Conference on Education at Geneva in 1960. He has written many articles and books. Dr. Brownell indicates what he believes to be the proper interrelationship between government and education in a "free" society.

Political scientists and professional educators have for some years had differences in their thinking about the proper place of education in the structure and processes of government. Some political scientists and governmental administrators have advocated that education be established as a branch of state and local government exactly in the same manner as are public works, public safety, and public welfare. They point to the fact that on the state level the budget for education and the laws governing education must be voted by the same legislature that prescribes for other public agencies, and they argue that the financing of education should be a part of over-all state fiscal planning and operations. They call attention to the fact that the taxes paid to support public safety, public works, and public education come from the pockets of the same local citizens. They, therefore, conclude that schools should be organized and operated as a department of municipalities and of states, run in similar fashion to the several departments, and responsible to the mayor or the governor in the same way.

On the other hand, educators generally contend that education is unique in many respects; some have gone so far as to suggest that it should be a fourth branch of government, in addition to the legislative, judicial, and executive branches. This group would recognize that—as is true for the executive and judicial branches—the policies (laws) governing the operation of schools and the funds available for them to

Reprinted by permission of Dodd, Mead & Company, Inc., from *Education in Urban Society* by B. J. Chandler, Lindley J. Stiles, and John I. Kitsuse (eds.), pp. 107–116. Copyright © 1962 by Dodd, Mead & Company, Inc.

do their work are dependent on legislative action. But within those policies and within that budget the executive and the judicial branches have a large degree of independence from the legislative branch and from each other. Many professional educators would have education equally autonomous.

It seems timely to examine relationships of education and government in view of increased recognition of the importance of education to the individual and to the nation, concern in many states as to the support and control of rapidly expanding higher education, and multiple proposals for federal support for schools and colleges.

FREEDOM FROM PARTISAN POLITICS

The history of education in this country presents several classic examples of what has happened when, in localities or in states, partisan political leaders have attempted to use schools or educational institutions to strengthen their political power, either by making educational appointments on political rather than professional qualifications or through spending school funds to influence partisan political ends rather than to achieve educational benefits. Sooner or later it has become apparent to citizens that such operations do not result in maximum educational returns for each taxpayer dollar. In such cases, students are denied full benefit of the money appropriated for schools because top priority in decisions as to staff and finances is predicated on spurious criteria. The remedy is for citizens to rebel and vote out those who are in power. This usually happens, as some governors, mayors, and political party leaders have learned to their sorrow. This type of citizen reaction comes more slowly in a large city than in a smaller community, but it happens just as surely.

A governor or a political party machine which tries to control college appointments may "get by" for a time. Then the situation is made a public issue. Citizens of this country time and again have demonstrated their conviction that partisan political considerations should not control the operation of education institutions. They place educational well-being above political party loyalty in cases of conflict. They recognize that those attending school are in most instances minors for whom the state has established lay member boards of trustees who are charged with the duty to see that pupils receive their heritage of good schooling. Most communities are allowed to pick their local trustees, and state board of education members are in a number of states selected by citizens. In turn, lay boards are given authority over the program and operation of the schools in their charge. The state, through legislation, sets up the limitations of power and indicates the obligations of these trustees, much as it does for the trustees who have responsibilities for minors in other ways. The educational trustees as the people's representatives are expected to safeguard the interests of minors who attend schools—not to protect or to advance vested or selfish interests of individuals or groups. Trustees of public education, generally, are readily and directly responsible to the people, so that they may receive the penalty of early removal from office if they fail to carry out the educational trusts vested in them by the citizenry.

One result of strong feelings about established traditions concerning education has been that many persons have said that education and politics must be kept completely separate. Such a notion reflects the misconception that politics means the use of governmental office to advance partisan political interests above the general welfare of the people. For what have been considered the best interests of education some have pressed this point of separation of education and politics, and with great success.

But candid observation reveals that in certain situations education and politics have been kept so completely separate that a different kind of problem has arisen.

At the state level, in some states, governors and legislators have not concerned themselves sufficiently with the problems of education to appreciate their importance. In such cases, it has been assumed apparently that educators and boards of education could solve all educational problems. Consequently, when educational needs were presented for consideration by educators and by boards of education, the proposals were looked upon as presentations of self-interest groups, especially when tax increases were requested. In such situations governors and legislators have sometimes resisted more or less automatically instead of examining carefully forward-looking educational programs. Thus, educational leadership has been denied to school executives and to state boards because they were so far separated from the executive and legislative branches of government. This situation is by no means universal, but it is a problem.

PROPER INVOLVEMENT OF EDUCATION IN GOVERNMENT

How can education have its rightful consideration in government and its appropriate support by governmental officials without being dominated or controlled for partisan political ends? Another way to state the problem is this: How can and should education be involved in politics?

The term "politics" is used here to describe the process by which the machinery of government operates. Politics may be beneficial or harmful in serving the interests of the people. Good politics result in good government for the people; bad politics bring about government detrimental to the best interests of the people. One major purpose of politics in a democracy is to make desirable opportunities and services available, not to a privileged few, but to all citizens. Good politics operates so that persons appointed to render public services and to purchase materials and services for governmental activities make appointments and award contracts on the basis of ability to perform the service or to deliver the best goods at the least cost rather than on the basis of "pull and power." Bad politics operates so that government is used as the means of securing privilege for the few at the expense of many.

Some use the word "politics" to describe corrupt practices and undesirable behavior of public officials. It is used in this sense to refer to governmental actions by which public money is used to reward the few who are friends of those in power because they are "politically" allied, not because they are the most competent or the most deserving on their merits. In this discussion politics that results in exploitation is referred to as "bad politics." What some people mean who advocate separation of education and politics is that schools shall be kept apart from *bad* politics.

It is necessary to bear in mind that there isn't one relationship of education to government; there are several. Different principles and, perhaps, different practices should be used to deal with these relationships. Comments will be made on the relationship of government to the operation of instructional programs in schools and colleges; on the relationships for getting proper provisions for education through governmental action; and, finally, on the relation of education to preparing good politicians, i.e., citizens who take an active part in government.

Several principles with respect to operating educational programs in schools and colleges have evolved. Some of these principles are discussed briefly in the following paragraphs.

Instruction by qualified teachers must be independent of control by government officials as to what is taught and how it is taught. This principle is important because there is danger that the power to control instruction might be used as a means of perpetuating individuals or their party in power. The danger is illustrated by what has happened in the use of control of instruction to establish and retain in power totalitarian governments. Educational institutions must be free to develop curriculum and instructional methods as a safeguard to individual freedom. Thus, generally, policies governing instruction in schools and colleges are entrusted to representatives of the people who are elected to boards of education in special, nonpartisan elections.

Instructional policies and procedures must be relatively stable and not be interrupted as the result of political changes. Education is for the benefit of *all* students, whatever their political ideas. It is a long process which needs to be continuous year by year. For this reason governing boards should not change majority membership precipitously.

Instruction must be closely integrated with and responsive to the ideas and ideals of the home and community. Formal schooling has been established to supplement and complement the education provided by the home and the community. Local lay boards for elementary and secondary schools and representative lay boards for higher education have been given broad authority over curriculum so that home and community ideas and ideals might be reflected in school and college educational programs. There is some danger that in carrying out this principle laymen may not accept, even when it would be wise to do so, the advice and leadership of trained people in specialized fields. But generally the principle has been accepted in the belief that it is a safeguard against control by professional educators.

Education must be readily and directly responsive to public action because of its importance to the individual and to the nation. This policy has led rather generally to having local and state school boards elected or selected separately from other government officials—evidence that a distinction between education and other governmental functions is made in the minds of many citizens. But more than that, it reflects the realization that schools are important to individuals whose education cannot be stopped or handicapped, and then at a later time remedied. If there are school conditions needing change, the people want to be able to get at them directly without having to vote out of office a political party that may be reasonably effective in other respects. Here is perhaps the strongest argument for having school boards that are responsible for operating instructional programs elected separately from other officials.

Now for a look at the relationship of education to government as it relates to securing the necessary policies and financial support for schools. It is important for schools that attention be given educational needs equal to that given other enterprises supported by and controlled through governmental action, and that executives and legislators be informed and concerned about educational problems. It is important that these officials accept as an important part of their responsibility the function of planning and providing for schools. They need the best educational counsel possible in evaluating policies and voting on legislation and appropriations affecting education. Educators have the responsibility to provide professionally sound advice. These conditions must be met if satisfactory educational legislation is to be formulated and enacted.

As school needs increase in significance and magnitude, as more people are actively involved in the study of educational problems and in legislation needed to improve education, executives and legislators are likely to realize that the actions they take on educational legislation are important to the political party they represent. They will see that their position will have an effect on how they as individual officials, and their party as a party, stand with the electors. This relationship is not unique to education. It is true about decisions they must make about roads, defense, vaccine, and taxes. Although political parties may agree that roads should be improved, that there should be a strong defense, that vaccine should be available to all who need it, and that taxes should be raised (or lowered) because these are of concern to people, each party often tries to get credit for popular legislation and to place the blame on the opposing party for unpopular programs. Similarly, if educational executives and boards are effective in making a case for school needs, one version of recommended programs may be pushed by one party, and another somewhat different plan may be pushed by the other party, although the end to be accomplished may be the same. The objective of educators and boards of education is to retain their role of professional advisership so that government officials respect it and call on it in the consideration of budgets and legislative programs without permitting partisan political considerations to take precedence over the educational well-being of children.

Definitive principles for determining action in this relationship have yet to be worked out. In practice, states are not uniform structurally in the way they handle the relationship, and maybe they shouldn't be. But here are a few suggestions.

The educational leader who serves as chief adviser to the executive and legislative branches should be a person of undoubted professional competence. If so, he can be relied upon to place educational well-being above partisan politics, just as the chief public health official or chief justice must be expected to place public health or justice above partisan ends.

The staff of the education office of the state or nation must be assured that professional competence, not partisan loyalty, will govern its tenure. Each person must be free to analyze and challenge or support proposals on their educational merits. Educational research and services should continue without staff changes based on political affiliation or the spoils system.

The educational executive should be kept as independent of reliance on the job as possible. He should not be tempted to sacrifice his independent judgment in order to continue in his job. This is true for anyone in a public educational administrative position.

EDUCATION'S RESPONSIBILITY TO GOVERNMENT

Now for the third relationship. Schools do not exist only because government machinery (politics) provides them. They, in turn, must educate so that good government machinery is provided. They must exemplify good government in their operation and prepare pupils to participate as good politicians in all aspects of government. In fact, the hope for *good* politics lies in training good practitioners of politics in our schools. This means that all students must understand how government machinery works, i.e., what "politics" is. They must also understand the importance to good government of active participation by individuals in the selection and support of those who operate government for the benefit of all. They need to be exposed to the vast range of human experience and ideas, so that they will have a basis for making intelligent choices. They must put this knowledge and appreciation into practice as citizens who will inform themselves about issues and candidates and who will vote on election day. They need to be active in political party organizations; they need to be willing to help get people to the polls or to work on election boards. They will be practitioners of good politics who will help to keep politics *good* politics, and politicians *good* politicians.

Students must learn that *good* politics start with the individual and in his commitment to efficient local government. Through school experiences, they should develop an understanding of the requirements of effective and efficient government, and they should learn to participate in self-government. This part of their education will be effective to the extent that it goes beyond the stage of lip-service acceptance and results in the development of practices that make it possible for children and youth gradually and naturally to become full-fledged, responsible citizens.

A much more realistic job is being done in this area than was the case twenty-five years ago. Many students have practice in school government and field experiences such as trips to state capitals and to Washington. They watch nominating conventions, Presidential news conferences, and other political events on television. Such experiences help them to gain insight into the workings of government. Yet opportunities which exist in all communities for governmental experience on an apprentice basis are not always used to good advantage. It would be good for community government and for young people if they were to be given real responsibilities, just as it is good in homes for children to take on home responsibilities. Furthermore, we have not done in any significant way what might be done to have those who teach government learn government operations beyond book knowledge, or to have those who operate government assist in the teaching of government.

It is hoped that this attempt to analyze three relationships of education to government may shed light on the premise that keeping education and politics separated is neither possible nor desirable. Instruction in schools and colleges must be free from partisan political control as a safeguard to individual freedom and for security against totalitarianism. The welfare of the minors whose educational heritage is a public trust must be safeguarded through vibrant, wholesome, and efficient government. Educational welfare and progress demand governmental officials who understand and are committed to quality education and who will develop and maintain policies necessary for the achievement of this goal. Finally, government in a democratic society can hope to serve the people well only if schools prepare ethical and informed political practitioners.

5-4   THE SCHOOL AS A CULTURAL SYSTEM

John H. Chilcott

John H. Chilcott received his A.B. in anthropology from Harvard University and continued his interest in anthropology while pursuing graduate work in education at the Universities of Colorado and Oregon. He has directed several National Science Foundation Summer Institutes in Anthropology and has written several journal articles which relate anthropology to professional education. In this essay Dr. Chilcott uses the anthropological approach to describe the operation of a school.

The technique and approach to investigation of human behavior presented in previous sections of this book permit an anthropologist to study the "school culture" in much the same way he studies the culture of the non-literate inhabitants of a remote Pacific isle. This approach may apply to an entire cultural system such as that of America, or to clearly distinguished social structures such as a factory or school, which are sometimes referred to as sub-cultures; for one can readily see that, although the school culture or sub-culture has developed unique social norms, it also possesses many of the characteristics of the surrounding dominant culture.

When the anthropologist lands on his remote island and encounters the natives for the first time, he must immediately solve the problem of communication; he must learn the language. He may not find the language of the school to be obviously different from that of the major culture, but closer examination will show him that the school culture has developed its own grammatical usage and vocabulary. The child is taught to speak "proper English," and in the primary grades he spends considerable time learning the meanings of words that describe objects and behaviors encountered for the first time. As the child progresses through school, he learns speech patterns unique to a variety of school situations. Thus he will use different speech patterns to communicate with his teacher, his peers, and his athletic coach. A child from a lower class neighborhood or a home where English is not spoken may find the school language a major obstacle to his progress.

Just as the anthropologist on the remote Pacific isle describes the natives' living conditions, dwellings, and associated behavior patterns, so, too, can he describe the "little red schoolhouse." In many cases the school grounds are separated from the neighborhood by a high fence—symbolic, perhaps, of the cultural isolation of the school. The arrangement of the buildings, playgrounds, and athletic fields is so traditional, especially at the elementary school level, that it is possible to predict the arrangement of most other schools after viewing just one.

Entering a school building, the anthropologist notes a series of rooms similar in size; in each, the furnishings are arranged so that the teacher's desk faces rows of students' desks or chairs and tables. This room arrangement appears to have a long historical basis, for the only difference between old and new schools is in the building materials. From his observations, the anthropologist concludes that school building arrangements are based on tradition rather than on function. (Only in newer secondary schools are some rooms arranged to suit the activities conducted therein.)

Each traditional schoolroom houses children of approximately the same age. This *age-grading*[1] forms the basis for the social structure of the school; as each child grows older, he automatically acquires more status. In the elementary school, for example, certain areas of the playground are assigned on the basis of age, and a younger child faces social disapproval when he crosses the "line" to an area either formally or informally allocated to older classmates. In the secondary school, folkways such as the "senior bench" have emerged. This age-grading practice has become so rigid that any attempt to regroup children on another basis, such as that of ability, is resisted by children, teachers, and even parents. Parental concern about proper age and grade has led to the practice of social promotion whereby a child is passed to the next grade whether or not he has mastered or completed all coursework for his current grade.

Rites de Passage[2] are social mechanisms that assist the child in moving from one level of school to another. Thus a child attends graduation ceremonies at the conclusion of elementary school, junior high school, and high school. In most cases these ceremonies have become symbolic in nature; their quasi-religious source has been lost in the dim past history of the school. Sometimes there are even initiation rites for new students which provide public recognition of their new status.

While a degree of status comes with age, even for the teacher, the class status system of the dominant culture can also carry over to the school "society." Children from the upper class often find avenues, especially in extra-class programs, to maintain their status positions. Children from the lower class or certain ethnic groups find it much more difficult to participate in status activities such as cheerleading or student government, although athletes can surmount the status barrier.

As in any native society, the newcomer to each school position, whether student or teacher, must learn certain role behavior. He must dress in a culturally prescribed manner or face administrative discipline; on occasion, a child or his parents have objected strenuously to these clothing taboos and made news copy. In addition to clothing, other classroom procedures such as raising one's hand to be called upon, promptness, and chair alignment are traditional to the school culture and resistant to change. The student or, occasionally, the teacher who is unfamiliar with or opposed to the culturally prescribed school role is classified as a "behavior problem"; he may encounter a variety of discipline techniques designed to coerce accession to his proper role.

An anthropologist describing the daily activities of the school culture will be impressed with the emphasis on schedules, routine procedures, and bells that rigidly segment the day. He will note that the segmentation becomes more pronounced at higher school levels. Within the segments, or class periods, additional uniformity is required; with few exceptions, a student repeats his behavior pattern in each class each day with monotonous regularity. Associated with regimentation of time is the compartmentalization of activities, or subject matter, within each class. The perceptive anthropologist would be hard put to explain why twenty minutes were devoted to "spelling" on Friday afternoons while fifty minutes were devoted to "reading" every morning at 9:30. Seeking an explanation for the relegation of activities to specific amounts of time, he could only conclude that, here again, tradition rather than function actuates the decision.

Like other societies, the school has a calendar that records special events of the "school year." Especially noteworthy are the various ceremonials to which the

---

[1] An anthropological term applied to societies which possess divisions of fixed age grouping.

[2] An anthropological term to designate a ritual connected with crises or "passing over" points in the individual's life cycle.

school adheres. Some of these are national and religious holidays such as Thanksgiving and Christmas, but the majority relate to the school culture itself. The typical day begins with a short ceremony of salute to the national flag and announcement of school activities that are deviations from the school routine. There are also special periodical rituals such as assemblies, pep rallies, and sporting events, all designed to intensify student loyalty. Special school songs, art forms—even totems such as the panther, eagle, and alligator are important to these rituals. At least once during the school year there is a special reward ceremony; school leaders, athletes (or warriors), and participants in the rituals and other activities hear speeches in praise of their contributions and receive cups, plaques, emblems, or pins to be worn as conspicuous prestige symbols.

As in many primitive societies, the school member is subjected periodically to trials or tests that determine his suitability for membership and promotion to a higher status or grade. Series of examinations determine the amount of information the student possesses about the "subjects" studied. Traditionally, these trials are held at the end of each semester or school year; attempts to reschedule them at the beginning of the school year, to determine what the student *needs* to learn, have been unsuccessful. A student who fails these trials is retained in the school society but "loses face" before his peers.

The trials, ceremonies, traditions, and folkways provide a means of controlling the behavior of the student; he must conform to a prescribed behavior because he has been conditioned to the rules. Behavior peculiar to the school has been so systematized and ritualized that most students acquiesce without question. The student who behaves otherwise is punished through adverse public opinion, for social control involves not only the rules set down by the teachers, but the conformity required by fellow students.[3] To a certain extent students also control a teacher's behavior through their acceptance of him; an unpopular teacher can be eliminated from the school society through student pressure on parents, administrators, and the teacher himself.

One of the most interesting characteristics of a culture is the process of change; since much of the school culture is based on tradition, change comes very slowly. Parents feel more comfortable when their children have experiences in school that are similar to those of past generations. In addition, the school regimentation tends to maintain and encourage juvenile behavior through its emphasis on conformity rather than responsibility. Consequently, there is often a marshalled resistance to change in school programs on the part of teachers, parents, and even students.

Since World War II many attempts have been made to make the school more functional. Buildings have been devised to suit the needs of the teaching process; course content has been revised to better meet the needs of modern youth. However, innovators are discouraged by the lack of widespread acceptance of such changes. A recent survey indicates that there is, on the average, a twenty-five-year lag between inception and acceptance of an educational change; in some cases this lag exceeds sixty years.[4] Nevertheless, school culture *is* changing, and the extent and direction of the change are causing considerable furor among teachers and parents.

In conclusion, study of an educational institution by analogy with a cultural system provides a rewarding approach; the "school anthropologist" can readily explain

---

[3]In the following essay by Jules Henry, the means whereby teachers create conformity is graphically described.

[4]Everett M. Rogers, *The Diffusion of Innovations* (Glencoe: Free Press, 1962), pp. 40–41.

both the derivation of current programs and the behavior of members of educational institutions. He may also learn why a child whose cultural background differs markedly from that of the school culture regards the school, teacher, and principal with hostility. This child will be a behavior problem, an under-achiever, and eventually a drop-out until the school culture is altered to coincide, in part, with his cultural background. He misbehaves in and repudiates the school because he does not understand school expectations or because he values rewards of his own culture more than those of the school.

This paper merely suggests the results that an anthropological approach may provide in the study of educational institutions. Much empirical evidence can be gained, through which future educational institutions can alter and improve their day-to-day activities.

5-5   DOCILITY, OR GIVING TEACHER WHAT SHE WANTS

Jules Henry

Jules Henry has done field work among the Apache Indians, the Kaingang of Brazil, the Pilagá of Argentina, and the Tarahumara of Mexico, and is one of the few anthropologists who have done field research in education in the United States. He is currently professor of anthropology at Washington University at St. Louis and was formerly a research associate at the Sonia Shankman Orthogenic School at the University of Chicago. His recent book *Culture Against Man* is one of the more significant books in anthropology during the past decade.

Section II described our cultural heritage as an all-engulfing force capable of molding and shaping individuals as society considers desirable. The following essay is a continuation of this hypothesis, limited to student-teacher relationships in the "average" American classroom. Dr. Henry's opening sentence bears emphasis; it sets the stage for the ideas he expresses: "This essay deals with one aspect of American character, the process whereby urban middle-class children in elementary schools acquire the habit of giving their teachers the answers expected of them."

This essay deals with one aspect of American character, the process whereby urban middle-class children in elementary school acquire the habit of giving their teachers the answers expected of them. Though it could hardly be said that I deal exhaustively with this matter, what I do discuss, using suggestions largely from psychoanalysis and communications theory, is the signaling process whereby children and teacher come to understand each other or, better, to pseudo-understand each other, within the limited framework of certain schoolroom situations.

I think it will be readily understood that such a study has intercultural significance and interesting biosocial implications. The smooth operation of human interaction, or "transaction," if one prefers the Dewey and Bentley décor, requires that in any culture much of the give and take of life be reduced to a conventional, parsimonious system of quickly decipherable messages and appropriate responses.

From *The Journal of Social Issues*, XI, No. 2 (1955), 33–41. Copyright © 1955 by the Society for the Psychological Study of Social Issues; reprinted by permission of the Society for the Psychological Study of Social Issues and the author.

These messages, however, are different in different cultures, because the give and take of life is different in different cultures. At a simple level, for example, a Pilagá Indian paints his face red when he is looking for a sexual affair with a woman, whereas were an American man to paint his face red, the significance of this to other Americans would be quite different. Behaviors that have been variously called signal, cue, and sign are as characteristic of the animal world as they are of the human, and in both groups tend to be highly specific both with respect to themselves (signs, signals, cues) and with respect to the behavior they release in those for whom they are intended. Since, furthermore, each culture tends to standardize these, it would seem that any study of such behaviors, or rather behavior systems, in humans in any culture would throw light on two problems: (1) What the signal-response system is; and (2) How humans learn the system.

Since in humans the mastery of a signal-response system often involves the emotional life, and since in this paper on docility I am dealing with urban American middle-class children, it will readily be seen that a study of the manner in which they learn the signal-response system called docility carries us toward an understanding of the character of these children.

When we say a human being is docile we mean that, without the use of external force, he performs relatively few acts as a function of personal choice as compared with the number of acts he performs as a function of the will of others. In a very real sense, we mean that he behaves mostly as others wish him to. In our culture this is thought undesirable, for nobody is supposed to like docile people. On the other hand, every culture must develop in its members forms of behavior that approximate docility; otherwise it could not conduct its business. Without obedience to traffic signals transportation in a large American city would be a mess. This is a dilemma of our culture: to be able to keep the streets uncluttered with automotive wrecks, and to fill our armies with fighting men who will obey orders, while at the same time we teach our citizens not to be docile.

It is to be supposed that, although the basic processes as outlined are universal, every culture has its own way of creating the mechanism of docility. It will be the purpose of the rest of this paper to examine the accomplishment of docility in some American middle-class schoolrooms. The study was carried out by several of my graduate students and me. Names of persons and places are withheld in order to give maximum protection to all concerned.

In the following examples I shall be concerned only with demonstrating that aspect of docility which has to do with the teacher's getting from the children the answers she wants; and I rely almost entirely on verbal behavior, for without cameras it is impossible to record non-verbal signals. The first example is from the second grade.

1

The children have been shown movies of birds. The first film ended with a picture of a baby bluebird.

Teacher: Did the last bird ever look like he would be blue?
The children did not seem to understand the slant of the question and answered somewhat hesitantly: Yes.
Teacher: I think he looked more like a robin, didn't he?
Children, in chorus: Yes.

In this example one suspects that teacher's intonation on the word "ever" did not come through as a clear signal, for it did not create enough doubt in the children's minds to bring the right answer, "No." The teacher discovered that her signal had not been clear enough for these seven-year-olds, so she made it crystal clear the second time, and got the "right" response. Its correctness is demonstrated by the unanimity of the children's response and the teacher's acceptance of it. Here the desire of the teacher, that the children shall acknowledge that a bird looks like a robin, is simple, and the children, after one false try, find the correct response.

In the next example we see the relation of signal to cultural values and context:

2a

A fourth grade art lesson. Teacher holds up a picture.

Teacher: Isn't Bobby getting a nice effect of moss and trees?
Ecstatic Oh's and Ah's from the children. . . .

2b

The art lesson is now over.

Teacher: How many enjoyed this?
Many hands go up.
Teacher: How many learned something?
Quite a number of hands come down.
Teacher: How many will do better next time?
Many hands go up.

Here the shifts in response are interesting. The word "nice" triggers a vigorously docile response, as does the word "enjoy." "Learned something," however, for a reason that is not quite clear, fails to produce the desired unanimity. On the other hand, the shibboleth, "better next time" gets the same response as "enjoyed." We see then that the precise triggering signal is related to important cultural values, and that the value-signal must be released in proper context. One suspects that the children's resistance to saying they had learned something occurred because "learned something" appeared out of context. On the other hand, it would be incorrect to describe these children as perfectly docile.

The next example is from the same fourth grade classroom:

3

The children have just finished reading the story "The Sun, Moon, and Stars Clock."

Teacher: What was the highest point of interest—the climax?
The children tell what they think it is. Teacher is aiming to get from them what she thinks it is, but the children give everything else but. At last Bobby says: When they capture the thieves.
Teacher: How many agree with Bobby?
Hands, hands, hands.

In this example the observer was not able to record all the verbal signals, for they came too fast. However, it is clear that hunting occurred, while the children waited for the teacher to give the clear signal, which was "(I) agree with Bobby."

In all the examples given thus far, the desired answer could be indicated rather clearly by the teacher, for the required response was relatively unambiguous. Even so, there was some trouble in obtaining most of the answers. In the example that follows, however, the entire situation becomes exceedingly ambiguous because emotional factors in the children make proper interpretation of teacher's signals difficult. The central issue is that teacher and children are seen to have requirements that are complementary on one level, because teacher wants the children to accept her point of view, and they want to be accepted by her; but these requirements are not complementary on a different level, because the children's emotional organization is different from the teacher's. Hence exact complementarity is never achieved, but rather a pseudo-complementarity, which enables teacher and pupils to extricate themselves from a difficult situation. The example comes from a fifth grade schoolroom:

4

This is a lesson on "healthy thoughts" for which the children have a special book that depicts specific conflictful events among children. There are appropriate illustrations and text, and the teacher is supposed to discuss each incident with the children in order to help them understand how to handle their emotions.

One of the illustrations is of two boys, one of whom is griping because his brother has been given something he wants himself—a football, I think. The other is saying his brother couldn't help being given it—they'll both play with it.

(Observer is saying that this sibling pair is illustrated by three boys: (1) The one who has received the ball. (2) The one who is imagined to react with displeasure. (3) The one who is imagined to react benignly and philosophically, by saying: My brother couldn't help being given the football; we'll use it together.)

Teacher: Do you believe it's easier to deal with your thoughts if you own up to them, Betty?

Betty: Yes, it is, if you're not cross and angry.

Teacher: Have you any experience like this in the book, Alice?

Alice tells how her brother was given a watch and she envied him and wanted one too, but her mother said she wasn't to have one until she was fifteen, but now she has one anyway.

Teacher: How could you have helped—could you have changed your thinking? How could you have handled it? What could you do with mean feelings?

Alice seems stymied; she hems and haws.

Teacher: What did Susie (a character in the book) do?

Alice: She talked to her mother.

Teacher: If you talk to someone, you often feel that 'It was foolish of me to feel that way. . . . '

Tommy: He says he had an experience like that. His cousin was given a bike, and he envied it. But he wasn't ugly about it. He asked if he might ride it, and his cousin let him, and then I got one myself; and I wasn't mean or ugly or jealous.

Here the process of signal development is intricate, and children and teacher do not quite manage to arrive at a mutually intelligible complex of signals and behavior. The stage is set by the presentation of a common but culturally unacceptable situation:

A child is pictured as envious of the good luck of his sibling. Since American culture cannot accept two of its commonest traits, sibling rivalry and envy, the children are asked by teacher to acknowledge that they are "bad," and to accept specific ways of dealing with these emotions. The children are thus asked to fly in the face of their own feelings, and, since this is impossible, the little pigeons never quite get home. This is because teacher and pupil wants are not complementary.

It will have been observed that at first Alice does well, for by docilely admitting that it is good to own up to evil, she correctly interprets the teacher's wish to hear her say that the ancient ritual of confession is still good for the soul; and she continues docile behavior by giving a story of her own envy. However, eventually she muffs the signal, for she says she was gratified anyway; she did get a watch. And the reason Alice muffs the signal is that her own impulses dominate over the signals coming in from the teacher. Teacher, however, does not reject Alice's *story* but tries, rather, to get Alice to say she could have "handled" her thoughts by "owning up" to them and talking them over with someone. Alice, however, stops dead because she *cannot* understand the teacher. Meanwhile Tommy has picked up the signal, only to be misled by it, just as Alice was. By this time, however, the matter has become more complex: Tommy thinks that because teacher did not reject Alice's story it is "correct." Teacher's apparent acceptance of Alice's story then becomes Tommy's signal; therefore, he duplicates Alice's story almost exactly, except that a bike is substituted for a watch. Like Alice he is not "mean" or "ugly" or "jealous," not because he "dealt with" his thoughts in the culturally approved-but-impossible manner, but because he too got what he wanted. So far, the only part of the message that is getting through to the children from the teacher is that it is uncomfortable—not wrong—to be jealous, etcetera. Thus the emotions of the children filter out an important part of the message from the teacher.

We may summarize the hypotheses up to this point as follows: (1) By virtue of their visible goal-correcting behavior the pupils are trying hard to be docile with respect to the teacher. (2) They hunt for signals and try to direct their behavior accordingly. (3) The signals occur in a matrix of cultural value and immediate circumstance. (4) This fact at times makes interpretation and conversion into action difficult. (5) A basis in mutual understanding is sought, but not quite realized at times. (6) The children's internal signals sometimes conflict with external ones and thus "jam the receiver." (7) Both children and teacher want something. At present we may say that the children want acceptance by the teacher, and teacher wants acceptance by the children. (8) However, it is clear, because of the mix-up that may occur in interpreting signals, as in the lesson on healthy thoughts, that the desires of teacher and pupil are sometimes not quite complementary. (9) Teacher must avoid too many frustrating (painful) failures like that of Alice, otherwise lessons will break down.

As we proceed with this lesson, we shall see how teacher and pupils strive to "get on the same wave length," a condition never quite reached because of the different levels of organization of teacher and pupil and the unawareness of this fact on the part of the teacher.

Two boys, the "dialogue team," now come to the front of the class and dramatize the football incident.

Teacher, to the class: Which boy do you think handled the problem in a better way?
Rupert: Billy did, because he didn't get angry. . . . It was better to play together than to do nothing with the football.

Teacher: That's a good answer, Rupert. Has anything similar happened to you, Joan?

Joan can think of nothing.

(Observer notes: I do not approve of this business in action, though I have not yet thought it through. But I was intermittently uncomfortable, disapproving and rebellious at the time.)

Sylvester: I had an experience. My brother got a hat with his initials on it because he belongs to a fraternity, and I wanted one like it and couldn't have one and his was too big for me to wear, and it ended up that I asked him if he could get me some letters with my initials, and he did.

Betty: My girl-friend got a bike that was 26-inch, and mine was only 24, and I asked my sister what I should do. Then my girl-friend came over and was real nice about it, and let me ride it.

Teacher approves of this, and says: Didn't it end up that they both had fun without unhappiness? (Observer notes: Constant questioning of class, with expectation of affirmative answers: that wasn't this the right way, the best way, etc., to do it?)

Here we note that the teacher herself has gone astray, for on the one hand her aim is to get instances from the children in which they themselves have been yielding and capable of resolving their own jealousy, etc., while on the other hand, in the instance given by Betty, it was not Betty who yielded, but her friend. The child immediately following Betty imitated her since Betty had been praised by the teacher:

Matilde: My girl-friend got a 26-inch bike and mine was only 24, but she only let me ride it once a month. But for my birthday my mother's getting me a new one, probably (proudly) a "28." (Many children rush in with the information that "28" doesn't exist.) Matilde replies that she'll probably have to raise the seat then, for she's too big for a "26."

This instance suggests more clearly, perhaps, than the others another possible factor in making the stories of the children end always with their getting what they want: the children may be afraid to lose face with their peers by acknowledging they did not get something they wanted.

As we go on with this lesson, we shall see how the children's need for substitute gratification and their inability to accept frustration prevent them from picking up the teacher's message. As we continue, we shall see how, in spite of the teacher's driving insistence on her point, the children continue to inject their conflicts into the lesson, while at the same time they gropingly try to find a way to gratify the teacher. They cannot give the right answers because of their conflicts; teacher cannot handle their conflicts because she cannot perceive them. The lesson goes on:

Teacher: I notice that some of you are only happy when you get your own way. (Observer noticed too, horrified.) You're not thinking this through, and I want you to. Think of an experience when you didn't get what you want. Think it through. (Observer wonders: Are the children volunteering because of expectations, making desperate efforts to meet the expectation even though they do not quite understand it?)

Charlie: His ma was going to the movies and he wanted to go with her, and she wouldn't let him, and she went off to the movies, and he was mad, but then he went outside and there were some kids playing baseball, so he played baseball.

Teacher: But suppose you hadn't gotten to play baseball? You would have felt hurt because you didn't get what you wanted. We can't help feeling hurt when we are disappointed. What could you have done? How could you have handled it? (Observer notes: Teacher is not getting what she wants, but I am not sure the kids can understand. Is this a function of immaturity, or of spoiling by parents? Seems to me the continued effort to extract an idea they have not encompassed may be resulting in reinforcement of the one they *have* got—that you eventually get the watch, or the bicycle, or whatever.)

Charlie: So I can't go to the movies; so I can't play baseball; so I'll do something around the house.

Teacher: Now you're beginning to think! It takes courage to take disappointments. (Turning to the class) What did we learn? The helpful way. . . .

Class: is the healthy way!

Thus the lesson reaches this point on a note of triumphant docility, but of pseudo-complementarity. If the teacher had been able to perceive the underlying factors that made it impossible for these children to accept delayed gratification or total momentary frustration, and had handled *that* problem instead of doggedly sticking to a text that required a stereotyped answer, she would have come closer to the children and would not have had to back out of the situation by extracting a parrot-like chorusing. The teacher had to get a "right" answer, and the children ended up giving her one, since that is what they are in school for. Thus on one level teacher and pupils were complementary, but on another they were widely divergent. This is the characteristic condition of the American middle-class schoolroom.

If we review all the verbal messages sent by the teacher, we will see how hard she has worked to get the answer she wants; how she has corrected and "improved" her signaling in response to the eager feedback from the children:

1. Do you believe it's easier to deal with your thoughts if you own up to them, Betty?
2. Have you any experience like this in the book, Alice?
3. What could you do with mean feelings?
4. What did Susie (in the book) do?
5. (Rupert says that Billy, the character in the book, handled the problem in the better way because he did not get angry.) That's a good answer, Rupert.
6. (Betty tells how nice her girl-friend was, letting her ride her bike.) Teacher approves of this and says: Didn't it end up that they both had fun without unhappiness?
7. I notice that some of you are happy only when you get your own way.
8. What could you have done (when you did not get your own way)?
9. Now you're beginning to think. It takes courage to take disappointments. What did we learn? The helpful way . . . . and the class responds, is the healthy way.

DISCUSSION AND CONCLUSIONS

This paper has been an effort to describe the mental docility of middle-class American children *in their schoolrooms*. It says nothing about the home or the play groups. The analysis shows how children are taught to find the answer the teacher wants, and to give it to her. That they sometimes fail is beside the point, because their trying so hard is itself evidence of docility; and an understanding of the reasons for failure helps us to see why communication breaks down and pseudo-understanding takes its place. When communication breaks down it is often because complementarity between sender (teacher) and receivers (pupils) is not exact; and it is not exact because teacher and pupils are at different levels of emotional organization.

We may now ask: Why are these children, whose phantasies our unpublished research has found to contain so many hostile and anxious elements, so docile in the classroom? Why do they struggle so hard to gratify the teacher and try in so many ways, as our protocols show, to bring themselves to the teacher's attention?

We might, of course, start with the idea of the teacher as a parent-figure and the children as siblings competing for teacher's favor. We could refer to the unresolved dependency needs of children of this age, which make them seek support in the teacher, who then manipulates this seeking and the children's sibling rivalry in order, as our unpublished research suggests, to pit the children against each other. Other important factors, however, that appear in middle-class schoolrooms ought to be taken into consideration. For example, our research shows the children's tendency to destructively criticize each other and the teacher's repeated reinforcement of this tendency. We have taken note, in our research, of the anxiety in the children as illustrated in the stories they tell and observed that these very stories are subjected to carping criticism by other children, the consequence of which would be anything but an alleviation of that anxiety. Hence the schoolroom is a place in which the child's underlying anxiety may be heightened. In an effort to alleviate this he seeks approval of the teacher, by giving right answers and by doing what teacher wants him to do under most circumstances. Finally, we cannot omit the teacher's need to be gratified by the attention-hungry behavior of the children.

A word is necessary about these classrooms as middle-class. The novel *Blackboard Jungle*, by Evan Hunt, describes schoolroom behavior of lower-class children. There we see them solidly against the teacher, as representative of the middle class. But in the classes we have observed we see the children against each other, with the teacher abetting the process. Thus, as the teacher in middle-class schools directs the hostility of the children toward one another (particularly in the form of criticism), and away from herself, she reinforces the competitive dynamics within the middle class itself. The teacher in the lower-class schools, on the other hand, appears to become the organizing stimulus for behavior that integrates the lower class, as the children unite in expressing their hostility to the teacher.

In conclusion, it should be pointed out that the mental docility (or near docility) achieved in these middle-class schoolrooms is a peculiar middle-class kind of docility. It is not based on authoritarian control backed by fear of corporal punishment, but rather on fear of loss of love. More precisely, it rests on the need to bask in the sun of the teacher's acceptance. It is not fear of scolding or of physical pain that makes these children docile, but rather fear of finding oneself outside the warmth of the inner circle of teacher's sheltering acceptance. This kind of docility can be more lethal than the other, for it does not breed rebellion and independence, as struggle against authoritarian controls may, but rather a kind of cloying paralysis; a sweet imprisonment without pain. Looking at the matter from another point of view, we might say that, were these children not fearful of loss of love, they would be indifferent to the teacher's messages. In a sense what the teacher's signals are really saying is: "This is the way to be loved by me; and this is the way I want you to love me."

CONCLUSION

Educational institutions are the patterns of action societies adopt to train their young. In more complex societies, these institutions become large enough to develop their own subculture system, which may or may not approximate the total cultural system.

One might ask: Can the American educational system, in its present legal and social framework, function adequately to meet the unprecedented educational needs of a rapidly changing society? Can the school, so entrenched in tradition, adjust quickly enough to the new demands made of it? What is or should be the relationship among professional educators, economists, and political scientists? Are philosophical and intellectual discussions in the classroom ludicrous and mundane in relation to the real issues in our society? Some answers are provided in the essays by Brogan and Brownell.

Formal education, as we know it, is a device supported by society to insure the transmission of its norms to future generations, as well as to impart the tools and knowledge necessary to the individual's constant adjustments for survival. Conversely, society will consistently reject any innovations the educational system encourages unless they are appropriate to rather clearly defined historical and social needs. Ironically, our society verbalizes its desire for the educator to develop intellectual, creative, and far-sighted individuals but condemns them if they stray from the expected conformity to societal norms. The paradox is evident.

ADDITIONAL READING

David A. Goslin, *The School in Contemporary Society* (Chicago: Scott,Foresman and Company, 1965). " . . . not only a discussion of the major functions of the school in society, but also an examination of the established ways in which influence is brought to bear on the educational process by the society and vice versa."

Margaret Mead, *The School in American Culture* (Cambridge: Harvard University Press, 1951). "Does each unique type of American school really provide the cultural setting in which all children learn how to cope with the unknown problems of the future?"

Hilda Taba, *School Culture* (Washington, D. C.: American Council on Education, 1955). Does the school have a culture of its own or is it a miniature of the larger social order? This book presents the results of a study of the school's social pressures and what these results infer for improved social interaction.

Glenn M. Vernon, *Human Interaction* (New York: The Ronald Press, 1965). An introductory textbook to sociology providing a "symbolic interactionist framework which emphasizes the manner in which the symbols man uses are related to his behavior."

6

Social Stratification/Ethnic and Racial Groups

SOCIAL STRATIFICATION: INTRODUCTION

Modern nations are structured vertically into two or more segments that are usually referred to as social classes. Although criteria for membership in these classes vary from one society to another, such factors as family status, wealth, and occupation are universally significant in determining social class membership. An educator should be aware of the criteria, for education can contribute to the movement from one social stratum to another.

Even more important to the educator is the influence of the social group on the socialization and education of its members. In a sense, each class has a subculture that provides group identity and cultural similarities among its members and, at the same time, creates cultural dissimilarity among students attending a multi-class school.

Considerable research evidence indicates that a strong relationship exists between income and education. The task of education, therefore, is not only to maximize the opportunity for self-actualization and fulfillment, but also to facilitate upward mobility. A knowledge of the school's tendency to reinforce social stratification is paramount if the educator wishes to eliminate those conditions that inhibit the educational development of *all* American youth. An analysis of social stratification in and out of the school is a prerequisite to determining local school policy.

American culture is characteristically heterogeneous and, therefore, America has no well-defined class system that crosscuts the total population. Consequently, the following articles on the influence of class differences on education are generalizations; they are not selected to reflect a static condition but rather to serve as a basis from which to examine local class situations as they influence the teacher-student relationship. The reader should not stereotype a child as "middle class" or "lower class" on the basis of these generalizations.

6-1   SOCIAL CLASS AND EDUCATION

Wilbur B. Brookover and David Gottlieb

Wilbur B. Brookover is professor of sociology and education at Michigan State University, where he also serves as assistant dean of Research and Publications. He earned his A.B. at Manchester College and his Ph.D. at the University of Wisconsin, and has published a number of books and articles on educational sociology and minority groups.

David Gottlieb is professor of sociology and anthropology at Michigan State, having obtained his Ph.D. at the University of Chicago. He taught at Northwestern University, served as a Peace Corps consultant, and has been research advisor and consultant to the United States Social Security Administration.

In this statement from their introductory text in educational sociology, Drs. Brookover and Gottlieb sum up the relationship between education and social class.

There are few sociological reports or texts which do not deal with the question of social class in American society. The importance of the class structure is widely accepted. Through mass media we are told how the middle class lives, what it drives, what it wears, and what it eats. We are reminded that if we want to be identified as an "influential," we should read such and such a book or magazine. Entertainers are cautioned by their agents to maintain a certain kind of "image" or risk the possibility of alienating a certain social class. Concern with how class background affects the consumer's habits has led to the pre-testing of popular music, movies, food items, and so on. There is general agreement that if we are to understand the dynamics of the family, voting behavior, socialization processes, and countless other behavioral phenomena, we cannot go far without considering social class as a crucial variable.

Education has not escaped this influence. Much of this concern undoubtedly arises from the American belief in a democratic society, with a relatively fluid social structure, and the common assumption that education is the means by which equality of opportunity and social mobility are guaranteed. Hence, though much is yet to be learned about the social-class system in American society, there is some basis for considering the relationship between the class structure and the educational system. But before we examine this relationship, we should consider the nature of the social-class structure in America.

THE NATURE OF SOCIAL CLASSES IN AMERICA

The concept *social class* has many diverse meanings, all of which have to do with differentiation in the population of a society. A critical examination of the numerous

From *A Sociology of Education* by Wilbur B. Brookover and David Gottlieb, pp. 153–156, 166–179, 187–192. Copyright © 1964 by American Book Company. Reprinted by permission of American Book Company.

bases for differentiation and of the development of a theory of social class is not intended,[1] but some general considerations may be mentioned.

At least three bases for differentiation of class groups can be noted. Perhaps the most common is classification according to *status* and *prestige*. A second, which is closely related but not identical, is differentiation by *power*. Persons or groups, such as American labor leaders, may have much power in the community, but they have relatively low status or prestige. A third basis is by *sentiments* and *interests*. In this sense a social class is a broad group of people with relatively similar sentiments and interests distinguishable from those of another class.

Much difficulty and confusion in the conceptualization of social-class theory arise because the above criteria, distinguishable in the abstract, are not so distinguishable in the minds of the people who make up the class system. Differences in status, power, and sentiments are in reality almost always involved in a total complex of differences.

One means of avoiding this problem in defining the nature of class differences is to have the people of a community delineate the different classes and identify the members of each. Warner and his associates have made most extensive use of this technique without actually defining the basis on which the differentiation is made.[2] This concept of social class ignores the theoretical basis for class differentiation and attempts to determine the stratification existing in the interaction among the people, for it is assumed that "they are the final authorities about the realities of American social class."[3]

This technique, which Warner calls *evaluated participation*, makes no attempt to distinguish between differences in status and differences in power or sentiments. It may be assumed that these are interrelated to some extent, and that all are involved in the stratification which members of the group conceive among themselves. But people in one community may stratify on a different basis from those in another. For this reason it is difficult to equate the class system delineated by this method in one community with that of another. Much of the research on education and social class is based on Warner's method.

Other studies have used various socio-economic criteria commonly correlated with social class position. Among these are occupation, amount and source of income, levels of educational attainment, religious affiliation, quality and size of house, area in which the residence is located, family origin, participation in organizational activities,

---

[1] For some of these analyses, see Max Weber in Talcott Parsons (ed.) *The Theory of Social and Economic Organization* (New York: Oxford, 1947); Kingsley Davis, "A Conceptual Analysis of Stratification," *American Sociological Review*, VII (1942), 309–321; Talcott Parsons, "An Analytical Approach to the Theory of Social Stratification," *American Journal of Sociology*, XLV (1940), pp. 841–842; Lucio Mendieta y Nunez, "The Social Classes," *American Sociological Review*, XI (1946), 166–176; Charles H. Cooley, *Social Organization* (New York: Scribner's, 1929); Herbert Goldhamer and Edward Shils, "Types of Power and Status," *American Journal of Sociology*, XLV (1939), 171–182; John F. Cuber and William F. Kenkel, *Social Stratification in the United States* (Durham: Duke University Press, 1958); Joseph Kahl, *The American Class Structure* (New York: Rinehart, 1957). Numerous other items may be found in Reinhard Bendix and Seymour Lipset, *Class, Status and Power: A Reader in Social Stratification* (New York: Free Press, 1953).

[2] W. Lloyd Warner, Marchia Meeker, and Kenneth Eells, *Social Class in America* (Chicago: Science Research Associates, 1949), gives the most recent and detailed account of the process used in the identification of the various classes. This volume also contains a bibliography of other works by this group and other studies of social class.

[3] Warner *et al.*, 1949, p. 38.

and numerous other symbols of position. There is no universally accepted method of identifying the social class of a person or family. Perhaps no particular criterion or combination of criteria is equally valid for all communities. In some cases, particularly in rural communities, it is difficult to delineate the class structure. In other cases there may be two or more parallel systems of stratification. Stone and Form report such a situation in Vansburg.[4] In this community the older residents and the newcomers were stratified in two distinguishable systems. These were sometimes confused and difficult to recognize. It may be added that the farm people living in the surrounding area interacted in a third, ill-defined but emerging, class system. This community demonstrates the possible error in positing a single hierarchical class system. It indicated also that there are varying systems of class stratification in American communities.

SOCIAL-CLASS DIFFERENCES IN FORMAL EDUCATIONAL EXPERIENCE

Any analysis of the relationship between class position and education must include variations in the amount and kind of formal school experience obtained by children from different strata. These will be examined in the light of school attendance, differences in the type of education provided, differences in educational aptitude, and teachers' classroom behavior in relation to children from different class levels.

School Attendance and Social Class Position

School attendance has been correlated with social class position. In many studies the highest grade level attained has been used as an index of social position. Warner, for example, found that the levels of school attainment and social class as determined by his *evaluated participation* technique were related to the extent of a 0.78 coefficient correlation.[5] Although not in itself predictive of social-class position without consideration of other factors, the highest level of school attended is definitely related to class. The correlation does not prove, however, as it is sometimes interpreted, that the acquisition of a higher level of education automatically provides the youth with a ticket to higher status. But on the average, persons with higher social position go farther in the formal school grades than those in lower classes. This relationship is also reflected in the high correlation between level of education and other indices of social class. Occupation, amount and source of income, residential area, self-evaluation of social class, and various symbols of class are all related to the level of educational attendance.[6]

At the elementary level there is little class difference in the proportion of children who attend school, but as the non-compulsory school-attendance age is approached, differences occur.

Table 1 shows the proportion of a given age group dropping out of high school, graduating, and entering college in a Midwestern city of 45,000. Nearly 90 percent of the dropouts are from lower-class families. And less than one third of the 27.5

---

[4]Gregory P. Stone and William Form, "Instabilities in Status: The Problem of Hierarchy in the Community Study of Status Arrangement," *American Sociological Review*, XVIII (1935), 149–162.

[5]W. Lloyd Warner, Robert J. Havighurst, and Martin B. Loeb, *Who Shall Be Educated* (New York: Harper, 1944), p. xi.

[6]Warner, *et al.*, 1949, pp. 165–169.

TABLE 1.

HIGHEST EDUCATIONAL LEVEL OF AN AGE-GROUP OF RIVER CITY YOUTH.[7] (PERCENTAGES OF AGE-GROUP)

Social Class	High-School Dropouts	High-School Graduates	College Entrants
Upper and upper-middle	0.5	1.5	7.5
Lower-middle	3.5	12.5	11.5
Upper-lower	15.0	15.5	8.0
Lower-lower	16.5	7.5	0.5
All Classes	35.5	37.0	27.5

percent who entered college came from such families. A larger proportion of the young people in many communities enter college than in this River City group, and the proportion from each class may not be representative of the nation as a whole. The proportion attaining higher levels of education has been increasing rapidly in recent years, and most of the increase must come from lower- and lower-middle-class families. The data in Table 2, though based on estimates, gives an indication of this trend. Although lower-class youth have not commonly completed high school or attended college in the past, the estimates in Table 2 indicate that college entrants from lower-class families now outnumber those from upper-middle and upper-class families, even though a much smaller proportion of the lower class go this far. Continuation of this trend will either modify the correlation between educational level and social class or alter the social class distribution in our society.

TABLE 2.

THE RELATION BETWEEN TRENDS IN COLLEGE ENTRANCE AND THE SOCIAL CLASS OF THE ENTRANTS' PARENTS.[8]

Social Class	Percent in Population	Percent of a Given Social-Class Group Who Enter College						
		1920	1940	1948 Males	1958 Males	1958 Females	1960 Males	1960 Females
Upper and upper-middle	10	40	80	80	75	70	85	70
Lower-middle	30	10	20	50	45	32	55	35
Upper-lower	40	2	5	15	20	17	25	18
Lower-lower	20	0	0	6	6	0	10	5

[7]From Robert J. Havighurst, "Social Class Influences on American Education," in *Social Forces Influencing American Education*, 60th Yearbook, National Society for the Study of Education (Nelson Henry, ed.; Chicago: University of Chicago Press, 1961), p. 122. Reprinted by permission of the University of Chicago Press.

[8]*Ibid.*, p. 123. Reprinted by permission of the University of Chicago Press.

Class Differences in Type of Education

The expansion of the secondary school through the attendance of youth from all class levels and interests has presented another source of class differentiation. The early high school curriculum was designed for the predominantly higher-class youth who expected to enter the professions. The traditional classical curriculum was not well adapted to the tremendous numbers from all levels who came into the secondary schools with the advent of compulsory education. New curricula were designed to meet the needs of those who did not intend to go on to college and professional schools. The resulting curricula have a variety of content and titles. Among these are commercial, general, vocational, and homemaking.

TABLE 3.

PERCENTAGE OF EACH SOCIAL CLASS IN ELMTOWN HIGH SCHOOL ENROLLED IN EACH OF THREE CURRICULA.[9]

Curriculum	Social Class*			
	I-II	III	IV	V
College preparatory	64	27	9	4
General	36	51	58	58
Commercial	0	21	33	38

I-II—Upper Class
III —Middle Class
IV —Upper-Lower Class
V —Lower-Lower Class

*The classification here is similar to that of Warner, et al.

The college preparatory curriculum is most likely to be taken by higher-status youth. The significant correlation, indicated by the distribution in Table 3, between class position and curricula shows that the relationship is present in at least one Midwestern community. Furthermore, it seems that "the prestige bias in the different courses is particularly clear among the girls." One Elmtown senior gave a concise description of the social orientation of the various curricula.

If you take the college preparatory course, you're better than those who take the general course. Those who take a general course are neither here nor there. If you take a commercial course, you don't rate. It's a funny thing, those who take college preparatory set themselves up as better than the other kids. Those that take the college preparatory course run the place. I remember when I was a freshman, mother wanted me to take home economics, but I didn't want to. I knew I couldn't rate. You could take typing and shorthand and still rate, but if you took a straight commercial course, you couldn't rate.

[9]Adapted from A. B. Hollingshead, *Elmtown's Youth*, p. 462. Reprinted by permission of John Wiley & Sons, Inc.

You see, you're rated by the teacher according to the course you take. They rate you in the first six weeks. The teachers type you in a small school and you're made in classes before you get there. College preparatory kids get good grades and the others take what's left. The teachers get together and talk, and if you are not in college preparatory, you haven't got a chance.[10]

This high school senior would find it rather difficult to adjust to the general or commercial course if she were straining to acquire high status or if she were a member of a high-status family. Even more difficult might be the adjustment of her parents if they felt as she does. Parents who envision high-status positions for their children generally insist on their enrolling in the college preparatory course. These parents may consider the general curriculum satisfactory for the children who are not likely to go to college and may even believe that lower-status children should be directed into such programs. Yet they insist that their own children must prepare for college.

The teachers also provide the model for status differentiation between curricula. Teachers, except some in trade or vocational schools, always have had college training, and they place high value on the type of education which enabled them to attain their positions. It is therefore not unusual for the teacher of English, mathematics, languages, or science to look with disdain on both teachers and students in the vocational courses. They may regard these students as inferior in both ability and status to those who concentrate in their fields of interest. Although the teachers of vocational subjects may have a somewhat different view, many of them also consider their students inferior. Frequently, a vocational teacher can command a higher salary because fewer persons are willing to accept positions in which they are expected to teach the lower-status courses. It is not unusual for cleavage to develop between the two groups of teachers over differences in status and salary. These disagreements and the differential evaluation of curricula made by teachers are readily recognized by students.

EDUCATIONAL APTITUDE, ACHIEVEMENT, AND SOCIAL CLASS

Many maintain that differences in secondary-school curricula are necessary because they are based on inherent differences in aptitude. The cold-war concern about talent waste has increased the emphasis on special curricula and even separate schools for those students thought to be endowed with superior "gifts." Much of this attention has been directed to the discovery of talent at an early age, on the assumption that the factors producing high achievement and success are relatively stable. The validity of this assumption is limited by evidence that measured abilities, aptitudes, attitudes, motivation, and other aspects of behavior change over time—either these factors are less stable than is commonly believed or our methods for measuring them are unreliable.

It is generally accepted that there is some correlation, though limited, between ability as measured by intelligence tests and school achievement, on one hand, and adult accomplishment on the other. But the variation in both IQ and school grades from time to time and the other factors associated with adult achievement make early talent identification extremely difficult. Social class and other family-background differences in emphasizing the factors associated with achievement are among the basic considerations in this area.

---

[10]*Ibid.*, pp. 169–170.

A number of investigators have noted that eventual expression of talent may be a product of differences in child-rearing practices. These investigators point out that need for achievement is strongly affected by parental attitudes and values. Exactly what there is in the family structure that may account for these differences in achievement need is not clearly established. Rosen discusses an "achievement syndrome," which he finds more prevalent in middle-class than in lower-class families.[11] He attributes variations in achievement need and intensity to differences in the values held by parents in the social-class groups. Middle-class parents are seen to place greater emphasis on mobility and success; hence their children are more likely to embrace achievement-oriented behavior. Strodtbeck concludes from his study of differences in achievement and incentive between boys of Italian and Jewish extraction that the higher motivation of the Jewish youth can be explained by family-power structure, cultural traditions, and parental attitudes.[12] These and other studies suggest that ethnic or religious values may cut across social-class lines and reduce the importance of the socio-economic background.

What, then, can be said about the importance of socio-economic background as a factor related to achievement? At this point, it would seem, not much. McClelland makes the following observation about socio-economic status, IQ, and achievement:

> Since probably no other single assumption is so widely held among both scientists and laymen as that intelligence, as such, regardless of background, is linearly associated with success both in school, and in life, the importance of clarifying the whole issue is crucial. It should be accorded high priority in any set of research projects undertaken to improve the predictive efficiency of test scores.[13]

Numerous studies indicate a limited relationship between family-social status and both intelligence-test scores and school grades.[14] In recognition of this, the fact that these correlations are relatively low is sometimes overlooked.

The data in Tables 4 and 5 show a typical relationship between social class and both measured intelligence and grade-point average. The children from higher-status families have higher IQ's and higher school grades on the average than the children from lower-status families. At the same time, it must be noted that over 30 percent of the lower-status students are high achievers. Furthermore, the high achievement of nearly 40 percent of the lower-class children in the high-achievement category was attained in spite of below-average IQ scores. This indicates that factors other than social class are affecting school achievement and suggests the avenue which lower-class youth can follow for upward mobility. In spite of the limited educational attainment and lower occupational status of their parents, a sizable proportion of youth from lower-class families are excelling in school.

[11]Bernard Rosen, "The Achievement Syndrome," *American Sociological Review*, XXI (1956), 203–211.

[12]Fred L. Strodtbeck, "Family Interaction, Values and Achievement," in David C. McClelland, *et al.*, (eds.), *Talent and Society* (New York: Van Nostrand, 1958).

[13]David C. McClelland, *et al.*, *op. cit.*, p. 14.

[14]W. W. Charters, Jr., "Social Class Differences in Measured Intelligence," W. W. Charters and N. L. Gage, eds., *Readings in the Social Psychology of Education* (Boston: Allyn & Bacon, 1963).

TABLE 4.

MEAN INTELLIGENCE-TEST SCORES, MEAN GRADE-POINT AVERAGES, AND FREQUENCY DISTRIBUTION OF SEVENTH-GRADE MALES IN A MIDWESTERN CITY BY SOCIAL CLASS OF FAMILY AND ACHIEVEMENT CATEGORIES.*

Achieve- ment Category	Higher Mean IQ	Mean GPA	N	Social Class Middle Mean IQ	Mean GPA	N	Lower Mean IQ	Mean GPA	N	Total N
High	123	3.27	85	117	3.17	104	111	3.14	58	247
Average	110	2.47	25	109	2.43	39	104	2.45	14	78
Low	101	1.93	37	96	1.73	109	97	1.58	93	239
Total Group	115	2.77	147	107	2.44	252	103	2.21	165	564

TABLE 5.

MEAN INTELLIGENCE-TEST SCORES, MEAN GRADE-POINT AVERAGES, AND FREQUENCY DISTRIBUTION OF SEVENTH-GRADE FEMALES IN A MIDWESTERN CITY BY SOCIAL CLASS OF FAMILY AND ACHIEVEMENT CATEGORIES.*

Achieve- ment Category	Higher Mean IQ	Mean GPA	N	Social Class Middle Mean IQ	Mean GPA	N	Lower Mean IQ	Mean GPA	N	Total N
High	119	3.48	92	115	3.45	119	112	3.45	53	264
Average	107	2.86	22	108	2.79	37	110	2.76	17	76
Low	102	2.23	32	99	2.08	118	98	1.96	97	247
Total Group	114	3.14	146	107	2.77	274	104	2.51	167	587

*The data are from a current study of school achievement directed by the senior author. The average achievement category includes only those students with grade-point averages within the range of one standard error of measurement above and below the total mean. Social class is based on father's occupation.

Social Stratification and School Segregation

The pattern of social stratification in many communities is reflected in separate schools for students of different strata. Americans have been most conscious of the racially segregated school systems which have prevailed in the South. School-attendance districts which follow racial or socio-economic class lines are also common in large cities and in metropolitan areas throughout the country. Many central city school-attendance districts are almost 100 percent lower-class and sometimes have a high proportion of racial and ethnic minorities. Many other areas, particularly the suburban, are essentially 100 percent upper and upper-middle class. Although some school systems have attempted to overcome this ecological segregation of social strata in the schools, the residential areas, coupled with the traditional neighborhood school-attendance districts, have produced schools segregated on socio-economic and racial or ethnic bases in the metropolitan areas. Such segregation is less likely in smaller cities and towns, where a school district generally includes people from several strata.

Class differences in academic interest, measured ability, and school achievement may be exaggerated in such schools. The lack of cross-class motivation and the inferior educational programs generally provided in underprivileged areas increase rather than decrease the difference. In a study of a large Midwestern city, Sexton found that average school achievement was significantly lower in low-income area schools than in high-income area schools.[15] Furthermore, she notes that the difference increased from the fourth to the eighth grade.

There is ample evidence that in the city studied by Sexton, as in other metropolitan areas, school programs do not operate to equalize the achievement and opportunities of lower-strata youth. Many assume that this difference in achievement reflects inherent differences in ability to learn. They cite intelligence-test scores to support such contention, but the evidence that these tests have a strong class bias makes such an assumption untenable.

. . . The contemporary tendency to segregate gifted students, identified by intelligence- and achievement-test results, is a type of segregation founded on social-class differences.

SOCIAL CLASS AND THE SCHOOL SOCIAL SYSTEM

The work of Warner, Hollingshead, and the Lynds shows how a student's social-class position affects his role within the social system of the school. These authors leave little doubt about the importance of social class in school achievement, school activities, cliques, and teacher-pupil relationships. More recent analyses of the social system and norms of behavior which characterize schools throw additional light on the effect of social class on education.

Coleman conducted a study of the "climate of values" among students in nine public high schools.[16] His data suggest that (1) adolescents do not always reflect the values and attitudes of their parents; (2) social class alone will not indicate the types of attitudinal orientations held by individuals; and (3) education-al institutions differ in "social climates," and these differences alter the impact of social class on values, attitudes, and behavior.

Other investigators have shown that variation in "social climates" is not

---

[15]Patricia C. Sexton, *Education and Income* (New York: Viking, 1961), pp. 25–28.

[16]James S. Coleman, "Academic Achievement and the Structure of Competition," *Harvard Educational Review*, XXIX (1959), 330–351; see also Coleman's *Social Climates in High Schools* (Washington, D. C.: U. S. Dept. of Health, Education and Welfare, Office of Education, Cooperative Research Monograph No. 4, 1961).

limited to high schools but also can be found in American universities.[17] Clark and
Trow have identified several types of college-student sub-cultures, characterized as
academic, collegiate, vocational and non-conformist.[18]

Clark and Trow report that contemporary trends and forces tend to
strengthen vocational orientations in higher education. The increasing number of
lower-status students in college is probably a major force in this process. Such
students view college education as an instrument for obtaining higher-status
occupations. Gottlieb, in a study dealing with graduate-student socialization, found
that the "academic climate" of the graduate department, rather than social-class
origin, plays a significant role in the changes in career orientation among graduate
students.[19] Among graduate students in the traditional arts and sciences, academic
standing, professional orientation of the faculty, and contact with the faculty are
more significantly related to career orientation than is the student's socio-economic
background.

Several other studies dealing with aspects of adolescent behavior support the
position that there are norms of school culture which cut across social-class categories.
Form and Stone found that adult attitudes and sensitivity to clothing vary sharply by
social-class identification.[20] Vener investigated differences in attitude toward clothing,
sensitivity to clothes, and other aspects of clothing behavior among secondary-school
youth in the Lansing, Michigan, school system in relation to the social-class background
of their families.[21] A scale measuring attitude concerning the importance of clothing,
awareness of clothing, and feeling of clothing deprivation was developed for these
adolescent groups. Except for a feeling of deprivation with regard to clothing, Vener
found no significant differences among the boys or girls from the various social strata
in any of their age groups. These findings indicate that, in spite of differences in family
background, adolescents acquire a relatively common set of attitudes about the
importance of clothing.

In a similar study of seventh-grade girls in Lansing, Michigan, Roach found no
differences in clothing behavior by social class.[22] Through interviews with the girls
and their mothers, she obtained a wide range of data on style, appropriateness, judgment
of quality, basis for selecting several sample items of clothing, and related behavior.
The only social-class difference obtained was from the mothers. Higher-stratum
mothers more often reported that they purchased their daughters' clothes at specialty
shops, while lower-class mothers more often shopped at the chain department stores.
Apparently in this community the socialization process for junior- and senior-high-
school youth has not followed social-class lines closely.

[17]C. R. Pace, "Five College Environments," College Board Review, XLI (1950), 24–28.

[18]Burton Clark and Martin Trow, "Determinants of College Student Sub-Cultures" (Berkeley: University
of California, Mimeographed Report, 1962).

[19]David Gottlieb, "Processes of Socialization in the American Graduate School" (Ph.D. Thesis,
University of Chicago, 1960).

[20]Gregory Stone and William Form, Clothing Inventories and Preference Among Rural and Urban Families
(East Lansing: Michigan State University, Agricultural Experiment Station Bulletin, No. 246, 1955) and
The Social Significance of Clothing in Occupational Life (East Lansing: Michigan State University, Agricultural
Experiment Station Bulletin, No. 247, 1955).

[21]Arther Vener, "Adolescent Orientation to Clothing: A Social Psychological Interpretation" (Unpublished
Ph. D. Dissertation, Michigan State University, 1957).

[22]Mary Ellen Roach, "The Influence of Social Class on Clothing Practices and Orientation at Early
Adolescence" (Unpublished Ph.D. Dissertation, Michigan State University, 1960).

Houser's study of ninth-grade students' attitudes toward minorities suggests that adolescent attitudes vary according to sociometrically identified reference groups rather than according to the social class of the families.[23] This analysis was stimulated by the findings of an earlier investigation in a southern Michigan county showing that though the attitudes of *adults* toward minority groups differed according to their occupational classification, the attitudes of sixth-, ninth-, and twelfth-grade students did not vary according to their parents' occupation.[24] Houser hypothesized that the family was not necessarily the relevant reference group for adolescents' attitudes toward minority groups—at least not for all adolescents. Using sociometric choice data, she identified "pure" groups of ninth graders whose families were in a given occupational category and who chose and were chosen only by students from the same category. Attitudes of students composing these "pure" groups were found to vary according to parental occupation in essentially the same way as those of the adults in the community varied. A student who chose and was chosen only by students from a different occupational background than his own, however, expressed attitudes like those in this sociometric reference group when they differed from those in his occupational group. The attitudes of students who chose another group but were not chosen by members of that group on the sociometric test fell between those of the two relevant "pure" groups.

This analysis indicates that within the adolescent school society there are relevant patterns of interaction which cut across socio-economic categories characterizing the youths' families. Perhaps a similar analysis of the clothing, dating, school activities, career aspirations, and other behavior of high-school students would reveal that such reference-group interaction is at least as important as the family's social class in molding the behavior of adolescents and young adults.

Certainly the comprehensive school which draws students from all social strata provides an opportunity for cross-class socialization. The possibility that such interaction produces a relatively different set of behavioral norms in the school than exists in the various adult strata has not been fully explored.

EDUCATION AND SOCIAL MOBILITY

... The common goals for education in America are the teaching of democratic ideals, getting ahead and getting a better job, and the hope that education will solve the society's problems and make "this a better place to live in." These educational aspirations are related to the expectation that education will function as an avenue for social mobility in American society. Certainly this has been an important aspect of the philosophy supported by most professional educators. This ideal, which has long been associated with the name of Thomas Jefferson, was historically based on the desire to avoid hereditary classes. It now applies to any rigid class system.

Jefferson thought that widespread opportunity for education was the best means for avoiding a hardened class structure, as well as for providing a competent

[23]Leah Houser, "A Socio-Metric Test of Reference Group Theory in a Study of Prejudice among Youth" (Unpublished Ph.D. Dissertation, Michigan State University, 1956).
[24]John Holland, "Attitude toward Minority Groups in Relation to Rural Social Structure" (Unpublished Ph.D. Dissertation, Michigan State University, 1950).

democratic electorate. Most educators agree with James B. Conant that this ideal is far from realized at present and that in recent decades certain educational forces have tended to further stratify our society.[25] Although a classless society is impossible, conditions may be set up to prevent rigid class distinctions, so that differences between the classes remain relatively invisible and ease of mobility from one class to another is maintained. All youth who are able to acquire the necessary skills should also have the opportunity to move into any social position they choose. Such an equality of opportunity requires a provision for universal acquisition of the skills, habits, and sentiments common to all levels of society. This is one of the functions of mass education.

Since 1870 there has been a phenomenal increase in the proportion of American youth attending school. Many interpret this development as a guarantee against rigid stratification and an assurance of a mobile social structure. The validity of this position depends on an analysis of the trends in American social stratification during these decades. Such an examination requires a distinction between two types of social mobility. First, an entire segment of society may change its position in relation to other segments. This is illustrated by the position of American industrial workers. Their increase in wages and the rise in their general level of living, along with other factors, have changed the relative position of this group in American society. The second type of mobility is that of individuals from one stratum to another.

There is little doubt that the improvement in the general level of living for the masses of Americans over the past few decades has not produced a major rearrangement of the social structure. As a rule, positions formerly considered to have lower status still have lower status. It may be maintained, however, that the social distance between the top and bottom has been reduced. To the extent that this is true, group mobility has continued and perhaps increased during the great growth in education.

A wide range of social forces, including increased production, governmental tax policies, and our democratic ideals, has contributed to this social change. Mass education has also been a major contributor. The fact that most lower-class as well as upper-class people have a minimum level of literacy reduces greatly their differences. The former can read some of the same newspapers and magazines and react to many other common symbols.

Trends in individual mobility are less easily determined. It is possible that the masses of people have improved their relative position in society, while the opportunities for individuals to move from lower- to higher-status positions have declined. Many Americans consider this individual mobility an essential goal of our educational efforts.

Level of School Attendance and Social Mobility

Many have assumed that increase in the years of school attendance among lower-class as well as middle-class children carries with it a concomitant increase in social mobility. Although there is still a large difference between the educational opportunities of the lower and upper classes, a general increase in the level of school attendance for all may not increase the degree of individual social mobility. We noted

---

[25]James B. Conant, "Public Education and the Structure of American Society," *Teachers College Record*, XLVII (1945), 145–161. See also his "General Education for Democracy," *ibid.*, pp. 162–178.

the increasing proportion of lower-class students who attain high levels of education. Although this does not guarantee high social status for all individuals, it indicates that education is highly valued by many lower-class youth. Certainly most perceive it as an avenue for "getting ahead."

Education and Downward Mobility

The analysis of education and social mobility would be incomplete without an indication that lack of education may result in downward mobility. This occurs less frequently than upward movement, but failure to attain the expected level of education is sometimes one factor in preventing higher-status youth from maintaining their family position.

Arthur Hughes was a leading physician and president of the Atlas school board, as well as the father of five sons. His father had been a leading physician in town and his brother was also a doctor. He and his family had a high status, which he hoped the sons would maintain. He expected them all to complete college and to enter professions, perhaps medicine.

In turn, each of the three older boys graduated from high school with mediocre records. Each in turn enrolled in college, but none earned a bachelor's degree. The fourth son entered military service directly from high school and has no college experience. Of these four sons, one directs a small local dance orchestra, two are farmers, and the fourth is a factory laborer. The youngest son is a student in medical school.

It is clear that only the youngest of the five Hughes sons is likely to maintain the father's social status. Lack of a college degree was not the only factor in this downward mobility, but failure to achieve satisfactory school grades was certainly one screening device. Higher-status youth frequently are able to maintain the family position in spite of school failure, but school success is one of the symbols of status. Without it the youth must compensate with success in other fields or lose the family position.

IMPLICATIONS OF SOCIAL CLASS ANALYSIS FOR EDUCATIONAL POLICY

There is ample evidence that social classes exist in American communities. This fact is increasingly recognized, but there is still an inclination to ignore the implications of class structure for educational policy and to think of a school program as if it were independent of society. Every study of the school clearly indicates that it is part of the social system and must function within its structure and culture. Regardless of the function that education is to assume in relation to the class system, it must always operate in relation to other forces in the society. It cannot extricate itself from society, nor can it function as a molder of social structure, except as it functions within the framework of that society.

Many Americans expect mass education to maintain approximate equality of opportunity in American society. This implies a relatively low degree of social stratification, low visibility of barriers between classes, and a high degree of mobility within the social structure. The educational expectation is based on the belief that equality of opportunity depends on educational opportunities. Consideration of such expectations of education, when compared with the actual role of the school in relation to the class system, causes one to ask: What are the social-class goals of education?[26]

1)   One answer to this question is that the educator must accept the class system as it is and organize the schools to prepare youth to live in it as effectively and as happily as possible. This position is a realistic one for the educator who is clearly aware of the difficulties involved in organizing an educational system which could achieve the traditional aims of equality and mobility. Many frankly believe that the school can have little or no impact on the social-class structure. This does not mean that the class system does not change. Neither does it imply that the present class system is rigid. This position is based on the belief that education can change the social structure very little. . . . There is much evidence to support this position. If the educator is to accept it, his task becomes one of designing a school system which will prepare youth to function in roles which their status makes available to them. There are, however, some difficulties involved in this program.[27]

First, such a program would require a major change in one of the most valued sentiments in our society—that we can provide for mobility and equality of opportunity. If it is difficult for education to modify the class system, it may be even more difficult for education to modify the belief that the schools should continually strive to counteract the development of class barriers. The advisability of such an educational program may be questioned on another basis. It is possible that the control and direction of American society may shift in future generations to those who would, in the present situation, be educated for lower-class positions. If labor, for example, were to assume a managerial function in society, it would seem unwise to educate its members for a laborer's role only. Although it may seem logical to prepare youth to live in their own class, there are forces which make it difficult and perhaps unwise, even in a highly stratified society. Such a program assumes that the society will remain stratified on the same basis. This in unlikely in a society that changes as rapidly as ours.

2)   The second alternative for educational policy as it relates to class goals is to attempt to maintain low class barriers and to increase social mobility. This has been the traditional verbalized aim of education for decades. The difficulty involved in counteracting the other forces which tend to stratify society is so great that education can achieve only limited success in this direction. The design of an educational system that would function successfully in this way has not yet been produced. Any program that would attain a more fluid class system would necessitate drastic changes in the present educational program. If education is to modify the class structure, much more fundamental knowledge of the function of education in society and of the nature of the experience provided by the schools will be required. At this point we have little basis on which to design a system of educational control, the type of curricula, or the method of teacher selection and training which would insure equality of opportunity in America.

---

[26]See W. B. Brookover, "The Implication of Social Class Analysis for a Social Theory of Education," *Journal of Educational Theory*, I (1951), 97–105, for a more elaborate discussion of this problem. The material in this section draws heavily from that paper.

[27]Foster McMurray, "Who Shall be Educated for What?" *Progressive Education*, XXVII (1950), 111–116, gives a pointed analysis of the difficulties and unlikelihood of this position prevailing.

3) The third alternative is a continuation of the policy in which the values of equality and mobility are verbalized and diffused as widely as possible, while the educational and noneducational process of stratification continues. We have seen how both processes have operated side by side in the schools: perpetuation and reinforcement of the class system on one hand, and stimulation for mobility on the other. This assumes that we can continue to teach the ideal of equality in a social system in which it has only limited applicability. The difficulties involved in the other two alternatives and the momentum of long practice suggest this as the probable future of educational policy.

SUMMARY

Earlier studies have led to an overemphasis on social class as the single factor which accounts for variation in attitudes, achievement, and other behavior relevant to the school system.

American schools, particularly comprehensive public schools, provide an arena for the common or cross-class socialization of children and youth. This is evidenced by common social norms and patterns of school behavior that are widely distributed across social class lines.

Variation in reference group, motivation, self-perception, school "social climates," teachers' and other adults' expectations of the school, and other factors may account for some differences in educational achievement and other school behavior which have been attributed to social class. Much more examination of such intervening variables is needed.

The large number of lower-class youth who enter and complete extended programs of higher education demonstrates that education provides a relatively clear opportunity for social mobility in American society. Although class differences exist, increasingly large proportions of undergraduate and graduate student bodies are drawn from the lower strata of the society.

The assumption that social classes differ in the value they attach to education is questioned. In contrast, the demand for equal educational opportunities indicates that lower socio-economic groups place a high premium on education. Differences in consumption of higher education may be due to the fact that lower-strata persons are less sophisticated in knowing how to operate in the educational bureaucracy and in relating specific educational programs to their aspirations.

6-2 EDUCATION AND SOCIAL CLASS IN AMERICA

William H. Burton

William H. Burton was, following his retirement from Harvard, consultant to the Oregon State University Department of Education and a part-time faculty member at Oregon College of Education. He studied at Oregon and Columbia Universities and received his Ph.D. from the University of Chicago. He taught in rural schools in Oregon; at the State College of Washington; and at Cincinnati, Chicago, Southern California, and Harvard Universities. He authored many books and contributed extensively to educational journals. In this paper Dr. Burton indicates the need for familiarity with both the psychological and sociological influences of growth and development on learning.

. . . Education for all the children of all the people without let or hindrance, without invidious distinctions of any kind, has been an aspiration and goal of life in our country from the beginning. The dream and the goal has already presented one challenge which we have partially met. A second and more fateful challenge may be emerging.

BRIEF HISTORICAL BACKGROUND

The first Americans lost very little time in setting up schools. The laws of 1642 and 1647 in Massachusetts Bay Colony requiring that free schools be provided in every village became the basis of our tax-supported schools. The early leaders, however, made no provision to compel parents to take advantage of the schools. We might speculate as to the causes. Was learning so respected that no one dreamed of failure to take advantage of schooling freely offered? Doubtless this was a factor along with other circumstances.

The first law requiring children to go to school was not passed until 1852, almost exactly two centuries after the first laws providing for schools. The last state to pass such a law did so in 1918 although practically all states had such laws by 1900. A process of lengthening the compulsory period and of sharply tightening these laws has gone on since approximately 1900 and particularly since 1915. We need not go into the causes for this, since our purpose for the moment is directed to the effects.

THE EFFECT OF COMPULSORY ATTENDANCE

The eventual effect was that from 1915 onward our democratic dream of education for all the children of all the people became, on the elementary level, an actuality. Therein lay our first and serious challenge.

The school of the United States, despite our aspiration, was until the present

From *Harvard Educational Review*, XXIII, No. 4 (Fall 1953), 243–256. Copyright © 1953 by the President and Fellows of Harvard College; reprinted by permission of *Harvard Educational Review*.

century an aristocratic or class school. It catered largely to the so-called "better" classes. Oversimplifying, we may characterize the early school as one organized:

a. for children who wished to attend or whose families wished them to attend.

b. for children with the interest and (generally) the ability to get along in the abstract and verbal schooling then offered.

c. for children who were probably going beyond the first levels and whose families supported the ambition for more schooling.

Now then, what happened? Into the school so organized came hordes of children who:

a. did not wish to attend and whose families often did not value education.

b. had no interest and little ability (generally) for the type of education offered.

c. were not going to school beyond the compulsory limit and whose families (generally) supported the exodus into some gainful occupation.

In addition to all the normal children came the lame, the halt, and the blind, the tubercular, the undernourished, the mentally deficient, the already delinquent.

Part 1. The First Challenge to Our Schools: To Develop a Minimum Literacy and Simple Fundamentals of Citizenship

For the first time in all history a nation and its schools were called upon to educate all the children of all the people—and do it in the school so far designed for the selected few. We accepted the challenge, but not at first.

The first reaction of the school was to maintain the historic and traditional materials and methods. This was education and had been for some centuries. The "best people" had long approved it. If the "new people" now coming to school could not master it, could not learn, they merely represented proof of an ancient belief that the common people were unfit for education. A sad and tragic era ensued. Elimination from school was shockingly great. The army and census figures showed that in 1914 less than fifty percent of adult Americans had finished the sixth grade. The harsh and unsympathetic treatment caused the elimination and must have been a factor also in much delinquency and bad citizenship.

One of the great glories of our democracy and of our educational leadership is that we eventually accepted the challenge to meet this unprecedented situation—to educate all the children of all the people.

The turn of the century saw the development of the first so-called intelligence tests and the first subject matter achievement tests. Faulty as the early instruments were, they opened great new vistas. The huge range and nature of individual differences, commonplace now, gave new purposes and directions to the school. Eventually great amounts of information became available showing that the intellectual ability to handle abstractions was not the only kind of intelligence. Other important mental, social, and motor abilities came in for consideration. The range and complexity of special abilities and of special disabilities was increasingly understood. Diagnostic methods and the increasing knowledge of causes of disabilities encouraged the development of so-called remedial measure.

A great body of new knowledge was also being developed in psychology generally, in learning theory and process particularly. Factors far outside the schoolroom were now known to affect achievement in class. Research supplied more new material on personality development, and eventually on causes of personal maladjustment. Controls of behavior such as behavior patterns, constellations of understandings, attitudes, abilities and skills came to be recognized as highly desirable products of education and of learning, along with the typical subject matter outcomes of the traditional school.

The dynamic nature of our democracy, together with far better understanding of democracy, not merely as a political process but as a social theory and way of life, increasingly affected our educational belief and practice.

The educational system of the United States, aided by the great resources in new knowledge, met the challenge, namely, to develop an education to serve the wide range of individual differences brought to the school by the influx of all the children of all the people. The most extensive revolution in curriculum content and in methods of instruction ever seen eventually emerged. An important fact, which becomes more important as we consider later the second challenge, is that the answer to the first challenge was aimed at the personal goal of minimum literacy with introduction to citizenship as the only social goal considered. Individual differences between and among persons was the key. This was simple business compared to the new challenge now emerging.

SUCCESS HAS BEEN FAR GREATER ON THE ELEMENTARY LEVEL THAN ON THE SECONDARY

The educational revolution to date is confined largely to the elementary school. The elementary level, both leadership and rank and file, is committed in theory and well on the way in practice to real adjustment to the range of individual differences. Hopelessly unfit curriculums and instructional methods persist, but the main battle has been won.

The challenge did not confront the secondary school until the 1930's and stemmed from a set of circumstances different from those which confronted the elementary school. The compulsory attendance laws did affect the secondary schools somewhat, but the huge increase in enrollment followed the depression and the fundamental change in the labor market. The application of the principles of democracy is having some effect but so far chiefly on theory.

The secondary school with approximately seventy percent or more of eligible students enrolled is now challenged as was the elementary school a third of a century earlier. The leadership in American secondary education is keenly aware of the facts and of the situations created. Individual secondary school staffs here and there are making magnificent efforts to meet the challenge. The secondary school generally, however, is relatively untouched by the developments of the first half of the twentieth century. Again we cannot digress into causes; we are concerned for the moment with the facts and possible effects. Conditions within the huge majority of secondary schools are similar to those in the elementary schools before the revolutionary changes. Curriculums and methods are still formal, abstract, verbal, and unrealistic. Students are not introduced in any sensible way to the century in which they live, to its truly great strengths and achievements, to its dangerous tensions, to its imminent and fateful decisions. Certainly they are given no guidance for the second half of the century in which they will live and participate in decisions. So far nothing much has happened beyond tinkering with curriculums and methods. Excellent theoretical proposals are available, but resistance on the practical level is unbelievably stubborn.

The second challenge, discussed below, affects chiefly the secondary school as the first did the elementary school, though both are vitally involved. Failure to meet this challenge may result in (a) the relegation of the present type of secondary school to the status of an extra-curricular activity with a new institution rising to meet the challenge, or (b) in a serious blow to the advancement of democracy in the United States. The first challenge was reasonably well met when all types and conditions of children were given the opportunity to achieve literacy and an introduction to our democratic citizenship. The second challenge is far more complex, aiming at that degree of cultural literacy, moral responsibility, creativity, necessary for the constant upgrading of democracy.

Part II. The Second Challenge Emerges: To Develop Cultural Unity within a Diverse Society Simultaneously with Development of Individual Talent

The scientific research and philosophic inquiries of the first quarter of the century made us aware of individual differences among learners, of the importance of personality development, and of the principles of democracy as applied to individuals. The second quarter of the century saw the development of another great body of new knowledge, this time in group dynamics, the democratic implications of group discussion and decision, in human relations and particularly in social and cultural anthropology. The anthropologists have demonstrated the social class structure of our society. The implications of these findings raise certain serious questions and present a basic challenge to our society and particularly to the schools.

The people of the United States have been committed from earliest times to a theory of society in which there are no classes, or at least no absolutely insuperable class barriers. Any man, we assert, is free to improve his status, that is, to move upward in the social structure. Education is one of the means, if not the chief means through which the individual may improve himself and his social status. All our far-flung structure of free schools flows from this, plus our insistence enacted into law that all must be exposed to education for a stated number of years.

As we shall see, a number of grave questions arise when we examine theory and practice both in social process and in educational practice. Before proceeding to these questions, let us examine some of the immediate facts, practices, and implications.

THE IMMEDIATE IMPLICATIONS FOR EDUCATION OF THE SOCIAL CLASS STRUCTURE

The culture in general and the particular segment of the culture within which the individual grows up influence learning and behavior in a fundamental manner. Teacher education, until recently, has neglected this vital factor affecting education.

Cultures impose upon their participants a basic set of values and social habits for controlling everyday life activities. Certain general roles are expected of all children as they grow up: a sex role, an age role, and in developed cultures a social class role. A caste role based on race, color, or creed may sometimes be present.

Each child brings to school a collection of values, beliefs, and attitudes, plus behavior patterns through which the values and meanings are expressed. Cultural factors over which he has no control play an important part in making him what he is. These factors are, of course, affected by and affect the biological processes of growth or maturation, the range of individual differences, the interests, purposes, and needs which the individual develops. The constellation of influences playing upon the child is complex; the effects of single components are difficult to trace. Influence is often subtle and hidden from casual observation. Anyone who rears or teaches children must, however, possess such facts as we have at this time. Equally one must be cautious in drawing generalizations, in attributing certain results to one or another factor without reference to the total picture. There is no such thing as "the child." Each one is "a child" with his unique collection of beliefs and behaviors.

The social classes differ materially in approving or stigmatizing certain beliefs, values, and behaviors and in their regard for education. Middle and upper classes particularly stigmatize, in the lower classes, what the upper classes call laziness, shiftlessness, irresponsibility, ignorance, immorality. Within the lower classes, however, some of these are accepted ways of behavior, possessing background and rationale. The lower classes are likely to resent in the upper classes what lower class individuals call "snootiness" or snobbery, good manners, proper language, lack of aggressiveness, or unwillingness to fight.

The middle and the upper-lower classes also believe in and impress on the children the value of "getting ahead" or of "bettering one's self" in life. Children in the middle class largely resist strongly the class values and habits imposed upon them, preferring the less controlled behaviors of the lower classes. Children in the lower classes quite generally accept the values and behaviors of their class. Significantly the latter group is often unaware that its language, manners, and standards are quite unacceptable within other groups.

The efforts of parents and teachers to socialize children precipitates constant conflict between the psychological drives of children and the pressures of the culture. The child's need for physical activity, for sensory enjoyment, for self-direction, and for prestige with age mates fights hard against restraints, controls, and demands for conformance.

Many of the conflicts between parents and children or teachers and children result from grave lack of insight into the nature and effects of constant pressure, open or subtle, to conform to social values and roles. Parents and teachers regard the procedures they use in socializing children as natural and desirable. The *adults* are not even aware that there is any pressure. The *children* are keenly aware of it. The emotional cost to both may be very high. Parents and teachers become irritated and angry. Children become destructive, antagonistic, or sullen, or retreat into periods of negativism. These are not manifestations of "original sin" or of an evil disposition; they are but defenses against the constant "cultural bombardment." The more social the requirements, the more arbitrary and unjust they seem to the "natural" child.

Certain further facts may be summarized briefly as follows:

First, it is important to know that the children in our schools are drawn from the social classes in approximately these percentages: three percent from the upper class, thirty-eight from the middle class, and fifty-eight from the lower class.

Second, the teaching body, in contrast, is drawn largely from the middle class. Many teachers simply cannot communicate with lower-class children and have no idea of the beliefs and motives of these children. The children in turn trying to communicate are abashed at criticism of their language and behavior which is quite acceptable within their own social group.

Third, the school has generally been geared to the aims, ambitions, moral or ethical standards of the white, prosperous middle class, Protestant, Anglo-Saxon population.

Fourth, the school is not organized to capitalize upon the nonverbal types of intelligence often found among children who have not had access to or constant contacts with books. The school often does not recognize the emergence of high intelligence and creative behavior in forms other than the abstract verbal type long fostered by the school.

The school generally attempts to impose middle class values upon huge numbers of lower-class children. Problems, assignments, projects set by the school are, therefore, not at all the same problems when tackled simultaneously by upper- and lower-class children. The motivations are not at all alike. Many lower-class children simply do not value the objectives and processes of the school, hence do not try. The school immediately dubs these children "unintelligent," "uncooperative," or "stubborn." The old class clichés may enter; the children are lazy, shiftless, irresponsible. The facts are that the school often simply does not meet their needs or ambitions, does not operate within their framework of values and motivations. The very tests of intelligence (so-called) and of achievement are now known to be heavily weighted toward middle-class experience, knowledge, values, and beliefs. The lower-class child, to use his own expression, "Can't win." The school does not give its typical rewards generally to lower-class children.

Fifth, the school achievements and the degree of understanding and loyalty to our society and culture are thus definitely affected by the class origins of the children.

The middle-class regime simply does not socialize the lower-class children. They are neither believers nor participants in the cultural heritage of middle-class society. The method of cultural training used by the school has basic effects upon children's *inward acceptance* of cultural objectives, as differentiated from outward conformance. The effects upon morality, delinquency, mental hygiene, and personality development generally are often not what the school thinks they are. We know now that learning situations wherein the child can identify himself with the total social group including adults are far more effective than methods of imposition and pressure.

Sixth, we should note, though this is not strictly a class structure matter, that the gifted child in our schools is often as sadly neglected and unstimulated as is the lower class child.

The school is challenged under the American faith to develop integration and unity within our diverse society; to develop persons possessing, in terms of their capacities, cultural insight, standards, taste, and above all moral responsibility; persons committed to the democratic process in our national life and in the world.

The eight-point discussion which follows is based upon acceptance of the historic American beliefs about society, the individual, and education. Certain very serious questions about the acceptance of these beliefs and the effect of changing beliefs upon education are reserved for the very end of this article.

Detailed development of this challenge would fill a volume. A series of statements with brief supporting discussion must suffice here.

1. All levels of educational workers should be familiar with the structure of our society; particularly with the summaries of the characteristics of the several social classes making up our society.

The processes of education, of learning, and of teaching can be based only upon the experiential background, the goals and motivations of the learner. This is a commonplace. Any extension of experience, improvement of goals and motivations can be achieved only by methods which do not ignore or insult the learner's origins and present value system, thus preserving his security while challenging to growth and improvement.

2. All levels of educational workers should be familiar with the structure of human personality and the conditions of its growth.

3. All levels of educational workers should be sensitive to efforts to state the over-all goal for our society and for education within that society; should constantly engage in critical analysis designed to keep these goals abreast of new knowledge about society and persons.

The desired goals in any dynamic society are in constant need of critical analysis, reassessment, and restatement. A common cultural background making for common aims, beliefs, and loyalties, together with provision for free development of individuality and creativity are essential to any society.

The values and beliefs of any one social class cannot be imposed upon the society. Several writers have pointed out that certain values and processes of the lower class, usually ignored, may well possess social value. The characteristics of a desirable personality, of desirable social process, desirable social institutions need to be restated constantly as new knowledge and insight appear. The implications of the general aim for the more immediate cultural and personal objectives need to be stated in far greater detail than heretofore and far more clearly. We will doubtless always have social classes, but equally important is the preservation of upward mobility and the development of necessary cultural integration and unity.

4. All educational workers should be constantly engaged in the reorganization of curriculum materials and instructional processes with special reference to our new knowledge concerning the nature of our society.

The curriculum movement has been under way for some time in our society and will continue under the impetus of new knowledge, which in fact has been the case always.

Several pages could be filled, at this point, with illustrations. Details of curriculum content and instructional procedures could be listed, all showing the almost complete neglect of the facts concerning the structure, problems, tensions, and maladjustments growing out of this special situation.

Books used in beginning reading practically never base content upon the experience known to the whole range of children using the books. The experience of the huge majority is, in fact, usually ignored. The very books designed to teach children to read actually cannot be read by some of the children. Not a single series of readers includes the experience of lower-class children. Certain authors of individual books for free reading by children have boldly broken with tradition and are presenting the lives of many different types within our society. Books such as *Steppin' and Family* by Hope Newell, and *Tobe* by Stella Gentry Sharpe tell of the Negro without caricaturing him. *New Broome Experiment* by Adam Allen portrays the stupidity of anti-Semitism, while John R. Tunis in *The Keystone Kids* aims at breaking down prejudice against any minority. *Blue Willow* by Doris Gate is the story of a family of sharecroppers, while Caroline R. Stone's *Inga of Porcupine Mine* tells of miners' families in Michigan. Eleanor Estes is the author of books dealing with people who are not especially prosperous. These are but promises of what must appear in all subject areas.

History and geography are often presented with no bridge from the backgrounds of meaning possessed by the children. The lack of background necessary to understand is usually ignored. Verbal presentations of places the children will never see are unrelieved by any aids toward reality. Equally, no attention is paid to the possible use and value of these materials in the lives of the particular children being taught.

Details, as stated, could be multiplied indefinitely. The result is an education consisting too largely of verbalisms about the nature and problems of our society, instead of experience with social organization and decision making. The outcomes are glib repetition of the verbalisms with no understanding and certainly no appropriate patterns of behavior.

A sweeping and fundamental revision in curriculum materials and instructional processes is needed. The important curriculum movement already present in our schools needs redirection. The attention given to individual differences in ability, in types of interest and endeavor, in achievement should now be supplemented with attention to the facts concerning differences between and among discernible groups.

The basic revision of the nature and distribution of the rewards of the school, marks, prizes, special recognition of any type, the methods of reporting and using evaluations is a part of this curricular development.

5. All educational workers should study the field and processes of the communication arts, with special reference to communication between and among groups of differing backgrounds, goals, and values.

6. All educational workers should be able practitioners of the group process, and of leadership therein.

7. All educational workers should work for increased school-community interaction.

This has always been important and is doubly so in light of the knowledge about the social structure of the community. Only through genuine interaction can educational workers understand the community (from local to international level), and the community understand classroom procedures and the purposes of education.

8. Education is challenged above all to be real.

An education based on words and gained through words has always been a poor preparation for a world of things and persons. Now it is doubly incompetent. Talking about the tensions and maladjustments of our society, of the effect on our society of differing class values and ambitions is not the same as participating in these problems. The strength and achievements of our society can be learned and will beget loyalty only through participation.

TEACHER EDUCATION AND THE NEW CHALLENGE

The sharpest focus in all this is on teacher education. A number of bold, creative efforts are appearing. New patterns of provocative and promising nature are under trial. In general, however, many engaged in teacher education are incredibly unaware of the nature of the society in which they live, incredibly unaware of the problems of many types of persons trying to live in our changing, insecure, and frightening world. The practice in the field is far too often a soggy mediocrity.

The public does not pay for the teacher or the teaching we need—and thereby may hang a disastrous story in the future. This should not prevent our stating goals and working for them.

The teacher should be an educated person, loyal to his own society but a part of the world society also. A teacher who is to inspire respect for the basic values of the society in which the learner is to live must know and believe in the long cultural history of that society. A teacher who is to aid learners to face courageously our changing, often insecure and frightening world, must know why society is in revolution currently; must know how human beings live and grow, must know their motivations and frustrations, their cultural likenesses and differences. A teacher fundamentally ignorant of the structure of his society, and equally ignorant concerning the growth of human personality, cannot aid individuals to become citizens of their world.

A teacher must not only know the moral and ethical values, the persistent truths of his society, but must have actively developed a code of values for himself. A teacher fundamentally ignorant of moral values, who has never developed any values or appreciations of his own, cannot possibly contribute to the growth of moral character. Giving devices for the development of "citizenship" to a teacher ignorant of the structure and process of democratic society is absurd.

We seem to be in a world-wide period of what may be called "unmorality." This characterizes many aspects of life from day to day, from person to person relationships to international relations. The struggle within and between groups intensifies all this. Understanding, tolerance, recognition of worth between and among all groups within our society and between societies must be achieved. "Civilization is (in truth) a race between education and disaster."

The most important factor in cultural unity and stability may be moral responsibility. It may even be the crucial factor in the integration or disintegration of a mobile, dynamic society. The teacher needs above all to know the place in life of a philosophy or a religion and to have developed one of his own. Achieving cultural unity within a diverse society is not impossible, but it will not come of itself. The challenge to education and to all agencies of enlightenment is unmistakable and not to be escaped or denied.

The problem is intensified by the world-wide "revolt of the masses." Individuals and groups now sit in places and control operations heretofore controlled by very different persons and groups. The new group brings its values and procedures with it. Condemnation of either group by the other is useless. The development of common values designed to achieve improvement of life for all groups should be our concern.

THE MORE REMOTE AND FATEFUL ASPECTS OF THE CHALLENGE

Education is a part of the social process, the school a part of the social structure. Education and the school cannot ever be free from the influences already at work in society, nor from trends which appear. The school reflects the society and culture within which it operates, and must participate in, and influence, any changes which occur.

The class structure within any society contains a number of factors quite apart from education which also affect mobility upward within society—or downward for that matter. Evidence exists, as stated earlier, that education as administered may actually interfere with social mobility and curtail opportunity—a direct reversal of the original faith and practice.

Educational leaders, both theoretical and practical, must be well informed concerning the life of their society, the factors and trends within it which bear upon the thing education was originally designed to do.

> *Question.* Is education at the mercy of the structure of society? Should we direct education openly toward acceptance of and integration with existing structure? Or, can education do something to influence trends within our society?

The actual situation within society becomes, in the light of these questions, a crucial matter. School leaders, practical and theoretical, are remarkably ill-informed concerning the *actual* philosophy and process of their society.

> *Question.* Should education accept and continue to operate on the basis of the typically accepted American tradition that any and all should aspire to life work within what are usually called the more favorable areas: the professions, skilled technologies, independent enterprise in business, or at least to top level directorial positions in industry and commerce?

Some of these areas are desperately overcrowded. Experience in European countries raises serious questions about the social utility of this procedure. A serious question, stated next, emerges at this point.

> *Question.* Do we as Americans *really* believe in our ancient faith—a relatively classless society, or one at least with relatively easy upward mobility for anyone, and surely with no artificial barriers to individual improvement?
>
> Have we in fact deserted our traditional faith in democracy and in the uniqueness of the individual and accepted uncritically the class structure and the placement of given persons in given classes without opportunity (or possibility) of movement from class to class?

Certain people become furiously angry upon hearing the question. Others cynically regard the question as foolish if to them the obvious answer is that we do not believe in or practice our original philosophy. The reaction of serious and loyal Americans is to look the facts in the face seriously and then to try to develop some answers.

We state *explicitly* in many places and on many occasions that we firmly uphold the faith, but the actual operation of social process and of education within the school gives cause to suspect *implicit* acceptance of a far different social and educational theory.

No one knows the answer, but our practices raise serious questions and dilemmas. Educational practices briefly mentioned in earlier pages are illustrations. The differentiation of curriculums which is a prominent characteristic of our secondary schools is ostensibly based on "differences in ability." The ability considered is always but one of the important abilities; namely, that required for abstract, verbal, academic work. Others are ignored. Worse than that, the differentiated curriculums are closely related to class differences within the population. The statement is made openly or by implication that certain individuals are destined for certain levels within society. If this is because of their class origins and not because of their "abilities," then we have a serious interference with democratic process. The cosmopolitan high school with a wide range of courses under one roof is often referred to as a "democratic" school. It is in fact not democratic at all. The basis is a design fundamentally different from democracy as American tradition has upheld it.

The developments in the secondary school have been generally produced by the "practical" schoolman, so-called. The operations of the "practical" man are usually based upon expediency, lack of information, and naive lack of critical insight. The theoretical leaders have also a professional error, namely, the promulgation of doctrinaire solutions due to ignorance of, or failure to recognize, the harsh limitations of reality. *Present unfavorable practices may, therefore, result not from any failure of our faith but from lack of ability and failure to pay attention to such facts as we have.* A number of current proposals by competent theorists and a number of practices developed by competent practical leaders may point the way to a better reassessment of both the extent of our faith and our ability to develop practices in accord with that faith.

Question. Should we not overcome our traditional antagonism to intellectual differences, outgrow our refusal to face the facts of intellectual differences? That is, should we not accept and operate upon knowledge that there are differences in intellectual ability?

Should we not recognize that (a) there are other abilities than the intellectual, with differences here also between persons, and (b) that the other abilities than the intellectual are necessary for the common life?

Granted these facts, we may then attack the two major problems (a) providing general education for all simultaneously with (b) provision for special or differentiated education in terms of individual talents within all of the abilities. One difficulty is to provide general education, common purposes and values, thus avoiding artificial divisions within society, and at the same time to maintain a level of quality in the general materials. The other difficulty is to select the various abilities and talents for special training without at the same time unwittingly introducing undesirable group distinctions.

All societies are differentiated except pioneer societies, and even there recognition is given to different contributing groups to the safety and development of the group. We propose here a recognition of differences in capacity on which a democratic system can be built.

Question. Have we the courage and the ability to develop curriculums based not on supposed differences in "ability" but on the hypothesis that we can provide experiences enabling all types and degrees of ability to achieve common cultural understandings, common values, and common understandings of the work of the world?

Have we the courage and the ability to develop curriculums for specialized training and to work for elimination of invidious distinctions between curriculums and their aims?

The answer to those questions turns upon the question that is probably basic to the whole discussion. It is:

Question. Should the leaders of our common life, together with the school workers, stand for a theory of society which would respect and honor any and all types of human endeavor; would regard any contribution to the common life as worthy, regardless of level of difficulty, skill, intangible or material rewards?

The implication is probably nearer to our ancient democratic faith than are most of the current statements and practices. Acceptance of the hypothesis would entail grave responsibility upon all who participate in any capacity in our social process. Particular responsibility rests upon all who are concerned with processes of enlightenment of any type. A long, slow, tedious process of developing and greatly expanding insights within the body politic is indicated, not to mention the tremendous task within the technical processes of schooling in particular and popular enlightenment in general.

A number of alternative conclusions seem to be apparent. We are now actually operating an educational system based on assertions and assumptions of democracy within society, opportunity for individual advancement, but actually showing practices which deny this. Do we wish to continue this or to substitute something else? The answer will depend upon a far more careful analysis of (1) the actual values and beliefs of our society, (2) the assumptions of our educational system, of the practices of that system, and more important, the relation between assumptions and practices.

1. Do we wish to continue a system based on one set of assumptions, but denying these in practice, at least in part?

(The cosmopolitan high school with differentiated courses actually operates on acceptance of the class stratification of society, in large part. The very small high school operates as if there were but one class in society, the others being blithely ignored.)

2. Do we wish boldly and aggressively to reaffirm our original faith in a democratic society, with opportunity and mobility, and then stand up and

fight for an educational practice in line with the faith? (This means the rejection of expediency and of the retreat into verbalism, and of the retreat from action. This calls for acceptance of a moral imperative, the avoidance of which will entail severe setbacks to education, and could conceivably contribute ultimately to a social disaster of considerable magnitude.)

3. Do we wish with equal boldness to accept stratification in society with its full and ultimate implications and go boldly about the business of education for it?

The latter would probably be universally condemned by our society—without awareness that we could fall into that very practice for lack of clarifying our assumptions and practices. The only legislative proposal for dual schools ever to emerge in our country aroused such a storm of opposition that it has never seriously appeared again. The practice, however, might easily slip up on us unawares.

Our choices depend upon answers to the several questions propounded. Facts relating to some of the questions do not exist. They will be secured in some instances with great difficulty. The writer does not know the answers. He does believe, however, that answers must be developed. Securing the answers must precede the answering of the great current challenge which is emerging. The rising generation of social and educational leaders will not join the ranks of the unemployed for some time.

6–3   WHO IS THIS LOWER-CLASS CHILD?

Robert J. Fisher

At the time he wrote this article, Dr. Fisher was an associate professor of education at Eastern Michigan University in Ypsilanti. He provides a timely warning to the social scientists and to teachers who may oversimplify the relationship between education and social class.

Many teachers have at last become aware of social class differences. It is not in vain that they have taken courses in sociology and the social foundations of education. Prior to this they tended to see each child as an individual, a being apart from his own background. But as a result of social class analysis they now have a new set of tags with which to classify children. They now recognize and shudder at the thought of that irreverent, undisciplined, non-motivated, and irrevocably handicapped lower-class youngster.

What is this lower-class child like? An image has been created. He lives in a city slum or in tents and shacks for impoverished migrant families. His parents care nothing about education. His parents neglect him. He suffers from malnutrition, lack

From *Journal of Educational Sociology*, XXXIV, No. 7 (March 1961), 309–311. Copyright © 1961 by the Payne Educational Sociology Foundation, Inc.; reprinted by permission of the Payne Educational Sociology Foundation, Inc.

of affection, and general misunderstanding. His achievement level is low. His grades are poor. The intelligence tests are biased against him. The teachers do not speak his language. And he fails dismally to meet the middle-class teacher's expectations. He swears. He comes to school dirty. He gets into fights. Sometimes he carries a razor or a switchblade. When he reaches high school, he wears a black leather jacket and allows his hair to grow unusually long. Perhaps he smokes marijuana and hangs around the streets in the company of potential delinquents or races up and down the highways on motorcycles or souped-up jalopies.

A new stereotype has emerged. Teachers now recognize what their college professors are talking about when they use the term lower class. The image which this stereotype awakens both frightens and arouses pity, but how much basis is there for it?

A group of prospective teachers took a field trip to a lower-class school. They knew it was a lower-class school, because the children who attended were living in a run-down, temporary, government housing project, and the families were among the lowest income groups. The children were both white and colored, and the faculty was integrated as well. They interviewed some of the teachers with questions designed to gain verification for the images which they held about lower-class children and their parents.

"Wasn't it true that these parents showed little interest in the school or their children's progress?"

"Oh, no," replied the teachers, "In fact, the parents turned out in large numbers to all school functions. The attendance at parent-teacher conferences was close to 100 percent. They seemed to have high hopes for what the schools might do for the children."

"Were the children unruly or hard to handle?"

The teachers did not seem to think so. They agreed that they did have to modify some of their conceptions about acceptable behavior, but the teachers did not feel any more plagued by discipline problems than they had been in other classrooms.

"Did they find the achievement level rather low?"

The teachers recognized wide differences in levels of achievement, and could see no distinction between classes they were presently teaching and ones that they had taught in more favored neighborhoods.

The prospective teachers came back to class somewhat disillusioned. They had not received confirmation for their stereotypes. Why didn't these lower-class children behave like lower-class children are supposed to behave? One of the difficulties seems to be that a term used as an ideal-type construct designed primarily for anthropological or sociological research has deteriorated to a set of assumptions and descriptions which lend themselves easily to over-simplification.

There can be no doubt that studies do uncover class systems based upon a differential hierarchy of status. There is no doubt that statistically significant differences exist between social class categories of children in relation to school success. The evidence is fairly conclusive that commonly used intelligence tests do, indeed, discriminate against the vocabulary and motivation of children classified as lower-class. But wherever statistically significant differences occur, they cover over the wide range of exceptional behavior within the groups being compared.

The argument here is not so much with the use of social class constructs in helping teachers to accept relevant differences. The real trouble comes with the realization that some teachers are swallowing whole the categories describing social class differences. This may well be doing more to place barriers in the way of better human relations than it does to overcome misconceptions.

It seems evident that our schools in many slum neighborhoods simply are not providing realistically for a large number of the children who attend. This does not mean that they fail with all of the children. They do offer the opportunity for many children to acquire some of the skills and attitudes which will enable them to use the schools as effectively as children in other parts of the city.

One trouble with stereotypes is that the lower-lower class child does not know that he is lower-lower class. He probably would not accept the classification if he did know it. He is just as apt to be insulted if someone thinks of him and treats him as if he were some kind of pariah.

Another trouble with the stereotype about slum children is that most people who live in slums would just as soon live elsewhere. The stereotypes about lower-class youth are applied by teachers to Negroes, Mexican-Americans, and Puerto Ricans whose families are frequently denied access to other neighborhoods. Members of groups who suffer from housing and employment discrimination frequently develop strong motivation to break out of the slums and to improve living conditions. Only when the avenues of escape are cut off by discrimination does apathy develop.

The parents of the children in the temporary housing development are not apathetic or hostile to the schools. As a matter of fact, they show great interest in the potential which the schools offer for their children and frequently hold unreasonable expectations of the hopes which education can fulfill.

In some ways the teacher who did not know about social-class differences had better attitudes about the varying needs of individuals than the teacher who categorizes people too easily. It may come to the point where professors have to spend as much time breaking down stereotypes about lower-class groups as they now do about racial and religious groups. A stereotype obscures differences. The basic democratic value that differences be respected should lead teachers to be very careful about applying ideal-type constructs too indiscriminately. Teachers *do* need to know the social-class background of the children they teach, but to know this is not enough. The next step must be to offer educational opportunities which will provide for the wide range of differences in abilities, interests, and goals which are found among *any* group of children.

6-4   THE ROLE OF SOCIAL CLASS DIFFERENCES AND HORIZONTAL MOBILITY IN THE ETIOLOGY OF AGGRESSION

Gerhard L. Falk

Gerhard L. Falk is in the department of social studies, State University of New York College for Teachers at Buffalo. In the following essay he suggests that lower-class children are more violent because their subculture is more violent rather than because they have criminal tendencies. He further indicates that the school authorities' harsh treatment of lower-class boys may reinforce their cultural conditioning.

It is the object of this paper to demonstrate that differential aggression patterns are the consequence of social class membership. From such a demonstration it may then be inferred that the consequences of aggression, such as homicide, assault, etc., are equally related to social class.

SOCIAL CONTROLS

That there is a difference in the adaptation of the social classes to their environment was already recognized by Aristotle.[1] The philosopher advises that one class is rich, another poor and the third "mean" and that the latter is "best." By this he meant that "he who greatly excels in strength, beauty, birth or wealth or is very poor, very weak or disgraced cannot follow rational principles." The two extreme groups, Aristotle tells us, are likely to become criminal, as those who have too much good fortune are neither willing nor able to submit to authority. They are never reared to learn the habit of obedience but commit "roguery."[2] "Evil begins at home," says the philosopher. We are also told that only the middle class of citizens can be relied upon to secure the state and to exhibit a stable and permanent influence. Aristotle also commented that children are treated in a differential manner with reference to socio-economic class.

This phenomenon is of course still true. Thus we find that the lower classes are more severe with regard to toilet training while American middle classes expect of their children a good deal of educational attainment.[3] The social classes also differ with respect to the feeding of infants, weaning and the use of pacifiers, bowel and bladder

From *Journal of Educational Sociology*, XXXIII, No. 1 (September 1959), 1–10. Copyright © 1959 by the Payne Educational Sociology Foundation, Inc.; reprinted by permission of the Payne Educational Sociology Foundation, Inc.

[1] Benjamin Jowett, *Aristotle's Politics* (New York: The Modern Library, 1943), p. 190.
[2] Jowett, 1943, p. 191.
[3] Robert J. Havighurst and Allison Davis, "A Comparison of the Chicago and Harvard Studies of Social Class Differences in Child Rearing," *The American Sociological Review*, XX (August 1955), 441.

control, and the assumption of responsibilities in the household.[4] In other words, the techniques employed in the care and rearing of children are culturally patterned and therefore tend to be similar within a social class.[5] Lower classes are reported to have a psychologically close hierarchical and rigid parent-child relationship, while middle classes are more ostensibly equalitarian and flexible in this regard.[6] At the same time lower classes tend to be more permissive with respect to outside activities than the upper classes. The middle class is more concerned with fostering parentally trained independence in their children by clearly defining the extent of outside activities that may be sought. Maintenance of supervision by the withdrawal of approval makes the middle-class child aware of the importance of "proper" behavior which may be defined as conformity to class standards.

Warner[7] indicates that life in the middle-class family proceeds according to strictly established rules with reference to the outside world and that children are vigorously supervised and brought up to value the achievement patterns and moral codes of their class. Discipline exists in the lower classes also, but it is often harsh, and there is little supervision of children outside the home.

DIFFERENTIAL CHILD REARING AND AGGRESSION

These differences in child rearing are not confined to the home. They are carried over to the schools as well.

This means that there are different controls upon children from different social classes in the schools of the country.[8] Thus, as schools are now constituted, controls fall more heavily on boys than on girls, and the hand of authority is much lighter upon the child of the upper and middle class than on the child of the lower class.[9] The tendency is to be harsh and rebuking to the child of the lower class, to make punishment more severe for such children and to minimize rewards for children categorized as "racial" or "ethnic" minorities. The same holds true of a child with a "bad" reputation.

The consequence of these class differentials in rearing children is of course differential personality organization as well. It is the predominant type of social relationship in a society or ethnocentric group which determines an individual's society-oriented identification, his status, his demands and his expectations.[10] To these he must conform in order to preserve his social relationships.

Thus the personality of an individual becomes the organization of his drives and motives as dictated by the unconscious aspects of mental behavior. This behavior differs from class to class and is largely determined by environmental pressures.

Thus we see that personality is a function of class differentials, a view which

---

[4]Allison Davis and Robert J. Havighurst, "Social Class and Color Differences in Child Rearing," *The American Sociological Review*, XI (November 1946), 698.

[5]Abraham Kardiner, *The Individual and His Society* (New York: Columbia University Press, 1939), p. 147.

[6]Henry Maas, "Some Social Class Differences in the Family Systems of Pre- and Early Adolescents," *Child Development*, XXII (September 1951), 145.

[7]Ruth Rosner Kornhauser, "The Warner Approach to Social Stratification," *Class, Status and Power* (New York: The Free Press, 1953), p. 233.

[8]George Psathas, "Ethnicity, Social Class and Adolescent Independence from Social Control," *The American Sociological Review*, XXV (August 1957), 442.

[9]H. Otto Dahlke, *Values in Culture and Classroom* (New York: Harper Brothers, 1957), p. 274.

[10]Jack P. Gibbs and Walter T. Martin, "A Theory of Status Integration," *The American Sociological Review*, XXIII (April 1958), 141.

is supported by the finding that there is a relationship between neurosis and social class.[11] This would indicate that if neuroses of all kinds are manifestations of underlying personality characteristics, there is some evidence that class differentials affect adjusted as well as non-adjusted persons.[12]

Adjustment is defined as emotional conditioning to class values. Since the pressures and constraints of one class differ so much from those of another class, it becomes evident that there is no objective criterion of well-adjusted or "neurotic" but that these terms must be sociologically interpreted with reference to the group in which the subject operates.

Thus, lower-class children are encouraged to express aggression freely and openly. The slum culture teaches a child to fight and to admire fighters.[13] Thus the child who shocks her middle-class teacher by telling how her uncle beat her aunt as a "Mother's Day Present"[14] gets approval from her own group for aggression while the teacher considers the same trait obnoxious. The reverse is also true. Middle classes praise children for being anxious to please, for keeping quiet, and for compliance with their requests. These same traits, however, are considered the attributes of a "schemer" by the lower class. Here outspokenness is considered important and aggression is considered a token of "honesty."[15] Readiness to "tell people off" is esteemed, and culture heroes are people who have long police records, particularly if they have been charged with murder.[16]

This aggressiveness is developed in children from two to five years of age so that they will be quick to fight and proud of their handiwork. Women expect their brothers, fathers and husbands to be cocky and aggressive.

Additional light is shed on this class differential by the fact that lower-class children have less of an opportunity to rise to a higher socio-economic position than is true for middle-class children. Therefore, the restrictions imposed by the middle-class parent on his children are purposeful because they lead to upward mobility. The lower-class child sees no such advantage and therefore resents restrictions more and is more willing to exhibit aggression or frustration.[17]

VALUES AND SOCIAL CLASS

In simple folk societies most people have a rather well defined status which is sustained and reinforced by direct participation in community life.[18] Thus social forces make for a good deal of rigidity of classes and give each individual a definitive guide for behavior. In American society, however, classes are less well defined than in

[11]Robert J. Havighurst, "Social Class and Basic Personality Structure," *Sociology and Social Research,* XXXVI (July 1952), 356.

[12]Robert B. Catell, "The Cultural Functions of Social Stratification," *The Journal of Social Psychology,* XXI (July 1948), 25.

[13]W. Allison Davis and Robert J. Havighurst, *Father of the Man* (Boston: Houghton Mifflin Co., 1947), p. 14.

[14]Davis and Havighurst, 1947, p. 15.

[15]Davis and Havighurst, 1947, p. 17.

[16]Davis and Havighurst, 1947, p. 19.

[17]Milton J. Barron, *The Juvenile in Delinquent Society* (New York: Alfred A. Knopf, 1955), p. 134.

[18]Elwin H. Powell, "Toward a Redefinition of Anomie," *The American Sociological Review,* XXIII (April 1958), p. 131.

caste societies.[19] This is particularly true in the urban community but is also true in urban-oriented groups. Even while some social forces have made for more rigidity, others have tended to counteract this. As a result many persons' notions of class have become confused and indistinct. This trend is further enhanced by the indeterminate state of the class structure as designed by such variables as occupation and economic success. Ours is an acquisitive and competitive society where individuals are admired by reason of prestige positions that are achieved. The roles which the person plays first as a child in the family and then in the peer group and finally as an adult are all functions of the rights and obligations of status, which is defined here as any position in any social system.[20]

These roles finally become incorporated into the structure of the self and are exhibited in self-discipline, the unconscious aspect of mental behavior.[21] Outside pressures, such as the demands of the job, the expectations of friends and relatives, and the relations to associates structure these roles even more closely and serve to keep the family together and control the individual.[22]

This then leads to the conclusion that the status of the adult white male in America depends primarily on occupation. Thus the vocation of an individual determines his general social status if determined either by himself or someone else.[23] However, status is not the same when subjectively determined or when objectively analyzed. In fact, differences arise here which are a function of class membership. Therefore, values are not the same from class to class.[24]

When differences between the values of people are analyzed by class, it appears that differing social classes will define values subjectively in a manner which may differ from the objective measure of their class membership. This means that the criteria of occupation and economic conditon, value judgments and other objective factors tend to classify individuals in a social class which is not always consistent with their self-conception of their status.

Thus class is defined both subjectively and objectively and differs on the basis of who classified an individual. Therefore, the attitudes of people are determined by the class in which they believe they are. For instance, different groups in a community have a differential amount of power, but this does not mean the same thing to everyone.[25]

The power relationship in society is instrumental in promoting the individuality of each member of the group. Thus, the master is more of an individual than the servant, the commander more than the common soldier. Individualism grows with power and with wealth, but also with responsibility. This responsibility consists both of the view which the individual has toward himself and also the opinion he has of those who make him responsible.[26]

---

[19]Gideon Sjoberg, "Are Social Classes in America Becoming More Rigid?" *The American Sociological Review*, XVI (December 1951), 783.

[20]Powell, 1958, p. 132.

[21]Havighurst, 1952, p. 358.

[22]August B. Hollingshead, "Class Differences in Family Stability," *The Annals of the American Academy of Political and Social Science*, CCLXXII (November 1950), 39.

[23]Powell, 1958, p. 132.

[24]Ivan D. Steiner, "Some Sociological Values Associated with Objectively and Subjectively Defined Social Class Membership," *Social Forces*, XXXI (May 1953), 328.

[25]Walter Goldschmidt, "Social Class in America—A Critical Review," *The American Anthropologist*, LII (October 1950), 484.

[26]Ferdinand Tonnies, "Stande und Classen," *Handworterbuch der Soziologie* (Glencoe: The Free Press, 1931), p. 58.

CLASS MEMBERSHIP AND THE FRUSTRATION AGGRESSION HYPOTHESIS

In modern western societies the "proletariat" and other classes are theoretical-ly considered equal before the law. Actually, however, and to some extent even legally, the totality of their rights and privileges is much more modest than that of other classes.[27] Thus, punishment for criminals with different social characteristics, such as social class and sex, varies according to the crime and its cultural significance for that class and sex.[28] The reason for this is that people with different life experiences are likely to make different judgments concerning the seriousness of an offense and the punishment that should be assigned for the violation of the law.

The deterrent and retributive effects of a given sentence can therefore be assumed to be different for different segments of the population. For instance, the lower-class Negro is characterized by attitudes and modes of behavior brought from the South. He has "a greater tendency to follow without anxiety an accommodative and stereotyped role with respect to whites, a more unstable and mobile employment status, and a fairly casual attitude toward family and institutional controls."[29]

Law, however, was developed, in an earlier and more integrated society and does not always reflect contemporary diversified values as outlined in the above quota-tion.[30] In addition to the differences in interpretation of social control as practiced by diverse socio-economic and racial groups, the agents of social control also differ in their interpretation of behavior, dependent, of course, on their class membership. Thus the background of judges is related to their judgments, and the punishments they assign for various offenses differ with the sex, socio-economic status, and size of the community concerned.[31] Therefore, punishments favored for criminals of different social classes and for the two sexes vary according to the crime and its cultural meaning in relation to class and sex.

Thus social controls of a legal nature are more stringent upon the less privileged groups than the more powerful groups. However, this is not the only area in which the deprivations of a low socio-economic status operate. The nature of the work done by the "proletarian" is often highly monotonous. It is boring and little calculated to stimulate thought, to say nothing of creativeness. His share of burdensome duties including subordination and dependence on others is disproportionately large. Thus, "to be poor means to be dependent on the grace and good will of the rich."[32]

Now the problem of the place of power in the social system shades directly into that of authority relationships. Both root in the fundamentals of social interaction and become meaningful when institutionalized expectations include the legitimization of coercive sanctions.[33] This means that authority is synonymous with superiority and control over the action of others. The nature and basis of such superiority may vary

---

[27]Pitirim Sorokin, "What Is a Social Class?" *The Journal of Legal and Political Sociology*, III (September 1947), 24.

[28]Arnold M. Rose and Arthur E. Prell, "Does the Punishment Fit the Crime?" *The American Journal of Sociology*, LI (November 1955), p. 248.

[29]Richard A. Schermerhorn, *These Our People* (Boston: D. C. Heath and Co., 1949), p. 148.

[30]Sorokin, 1947, p. 25.

[31]Rose, 1955.

[32]Tonnies, 1931, p. 62.

[33]Talcott Parsons, "The Theory of Social Stratification," in R. Bendix, and S. Lipset, eds., *Class, Status & Power: A Reader in Social Stratification* (New York: Free Press, 1953), p. 96.

widely. However, whatever its source, the superior-inferior relationship promotes a feeling of frustration on the inferior individual and generates a strong motive for conflict by imputing to the superior class responsibility for the injustices under which the inferior suffers.[34]

This does not imply that frustration for the lower classes in American society is imaginary. Instead, it is very real and self-perpetuating. Poverty means hardship. By reason of low income or dependence on relief, undernourishment is common.[35] Clothing, furniture and utensils cannot be replaced when they wear out. Life is thus a nightmare of fear and hunger, evictions and a pauper's grave. The burden of debt holds many families in poverty even if their income might otherwise be adequate. This perpetuates the deprivations of the lower-class community and creates a sense of despair. Such despair is founded on experience as a vicious circle enmeshes the poor. Their health is generally poor. Therefore their stamina is low. In addition they are culturally deficient as they lack education. Consequently, employers are unwilling to hire them except for the most routine jobs. These are the least stable and most subject to business cycles, so that the lower-class worker is the last to be hired and the first to be fired. This in turn results in cheap rental living, overcrowded rooms and family instability.[36]

"The lower-class family pattern is unique. The husband-wife relationship is more or less an unstable one even if the marriage is sanctioned by law. Disagreements leading to quarrels and vicious fights followed by desertions by either men or women are not uncommon."[37] Thus broken homes are frequent, and children begin their lives under such circumstances. This leads many lower-class persons to assume that their circumstances are hopeless, that respectable people sneer at them and that the social controls are unjust.

Admittedly, social controls always have their limitations. Abel describes how even the rulers of a concentration camp cannot insure a "foolproof" organization but must contend with the unforeseen and the weaknesses of human nature.[38] That is to say that humans cannot be molded like robots. Thus any ruling personnel is dependent on its subject population, and this dependence insures that controls can never be complete. Nevertheless there appears to be some evidence that frustrations consequent to social controls may lead to aggression.[39]

The frustrations inherent in any vertical relationship produce a number of different possible responses, one of which may be some form of aggression. Even when no specific frustrating agent is present, some object may be created for the purpose of relieving aggression arising from frustrating situations.[40] This need varies with the tolerance to frustration which a thwarted individual may have. However, such frustration is often displaced upon a person or group representing a constellation of ideas that evoke hostility. Such aggressive responses as are then evoked may be spectacularly dangerous to society.

---

[34]T. H. Marshall, "The Nature of Class Conflict," *Class Conflict and Social Stratification* (New York: The Institute of Sociology, 1938), p. 108.

[35]James Ford, *Social Deviation* (New York: The Macmillan Co., 1939), p. 290.

[36]Joseph A. Kahl, *The American Class Structure* (New York: Rinehart and Co., 1957), p. 211.

[37]Kahl, 1957, p. 212.

[38]Theodore Abel, "The Sociology of Concentration Camps," *Social Forces*, XXX (December 1951), 154.

[39]John Dollard, *Frustration and Aggression* (New Haven: Yale University Press, 1950), p. 134.

[40]Neal E. Miller, "The Frustration Aggression Hypothesis," *The Psychological Review*, XLVIII (July 1941), 340.

Periodically attention is focused on a person who has committed an extremely aggressive crime.[41] Such crimes are often committed by persons feeling inferior either with regard to society in general or with regard to a specific person with whom there exists frequent face to face contact. In such cases murder may be the result of a wish to get rid of the real or imagined domination of another person, thereby removing the inferiority suffered.

Alexander[42] describes such a case, a situation which resulted in fratricide: "In the course of a quarrel Mark, who was nineteen years old, shot his brother William, who was two years younger than he, and his friend Ferdinand, approximately the same age. The psychological problem that the criminal act of this boy imposes on us consists fundamentally of how this weak, somewhat introverted, not especially aggressive young man with a constant feeling of inferiority committed such a deed which no one thought him capable of.

. . . his younger brother William was physically stronger and had beaten him brutally . . . he began to give way to the feeling of being constantly the underdog. In phantasy his brother continually struck him. When he got into a controversy with anyone this picture appeared, paralyzing his power of resistance. The resulting tension caused his hatred of his brother and the shooting." This murder occurred within a family group.

DIFFERENTIAL MOBILITY

An important function of our class-oriented society is horizontal and vertical mobility. This presents the individual with the necessity of adapting to various social strata and different conditions in time and place throughout a lifetime.[43] Consequently a good deal of mental and emotional strain accompanies this mobility, while intensive shifting from place to place also hinders considerably the promotion of rigid habits and stable morals. Thus we find that stratification creates hostility and horizontal mobility fosters the opportunity to express it. Therefore, an inverse relationship exists between the degree of horizontal mobility and the strength of the social controls.

Anyone who has read *The Grapes of Wrath* by John Steinbeck finds therein an example of this relationship. This is further underscored by the high delinquency and crime rates in the slums of New York and Chicago and other large cities where high mobility is accompanied by truancy, runaway children, vagrancy and crimes of all kinds.[44]

Thus, both urban and rural mobility promotes disorganizaton. The country boy who comes home from the city with alien notions is a less frequent example of disorganization than the city boy who has been exposed to differential culture patterns. Nevertheless, the effect is the same and maladjustment is the result.[45]

---

[41] August B. Hollingshead, "Selected Characteristics of Classes in a Middle Western Community," *American Sociological Review*, XII (June 1947), 385.

[42] Franz Alexander, "A Double Murder Committed by a Nineteen-Year-Old Boy," *The Psychoanalytical Review*, XXIV (June 1937), 113.

[43] Pitirim Sorokin, *Social Mobility* (New York: Harper and Bros., 1927), p. 510.

[44] Harry Elmer Barnes and Negley K. Teeters, *New Horizons in Criminology* (New York: Prentice Hall, 1947), p. 154.

[45] Barnes and Teeters, 1947, p. 154.

A study of mobility in Seattle connects high labor turnover with juvenile delinquency, low school attendance and court appearances. Thus it can justifiably be concluded that delinquency varies directly with horizontal and vertical mobility. An illustration of the degree of spatial mobility with which our society must deal is given by Sutherland.[46] Relating the circumstances of the Urschel kidnapping he says, "The Urschel kidnapping occurred in the state of Oklahoma, the victim was held captive in a remote rural section of Texas, the ransom money was paid in Missouri, a portion of the money was exchanged in Minnesota, another portion was hidden in Texas, one of the guilty parties was located in Colorado and the others in Tennessee, Minnesota, Texas and Illinois."

CONCLUSION

We have shown that aggressive patterns are learned as part of early childhood education and are reinforced by class membership. Consequently, violent crimes are equally related, and learned. It can thus be adequately concluded that the preponderance of violent offenses in the lower classes is related to a *generally more violent* environment, rather than to any "criminal tendencies." Since crimes of violence are more subject to publicity, however, than crimes of a more subtle nature, it is easy to believe that crime is *per se* more frequent in lower than middle or upper classes.

This view we have thus refuted.

[46]Edwin H. Sutherland, *Principles of Criminology* (New York: J. B. Lippincott Co., 1947), p. 248.

6-5 SOCIOECONOMIC POSITION AND ACADEMIC UNDERACHIEVEMENT

Richard A. Cloward

Richard A. Cloward is professor of social work, New York School of Social Work at Columbia University. He studied at the University of Rochester and obtained his Ph.D. at Columbia. He has written extensively on criminology, delinquency, penology, and social perspectives of behavior. His essay is an excellent summary of the effect of social class membership on school programs.

What we do about a persisting social problem, such as poor academic achievement, depends in large part on our assumptions about the forces that produce it. Every approach to this problem is based on certain assumptions, explicit or implicit, about why the problem it is seeking to solve exists in the first place. In this paper, I shall set forth some ideas which I hope are helpful in

---

Mimeographed, December 1961, pp. 1–22. Reprinted by permission of the author.

accounting for the problem of poor academic performance among certain categories of children.

At the outset, I should like to note that the problem I have been asked to focus upon is that of the generally direct correlation between socioeconomic position and academic achievement. There are, of course, important qualifications which should be noted when this correlation is discussed. Although the correlation holds generally when the various strata of our society as a whole are compared, it may not necessarily hold for certain important subgroupings; some ethnic groups may tend to perform well despite their low socioeconomic position; some groups may tend to perform poorly despite very high socioeconomic position. My point is not that the correlation is unvarying whatever the specialized status categories one compares, but rather that it tends to hold for very large aggregates of the population despite these internal variations. By defining the problem in these terms, it should be noted that I am excluding from consideration in this paper the problem of the low achiever as he may be found other than in the low economic segments of our population.

For all practical purposes, I am inclined to dismiss the possibility that this correlation can be accounted for in terms of native endowment, although I am aware that there are distinct differentials by income level in intelligence test performance. My objection here is the not uncommon one that such tests probably do not differentiate social influences from native endowment well enough, and thus probably measure achievement as well as endowment. Even if, by a process of selective social mobility, a correlation between endowment and social position does exist, then I would still be inclined to take the view, until contrary evidence is produced, that this factor alone is not enough to explain the general correlation between income level and academic achievement. I would still assume, in short, that the achievement-income correlation would persist, although perhaps in a weakened form, if native endowment were held constant.

The use of the term "under-achiever" may obscure more than it illumines. Like many other terms which designate gross social problems, such as juvenile delinquency, it is necessary to ask whether the term subsumes behavior which is all of a piece or whether discrete types of behavior are not otherwise lumped together. With respect to underachievement, I am inclined to believe that there are at least two general types: those whose underachievement is not inconsistent with the beliefs, values and norms of those with whom they interact, and those whose underachievement is inconsistent with the beliefs, values and norms of those with whom they interact. In the first case, underachievement is socially structured; that is, high achievement does not receive strong support in the milieu of the actor. In the second case, however, underachievement is idiosyncratic; it is an isolated instance of aberrant behavior which receives no support and may be condemned in the milieu of the actor.

I have the distinct impression that these two forms of underachievement are differentially distributed in the social structure. If we ask how support for underachievement is distributed, we would probably answer that it is more likely to be found in the lower socioeconomic strata of our society, for a great deal of evidence suggests that there is less emphasis here upon educational performance than elsewhere in the society. Although education is widely valued in our society, it is not equally valued among the several social classes. Hyman has summarized a national survey in which a sample of youths was asked: "About how much schooling do you think most young men need these days to get along well in the world?'' The results are shown below:

**CLASS DIFFERENTIALS IN EMPHASIS ON THE NEED
FOR COLLEGE EDUCATION
(201 Males Aged 14 to 20)** *

Socioeconomic Position of Family	Percent Recommending a College Education	Number of Respondents
Wealthy and prosperous	74	39
Middle Class	63	100
Lower Class	42	62

*H. H. Hyman, ''The Value Systems of Different Classes: A Social-Psychological Contribution to the Analysis of Stratification,'' in Reinhard Bendix and S. M. Lipset, eds., *Class, Status and Power* (Glencoe, Ill.: Free Press, 1953), p. 432.

These data, like others that Hyman presents, show that a sizable proportion of persons at each point in the social structure consider a college education desirable. Even in the lowest level of society, the proportion who emphasize the need for education is not small. But it is also true that there are strong differences from one stratum to another. In general, the proportion recommending higher education increases with each upward step in the socioeconomic hierarchy.

The task confronting the educational enterprise obviously differs greatly depending on which of these forms of underachievement it must overcome. In the case of socially-structured underachievement we probably face the more difficult task, for we must deal not only with an actor who deviates from official educational prescriptions but with a milieu which buttresses such behavior as well. Since the matter of social support may lie at the heart of lower-class underachievement, it is to some thoughts about this particular problem that I shall address myself. What I shall have to say, then, will not go to the important question of the more idiosyncratic forms of underachievement, for I do not believe that a single explanation can encompass the various forms of underachievement which confront us. It is one thing to ask why cultural values arise at certain points in the social structure which, if only inadvertently, tend to support underachievement; to the extent that the underachievement of a given person represents conformity with those values, the salient question then becomes one of explaining the origin of the values rather than the behavior of the individual. It is quite another thing to ask, however, why some persons fail to attain good academic records when the milieu in which they find themselves condemns such failure. Although I shall limit my remarks to the first question, the second also calls for answers.

LIFE CHANCES AND EDUCATIONAL ACHIEVEMENT

Given the fundamental importance of education to social advancement, how are we to account for these class differentials in emphasis on the value of education? Why is it that a substantial proportion of lower-class males aged 14 to 20 do *not* orient themselves toward educational achievement? What are the special pressures impinging upon youth in city slums to which deviant patterns—such as educational failure—are a logical outcome?

It is my view that one very important pressure toward underachievement in this group arises from discrepancies between their social and economic aspirations and their opportunities to achieve these aspirations by legitimate means. The aspirations are the result of socialization in a society that places great emphasis on economic and occupational achievement and whose ideology stresses the possibility of achievement by all its members, irrespective of their ethnic or socioeconomic backgrounds. Members of low socioeconomic or minority groups, however, are subjected to discriminatory practices which have the effect of restricting access to the usual means (e.g., education) of rising in the social and occupational scale. Slum youth, therefore, share the aspirations of youth located elsewhere in American society but, for reasons largely beyond their control, are much less likely to achieve these goals.

The emphasis on upward mobility for all members is a unique characteristic of industrial societies. Something in the organization of life in such societies must therefore require that the members make a virtue of dissatisfaction, of discontent with their present positions. If we can identify this "something," we shall be on our way to understanding an important feature of American life, and, furthermore, we shall have taken an important step toward an explanation of lower-class patterns such as educational underachievement.

All societies, industrial or not, must solve the problem of perpetuating themselves or else disintegrate. In many societies it is enough that the young work alongside their parents, acquiring through these intimate associations the values and skills that will enable them to engage successfully in adult occupational and family activities. The occupational systems in such societies are relatively simple and undifferentiated; most of the major work roles can be passed directly from father to son. The transmittal of occupational skills is a more difficult problem in our society, with its vastly proliferated structure of extremely technical work roles. We cannot depend upon the vagaries of birth to determine who will occupy each role, for we cannot assume that the son of a physicist will be a competent successor to his father. Nor can we require the father to transmit highly specialized knowledge to his son in the context of the family, for this would divert the father's energies from the primary work role that he is supposed to perform. The family, in other words, is not a satisfactory environment for the learning of specialized occupational skills. The industrial society must organize itself in such a way that it can allocate people to roles more or less on the basis of merit and endowment rather than on the basis of social origins, and it must provide— outside the family—the formal learning experiences that are prerequisites to occupational performance.

A crucial problem in the industrial world, then, is to locate and train the most talented persons in every generation, irrespective of the vicissitudes of birth, to occupy technical work roles. Whether he is born into wealth or poverty, each individual, depending upon his ability and diligence, must be encouraged to find his "natural level" in the social order. This problem is one of tremendous proportions. Since we cannot know in advance who can best fulfill the requirements of various occupational roles, the matter is presumably settled through the process of competition. But how can men throughout the social order be motivated to participate in this competition? How can society generate the ambition and persistence that are necessary if the individual is to make his way in the occupational world? How can we persuade the young to invest their resources, time, and energies in acquiring specialized knowledge and complex skills? It is not enough for a few to make the race; all must be motivated to strive, so that the most able and talented will be the victors in the competitive struggle for high status.

One of the ways in which the industrial society attempts to solve this problem is by defining success-goals as potentially accessible to all, regardless of race, creed, or socioeconomic position. Great social rewards, it is said, are not limited to any particular segment or segments of the population but are available to everyone, however lowly his origins. The status of a young man's father presumably does not put an upper limit on the height to which the son may aspire; in fact, he is exhorted to improve his status over that of his father. The industrial society, in short, emphasizes *common* or universal success-goals as a way of ensuring its survival. If large masses of young people can be motivated to reach out for great social rewards, many of them will make the appropriate investment in learning and preparation, and a rough correlation between talent and ultimate position in the occupational hierarchy will presumably result.

One of the paradoxes of social life, however, is that the processes by which societies seek to ensure conformity sometimes result in nonconformity. If a cultural emphasis on unlimited success-goals tends to solve problems in the industrial society, it also creates new ones. A pervasive feeling of position discontent leads people to compete for higher status and so contributes to the survival of the industrial order, but it also produces acute pressure for aberrant behavior if large sectors of the population are denied equal opportunity to achieve high status.

Let us turn then to a discussion of barriers in access to educational facilities which confront low income groups in our society.

Relationship of Educational Achievement to Occupational Achievement

"Education," Lipset and Bendix have remarked, "has become the principal avenue for upward mobility in most industrial nations," particularly in the United States. The number of nonmanual occupations that can be fruitfully pursued without extensive educational background is diminishing and will doubtless continue to do so as our occupational structure becomes increasingly technical and specialized.[1]

It should be pointed out, however, that educational attainment does not necessarily enable the lower-class person to overcome the disadvantages of his low social origins.

> Thus workers' sons with "some college" education are about as well off [financially] as a group as the sons of nonmanual fathers who have graduated from high school but not attended college. Similarly, high school graduation for the sons of workers results in their being only slightly better off than the sons of nonmanual workers who have not completed high school.[2]

---

[1] S. M. Lipset and Reinhard Bendix, *Social Mobility in Industrial Society* (Berkeley and Los Angeles, Calif.: University of California Press, 1959), p. 91.

[2] *Ibid.*, p. 99.

To the extent that one's social origins, despite education, still constitute a restraining influence on upward movement, we may assume that other objective consequences of social position intervene, such as the ability of one's family to give one a start in a business or profession by supplying funds or influential contacts.

The influence of social class as a deterrent to social mobility, despite the possession of education, becomes all the more important when coupled with influences stemming from race and nationality. It hardly needs to be said to an audience of this kind that race frequently acts as a major barrier to occupational mobility no matter what the educational achievement of the person involved. This situation is easing, to be sure, as progress in fair employment practices for all racial groups is slowly achieved. Nevertheless, it would be grossly inaccurate to say that a Negro youth in our society has the same chance as a white youth to become upwardly mobile given an equivalent level of education. It is not in the least uncommon to find Negro youth with college training forced to take employment in semi-skilled and lower white collar positions. Among the professions, only teaching and social work have been readily available to them.

The point is, of course, that the major inducement to educational achievement in our society is the promise of future occupational rewards. If, however, it is known in advance that these rewards will be largely withheld from certain socioeconomic and racial groups, then it is unlikely that high levels of educational achievement can be sustained in such groups. Thus academic performance may be devalued because the young in such groups see no relationship between it and the realities of their future.

What we have been saying about the relationship between educational performance and occupational rewards assumes, of course, that discrepancies between the two tend to be perceived by low income and minority groups in our society. Generally speaking, the evidence available does suggest that perceptions of opportunity do accord with the reality. In this connection, Hyman summarizes data which show that there are distinct differentials by socioeconomic status in judgments regarding the accessibility of occupational rewards. Thus 63 percent of one sample of persons in professional and managerial positions felt that the "years ahead held good chances for advancement," while only 48 percent of a sample of factory workers gave this response. Furthermore, the factory workers were more likely to think that "getting along well with the boss" or being a "friend or relative of the boss" were important determinants of mobility; professional and executive personnel were more likely to stress "quality of work" and "energy and willingness."[3] Such findings suggest that low-income persons do indeed perceive the impact of social origins upon their life changes. If these are the perceptions of occupational mobility held by parents in such groups, it is hardly likely that children in such families would hold contrary views on a wide scale. Under such circumstances, the perception of the role of education as a determinant of mobility may fail to assume the importance which we might otherwise wish.

Equality in Access to Educational Facilities

It is doubtful that lower-class persons are unaware of the general importance assigned to education in our society or of the relationship between education and social mobility. But they are probably also very much aware of their limited

---

[3] *Op. cit.*, p. 437.

opportunities to secure access to educational facilities. Educational achievement is not just a matter of favorable attitudes; opportunities must be available to those who seek them. For many members of the lower class, struggling to maintain a minimum level of subsistence, the goal of advanced education must seem remote indeed. In a family that can scarcely afford food, shelter, and clothing, pressure is exerted upon the young to leave school early in order to secure employment and thereby help the family. In a recent study of an extensive sample of adolescents in Nashville, Tennessee, Reiss and Rhodes found that most adolescents who quit school did so because they wanted to go to work immediately. Quitting school, their data show, is not necessarily a negative or rebellious response to compulsory-attendance laws but may be a necessary response to economic pressures.[4]

In the past few decades, a variety of studies have concluded that there are marked class differentials in access to educational facilities.[5] The lower the social position of one's father, the less likely that one can take advantage of educational opportunities. Furthermore, class differentials in access to educational facilities are not explained by differences in intelligence. If children from various social classes who have the same general intelligence are compared, differentials in chances to acquire an education still obtain.

The influence of economic barriers to education can be inferred from studies of situations in which these barriers have been temporarily relaxed. Warner and his associates, for example, observed a "sharp increase in college and high school enrollment [resulting from] the establishing of the National Youth Administration student-aid program in 1935."[6] In a more recent study, Mulligan examined the proportions of students from various socioeconomic strata enrolled in a Midwestern university before and during the G. I. Bill of Rights educational program. Not surprisingly, his data show that as a result of the government-aid program a larger proportion of students were drawn from the lower echelons of the society. This strongly suggests that the lower class contains many persons who desire higher education but cannot ordinarily afford to acquire it.[7]

Commenting on financial barriers to high-school attendance, Warner and his associates note: "There is a substantial out-of-pocket cost attached to attendance at a 'free' high school. . . . Students can go to school and spend little or no money. But [the poor] are barred from many of the school activities, they cannot even take regular laboratory courses, and they must go around in what is to high-school youngsters the supremely embarrassing condition of having no change to rattle in their pockets, no money to contribute to a party, no possibility of being independent in their dealings with their friends."[8]

---

[4] A. J. Reiss and A. L. Rhodes, "Are Educational Norms and Goals of Conforming and Delinquent Adolescents Influenced by Group Position in American Society?" *Journal of Negro Education* (Summer 1959), pp. 262–266.

[5] See W. L. Warner, R. J. Havighurst, and M. B. Loeb, *Who Shall Be Educated—The Challenge of Unequal Opportunities* (New York: Harper & Bros., 1944); Lipset and Bendix, *op. cit.*; Elbridge Sibley, "Some Demographic Clues to Stratification," *American Sociological Review*, VII (June 1942), 322–330; and George F. Zuok, "The Findings and Recommendations of the President's Commission of Higher Education," *Bulletin of the American Association of University Professors*, XXXV (Spring 1949), 17–22.

[6] W. L. Warner *et al., op. cit.*, p. 53.

[7] R. A. Mulligan, "Socio-Economic Background and College Enrollment," *American Sociological Review*, XVI, No. 2 (April 1961), 188–196.

[8] W. L. Warner *et. al., op. cit.*, pp. 53–54. For a further discussion of these and related matters, see A. B. Hollingshead, *Elmtown's Youth* (New York: John Wiley & Sons, 1949).

Aside from economic barriers in access to education, there is the further fact of inequality stemming from the organization of educational facilities for low-income youth. One problem is that of differentials in teacher turnover. For a variety of reasons, many teachers are reluctant to teach in the slum school. A study of the career patterns of Chicago public-school teachers documents the fact that teachers normally begin their careers in lower-class neighborhoods, where there are more vacancies, and transfer out as soon as they can.[9] Thus teachers in slum schools are generally less experienced.

The effect of this situation is especially unfortunate when one considers the characteristic instability of many slum communities, not to mention the economic uncertainties of slum youngsters' lives and the frequent changes in the composition of their families. It is important that the school, as represented by its teachers, be a constant, stable, omnipresent force in the community.

Because of the greater control problem posed by lower-class pupils and the greater turnover of teachers in slum schools, lower-class youngsters receive less actual instructional time than do school children in middle-class neighborhoods. Indeed, one study of a deprived-area school indicated that as much as 80 percent of the school day was devoted to discipline or organizational detail; even with the best teachers this figure never fell below 50 percent.[10] While these figures may be high, or unique to the particular school which was studied, problems in discipline and teacher turnover must inevitably limit instruction time in lower-class schools. In such instances, the role and self-image of the teacher may be transformed from instructor to that of monitor.

The generic problems of the school system—i.e., oversized classes, split shifts, inadequate staffing, the dearth of specialized services, etc.—are especially problematic for lower-class youngsters. For example, while an accepted New York State standard is 300 pupils to 1 guidance counselor in junior and senior high schools, ratios in New York City are 637 to 1 in the high schools, 1,710 to 1 in junior high schools. Still larger guidance loads are usual in elementary schools, with many such schools having no guidance person at all. In vocational high schools, which as a rule serve children from deprived backgrounds, counselors are assigned as many as 1,000 pupils each. Other specialties are similarly understaffed. In these and other ways, then, the accessibility of education is greatly influenced by socioeconomic factors. Inadequate educational performance among the poor can be understood in part as a response to restrictions in the availability of education and in part as a response to the inferior quality of the education which they do get.

If traditional channels to higher position, such as education, are restricted for certain categories of people, then pressures will mount for the use of alternative routes. Thus some lower-class persons orient themselves toward occupations in the fields of entertainment and sports. People of modest social origins who have been conspicuously successful in these spheres often become salient models for the young in depressed sectors of the society. The heavyweight champion, the night-club singer,

---

[9] Howard Becker, "The Career of the Chicago Public School Teacher," *American Sociological Review*, XVII, No. 7 (July 1952), 470–476.

[10] Martin P. Deutsch, *Minority Group and Class Status as Related to Social and Personality Factors in Scholastic Achievement* (New York: The Society for Applied Anthropology, Monograph No. 2, 1960), p. 23.

the baseball star—these symbolize the possibility of achieving success in conventional terms despite poor education and low social origins. The businessman, the physicist, the physician, on the other hand, occupy roles to which the lower-class youngster has little access because of his limited educational opportunities. By orienting himself toward occupations which offer some hope of success in spite of poor social origins and education, the lower-class boy follows a legitimate alternative to traditional avenues to success-goals.

But the dilemma of many lower-class young people is that these alternative avenues to success-goals are often just as restricted as educational channels, if not more so. Of the many lower-class adolescents who go into the "fight game," hoping to win social rewards—money and glamor—by sheer physical exertion and stamina, a few succeed, but the overwhelming majority are destined to fail. For these lower-class youth there seems no legitimate way out of poverty. Thus they experience desperation born of the perception that their position in the economic structure is relatively fixed and immutable—desperation made all the more poignant by their exposure to a cultural ideology in which failure to orient oneself upward is regarded as a moral defect and failure to become mobile as proof of it. In a society that did not encourage them to set their sights high, they might more easily adjust to their impoverished circumstances; but since social worth is so closely identified with social position in American society, discontent and alienation are experienced by many youth in the lower reaches of the social order. Here, then, is one general source of a lack of emphasis among low-income people upon the value of education.

SOCIALIZATION AND EDUCATIONAL ACHIEVEMENT

Various elements in the socialization of lower-class youth also help to account for poor educational performance. In general, these elements stem from two related sources: the character of lower-class occupations and the content of various ethnic and nationality values found in large segments of the lower class. Both of these forces markedly influence the nature of socialization in the lower class and help to account for the lower emphasis upon education and for the relatively poorer academic performance found there.

Occupation and Inadequate Socialization

Low income produces inadequacies in socialization, and this in turn has implications for educational achievement. In the lower-class family, the need to concentrate upon economic survival severely limits the amount of attention parents can allocate to the "non-essential" activity of stimulating their children's intellectual growth or planning their educational future. Further, the crowding, lack of privacy, and disorder characteristic of family life in many slums are poor preparation for the quiet, orderly classroom. Differentials by social class in this respect have been described by the Institute for Developmental Studies: "The lower-class home seems to be characterized by a lot of noise and very little sustained verbal communication, while the middle-class environment seems to be almost the reverse. Thus, the lower-class child entering school is ill-prepared for the classroom setting in which he is continually called upon to speak or be spoken to."[11] With less demand made upon him in the home, the lower-class youngster has less need to develop a sustained attention span or a high degree of articulateness; since thought processes are dependent upon the use of language, the result is underdevelopment of abstract thinking processes.

Intellectual stimulation in the form of books, recordings, trips, and the like is lacking in the lower-class home, for purely economic reasons if not for others as well. The youngster who has seen his parents read books, as have most middle-class children, enters school identified with people who are literate. His lower-class counterpart is less often exposed to experiences that whet his intellectual curiosity.

The lower-class child is also handicapped educationally by the inexperience of his parents, which limits their ability to prepare their youngster for school success; for example, they often lack the knowledge as well as the time to help with homework. Shyness and suspicion further inhibit the lower-class parent from demonstrating his interest by visiting the school, discussing his child's progress, and, when necessary, intervening in the child's behalf. The child may therefore receive little support in his attempt to bridge these two adult worlds.

The problems in socialization for education characteristic of lower-class children generally are most acute in the very bottom economic groups. The lower class is not all of a piece; there are distinctive subgroupings within it, and the extent of the problem in these various groups differs.

From the standpoint of economic stability, it is possible to conceive of the lower class as being composed of two broad groupings. The first is composed of those who are more or less regularly employed (excepting severe recessions, strikes, and the like) and may be called the "stable working class." Persons in this category engage in manual occupations of a semi-skilled or skilled character. The second broad grouping consists of those who are irregularly employed—the transient, casual, intermittent, seasonal, and occasional workers who engage in essentially unskilled forms of employment.

One of the major consequences of these economic differences is the character of family structure in the two groupings. The stable working class generally exhibits a solidary, patriarchal, sometimes extended kinship system. By contrast, the large grouping of irregularly employed persons generally exhibits a female-centered household characterized by much illegitimacy and frequently transient adult males. Both groups exhibit a variety of values in common, including an emphasis on security rather than risk, expressive rather than instrumental orientations (including a strong person orientation rather than a task or function orientation), traditionalism, pragmatism and anti-intellectualism. It is important to note, however, that these emphases are found more strongly in the irregularly employed class than in the stable working class. Indeed, it would be accurate to say that the stable working class stands more or less midway between the transient labor subculture and the middle class.

The importance of this socioeconomic distinction stems from the observa-

---

[11]Institute for Developmental Studies, *Descriptive Statement* (New York: New York Medical College, 1960), p. 2. For some related essays on lower-case socialization and education, see the following:

Allison Davis, "What Are Some of the Basic Items in the Relation of Intelligence Tests to Cultural Background?", *Intelligence and Cultural Differences*, Eells *et al.*, eds. (Chicago: University of Chicago Press, 1951), p. 26; Donald Super, *The Psychology of Careers* (New York: Harper & Bros., 1957), p. 108; Robert J. Havighurst and Bernice Neugarten, *Society and Education* (Boston: Allyn and Bacon, 1957), p. 265; Martin P. Deutsch, *op. cit.*, p. 25.

tion that the irregularly employed subgrouping within the lower class contributes disproportionately to underachievement and drop-outs. Persons socialized in this group experience the greatest discrepancy between socially-induced aspirations and socially-structured life chances. They are least likely to have been exposed to familial systems which can successfully inculcate values and skills essential in achieving upward mobility. For example, boys socialized in this sector of society are not likely to have had stable father figures who held stable occupational positions, and thus opportunities for identification with occupational roles are limited if not absent. Such identification is crucial to achievement, and it is difficult to make such identification in the absence of appropriate role models. In view of these facts, frustrations ensuing from discrepancies between aspirations and life chances are acute, and alienation from the school and other middle-class institutions is the consequence.[12]

As these cultural patterns emerge in response to economic life circumstances, persons who are exposed to them become all the more unable to negotiate channels of mobility. In primary and secondary schools, for example, the children of the poor find themselves at a competitive disadvantage with those from higher strata, for verbal fluency, a capacity for deferred gratification, a sustained attention span, and other attributes which facilitate academic achievement are more closely integrated with socialization in the middle-income than in the low-income strata of our society. The result is that many lower-income youngsters come to compare themselves invidiously with middle-income youngsters because the latter succeed more readily in school. Subsequently, some former adolescents may become estranged from the school and join the ranks of the dropouts. Continued exposure to the cultural patterns may even affect IQ scores adversely.

The major problem in dealing with self-defeating adaptations is that they generally become "functionally autonomous"—that is, once they come into existence, they tend to persist quite independent of the forces to which they were initially a response. The adaptation itself becomes elaborated and refined as a way of life into which people are directly socialized from birth. Hence they become carriers of the cultural system even before they have themselves experienced some of the frustrations discussed in the earlier part of this paper. Instead of developing a capacity to need and enjoy long-range accomplishments, for example, they may learn to need and enjoy immediate achievements; instead of developing satisfaction from risk-taking, they learn to derive satisfaction from successfully organizing their limited resources in a way that provides maximal security; instead of stressing instrumental skills, they may stress elaborate and stylized expressive modes of behavior. Once stabilized, in

---

[12] Work with the irregularly employed grouping within the lower-class should not necessarily be aimed at opening channels for them to middle-class status. Perhaps some can make the transition, and they of course should be afforded the opportunity to do so. But it appears to be true that the movement of groups out of this unstable economic situation to the middle class occurs in stages, the most important of which is the formation of a stable working-class culture. To move into this intermediate stage depends upon educational opportunities to acquire some middle-class values and upon economic opportunities to form a stable monogamous kinship system. Once this stage of socioeconomic development has been achieved, a base for subsequent movement into the middle class then exists. From the standpoint of educational policy, therefore, it follows that goals or aspirations for differing socioeconomic groupings should vary. In the case of the least economically stable groups, the achievement of a stable working-class culture should be the aspiration. Programs leading to middle-class status, however, would seem realistic for those who already have been socialized in the working-class world, and they should be encouraged in such aspirations.

other words, these patterns of living become capable of maintaining themselves in part through the induction of the young who learn to satisfy their needs through them. When the children of the poor eventually come to experience dissatisfaction with their lot in life as the larger society reaches them and generates status discontent, they then find that they are imperfectly socialized for competition in the middle-class world. Although they may have high aspiration, they do not have the values and skills which would permit them to compete effectively in the middle-class world. The task, then, is to institute programs which will permit the effective re-socialization of such youth— effective in the sense that they will enable them to acquire traits useful in the exploitation of new opportunities.

DIFFERENTIAL SOCIALIZATION AND EDUCATIONAL ACHIEVEMENT

It would be a mistake, however, to say that the problem of socialization in some parts of the lower class is a problem simply because it is deficient, inadequate or incomplete. There is the further problem of differential socialization, and it may well be that we have been insufficiently attentive to the task of taking these differential values into account in the structuring of educational programs.

The problem of differential socialization vis-à-vis educational achievement can best be seen by looking at certain ethnic and nationality values. By and large, immigrant groups historically have entered our social structure at the bottom, and thus it is in the lower class that one finds the greatest impact of such values. In many of the groups which have come to this country, distinctive systems of values were already well established and thus tended to persist for a number of generations here. Although the more superficial aspects of the American middle-class value system may have been acquired rapidly, the more subtle and deeply embedded aspects of the Old World values were abandoned less readily. Indeed, there is good reason to think that many of these values continue to exert a profound influence upon the behavior of many persons in the second and third generation.

The point to be made about these persisting value orientations is that they do not always facilitate success in the school. Our system of education places a strong stress upon doing rather than being, upon a future orientation rather than an orientation toward the present or the past, upon the notion that man is superordinate to nature rather than in harmony with it or subjugated by it, upon the notion that man is flexible and plastic and capable of change rather than that he is essentially evil and perhaps immutably evil. A child who has not acquired these particular value orientations in his home and community is not so likely to compete successfully with youngsters among whom these values are implicitly taken for granted. In a number of ethnic and nationality groups, a strong emphasis upon the value of being, on the present and the past, and the like can be detected. These values are rooted in traditions many centuries old, and can be expected to be extinguished only through successive generations of assimilation in this culture. Although the values may, after several generations, be greatly weakened, they nevertheless continue to exert a subtle influence in many spheres of role behavior, including educational performance. Part of the problem of under-achievement among some lower-class persons may therefore be attributed to the existence of these alternative value orientations to which the young are differentially socialized. This is a further sense, then, in which underachievement is supported in some ethnic and nationality subcultures in the lower class.

In conclusion, I would like to make a brief statement about the problem.of equality of opportunity in education. I take it that there are at least three respects in which equality can be understood. First, equality means that equivalent educational facilities shall be available whatever the socioeconomic position of the child. Second, equality means that individual differences in learning patterns shall be taken into account. Finally, equality means that the educational system shall not be organized in such a way as to favor children who are socialized in one rather than another part of the social structure. Differentials in socialization, arising from socioeconomic position and ethnic origins, must, like individual differences in learning, also be adjusted to by the school system. If the educational enterprise is simply an extension of the middle-class home, then it follows that only middle-class children will tend to do well in it. If the school fails to practice equality in these several respects, then it can be understood as contributing to the very problem which it otherwise deplores.

6-6   SOCIAL STRATIFICATION AND MOBILITY PATTERNS

Carson McGuire

Carson McGuire is professor of psychology at the University of Texas at Austin. He earned his Ph.D. at the University of Chicago. Professor McGuire is co-author of *Democracy in Jonesville* and *Growing Up in an Anxious Age* and author of *Talented Behavior in Junior High School* and many articles.

As a concluding statement on social stratification and education, Dr. McGuire discusses mobility patterns and orientations and the function of education in social mobility.

This is a paper on certain aspects of the general theory of social stratification with special reference to status and mobility in American society. Working hypotheses are embodied in the paper, and some are reinforced by brief summaries of selected research findings.[1] Particular attention is paid to the structural-functional variables[2] necessary for the comparative study of contemporary communities. Most of the structural phenomena may be ordered within a frame of reference which has key,

---

From *American Sociological Review*, XV, No. 2 (April 1950), 195–203. Copyright © 1950 by American Sociological Association; reprinted by permission of American Sociological Association and the author.

[1]My assignment is to make particular reference to the team research of W. Lloyd Warner and our associates in the so-called "Chicago group." The reader may detect consideration of the theory and findings of others whose work has not been cited.

[2]The search for variables (and their values) fitting a structural-functional theory parallels the approach of Talcott Parsons in, for example, "The Present Position and Prospects of Systematic Theory in Sociology," *Essays in Sociological Theory: Pure and Applied* (Glencoe, Ill.: The Free Press, 1949), pp. 17–41.

interrelated variables for analysis of the contexts of human behavior. The framework is a starting point for the functional or dynamic analysis of the major processes that appear to be operating. To illustrate this, a functional aspect of stratification is demonstrated in terms of patterns of mobility behavior.

From a theoretical point of view, social stratification is a special case of principles of inclusion and exclusion which characterize systems of human behavior. Two other structural elements, age and sex, are based upon visible biological distinctions. Patterned expectations according to age-grade and generalized social-sex role have predictable influences upon the behavior of individuals and upon their shared idea-systems. A third principle, that of segmentation or the status-ranking with which we are concerned, appears to order both distant and intimate social relationships. Experience in the resultant social matrix through time seems to affect the personality make-up of people, especially their preferred perceptions and relatively enduring value-attitudes. Finally, among people of similar status or between groupings at several status levels, there may be discrepant definitions of the situation where interest operates as a principle of inclusion or exclusion. The seeking efforts of individuals changing status and of competing interest groups have a mobile character.[3]

Only selected phases of such segmentation phenomena focusing upon status-mobility theory can be discussed within the limits of a paper. My first step is to clarify current misunderstandings about the social class concept.[4]

SOCIAL CLASS REALITY AND SCIENTIFIC CONSTRUCTS

Social class is a reality of American social stratification if the primary data of contemporary community studies are to have any meaning. Persons and families act and react toward one another as equals, superiors, and inferiors within the contexts of community behavior. Men and women, young and old, talk of themselves or their families in relation to other persons and their folks in a frame of reference characterized by rank. Just as in England, Canada, and other complex societies, there are valued symbols of status which one may have or achieve. Americans—and people all over the world—not only refer to their own relative position, either directly or indirectly, but also they "place" others in terms of differentially valued symbols and commonly understood levels of social participation and moral reputation. These persistent differentiations (and the way people behave in accord with them) form a crucial element of social class—a key concept in understanding American status-structure.

The essential reality of social class (the entity) is such that it can be approximated in a scientific manner. The descriptive categories used by Warner and his associates[5] are known to most social scientists and often are employed by laymen. The terms "lower class," "middle class," "upper class," and their subdivisions have

---

[3]Social mobility, change of status, is a neglected dimension in many otherwise brilliant analyses; for example, Herbert Blumer, "Sociological Theory in Industrial Relations," *American Sociological Review*, XII (June 1947), 271–278.

[4]The term "social class" as employed in American research has a certain equivalence to the term "social status" (or "*stratum*" stand) used by Max Weber, *The Theory of Social and Economic Organization* (New York: Oxford University Press, 1947), pp. 428–429.

[5]For example, W. Lloyd Warner and Paul S. Lunt, *The Social Life of a Modern Community* (New Haven: Yale University Press, 1941); Allison Davis, Burleigh B. Gardner and Mary R. Gardner, *Deep South* (Chicago: University of Chicago Press, 1941).

definite referents in the minds of many persons as well as commonly-accepted meanings. These social class categories have been employed in our study of Jonesville and other communities as values of a major variable in the analyses of their structure.[6] Jonesville, for instance, is typical in the sense that all of the interrelated status-mobility variables are present. The exact values of each variable for Jonesville are not necessarily the same as for any other community whether it be a country unit, the small town, a middle-sized city, or the varied and sometimes superimposed communities of a modern metropolis.[7]

Clarification of concepts usually moves from description and classification to the derivation of indices which enable the scientist to manipulate and assign meaningful values to the variables being studied. This has taken place in stratification research. The *index of status characteristics* is a construct, a product of multiple regression analysis.[8] Warner's I.S.C. attempts to approximate, with a minimum of error, the ascribed (or achieved) and very real *social class* status of a person or a whole family.[9] The intervening operation has been to obtain the *evaluated participation* of people in a "blue ribbon sample" to establish the index. Instead of Warner's E.P. technique as an intervening operation, some class analysts prefer to employ "prestige judges" and rating procedures.[10] Others start with the quantification of variates believed to define status, making the assumption that social status is what their test or technique measures.[11] Either of the first two procedures would seem to be acceptable in status analysis, but the last is questionable on obvious grounds.[12]

A fundamental notion of reciprocal relations among stratification theory, empirical data, and methods of study has been illustrated with reference to the social class concept. It is an analytical element[13]—a variable which represents emergent

---

[6] W. Lloyd Warner and Associates, *Democracy in Jonesville* (New York: Harper & Bros., 1949). The book is a product of team research under the auspices of the Committee on Human Development at the University of Chicago.

[7] Team research, lending credence to this proposition, has extended over the several kinds of communities. Some investigations have been reported; others are still in process. Tentative findings suggest emphasis upon variation among common variables in "city," "town," and, "country" and avoidance of an explicit "rural-urban" dichotomy.

[8] W. Lloyd Warner, Marchia Meeker, and Kenneth Eells, *Social Class in America* (Chicago: Science Research Associates, 1949).

[9] The Warner I.S.C. is computed from ratings on scales for (1) occupation, (2) source of income, (3) area lived in, and (4) house type. Alternate scales (suited to various purposes and situations where different kinds of information are available) are being developed for education attained, religious affiliations, and to correct for ethnicity. These scales are used to modify or replace certain components in the original Warner index.

[10] For instance, August B. Hollingshead, *Elmtown's Youth* (New York: John Wiley & Sons, 1949), pp. 25–41. The Hollingshead procedure in the same community separates out the same five classes as the Warner technique with close case by case agreement on an overlap of families in the two studies.

[11] For example, F. Stuart Chapin, *The Measurement of Social Status by the Use of the Social Status Scale* (Minneapolis: University of Minnesota, 1933); Harrison G. Gough, "A Short Social Status Inventory," *Journal of Educational Psychology*, XL (January 1949), 52–56.

[12] Proposals to employ either the Alba Edwards or N.O.R.C. occupational classifications are also questionable. First, Warner's scale for "occupation" has several levels for each kind of occupational category found in either set of classifications. Second, the high correlation in the Warner study between "occupation" and "social-class placement for Old Americans" is for a "blue ribbon" sample. In random samples, the "occupation" component only accounts for about half of the variation. Hence it is wiser to use a multiple component index wherein the several scales correct for each other.

[13] The term is elaborated in Talcott Parsons, *The Structure of Social Action* (New York: McGraw-Hill, 1937), pp. 34–35, 616–624, 738–752.

properties of individuals or of social groupings within complex systems of motivated human behavior. Coping with actual data forces the social scientist to clarify and recast his theoretical ideas. Moving from descriptive categories of status reality to observable indices, by successive approximations, results in constructs which enable him to employ the variable economically in various kinds of research.

COMMUNITY STATUS-STRUCTURE

Social class is only one of a number of interdependent variables involved in status-mobility theory and investigation. A schematic diagram (Figure 1) shows values of the social class variable and how they fit with other analytical elements in community status-structure. A majority of present-day communities have all of the structural, class, ethnic, and color caste elements of the "ideal type" chart.[14] Some will lack an upper, or even an upper-middle class. Although informants often talk of certain families within a community as "society," the ones referred to may have "middle-class goal structures" (to use the Kluckhohn phrase) rather than the class orientations and shared beliefs and values of the general American upper class. Other localities, especially certain suburbs of large cities, will have a relatively small lower-class population. Again, places like Jonesville have very few members of a subordinated caste-like, dark-skinned segment. The actual ethnic or minority groupings differ from community to community. These variations make the conceptualization valuable for they facilitate both comparative and intensive analysis.

The schematic diagram depicts seven social structures or systems of social relations.[15] The family is a basic social unit. It is a person's family (of orientation) that identifies him as being affiliated initially with a status and a culture pattern. The informal associations (social cliques, street-corner gangs, etc.) and the formal organizations (for instance, Rotary or the P.T.A.) are recurrent contexts of behavior. Being a structured situation, a formal organization permits its members to have contacts with people of various class positions without the necessity of intimacy. Acceptance within relatively unstructured informal associations is the crux of status reputation.[16]

The other four social structures are the basic situational institutions, outside of the family, influencing status and role (the functional aspect of status). The political, economic, religious, and educational institutions are relatively separate but interdependent status hierarchies. No matter how similar their behavior may be in the several situations, people tend to think of their roles in business, in government, in

---

[14] At least three kinds of class culture patterns or shared value-attitude systems also may be present: upper (ego-oriented?), middle (superego-oriented?) and lower (impulse-oriented?). Class orientation of a person or family does not necessarily coincide with status reputation or participation, nor with socio-economic position. This, as we shall see, is a fundamental set of discrepancies underlying mobility patterns in American society.

[15] To conserve space, material in the original draft of the paper dealing with the several social structures has been omitted.

[16] When new families come to a community, tentative appraisals are made. Variations of the following questions are asked: What do you do? Where do you work? Where do you live? Who lives near there? What is your church? Where did you go to school? The index of status characteristics is, in a sense, a set of scales which appraise answers to such questions. There are "errors of placement" because the critical test of status reputation is membership in and reference to formal and informal associations, or the lack of such affiliation (including potential family interaction).

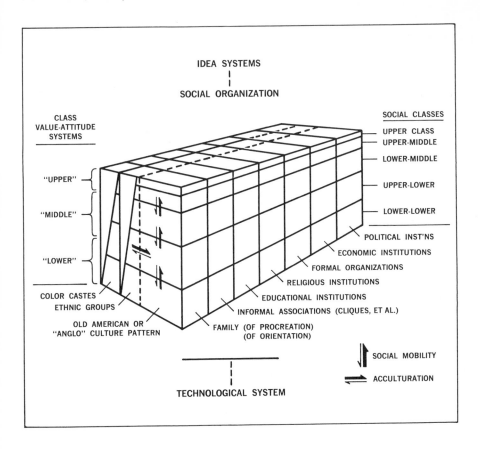

Fig. 1. Schematic Diagram of Community Status-Structure

the church, and with regard to education, as somewhat separated identities. In America, we feel that democracy is threatened when persons or "interest groups" within one of the vertical hierarchies attain "too much power." Differential attitudes within communities and in the total society toward "boss rule," "big business," and "government control" are cases in point. Among people at relatively the same status level and within an institutional pattern (for instance, between "management" and "top labor leaders"), the conflict of interests assumes paramount importance. One means of achieving status, of becoming socially mobile, is by activity within and on behalf of an interest grouping.

Understanding of structure or a pattern of contexts permits conceptualization of function or sets of processes which constantly are operating or which intrude under certain conditions. The schematic diagram conveys the loci of changes involved in two of the processes associated with stratification. Movement vertically from one class to another—up or down, and usually at uneven rates among the seven structures—is social mobility.[17] Movement across from an ethnic to the "old American" (or "Anglo") culture pattern is acculturation (or assimilation). Both social mobility and acculturation are assessed ultimately in terms of variations from the original family status.[18] Acculturation often is followed by upward or downward mobility. In studying these processes, the diagram merely guides the investigator. He is reminded to look for movement in the several contexts, for the acquisition of status symbols (including residence), and for changes in social behavior and underlying value-attitudes.

MOTIONS OF STATUS AND MOBILITY

The problems of theory and research with regard to social mobility as a functional aspect of stratification phenomena are clarified somewhat when at least three notions of status are considered. First, inherent in the social organization, there is *social class* status. This marks the beginning and the end of mobility. Second, *socioeconomic* discrepancies clearly are observable. Occupation and income are important elements of social position, provided wealth is translated into appropriate symbols of status-rank and accompanied by acceptable behavior in the several community contexts. Education opens up opportunities and sets limits upon socioeconomic status. The tendency to classify by socioeconomic status, an external attribute, does not seem as great a contradiction of the American cultural belief that "all men are equal" as does differentiation by total life style—social class. Finally, class culture patterns or shared *value-attitudes* partially segment the American idea system, at least, into two competing (upper and middle class) and one alternative (lower class) cultural orientations.

The several social classes have evolved, through time and with regional variations, typical modes of behavior accompanied by characteristic beliefs and sentiments. From the Jonesville and other data, it would appear that shared class value-attitudes underlie these observable differences. As attitudes are learned within the family, among age-mates, and in community contexts (largely through reality testing, imitative identification, and insight with subsequent introjection), preferred class-typed meanings as well as symbols are attached to them. During childhood and adolescence, social learning at home, among same-age friends, and in school and church is oriented to a way of life. Given an opportunity to affiliate with youth from the "better" family backgrounds, lower status young people can and do learn much of the "higher" life style. The private as well as the shared value-attitudes of the upwardly mobile person are, in many respects, much like people in a social class above him.[19] By and

---

[17] The term "social mobility" is defined as "transition of an individual from one social position to another," by Pitirim A. Sorokin, *Social Mobility* (New York: Harper & Bros, 1927). Population mobility enters into consideration only insofar as in- and out-migration of people among communities facilitates their social mobility.

[18] Means of appraising social mobility and assessing acculturation from case data have been worked out by Martin Loeb; cf. Jurgen Ruesch *et al*, *Chronic Disease and Psychological Invalidism*, Psychosomatic Medicine Monographs (New York: Paul Hoever, 1946), pp. 102–124; Jurgen Ruesch *et al*, *Acculturation and Illness*, Psychological Monograph No. 292 (Washington: A.P.A., 1948), 1–40.

[19] The evidence for these general statements and an analysis of the processes involved will appear in later reports of research.

large, the climbing, striving, clinging, or declining behavior of the mobile person is a function of discrepancies among social class, socioeconomic, and value-attitude attributes which may be regarded as variables. The discrepancies, in a sense, are indices of internal and external forces pressing upon the mobile individual.

It would appear that there are dynamic processes in the American social structure which operate to forge persevering, motivating, guiding aspects of individual personality. Variations in overt and covert behavior are related intimately to status situation and mobile or conforming behavior. The overt, social aspects of *mobility orientation* are recognized, either directly or indirectly, when people are encouraged to talk about one another.

> *Climber:* "He's really getting along in the world." "Oh! She made a good marriage and finally got out of that mess at home."
> *Strainer:* "He's really trying to get ahead—but I don't think he's got what it takes." "She's doing her best to get in. . . ."
> *Static:* (non-mobile): "Like father, like son." "She's a nice, quiet person like her mother." "He'll follow in his father's footsteps." "She's not much interested in things—stays at home."
> *Clinger:* "He's trying to follow in his father's footsteps, but he's not doing so well." "Her folks didn't leave much—she's going to have a hard time." "They're just managing to hang on."
> *Decliner:* "Just a backslider." "She dropped out of things—we never see her anymore." "The family's hit the skids—the kids are delinquent." "Maladjusted." "Alcoholic."

These categories have been adopted as tentative values of mobility orientation, an analytical element in exploratory studies of mobility patterns.

SOCIAL MOBILITY IN AMERICAN SOCIETY

Social mobility is a process which has meaning only in stratified contexts. From both the social and the psychological point of view, generalized mobility orientations are a function of a situation wherein there is a status system in the social organization and an "American Dream" in the idea system. The "American Dream" says in part that everyone has "the right to succeed" and that each should do his best "to reach the top." Is this theme in accord with the realities of American social stratification? Is there a pattern of mobility and conformity? How much social mobility actually occurs?

Provisional answers to these questions may be derived in two ways. First, it is possible to work out a set of estimates for the total American society based upon census data. Second, in the Jonesville research, 300 young people have been studied through the teens to adulthood, and patterns of mobility and conformity are clearly evident.[20] For what it is worth, the estimate and the sampling study appear to corroborate one another.

---

[20]The samples included nearly all persons in Jonesville town and Abraham county born in two separate years of the 1920's. Among the 300, including 143 males and 157 females, are those who left Jonesville for higher education and those who migrated elsewhere in later youth and adulthood.

The estimates of Table I have been obtained by employing "social mathematics" and collating census data in terms of indices of status. In this manner it is possible to approximate the social class distribution of the population for a particular period. The class reproduction rates vary in such a way that more than sixty percent of all children are born into lower-class families. Hence, a balance of upward mobility is required to maintain the overall status-structure. Insofar as the table is a good estimate, it would seem that at least twenty percent of the American population moves upward in social class status each generation.

TABLE 1.

PERCENT OF SOCIAL MOBILITY IN AMERICAN SOCIETY BY STATUS*

Social Class	Population Distribution by Status	Population by Net Rate of Reproduction	Net Social Mobility Required	Percent of Mobility from Status Below
Upper Class	3.0	2.5	+ 0.5	+ 7.7
Upper-Middle	9.0	6.5	+ 3.0	+ 10.7
Lower-Middle	36.0	28.0	+ 11.0	+ 28.2
Upper-Lower	35.0	39.0	+ 7.0	+ 29.1
Lower-Lower	17.0	24.0	—	—
Totals	100.0	100.0	+ 21.5	—

*Space does not permit explanation of the methods of social mathematics, of the relative reproduction rates employed, or of the projection of trends which indicate an increasing middle-class segment in American society. Similar tables have been calculated independently by Robert J. Havighurst.

To comprehend the table, the figure "+ 3.0" mobile to upper-middle in the third column is the difference between "9.0" in column 1 and the "6.0" left in column 2 when "+ 0.5" percent of a generation move into upper class. The fourth column indicates the percent of young people in the social class just below (or others from farther down) who will have to move up in class status to maintain the composition of the American status-structure.

These estimates may be compared with data from the Jonesville research where family social background and present adult status of the 300 young people are known. For our present purposes, differences between the distribution of all Jonesville families by status and the distribution of youth born into the two age-groups by status permit a calculation of "net social mobility required." In Table 2, although Jonesville has a relatively greater proportion of people in upper-lower class, the pattern of figures is similar to that for Table 1. The net upward mobility "required" takes the same form as the estimated mobility pattern for the total society. Since there seems to be about five percent downward mobility, and each person who drops in status has to be replaced, the estimate and the sample data indicate that total upward mobility in American society is approximately twenty-five percent of each generation.

TABLE 2.

PERCENT OF SOCIAL MOBILITY "REQUIRED" AMONG 300 MEMBERS OF TWO AGE-GROUPS OF JONESVILLE YOUTH

Social Class	Distribution by Status (Jonesville)	Age-Groups by Family Status	Net Social Mobility Required	Percent of Mobility from Status Below
Upper Class	2.8	1.0	+ 1.8	+ 31.5*
Upper-Middle	7.9	5.7	+ 4.0	+ 13.7
Lower-Middle	35.1	29.0	+ 10.1	+ 21.4
Upper-Lower	41.2	47.3	+ 4.0	+ 23.5
Lower-Lower	13.0	17.0	—	—
Totals	100.0	100.0	+ 19.9	—

*At the upper-class level, where small numbers are concerned, there are fluctuations according to the community and age-group studied.

The tables would suggest a working hypothesis that the proportion of social mobility is much greater from lower-class family backgrounds. To sharpen the focus, twin propositions might be stated about the function of education in a complex, stratified society.

(1) The function of the public schools is to make certain that only a minimum number of young people from middle-class homes decline in status and, at the same time, to recruit the necessary proportion of youth from lower-class families into a middle-class way of life or—at least—into assuming responsibilities for productive work and conforming citizenship.

(2) The function of higher education is to make certain that only a minimum number of young people from upper-middle and upper-class homes decline in status and, at the same time, to recruit "promising" youth from lower-middle and lower-class backgrounds into an upper-middle class way of life or—at least—into being informed, contributing citizens.

In a sense, these statements are calculated to provoke controversy. This is so because the beliefs and idea systems of the culture ("what ought to be") tend to vary somewhat from the realities in the interaction systems of American society ("what really is"). Nevertheless, these twin propositions would seem to express precisely what we are requiring of our educational system. Variations on the same theme underlie present concerns about "the American family."[21] Perhaps community agencies and programs of mental hygiene, social welfare, and so forth are set up (in reality) to control mobility

[21] Probably there is no such entity as "the American family." Structurally, the lower-class family is "extended," the middle-class "immediate," and the upper-class family is "interconnected." Functionally, the family orientation may be "conforming" in terms of the class-typed value attitudes of both parents, or "mobile" when emphasis is upon climbing behavior, or "divergent" when father and mother vary in terms of preferred culture patterns and status affiliations.

patterns. Some of the propositions that could be made would be obvious were it not for the fact reality often is clouded by emotional and ideological blocks in our perception.[22]

Mobility patterns already are evident among members of the two Jonesville age-groups studied. Table 3 has been constructed to show variations from the original family social class status compared with the index of adult status achieved by these young men and women upon their transition to the adult world.[23] It indicates the number and percent of upward mobile behavior, of those conforming to family status, and of persons who may be or who actually are moving downward. Most of those moving upward are climbers in mobility orientation, but a number of strainers (psychologically speaking) are included. By and large the non-mobile are static persons, but some would be classified as strainers or clingers. Some of the downward mobile have been

TABLE 3.

FAMILY SOCIAL CLASS AND INITIAL ADULT STATUS IN TWO AGE-GROUPS

Initial Adult Status	Social Class of Family					Total	Percent
	LL	UL	LM	UM	U		
Upper Class	—	—	—	1	3	4	1.3
Upper-Middle	—	4	19	15	—	38	12.7
Lower-Middle	2	33	63	1	—	99	33.0
Upper-Lower	11	97	3	—	—	111	47.0
Lower-Lower	38	8	2	—	—	48	16.0
Total	51	142	87	17	3	300	
Percent	17.0	47.3	29.0	5.7	1.0		100.0

PERCENT OF MOBILE AND CONFORMING BEHAVIOR

Upward social mobility	25.5	26.0	20.8	5.9	—	(70)	23.3
Non-mobile or conforming	74.5	68.4	73.5	88.2	100.0	(216)	72.1
Downward social mobility	—	5.6	5.7	5.9	—	(14)	4.6
Net upward mobility	25.5	20.4	15.1	—	—	(56)	18.7*

*Since initial adult status is measured, in part, by early adult occupation and source of income, young people who later improve their socioeconomic status will not be included in this approximation of incipient net upward mobility.

[22] A case for examining supposedly obvious facts is made by Gustav Ichheiser, "Misunderstandings in Human Relations: A Study in False Social Perception," *American Journal of Sociology*, LV (September 1949), part 2, 1–70.

[23] The index of initial adult status is a tentatively validated construct derived from scales for (1) subject's occupation, (2) source of income, (3) education attained, and (4) religious affiliation.

categorized as decliners, but others appear to be clingers. Mobility into the upper-middle and upper classes does take time to establish the necessary socioeconomic base as well as social participation and status reputation. Hence some of the incipient upper-middle class persons, especially the strainers, actually will fail in their attempt to achieve that status. On the other hand, there is reason to believe that more than one upper-middle class individual eventually will attain upper class status and that the proportion moving from lower to lower-middle class will be greater than shown in the table. For instance, some of the young men from lower-class homes with a high school education are learning skilled trades which eventually should support a "good" middle-class home, providing they make the "right" marriage.

These mobility patterns are manifest functions (objective consequences)[24] of discernible processes which operate in the total American status-structure. The alternative patterns appear, in part, as resultants of differential social (as well as intellectual and emotional) learning within specific community contexts. Paralleling the patterns, there are personal motivations which have been termed mobility orientations—climber, strainer, static, clinger, and decliner. Since motive and function are independent variables, persons of climber mobility orientation do not necessarily constitute all of those who succeed in an upward mobility pattern. The latent function (generally unrecognized consequences) of mobility patterns is the occurrence of discrepancies between individual orientations and places in the status-structure which contribute to maladjustment, neurotic behavior, or compensatory action.

The realities of the American stratification system allow a substantial proportion of the population to live in accord with the "American Dream." At least the proposition seems to be in accord with the available data. The "room at the top" appears to be a result of not less than three phenomena. First, there is a differential birth rate, with the lower-class families producing relatively more children than families of social classes above. Second, there has been a long-term shift in social structure, with "places" for more middle-class people (accompanied by an increasing demand for secondary and higher education). Third, there is the downward mobility of some persons in each generation. Paralleling these phenomena of American stratification, there is the "push" of the ideology toward cultural attainment and a "higher" way of life (usually coupled with increasing productivity in the technological system).

However, all of this could be changed. If the class birth rates were equalized, if the structure were to become static, or if declining behavior were checked completely by therapy and other measures, we might expect upward mobility to decrease sharply. The dynamic processes now at work in American society no longer would operate. The "open class" stratification and the mobility patterns of our society would tend to disappear.

---

[24] Robert K. Merton, "Manifest and Latent Functions," *Social Theory and Social Structure* (Glencoe, Ill.: The Free Press, 1949), pp. 21–81.

ETHNIC AND RACIAL GROUPS: INTRODUCTION

In most modern societies that contain a variety of races and ethnic groups, racial and ethnic identity is often maintained through prejudice directed toward the minority groups by the dominant racial and ethnic group(s). Strong motivations for upward social mobility may minimize the difficulties of minority groups in adjusting to the dominant cultural group, but, even then, there is evidence that for cultural cohesion and identification these subgroups cling to residual characteristics that inhibit their full participation in the dominant culture.

Teachers and administrators working with representatives of these groups must make decisions similar to those regarding social class differences. Related to the encouragement of upward mobility and economic self-sufficiency is the responsibility of determining whether the elimination of cultural characteristics may lead to psychological disintegration and social dysfunction. As illustrated in previous readings, cultural pluralism can only result when individual differences are acknowledged and treasured, but all too often school success is measured in accommodation and achievement that reflect the middle-class social ethic. To solve this dilemma, the educator must assist individuals in retaining those cultural traits that provide self-satisfaction without hindering full participation in the dominant culture. The educational program should be designed to avoid both withdrawal from participation and overidentification with the dominant group.

The following selections focus on cultural differences and similarities. Some attention is given to the Negro, the American Indian, and the Mexican-American as three subgroups that have encountered the most difficulty in adjusting to the dominant Anglo-American cultural pattern. To examine the literature on all minority groups in America would be an impossible task. The general approach suggested in this section, however, may also apply to racial and minority groups in the reader's community. Details of other minority groups may be found in social science literature; the educator must understand such details in order to provide an effective program.

As with social class membership, the reader is warned against using these generalizations to stereotype members of racial and ethnic groups. There is no "typical" Negro child, Indian child, or Mexican-American child. Within each group there is tremendous individual variation; consequently, the teacher should diagnose individual rather than group difficulties. The following statements about racial and ethnic groups are merely guidelines to aid in diagnosis of individual problems of adaption to the dominant culture.

6-7   ETHNIC DIFFERENCES

Otto Klineberg

Otto Klineberg is a professor of social psychology at Columbia University. He received his M.A. from Harvard and his Ph.D. at Columbia. He studied in France with the United Nations Education, Science, and Culture Organization as a recipient of a Guggenheim Fellowship. Dr. Klineberg is the author of numerous articles and several books, including *Social Psychology, Race Differences*, and *Tension Affecting International Understanding*. In this article he dispels many myths concerning race and ethnic group membership.

INTRODUCTION

The problem of psychological differences between ethnic groups—"races" and nations—has always been of interest to the social psychologist. At various times and in many countries it has obtained a practical application and a political significance which have made it far more than an academic question. Since these practical applications have been justified in the name of science, it is especially important to know with some precision the findings of scientists who have worked in this field. It is a field in which objectivity is rare, but for that reason all the more important, and it has become the real duty of the student of social science to inform himself as to what may legitimately be said on so controversial a topic.

The notion that racial classifications may be artificial and arbitrary is not a new one. In 1843 Pritchard[1] expressed the opinion "that all mankind constitute but one race, or proceed from a single family." The French naturalist Buffon[2] wrote, "Species, orders, and classes exist only in our imagination. They are merely conventions. Nothing really exists but the individual. Nature does not recognize our definitions: she has never classified her work by group or kind." The German philosopher Herder[3] also protests against the use of the term "race" in connection with man, since there are always transitional forms between one alleged race and another. Even Blumenbach insists that "the various types of men differ from each other in degree and not in kind and are connected with each other by innumerable gradations."[4]

The discrepancies in the racial classifications, the fact that transitional forms may always be discovered, and the marked degree of overlapping in physical characteristics between one group and another, appear to justify the conclusion that human races, in any strict sense of the term, exist only in the mind of the classifier. It may be that at some future date new methods in the field of physical anthropology

From *Social Psychology*, Revised Edition, by Otto Klineberg, pp. 291–324. Copyright © 1940, 1954, Holt, Rinehart and Winston, Inc. Reprinted by permission of the publishers.

[1] Pritchard, A., *The Natural History of Man*, 1843.
[2] Buffon, G. L., *Histoire Naturelle*, 36 volumes, 1749–1788.
[3] Herder, J. C., *Ideen zur Philosophie der Geschichte der Menschheit*, 1784–1791.
[4] J. S. Huxley and A. C. Haddon, *We Europeans*, 1935, p. 27.

or genetics may make it possible to reach a sound differentiation, but the techniques at present available hold little hope in this direction. When the method of blood groupings was first applied to race by the Hirszfelds,[5] it was thought that it might eliminate the difficulties inherent in other approaches and make it possible to arrive at an objective and scientifically acceptable classification. This hope has now been shown to be unfounded, and the complications in the use of the blood groups are at least as great as those found with the more usual physical criteria. Although many anthropologists insist upon retaining the concept of human races, and many new classifications still appear, by far the most reasonable position seems to be that there is only one human race, and that the distinctions found within it are relatively unimportant. For that reason the present writer prefers, when referring to existing populations, to use the term "ethnic group," which may be distinguished by inherited physical type, or by culture, or by nationality or by any combination of these.

Even if this position is accepted, however, the problem of the meaning of physical differences still exists and requires more direct consideration. Although the usual distinction between the Negro and the Caucasian may have little significance in terms of a scientifically valid classification, it is certainly taken seriously by the large majority of people. On the basis of the customary racial classification, a great deal of research has been carried on, and there is now a voluminous literature on the question of the psychological and cultural implications of race differences. Most of this has centered upon the problem of ethnic differences in ability, and we turn now to an appraisal of the arguments which have been used in this connection.

THE BIOLOGICAL ARGUMENT FOR "RACIAL" SUPERIORITY

One type of argument heard with some frequency is that "races" differ in their degree of "primitiveness"—more specifically, that one physical type, for example, that of the Negro, may have developed earlier from the ancestral anthropoid stock and represents therefore a species inferior to the later evolved Caucasian or Mongolian. This assumption determines the nature of the developmental or genealogical trees found in books by Osborn, Warden[6] and others. It rests upon the observation that in certain physical characteristics, for instance, the wide flat nose, the long arms, etc., the Negro resembles the anthropoid more than do either of the other two racial stocks. This argument has been examined in detail by Boas, Kroeber,[7] and others. As they have pointed out, this hierarchy of physical types depends upon the nature of the criteria used. There are many characteristics in which the Negro resembles the anthropoid less than do other physical types. As Kroeber points out, there is an approximately equal number of ape-like characteristics in the three stocks, and no decision is possible as to which is the most primitive.

It is frequently argued that the physical differences create a presumption in favor psychological differences. Kroeber[8] states that there is "no sound reason to expect anything else but that races which differ anatomically also differ in some

---

[5] L. Hirszfeld and H. Hirszfeld, "Serologic Differences Between the Blood of Different Races," *Lancet*, II, No. 5016 (1919), 675–678.

[6] H. F. Osborn, *Men of the Old Stone Age*, 1918; C. J. Warden, *The Evolution of Human Behavior*, 1932.

[7] Franz Boas, *Anthropology and Modern Life*, 1928; A. L. Kroeber, *Anthropology*, 1923.

[8] A. L. Kroeber, "Cultural Anthropology," *The Problem of Mental Disorder* (edited by M. Bentley and E. V. Cowdry), 1934, p. 352.

degree physiologically and psychologically." Franz Boas[9] wrote in the first edition of *The Mind of Primitive Man* in 1911: "It does not seem probable that the minds of races which show variations in their anatomical structure should act in exactly the same way. Differences of structure must be accompanied by differences of function, physiological as well as psychological; and as we found clear evidence of differences in structure between the races, so we must anticipate that differences in mental characteristics will also be found." It is significant that this passage does not appear in the later edition (1938) of the book, and it seems highly probable that Boas changed his mind on this point.

The fact is that there is no sound reason to expect any such relationship. Races differ anatomically by definition; if they did not differ anatomically, they would not be different races. Before we may assume that this has any psychological significance, however, we must have independent evidence of some genetic or other relationship between psychological characteristics and those anatomical features used in racial classification. Differences in skin color, for example, may have arisen in response to the direct or indirect effect of the physical environment. It is possible, as Linton[10] suggests, that the different skin color in tropical and in cold regions may be related not to differences of heat, but of light intensity. The actinic rays of the sun are beneficial in small quantities, but harmful in large ones. The skin pigment seems to act as a ray filter, its efficiency being related to the depth of color. In the tropics a dark skin color is an advantage since it prevents the absorption of too great a quantity of actinic rays; in cold regions a light skin color aids in the absorption of the necessary amount. Under these conditions a process of natural selection may help to fix one or the other skin color as a racial trait. If this interpretation is correct, there is no reason to suppose that psychological factors are in any way involved in the process of selection. The dark skin would simply be more advantageous in one physical environment and would therefore survive. Unless there is some other reason to assume an original relationship between skin color and psychology, the probabilities are that this form of natural selection would have no psychological significance whatsoever.

In the second place, Kroeber's argument assumes that there is in general some necessary connection between physical and psychological characteristics. This is a problem which has interested psychologists and physiologists throughout the history of their research, and a large amount of material has been accumulated. There have been studies of the possible psychological significance of various physiognomic features, including skin color, shape of the head, size of the nose, height of forehead, convexity and concavity of facial profile, glandular make-up and general bodily constitution. Some of these attempts, for example the last, have for a time held out promise of the establishment of a positive relationship, and in particular the theories of Kretschmer and Sheldon[11] concerning the relation between constitution and personality have received considerable attention. In any case, such constitutional typologies do not involve to any important degree the specific characteristics—skin color, head shape, hair texture, etc.—that have been used in racial classifications. As far as such characteristics are concerned, the careful examination of the research data by Paterson,

---

[9] Franz Boas, *The Mind of Primitive Man*, 1911.

[10] R. Linton, *The Study of Man*, 1936.

[11] E. Kretschmer, *Physique and Character*, 1925; W. H. Sheldon, S. S. Stevens, and W. W. Tucker, *The Varieties of Human Physique*, 1940; Sheldon and Stevens, *The Varieties of Temperament*, 1942.

Anastasi and Foley,[12] and others justifies the conclusion that not a single one of them has proved any positive relationship between physique and mentality. This means that we have no right to assume a relation between physical and psychological differences and to treat the problem of race differences as if this assumption had been verified. (The problem of sex differences is, of course, in a different category.)

There is one physical feature which requires somewhat more detailed consideration—namely, the size and shape of the brain. As far as size is concerned, the earlier studies apparently demonstrated certain differences in averages, the brain of the Negro being somewhat smaller than that of the White. Some significance has been attached to this difference. It must be borne in mind, however, that the overlapping is very great, so that there are a great many Negro brains larger than the White average. In addition, the fact that the brains of certain Negro groups like the Kaffirs and the Amaxosa are on the average larger than those of certain White groups like the Scots makes it difficult to assume any significant "race" difference in this respect. It is probable that general body contours as well as physical well-being also play a part in determining brain size. Most important of all, a very careful study of Negro and White brains from similar (low) socio-economic status made by Todd and Lindala[13] revealed "no significant stock differences." Finally, the fact that studies of brain size within the White group have failed to show any close correspondence with level of mentality, and the added fact that the brain size of women is both relatively and absolutely inferior to that of men, throw further doubt on the psychological significance of possible group differences in this respect.

In connection with the qualitative characteristics of the brain, the early investigations of Bean[14] have focused attention upon possible Negro-White differences. In a series of studies Bean arrived at the conclusion that the frontal area of the brain was less well-developed in the Negro than in the White, and the posterior area better developed. He believed that this difference paralleled the "known fact" that the Negro is inferior in the higher intellectual functions and superior in those concerned with rhythm and sense perception. Another important difference was in the depth of the convolutions of the cortex, those of the Negro being much shallower and more "childlike" than those of the White. There were also differences in the shape of the corpus callosum, which connects the two hemispheres of the cerebrum, and in the temporal lobe, but these were not regarded as having any direct psychological significance. It happened that these studies were carried out at Johns Hopkins University under the direction of Professor Mall, head of the Department of Anatomy. Mall was for some reason uncertain of Bean's results, and he repeated the whole study[15] on the same collection of brains on which Bean had worked; he took the precaution, however, of comparing the brains without knowing in advance which were Negro and which were White. When he and his associates placed in one group

---

[12]D. G. Paterson, *Physique and Intellect*, 1930; A. Anastasi and J. P. Foley, Jr., *Differential Psychology*, 1949.

[13]T. W. Todd and A. Lindala, "Dimensions of the Body; Whites and Negroes of Both Sexes," *American Journal of Physical Anthropology*, XII (1928), 35–119.

[14]R. B. Bean, "Some Racial Peculiarities of the Negro Brain," *American Journal of Anatomy*, V (1906), 353–432.

[15]F. P. Mall, "On Several Anatomical Characters of the Human Brain," *American Journal of Anatomy*, IX (1909), 1–32.

those brains which had rich convolutions, and in another those with convolutions which were shallow, they found exactly the same proportion of Negro and White brains in the two groups. When further they measured the size of the frontal and posterior lobes in the two groups of brains, they found no difference in their relative extent. As a consequence Mall came to the conclusion that Bean's findings had no basis in fact, and that it had not been demonstrated that Negro brains differed in any essential manner from those of Whites. Incidentally, these two studies taken together illustrate in a very significant manner the importance of stereotypes and "mental set" in determining what one will see in any given situation. There can be no doubt that Bean was sincere in his belief that he had observed these differences between the two groups of brains. It seems clear, however, that because of the expectation of finding signs of inferiority in the Negro, and because of his knowledge of the origin of the brains he was examining, he actually "saw" differences which did not exist. In any case Mall's more carefully controlled study testifies to the fallacy of the popular assumption that one can recognize a Negro brain by the presence of certain definite inferiorities.

THE CULTURAL ARGUMENT

A second group of arguments in favor of the superiority of certain ethnic groups over others centers upon the question of their relative contributions to culture or civilization. This is the type of argument made popular by Gobineau and used by many writers who more of less followed his example. Gobineau spoke of the superior "race" as the Aryans; Houston Stewart Chamberlain[16] glorified the Teutons; Madison Grant[17] and Lothrop Stoddard[18] and many others have spoken of the supremacy of the Nordics. Throughout the variations in terminology there is the common tendency among these writers to regard as superior the North European, usually conceived as tall, blond and blue-eyed; the other European groups are regarded as having made relatively inferior contributions, but they are still superior to the Mongolians, and even more markedly to the African Negroes. This point of view has been developed so frequently during the past century that it is customary to think of the problem mainly in terms of the alleged superiority of the Nordics.

The first important consideration in connection with this type of evaluation is the need to place it in proper historical perspective. It is necessary to keep in mind that we have no right to argue from a temporary to a biological and permanent superiority. It is illuminating in this connection to examine some of the judgments of "racial" ability found in the earlier literature. We know that Aristotle,[19] for example, basing his argument mainly upon the effects of climate, regarded the North Europeans as barbarians incapable of a creative culture, particularly in the field of politics. The Roman Vitruvius[20] took a similar position. At the time these men wrote, no one could possibly have made a reasonable case for the superiority of the Nordics. Even in fairly recent times there is by no means unanimity in connection with this judgment.

---

[16] H. S. Chamberlain, *The Foundations of the Nineteenth Century*, 2 volumes, 1911.

[17] M. Grant, *The Passing of the Great Race*, 1916.

[18] T. L. Stoddard, *The Rising Tide of Color Against White World Supremacy*, 1920.

[19] Aristotle, *The Politics of Aristotle*, 1885.

[20] P. Vitruvius, *The Ten Books on Architecture*, 1914.

Writers like Huntington and Dixon[21] regard the contributions of the Alpines as superior. Sergi, Elliott Smith,[22] and Huxley and Haddon[23] believe that the Mediterraneans had laid the foundations of European civilization long before the Nordics came upon the scene, and that the contribution of the latter is relatively insignificant. Elliott Smith in particular thinks of civilization as having originated among the Mediterranean Babylonians, Sumerians and Egyptians, and having later traveled through the world from that source. W. I. Thomas[24] points out that our Western European civilization is a composite containing contributions from peoples all over the world, including those of Asia and Africa, and that to think of it as exclusively or predominantly Nordic in origin indicates merely regional or national chauvinism. We see that even within the framework of our contemporary Western civilization there is by no means unanimity of judgment as to which group has made the most important contribution.

In the second place, however, the argument becomes even more tenuous when we remember that other groups may legitimately protest against our judging them in terms of our own criteria. We tend to think of the Eskimos or the Africans as inferior because they have failed to develop our type of civilization. There is, however, no universal criterion which enables us to determine the superiority of one culture or civilization over another. Marco Polo may have ridiculed the Chinese for wasting their discovery of gunpowder on firecrackers, but they with at least equal right might have questioned the intelligence of using it for the destruction of human beings. Rivers[25] in an amusing passage imagines the effect of our civilization upon a Melanesian; he suggests that to the Melanesian our failure to keep clearly in mind the degrees of consanguinity of all our relatives would certainly indicate our incapacity, since to him nothing is more important than social and family relationships. Lips[26] has collected many illuminating examples of the manner in which members of primitive groups have reacted to the presence of Whites among them. There are cases in which the Whites are admired, but frequently they are despised and hated as criminals and oppressors. LaPiere and Farnsworth[27] quote from a letter written by a Chinese of the 17th century, following upon the first visits of Jesuits to his country, in which doubt is expressed that these "Ocean Men" are human in the same sense as are the Chinese. Nansen's example of the Eskimo who wished to send medicine men as missionaries to the Whites in order to teach them the advantages of peace may again be cited in this connection. As has been pointed out many times, Western man has shown the greatest skill and ingenuity in his mechanical inventions and in his conquest of physical nature generally, but he has so far not succeeded in devising a satisfactory formula for living. The one fact that we are in constant fear of the destruction by war of everything we have created makes it impossible in any objective sense to regard our civilization as superior.

A third reason for questioning any intimate relation between physical type and culture is the great amount of variability found within any one type in this respect. The most cultivated Chinese and the simplest tribes of Siberia are of the same inherited physical type; the same is true of the Incas of Peru and the

---

[21] E. Huntington, *The Character of Races*, 1924; Osborn, 1918.
[22] G. Sergi, *The Mediterranean Race*, 1895; G. E. Smith, *Human History*, 1929.
[23] Huxley and Haddon, 1935.
[24] W. I. Thomas, *Primitive Behavior*, 1937.
[25] W. H. R. Rivers, *Psychology and Ethnology*, 1926.
[26] J. Lips, *The Savage Hits Back*, 1937.
[27] R. T. LaPiere and P. R. Farnsworth, *Social Psychology*, 1936.

Mayas of Yucatan on the one hand, and the rude communities of the California Indians on the other. These wide divergences make it impossible to assume that physical type is in any direct way the cause of culture. They indicate rather that we must take into account a whole host of geographical and historical factors which are relatively independent of physique, which make it possible for one society to reach the height of complexity in its cultural and social life, and which keep another at a relatively simple level. Individuals within various groups may differ in their biological make-up, but in the examples cited above they are "racially" homogeneous.

The frequent contrast in the data supplied by social statistics regarding different sub-groups of the same inherited physical type also argues in this direction. McDougall[28] believed that suicide occurs with greater frequency among peoples of Nordic ancestry because of their tendency toward introversion, which causes action to be directed to oneself in any crisis situation. He cited figures to prove that this was an essential Nordic characteristic. More complete statistics showed, however, that this was by no means necessarily true; the figures for Norway, to take only one example, were among the lowest, in spite of the marked predominance of the Nordic component among Norwegians; both France and Switzerland, with the Alpine the most frequent physical type, had very high rates of suicide.[29] The alleged frequency of homicide among Mediterranean peoples has also been linked to their genetic origin, but quantitative studies have shown[30] that the apparent homicidal tendencies of Italians in America are markedly reduced after the passage of one generation, and that American-born sons of Italian parents have a homicide rate closely approaching that of the American population in general.

The same variability within each group holds for other characteristics of culture and of personality. The American Indians of the Plains were warlike, and their whole social structure depended upon war as an institution; the Pueblos of the Southwest, at least in recent times, were a peaceful group who fought only in self-defense. The American Negroes are said to be musical, but there are many tribes in Africa for whom ethnologists have reported little or no music. The plastic art of Benin and Dahomey is famous the world over, but there are large areas in Africa where this type of art is unknown. It is difficult to understand this great variability on the assumption that these aspects of culture are directly associated with inherited physical type.

TESTS OF INTELLIGENCE

There have been many reviews of the literature dealing with the application of mental tests to the study of racial and national differences in intelligence. The reader will find extensive discussion of the techniques and results in the books by Anastasi and Foley[31] and Klineberg.[32] At this point we shall attempt only a brief summary of what seem to be the more important considerations.

---

[28] W. McDougall, *Is America Safe for Democracy?*, 1921.

[29] F. H. Hankins, *The Racial Basis of Civilization*, 1926.

[30] E. H. Stofflet, "A Study of National and Cultural Differences in Criminal Tendency," *Arch. Psychology*, No. 185 (1935).

[31] Anastasi and Foley, 1949.

[32] O. Klineberg, *Race Differences*, 1935; *Characteristics of the American Negro*, 1944.

Marked changes in viewpoint may be noted among the investigators in this field since the work of testing group differences in intelligence on a large scale was begun during World War I. The analysis of the results of this study by C. C. Brigham[33] came to the conclusion that there was clear evidence for the innate intellectual superiority of Whites over Negroes, and of North Europeans or Nordics over Alpines and Mediterraneans. These conclusions were widely quoted and generally accepted by psychologists at the time of their appearance, although criticism, especially at the hands of anthropologists, was by no means lacking. As the result of further critical analysis, doubt was thrown not only upon the racial distinctions used in the study, but also on the capacity of the tests themselves to measure native intelligence apart from the effect of environment. More refined statistical analysis of the nature of the Army Alpha tests supported the growing conviction that these conclusions were invalid. Brigham himself in a later publication[34] carried certain of these criticisms to their logical conclusion, and with fine scientific and objective candor withdrew completely from his earlier position, stating that all the studies which had appeared to demonstrate racial differences by means of intelligence tests, including his own, fell completely to the ground. In Brigham's own change of attitude may be seen the reflection of a change typical of a great many psychologists. It is unfortunate that so many people have been influenced by the original study, whereas relatively few know of the recantation.

A further example of this change in point of view is represented by Goodenough,[35] who published an article in 1926 on ethnic differences in the intelligence of school children. She used her own "Draw-a-Man" test, in which achievement is measured in terms of how accurately the figure is drawn, without regard to the esthetic qualities of the drawing. Since the test makes no use of language or information, she believed it could be regarded as a measure of native intelligence, independent of culture or previous experience. Her groups did differ in economic background, but she regarded this fact as irrelevant. She wrote: "It seems probable upon the whole, that inferior environment is an effect at least as much as it is a cause of inferior ability. . . . The person of low intelligence tends to gravitate to those neighborhoods where economic requirement is minimal. . . . His children inherit his mental characteristics."

In 1950 Goodenough, writing with Morris[36] reviews many of the investigations made with her test and concludes that there is a definite indication of the influence of culture and previous training on the results obtained. The test is not so "culture-free" as was formerly believed. The investigators state that they "would like to express the opinion that the search for a culture-free test, whether of intelligence, artistic ability, personal-social characteristics, or any other measurable trait is illusory, and that the naive assumption that the mere freedom from verbal requirements renders a test equally suitable for all groups is no longer tenable." In a brief footnote Goodenough adds that her own earlier study reporting differences among the children of immigrants to the United States is "certainly no exception to the rule. The writer hereby apologizes for it!"

---

[33] C. C. Brigham, *A Study of American Intelligence*, 1923.

[34] C. C. Brigham, "Intelligence Tests of Immigrant Groups," *Psychological Review*, CXXXVII (1930), 158–165.

[35] F. L. Goodenough, "Racial Differences in Intelligence of School Children," *Journal of Experimental Psychology*, IX (1926), 388–397.

[36] F. L. Goodenough and D. B. Morris, "Studies in the Psychology of Children's Drawings," *Psychology Bulletin*, XLVII (1950), 369–433.

These honest and courageous admissions on the part of distinguished scholars are mentioned here because they represent in clearest form the development which has taken place in this whole field of inquiry. When the tests were first applied to representatives of different ethnic groups, it was usually in the belief that the method was capable of measuring native ability and that the results could be so interpreted. Voices of caution and criticism were raised from the beginning, but for a time, at least among psychologists, they were in the minority. The history of the mental testing of ethnic or "racial" groups may almost be described as a progressive disillusionment with tests as measures of native ability, and a gradually increasing realization of the many complex environmental factors which enter into the result. As between Terman's[37] earlier position that the tests were a true measure of native capacity and the insistence of Garrett and Schneck[38] that "the examiner must always remember that comparisons are permissible only when environmental differences are absent, or at least negligible," there can be no doubt that at present most psychologists would accept the latter position. . . . It is essential to keep in mind the effect of previous experience.

In the field of ethnic comparisons, a number of environmental considerations have been regarded as important. The relationship of the subjects to the tester, or the degree of rapport between them, may obviously differ in the case of two ethnic groups. Their motivation, or their anxiety to do well on the test, cannot always be presumed to be similar. The discussion of occupational differences in intelligence has shown that even within one race, socio-economic and educational factors are of importance; their weight is all the greater in any comparison, for example, of Negroes and Whites, who differ so greatly in economic opportunities and in the nature of schooling and other education available. The frequent reliance in the intelligence test upon speed as a measure of capacity has also been shown to be unfair to those groups outside of our own culture who place no premium upon getting things done in a hurry. There may also be, as Porteus has pointed out,[39] an actual misunderstanding of the purpose of the test on the part of those who are not accustomed to being tested. There are varying attitudes and points of view which we collectively call "culture," which may produce such different reactions as to make direct comparison of two racial or cultural groups scientifically valueless.

We are not suggesting that there are many studies of ethnic differences in which all of these environmental factors enter. It is hard to imagine an investigator so naive that he would compare two groups differing in all of the above respects. It is more probable that some of these factors operate in one investigation, but not in another; one group may be handicapped by linguistic disability, a second by poor schooling, a third by lack of adequate motivation, a fourth by a combination of any of these, and so on. Taken all together, these environmental factors may account for a good part if not all of the differences found in the mental test performance of racial and national groups.

Even if the two groups are adequately equated in these respects, there still remains an important source of error—namely, the factor of sampling or selection. Obviously an investigator or a team of investigators cannot test all the members of any two groups which are being compared, and only a relatively small proportion of each may possibly be examined. This raises the question as to the degree to which

---

[37] L. M. Terman, *The Measurement of Intelligence*, 1916.
[38] H. E. Garrett and M. R. Schneck, *Psychological Tests, Methods and Results*, 1933, p. 24.
[39] S. D. Porteus, *Primitive Intelligence and Environment*, 1937.

this sample is truly representative. To take a specific instance, the comparison of Scottish and Italian children in New York City, even if all of the environmental factors have been adequately considered, may still not hold for Scots and Italians generally, since the migrants to this country may not represent similar samples of the total Scottish and Italian populations. This makes it necessary to restrict the conclusions to the particular samples studied. An investigation by Franzblau[40] indicates that the superiority of Danish over Italian children in this country does not extend to Danish children in Copenhagen as compared with Italian children in Rome. In spite of statistical and other checks on the validity of a sample, this remains a constant problem and a possible source of error in all group comparisons.

. . . An investigation by Army testers showed the superiority of White recruits over Negroes in general, but it also indicated that Negroes of certain northern states during World War I were superior to the Whites of certain southern states. This was especially true for those who took the Army Alpha examination, which is a test involving the use of language. In this test the Negro recruits from Ohio, Illinois and New York obtained higher scores than did the Whites, for example, from Mississippi, Kentucky and Arkansas. In previous discussions of this comparison (including those by the present writer), it was not made sufficiently clear that these comparisons referred only to the Army Alpha. Since this is a "language" test which was not taken by all the recruits, a fairer statement would run somewhat as follows: that the literate Negroes from certain northern states, who took the Army Alpha, obtained higher average scores than the literate Whites from certain southern states who were examined by means of the same test.

The fact is, however, that the scores obtained with the Army Beta, a non-language test, support the conclusions indicated above. In some cases, groups of northern Negroes were superior to groups of southern Whites on both tests. This was true for Negroes from Ohio and Indiana, for example, in comparison with Whites from Kentucky and Mississippi. The conclusion is therefore justified that the Negro recruits from some of the northern states did obtain higher scores on the Army intelligence tests than the Whites in some of the southern states.

This raised the question as to whether the superiority of the northern Negroes was due to the better educational and economic opportunities available to them in the North, particularly in the large cities, or whether there had been a selective migration of superior Negroes from South to North. The Army testers did not commit themselves to either of these alternatives. A study by Peterson and Lanier[41] of twelve-year-old Negro and White boys found the Whites superior in Nashville, slightly superior in Chicago and equal to the Negroes in New York. The investigators decided that selective migration to New York was responsible, although their evidence does not seem to support this conclusion. In a more direct attack upon this problem[42] there appeared to be no indication of a selective migration to the North, since the school records of the migrants were not in any way superior to those of the non-migrants; on the other hand there was definite

[40] R. N. Franzblau, "Race Differences in Mental and Physical Traits: Studied in Different Environments," *Arch. Psychology*, No. 177 (1935).

[41] J. Peterson and L. H. Lanier, "Studies in the Comparative Abilities of Whites and Negroes," *Mental Measurement Monograph*, No. 5 (1929).

[42] O. Klineberg, *Negro Intelligence and Selective Migration*, 1935.

indication of an improvement in the intelligence test scores of southern Negro children living in New York City, which was clearly related to the length of time during which they had lived in the superior environment. There was direct evidence of an environmental effect, but no indication of selective migration. Since the average test scores of the Negroes even in New York City were slightly inferior to the White norms, this study cannot be regarded as disposing of the question of group differences. It must be borne in mind, however, that even in New York City the environment of Negroes cannot be regarded as completely equal to that of Whites. The study does at least indicate that as the environment of the Negro improves, his test scores rise correspondingly. It seems to the writer highly probable, if not certain, that with complete environmental equality, the present difference in test scores between Negroes and Whites would entirely disappear. It should be added that an investigation by Lee[43] in Philadelphia, closely paralleling the study just described but following the *same* pupils for several years after their migration from the South to that city, also demonstrated a gradual improvement in test scores accompanying the longer sojourn in a more favorable environment.

An approach designed to avoid the difficulties discussed above is represented by a study of very young children, presumably before they have been subjected to any influences from the social environment. This was attempted by McGraw,[44] who studied White and Negro infants in the first year of life, administering to them the "Baby Tests" devised by Hetzer and Wolf under the direction of Charlotte Bühler at Vienna. The results showed the White babies to be on the average definitely superior to the Negro. The author concludes: "It is significant that with even the very young subjects when environment factors are minimized, the same type and approximately the same degree of superiority is evidenced on the part of the White subjects as that found among older groups."

The difficulty with this conclusion is that environmental factors, even at this early age, are by no means "minimized." The performance of an infant on these tests is markedly influenced by general physical development, which in turn depends on adequate nourishment. In this respect the Negro children were definitely at a disadvantage. They came from economically inferior homes and were relatively deficient in weight. These facts are not irrelevant simply because the children were young; on the contrary, the linkage between physical and mental development should be at least as striking at the beginning of life as later.

This interpretation is supported by a study of Negro and White babies in New Haven, Connecticut, by Pasamanick[45] under the direction of Arnold Gesell of Yale University. This time the Negro infants revealed a physical and psychological development equal to that of the Whites; the tests showed no significant differences between the two groups. The investigator points out that, as the result of careful dietary controls introduced during World War II, the Negro mothers in this group received adequate

---

[43] E. S. Lee, "Negro Intelligence and Selective Migration: A Philadelphia Test of the Klineberg Hypothesis," *American Sociological Review*, XVI (1951), 227–223.

[44] M. B. McGraw, "A Comparative Study of a Group of Southern White and Negro Infants," *Genetic Psychological Monograph*, X (1931), 1–105.

[45] B. Pasamanick, "A Comparative Study of the Behavioral Development of Negro Infants," *Journal of Genetic Psychology*, LXIX (1946), 3–44.

nourishment and in fact were not markedly different from the White mothers in this respect. The general economic level of the Negro group had also improved as a consequence of the opportunities opened up by defense industries. These Negro infants started out, physically, on equal terms with the Whites; they also, in parallel fashion, showed no inferiority or retardation in psychological development. With the equating of environmental opportunities, the difference between the two groups disappeared.

It is important to remember that when it is alleged that Whites are superior to Negroes, it is a superiority *on the average* which is being defended. In other words, even if there is a difference of this type, it is still true that a great many Negroes are superior to a great many Whites. Any restrictions therefore upon the education or occupation of Negroes on the basis of the results of psychological studies is unwarranted. In this connection it is interesting to consider some of the cases of gifted Negro children described by Witty and Jenkins.[46] One of these, a young girl of nine, of almost unmixed African ancestry, had a Binet I.Q. of 200 with correspondingly high scores in a number of other intelligence tests. This score has been matched by very few indeed of the thousands of White children tested. It goes without saying that any restrictions placed upon this girl on grounds of race have no foundation in the science of psychology.

American Indians in general obtain low test scores; on the average, the Indian I.Q. is in the neighborhood of 80. This result is not difficult to understand. Not only do most American Indians occupy an inferior economic position in comparison to the rest of the population; but, in addition, their whole background and culture are so different from those of White Americans that they can hardly be expected to do equally well on tests that have been standardized on the latter group.

In an important study, Garth[47] attempted to discover what would happen if American Indian children were placed in a "White" environment. He reported that a group of Indian foster children living in White homes obtained an average I.Q. of 102, which is certainly a remarkable improvement over the general Indian average of 80. This result would be conclusive evidence of the effect of the environment on group differences if it were not for the possibility that the Indian children living in White homes were exceptional to begin with. It may be that when White families pick Indian children, they choose those who have superior intelligence. This is the hypothesis of "selection" in a different context and in another form. Garth attempted to answer this criticism by testing also the brothers and sisters of the foster children; these siblings were still living on the reservation. Their average I.Q. was only 87.5. This suggests that the superiority of the foster children is in fact due to their more favorable environmental opportunities, but the proof is not complete.

An even more convincing result is represented by Rohrer's[48] study of Osage Indians in Oklahoma. These Indian children live under social and economic conditions quite similar to those of the White children with whom they were compared. This is largely due to the fortunate accident that, on the land which was ceded to them by the American Government as a reservation, oil was later discovered. As a consequence, these Indians became relatively well-to-do, and were able to create for them-

---

[46] P. A. Witty and M. D. Jenkins, "The Case of 'B,' a Gifted Negro Girl," *Journal of Social Psychology*, VI (1935), 117–124.

[47] T. R. Garth, "A Study of the Foster Indian Child in the White Home," *Psychology Bulletin*, XXXII (1935), 708–709.

[48] J. H. Rohrer, "The Test Intelligence of Osage Indians," *Journal of Social Psychology*, XVI (1942), 99–105.

selves and their families living conditions far superior to those of other Indian communities. With this fact in mind, it is illuminating to look at the results obtained by Rohrer. On one test, the Goodenough "Draw-a-Man" test, the White children obtained an average I.Q. of 103, and the Indian children, 104. On a second test, which made use of language, the White score was 98, the Indian, 100 (these differences are of course so small as to be insignificant).

There can be no doubt in this case that when American Indian children have environmental opportunities comparable to those of Whites, their apparent inferiority disappears completely. Nor can this result be explained by selection. It was *after* they had been given their land that oil was discovered; they did not seek out this particular region. Their good fortune gave them opportunities denied to other Indians. This is reflected not only in their economic success, but also in their ability to solve the problems presented by the intelligence tests.

As far as nations within the White race are concerned, there is almost complete unanimity among psychologists that biologically determined differences between them have never been proven. As we have seen above, the most extensive investigation in this field has been repudiated by its author. It may be added that an attempt to compare groups of Nordic, Alpine and Mediterranean children, selected in Europe according to the most rigid anthropological criteria, failed to demonstrate any significant differences between them. To speak of national instead of racial differences really begs the question, since nations are political and not biological entities.

As an indication of the change in attitude among social scientists on this question, we may cite in conclusion a statement by Odum[49] that among "the errors of sociology" is "the assumption that races are inherently different rather than group products of differentials due to the cumulative power of folk-regional and cultural environment." This statement is all the more significant in view of the fact that Odum himself in an earlier work on the social and mental traits of the Negro[50] expressed the very definite conviction that Negroes are constitutionally inferior to Whites.

The conclusion of this discussion is that there has as yet appeared no adequate proof of inherent "racial" differences in ability. The various arguments used in support of such differences are not scientifically valid. This does not mean that we rule out heredity as an explanation of certain individual and possibly even group differences. . . . It is perfectly consistent to regard the differences between large groups, socio-economic or ethnic, as due to environmental factors, while insisting that within each of these groups the individual differences may at least in part be determined by heredity. In connection with race, the differences between Whites and Negroes in present achievement may be explained in terms of the background of the two groups, but the tremendous variations within the Negro and within the White group may still reveal the influence of hereditary factors. Expressed differently, a White superiority of ten or twenty points in average I.Q. may be explained by the environment, but a range of at least 100 points between the best and the poorest members of each group may hardly be accounted for in the same manner. This does not mean that the environment plays no part in the causation of these individual differences, but it is certainly not entirely responsible for them.

---

[49] H. W. Odum, "The Errors of Sociology," *Social Forces*, XV (1936–37), 327–342.
[50] H. W. Odum, *Social and Mental Traits of the Negro*, 1910.

THE MEASUREMENT OF NON-INTELLECTUAL TRAITS

It has sometimes been argued that the essential differences related to inherited physical type are in the realm of personality rather than intelligence. The criticisms that we have leveled against the use of intelligence tests in this field apply even more strongly in the case of tests of non-intellectual characteristics. In addition, the results conflict to such a degree that any conclusion from them is unwarranted. This is true, for example, of tests of musical ability, in which even the alleged superiority of the Negro in rhythm is by no means a consistent finding. There are, however, a few studies in this field which raise problems of special interest in this connection.

One of the most significant of these is the investigation by Efron[51] which deals with the gestural patterns sometimes regarded as being inborn group characteristics. By means of very careful sketches and motion picture recordings it was possible to compare in great detail the gestures used by Jews and Italians in a large variety of social conditions. There were marked differences between the two groups, the Italian gestures being much more frequently symbolic and conveying a definite meaning, whereas those of the Jews were rather a running accompaniment to speech, but without significance when taken by themselves; there were differences also in the nature of the movements employed, those of the Italians tending to extend laterally away from the body, and those of the Jews forward toward the person addressed. The interesting finding was, however, that in spite of these marked differences between the immigrant Jews and Italians, the gestures almost entirely disappeared with the passage of one generation. There was clear indication, therefore, of the temporary and cultural rather than of the native character of the gestures.

The problem of speed is also of interest in this connection. Not only is it of significance in relation to intelligence test scores, but it has also some direct bearing on the general question of personality differences. It has been suggested that groups may differ in this respect because of the direct effect of physiological factors. In connection with the apparently more easy-going tempo of the Chinese, for example, Earle[52] has suggested that a difference in basal metabolic rate between the Orientals and the Whites may be responsible. This seems unlikely for several reasons—first, because the basal metabolism is affected by factors of diet, climate, occupation and other environmental circumstances; second, because the metabolism of members of the same race living in different environments may vary greatly; and third, because experimental methods have failed to reveal any direct relation between basal metabolism and speed of behavior in normal subjects.

The more direct approach to the question of differences in speed by means of reaction-time experiments as well as measurement of rate of movement have revealed marked variations between groups, but apparently not determined by inborn factors. Indians on the Yakima reservation, for example, moved very slowly in the test situation and showed a corresponding decrease in the number of errors during the solution of a performance test; this qualitative difference between Indians and Whites did not obtain in the case of pupils at the Haskell Institute, where the Indian children are

[51] D. Efron, *Gesture and Environment*, 1941.
[52] H. G. Earle, "Basal Metabolism," *The Caduceus*, I (1922), 81–85.

brought up in a manner comparable to Whites generally.[53] The conclusion that differences in speed are cultural, not innate, is supported by the careful study by Foley,[54] who showed a relationship between type of occupation and speed of movement in a variety of test situations. It is true, however, that this study did not entirely control the factor of selection, and there is the possibility that those who prefer a quicker tempo find their way into certain occupations. Foley prefers the conclusion that tempo is determined by habits acquired by the individual.

The use of personality tests of the usual type, including those of the paper-and-pencil and of the performance variety, have failed to reveal any significant group differences. One study[55] involved the application of the Bernreuter inventory, the Allport-Vernon Study of Values, a persistence test, a test of suggestibility, and an honesty test to students in a number of academic institutions in New York City and vicinity. These were divided according to their "racial" characteristics into Nordic, Alpine and Mediterranean groups, as well as into Jews and non-Jews. The results showed these "racial" differences to be insignificant, although there were rather marked variations among sub-groups of the same "race" in different academic institutions and different socio-economic classes. This result finds support in an earlier observation by Hartshorne and May,[56] who in their *Studies in Deceit* noted that Jewish children in a poor neighborhood cheated more frequently than the average, and those in a good neighborhood less frequently. Their conclusion is that honesty in these situations appears to be a function of intelligence and background and not of ethnic origin.

Personality tests are so deeply impregnated with the culture in which they have originated that their direct application to other groups and other cultures yields results that may be very misleading. To mention one specific example, the Pressey X-O Test, which is designed to measure emotional responses, was administered to Indians of varying tribal origin, now living in Nebraska, Montana, California, New Mexico and Oklahoma.[57] The investigators report that the Indians were less mature emotionally than the Whites with whom they were compared. "The Indian tends to remain immature; either he is incapable of a more mature adjustment, or else his environment has been so simplified that adjustment on a childish level is good enough." In view of the obvious cultural relativity of the concept of emotional maturity, this statement does not seem especially meaningful. The investigators themselves realize this at least in part, for in a subsequent study[58] they point out that the tribes with the greatest degree of White contact (like the Crow) are "less retarded emotionally" than those who have remained relatively isolated (like the Hopi). This conclusion closely parallels the findings in the case of intelligence tests, that the more similar

---

[53] O. Klineberg, "An Experimental Study of Speed and Other Factors in 'Racial' Differences," *Arch. Psychology*, No. 93 (1928).

[54] J. P. Foley, "Factors Conditioning Motor Speed and Tempo," *Psychology Bulletin*, XXXIV (1937), 351–397; "An Experimental Study of the Effect of Occupational Experience upon Motor Speed and Preferential Tempo," *Arch. Psychology*, No. 219 (1937).

[55] O. Klineberg, H. Fjeld, J. P. Foley, unpublished study.

[56] H. Hartshorne and M. A. May, *Studies in Deceit*, 1928.

[57] S. L. Pressey and L. C. Pressey, "A Comparative Study of the Emotional Attitudes and Interests of Indian and White Children," *Journal of Applied Psychology*, XVII (1933), 227–238.

[58] S. L. and L. C. Pressey, "A Comparison of the Emotional Development of Indians Belonging to Different Tribes," *Journal of Applied Psychology*, XVII (1933), 533–541.

the environments of the groups compared, the smaller the difference in their average test scores. Any inference to inherited group differences is completely unjustified.

There is, however, as in the case of measures of intelligence, ample room for heredity to exert a significant effect upon the range of variations among individuals within any community and in all probability these variations do have in part a biological origin. Our negative conclusion with regard to hereditary factors applies again, therefore, not to individual, but to group differences.

In what has been said here, there is no implication that all ethnic groups are alike in their behavior. Obviously they are not alike; or rather, they are alike in some respects and not in others. The differences that emerge, however, cannot be attributed to the physical or anatomical characteristics associated with racial classifications. It is not easy to determine just what is responsible. The causes may lie deep in history; they may be due to socio-economic factors; they may be related to the physical environment, to contacts with surrounding peoples, to the inventions and discoveries of individuals, to the problems which had to be solved, and to the ways hit upon, sometimes by accident, for their solution. In any case, there is no evidence that they are innate.

SUMMARY

The word *race* refers to a group of people of similar physical type and common heredity. In popular usage it is frequently confused with nation, which is a political grouping consisting of individuals heterogeneous in origin and in physical characteristics; there is no German or Italian or American race. Another type of confusion is with language; the terms *Latin, Semitic,* and *Aryan* all refer to families of languages, and not to race. Similarly, there is no Jewish race.

The very concept of race as applied to man has been challenged because of lack of agreement as to the criteria of classification. Subdivisions based on skin color are in conflict with those based on cephalic index, and there appears to be no means of deciding which is to be preferred. This supports the notion that "all mankind constitute but one race."

The physical differences which do exist have often been regarded as having psychological implications. It has been urged, for example, that the characteristics of the Negro are more primitive than those of other races, but ape-like features occur with equal frequency in all groups. The brains of Negroes and Whites appear to be approximately equal in size and to have the same conformation. In general, there has been no demonstration that psychological differences of any significance are associated with the physical features used in race classification.

The cultural argument for racial superiority is unsatisfactory because of the great variations in the cultural level of the same ethnic group at different times in history, as well as of different sub-groups of similar physical type, and also because there is no acceptable criterion which may be used in judging all cultures. As far as intelligence tests are concerned, it was formerly believed by many psychologists that racial differences had been demonstrated, but the present consensus is to the effect that so many environmental factors enter into the comparisons that no conclusion as to innate ability is justified. The superiority of northern over southern Negroes argues in favor of the environmental determination of the test scores, since there is no definite evidence for the selective migration of a superior group. The discovery of individual

Negro children with intelligence quotients at the extreme upper end of the distribution, the excellent showing made by American Indian children adopted into superior White homes, as well as the marked improvement following a rise in economic level and educational opportunities, also testify to the absence of innate ethnic differences in intelligence.

The measurement of traits of personality has yielded mainly negative results in this field, partly because of the nature of the tests used, and partly because of the inconsistency of the findings. In this respect also, sub-groups within the same ethnic population differ markedly according to variations in the socioeconomic and cultural environment.

Miscegenation has been on the one hand opposed because of the physical disharmonies which are alleged to result, and on the other hand advocated because of the phenomenon of hybrid vigor. Neither argument appears to be particularly significant. The results of mixture depend upon the nature of the individuals who participate in the crossing, and upon the attitude which society adopts toward the hybrid.

There has been a striking change in the position adopted by social scientists with regard to inherited ethnic differences. Many investigators who formerly accepted the idea of such innate differences now regard them as unproven.

6-8   CULTURE AND THE PERSONALITY DEVELOPMENT OF MINORITY PEOPLES

Regina M. Goff

Regina M. Goff is professor of education at Morgan State College, Baltimore. She obtained her B.S. at Northwestern University, her M.A. and Ph.D. at Columbia. She has taught at Lincoln University and Florida A. & M. In 1950 she was consultant to the Ministry of Education in Iran. Dr. Goff has traveled extensively and contributed numerous articles to journals of education, applied anthropology, and social psychology. In the following essay she extends the notion of culture and personality to problems of a racial minority. Her conclusion: "The continuing task of education is the encouragement of social emancipation . . . and the advancement of liberalism."

I. THE BIO-SOCIAL BASIS OF PERSONALITY

As is generally recognized today, complex behavioral patterns are learned. Persistent traits and modes of responses, reflecting among other things an integration of interests, attitudes, capacities, and abilities, become associated in a totality referred to as personality. Individual modes of perceiving, culturally determined, are accom-

From *Negro Education in America* by Virgil A. Clift, Archibald W. Anderson, and G. Gordon Hullfish (eds.), pp. 124–150. Copyright © 1962 by Harper & Brothers. Reprinted with the permission of Harper & Row, Publishers, Incorporated.

panied by dynamic mental functioning which activates bodily energy later discharged in response. Uniqueness in perceiving and responding gives meaning to individual personality.

The biological features of development make possible perceiving, feeling, and responding, all of which are aspects of experiencing. As Sullivan[1] points out, "Experience is, in its last analysis, experience of tensions and experience of energy transformations." Personality functions as a correlate of those particular provisions or controls of the culture which determine for individuals how tensions may be reduced and energy directed toward the satisfaction of needs. Good adjustment, the product of a so-called normal personality, is best tested by noting the direction of energy exerted in tension-arousing experiences. A requirement is constant restoration of balance and continuous social equilibrium.

Behavior does not originate within the individual, subject solely to personal peculiarities. Motivation to act, as well as the goals toward which action is directed, are as much recognition of current social phenomena and demands as they are responses to inner drives and past experiences. When current demands and potentialities for meeting them are compatible, satisfaction and end product reinforce and finally establish the accepted pattern of action. When barriers produce failures in response to demands, dissatisfaction results in behavior often punishable as an offense against social requirements. Fortunately, in the constant interpersonal interaction of experience there is capacity for adaptability despite the persistence of recurrent modes of response.

The aggressively competitive and stratified American culture places value on personal achievement, independence, liberty, and power. The esteem in which the individual holds himself is directly proportionate to his feelings of mastery of circumstances, power over events, and prestige and acceptance among men. Such cultural demands, established values, have direct bearing on personality, being, in fact, motivators of behavior.

From birth, events, people, and laws influence what is learned by way of response. Since there is no common environment, there are no specific learnings which are universally shared. Personality is a function of special features of individual experiencing, and childhood is a determining stage in establishing the basic features of personality. Davis[2] points out the relationship between class position, methods of training in early childhood, and emergent behavior patterns. Variations in method and cultural exposures result in differences in specific learnings, motivations, and responses to varying folkways. Further, as shown in a study by Davis and Havighurst,[3] differences in personality may be traced less to race than to class training. Cultural differences in personality in middle-class and lower-class children, according to the study, are more pronounced than differences between Negro and white children of the same class. It is thus conceivable that much behavior stereotyped as racial is in reality class-patterned. Similarly, Linton,[4] speaking of culturally determined differences in

---

[1] H. S. Sullivan, "Multidisciplined Coordination of Interpersonal Data in Personality and Culture," S. Stansfeld Sargent, ed., *Wenner-Gren Foundation* (New York, 1949), p. 175.

[2] Allison Davis, "American Status Systems and the Socialization of the Child," *American Sociological Review*, VI (1941), 345–356.

[3] Allison Davis and R. J. Havighurst, "Social and Color Differences in Child Rearing," *American Sociological Review*, XI (1946), 648–710.

[4] R. Linton, "Problems of Status Personality in Personality and Culture," S. Stansfeld Sargent, ed., *Wenner-Gren Foundation*, (New York, 1946), p. 163.

personality, draws upon the findings of several studies which illustrate the tie between techniques of child care and particular features of the "modal personality" or personality norms of societies.

In general, it is conceded that although new learnings may be incorporated into new or revised action patterns, the early formative years with their attendant experiences are basic to the nature of maturity. In addition to the overt manipulation of the infant's body, which involves communication, there are intentional social practices on the part of the parent which, from the earliest awareness of the child, are for the latter the raw material out of which specific concepts develop: rudimentary understandings of preferences in social acceptance, codes of morality, and areas of freedom and constriction. For the Negro child, particular learnings come about because of the economic and social position of the family and of the social taboos of the South and the discriminatory designs of the North.

In childhood the individual begins to build meaning for his world. Impressions deepen and are extended as his interaction with the environment proceeds. His progressive socialization carries with it learnings the family prizes in compliance with the expectations and demands of superordinate members of the culture. In conjunction with this, of course, crystallization of feelings occurs in relation to the self. The future promises less need of conformance to deferential behavior patterns and, to the growing minority members, more by way of equalitarian reactions. But the ideals of the culture which appear visionary to minority members will remain so unless impregnable social barriers are removed. The initial motivation to achieve acceptable social goals will persist, however, if such goals appear to be attainable. Otherwise, a disheartening apathy may arise, or a useless dissipation of energy in socially unrewarding endeavor may follow. In either case, the bright promise of early growth will fade with serious consequences for the developing self.

II. THE EMERGENCE OF THE SELF

Clark,[5] Horowitz,[6] and Lasker[7] point out that consciousness of the self for the Negro child develops in the pre-school years. Davis found that in the South children begin to learn caste controls which differentiate them before they enter school. In these and other studies, the special features of the wider culture, which impinge upon the Negro child and cause negative feelings that have a bearing on self-perception, have been identified.[8] These include direct ridicule, name-calling, disparaging or belittling statements, physical ill-treatment, threats of violence of white adults, aggressive behavior by white children, and the more subtle effects of discrimination and discourteous or ill-mannered treatment, and indirect disparagement reflected in mass media productions, from movies to publications.

The extent to which actual first-hand intergroup interactions have influenced the child to differentiate the self from others by pre-school age has not been established,

---

[5] Kenneth B. Clark and M. J. Clark, "The Development of Consciousness of Self and the Emergence of Racial Identification in Negro Pre-School Children," *Journal of Social Psychology*, X (1939), 591–599.

[6] R. Horowitz, "Racial Aspects of Self-Identification in Nursery School Children," *Journal of Psychology*, XI (1940), 159–169.

[7] B. Lasker, *Race Attitudes in Children* (New York: Henry Holt, 1929).

[8] R. M. Goff, *Problems and Emotional Difficulties of Negro Children*, Contributions to Education, No. 960 (New York: Bureau of Publications, Teachers College, Columbia University, 1949).

however. Horowitz conceives of group consciousness and identification as an "intrinsic aspect of ego development. . . . Before the ego has been completely formed, in the very process of becoming, we find it subtly approximating a visible symbol that has been socially institutionalized to aid it in marking itself off from the not-self." According to this view, racial identification, culturally prescribed, is in essence a developmental feature accompanying other aspects of growth. Radke, Trager, and Davis[9] state that Negro children reveal most vividly and often the feeling of insecurity resulting from anticipated rejection and insult from white children and that "adult values and interpretations have a greater bearing on the child's attitude than his actual experiencing with other groups." Thus, in the absence of concrete experiencing, social thought, nevertheless, is a force of great power in shaping projected attitudes on personality development. Symonds,[10] in his discussion of the ego and the self, speaks of three distinct elements of the ego. He refers to the ego as a receiver of impressions, an organizer of impressions into action plans through symbolic processes, and a doer or activator of the plans toward satisfying ends. This view supports Horowitz' suggestion that racial identification is an intrinsic aspect of ego development. There is, of course, uncritical acceptance on the part of the child of the thought content of parental attitudes and, thus, the Negro child, as perceiver, may develop an early sensitivity to color meaning.

Rose,[11] in a thorough historical exploration of Negro group attitudes and reactions, points to the movement from the initial diversified and disorganized pattern of slave behavior, later welded into open group revolt and mutinous rebellion, to the positive protest patterns that are still current. All of this is indicative of the gradual trend toward strong group identification—a concomitant of sociological and psychological factors. Residuals by way of strains in attitudes are still present: group pride and loyalty or, negatively, shame because of membership. To the extent that these are operative and are generated in relationships with the child, they form part of his social heritage and contribute to his image of self and of it in relation to others.

Implications of Color

There always have existed interferences to complete unity in group identification. In this area skin color is prominent, as several studies have shown. Goodman,[12] in a study of Negro children aged 2–4 years, found expressions of uneasiness, tension, sensitivity, and gregariousness accompanying self-identification. The degree to which tension and sensitivity is due solely to color is difficult to isolate, however, since there are so many possible contributing factors. Clark and Clark,[13] working with children aged 3–7 years, found that a negation of the color brown was associated with the conflicting need of identification with this rejected factor. Attempts to resolve the conflict were achieved through wishful thinking and fantasies. Some indications of

---

[9] M. Radke, H. Trager, and H. Davis, "Social Perception and Attitudes of Children," *Genetic Psychology Monograph No. 40* (1949), 327–447.

[10] P. M. Symonds, *Ego and the Self* (New York: Appleton-Century-Crofts, 1951).

[11] A. Rose, *The Negro's Morale* (St. Paul, Minn.: The University of Minnesota Press, 1949).

[12] M. E. Goodman, "Evidence Concerning the Genesis of Interracial Attitudes," *American Anthropologist*, XL (1946), 624–630.

[13] Kenneth B. Clark, "Emotional Factors in Racial Identification and Preferences in Negro Children," *Journal of Negro Education*, X (1950), 341–350.

acceptance of identification were noted around the seventh year. If the growing individual receives no mature support in willing acceptance of his group identity, ambivalent attitudes toward the self emerge. The result is a vacillating adult personality—an individual who wishes to retain an unrealistic ego image, though the actuality of fact is inescapable. These studies make it clear that color connotations arise in the pre-school years.

The studies of Bovell[14] and Parrish[15] indicate that individual reactions toward one's own color are paralleled by in-group preferences and discriminations. Parrish reported that three out of every five persons approached considered black the worst color and associated it with low status. The dominance of white standards is reflected in the attitude. The assumed utility of specific gradations of color was investigated by Seeman.[16] His concern was with the operational importance or function of skin color in choices of friends and of reputation in the group. In two out of three all-Negro school classes, skin color was found an important variable, with light color leading in acceptability and reputation. In pointing to the emotional counterpart of reactions to color, a study by Meyers[17] supports those of Frank[18] and others which show that Negro psychotics are preoccupied with color. This fact, according to Meyers, may be attributed to their role in the community at large and to notions prevalent in the Negro community.

Warner, Junker and Adams[19] contend that, while skin color is not the most significant factor for every individual in the development of social personality, it is nevertheless definitely associated with social position and, as such, is the most potent single element determining the good or poor development of Negro character. Color, without doubt, figures prominently in both class and caste. It may prevent the emergence of feelings of belonging in chance social groups, as well as in primary groups from which one cannot easily escape. To the extent that feelings of isolation persist, ultimate adjustment is affected. A feeling of group acceptance is a basic psychological need, requisite to good adjustment.

Mechanisms to defeat group inclusion are not unusual. Brenman's[20] study on defenses against identification devised by a group of urban middle-class girls revealed three approaches—namely, conscious rejection of racial identification, awareness accompanied by in-group rebellion and pride, and awareness accompanied by deep anxiety.

Reactions toward this physical characteristic result from reflective processes in which images are perceived and categorized as acceptable or objectionable, followed by the inescapable placement of the self somewhere along the color continuum and the adoption of responses appropriate to the feelings elicited. Feeling becomes integrated in the total self-system and emerges in characteristic traits which distinguish the

[14] G. B. Bovell, "Psychological Considerations of Color Conflicts Among Negroes," *Psychoanalytic Review*, XXX (1943), 447–459.

[15] C. H. Parrish, "Color Names and Color Notions," *Journal of Negro Education*, XV (1946), 13–20.

[16] M. Seeman, "Skin Color Values in Three All-Negro School Classes," *American Sociological Review*, XI (1946), 315–321.

[17] I. M. Meyers, "A Study of Anti-Negro Prejudice," *Journal of Negro Education*, XII (1943), 709–714.

[18] J. D. Frank, "Adjustment Problems of Selected Negro Soldiers," *Journal of Mental Disease*, CV (1947), 647–660.

[19] W. L. Warner, B. Junker, and W. A. Adams, *Color and Human Nature* (Washington, D. C.: American Council on Education, 1941).

[20] M. Brenman, "The Relationship Between Minority Group Membership and Group Identification in a Group of Urban Middle-Class Girls," *Journal of Social Psychology*, XI (1940), 171–197.

individual. It would be fallacious to conclude from the foregoing, however, that, solely from this basis, every dark-skinned person develops lowered feelings of self-esteem. Consciousness of color may be absorbed by strong interpersonal bonds in the home and with later associates, as well as by motivation in areas where power and ability have been demonstrated through success. Since light skin as a value grows out of white dominance, desegregation in all areas of American life, with a subsequent leveling of the white-black hierarchy, should in time lead to the disappearance of the color factor as a status symbol.

White Attitudes

Present-day majority group standards and selection are reflected also in the attitudes of the young. Ammons[21] found evidence, in a study of white boys aged 2–6 years, of discrimination in skin color as early as the second year, and the existence of active prejudices at the fourth year. Melzer,[22] concerned with nationality preferences of white children, found that white children rank Negroes in twentieth place. Likewise, Blake and Dennis,[23] in an investigation of stereotypes held by children in grades four through eleven, found that young children attributed nothing favorable to the Negro. With increased age and experience, according to the latter study, adult stereotypes were acquired which, while predominantly unfavorable, did attribute some "good traits" to the Negro, such as religion, cheerfulness, and dancing ability.

In an attempt to distinguish individuals who change their attitudes from those who do not, Mussen[24] experimented with planned intergroup camp experiences. White and Negro boys were housed in the same dormitories and engaged in the same activities. The socio-economic level of the groups was considered comparable. Measures taken on each of the white boys before and after the exposure showed "no change in attitude in the group as a whole." Similarly, Meyers presented to a group of college students at the third and eighth meetings of the class fifteen statements designed to elicit ethnic attitudes. There were ten hours of lecture and assigned reading between the two periods. The second administration showed a change from more liberal to less liberal attitudes. The change was attributed to the increased honesty of the second reactions.

The findings of Mussen contrast with those of studies which have shown a positive influence of intergroup experience under favorable circumstances. Watson,[25] for example, studying means of changing prejudices, found that personal contact with out-group members was considered a major factor in the change in 81 percent of the cases and a contributing factor in 18 percent. Contrary to the findings of Meyers, the same study revealed that school and college teaching were considered a major factor

---

[21] R. B. Ammons, "Reaction in a Projective Doll Play Interview of White Males Two to Six Years of Age to Differences in Skin Color and Facial Features," *Journal of Genetic Psychology*, LXXVI (1950), 323–341.

[22] H. Melzer, "Nationality Preferences and Stereotypes Concerning the Negro," *Journal of Genetic Psychology*, LV (1939), 403–424.

[23] R. Blake and W. Dennis, "The Development of Stereotypes Concerning the Negro," *Journal of Abnormal and Social Psychology*, XXXVIII (1943), 525–531.

[24] P. H. Mussen, "Some Personality and Social Factors Related to Changes in Children's Attitudes toward Negroes," *Journal of Abnormal and Social Psychology*, XLV (1950), 424–441.

[25] G. B. Watson, "Changing Prejudices," mimeographed data (New York: Teachers College, Columbia University).

in dispelling prejudice in 16 percent of the instances, and a contributing factor in 25 percent of the cases. The objects of prejudice in this study included, in addition to the Negro, the Jew, the white, the Protestant, and persons of other nationalities. The important fact revealed was that change occurred as the result of specific experiences.

III. PREJUDICE AND ITS SOURCES

Prejudice is no respecter of ethnic groups. This was illustrated in a study by Berdie[26] on attitude patterns accompanying infiltration by Negroes into white neighborhoods. Though there were few Jewish children in the block studied and contact with them was limited, newly arrived Negro children held more favorable attitudes toward non-Jewish white children than toward those of Jewish parentage. The reaction was attributed to ". . . unconsciously held but subtle and pervasive stereotypes." This differentiation between groups of the white world, carrying even greater negative feelings in one instance, intensifies already existing in-group consciousness because it narrows the field of outgoingness. As areas of contrast multiply, it appears that differentiation of the self sharpens.

Attitudes evolve from perception and feeling. Feelings provide the motivation which eventuates in response and, hence, they give content and expression to the self. The individual, an embodiment of a particular self-system, must relate himself, of course, to the larger world of other persevering selves. Because of its negative emotional aspect, prejudice prevents the emergence of conjunctive forces in human relations. Since prejudice is a part of the total personality structure, much attention has been focused on the probable causes of its occurrence.

Bayton[27] holds the view that the psychological sources of prejudice are to be found in the quality of parental control persisting through the formative years; that coercive, authoritative, and capricious control creates personality problems which have their outlet in active prejudices. The source is thus not related directly to the object or group toward which prejudice is directed. An indication of personality features involved in prejudice is given in a study by Gough, Harris, Martin, and Edwards.[28] They found a relationship between traits of prejudice and intolerance and emotional factors of fear, veiled hostility, and insecurity. An exhaustive investigation of anti-Semitism by Adorno, Frenkel-Brunswick, Levinson and Sanford[29] reveals the roots of prejudice within specific personality needs. Subtle displacement veiled actual pivotal factors. Lack of free affiliative relations at home and unresolved and unadmitted hostility toward parents were found to be reflected in anti-Semitism. Among the many findings presented by Allport and Kramer,[30] in their intensive study of the background of prejudice, was the evidence that individuals who had unpleasant childhood experiences with members of a particular group held generalized prejudices toward the group as a whole. Incidentally, contrary to a popular supposition, religious training was not an

---

[26]R. F. Berdie, "Infiltration and the Attitudes of White and Negro Parents," *Journal of Abnormal and Social Psychology*, XLVII (1952), 688–699.

[27]J. A. Bayton, "Personality and Prejudice," *Journal of Psychology*, XXII (1946), 59–65.

[28]H. G. Gough, D. B. Harris, N. Martin, and M. Edwards, "Children's Ethnic Attitudes: Relationship to Certain Personality Factors," *Child Development*, XXI, 83–91.

[29]T. W. Adorno, E. Frenkel-Brunswick, O. J. Levinson, and R. N. Sanford, *The Authoritarian Personality* (New York: Harper and Brothers, 1950).

[30]G. W. Allport and B. A. Kramer, "Some Roots of Prejudice," *Journal of Psychology*, XXII (1946), 9–39.

active influence in its elimination. Individuals holding church membership were the least tolerant group, while people with no religious affiliation were the most liberal. This is an interesting commentary on the discrepancy between belief and practice, not a reflection on religion itself. Prothro,[31] in an investigation of ethnocentrism, found a relationship in attitudes held by a single individual toward different minorities; those who were unfavorable towards Jewish people were unfavorable toward the Negro. A large percentage of those low on ethnocentrism, however, were definitely anti-Negro. This finding shifts the emphasis of the previous studies. Historical, cultural, and situational factors, rather than personality dynamics alone, must be viewed as of major importance by those who seek an answer to the American dilemma.

Watson has called attention to types of prejudices which are products of particular motives. These are referred to as conforming, projecting, generalizing, and profiting. In some instances, they may exist as unexamined or unattended remnants of early exposures to social attitudes and practices. Jersild[32] cautions that a child of any ethnic group, who is protective of the self and defensive toward out-group members who have injured him, holds realistic attitudes which should not be labeled irrational prejudices. Participation in a single group, the result of friendships growing out of normal events and circumstances, should not be considered as rejection of other groups. Prejudices involving attitudes of bias, hatred, and distrust, however, are projections indicative of personal difficulties which prevent relatedness with others and which reflect the limited esteem with which the self is held. This view finds support in the study by Trent[33] who, in an investigation of Negro children, found a relationship between self-acceptance and acceptance of others. Children who held themselves in low esteem, the result of barrenness, lack of warmth and sympathy in interpersonal relations, and who were the least self-accepting, were rejecting toward both Negro and white children. The reverse was true in the instance of children who were most self-accepting.

These findings in general contribute to the understanding of the psychological basis of misanthropy and have wide implications for personality development and inter-group relationships. The person with irrational prejudices in any ethnic or socioeconomic group is propelled by unhealthy mental states which lessen his capacity for equalitarian relationships. Prejudice shown toward the Negro lowers his self-esteem. It is probable that the major source of security against ego-deflation is within the individual himself. Latent features of personality may be developed and augmented by interpersonal relationships between family members and, later, by ever-widening positive experiences with others. The emergence of strength to offset socially mobilized anxieties is proportionate to the building of early security through affective relationships. It would be amiss to assume that psychological factors which prompt irrational prejudices are merely personal matters that are unrelated to features of the culture. Undoubtedly, a culture of stress and competition, one with the historical and social history of America, will have within it stresses which mobilize anxieties to which all members are susceptible. Insecure parents, disquieted because of their own unfulfilled needs, project their dissatisfactions in their children.

---

[31] E. T. Prothro, "Ethnocentrism and Anti-Negro Attitudes in the South," *Journal of Abnormal and Social Psychology*, XLVII (1952), 105–108.

[32] A. T. Jersild, *Child Psychology* (New York: Prentice-Hall, Inc., 1954).

[33] R. Trent, "The Correlates of Self-Acceptance among Negro Children," unpublished dissertation (New York: Teachers College, Columbia University).

IV. PROBLEMS OF PERSONALITY FORMATION

The Role of Symbolization

In the course of on-going interactions with the environment, the individual learns specific responses to particular cultural features. Meanings attached to cultural forms evoke responses appropriate to the level of his understanding. The red signal of the stop light, the warning blast of an air raid siren, the badge and uniform of the police officer, the passing flag, and the national anthem evoke, after continuing exposure, immediate reactions. But such a function of symbols does not necessarily imply the blindness or lack of insight associated with conditioned responses. Nor does it refer to symbols as labels or marks of identification. These responses have a subjective, emotional aspect as well as an intellectual one. Overt manifestations, where there is no penalty attached to behavior, give expression to inner attitudes and conceptions which eventually become part of the personality structure.

The study of Lewin, Lippitt, and White,[34] for example, illustrates the operation of learning mechanism is social situations. Specific types of leaders—authoritarian, *laissez faire*, and democratic—became symbols that evoked specific and recurrent forms of behavior in members of the group to which they were assigned. In everyday occurrences, the presence of certain individuals, or knowledge of behavior expectations under certain conditions, elicits specific reactions out of a repertoire of many possible responses.

The concept of symbolization is found in several studies. Kardiner,[35] in his discussion of slave psychology, infers that the plantation owner or master was a symbol of protection, therefore to be revered; but he was also an obstacle to freedom and, therefore, to be hated. The "Uncle Tom" behavior was an accommodation to ambivalent feelings. Both Mandelbaum[36] and Stevens,[37] observing the effect of Army segregation on the Negro soldier, found that such arrangements were damaging to motivation and morale. "Perhaps the main reason for this is that the fact of segregation increases the lack of confidence in each other as Negroes, a distrust which is held and implanted by potent sections of the larger society. And under battle stress, when the demand for mutual support is greatest, this undermining of confidence sometimes collapses the strength otherwise engendered in the primary group." The observation in this study of the negative response of Negroes to all-Negro assemblages is significant. Paradoxically, a sharing of feelings was offset by an inability to generate a common confidence. We infer here, also, the power of the symbol of the white man which, since it has endured through time, evokes feelings of security rather than of suspicion and distrust in specific circumstances. These findings call attention to the situational aspect of reaction patterns, the lack of air-tight fixity in behavioral responses, and the occurrence of change in reactions in terms of current needs and satisfactions.

The acceptance of white standards as right and desirable is further shown

---

[34]K. Lewin, R. Lippitt, and R. White, "Patterns of Aggressive Behavior in Experimentally Created 'Social Climates'," *Journal of Social Psychology*, X (1939), 271–299.

[35]A. Kardiner and L. Oversey, *Mark of Oppression* (New York: W. W. Norton & Company, Inc., 1951).

[36]D. G. Mandelbaum, *Soldier Groups and Negro Soldiers* (Berkeley, Calif.: University of California Press, 1952), pp. 89–90.

[37]R. B. Stevens, "Racial Aspects of Emotional Problems of Negro Soldiers," *American Journal of Psychiatry*, CIII (1947), 493–498.

in a study by Bayton.[38] In this study, 100 students in a southern Negro college were compared with 100 at Princeton University with respect to stereotypes. The Negro students assigned characteristics to themselves which were different from those they assigned to a typical Negro, with whom, therefore, they did not identify. As a result, a high degree of similarity existed between these Negro and white students with respect to the stereotypes of various racial and national groups they possessed. The study emphasized, as did those of Negro troops, the absence of intragroup morale. Brunschwig[39] made an analysis of the listings of famous Americans by Negro students in a southern college. The number of whites listed exceeded the number of Negroes mentioned. Responses indicated majority group members as evident symbols of prestige. A parallelism is seen in the Jewish group. Lewin[40] refers to the tendency of underprivileged groups to accept the values of the dominant members of the culture. Jewish anti-Semitism results from sensitivity to in-group standards which are a departure from accepted values of the wider culture. Group denial may express itself in rejection of Jewish institutions, mannerisms, and ideals, but though the tension level may be strained, fraught with fear and inferiority, expressions of group and self-hatred are typically subtle. A further example of symbolization is seen in an analysis of the fictional character "Bigger Thomas" in Richard Wright's *Native Son*. Charles[41] characterized Bigger as a neurotic individual to whom the white man was a symbol of fear. Final responses on the part of Bigger were interpreted as the result, in part, of the white man's low expectation of him by symbolizing him as an aggregate of primitive impulses.

The factor of previous conditioning is important to consider in describing learned reactions of this nature. Lower-class Negroes, according to Catharn,[42] because of their specific experiences, are more unfavorable in their stereotyped conceptions of white people than either the middle or upper classes, while middle-class members possess most favorable conceptions. Action patterns in the presence of white individuals vary in terms of the meaning attached or the nature of the conceived symbolization. Lack of security in self, revealed in practicing in-group discrimination, rejecting identification, and viewing the group as an alien division symbolizing weakness, is most likely a feature of a total pattern of insecurity. In its inception this pattern is related to decisive factors in the immediate environment but, as subsequent cultural pressures multiply, is enlarged and deepened.

The above studies illustrate the influence of subtle social learnings in the development of traits which become characteristic features of personality. In particular, the significance of symbolization in interpersonal relations is revealed. The social implications of the 1954 Supreme Court decision, however, foreshadow a psychological change in the designation of symbols traditionally deemed superior. As Rose[43] pointed out, recent concerted action for democratic practices, support of protest groups, and more widespread use of the ballot give evidence of an ever-increasing high morale within

---

[38] J. A. Bayton, "The Psychology of Racial Morale," *Journal of Negro Education*, XI (1942), 150–152.

[39] L. Brunschwig, "An Analysis of the Listings of Famous Americans by a Group of Negro College Students," *Journal of Psychology*, IX (1940), 207–219.

[40] K. Lewin, "Self-Hatred Among Jews," *Contemporary Jewish Record*, IV (1941), 219–232.

[41] C. V. Charles, "Optimism and Frustration in the American Negro—Negro Literature," *Psychoanalytic Review*, XXIX (1942), 270–299.

[42] T. Catharn, "Negro Conceptions of White People," *American Journal of Sociology*, LVI (1951), 485–467.

[43] Rose, 1949.

the Negro group. As the acceptance of the Negro becomes more general, as equal respect is shown, and as the Negro sees himself along with other groups engaged in the attainment of common goals of a democracy, black and white should eventually symbolize a common humanity.

The Influence of Role Assignment

The nature of the functioning of the individual in the culture is, of course, contributory to personality formation. What the individual does influences his perception, and his subsequent structuring, of the world. The elements which contribute to initial feelings of self-worth and final self-acceptance or depreciation occur within the framework of anticipated functioning and actual role assignment. The Radke study[44] showed that as early as the pre-school years, white children ascribed to Negroes inferior roles and low status. Without doubt, the attitude persists to later years in many instances. Considering the attitude of the Negro toward himself and his proposed work, Lawrence[45] discovered that Negro youth in California exhibited a lack of realism between occupational choices and availability of training. In addition, but one-half of the group had confidence they could achieve their goals. Poor school counseling was blamed for the discrepancy between aspirations and probable attainment. It is important to note that, while goal setting was not tempered by reality in terms of training possibilities, it was nevertheless realistic in terms of cultural values. The common trait of ego enhancement, guided by what society dictates as respectable functioning, is apparent.

In a study of aspiration levels of two groups of Negro children in North Carolina, aged 8–10 and 14–16 years,[46] little similarity was revealed, particularly in the low-income group, between the occupations of parents and the ambitions of children. Children chose areas of respectability in which inroads are of comparatively recent origin for Negroes, such as big league ball players and movie, radio, or television performers. There was generally a decrease in the confidence level, however, with increase in age, with low-income girls holding least hopes of success. The discrepancy between early goals and later achievement attests not only to cultural controls which interfere with strivings, but also to psychological omissions in training which result in timorous fibers in character structure and lack of strength in confronting barriers. It is conceivable, of course, that some individuals use the excuse of social restraints as a way of escape from serious endeavor. Incidentally, the study mentioned earlier that concerned emotional difficulties of Negro children, and the study by Trent, agree with the above findings in pointing to the greater sensitivity of girls to social pressures and to their tendency toward self-rejection.

NcNeil and Easton,[47] presenting research on the urban Negro, speak of the interaction of fixed status and free competition. "Fixed status places the role of the Negro in certain spheres of social life; competition allows him to widen the area in which he participates." Participation is one avenue toward integration. Widened opportunities

[44]M. Radke and H. Trager, "Children's Perceptions of the Social Roles of Negroes and Whites," *Journal of Psychology*, XXIX (1940), 3–33.

[45]P. F. Lawrence, "Vocational Aspiration of Negro Youth in California," *Journal of Negro Education*, XVI (1950), 47–56.

[46]R. M. Goff, "The Influence of Rejection on Aspiration Levels of Minority Group Children," *Journal of Experimental Education*, XXIII (1954), 179–183.

[47]E. O. McNeil and H. R. Easton, "Research on the Urban Negro," *American Journal of Sociology*, XLVII (1941), 176–183.

develop feelings of belonging and acceptance, and these advance reactions of personal worth.

It is clear that the pattern of segregation has resulted in in-group status roles which serve either to augment or further to depress feelings of esteem. In some instances, members of the small minority of the upper class find compensatory relief in roles of importance within the group and, from this status, reject lower-class members. Those at the bottom, suffering a two-fold rejection, are often as distrustful and suspicious of the sincerity of the upper-class Negroes as they are of whites. The degree of reward or felt satisfaction accruing from top in-group status not only determines the power of the impact of rejection of the larger world; it is also a factor determining which role is most functional in total personality. Complete satisfaction may result in an insular personality which rejects integration. This will occur most likely, however, for a person in conflict, his security in one area being threatened by his lack of confidence in handling the other.

Culturally approved or assigned tasks reflect society's image and evaluation of specific group members. These evaluations projected in behavior are then internalized by the members themselves. They come to see themselves as the culture sees them, depending on their individual strengths. Some persons accept stereotyped notions of themselves; others reject them. Whatever the reaction, it becomes a part of the intricate complex of feelings and of one's final judgment of worth of self.

V. FEELINGS, ATTITUDES, AND RESPONSES

It is evident from the preceding exploration that the Negro grows up in a symbolic world. This is perceived in terms of early learnings and meanings that are abstracted from continuous experiencing of a specific nature; learnings which involve group identification, status position, and meanings of cultural features. In a survey of opinions of social scientists[48] on the psychological effects of segregation, ninety percent agreed the effects were detrimental. Consequences by way of inferiority feelings, including shame and embarrassment and the negative emotions of hostility and fear, are revealed in a series of studies on the subject. McLean[49] gave great weight to the presence of fear, noting that psychoanalysis of the Negro revealed a deep unconscious fear of the white man and associated guilt feelings, which resulted in deprecating feelings of self-loathing and self-hate. Such intensity in self-reference, as stated in this view, may be appropriate to disturbed individuals; it would be fallacious, however, as a generalization applied to Negroes as a whole.

Johnson[50] found an absence of emotional security, resulting mainly from conflicts in areas of status and occupation, in his investigation of the effects on adolescents of growing up in the South. Atwood, Wyatt, and Davis[51] found economic status to result in a corroding frustration which penetrated, in a variety of ways, all aspects of living. Frazier points out that the comparative isolation of the Negro youth

---

[48]M. Deutcher and I. Chein, "The Psychological Effects of Enforced Segregation, a Survey of Social Scientists' Opinion," *Journal of Psychology,* XXVI (1948), 259–287.

[49]H. V. McLean, "The Emotional Health of Negroes," *Journal of Negro Education,* XVIII (1949), 283–290.

[50]Charles S. Johnson, *Growing Up in the Black Belt,* (Washington, D. C.: American Council on Education, 1941).

[51]J. H. Atwood, D. W. Wyatt, and V. J. Davis, *Thus Be Their Destiny* (Washington, D. C.: American Council on Education, 1941).

because of his restricted participation in the larger community has an influence on attitudes and behavior. The home becomes a focal point and, accordingly, personality is considered a response to the family situation. Davis and Dollard[52] point to the rise of patterns of aggression. While granting, as earlier mentioned, significance to factors of caste, class controls make the greatest impact on personality development. The four preceding studies were concerned with youth in that stage of development where the normal growth process elicits conflict patterns. Additional tensions at this stage of development accentuate biological, emotional, and social problems, and this is of crucial importance in terms of later adjustment.

The following abbreviated account is illustrative of cultural influences on intra-family relationships and subsequent feeling reactions.

> Ten-year-old Ted was brought to a behavior clinic by his mother, who reported concern over his hostile, aggressive behavior toward all family members and his threat of committing suicide. Ted was medium brown, as was his mother. His younger brother was light. The father, the least Negroid in appearance, was obsessed with the idea of the possibility of white parentage. The mother had finished college, but the college career of the highly ambitious father was interrupted by the pregnancy of the young woman he later married.
>
> Interviews with the father centered, of his own accord, mainly around the subject of "passing" for white. "I try to be certain when I cross the line. I can't stand a rebuff. It makes me sick. Ice picks start jabbing at my heart. I have to go to bed because I'm really downright sick." When the mother accompanied him downtown, she walked accommodatingly two blocks behind. When at home, she dutifully bathed him and catered to his every wish. The light son, William, was referred to as "my heart." Of Ted the father stated, "He has his limitations; he's just normal, not even above average. I'm frightened, really frightened. He makes me think of the ole Negro in the South who just sits on a box with his feet dangling down, doing nothing. He just can't do much. I don't think he'll ever amount to much." The mother, sharing the father's lack of enthusiasm, elaborated on the contrast between the two children and highlighted the intelligence and virtues of the younger child. Meanwhile, Ted spent his time going about chanting, "Everybody hates me. Everybody hates me. I wish I was dead." Later he changed to, "I hate William. I hate William. I wish he was six feet under."

The antecedent of the attitudes and behavior observed in the child, of course, was the dominant white world. The more decisive factor was the immediate home. The father attempted an unrealistic escape from a biological reality—the self which was Negro. He broke before the pull of the culture which designated him as both white and non-white, according to the situation in which he was functioning, but which punished him for either role. Restrictive measures placed on him as Negro were interpreted as punitive. When he escaped through "passing" or crossing the caste line, realization that the new world was fictional not only sharpened the prick of reality, but generated a constant fear of unexpected exposure. When goal-directed sequences were threatened, that is, when there was interference in achieving white status, negative emotions

---

[52]Allison Davis and John Dollard, *Children of Bondage* (Washington, D. C.: American Council on Education, 1940).

and concomitant physiological reactions followed. Emotional dangling and insecurity were partially compensated for through status demands in the home—particularly in requirements of the mother. The affectional needs of Ted were ignored and, in fact, there was probably an inability to meet them. The father stated, "I'm a very inadequate father. I'm a much better husband, and that's the role I prefer."

The mother, born into a caste arrangement from which she could not escape, held the same goals, nevertheless, as her husband by way of status and prestige. The need of a feeling of worth of self was heightened by her awareness of her husband's depreciation of the Negro group. The need for her husband's affection induced the necessity of catering to his whims and desires and identifying with his choices. The end result was her rejection of the child toward whom the father evinced no paternal feeling.

The conscious or unconscious assignment of Ted to a subordinate position naturally resulted in feelings of rejection on his part. Inter-group conflicts, reported by him, created further sensitivity to color meaning. The arrival of a light-skinned brother did nothing to help him in his strivings for self-esteem. The family structure for him was reduced to a mere proximity of people who offered no satisfactions or rewards and from whom he wished to escape. The result of the total situation was family psychological disunity and maladaptive behavior on the part of the child. The entire situation was grounded in the fact that color makes a difference in feelings and reactions.

In some cases, responses are channeled in the form of in-group aggression and crime. Moses,[53] studying differentials between Negro and white crime rates in Baltimore, for example, found felony and juvenile delinquency rates markedly higher for Negro areas. All murder and manslaughter offenses during a given period were committed by Negroes. "Due to low socio-economic status accentuated by racial proscription, Negroes do not have freedom of wholesale expression comparable to that of a similarly situated white group." This situation is prevalent generally. It is probable that much in-group aggression is misdirected hostility, a blind striking back at available scapegoats in the face of an inability to handle the larger white world.

Compensatory behavior is further seen in obvious display of material objects and varying forms of out-group aggression. A New York columnist facetiously stated there were more Cadillacs in one square block in Harlem than in any other square mile in the world. The roar of a high-powered car, with muffler deliberately bent to increase the fractious noises, and the handling of brakes so as to screech to a halt at busy intersections, are but subtle methods of indicating equality, or even superiority, in this area of ownership and control. Power is demonstrated over a mechanical aspect of the environment, at least. While there may be relief in abandonment and release of aggressive drives, and temporary bolstering of the ego in an assumed position of importance, little disguise is thus effected of the deep-seated feelings of inferiority. The practical realist finds the behavior childish. The student of human behavior sees it as an immature pattern of adjustment; nevertheless, he understands the underlying motives.

The pervasive influence of class on the nature of responses is again noticeable. Yet it would be an error to interpret behavior in the light of one's particular position, to ignore the fact that values and standards are relative, and to condemn individuals for techniques of adjustment which may be the best they can devise with the knowledge

---

[53]Earl R. Moses, "Differentials in Crime Rates Between Negroes and Whites Based on Comparisons of Four Socio-Economically Equated Areas," *American Sociological Review*, XII (1947), 411–420.

and aids available to them. The lower-class Negro whose image of himself is in a descendent position to all others seeks only to exist. He is passive toward wider social goals and uses aggressive defenses toward a hostile world. Occasionally, one endowed with the virtues of humor gets rid of his hostility through good-natured attacks, as did the cook who told her employer with a half chuckle, "You all supposed to be good folks and keep the Commandments, but the Lord say six days you work, and the seventh, ain't no work. But I works every day and Sunday too, and that ain't right." When the employer left, she added, "Don't come throwing slop in my face and call it water." When time off for church was granted, she calmly smiled, "Thank you, Jesus."

Middle- and upper-class individuals are sensitive to their position in the wider social hierarchy; yet, facing the problems inherent in limited participation and incomplete expression, they continue to strive for the attainment of larger cultural values.

The group studies reported here give general trends. All along the continuum individual reactions toward the self determine the designation of goals and the extent of continued push toward the achievement of them. Motivation may stem from feelings of self-confidence and esteem or may be compensatory simply, arising from felt inadequacies.

VI. IS THERE A NEGRO PERSONALITY?

Kardiner and Oversey,[54] in an extended treatise on the Negro, explain that continuous childhood frustration, plus pressures to adapt to a white culture, coupled with an inability to achieve standards, result in personality which, among other things, is devoid of confidence in human relations. It reflects a loss of efficiency, also, by virtue of its preoccupation with factors that have a prior claim to attention. These investigators believe there is a basic Negro personality, which is a caricature of the corresponding white personality. Realistically, of course, a liberal person or a bigot may be either black or white and, whichever is represented, we assume similarity in attitudes and action patterns. Certain feeling reactions, such as inferiority, and certain impulses toward the environment, such as hostility, which end in response patterns of withdrawal, avoidance, or aggression may appear, if it is true, more frequently within the Negro than within the white group. Caste arrangements are not without effect. If, however, we use this basis to refer to a unit personality which is Negro (this may not have been the intent of the authors), there is the implicit assumption that expressed behavior is a reflection of personality.

Behavior may or may not with certainty reflect an inner self. It may be an accommodation to the particular field of operation. The northern-born and reared Negro, when in the South, conforms with the controls operative at the moment, but in the more permissive environment of the North the same individual is more free to behave in terms of the dictates of the true self-system. He may then be very unlike his southern-born counterpart who occupies the same status position. Sullivan refers to learned accommodations in behavior as the sub-personality. That is, there is an adjustment to the assumed demands of a specific group. Such adjustment may demand that consciously held convictions be held in temporary abeyance. Further, since there are greater class differences within the group than there are caste differences between comparable groups, reference to a generalized Negro personality is questionable.

[54]A. Kardiner and L. Oversey, 1951.

VII. EDUCATIONAL SIGNIFICANCE OF THE FINDINGS

A social order which breaks the spirit and trammels the selfhood of any segment of its population implies that those so treated have nothing to contribute to its greater good and strength. The present movement toward modifications of pressures and reforms in antisocial practices promises control over previous circumstances which prevented all citizens from enjoying a full measure of democratic participation. The movement to integrate all pupils in public schools is a test of the concreteness of the theory we have espoused. If the test is met, democratic sharing, planning, and participation in purposeful classroom activities on the part of white and Negro children will become instruments for the development on the part of all respectability of self and concern for the welfare of others.

Students of education, working within the framework of scientific method, have made certain assumptions concerning the nature of the organism, the learning process, and the nature of society. One assumption is that passing on the cultural heritage, diffusion of knowledge, and the development of tools for clear communication will result in personal power and efficiency in interpersonal relationships. Realization of the goal is dependent upon capacity to profit from experiences designed to advance it. Many Negro children, however, are early subjected to traumatic emotional upsets by virtue of illegitimate birth and subsequent rejections, exposures to adult insensitivity to cultural mores, and growth in homes harassed by financial insecurities and attending deprivations. Their motivation toward the acquisition of prescribed learning is dulled; the demarcation between content of school subjects and actualities of personal pressures is too wide.

A slow-learning child may or may not be retarded, just as a mentally ill person may be bright or dull. Many children work below their capacity because of distracting, often soul-breaking, experiences for which no relief has been granted. Marie, for instance, a fifteen-year-old girl, stuffed into a third-grade seat in a school located near a migrant camp area, sat motionless, listlessly gazing out of the window. The night before, her drunken father had kicked her pregnant mother to death and that morning had attempted to rape her on the front porch. Psychopathic personalities are privileged with fatherhood, but unless discovered, no defenses are developed against the anxieties and tragedies which they mobilize. School was the only refuge for the hapless girl. Yet the teacher went blithely on with abstract subject matter, later revealing no knowledge of social agencies she might contact nor even showing an interest in what would happen to the girl at the close of the school day. Such instances, equally tragic, could be multiplied. What all would reveal, however, is that neglect of the fundamental features of growth and of social and emotional problems, together with the setting of goals unrelated to basic pupil needs, result in an unhealthy psychological state, resistance to learning, and a conflict in pupil-pupil, as well as in teacher-pupil, relationships. The unwitting behavior of middle-class teachers in imposing their standards on lower-class children, who make up the bulk of the public school population, is clearly presented by Davis.

This does not suggest that we ignore the importance of diligence in the performance of tasks within the range of individual capacity. Mastery of abstract symbols and successful transformation of the environment through manipulation of aspects of the physical world, where appropriate to the developmental levels of children, and when congruent with their interests, nurture a feeling of confidence in self. If we learn what we live, mastery of problems through attention to details, which makes for thoroughness of the whole, engenders a feeling of equality with situations. The Negro child, in particular, should be helped to realize his potentialities for the development of insights and understandings. He is in need of the support which may thus be given to a self that may, otherwise, too easily evolve into a suppressed promise of "what might have been."

A second assumption is that the biological basis which makes learning possible also provides for adaptation to change as experience warrants. The work of Axline[55] points to change in attitudes and behavior through social interaction in play sessions. In a group which included Negro, Jewish, and white children, an atmosphere was provided which permitted free expression of feelings and in which consequences of behavior were accepted as personal responsibilities. Changes in behavior in the form of respect for individuals as persons were noted. The permissive atmosphere provided opportunities for social learning that could not be achieved under conditions of repression and undue constraint. Unfortunately, not all teachers are secure enough themselves to follow the leads of the psychology they know. In some settings, therefore, rather tight initial control, moving to a gradual lessening of routine disciplines, may be necessary. However achieved, freedom within rules provides means for the growing individual to learn for himself the meanings of the language of the democratic creed.

The desirable teacher not only uses the classroom and recreation centers as laboratories for the study of behavior; he makes a constant appraisal of his relationship with pupils, also. Friendly communication, given by way of gesture, if not verbalization, and exemplification of good will contribute substantially in changing aggressive, antagonistic behavior, in which bigotry and unkindness are rooted, to behavior that is outgoing and trustful of others. Sympathy, understanding, friendliness, are learned more from example than from maxim and command.

A third assumption is that critical thinking and values can be taught. A corollary is that reason should control human behavior and social action. Despite the most careful research, attention to truth, and accuracy in subject content, there yet remain bright people who retain the prerogative of emotionalized attitudes and who see as right social inequalities that are based on such abstractions as skin color and historical status. Not all Southerners, not even all political leaders of the South, are dull.

Democratic behavior does need the force of intelligence. But it needs more. Facts in themselves do not bring release from human tensions nor do they fulfill felt needs. Since social arrangements are as much a product of individuals as individuals are a product of society, it is important to consider the totality of factors which interfere with the emergence of democratic attitudes and practices. Critical thinking and reasoning on social issues are functional in social action and betterment when they are congenial to the total complex of the personality. Stereotypes and emotionalized, irrational attitudes control human behavior when they serve the purpose of satisfying psychological needs. Verbalization, the printed page, even well-planned experiences do not necessarily lift the individual to a sense of human values. A criticism of the Lewin study on the influence of various types of leadership is that it does not go far enough. After discerning group behavior which followed each type of leader—authoritarian, *laissez-faire*, democratic—inter-group interaction was not reported. Democratic members, however, were noted to have been hostile on some occasions toward members of other groups, as were those who had not had the "democratic" exposure. Emotional reconditioning, more easily attained when there is intelligent understanding of basic causes of reactions, is imperative.

---

[55]V. Axline, "Play Therapy and Race Conflict in Young Children," *Journal of Abnormal Psychology*, XLIII (1948), 300–310.

Along with experience, there must be continuous appraisal of interpersonal relationships within the total situation so that insights may be gained into personal inner forces active in determining the nature of relationships. Critical observation and evaluation will disclose the acceptance of facts and knowledge as these arise and function in the context of living.

A fourth assumption is that continuous reevaluation of experiences and co-operative intelligent planning in terms of the democratic ideal will eventuate in the good life for all. Bode[56] states, "The school is peculiarly the institution in which democracy becomes conscious of itself." It is also an institution which, by virtue of this consciousness, becomes critical of itself. If democracy is a distinctive way of life, if things learned "must be translated into terms of emotion and conduct if they are significant," the school must exemplify what it teaches. The Supreme Court decision in 1954 repudiated the fallacy that democracy can be taught in segregated settings.

In addition to present objectives, education should turn attention to the building of psychological strength—preventive therapy—in order to offset human entanglements. This need should have been apparent throughout this discussion. The roots of democracy spring from an inner potential; the potential of a congenial out-goingness to an ever-widening circle of persons. Such a potential emerges in response to the human environment which nurtures it and, paradoxically, is embedded in the same raw material from which aggression and hatred spring. The challenge before the school is to devise the best means of developing those latent qualities for decency which, if unawakened, remain doomed to obscurity.

The continuing task of education, then, is the encouragement of social emancipation, the restoration from morbidity of thought which yields to bigotry, and the advancement of liberalism as decreed by law that has as its sustaining ground the Constitution of our country.

[56]Boyd H. Bode, *Democracy As a Way of Life* (New York: Macmillan and Company, 1939).

6-9 WORLDS APART

Edward H. Spicer

Edward H. Spicer is professor of anthropology at the University of Arizona. He earned his Ph.D. in anthropology from the University of Chicago, received two Guggenheim fellowships for study and writing in Mexico, was visiting professor at Cornell and the University of California and editor of the *American Anthropologist*. He has worked extensively in Mexico and among the Indians of the Southwest. His numerous articles and books include *American Indian Culture Change; Pascua, A Yaqui Village in Arizona; Cycles of Conquest*; and *Human Problems in Technological Change*. In this essay, Dr. Spicer suggests that assimilation of ethnic or racial groups may be a long and complicated process.

First, ... I raise the question as to whether there are now ... cultural differences of any consequence here in the Southwest. I suspect that the asking of this question immediately divides most of you into two camps. For some who

From *Arizona Quarterly*, XIII, No. 3 (Autumn 1957), 198–208, 228–230. © 1957 by *Arizona Quarterly*. Reprinted by permission of *Arizona Quarterly* and the author.

have had intimate contacts with the various peoples of the Southwest, I am sure you would prefer that I get down to business and discuss the nature of the differences; you have long been convinced that they exist. On the other hand, I would guess that there are others who have travelled widely in the region, have spent some time talking with Indians and others, and who believe that cultural differences, where they exist at all, are rather superficial.

It seems to me that the latter view is widespread among those who have considered the matter at all and that it is based on a good deal of accurate observation. On the one hand it seems often to grow out of the experience of encountering so many Indians who speak English. Tribal council leaders and others who meet visitors to reservations, silversmiths who sit in craft shops, young men and women attending schools and colleges, and even the casual acquaintances that one meets on or off reservations often chat in easy English, crack jokes, and show a familiarity with the language that misleads. It leads one to infer that, since communication is not too difficult with even numerous elderly people, there must be no great gulf separating the Indians' way of life from ours. But before one accepts such a conclusion it should be remembered that the Rio Grande Pueblos, who have about the same literacy rate as non-Indians in the Southwest, maintain the most vigorous and the best integrated round of native religious ceremonies of any people in the region. Some of the most thoroughly literate Hopi Indians are the most active in conscious efforts to further the native religious life and the old forms of village organization; they in fact send through the mails regularly printed bulletins in English, to explain their ideas and to convince non-Indians of the truth and rightness of what they have come to call, in English, the Hopi way. The fact is that this use of English is no more an indication of abandonment of long-standing cultural values than is the knowledge of English displayed by visitors from other countries who learn in an effort to get along satisfactorily with Americans. English-speaking Indians are also speakers of Apache, Navajo, Papago, Hopi, and the fifteen other Indian languages of the region. A better index for indicating cultural assimilation would be the number of Indians who know *only* English and no Indian language; and this number on any reservation in the Southwest today is very small.

The view that Indian cultural differences are non-existent or superficial rests perhaps even more solidly on the observation that Indians are using so many of the same *things* that everyone else is using in the Southwest. The blue jeans, the dresses, the hats, the shoes of young people and even of older people are bought obviously at Sears and Penney's, with perhaps only some tribal mannerism in the wearing. Many houses or hogans on the reservations have glass windows, hinged doors, padlocks; inside there is overstuffed furniture, and outside there is so often a car or a pickup. One goes to a sing deep in the Navajo country and there are dozens of red, blue, and perhaps orchid pickup trucks and only occasionally a wagon. It is very clear that even to a greater extent than in the adoption of an additional language there has been acceptance of our material goods. But again to infer that this means a corresponding acceptance of the deeper values of our social and religious life is dangerous.

Let me illustrate the dangers of this view that acceptance of white man's technology is an index of cultural disintegration. It has been held by white observers of Indian life for more than a hundred years. The great majority of such observers from the 1850's to the 1950's have, with great regularity, on the basis of observations of changing clothes and tools, predicted that it would not be long now until the old ways would be gone and Indian cultures would have disintegrated. Most observers of the

1950's have about the same report to make as those of the 1850's. They may be inclined to state it in more sophisticated terms, such as that "assimilation is inevitable," but it is the same one-hundred-year-old viewpoint. It is an integral part of the outlook that the majority of us have as the currently dominant group.

Before I embark, however, on the precarious task of prediction, I wish to make some other points. One of these is that the recurring renewal of this prediction should be a constant reminder that Indians have, during the three hundred years of intensive contact with white men, regularly poured the old wine of their way of life into the new bottles of the material trappings of Spanish and Anglo civilizations. The fact that the predictions of disappearance have to be *re-made* so *frequently* testifies to the continued vigor of Indian cultures.

If the indexes of language and technology are not reliable, what criteria can we use—other than the assertions of anthropologists who might be expected to be somewhat biased in this matter? One that I regard as well worth consideration is that of the experience of Indian Bureau personnel who work not in area offices but directly on the reservations. Recently a superintendent of a Southwestern reservation with long experience and a record of considerable achievement told me that the characteristic response of Bureau employees after three to six years' service was one of resigned frustration. If such a worker begins with the hopeful objective of transforming Indian life, the usual result is rather the transformation of the employee. In direct proportion to his beginning hopefulness, the Bureau worker by the end of his fifth or sixth year at the very latest becomes frustrated and develops a more or less intense conviction of the inherent distinctness of the Indian mind from that of the white man. In part, this is a reaction to the limited scope for activity in a government bureau ill-adapted to the bringing about of any sort of consistent change in individual lives. But it is also, according to our superintendent, a result of the encountering by the employee of a way of life oriented to values different from and often antithetical to our own. Wholly unprepared for such a reality, the employee becomes antagonistic to Indian spokesmen for these values and settles down to the minimum activity for holding his job. In the superintendent's view, this is not an indictment of the principle of federal assistance in Indian adjustment, but rather a criticism of the preparation of Indian Bureau employees for the situations in which they have to work. Their training, he believes, ought to include some learning of facts about the underlying premises of thought that characterize the viewpoints of the Indians of the different Southwestern reservations. They would not then come to their work believing that they were dealing with people who differ from themselves only in superficialities of dress and manner.

There are other lines of evidence indicating the reality of fundamental cultural differences. In Sonora, which is really part of our Southwestern region so far as its cultural make-up goes, this past summer and up to a few months ago there were rumors of war—of a renewal of the bloody fighting between Yaqui Indians and Mexicans which had characterized Sonora for over a century. The last actual fighting took place . . . in 1927. These wars far overshadowed, in terms of lives lost and property destroyed, the Apache wars of Arizona. They focused around the issues of Yaqui resistance to the Sonoran government's program for incorporating the Yaqui communities into the state. Yaquis fought for management of their land and autonomy in their village affairs. They wanted to maintain their own kind of unified village and religious government on what they regarded as their sacred tribal land. For many years the Sonora government was too weak to impose successfully its program for breakup of land holdings on the Yaquis, and during this period the Yaqui devotion to their institutions intensified. As Mexican national strength grew, little by little, like Indians in the United States, Yaquis had to yield. The rumors of war last summer were an indication that the long-standing conflict over fundamental cultural differences is not over, even though Yaqui military power has been almost erased.

A conflict almost identical in its bases exists on the Hopi reservation in Arizona, where conservative Hopis maintain much the same values as conservative Yaquis with respect to land and local government. Here it involves no threat of war, since Hopis are so few in number and since Hopi leadership has been forced long since to adopt such a different approach from the Yaqui. Nevertheless, the same issues are there, and they have by no means been resolved up to the present moment. Insight into them can be gained from thumbing the hundreds of pages of reports on hearings which the Indian Bureau has published during the past two years. I do not propose to summarize these piles of documents, but merely to point out that there is abundant documentary evidence here and elsewhere of the cultural differences and their political and administrative implications. Most of us know little of these, but they exist as concrete evidence of cultural differences just as extreme, if not so potential of overt warfare, as those between the Yaquis and the Sonorans.

We shall have to let this mention of a few lines of evidence do as suggestive of the persistence of cultural differences in the Southwest down to the present. What, then, are these differences dimly felt and largely misunderstood by a century of more or less casual observers and encountered with such frustrating definiteness by Indian Bureau workers of the present day? Somewhere between the views that they consist in colorful externalities of costume and behavior and that they consist in unfathomable spiritual orientations lies, I think, the truth of the matter.

To speak generally of all the cultures of the Indians of the Southwest is difficult, because of their diversity. Yet I believe that it is possible to make some generalizations that apply to all, and in the effort to do so, a better understanding of the Southwestern situation as a whole emerges. It is a mistake to expect to find that the most significant differences consist in elements somehow preserved unchanged from the isolated folk cultures of the days before white men came on the scene. No Southwestern Indian culture has been untouched by the succession of events of the past four hundred years.

And one of the striking characteristics of the world-views of Indians today is some kind of awareness of those events and of the succession of peoples who have entered the Southwestern region. There is a difference between *them* in this respect and the recently arrived Anglos. The vast majority of Anglos have come into towns, cities, and ranches already established in the patterns of their own tradition. As they settle in, they remain insulated by their own numbers from the Indian cultures and even from the older established Spanish-speaking peoples. Generally unaware of the processes by which their own dominance has come about, they have developed no historical traditions which link them, except perhaps in a vague consciousness of the Apache wars, with other people in the Southwest.

On the other hand, for each of the Indian groups, struggles and alliances with white men and with other Indians have been the stuff of their lives. Their fathers and grandfathers have told them of their parts in these events, and each tribe has its traditional history—the Navajo Long Walk to and from captivity at Fort Summer, the Hopi versions of the Bahana myth, the Yaqui deportations to Yucatan, the Papago defense villages against the Apaches, the Pima loss of the Gila River irrigation water, and so on. The result is an intense awareness of the balance of interests and purposes among the people of the Southwest. Indians have their traditional evaluations of the behavior of the early Anglos, of the Indian Bureau people, of the post-World War I agricultural migrant workers, and all the other strata of comers to the Southwest. If you go yourself, with enough background in the history of the region to understand what is said to you, and really find a way to communicate with older men and women on the reservations, you are sure to find your information illuminated in a lively way—from the Papago or the Navajo or the Apache or the Pueblo point of view. True enough, it may seem to you that the tribal traditional history is naive with respect to many aspects of Anglo civilization, but generally, I think, *far less naive* than the view of *Indian history* that *you* had before you began your discussions. What you find repeatedly is that the reservation dweller generally has a fuller understanding of the succession of events in the development of at least his section of the Southwest and a more realistic view of both local Anglo and Indian behavior than you have had of either.

Along with this historical sense of the region goes an awareness of themselves as one people among many. Watching the successive waves of newcomers, noting closely the veerings and shifts in Indian Bureau policy, listening to the various theologies preached by the ever-increasing missionary sects; a definite sense of distinct identity and of the boundaries of their own way of life has developed among Indians. This sense of identity is much sharper and clearer than among Anglos, who push on with their myriad projects quite unconscious of themselves as bearers of one tradition among many which might be seriously questioned or which might conceivably lead to dead ends of the spirit.

Individual Indians, of course, respond in different ways to this heightened sense of identity. For some the response is merely to reject the ways of, as they say, "those Indians" and to try to be like whites; for others there is dogged and dogmatic rejection of the Western civilization rolling against them. But for all, conscious or not, there is a constant effort to adjust divergent religious beliefs—to reconcile varying viewpoints.

The processes of individual adjustment often go on with a sense of confusion and uncertainty—of groping with respect to the elements of the white man's identity with which reconciliation must be made. The over-all effect is the creation of conditions which have in them the seeds of new growth, of a creativity of a different order from that which exists in the dominant peoples' laboratories, schools, and churches. It has been from various minority groups in similar situations that some of our greatest insights into existence, the world religions, have come in the past.

Now I realize, as I say it, that this idea in the context of our Southwestern reservations may seem fantastically far from the reality. The often battered and directionless chairmen of Tribal Councils hardly present a picture of significant new developments. The sometimes hard-drinking young veterans of our wars and their often poverty-stricken households don't look like seed-beds of a brave new spiritual world. Nevertheless, the reconciliation of traditions is always going on in these places. It has resulted in small new religious movements from time to time which have sought to bring the Christian and the Indian traditions into some meaningful relation to one another. The Silas John Holy Ground religion among the Apaches, which spread to several tribes, and the Native American Church among the Taos Pueblos and the Navajos have been movements of this kind, and their force has not died out. They are examples of the sort of creativity which exists in these situations where the need to reconcile contrasting cultural values has arisen.

I do not say that either of these holds much direct significance for the rest of us. We perhaps come closer to a movement of more general significance among the Hopis today—where some leaders are intensely conscious of both their own native religious teachings and those of some of our Christian sects. Here a genuine religious movement, of small scope but great intensity, brings some Anglos and some Hopis together. It seems doubtful at the moment whether it will grow or whether it has yet formulated its position with sufficient clarity to influence more than a few. But its existence is undeniable, and it is merely one among the several fusions of tradition which have marked the contacts of whites and Indians through the years down to the present. The creative forces are there and may be channeled in various directions. One result of the situation is rather well-known and may be mentioned here as an indication of the possibilities. This is the growth of the Southwestern Indian School of Painting, a fusion of traditions which has in at least a minor way enriched American culture. It was possible, of course, because a few in our society became almost as conscious of Indian background and culture as Indians usually are of ours.

What I have discussed so far, you may say, are not cultural differences. They are merely differences of situation contributing to different points of view. This is true, but the heightened sense of their own identity in a world of contrasting and often conflicting values constitutes the framework within which the Indians maintain the more formal and more traditional features of their ways of life. It is these latter which we shall now discuss. It seems to me that we can consider them, inseparable as they actually are in Indian life, as two different aspects of the Indian cultures: on the one hand, the form and conception of community life; and on the other, the nature of what we call religious belief and practice.

It is an interesting fact, and one which seems to me of immense significance in attempting to predict the future of Southwestern Indian life, that those tribal groups who have had the longest and most intensive contacts with Western civilization are those who exhibit the clearest differences from ourselves today and who show the most definite determination to maintain their differences. These are the Rio Grande Pueblos. Over 350 years ago, before the east coast of the United States was settled by Europeans, the Spaniards built a capital in one of their villages in 1598. Within a year the Indians who lived in that village moved across the river to separate themselves from the Spaniards. This separation is symbolic of the relationship between Pueblos and Europeans throughout their history. . . .

Finally, the burden of what I have said is this: The Indian cultures do persist— ideals regarding community life and of religious thought is constantly poured into new bottles. It changes with the pouring from generation to generation but still retains a distinctive savor. Some of the changes are easy for us to see, and we incline to interpret the whole direction of change in terms of these few factors. I am inclined, for example, to think at times that there are two conditions which would lead to the progressive disappearance which almost everyone assumes is taking place.

One would be the re-institution of the Indian Bureau's old policy of destruction of Indian cultures, including the systematic breakup of the reservations, and the public acceptance of this. While there are some strong tendencies in this direction in present Bureau policy, it seems unlikely that general public acceptance could be obtained for a full-scale and deliberate program of this sort. On the other hand, public support can be obtained for a policy creating another sort of condition which could lead to the disappearance of Indian ways of life. This would consist in making that great instrument for cultural assimilation, the American public school system, completely effective on all the reservations. We have in fact just entered a phase in which this possibility appears. If this trend continues, one might guess that before the middle of the twenty-first century—say, in another three generations—we would see the disappearance of the Indian cultures.

However, I have little confidence in such predictions. We know that individuals leave the Indian societies, but we also know that at the same time individuals who have tried Anglo society return to reservations. It is by no means clear that there is a steadily diminishing number of Indians who participate in the Indian cultures. There certainly is no simple direct correlation between the use of English and our technology and the rejection of Indian ways. I do not believe that anyone is in a position to state with adequate evidence for support that there are today fewer communicants of Indian religions than there were fifty years ago. My own opinion is that there are many more. We are seduced into making easy predictions of disappearance by our general lack of knowledge of what is really taking place in Indian cultural adjustment. We remain profoundly isolated. It is the nature of that isolation which has been the theme of this paper.

6-10 SOME PERSPECTIVES FOR TEACHING FIRST GENERATION MEXICAN-AMERICANS

John H. Chilcott

John H. Chilcott, who has conducted field work in Mexico, utilizes the socio-cultural approach toward the resolution of ethnic and social class factors affecting the school performance of a major ethnic group in America.

God Made People

God made the people
God made them at night
God made them in a hurry
He forgot to make some right.—Bill[1]

Her Eyes

Her eyes are like cat eyes
Gleaming in the night.
Her eyes remind you of a star
And all its sparkling light.
Her eyes have the image of the moon
And all its light.
Her eyes are like a cavern
With a crystal for its only light.
Her eyes are like a song
With lovely tone and its delight.
Her eyes are the color of the sky
With all the clouds in flight.—Juan[1]

---

[1] Marianna Wolman, "Cultural Factors and Creativity," paper presented at the spring meeting of the Southwestern Anthropological Association, Pomona College, March 1960. Mimeographed.

The writers of these two poems have much in common. Both Bill and Juan speak English as a "second language." Both have IQ's under 80, according to school records; both scored at the zero percentile on the English Cooperative Test. Both have been stereotyped by their teachers as sullen, troublesome, dirty, lazy, and disinterested in school; only their English teacher describes them as alert, intelligent, and responsive. Both will probably drop out of school before graduating. Both live in a segregated neighborhood. The parents of Bill and Juan were born in Mexico, cannot speak English, cannot read or write Spanish, and are classified as unskilled laborers. In short, Bill and Juan are first generation Mexican-Americans.

The more than 10,000,000 Mexican-Americans[2] have withstood assimilation by our Anglo-American society more completely than any ethnic group except the American Indians. The public schools have been fairly efficient in amalgamating other ethnic groups, but with the Mexican-American they have failed in more cases than they have succeeded. In some areas up to ninety percent of the Mexican-American students fail to complete secondary school. To be sure, there are Mexican-Americans who can be found at every stage in the acculturation process, but as a group they remain closer to their Mexican heritage than to Anglo-American society. Three interrelated conditions are hindering the assimilation process: culture conflict, Anglo-American prejudice, and the Mexican-American's lower socio-economic class membership.

Although it is difficult to discern at what stage of the acculturation process the greatest disturbance occurs, every stage can be ameliorated if the first stages of acculturation are better understood. School authorities report that second and third generation Mexican-American children have an easier time in school because the school is not as strange to their parents as it was to their Mexican-born grandparents.[3] Certainly formal education is not a panacea for minority group problems; nevertheless, the school, if properly oriented, can serve as a more important acculturating vehicle for Mexican-Americans, especially those of the first generation.

Lest this paper replace one stereotype of the Mexican-American with another, the reader must realize that the following conditions of acculturation, although resident in the acculturation process, are not universally present. Each Mexican-American student is an individual and should be treated as such. For purposes of analysis, however, the teacher and counselor should know that there are some general conditions which contribute to his individuality and, in varying degrees, affect the assimilation of Mexican-Americans as a group. The Mexican-American population itself appears to have regional variations based on both the area in Mexico from which that population emigrated and the area in the United States in which it settled.[4] For example, the recent arrivals in Southern California have come primarily from south-central Mexico, a region highly populated by Indian cultures. The Arizona Mexican-American population, however, emigrated primarily from Sonora in northern Mexico. The Sonorans, because of Apache raids and a mining economy, are more urban than rural in character; consequently, they make an easier adjustment.

The following generalizations, therefore, must be considered in the light of the heterogeneity of the Mexican-American population. They merely provide a point of departure; they are perspective, not directives.

---

[2] Since census figures are not available for the Mexican-American, this figure is an approximation.

[3] Ruth Landes, "Cultural Factors in Counselling," paper presented at the meeting of the Southwestern Anthropological Association, Pomona College, March 1960. Mimeographed.

[4] This is a hypothesis on the part of the writer; it has yet to be verified through research.

PROBLEMS ARISING FROM CULTURE CONFLICT

The Anglo-American culture, characteristic of the dominant group in the United States, was derived primarily from northern European cultures and was little influenced by contact with the indigenous population. Furthermore, the majority of the colonists brought their families with them or married girls sent to the colonies to maintain and increase the European population. Mexican culture, on the other hand, was derived from southern European and northern African cultures and was considerably influenced through contact with the more "civilized" indigenous population of Mexico. In addition, Spanish colonists married Indian women. The resulting *mestizo* culture possesses many characteristics which are not found in Anglo-American culture. Consequently, when the Mexican-American school child seeks to learn the Anglo-American culture from his teachers, he can draw upon few similarities in his own culture. A teacher can easily "talk over the child's head" unless he is aware of the discontinuity between the two cultures.

To illustrate this discontinuity, a comparison between the Mexican and Anglo-American child's concept of self is useful. The rugged-individualism ideal of the Anglo-American child, with its emphasis upon self-assertion, individualism, and aggression contrasts dramatically with the Mexican child's *personalismo* ideal which requires a series of close, primary, dependent associations with friends and relatives.[5] The Mexican child conceives of himself as a member of a group. He cannot "go it alone"; he is not sufficient within himself. Rugged individualism is simply an impossibility for him without explanation and observation. This difference in cultural ethos is not insurmountable, but the teacher must always be aware of it.

The most obvious difference between the two cultures is language. A recent arrival from Mexico or a child raised in a rigidly segregated neighborhood, arriving at school for the first time, not only experiences normal fear of a new and strange situation, but also encounters what to him is a foreign language. A strange culture, a strange situation, and a strange language; no wonder this child is often absent.

Closely associated with language are body posture and gestures, some of which reinforce the strangeness of the language. In some parts of Mexico, for example, pointing a finger is considered vulgar. This gesture is common to many Anglo-American teachers, especially if they do not know a child's name or are having difficulty in communicating with him. The phonetic nature of the Spanish language can create problems also; the Mexican-American child will refer to his teacher as *Mees* Wilson (*i* is pronounced *ee* in Spanish), an inflection which she may consider derogatory.[6]

The language barrier not only creates difficult teaching situations; it renders almost useless the major method for evaluating pupil progress in American schools— the written examination. The combination of strange terms and strange cultural situations described in these tests causes the Mexican-American child to achieve poorly and creates the impression that he is innately dull. The average IQ test score for Mexican-American children is 80.[7] Teachers that understand the language barrier

---

[5] Howard M. Jones, *The Scholar as American* (Cambridge: Harvard University Press, 1960), p. 11.

[6] Simon J. Chavez, "Preserve Their Language Heritage," *Childhood Education*, XXXIII (December 1956), 165.

[7] Arthur R. Jensen, "Learning Abilities in Mexican-American and Anglo-American Children," paper presented at the annual meeting of the California Educational Research Association, Palo Alto, California, March 1961. Mimeographed.

realize that other means of evaluation such as oral quizzes and performance tests must be used and that IQ and achievement tests must be cautiously evaluated.

A language barrier exists when the child's knowledge of Spanish exceeds his knowledge of English. This index provides a good indication of the degree of acculturation. A number of programs have been employed to overcome the language barrier. One program enrolls the five-year-old Mexican-American child in school with the specific purpose of teaching him English for a year before he becomes a regular student.[8] In another program, the first-grade language is Spanish, and English is gradually introduced.[9] In some school districts a traveling teacher gives individual help to each student who enters school at a higher grade. Still another program segregates the student into special classes to teach him English and Anglo-American culture until he is ready for regular classes.[10] Unless it succeeds immediately, this program can cause parents to resent the school's "discrimination" against their child.

One of the more promising programs for the older Mexican-American child includes him in academic Spanish classes. This not only provides some security, but also permits him to increase his knowledge of his own language.[11] Since parents often are illiterate in their native tongue, the child's rapid achievement in the literacy skills of the Spanish language can be a source of satisfaction for both parent and child. Mexican-American parents are also bothered by their child's grammatically imperfect Spanish—phonetic spelling of Spanish words and incorporation of English words into Spanish sentences. However, counselors should carefully consider proper orientation to this program, as there is evidence that *second* generation Mexican-American students have little success when placed in academic Spanish classes.[12]

Some schools with large Mexican-American populations forbid the use of Spanish in school or on the playground in an attempt to force students to speak English. Unfortunately this practice may restrict acculturation in other areas of Anglo-American culture by suggesting that Spanish is "bad." In other schools fights erupt when an Anglo-American child, who does not understand Spanish, thinks he has been insulted by a Mexican-American.[13] The Mexican-American finds security in his own language; he feels that he can say so much more in Spanish than in English.

A Spanish accent quickly identifies the Mexican-American as a minority group member and can hinder the process of acculturation. In English classes or during the period devoted to English in the elementary school classroom, teachers should provide opportunities for Mexican-American children who have language difficulties to hear good English and try to imitate it.[14] The child who has attended school in Mexico is accustomed to reading aloud.[15] If oral reading were permitted, teachers or other students could watch for and assist in correcting mispronunciations. If a child speaks no English, the teacher may assign another child in class—perhaps a

[8] William R. Holland, "Language Barrier as an Educational Problem of Spanish-Speaking Children," *Exceptional Children*, XXVII (September 1960), 50.

[9] Holland, "Language Barrier," p. 46.

[10] John H. Burma, *Spanish Speaking Groups in the United States* (Durham: Duke University Press, 1954), p. 76.

[11] Jack E. Davis, "Teaching Spanish in a Bi-Lingual Area," *Hispania*, XL (May 1957), 207.

[12] Burma, *Spanish Speaking Groups*.

[13] Ruth D. Tuck, *Not with the Fist* (New York: Harcourt Brace & Co., 1946), p. 97.

[14] Louise Gurren, "Foreign Children Like to Sound American," *Instructor*, LVII (January 1958), p. 82.

[15] John H. Chilcott, "Formal Education in a Mexican *Ejido*." Unpublished manuscript.

Mexican-American—to help him. In Mexico older siblings play an important role in educating their younger brothers and sisters.[16] Thus a big-brother or big-sister arrangement is within the experience of the Mexican-American child and can assist the teacher in reducing the time allotted to personal direction and exploration.

The child from a Mexican school is accustomed to copying and memorizing material from texts and chalkboard; consequently, his Anglo-American teachers should permit him to copy and memorize work from his fellow students' papers and text-books and from the chalkboard. Manual manipulations are most effective until the Mexican-American child learns enough English to participate in verbal activities. However, the Mexican-American child is embarrassed when he lags behind his Anglo-American classmates, so teachers should not overemphasize the differences caused by the language barrier. Much of the literature on problems of educating Mexican-Americans is devoted to language problems. The main reason the suggested programs fail is that only language is considered, while other barriers to accultura-tion are overlooked. The child must learn new behavior as well as a new language.[17]

One of the characteristics of the Mexican-American child most exasperating to an Anglo-American teacher is his complete lack of interest in promptness—in arrival, in completing assignments, and in developing aspirations for the future. The Mexican concept of time is entirely foreign to the Anglo-American school system, which in-cludes bells, charts, timetables, and long-range planning. For Anglo-Americans, time is horizontal and advancing; it moves from the past to the present and into the future. For the Mexican, time is vertical and stationary; it stays within a given space.

The Mexican lives in the present, which contains all the time there is. The past is not behind him, but around him; the future is part of today.[18] He realizes he cannot possibly do everything he should or would like to do in one lifetime. There simply isn't enough time, so he lives each moment and each day to the fullest extent; tomorrow does not concern him. Engaged in an interesting activity, he will pursue it until he is bored. He will not stop because of a bell or a schedule. Life is to be lived and loved, not planned.[19] A Mexican-American child will linger over his breakfast and then blame the school bus driver for not waiting for him.[20] The *mañana* promise is an attempt by the Mexican-American child to compromise between his cultural concept of time and his recognition of pressures to accept the American concept. School authorities must learn to accept the Mexican concept of time and expect the Mexican-American child to be late to class, to "forget" his homework assignments, and to fail to appear for after-school activities. The child raised in rural Mexico has perhaps never seen a clock, much less learned how to "use" it.[21] Once it has accepted these characteristics as "natural," the school can pursue a program to help the child understand the significance of time in Anglo-American society.

In Mexico the family is the strongest social unit. Not only does the family develop strong personal ties with uncles, aunts, and cousins, but it also extends

---

[16] John H. Chilcott, "Enculturation in a Mexican Rancheria," *Journal of Educational Sociology*, XXXVI, No. 1 (September 1962), 42–47.

[17] "Teacher's Guide to the Education of Spanish-Speaking Children," *California Department of Education Bulletin*, XXI (November 1952), p. 11.

[18] Helen Augur, *Zapotec* (Garden City, New York: Doubleday, 1954), pp. 273–274.

[19] Landes, "Cultural Factors in Counselling."

[20] Simon J. Chavez and Turila L. Erickson, "Teaching American Children from Spanish-Speaking Homes," *The Elementary School Journal*, LVII (January 1957), 198.

[21] Chilcott, "Enculturation in a Mexican Rancheria."

family membership through the custom of *compadrazgo*, wherein god-parents are treated as another set of parents.[22] Second generation Mexican-Americans, who have lost their family ties and not yet been accepted into Anglo-American culture, rely on their peer group for security and direction. Thus, teachers of second generation Mexican-Americans can find in the peer group cues to student behavior. But the first generation Mexican-American is caught between his home traditions that emphasize dependence and the Anglo-American ideals of family life, presented at school, that emphasize independence. In Mexico the stability of the family is maintained with increased individualism on the part of the children.[23] The school's task is to assist the Mexican-American child in accepting the nuclear Anglo-American family without losing the personal relationships of his own family.

The nature of the Mexican family and society is authoritarian. Both adults and children are accustomed to being told what to do. Thus, when confronted by a "democratic" classroom and a permissive teacher (or a counselor using non-directive techniques), the Mexican-American child is dumbfounded. When a teacher asks him what *he* thinks, he can only shrug his shoulders or say meekly, "I don't know." As a consequence, the Anglo-American teacher characterizes the child as unresponsive. The teacher and counselor may find authoritarian techniques more effective with the Mexican-American child. Even nagging can be an acceptable procedure.

Although he may contribute economically, the child has little status in the Mexican family. School notices sent home through the children may be disregarded. Similarly, parents do not support or follow through on homework. The vocational choice of the Mexican-American child should be cleared with his parents. Because parents consider the child an inferior and do not understand the school's goals, they may keep the child at home when he is needed. In rural Mexico one may find a child of thirteen in the first grade because his parents "kept" him at home.[24] This attitude, combined with a fear of the strange "gringo" school, causes high absenteeism. School authorities who wish to improve the attendance record of a Mexican-American child must interpret the goals of the school to his parents and develop a program for the child that provides immediate benefits.

Mexican-American parents who are illiterate in their native tongue, speak no English, and have little or no formal education cannot be reached through the usual channels of school-parent communication. For obvious reasons, they do not attend PTA meetings and rarely respond to a school summons. The parents must have a purpose in visiting the school. To achieve some success with the child, the school must design an adult education program to acculturate the parents. New York City schools were unsuccessful in educating the children of Puerto Ricans until their parents were included in adult education programs.[25] Through such programs conflict between school and the tradition-steeped Mexican-American family can be reduced. However, in organizing an adult education program, school authorities must realize that parents are unaccustomed to change; suggestions for change should be presented gradually and should be based on experiences familiar to the parents.

In general, Mexican-American parents have low regard for education as a

---

[22] Nathan L. Whetten, *Rural Mexico* (Chicago: University of Chicago Press, 1948), p. 398.

[23] Oscar Lewis, "Tepoztlan Restudied: A Critique of the Folk-Urban Conceptualization of Social Change," *Rural Sociology*, XVIII (June 1953), 127.

[24] Chilcott, "Formal Education in a Mexican *Ejido*."

[25] Board of Education, New York City, *The Puerto Rican Study, 1953–1957*, pp. 152–153.

means of upward mobility.[26] Since middle and upper class Mexicans fare better economically in their own country and prefer to remain there, most Mexican-Americans are members of the peasant class. These people have lived for generations under a feudal system, have accepted their "place" in the world, and have little desire to change their status. Instead, they are content to lead the "good life"—to have family relationships and many good friends (not merely acquaintances), to sit and talk, to enjoy life as it is. They are not interested in acquiring material wealth or high-status occupations; in short, they have few of the Anglo-American middle class goals that the schools represent. Education is not necessary to the good life, nor is the good life found in the schools.

The Anglo-American ideal of equality of the sexes can create further tensions between home and school. In the Mexican family the father maintains a position of authority. The mother does not enjoy high status, due in part to the lowly position of the Spaniards' Indian wives. Thus it is difficult for a male in Mexico to accept a woman in a position of authority.[27] Similarly, the Mexican-American child may subconsciously reject his female teacher. The school would be wise to use male staff members for all contacts with the Mexican-American home.

Many times the child shows a complete disinterest in American ways of life. The typical school curriculum, especially the social studies program, includes nothing from his Mexican heritage. He hears of Anglo-American heroes and Anglo-American history; he reads Anglo-American literature; but he hears and reads nothing of Mexican heroes, Mexican history, Mexican literature, or Mexican music.[28] His own history's image of the "gringo" American is quite different from that of the American school. Defeated in war, dominated economically, the Mexican conceives of the American as a hostile figure. Few school curricula do anything to overcome this concept.

Although many Mexicans are not active Catholics, they nevertheless consider themselves Catholics.[29] One week they may throw rocks at a visiting priest, and the next participate in a religious procession to the local church, using lay leaders as surrogate priests. The average Mexican resents the proselytizing of his Catholic countrymen by American Protestant missionaries. Thus, the Puritan Protestant ethic central to Anglo-American culture is not only alien, but represents a hostile aggressive element which Mexican-Americans resent. Protestant Mexican-Americans are rejected by their own ethnic group.[30] The American tradition of separating church and school precludes, in addition, the cooperation of the local Catholic priest with school authorities.[31]

To the Mexican, life is dramatic. He has a great love of color, movement, and sound; he delights in the bullfight and fiesta. His goals for life are non-material. The emotional flow of his culture reassures him; the impersonality and materialism of Anglo-American society irritate him. To the Anglo-American, the Mexican-American is a child in an adult environment, while to the Mexican-American the Anglo-American is too matter-of-fact; he lacks sentiment and joy.[32]

---

[26] Norman D. Humphrey, "The Cultural Background of the Mexican Immigrant," *Rural Sociology*, XIII (September 1948), 251.

[27] Landes, "Cultural Factors in Counselling."

[28] Landes, "Cultural Factors in Counselling."

[29] Whetten, *Rural Mexico*, p. 454.

[30] Burma, *Spanish Speaking Groups*, p. 83.

[31] Landes, "Cultural Factors in Counselling."

[32] Emory S. Bogardus, *The Mexican in the United States* (Los Angeles: University of Southern California Press, 1934), pp. 57, 67.

The Mexican *la raza* idealization of Latin culture retards the acceptance of Anglo-American culture, since parents and child feel the old ways are better.[33] Thus the Mexican-American, unlike many other ethnic minorities in the United States, does not anglicize his name to hide his ethnic background.[34] Instead he is proud of a name which identifies him with his Latin background. Unlike other Spanish-speaking ethnic groups, the Mexican-American can and does visit his homeland frequently. In addition, family and friends from Mexico visit him in the United States. This contact reinforces his idealization of the Mexican culture and provides a security he cannot find in the Anglo-American culture, thus intensifying the culture conflict which the school may be attempting to ameliorate.

PROBLEMS ARISING OUT OF PREJUDICE

Segregated at home (and in some cases at school as well), stereotyped with uncomplimentary adjectives, and treated with hostility by members of the dominant Anglo-American culture, the Mexican-American child perceives the school as a strange and fearful world. Through body postures, word intonations, and in some cases overt behavior, school authorities often express hostility. And the cultural ineptitude of many children, generally caused by their alienation, contributes to this hostility.

When exposed to this strangeness and hostility, the Mexican-American pupils typically withdraw—a common reaction to discrimination. Having withdrawn, the Mexican-American child seeks security in his own group. Thus it is not uncommon during recess periods and lunch hours to find Mexican-American children speaking to one another in their native tongue. Anglo-American teachers misinterpret this withdrawing and ethnic separateness as lack of initiative and passivity, both of which are neither accepted nor rewarded in the middle-class Anglo-American culture.

Adding to the misunderstandings which confuse and disturb the Mexican-American child is the common practice among Anglo-American teachers of maintaining an objective and oftentimes impersonal relationship with their students. Although the Mexican-American child does not show affection outwardly, he is accustomed to intense personal relationships with his family and his friends. The impersonality of Anglo-American urban society and especially the impersonality of the teacher with whom the child interacts continuously during the day can easily be misinterpreted by the child as hostility. Although he may not be overtly aware of this reaction, he subconsciously reacts to it in a negative fashion.

Prejudice becomes *overtly* manifested when the Mexican-American seeks Anglo-American vocational goals. Not only is it difficult for the Mexican-American child to develop long-range goals, not only does he have a difficult time developing educational aspirations, but he soon becomes aware that not all the vocational goals aspired to by his Anglo-American friends are available to him because of discrimination. The descriptions by parents and friends of discriminatory practices against them in the vocational world are far stronger influences than the idealistic implorations of teachers and counselors. And, in some cases, school authorities intentionally discourage Mexican-American children from selecting educational programs which lead to middle-class vocations. One of my former Mexican-American students told me how he tried seven times to persuade his high school counselor that he wanted to enter the college preparatory program. He now holds an A.B. and a fifth-year teaching certificate.

[33] Landes, *ibid.*
[34] Tuck, *Not with the Fist*, p. 134.

Most Mexican-American youngsters with less tenacity would have given up on their first refusal.

Since prejudice and discrimination are based upon ignorance, school authorities and Anglo-American students can remedy the problems somewhat by learning more about Mexican culture. A teacher who can speak a few Spanish phrases, who can discuss with appreciation some of the objects, behaviors, and values of Mexican culture, who can indicate an interest in each Mexican-American child on a person-to-person basis, can do much to reduce hostility. School counselors need to search for successful Mexican-Americans (in terms of middle-class vocations) and include them among the speakers on Career Day. At the elementary school level, especially in those districts where Mexican-Americans are rigidly segregated, the school should increase their "life space" through visits to parts of the community with which they are not familiar. Each teacher and counselor must conscientiously analyze his own subtle manifestations of prejudice. Not until prejudice is recognized is it possible to overcome it. Finally, in all attempts to solve the problems of prejudice, the school must be cautious not to approach the Mexican-Americans as if they are basically different, for this approach can offend group loyalty and negate all efforts to acculturate the Mexican-American children.

PROBLEMS ARISING FROM LOWER SOCIO-ECONOMIC CLASS

Mexican immigrants come primarily from rural villages and urban slums. In the United States they become *braceros*, working by the day or by the season. Their sons and daughters must overcome not only the obstacles of cultural discontinuity and prejudice, but the problems of extreme poverty. Ill-fed, housed under unsanitary conditions, periodically without money, these children must attend a school that bases its expectations on the materially secure middle-class Anglo-American home. The typical Anglo-American school does not recognize the problems of deprivation that hinder the Mexican-American child's acculturation.

Living in two- or three-room tenements or shacks, sleeping on the floor or in a communal bed, sharing limited or obsolete toilet facilities, this child has little understanding of school health programs. Mexico largely lacks modern sanitary conditions, so the Mexican-American child has no background to draw upon when health programs are presented.[35] The school health program needs to consider this background and the existing facilities of the Mexican-American home and start with this stage rather than from an advanced stage not yet available to these children. The health program is further handicapped by the many superstitions which surround health in the Mexican-American culture.[36] One example is the belief that illness is caused by an imbalance of hot and cold in the body. The teacher must recognize that resistance to modern health practice is not caused by the indolence of a Mexican-American child, but by his lack of experience with modern health practices and his confidence in folk medicine.

The concept of preventive medicine based on "germ theory" is especially foreign to the Mexican-American child. In his own culture sickness is a result of divine intervention. "It is God's will that our child sickens and dies." Closely allied to his concept of time and his indifference to the future is the feeling that

---

[35] Chilcott, "Enculturation in a Mexican Rancheria."

[36] Margaret Clark, *Health in the Mexican-American Culture* (Berkeley: University of California Press, 1959), p. 163.

he need not think about sickness until he becomes sick. A Mexican-American doesn't worry about his teeth until he gets a toothache.

Within the lower socio-economic class in America, sex behavior is more overt than among other classes.[37] When adults and children share the same sleeping quarters, the children at an early age hear and see adult sex activities. In Mexico the male sex role requires promiscuous behavior before and after marriage. The Mexican male brags about how many children he has fathered outside of the family. He is honestly faithless.[38] The *machismo* concept of manliness is synonymous with sexual virility.[39] The Mexican male distinguishes between love, which is a mystical experience, and sex, which is a necessity.[40] In rural areas of Mexico the marriage age is 14 for girls and 16 for boys.[41] Thus, the Mexican-American child has a cultural ethos for early aggressive interest in sex. Overt sexual behavior, even constant teasing of the girls, is shocking to Anglo-American middle-class teachers, who classify as bad the sex behavior that the Mexican-American child considers normal.

In spite of the overt acts of sexuality of her boys, usually enacted away from the home, the Mexican-American mother is shocked by the school's sex education program. She is embarrassed by the questions her children raise as a result of it and resents the school for placing her in an embarrassing situation. Sex education in the Mexican-American home is limited to a mother telling her daughter to "stay away from boys."[42] The double sex standard of Mexican culture, which provides freedom for males but restricts women, creates anxiety among Mexican-American women when they encounter the *casual* and scientific Anglo-American approach to sexual behavior.

Most common-law marriages in the United States exist among the lower socio-economic classes. In some areas of rural Mexico, free-union marriages are far more common than secular or church marriages.[43] If a young Mexican couple cannot afford the expense of a church or secular marriage, they may enter into a free-union marriage, anticipating that some day they will be married by a priest. For most, this day never arrives. Thus, American law and mores may brand children of recent arrivals from Mexico illegitimate, adding the stigma of illegitimacy to that of ethnic affiliation. Often the Mexican male tires of his wife and the responsibilities of his home and deserts them both, leaving his wife to "take up" with another man who may father other children. Consequently, children of the same mother may have different fathers. To the Anglo-American, the person who procreates a child is the father even though he abdicates all responsibility for raising the child and is absent. Other societies, however, define father as the person who assumes responsibility for raising the child. School authorities could better cope with the problem of the illegitimate Mexican-American child by accepting the latter definition of father.

The violent nature of Mexican society is reinforced by membership in the lower socio-economic "culture" wherein physical aggression, rather than arbitration, is the accepted means of settling arguments.[44] The "don't care, don't show physical weakness,

---

[37] Allison Davis and Robert J. Havighurst, *Father of the Man* (Boston: Houghton Mifflin, 1947), p. 26.

[38] Humphrey, "Cultural Background of the Mexican Immigrant," p. 25.

[39] Henry P. Anderson, *The Bracero Program in California* (Berkeley: University of California Press, 1961), p. 259.

[40] Anderson, *ibid*.

[41] Chilcott, "Enculturation in a Mexican Rancheria."

[42] Clark, *Health in the Mexican-American Culture*, p. 136.

[43] Whetten, *Rural Mexico*, p. 376.

[44] Davis and Havighurst, *Father of the Man*, p. 186.

just beat somebody up" aspect of the Mexican male *machismo* concept is tolerated and even encouraged by male contemporaries in the lower socio-economic class in the United States.[45] On the school grounds, however, such behavior is unacceptable. The Mexican-American child may solve the resulting conflict by withdrawal.

It is a common practice for school children to compare and even share their school lunches. Here the food habits of the Mexican-American differentiate him from other children. Even after he has grown accustomed to Anglo-American foods, the Mexican-American child may be unable to afford an American lunch. Consequently, he is embarrassed when he brings his *refritos* and *tacos* to school. Through a program designed to develop an appreciation for both Mexican and Anglo-American foods, and through free lunch programs during periods of privation, school authorities can improve dietary habits among Mexican-American children.

In an environment of poverty, a child takes little interest in arts and crafts or in reading for pleasure. School authorities should allocate funds for encouraging these activities in the school environment and for the pursuit of cultural enrichment programs by community agencies. Whatever the program, its materials should include elements of both Mexican and Anglo-American culture.

Poverty and lower class status are not new to the Mexican-American. The Mexican *pelado*[46] distrust of strangers and the modern scientific world—in fact, of all men, including himself—stems from centuries of frustration and domination by "superior" individuals. His membership in the lower class stratum in the United States encourages his continued distrust of persons in authority. The school must devise a program to develop confidence in himself and other members of our society.

In spite of cultural conflict, prejudice, and lower socio-economic class membership, the Mexican-American child can and does become an acculturated, successful middle-class American. There is an expanding Mexican-American middle class today, due in part to opportunities provided in the armed services.[47] With middle-class membership come new behavior patterns—the decline of male sexual aggressiveness, new dating habits, an elevation of the wife as both marriage partner and wage earner, all of which create still other problems for first-generation Mexican-Americans. Thus, the public school must provide programs based on a greater understanding of Mexican-American culture as it exists today. The Mexican-American should be encouraged to retain the best of his heritage and, at the same time, contribute to American democracy by becoming an intelligent and productive citizen.

In order to accomplish this with the first-generation Mexican-American child, school authorities must consider each child as a distinct personality in a different stage of the acculturation process. The successful teacher will determine the particular technique to be used with each child at each stage. He must realize that the use of Spanish at one stage may provide security, while at another it may evoke hostility. He must also work with the parents as well as the child. When the teacher evaluates his personal feelings about Mexican-Americans, when he understands Mexican-American viewpoint, when he accepts the professional goal that each child will have an equal opportunity to achieve to the limits of his capacity—then he will be able to work effectively with Mexican-American children.

---

[45] For a good description of *macho*, see the story of Roberto in Oscar Lewis's *The Children of Sanchez*.

[46] Roughly translated as "plucked" or "penniless." See Samuel Ramos, *Profile of Man and Culture in Mexico* (New York: McGraw-Hill Book Company, 1963), pp. 57–63.

[47] William Madsen, *The Mexican-Americans of South Texas* (New York: Holt, Rinehart, and Winston, 1964), p. 35.

6-11   CHILDREN, TEACHERS, AND ETHNIC DISCRIMINATION

I. Roger Yoshino

I. Roger Yoshino is at present associate professor of sociology at the University of Arizona. He received his B.A. from Denver University, where he was elected to Phi Beta Kappa, and his Ph.D. from the University of Southern California. In 1952 he was a Ford Foundation Fellow in Japan, where he completed a village study. In 1964–65 he was a National Science Fellow at Harvard University. Professor Yoshino has written extensively about minority groups in the United States. In the following article he describes the role the teacher can play in eliminating the "disease" of ethnic prejudice.

Research on the attitudes of young children indicates that basic ethnic values develop quite early in life and are mainly molded by the family, other primary groups, the community, and to a considerable extent by the schools.[1] However, there is a paucity of current studies pertaining to children's awareness of ethnic differences and the effects of early school experiences on prejudice and discrimination.[2] Since the Supreme Court decision of 1954 desegregating public education, there have been changes in the covert and overt behavior of the general population in the area of ethnic relations. Are similar changes in evidence in the thinking and behavior of this generation's children?

This paper is a descriptive exploration of (1) the ethnic feelings of young children today and (2) the teacher's influence in channeling ethnic attitudes and discriminatory behavior.

How do past research findings relate to current observations of the relationship in school between children of different racial and cultural backgrounds?

Criswell, after comparing several studies, summarizes:[3]

" . . . we may conclude provisionally that children enter school with race preferences already in the process of formation. They may at this age have little

---

From *Journal of Educational Sociology*, XXXIV, No. 9 (May 1961), 391–397. c 1961 by the Payne Educational Sociology Foundation, Inc.; reprinted by permission of the Payne Educational Sociology Foundation, Inc.

[1] For example see E. Frenkel-Brunswick, "A Study of Prejudice in Children," *Human Relations*, I (1941), 294–306; E. L. Hartley, M. Rosenbaum and S. Schwartz, "Children's Use of Ethnic Frames of Reference: An Exploratory Study of Children's Conceptualizations of Multiple Ethnic Group Membership," *Journal of Psychology*, XXVI (1948), 387–398; E. L. Horowitz, "The Development of Attitude toward the Negro," *Archives of Psychology*, XCIV (1936); B. Lasher, *Race Attitudes in Children*, Henry Holt and Co., 1924.

[2] Some noteworthy studies prior to the desegregation decision are: J. H. Criswell, "A Sociometric Study of Race Cleavage in the Classroom," *Archives of Psychology*, CCXXXV, (1939); M. B. Goodman, *Race Awareness in Young Children*, Addison-Wesley Press, 1952; A. F. Manshe, *The Reflections of Teachers' Attitudes in the Attitudes of Pupils*, Columbia University, 1935; P. W. Schlorff, *An Experiment in the Measurement and Modification of Race Attitude in School Children*, New York University, 1930.

[3] Criswell, 1939, p. 11.

understanding of the concept of race, but they have already perceived physical differences between races and absorbed some hostile attitudes from parents and other members of their community. From kindergarten through high school, the attitudes of white children, at least, show development.

In Criswell's empirical research she found that cleavage between the sexes was greater than racial cleavage. She states, for example, that a white boy would almost invariably prefer a Negro boy to a white girl.[4] It is her belief that race consciousness is a gradual process, having a direct and positive relation to the age of the child.

In an early study, Lasher says that the child does not specifically become conscious of membership in a certain racial group until adolescence.[5] According to Gordon Allport, very young children are not cognizant of racial differences. The story is told of Tommy (white), aged 6, who asked his mother if he might bring Sammy home to lunch some day from school. The mother, knowing that Tommy attended a "mixed" school, asked if Sammy were white or colored. Said Tommy, "I don't know, but I'll look next time I see him and tell you."[6]

Goodman used a number of projective materials to test for prejudice in young children.[7] After rapport had been established with a group of children in a biracial nursery school, they were invited, one at a time, to play with some new things. Each child eventually received several such invitations, and in the course of the "play interviews," each was introduced to four sets of projective materials.[8] On the basis of this experimentation, Goodman shows that a child's awareness of racial difference is directly related to his environment and its prevailing attitudes.

Ethnic attitudes of children evolve from a complex of societal and personality characteristics which reveal themselves in interrelationships of various sorts, including parental attitudes toward children and preferred practices in child-rearing.[9] A child's world is full of new experiences. Not only is he influenced by members of his family and his play group; he learns upon going to school that he must mind his teacher. In today's society of changing ethnic attitudes and behavior, how effective is the teacher in influencing the children's ethnic attitudes?

Although Criswell realizes the primacy of the influence of the wider social pattern of which the children are a part, she believes that the teacher, curriculum, and experience with fellow students may somewhat modify racial attitudes.[10] Underscoring this point, Montague asserts:[11]

> It is the educators, and the parents, who are capable of changing all this, of making truly human beings of the wards in their charge. The enterprise must be a joint one, between parents and teachers. But where parents have failed, the teacher should not also fail. Parents of the coming generation must be taught to love their children, to endow them with that sense of inner security

---

[4] Criswell, 1939, p. 18.

[5] Lasher, 1924, p. 34.

[6] Gordon Allport, "Some Roots of Prejudice," *Journal of Psychology*, XXII (1946), p. 31.

[7] Goodman, 1952, see Appendix B, "The Methods of Study," pp. 230–257.

[8] The four sets of projective material were (1) jigsaw puzzles, (2) a doll house with its furnishings and miniature doll families, (3) a set of pictures, and (4) a collection of dolls of several types.

[9] E. L. Hartley *et al.*, 1948, pp. 387–398.

[10] Criswell, 1939, p. 11.

[11] M. F. Ashley Montague, *Man's Most Dangerous Myth*, Harper and Brothers, 1952, pp. 280–281.

which will fortify them against all exterior assaults upon their integrity, and by loving them thus teach them to love others. But this is where teachers must take the lead. It is this which they must teach those who are to become parents and those who are already parents. We shall have neither peace nor harmony in the world until we have made human beings with peace and harmony in themselves.

It has been generally known that attempts to promote more favorable ethnic attitudes have been most successful with younger children, especially those on the elementary school level. On this point, Goodman states:[12]

> We can have "America for everybody" a little faster if we do something about those childhoods. There is little hope for our grownups, but in our children lies the big hope. While they are very young and suggestible, before their thinking jells and their feelings curdle, we can give them some tools for buildings "America for everybody."

She points out that ethnic attitudes are generated in each child out of the personal, social, and cultural materials he happens to possess. There are, therefore, many points of attack. But since attitude becomes more resistant to change as one grows older, it is imperative to influence attitude formation while the personality is still malleable, even before the generation process is well under way.[13]

Montague presents his approach to the matter of attitude formation in this manner:[14]

> What the educators must do is, I think, obvious: they must become aware of their strategic advantage, and they must, alone or in cooperation, take it upon themselves to reorganize the education of the young along the lines I have indicated; to teach humanity first and to regard all other education as subordinated to this.

He further emphasizes the role of the teacher in forming favorable attitudes by pointing out that "good teachers are more important than anything they teach."[15]

In short, the teacher plays a most important role during the children's early years of attitude formation. Two of the better laboratories in which to practice human relations, regardless of color of skin, creed or religion, are the classroom and its adjunct, the play period.

Recently, during an interview with the principal of a grammar school in the Southwest where there is a mixture of whites, Mexicans and some Negro children, the following comment was made: "The whites don't like the Mexicans and the Mexicans don't like the colored." Did this general statement apply to children of the lower grades? An interview with a young first grade teacher in the same school helped to clarify the query. She stated that, while the children displayed no awareness of ethnic differences, nevertheless she believed that especially among the darker Mexicans, the Negroes and the fairer whites, some children were

---

[12] Goodman, 1952, p. 190.
[13] For a discussion of the process of attitude generation see Goodman, 1952, pp. 217–220.
[14] Ashley Montague, 1952, p. 281.
[15] Ashley Montague, 1952.

vaguely aware of racial differences. However, she added: "I think the children very, very rarely even give a thought to this variance in color." Her daily observations led her to believe that her pupils get along well with one another, both in the classroom and on the playground. Furthermore, the children display no ethnic discrimination in situations in which they choose partners. On the playground, in less controlled situations, her pupils seem to choose playmates according to their ability in the particular activity, with apparent disregard for ethnic differences.

Shifting the scene to the Northwest, several years ago in a local paper of a community undergoing rapid population growth and metamorphosis, a columnist wrote an article welcoming a new group of teachers.[16] Several weeks later, the paper carried this follow-up editorial comment:

> Now that the new teachers have been here for awhile and have gotten settled, I wonder what they'll teach our kids? I wonder what our kids will teach them?

A partial answer is implied in the experiences of a young new teacher who taught in one of the new schools where the majority of children were of Caucasoid descent (gentiles) with about 5 percent of the population consisting of Mexican-Americans, Japanese-Americans, Negroes, and Amerinds.

> I was asked by several grade-school classes to come visit them and tell them about guppies. This was brought about by the fact that my guppies in the school aquarium were so prolific, and as a result I had furnished several classrooms with fish. One classroom I visited, rather typical of the system, brings to mind this experience. It was a third grade class bouncing and full of enthusiasm with great interest in what I was to say. They were trying to relate everything I said to their world around them. It was a world centered around the family and immediate community that appeared yet free from racial prejudice. A number of questions such as these were asked:
>
> "Do you think guppies would like rice? We eat rice at our house." (By a Japanese-American child)
>
> "I can bring a tortilla. Do you think the fish would eat it?" (By a Mexican-American child)
>
> When the bell rang everyone went to recess. The color of their skin made no apparent difference in their play. Each was proud of his family, his teacher and classroom, his friends and classmates, regardless of such a thing called skin color or prejudice which apparently did not exist in the minds of the primary school student.

According to this elementary school teacher, there were no evidences to his knowledge of racial discrimination and very little outward awareness of ethnic differences on the part of the primary school children. However, he observed that in the same school system, the social relationships are modified in the junior high school

---

[16] The community referred to is Moses Lake, located in the north central part of the state of Washington. One of the daily newspapers which serves this area is the *Columbia Basin Herald*, which contained the above mentioned article.

Students add new words to their vocabularies, including such derogatory terms as nigger, jap, dirty Mexican, and kike.

This observation generally supports the findings of previous studies such as Criswell's, which points out that the fifth grade level stands out as the point at which mutual withdrawal of races "crystallizes as the characteristic group pattern."[17] Awareness of physical and cultural differences which influence ethnic attitudes, for the most part, does not manifest itself until early adolescence.

However, the question of why children begin to discriminate is still open to considerable controversy. There are a number of theories of prejudice and discrimination ranging from fear of color and social differences to economic rivalry and the scapegoat need. However, they do not fully account for the ethnic attitudes and behavior evident in youth. Perhaps one plausible hypothesis may be the young adolescent's need to belong to a peer group. In the in-group out-group relationship, the young may be under duress to discriminate.

This exploratory paper makes no pretense of delving into the question as to why children begin to discriminate. However, it is hoped that students in the field of educational sociology and social psychology can utilize this report as a point of departure for serious research. More research is needed in ascertaining the degree of prejudicial and discriminatory behavior in various sections of the United States, especially of children whose attitudes have not yet hardened into a set pattern.

In the meanwhile, the hope of overcoming the "American dilemma"[18] lies in the joint efforts of teachers, parents and the community as suggested by the following letter, which might well have been written in response to the Moses Lake newspaper's editorial query:

Dear Editor:

We'll teach your children things that will better prepare them for the future. We'll try to show them the importance of the family, of friends, of being creative, of furthering interests, of developing better human relationships, and the need to develop one's ability to think.

We will try to instill the cooperative spirit into each child as he interacts in group situations. We will try to bring out in each child the value of personal inner self-respect and a concern for the dignity of the individual. This will mean a whole re-emphasis on the worth of the individual, Mexican, Negro, Oriental or Indian.

We'll do as teachers the best we can, but we'll need your help, your support. If we, as teachers, can make students and parents aware of the ethnic problems existing in their community, this would be a step in the right direction.

If we are to resolve just this one problem of ethnic discrimination, we'll have to start in our own back yards. Maybe you and other parents and leaders

---

[17] Criswell, 1939, p. 81.

[18] See Gunnar Myrdal, *An American Dilemma; The Negro Problem and Modern Democracy*, Harper & Brothers, 1944.

of the community will have to alter a few of your attitudes and follow the example set by your primary school children.

We're learning a lot from your children; are you?

Yours sincerely,

A New Teacher

Ethnic prejudice is a disease that is contracted during childhood, and one for which there is no common remedy in adulthood. Adults pass on their attitudes to children, and the young become powerful carriers of this contagious social virus. Teachers can play a most important part by helping to immunize children against ethnic discrimination, a curable un-democratic disease.

CONCLUSION

The influence of social stratification and of ethnic and race membership on a school program has been suggested by the readings in this section. The task of the school is to isolate those factors that impinge on the educational progress of youth, to ameliorate such influences, and to develop an instructional program that motivates and prepares students for upward mobility. This requires an identity with the dominant culture group and a rejection of former patterns of behavior.

The philosophical aspects of education as a cultural determinant have not been considered. The sociological and anthropological data are provided to arouse in educators a sense of commitment to providing a choice of cultural alternatives to a large portion of the American people. An understanding of the complexity of the social structure and the cultural groups that comprise American society helps to provide direction and purpose for both education and educator. The role of the teacher is vital if the ideal of a classless American society, providing for maximum social mobility, is to be achieved.

Another purpose of Section 6 is to emphasize that stereotyping is dangerous and unscientific; it must be avoided when preparing an instructional program for *all American youth*. Ideally the instructional program should focus on individuals and their problems rather than on groups representative of race, ethnic minority, or social strata. Achieving the dignity of man is an individual rather than a group process.

ADDITIONAL READING

Allison Davis, *Social Class Influences on Learning* (Cambridge: Harvard University Press, 1949). A concise and excellent presentation of factors which tend to inhibit certain social classes from obtaining maximum benefit from learning experiences provided in school.

Edw. Franklin Frazier, *Black Bourgeoisie* (Glencoe, Illinois: Free Press, 1957). An excellent sociological description of the Negro in America.

John Howard Griffin, *Black Like Me* (New York: Signet Books, 1962). By using pills and skin dye, a white newspaperman moves into the Negro world of the South. A white man's interesting, if subjective, impression of what it means to be a Negro.

Alan P. Grimes, *Equality in America* (New York: Oxford University Press, 1964). The role of American politics in earning equality for religious and racial minorities.

A. B. Hollingshead, *Elmtown's Youth* (New York: Wiley, 1949). A case study approach to the analysis of social class differences and participation at the secondary school level.

Oscar Lewis, *Five Families* (New York: Basic Books, 1959). An interesting anthropological approach to the analysis of five Mexican families, each on different levels of social stratification.

Robert K. Merton, *Social Theory and Social Structure* (Glencoe, Illinois: Free Press, 1957, Revised). A theoretical and well presented analysis of social structure.

Thomas F. Pettigrew, *A Profile of the Negro American* (New York: D. Van Nostrand Company, Inc., 1964). An excellent attempt to dispel many of the myths surrounding the American Negro.

Patricia C. Sexton, *Education and Income* (New York: Viking Press, 1961). The influence of income on the educational development of portions of American society. Particularly significant for those interested in teaching in urban areas.

W. Lloyd Warner, *Social Class in America* (Chicago: Science Research Associates, 1949). A classic in social class analysis.

Wm. F. Whyte, *Street Corner Society: The Social Structure of an Italian Slum* (Chicago: University of Chicago Press, 1943). An "inside" description of the organization, values, and behavior of an Italian street gang in New York City.

7

The Family and Peer Group in American Society

INTRODUCTION

Few would deny that the social institution exercising the greatest influence on the socialization process and personality formation of any individual is the family. No one chooses his parents, his environment, or the culture into which he is born. Within a very short time the individual internalizes the responses acceptable to those around him, and the process of accepting and rejecting is almost entirely controlled by the family environment. By the time the individual is capable of making important decisions, his personality and corresponding thought processes have largely been culturally conditioned.

In a comparatively short time America has changed from a rural to a highly specialized industrial economy. The family alone no longer orients the individual to the expected ways of life. While still in the formative years, young people are subjected to considerable pressure from the peer group—which may replace the family as the most influential force governing adolescent behavior—and many other social agents of the society as a whole. The American child often experiences anxiety caused by conflicting role expectations of the family, peer group, mass media, and youth-serving agencies in his community.

This section describes the nature of the American family and peer group, and, at the same time, demonstrates the changing relationships between the school and these groups. As the American economy and social mores continue to change because of dramatic technological advances, we can expect to see corresponding changes in family and adolescent behavior.

7-1   THE FAMILY

Ralph Linton

Anthropologist Ralph Linton, who has contributed three earlier essays to this book, describes the two major types of families found in human society. He indicates some of the advantages and disadvantages of each type for satisfying the psychological and social needs of the individual and the society.

All societies recognize the existence of certain close-knit, internally organized coöperative units intermediate between the individual and the total society of which he is a part. Theoretically, every person is assigned to one or another of these units on the basis of biological relationships established through mating or common ancestry. Actually, membership may also be ascribed on the basis of recognized substitutes for such relationship, such as presumptive paternity and adoption. Such units always have specific functions with relation both to their members and to the total society. Membership in the unit entails upon the individual specific rights and duties with regard to other members and also a series of rather clearly defined attitudes. The unit is expected to be the primary focus of its members' interests and loyalties. Those who belong to it are in duty bound to coöperate with and assist each other and to place each other's interests above those of outsiders. The interaction of the personalities within the unit is close and continuous, and their mutual adjustment is expected to be correspondingly complete. Ideally, the members of a family are bound together by ties of affection as well as by those of common interest, and quarrels between them are considered more reprehensible than quarrels between members and outsiders.

There can be little doubt that all such units are derivatives of the primitive, biologically determined grouping of mates and offspring. However, they are widely variable in both form and content. The most constant feature in connection with them seems to be the general attitudes enjoined upon their members. Both their personnel and their functions differ so much in various societies that we are forced to conclude that these features are now determined by cultural factors. In other words, the family, although it began as a biological phenomenon, a primate reproductive unit, has evolved into a social phenomenon, something more nearly comparable to such units as a monastic order or a craft guild than to its own remote ancestor. Although the biological factors which first brought the human family into being are still operative, their influence on families as social institutions appears to be about on a par with the influence on the innate qualities of members of particular sex or age categories upon the statuses and rôles actually assigned to members of such categories.

It is hard for Europeans to realize the sharp distinction which exists in many social systems between the reproductive unit composed of mates and their offspring and the authentic, institutional family. It happens that in our own society these two units coincide much more closely than in most. As a result, European students have shown a

From *The Study of Man* by Ralph Linton, pp. 152–154, 155–163. Copyright, 1936 by D. Appleton-Century Company, Inc. Reprinted by permission of Appleton-Century-Crofts.

strong tendency to assume that any grouping composed of father, mother, and children must constitute the social equivalent of the family among ourselves. Actually, such groupings play an insignificant rôle in the lives of many societies, while at least one society refuses to give them any formal recognition. Nevertheless, all these societies which minimize the importance of the reproductive unit have other units which show a general correspondence in their social significance to the family among ourselves. These units agree with our own families in the attitudes enjoined upon their members and, less closely, in the functions ascribed to them. To the student of society and culture the functions of these units are vastly more important than their personnel. Their social significance lies in what they do for their members and the total group rather than in what they are. If we can get a fairly clear picture of these functions, we will be in a better position to understand why the membership of such units can be so variable.

Every society has assigned certain functions to its family units. In nearly all cases some of these derive from the biologically determined functions of the ancestral mating group, but such derived functions cannot be considered a part of the family pattern unless they are given social recognition and approval. Even the most intimate physiological aspects of the mate relationship are often controlled by culturally established patterns. Practically all societies have taboos on sexual intercourse between socially recognized spouses under certain circumstances. Thus most of the Madagascar tribes prohibit it for three months after the birth of a girl and for six months after the birth of a boy. Some societies also prescribe it at certain times. The modern Maya require it at the time of corn-planting to ensure the success of the crop. Thus even the oldest of all family functions, that of providing the spouses with satisfaction of their sexual needs, has been shaped and modified by cultural factors. . . .

There is a tendency in nearly all societies for certain aspects of child training to be taken over by agencies outside the family, such as schools and initiation groups. However, the physical dependence of the young child on its mother sets an age limit below which these agencies cannot operate. Conditioning to social life begins so early that much of the groundwork of the personality is laid before such extra-family agencies can be brought into play. It has been said that it takes three generations of education to eliminate an error of grammar from a family line. It is conceivable that with further advances in scientific knowledge the mother may be rendered unnecessary from birth on and the child-rearing function may be completely divorced from the family, but this is still far in the future. The family unit still remains the most effective mechanism so far devised for the care and rearing of children, and these functions are still left to it in all societies.

In addition to these functions which derive directly from conditions present in the original biological family, each society has selected and ascribed to its family units a series of other functions. These are culturally determined and in no society do they exhaust the unit's potentialities for function. Thus in our own society the family is not used as a basis for the religious cult. In China it is utilized for this purpose, the family's worship of its ancestors taking precedence over all other forms of religious devotion. Again, our families do not, as units, assume responsibility for the conduct of their adult members. An American business man can transfer his assets to his wife and then, after an interval, "fail" with impunity. Many other societies do make the family responsible, thus assigning to the unit highly important functions in relation to social control.

Among these socially ascribed functions of the family unit the most important

seem to be those connected with economic production. Our own culture is witnessing a
rapid diminution in the importance of these, but our own situation is quite atypical
for mankind as a whole. In all societies the family is normally the smallest organized
unit for both production and consumption and tends to be self-sufficient as far as its
members' ordinary needs are concerned. The labor involved in satisfying these needs
is apportioned among its members in such a way that the activities of each individual
supplement those of the rest and all share in the benefits. The male members do certain
things and the female members other things, and the specialization is usually so
complete that persons of each sex have only a vague general knowledge of the techniques
employed by the opposite one. The difficulties of the average American husband when
called upon to cook and look after the children in his wife's absence are familiar to
most of us. This specialization and the organization which is its necessary accompaniment are of tremendous importance in ensuring the continuity of the family. Neither a
man nor a woman can provide for all wants when alone, and when marriage is utilized as
the core of the family unit, realization of the discomforts inevitably resulting from
separation make for tolerance of a partner's foibles. Similarly, when the unit rests
on some other type of relationship the loss of a member means the disorganization of
its coöperative system and will be prevented whenever possible.

The care of aged and infirm members is also an almost universal function of the
family. There is no society in which the individual's connection with his family group
is severed as soon as his usefulness to it is passed. Having given service, the old are
entitled to receive service in return. There are certain societies which lighten the
family's burden in this respect by killing the old, but such acts are usually rationalized
in terms of the best interests of the old themselves. It is said that in ancient Fiji
it was the duty of a good son to watch his father and to kill him when he showed signs of
approaching senility or extreme decrepitude. Since the condition of the soul in the next
world corresponded to that of the individual at the time of his death, it would be cruel
to do otherwise. In any case the family has an obligation to provide its aged members
with good funerals and to look after their well-being in the next world.

Another universal function of the family is that of protecting its members'
interests against outsiders. This function varies rather in degree than in kind. There
are societies in which the individual can feel sure of his family's support no matter
what the nature of his trouble with outsiders may be, where the fault lies, or what the
cost to his relatives. In certain Madagascar tribes the possession of land was vitally
necessary to the family's survival, yet it would be sold to ransom a relative who had
been captured and enslaved. The family honor required that he be redeemed even though
the act entailed hardship for generations to come. Again, in some tribes which
have the pattern of vendetta a murderer's relatives must shield him at all costs and
fight for him even when they know that to do so means almost certain destruction for
the family. More commonly, there are socially defined limits to the demands which the
individual may make upon his family. Thus a murderer's relatives may be forbidden to
shield him from vengeance by force, which would lead to additional killings, but
they are free to aid his escape, try to compound the murder, and contribute to payment
of the damages. In some societies the pattern of mutual assistance between family
members has been reduced to the point where it is almost meaningless. They are
expected to have a certain feeling of solidarity, but the expressions of this feeling are
left mainly to the judgment of the component individuals. For example, we ourselves
have no patterns governing assistance to relatives as distant even as first cousins. There

is a feeling that we should help them, but the kind and degree of assistance always depend upon personal factors.

If we take the universal functions of the family, we find that there are only two absolute prerequisites for their successful performance. The family unit must include able-bodied adults of both sexes, and the association between these adults must be close enough and prolonged enough to permit of their training and their organization into an effective coöperative unit. Unless they live and work together for some time, they will not be able to reach satisfactory personality adjustments or to reduce their complementary activities to matters of habit. It is obvious that until such adjustments have been made and coöperation has become more or less automatic the family unit cannot perform its socially ascribed duties with any high degree of efficiency.

Such prolonged associations between individuals of opposite sex can be assured in either of two ways. A society may capitalize the sexual attraction between adults and do all it can to give permanence to mated relationships, or it may capitalize the associations formed on an asexual basis during childhood, reinforcing them and continuing them into adult life. Such asexual associations are most readily established between individuals brought up in the same functional family unit, i.e., real or socially designated brothers and sisters. In other words, the association of adults which is the necessary nucleus of any family as a functional unit may be based on either a conjugal or a consanguine relationship. Our own society has stressed the conjugal relationship as the foundation of its functional family unit to such a degree that we tend to think of marriage and the family as inseparably linked, but many other societies draw a clear distinction between the two.

In societies organized upon the conjugal basis we can picture the authentic functional family as consisting of a nucleus of spouses and their offspring surrounded by a fringe of relatives. In those organized on the consanguine basis we can picture the authentic family as a nucleus of blood relatives surrounded by a fringe of spouses. Under the first system it is the fringes of relatives which interlock and connect family with family. Under the second it is the marriages which, by their interlocking, link family to family. Under the first system the blood relatives of the spouses are of only incidental importance to the functioning of the family unit. Under the second, the spouses are of only incidental importance.

Both these systems represent modifications of the original, biologically determined human family group. If we may judge from the sub-human primates, the earliest human families probably corresponded to the nucleus of present families of the conjugal type. There was no recognition of blood relationships between adult individuals. Recognition of such relationship and its use as a basis for the ascription of social statuses must have been the first step in the evolution of families as we know them. It would seem justifiable, then, to consider those societies which organize their families on the consanguine basis as representing a higher point of evolution, in this respect, than those which cling to the conjugal basis.

Families organized upon the conjugal basis have certain inherent disadvantages for the performance of the functions universally ascribed to the family. Sexual maturity comes late in man, and actual mating is usually still further delayed by cultural and especially economic factors. This means that the individuals who must form the nucleus of the new conjugal family come to it with their personalities and habits already rather completely formed. There always has to be a period of adjustment, and some time must pass before the new family unit can begin to function effectively. Offspring of the union, as they grow up, are more and more integrated into the family unit. They begin to do part of the family's work very early. Even in our own rural communities the child of eight is already a distinct factor in the family's economic coöperation. The importance of children increases with age, and by the time they are fully grown their contribution is often as important as that of their parents. Whenever one of them marries and leaves the family, the coöperative unit is weakened and temporarily disrupted. Families built upon the conjugal basis are too variable in content to lend themselves to close and relatively permanent organization.

With relation to such functions as care of the aged, protection of its members' interests against outsiders, or most of the special functions, the disadvantages of the conjugal basis are even more marked. Conjugal families are strictly limited in size and come to an end with the death of the original partners. This means that the old may be left without support and that the individual may have insufficient backing or find himself with none at all. The short duration in time of conjugal families also makes them unsatisfactory agencies for the ownership of either property or privilege. When a society is organized on this basis, both must be reassigned in each generation, being either subdivided or passed on to some one of the offspring to the detriment of the rest. Repeated subdivisions of property, especially land, soon reduce the separate holdings to the point where they are almost valueless, while a corresponding distribution of privilege soon disseminates it so widely that it loses all social significance. If Europeans had allowed titles to be inherited by all children and passed on to all their children, every one of us would be a king a dozen times over. The short duration of families organized on the conjugal basis also deprives them of much of their potential value as reference points for establishing the status of individuals with regard to society as a whole. This function of the family is of little importance in simple societies but may become of great importance in complex ones where the rôles of individuals are clearly defined and require a considerable amount of preliminary training.

Most of the difficulties with regard to function which are inherent in family units of the conjugal type disappear when the nucleus of the family is made a group of real or socially ascribed brothers and sisters. In such units no time need be lost in the adjustment of adult personalities to each other. Such adjustments begin at birth and are completed during the formative period of the individuals involved. By the time brothers and sisters are grown up and ready to assume the nuclear rôles in the family unit, all questions of dominance and mutual adaptation will already have been settled and they will be in a position to work together smoothly and efficiently. The emotional attachments between them may be less strong than those existing between husbands and wives, but their association and coöperation will have the reinforcement of habit. Adult brothers and sisters may quarrel, but their disputes lack the vigor of those between husband and wife and are much less likely to lead to the disruption of the family unit.

The idea of unilinear descent seems to be almost inseparable from that of consanguine family organization. It is strongly stressed by nearly all societies which recognize the consanguine group as the nucleus for their authentic family units. The reasons for this linkage will be discussed later. With unilinear descent the consanguine family achieves a continuity which makes it admirably adapted to the performance of all functions. It persists for generations, its active nucleus being constantly recruited from below, and it can be extended to include a much larger number of persons than can any family organized on the conjugal basis. It can thus ensure support of the old and adequate backing to its members and is better adapted than the conjugal family to exploitative activities which require the coöperation of a large number of individuals. Its continuity makes it the ideal agency for the retention of property and privilege and a constant reference point for ascription of individual status.   *Kennedy*

Families organized upon a consanguine basis can, therefore, perform all the functions possible to those organized upon a conjugal basis, with the exception of the satisfaction of sexual needs and the production of children. These functions are ruled out by the universal human pattern prohibiting incest. The consanguine groups can even perform most of the family functions more successfully. Nevertheless, the Nayar appear to be the only group who have taken consanguine relationship as the exclusive basis for their family organization. This is presumably because the factors which brought the conjugal family into existence at the sub-human level are still operative. Social systems have changed and evolved, but the innate qualities of human beings have remained very much the same. The consanguine family may be a more efficient functional unit as far as society is concerned, but it is less emotionally satisfying to the individual than is the conjugal unit. Man shares with other primates sexual jealousy and a desire for the exclusive possession of a mate. These tendencies can be inhibited by training, but they remain strong enough to ensure the continued existence of conjugal units side by side with consanguine ones in practically all societies.

Although nearly all societies recognize both conjugal and consanguine groupings, most societies tend to put their emphasis on one or the other, making it the basis for the authentic, functional family as far as their own social system is concerned. On the basis of shifting emphasis, it might be possible to arrange societies in a graded series with such devotees of conjugal organization as ourselves and the Eskimo at one end of the scale and the exclusively consanguine Nayar at the other. Most societies would fall between these two extremes but with a recognizable leaning toward one grouping or the other as the focus both for family functions and individual loyalties. Thus the Malagasy marriages are attended by a ceremony as formal as our own, and there is nearly as much effort to give them stability. In fact, the divorce rate is probably lower than it is in the United States. At the same time, the consanguine unit to which each partner belongs is the focus for loyalty and for a good deal of coöperative activity. Husband and wife have no rights over each other's property, although relatives do have such rights, and the woman usually sends any money she makes back to her own family to be taken care of. Each partner will work for the interests of his or her own relatives against those of the other partner, and even the children feel only the slightest bonds with their mother's family. In one legend the mother's brother takes in her supposedly orphaned son, treats him well, and rears him to manhood. The son reciprocates by returning to his father's family and taking his benefactor's cattle with him, thus giving an edifying example of family devotion.

7-2   FAMILY AND NEIGHBORHOOD

Philip Cox and Blaine Mercer

Blaine Mercer is associate professor of sociology at the University of Colorado. Among his many published works are *The American Community*, *Education and the Social Order*, and *Study of Society*.

Philip Cox is professor emeritus of education at New York University. He, too, has published numerous books on education, including *Basic Principles of Guidance*, *High School Administration and Supervision*, and *The Junior High School and Its Curriculum*.

This article suggests that the family and the neighborhood have become equally important in the socialization process of the child. At times they reinforce each other; however, other social institutions and societal pressures frequently force the child to make what appear to be conflicting choices between the values held by his family group and those of his peers.

THE FAMILY AS A UNIVERSAL INSTITUTION

One of the institutions common to all mankind is the family. It varies greatly in specific form and function from one society to another and even from one group to another within the same society, but it exists in some variation everywhere and among all people. The dependence of the infant on the protection and nurture of older persons assures very intimate associations of the child with parents and, usually, with siblings during his early, most formative years.

Both biological adaptation and social learning take place in the young child from hour to hour. His learning is chiefly by trial and success or error, but his biological equipment is such that these successes and errors are largely functions of his intimate relationship with older associates.

Babies differ by nature in spontaneous bodily movement (mobility) and in emotional expression (temperament). Their patterns of interaction with other human beings and with material objects, as well as with their physiographic environments, are learned through practice. Habits of adjustment (which appear about the fourth month) are, therefore, products of learning, but biologically inherited predispositions determine in considerable degree which habits will be learned and which rejected.

In a relatively homogeneous society, the sum total of interactions results in behavior patterns that are more alike than unlike because the social environment to which individual children must adjust is similar. The student of the social foundations of education deals with personality traits which are common to all normal persons just as he does with any other facts of human development.

Nevertheless, the specialist in this field is usually peculiarly cautious where such generalizations are concerned. Two reservations are in order. First, he is keenly

From *Education in Democracy* by Philip Cox and Blaine Mercer, pp. 62–73. © 1961, McGraw-Hill Book Company. Used by permission.

aware that some patterns which are almost universal in one society may be unusual or nonexistent in another; consequently, they must be treated with reference to social conditioning in the family and the community rather than the biological equipment. Second, in common with modern psychologists, he is skeptical of any specific cause-and-effect relationship that might be inferred from the relating of feelings to behavior.[1]

X   Innate capacities are widely agreed to be less potent drives to human conduct for the great preponderance of men than are the social customs that condition the individual. "Men spring from culture."[2] These reservations do not mean the denial of the universality of certain equipment or the reality of the driving effect of emotion. They do mean that biological inheritances are frequently less important than culture in determining individual and group attitudes and conduct. The student of personality formation finds a major concern, therefore, in drives which have to do with the way men relate to one another, whether these drives spring primarily from the inherent nature of the person or the customs and taboos of the social group.

Approached in this way, the questions of what comes first in time and in importance, nature or nurture, and of the actuality of three, a hundred, or no inherited patterns of behavior become academic. Fear, anger, sex feelings, and other emotions are realities, and to understand personality is to understand the characteristics, the causes, and the effects of their varied manifestations in the social environments where they occur. *Effects are further causes*—there is a chain reaction. Each type of manifestation is to be evaluated in terms of its probable influence on individual and, for the educator, on social welfare.[3]

THE AMERICAN HOME

The family, functionally and structurally, is the most important conditioner of the child's personality. The infant comes into the world with relatively few inherited behavior patterns and with a great capacity for variety in adaptation to his environment. The acculturation process in the family depends upon the plasticity of the child.

It is almost inevitable that there should be considerable conformation of the baby's habits and attitudes to the family's functional requirements. Feeding, sleeping, dressing, comforting, and all other aspects of infant care involve human beings and their natural and acquired traits. Some of these traits relate to voice, skills, gestures, moods, and standards of hygiene, noise, orderliness, and other behavior characteristics.

There is, of course, great diversity in these matters, not only among different homes, but also within any home from one time and occasion to another. In most American families, home regimen and domestic values are not inherited en bloc from ancestral customs and standards. Home life is itself plastic, reflecting not only the

---

[1] Clyde B. Moore and William E. Cole, *Sociology in Educational Practice* (Boston: Houghton Mifflin Company, 1952), pp. 57–78.

[2] Leonard W. Doob, *Social Psychology* (New York: Henry Holt and Company, Inc., 1952), p. 46.

[3] For more detailed and comprehensive treatment of original nature and social conditions, see Gordon W. Allport, *Personality: A Psychological Interpretation* (New York: Henry Holt and Company, Inc., 1937); Charles Horton Cooley, *Human Nature and the Social Order* (New York: Charles Scribner's Sons, 1902); John Dewey, *Human Nature and Conduct* (New York: Henry Holt and Company, Inc., 1922); Clyde Kluckhohn and Henry A. Murry, eds., *Personality in Nature, Society, and Culture*, 2d ed. (New York: Alfred A. Knopf, Inc., 1954); L. P. Thorpe, *Psychological Foundations of Personality* (New York: McGraw-Hill Book Company, Inc., 1938).

frequently unlike mores of parents and other adults, but also the many other factors that arise in the modern society. Among these factors are various technological gadgets in the home (such as nursing-bottle warmers, thermostatic controls, portable telephones, cooking timers, and plastic toys and containers) and also the influence of individuals and agencies concerned with child welfare. At one time, child specialists and agencies recommend early habit formation and impersonality in child care. A few years later, they advocate flexibility of schedule, postponement of some aspects of training, and much mothering (fondling, singing, talking) by adults.[4]

Nevertheless, these variations are but deflections of the stream of acculturation by which most children learn the conventional practices and standards of American life (for example, eating at a table, sleeping in a bed, control of elimination, cleanliness, dress, and forms of address). And the child's nervous and organic system responds to this inculcation of culture in such ways that his personality emerges as a pattern of habits, adjustments, standards, and beliefs. This pattern is, for good or for ill, not fixed in childhood or even in adulthood; but it does underlie the feeling of "fitness" or "unfitness" by which many later experiences and standards are judged.

Growing up is an age-old and very complex business for the human being, endlessly varied as the individual experience is. The regimen of child-care institutions, however intentionally and intelligently organized and administered, has not been so successful as home rearing has been. Despite the frustration, disharmony, punishment and reward according to whim, and the frequently un-hygienic conditions of home life, somehow the child who grows up in his home is more likely to survive as a reasonably normal individual than one brought up in a child-care institution.[5] There are subtleties in the relationships and mutual adjustments of the child-parent-sibling complex that seem almost to defy analysis.[6] These subtleties are parts of the social inheritance, through which responsiveness, security, adventure, and recognition are sought and found, hour by hour and day by day. Ego shapes itself in a world it never made but which it in part accepts and in part rejects progressively, experimentally, selectively, and continually.

INTERRELATIONS OF FAMILY AND NEIGHBORHOOD

Neighborhood Influences

What has been said regarding family life is, in greater or lesser degree, true of the neighborhood. Of course, the relatively homogeneous neighborhood, where most families have similar customs, values, antagonisms, and fears, reinforces the individual family's patterns more strongly than does the more heterogeneous neighborhood. But whether a neighborhood is fragmented or unified in any and all respects, other than nearness of residences, it affects people's attitudes and behavior. Propinquity to play areas, gang hangouts, churches, and police stations, for example, deserves serious attention in the study of forces which stabilize or disorganize family life.

[4] Martha Wolfenstein, "Trends in Infant Care," *American Journal of Orthopsychiatry*, XXXIII (1953), 120–130.

[5] James H. S. Bossard, *The Sociology of Child Development* (New York: Harper & Brothers, 1954), pp. 51–72. See also Rene Spitz, "Hospitalism," in *The Psychoanalytic Study of the Child*, Vol. I (New York: International Universities Press, 1945).

[6] Bossard, 1954, pp. 91–118.

No neighborhood exists in a social vacuum. Generally, indeed, the standards and behavior of the cohesive neighborhood are more varied and responsive to the patterns of the general community culture than those of any one family are likely to be. Even if all residents are Negroes rather than whites, Orthodox Jews rather than Protestants, or middle-class rather than lower-class, they share many interests and experiences with residents of other neighborhoods. Many of them see the same movies and television programs, follow the same comic characters in the same newspapers, root for the same athletes, are confronted with the same advertising displays, are allured by the same factions, and are appealed to by the same political devices.[7]

Moreover, the same individualistic impulses and urges that make growing children respond by a mixture of acceptance and rejection to the standards and practices of home life, characterize their maturation as members of local groups. The neighborhood usually provides the early out-of-home environment wherein the adaptation mechanisms are developed in contrast to those patterns learned in the family circle. Here, the family patterns are modified, avoided, or vigorously asserted. Experience is often a tough school, with frustration, deprivation, and physical pain exacted as the price for gaining status in one's age group. In extreme cases, indeed, the experience compels the child to lead a double life or, more accurately, multiple lives.

He may be timid, but compensate for it by "acting tough" or "covering up." He may be a gentle, cooperative brother and yet belong to a destructive, callous gang. He may be a devout "Christian" and yet hate all who are not recognized as members of his own groups. He may be a bitter rebel in his own home, and yet a docile member of his team, class, or "set." He may be meticulously honest under one set of conditions but a liar and thief under another set.

Family and Neighborhood Influences Not Clearly Distinguished

The dilemmas related to conflicting and evanescent selves are exceedingly complex and often lead to frustration. Both the family and the neighborhood are human environments into which practically all children are introduced for development. They provide the face-to-face relationships that serve as a nexus between infancy and maturation.

The means by which acculturation is fostered provide one way of distinguishing family processes from those of neighborhoods. Means characteristic of the family are sibling- and parent-child relationships, sleeping, eating, and dressing customs, expressions of affection, scolding, and rewarding. Processes of the neighborhood are those connected with church, school, gang, team, corner gossip groups, play field, movie theater, parties, and excursions. Obviously, there is much interpenetration between family life and neighborhood life. Older brothers and sisters, and sometimes parents, may participate in the same neighborhood institutions and practices as does the individual child who is striving for his own adjustment.

As has already been pointed out, moreover, both family and neighborhood absorb many of the values and stereotypes that are "American." The climate of opinion, in so far as it fosters attention to personal appearance, social and economic rivalry, self-assertion, and voluntary conformity to language, dress, and other behavior

---

[7] Although the neighborhood exemplifies the local community, it is the intensified *process of communication* due to propinquity that must be emphasized. Neighborhood and family mediate between the community's values and behavior and those of individuals.

patterns, controls in large degree the standards that are exalted in the home and the neighborhood.

Even within families and relatively homogeneous neighborhoods, the inevitable conflicts between the values and the practices approved by adults (many of which are likely to be accepted by children as standard patterns) often have serious repercussions on group unity, loyalty, and authority. In the American melting pot, the potent instruments of communication penetrate almost irresistibly the ego ideals of young and old.

Variety of Family and Neighborhood Acculturation Processes

If the individual child were standardized in native equipment and early experience, it might be possible to classify the processes and effects of family and neighborhood upon his development. Of course, this is not the case. The securities and insecurities of childhood, the fears and frustrations, the affectional experiences and the successes, the early or late development of abilities to walk, speak, and read, and the successive states of health of any individual are too numerous and varied for it to be possible to make other than very crude categories of environmental settings or of types of personality development.

Nevertheless, such classifications aid in understanding the ways in which primary group processes condition the mental, emotional, and physical growth of the individual. It should be kept in mind that there are some important constants in these interpersonal processes: the helplessness and consequent dependence of the young child; the plasticity of the human infant and his potential for conditioning and learning; the mores that exalt obedience, affection, kindliness, parental authority, individualism, and conformity; and the moral drive of habits and standards built into the individual mind of childhood, chiefly by parents and their substitutes.

The varied, and often elusive, effects of family and neighborhood influences on the development of the individual personality are further complicated by the patterns of mobility in the United States. Transiency of residence in a neighborhood is one form of mobility. Identification of self with a coterie not confined to the home community is another form of mobility. School attendance and membership in youth-serving organizations selectively enlarge the neighborhood experiences of boys and girls and constitute still another form.

The efforts of the larger community's constructive social agencies (such as governments, churches, and welfare agencies) are necessarily adapted to the conditions and trends of family and neighborhood life. There are two major reasons for this. In the first place, the effects of their homes and neighborhoods on young people determine in large part the occasions and opportunities for these agencies to function. In the second place, the success of the methods available to meliorative agencies depends on the primary groups' understanding of, and support for, their ends and efforts.

SIGNIFICANT MOTIVATIONS CONDITIONING FAMILY AND NEIGHBORHOOD

In the modern world, no family lives to itself. Its internal relationships and practices merge with the social organization and the general style of life which characterize the community. The family in a depressed neighborhood adapts itself to slum facilities, standards, and emotionalized attitudes; its members may accept or reject, but they cannot ignore, their neighbors' ways of life. The same holds true for families in other types of residential areas. Children who grow up in one type of social and economic environment are in varying degrees products of their neighborhoods as well as of their families.

Most of the social-class characteristics identified by recent sociological investigators are products of such adaptations. They are the result of the interactions of individuals and groups in the context of the customs and value systems of their neighborhoods. The personality outcomes, though individually unique, are similar enough to justify classification. And the advantages are not all with middle- and upper-class neighborhoods.[8] The lower-class environment, in general, favors "more gratification and easier outlet for children's organically based drives"—rage expressions, aggressive behavior, and sex expressions. The middle-class neighborhood mores restrict physical aggressions to patterned forms, either rule-controlled contests or subtleties of posture or gesture. Overt sex expression and fist fighting are discountenanced and so over-controlled that children's personality problems focus about aggression and sex. Compensations and sublimations for these repressions take many forms, among them initiative and skill in social and economic competition, ambition for class prestige, and fear, anxiety, and guilt about sexual and crass physical behavior.[9]

Among the small[10] and rather esoteric upper class, "good form" in manners, taste, and accomplishments outweighs overtly expressed competitive ambitions. Family pride and class awareness, subtly transmitted, make for dependency on parental approval. Upper-class neighborhoods tend to be coteries or cliques, self-sufficient and mildly individualistic, influential in artistic and intellectual affairs, but somewhat outside the stream of the dynamic social life of the community. Boys and girls are frequently trained and educated separately, especially during adolescence. Engaging in competitive behavior which is obviously for self-advantage is "not done"; etiquette, "honor," and discretion are mandatory.

Numerous sociological researches have shown that, while social-class membership has especially important ramifications in the lives of children and youth of the lower and middle classes, as compared to the upper class, it is, nonetheless, important in the lives of all three. Although the findings of research on child training,[11] as it is

---

[8] Allison Davis and Robert J. Havighurst, *Father of the Man* (Boston: Houghton Mifflin Company, 1947), pp. 17–29.

[9] Davis and Havighurst, 1947, pp. 24–25.

[10] W. L. Warner and P. S. Lunt report that, in Yankee City, the upper-upper class contained 1.4 percent, and the lower-upper class 1.6 percent, of the population, *The Social Life of a Modern Community* (New Haven, Conn.: Yale University Press, 1941). "Five percent of the respondents in a Gallup Poll said they were upper-class," George Gallup and Saul F. Rae, *The Pulse of Democracy* (New York: Simon and Schuster, Inc., 1940), p. 169. Similarly, Richard Centers found that five percent of a cross section of American males categorized themselves as "upper-class," *The Psychology of Social Classes* (Princeton, N. J.: Princeton University Press, 1949), p. 77.

[11] Studies of Chicago and Boston families, while revealing some disagreements, showed a much clearer relationship between social-class and child-rearing practices (for example, greater severity with respect to toilet training among lower- than among middle-class families) than indicated by other studies in New Haven, San Francisco, and Eugene, Oregon. See Allison Davis and Robert J. Havighurst, "Social Class and Color Differences in Child-Rearing," *American Sociological Review*, II, No. 6 (1946), 687–710; Robert R. Sears and others, *Patterns of Child Rearing* (Evanston, Ill.: Row, Peterson and Company, 1957); Martha Sturm White, "Social Class, Child Rearing Practices, and Child Behavior," *American Sociological Review*, XXII, No. 12 (1957), 704–71; George Psathas, "Ethnicity, Social Class, and Adolescent Independence for Parental Control, *American Sociological Review*, XXII, No. 8 (1957), 415–423; and Richard A. Littman, Robert C. A. Moore, and John Pierce Jones, "Social Class Differences in Child Rearing: A Third Community for Comparison with Chicago and Newton," *American Sociological Review*, XXII, No. 12 (1957), 694–704.

influenced by social class, are somewhat conflicting, there can hardly be doubt of the general significance of class to the life ways of American young people. Irregular employment in a slum area makes hunger, cold and sickness experiences to be dreaded and compensated for. Hence, the neighborhood tolerates acts and attitudes that shock the prudent and responsible bourgeoisie. Children running loose, violence and disorder in the crowded homes, recourse to orgies, predatory gangs, cleavages and segmental prejudices, narrow loyalties to leaders and institutions, all these complicated and inconsistent phenomena have survival values within some neighborhood frames of reference. Where and under what conditions one develops and adapts determines what his personality will be far more truly than the reverse.

Many questions that are matters for individual decision in the middle-class neighborhood are economically resolved among the poor. Woman's place is more likely to be where she can help stave off hunger and cold. Children more frequently must care for themselves and for their younger brothers and sisters if there is to be any care at all. The sacredness of private property is little esteemed among the propertyless. Law-enforcement officers are often resented as representative of middle-class standards that seem to have little application to slum neighborhoods. This attitude is accentuated among immigrant groups who retain a fear of governmental supervision.

Status and Role as Determinants of Choice

An urge for self-expression is an attribute of every human being. Indeed, several selves generally characterize an individual, one being dominant in one situation, another in a different circumstance. An aggressive star on the athletic field may become a gracious host in the evening. One selects the role that he will assay in the light of his estimate of his capacities, his "audience's" supposed receptivity, and some ego ideal that he hopes to achieve. Success in fulfilling his chosen role, he expects, will in degree bring recognition by whatever "audience" he courts.

The "audiences" which are valued vary for different individuals and for the same individuals at different times and in different settings. The often-heard generalization that the individual tends to be group-satisfied must be cautiously applied. The specific group settings to which he responds are ephemeral and varied. On occasion, the dominant group influence may be that of a coterie (a gang, clique, an ethnic or religious segment). At another time or in another mood, group satisfaction may be sought somewhat imaginatively and vicariously in a group ideal, myth, or stereotype (behavior believed becoming for a Baptist, a musician, or a spaceship pilot).

To be sure, all the varied forms of approval which the individual seeks are conditioned by his culture and so, in a broad sense, group satisfactions are implicit. Roles and statuses that arouse individual enthusiasm in a slum quarter are likely to be different from those that stimulate members of an upper-class neighborhood. In neither case, however, is there uniformity for all persons in the neighborhood.

The concept of the special potency of the peer group in influencing an individual's attitudes, beliefs, and behavior is fruitful in that it properly emphasizes a somewhat specific in-group acceptance and toleration. But here, too, caution is needed, for the individual usually belongs to several peer groups, the members of each of which may be superiors or inferiors in other settings. Football peers are not necessarily social-class peers or musical peers.

Irrational Authority of Group and Institutional Figures

Habitual behavior and its accompanying attitudes are generally unreasoned, though they may be reasonable or, at least, amenable to rationalization. They are adopted and practiced because conformity to the ways of the family, neighborhood, and other groups with which the individual identifies himself maximizes security. "Right" and "wrong," "fitting" and "unfitting," "loyal" and "disloyal" are terms of great moral significance. But they reflect the essentially irrational authority of the mores. Affection, approval, and hence security within family and other primary associations require at least some compliance with the standards accepted by the groups. Failure to conform is met with disapproval, perhaps by punishment; certainly it results in social isolation, at least temporarily.

The moral structures of the family, the gang, the athletic team, and ethnic, religious, and occupational groups are not altogether compatible. So each person learns to differentiate among the "right" and "fitting" behaviors and the "wrong" and "unfitting" ones for each occasion. To tell the truth, for example, is moral in general. In specific situations, however, withholding the truth or even lying to protect one's fellows is morally approved; in such cases, loyalty supersedes honesty, becomes "more moral." Moral development, then, comes out of the subtle process of compromising and resolving the conflicting, irrational elements of the moral structure the individual necessarily obtains from his social experience.

Irrational and incompatible as these complex adjustments are, they are of prime importance. Throughout history, the family and its immediately associated groups have been universal conditioners of individual personality patterns. The subtleties of human adjustment to the ways of life of parents, siblings, and neighbors are neither clearly nor completely understood. It is known only that stable home and neighborhood conditions are necessary for the preservation of the texture of stable societies.

The conflicting currents of rapid social and cultural change often disorganize long-established family and neighborhood patterns and so sacrifice something of their stabilizing influence. The effects of these disorganizing forces are, however, ambivalent. Outmoded in-group prejudices and narrow loyalties may help the individual in identifying with his childhood and parochial peer groups, but they are likely to unfit him for membership in the broader community which is characterized by diversity of association and outlook. Nevertheless, family and neighborhood conditionings are so potent that social changes are likely to be insignificant unless they affect, or find support in, these primary groups. Hence, the efforts of reformers, merchandisers, social workers, and educators, are likely to fail if they do not gain the cooperation of families and neighbors.

The interpenetration of broader social movements and organizations and of local communities has gone so far in the modern world that some authorities believe it is almost necessary to initiate reforms in family and community patterns before attempting to interpret them as general social norms.

Ideas crystallized in national and world organizations are in many cases hatched and nourished in numerous small communities. Some totalitarian states have quite successfully used the concept of planting germinal ideas in small communities so that they may "catch fire" and appear later in national concepts. The Russian rulers may still be pondering why the Ukrainian farmers have not wholeheartedly taken over the notions of collectivized agriculture injected into their centuries-old way of life, which is characterized by a closely knit family-neighborhood-community structure. Some effort has been made, of course, to identify the collective farm with the historic *mir* (village) in the minds of peasants. In Nazi Germany, slogans and rituals were effectively related to warmly remembered village ceremonials and traditions. The father concept and the authoritarian patterns of German family life are reflected in the words patriotism and fatherland; the priest and the monarch are "father figures." The term "fireside talks," popularized by President Roosevelt in the 1930's, was analogous to the family council.

Most successful state reforms have come through the local channels first. Historic examples of this sequence are those of the Gracchi brothers of Rome, the Napoleonic Code in France, the socialization of Mexico, and the breakdown of the sharecropping system in the Deep South. The degree of success of the reforms has depended largely upon the amount of interpenetration existing among the local communities involved.

National policies, if they are to become permanent and basic to the life of the people, must have their roots in local community organization. Open forums and town halls are still necessary and basic to the "jelling" of concepts due to become national issues.[12]

SUMMARY

To understand youth and its world, it is almost an absolute necessity that the chief concern be with processes since young people's interests most surely lie in the future. An understanding of the dynamics of social and cultural change is indispensable to the educator who seeks to know how the family experiences of young people link them to peers and adults outside their own families. The family, the school, and the community exemplify constantly changing and intricately interwoven life processes.

It is obviously impossible, in a short treatise such as this, to treat in full the family influence upon an individual's development. The intent has been to orient the reader in the areas of family and neighborhood organization as the essence of human society in general and to show some of their important influences upon the individual in particular.

---

[12] Recent communications research indicates the importance of group memberships and communication in the acceptance or rejection of messages which come to an individual via the mass media. Group norms and the patterns of person-to-person communication (especially through "opinion leaders") suggest the importance and potentials of public forums in a democracy. Elihu Katz and Paul F. Lazarsfeld, *Personal Influence: The Roles Played by People in the Flow of Mass Communications* (Glencoe, Illinois: Free Press, 1955), pp. 130ff, 331–332.

7-3   THE SCHOOL, THE PEER GROUP, AND ADOLESCENT DEVELOPMENT

Richard L. Simpson and Ida Harper Simpson

Richard L. Simpson is associate professor of sociology at the University of North Carolina. He obtained his Ph.D. at the University of North Carolina, has taught at Pennsylvania State and Northwestern Universities, and has written extensively in the fields of sociological organization and theory.

Ida Harper Simpson is assistant professor of sociology at Duke University. She earned her Ph.D. at the University of North Carolina and has taught at the College of William and Mary, Pennsylvania State University, and the University of Illinois. She and her husband, Dr. Richard L. Simpson, have co-authored several books and articles.

Although adolescents whose actions are approved by the adult society are considered "devoted, dedicated, and intelligent young people upon whom the future of the society rests," much of the literature on adolescent youth is, unfortunately, negative. The stereotyped adolescent is in a constant state of rebellion and acts disrespectfully toward the older generation and society as a whole.

A young individual who creates overt or emotional disturbances in the larger society is looked upon with great disapproval and suspicion. Generally unacceptable adolescent behavior ranges over a wide area of thought and endeavor; some actions are accepted as part of the normal maturing process while others are viewed with foreboding and premonition. However, adolescents in any society are products of the culture in which they live. Growing youths reflect the society; their assertions of individuality and dissatisfaction with the adult world are as much a part of the culture as are their approved actions.

Richard and Ida Simpson use the following essay to support their hypothesis that the peer group, especially that associated with the school, becomes increasingly influential in the child's socialization process as he grows older.

INTRODUCTION: STATUS OF THE ADOLESCENT IN THE UNITED STATES[1]

Human biology dictates that in all societies there be a period of adolescence, during and after puberty. Societies vary, however, in the extent to which they recognize adolescence as a separate age category and provide a distinct pattern of behavior for it. Some distinguish adolescence sharply from childhood and adulthood, others do not.[2] In our own society, adolescence is known as the "awkward age," while in some societies

From *Journal of Educational Sociology*, XXXII, No. 1 (September 1958), 37–41. © 1958 by the Payne Educational Sociology Foundation, Inc.; reprinted by permission of the Payne Educational Sociology Foundation, Inc.

[1] The ideas developed here grew out of discussions connected with a study conducted by Ida Harper Simpson under the direction of Professor M. E. John at the Pennsylvania State University. Ida Harper Simpson, "Adolescent Behavior and Food and Beverage Patterns," Report No. 1, Social Science Research Center, Pennsylvania State University, University Park, Pennsylvania, April 1957.

[2] Ralph Linton, "Age and Sex Categories," *American Sociological Review*, VII, 589–603.

this period is relatively tranquil and devoid of problems.[3] This fact indicates that the problems of adolescence, where they exist, are not biological but social in origin. A comparison of various cultures suggests that our own problems of adolescence stem from the position of the adolescent in our social structure. We consider adolescents a distinct category, neither children nor adults, and we keep them in the adolescent category well into the years of biological maturity. Yet we do not provide explicit or compelling norms to guide adolescent behavior.

In some societies, the beginning and end of adolescence occur at definite times, and are celebrated by collective rites of passage. Throughout Polynesia, for example, adolescents are sharply differentiated from children and adults. They are formally organized into age groups and, relieved of most social and economic responsibilities, are left free to pursue the tasks of courting and personal adjustment. The primary function of the adolescent groups is to entertain themselves and others.[4]

Our own society, in contrast, does not clearly specify the onset and end of adolescence, or the proper behavior during this period. This vagueness is at the root of our adolescent problem, since people adjust most easily to those situations in which their expected behavior is most clearly defined and understood.[5] The social role of the American adolescent is not clear. In school, for example, he is expected to be a diligent worker, but his peer group may prefer that he be an irresponsible pleasure-seeker.

The adolescent plays numerous roles in numerous groups. Studies which have emphasized the "trauma" of adolescence have usually focused on only one status of the adolescent: his status in the parental family in Freudian writings, and his status in his peer group in most other writings. Yet the very diversity of statuses occupied by the adolescent in modern society may account for his insecurity. He has no single "core status" or dominant role whose expectations take priority over the demands of other statuses.[6] Viewing this situation psychologically, one might say that the adolescent lacks an all-pervasive self-concept. He does not know exactly who he is or who he wants to become.

THE PEER GROUP AND ADOLESCENT SOCIAL NEEDS

The social striving of the American adolescent centers around the need to develop a clear status and a gratifying self-concept which will equip him for adult life. To satisfy this need, the adolescent must do several things. He (or she) must gain social recognition on the basis of his own achievements, and in terms of the values of his age group; no longer may he depend on the assured recognition which his family gave him in childhood. He must develop a self-concept, and the behavior patterns which support this self-concept, which will differentiate his behavior clearly from that appropriate to the

---

[3] Until 1928, most writers agreed with Clark Hull's view that the "trauma of adolescence" results from the physiological changes attending puberty. The "social" explanation of adolescent behavior has gained sway since Margaret Mead, in *Coming of Age in Samoa* (New York: William Morrow, 1928), described a society in which adolescence took place without trauma. This approach holds that adjustment to the biological changes of adolescence is helped or hindered by the culture's interpretation of these changes.

[4] Ralph Linton, *American Sociological Review*, VII, 589–603.

[5] Leonard S. Cottrell, "The Adjustment of the Individual to His Age and Sex Roles," *American Sociological Review*, VII, 617–620.

[6] The concept of core status was suggested to the writers by Professor Harvey L. Smith of the University of North Carolina.

opposite sex.[7] Finally, he must develop certain habits or qualities needed for successful adult living, such as initiative, responsibility, and self-reliance.

Much of the burden of adolescent socialization is placed upon the school. The adolescent spends many of his waking hours in school, or in activities connected with the school. The formal program of the school, however, is not sufficient to meet all of the adolescent's developmental needs. The demands of the curriculum make no distinction between the statuses of boys and girls, with the exception of minor portions of the curriculum such as physical education, shop work, and home economics; therefore the school program contributes little toward differentiating the sex roles of adolescents.[8] Moreover, the values of the school—diligence in study, respect for the social etiquette and moral codes of the middle-class adult world—are not necessarily those of the adolescent; and the adolescent may or may not derive great satisfaction from achievements in terms of these adult values. He needs to attain recognition on the basis of values peculiar to his own age group.

Unlike the formal program of the school, the peer group enables the adolescent to gain social recognition through his personal qualities and achievements. Its dating pattern, athletic contests, and other activities build a clear-cut sex role into the self-concept of the adolescent. The individual wins recognition for his sense of humor or his loyalty to friends. The boy asserts his maleness in athletics, or by swearing and telling sexual jokes. The girl competes for prestige through dating, and pays homage to her sex by giggling over the latest Elvis Presley record. In these ways the peer group, far more than the formal school program or even the home, defends the individual against the uncertainties of adolescence through the security of group membership. The importance of the peer group for adolescent adjustment is shown in a study of young adult schizophrenics, by N. J. Demerath. The subjects, before their schizophrenic conditions developed, had seldom participated in intimate, informal group activities. They had lacked the ability to associate with their fellow students, had felt socially rejected, and had identified with the adult norms of scholarly excellence, moral perfection, and submissiveness. Demerath concludes that the person who successfully adjusts to adult demands must first prepare himself in the informal group life of adolescence.[9]

THE ROLE OF THE SCHOOL IN ADOLESCENT DEVELOPMENT

Despite the value of the peer group for adolescent development, it has its limitations. To the adolescent peer culture have been ascribed such characteristics

[7] Some writers maintain that the need for sex differentiation is subsidiary to the more general need for personal achievement and the approval of the peer group. In this view, the wish of the adolescent to be desired as a date, or to be a football hero, stems from the more general wish to achieve social eminence in the peer group. It has been noted, for example, that a high school or college girl may be more interested in what dress she wears to a party than in whom she accompanies as a date, provided that the boy is socially presentable. On this general point see Margaret Mead, *Male and Female* (New York: William Morrow, 1949), pp. 284–288. Whether the needs for personal achievement and sexual differentiation are in fact one or two needs is a question that can remain open without damage to the present analysis.

[8] See Talcott Parsons and Robert F. Bales, *Family, Socialization, and Interaction Process* (Glencoe, Illinois: The Free Press, 1955), p. 116; and Talcott Parsons, "Age and Sex in the Social Structure of the United States," *American Sociological Review*, VII, 604–616. Parsons suggests that adolescent sex roles are not significantly differentiated in the family, the community at large, or the school, and that the burden of change and differentiation of sex roles is therefore thrown almost wholly on the peer group.

[9] N. J. Demerath, "Adolescent Status Demands and the Student Experiences of 20 Schizophrenics," *American Sociological Review*, VIII, 513–518.

as irresponsibility, distaste for constituted authority and established moral codes, blind conformity to group values, and a purely hedonistic approach to life.[10] If this description of the peer culture is in any degree accurate, one might question its ability to develop such habits as self-reliance, initiative, and responsibility.

The demands of the school curriculum help to meet the need of the adolescent to develop habits of self-reliance and responsibility. Schoolwork requires concentrated effort and abstention from other activities until the assignments are completed, and it represents striving for a distant goal. Where the academic program falls short is in its inability to harness the adolescent's desire for achievement and recognition among his peers. But perhaps the school is not entirely helpless in this regard. Through its extracurricular activities program, it can enable its pupils to work willingly, in natural and intimate groups, toward goals which they themselves value highly, and in ways which develop such qualities as responsibility and the facility for making vital decisions. The student council, the dance committee, even the home room clean-up committee bring adolescents together in useful or harmless projects where leadership is exercised, mutual obligations are met, and camaraderie is developed. In the extracurricular program, the benefits of the peer group and the school are combined. A balance is struck between free initiative and guidance from above, between play and work, between individual achievement and group obligation.

To be sure, the adolescents in their extracurricular activities will adhere to the values and mores of their peer culture. No more than at the corner drugstore or the bowling alley will they overstep the bounds of conformity to group standards. There is a difference, however, between passive conformity to the behavior patterns of the herd and active problem-solving within the framework of group values. Listening to some popular singer because one knows that one has to like this singer is passive conformity. Deciding which orchestra to employ for a dance, or how to finance the affair, is active problem-solving behavior, within the value framework of the group but requiring creative thought and initiative nonetheless. Conformity to group mores is with us all our lives, and must be with us if society is to proceed in an orderly fashion; but there are different kinds of conformity.

Like anything else, extracurricular activity programs are limited in their effectiveness. They are not a substitute for the study of books. They usually reflect the class stratification of the community with students from the more well-to-do families monopolizing the leadership and those less economically fortunate often left out or relegated to minor positions.[11] They may have little appeal to some pupils in under-privileged neighborhoods, among whom the thought of any activity connected with the school arouses feelings of dread or contempt. It seems reasonable, however, to claim some efficacy for them, as one way in which the adolescent can achieve a secure status among his fellows and develop habits of responsibility at the same time. At best, active participation in extracurricular affairs can draw together the separate roles of "student" and "member of the peer group," thus helping to clarify the uncertain status of the

---

[10] See, for example Edward Y. Hartshorne, "Undergraduate Society and the College Culture," *American Sociological Review*, VIII, 321–331; Talcott Parsons, 1955; Robert J. Havighurst and Hilda Taba, *Adolescent Character and Personality* (New York: John Wiley and Sons, 1949); and Arnold W. Green, "Young America Takes Over the Colleges," *Commentary*, VII, 524–534. For an opposing view see Frederick Elkin and William A. Westley, "The Myth of Adolescent Culture," *American Sociological Review*, XX, 680–684.

[11] A. B. Hollingshead, *Elmtown's Youth* (New York: John Wiley and Sons, 1949).

adolescent. It may even, in some cases, give him something resembling a "core status" as "member of the school community."

One conclusion from this analysis is that we need not, in the current clamor to tighten discipline and produce a generation of intellectuals, lose sight of the function which extracurricular activity programs may fulfill.

7-4   THE UNDERSTOOD CHILD

Harold Taylor

Dr. Taylor obtained his doctorate in philosophy at the University of London. As president of Sarah Lawrence College for fourteen years, he developed many experimental programs in education. He has written more than two hundred articles on philosophy and education in addition to his books *On Education and Freedom, Art and the Intellect*, and *Essays in Teaching*. He is the founder of the National Research Council on Peace Strategy.

The following article is refreshing. Unlike so many others that discuss the teenager in negative terms and see dire consequences for society because of his lack of responsibility, this selection emphasizes the positive influences of a social climate in which the young are forced to mature rapidly and thereby to create their own miniature adult world and to assume responsibilities and patterns heretofore attributed only to adults. After reading the essay, one cannot help but ask: "Are we doing modern youth a disservice by comparing their actions to those of days gone by? Should we rather evaluate present actions in terms of present needs and impinging societal pressures?"

We have not yet realized the effect our national attitudes have had on the younger generation over these past ten years. We have assumed that schools and colleges are places where the young should be insulated from political and social controversy, and that college students are to be suspended between two worlds, the world of adolescence and the world of adulthood. We have thought of the home as a shelter against psychic shock, a center of warmth, understanding, and togetherness. We have thought that relations between people must always be free of tension, that children and parents must always understand each other.

We have then wondered why the young have been so silent, why they didn't show more initiative, why they seemed to settle for so much less than they could try for, why they sailed along with the tide and weren't interested in bucking it. We assumed that because they were quiet, they were acquiescent. They were not. They simply did not care to speak of what they knew.

What they were doing, in fact, was growing up in a world that mixed security and danger in so clever a way that at every step they were counseled by the older generation to be careful of what they said and what they did, to do what everyone else was doing

From *Saturday Review*, XLIV (May 20, 1961), 47–49, 66. Copyright © 1961 by Saturday Review, Inc; reprinted by permission of Saturday Review, Inc., and the author.

so that they would not be criticized and become unpopular or be marked as an outsider. A member of this generation has said of the attitude of the older generation that "everyone was required to be well-rounded; well-rounded in the sense that all the sharp edges are to be rubbed off until one is perfectly round, like a tennis ball, with a little friendly fuzz on the top." Or, as another student has put it, "We are the generation of the third eye, the eye of self-consciousness. ..."

At every step members of the younger generation have been cautioned, watched and studied, treated as subjects for analysis. They are the children of understanding parents. They have learned to live with the handicap of being understood, and in the process have understood more than we have realized.

The younger generation now presents a new attitude, and a degree of self-understanding unknown in previous generations of the young. Coupled with this has come a higher degree of social sophistication and new high school patterns of social behavior which were formerly the patterns of college students. Social relations and the whole apparatus of dating, pinning, going steady, telephoning, and party-going have been brought into the lower age groups—to the fourteen-year-olds rather than the seventeen- and eighteen-year-olds of former years—with a lowering of the average marriage age by approximately two years.

Two things have happened. One is that the young have already learned to practice in their own way what there is to know about the social life and customs of adult society. The other is that the younger generation has separated itself from the older by a shift in attitude toward parental authority, a shift that has come about largely through the modern attitude of parents toward their children. The young have now established their own quasi-adult society with its own vocabulary, emotions, heroes, attitudes, and customs. They have become self-sufficient and independent as a group, but in a curious way less identifiable as individuals, more easily classified as groups with common customs and ideas. They take their cues from the attitudes of their own kind, rather than from individual models provided by their parents.

The growth of a new attitude toward child-rearing has meant that most parents in bringing up this generation have made a genuine effort to understand their children and not to impose parental authority in ways that might inhibit the young child.

As a result, it is extremely difficult for the child to rebel, since he is understood rather than repressed. This has its consequence in giving him nothing but feather pillows to fight, and in developing an attitude of self-understanding before there is a great deal of self to understand. We have all heard fifteen- and sixteen-year-olds discussing with their parents and among themselves the correct way of handling sixteen-year-olds, including their own relation to the authority of their parents. If an effort is made by parents to assert authority, it is usually rejected, since both parents and child know that there is little the parent can do about a refusal to accept authority. The modern parent is unlikely to threaten the sixteen-year-old with bodily harm, and threats to withhold money or special privileges very often produce more tensions and problems than they solve, since they set conditions which it then becomes almost impossible for the parent to meet when the showdown comes.

Most sixteen-year-olds are sufficiently sophisticated not only to know the limits of power possessed by their parents if it were to be put to the test, but are also prepared to live an independent emotional life by depriving the parents of a return of affection, by appearing a minimum amount of time at home, by surface conformity to demands, or by simply leaving home altogether. With the removal of the concept of parental authority, the balance of power in family life shifted to the young.

In a relationship at once informal, friendly, and mutually accepting, the parents become not objects of filial piety, but adult friends with whom one may have a deep or fairly superficial relationship and who have certain obligations toward their children. Having dropped the attitude of parental authority, and with it the necessity of obedience to parental wishes, parents now find themselves with a new set of consequences for which in many instances they had not been prepared. Having staked everything on a warm and affectionate relationship with the child, parents cannot then resort to older methods of authority with any expectation of respect and obedience.

In this situation, the strongest force that parents usually exert is an attempt to produce a feeling of guilt on the part of the child in causing distress to the parents whose requests are disregarded, a guilt that may from time to time have its own aggressive manifestations in a confused rebellion and a sense of frustration on the part of the child. A new syndrome thus emerges in which there is no longer a clear-cut authority-freedom issue for the adolescent, but instead there are ambivalent feelings of obligation, responsibility, and guilt. Whatever satisfaction there may be in open rebellion is stifled at the source. The adolescent is unable to rebel, since before overt rebellion occurs his parents will no doubt demonstrate their "understanding" of his wish to rebel by assuring him that it is perfectly natural. The tension of opposites, so often a necessary part in the healthy emotional situation of the adolescent, disappears in a warm bath of parental affection. The parent in fact has no control over the child; the child often has not yet had sufficient experience to exert control over himself.

This underlies and creates a new and different attitude on the part of high school and college students to the authority of their parents. It also creates a different attitude on their part to the authority of the school and college. The shift has been foreshadowed by a change in the social structure of the high school and preparatory school. In place of the disciplinary methods of twenty-five years ago has come a philosophy of student responsibility, worked out in the early progressive schools and spreading from there to the rest of the school system. There is a great deal more structure than before in the social organization of the American high school, partly because it has been asked to assume more and more duties that were formerly attached to the family—out-of-school play, entertainment, musical skills, sports, and outings. Much more is arranged for the students, in many more areas, and students learn to move from one social group to another in regular ways. At the same time, students are given more responsibility for sharing in educational and social policy-making. Added to this is the provision of entertainment by football games, television, radio, mass magazines, and community projects. The young person's attitude toward entertainment in general becomes that of a spectator; he no longer takes up with the same enthusiasm his opportunities for self-expression. Faced with the alternative of accepting the social patterns already arranged for him by parents and schools, or of inventing a life of his own by his own efforts, he has been persuaded to rely on the easier way of letting others do it for him.

At the same time, in its wider dimension, American culture has become fascinated with its own self-analysis; its novels are introspective, almost totally concerned with personal questions and relations; its theatre and poetry have turned to the emotional content of human life and away from the biggest human issues; its social comment has to do with the nature of the American character. It has become a self-absorbed culture; its intellectuals are more interested in analysis than in synthesis, in probing and investigating rather than in acting. It is a country of committees, of questions, and whenever an action is proposed or an idea is held it is first given a going-over to decide in advance whether the action will be approved or the idea accepted. Whenever anything is suggested a thousand little men run out from behind things to say why it can't be done or how it might fail. There is such a deal of peering, peeking, probing, and harassing on all sides that it is a wonder that anything gets done at all. As Christopher Fry once said, "Everywhere we hear the patter of tiny criticism. . . ."

The total influence of the culture is therefore to teach the young to run in groups, as if America were one consecutive series of committees of which no one wanted to be chairman, and in which everyone must be included.

What, then, are the forces at work in the schools and colleges?

The research on students' values shows that in most cases there is little relation between what the student studies in school and college and what he learns to admire and respect. That is to say, the effect of the formal teaching program is minimal and the effect of social habit, group pressure, and conventional ideas of American success is dominant. The student does his school and college work in order to gain his grades and academic credits. That is what he conceives school work to be. The rest of his life is lived in a social order that has been arranged for him and into which he fits.

There is accordingly a general type of "American high school student," identified by foreign visitors and others who look at our educational system from the outside. He has absorbed the influences of an extroverted community in his home town, particularly in the urban and suburban areas, and models his conduct to a large extent on a young American type, itself a product of the movies, the magazines, the television, the radio, and phonograph records. The boys and girls have a coeducational attitude to teen-age life and a complicated ritual of dating, pledging, riding in cars, attending sports events, along with a common vocabulary of popular phrases. They provide the material for the concept used by social workers, journalists, and parents—the teen-ager. They also provide the mass market for commercial exploitation by clothing manufacturers, record companies, and television networks. The values are for the most part accepted uncritically. The model for the boy is of a star athlete who has a straight A record, is popular with girls and elected to student office by popular acclaim. The model for the girl is one who is pretty, popular, having a B-plus record so that it will not be a threat to her popularity with boys, who likes sports, popular records, movies, has a well-knit social life, and is neither arty nor too brainy nor too intense about anything.

The over-all value is to think of school as a place where you learn to get along with people, prepare either for getting into college by taking subjects and getting grades that will do that, or preparing for a job or for marriage following the years of high school. The actual content of the curriculum is designed for one or the other of these ends and the school program consists of organized studies and social events related to them. The family income and social situation varies from lower and middle income to well-to-do, with some suburban communities supporting what amount to private schools for community children of well-to-do parents. Tolerance and a democratic spirit prevail. On the whole, students consider bigotry, prejudice, and autocratic attitudes taboo, and show a respect for each other, and a concern for mutual adaptation. There is usually demonstrated in school life a genuine loyalty to democratic values. In many segregated suburban communities, these students have no opportunity to meet those who are not white, Protestant, and moderately well-to-do, with a consequent innocence and ignorance of social problems and major social issues.

With the shift of the country's population to the suburbs from the cities, and the shift from small towns to cities, the large high school is now the dominant social force in the lives of young Americans. The values developed there are carried into the universities and into the working areas of American life. We need to question not merely the science and foreign language curriculum taught in our high schools but the attitudes developed there and the reasons they have developed as they have.

2) Another style of student values we can identify as the "prep" or "shoe" system, to be found largely in the private schools of the East Coast, for boys or girls, where a combination of residential facilities, small classes, a well-organized community life, and a serious program of academic studies designed to prepare the pupil to compete for admission to Eastern colleges, produces a coherent pattern of life and attitude. A major aspect of this value system is the social status of the school; attendance at such a school is in itself a mark of a particular status. It is to be expected, therefore, that a feeling of belonging to an in-group, or of occupying a known position in one's society, should be important here.

Since the private-school pupil lives twenty-four hours a day in an educative community, the seriousness with which he conducts his academic studies can be much greater than the public-school student who is in class for only part of each day. For some, the "prep school" culture develops a form of intellectual and social snobbery, for others a genuine concern for intellectual matters, and, on the whole, an uncritical acceptance of the social forms, social customs, and aims of an upper-income, established American society. For most, the prep school becomes an initiation into the fraternity of the well-mannered and the well-to-do.

The model of the student in this case is of one who knows how to dress well without looking as if he cares, knows his way around New York, might be mistaken for a Yale freshman or sophomore, is a good athlete, can spend money well and easily, and talks with a special vocabulary for initiates. Since these schools are usually not coeducational the attitude of the boys toward girls is for the most part pre-adult; that is, one that gropes for the sophistication of the intelligent adult male, but is actually shy, hesitant, and formal. In the case of the girls' schools, there is great loyalty to the school itself, a respectful and accepting attitude toward academic study and to social norms, an interest in social life, and on the whole a greater value placed on personal independence, serious intellectual pursuits, and involvement in the arts and literature.

The family influences are perhaps greater in the private-school system than in the high school, since they coincide in character most often with the influences of the private school. For the established family the school can be thought of as a continuance of an established educational pattern; for the newly rich family, or for the scholarship family, it is a movement ahead, with a greater opportunity for learning how to behave, both intellectually and socially. But in either case the motivation of the parents in sending the child to a private school is to achieve a "better education" with a stronger and more rigorous academic program and a better environment for achieving a set of values with which the parents can live.

3) There is another kind of student, sometimes to be found in the private school or the high school, more often in the progressive private school. His style is slightly different from the "shoe" attitude in the clothes he favors and in some of the books and

ideas that are considered fashionable. But the style is similar in its in-groupness and its own kind of togetherness. The togetherness shows itself in a special form of intellectual attitude—a serious concern for adult ideas and a rejection of the "high school" pattern, a highly developed critical point of view about almost everything. This often results in the progressive student dismissing all other American youth as either "prep-school" or "teen-ager," and in coming down hard on mass culture and mass education.

The model for the progressive is the person who wears jeans and shirts with careless style, has read widely, knows his way around the Village, understands women and Freud (the progressive girl understands men and Freud), loves folk-singing, jazz and classical music, modern dance *and* ballet, is a liberal in international affairs, is critical of practically everything, hates the bomb, Madison Avenue, television, and popular writers, and has got most of the major issues settled.

An additional characteristic of the style is that this student has a genuine concern for the rights and individuality of others, and a genuine independence of mind that carries over to life in college and after it. In the search for identity, this student is clearly concerned with finding an answer, and this clearly means a more intense and complicated struggle than for those who have not undertaken the search. You pay a price for that kind of searching. But the values held are those of equality for all creeds, colors, and countries, a sense of social justice, and a love of art and learning.

It is here that I come to the reforms to be accomplished in our educational system—the reforms that can help to recreate the American ideal of the individual as democratic man. We seek individuals, not mass men. We seek independence, creativity, imagination, enterprise, initiative, not caution, security-mindedness, materialism, me-too-ism, conservatism. In seeking these values, we must pit ourselves and our resources against major tendencies created by an industrial managerial society which looks to its youth to maintain the present establishment.

The present establishment is dominated by military and economic struggle with foreign countries. But the purpose of a democratic educational system is not to act as an instrument of national policy. Its purpose is to liberate the talents and to stimulate the thinking of its citizens so that they may share fully in the creation of national policies. The United States is the leader of the democratic world. The American educational system exists to bring into being the model of a democratic society that can serve the needs of the modern world, that can bring the privileges and the material well-being of a successful industrial society to the peoples of that world.

How then are reforms to be accomplished?

First, by conceiving the role of the parent and the school not merely to be that of understanding children and protecting them from social reality, but by insisting that certain ideals are better than others, that certain acts are higher in value than others, and that the older generation has both a right and a duty to act for social justice. As of now, the schools are reinforcing the prevailing social and political attitudes of the culture.

During the McCarthy period, it was not enough to understand McCarthy; it was necessary to fight him, to hold up the standards of honor and integrity. A school or college that wishes to serve its country and to teach its youth will use the instruments of educa-tion to make the society honest, rather than rest content with reflecting the prejudices of a confused society.

I suggest that we take full account of the leadership already being provided by the youth of this country, those who have until recently been quiet about themselves and their ideas. In Korea and in Turkey the students were the ones who sought independence from an oppressive power, and in fact achieved it. In the United States the students in Negro colleges and high schools are the ones who have taken the leadership in the expression of American freedom and in cleansing American society from the disease of racial prejudice. The patience, tolerance, dignity, and idealism of those Negro students who have quietly exercised their rights by asking to receive the simple privilege of being served at lunch counters, those students—more than 1,800 of them— who have been arrested for engaging in peaceful demonstrations, the students who have put their lives, their careers, their futures in jeopardy without thought of personal gain, often against the wishes and advice of their parents and teachers, always against the forces of their society—these qualities truly represent the ideals of America.

James Baldwin, the distinguished Negro writer, in commenting on the example of the Negro students, has this to say about their situation:

> These are all very serious matters, made the more serious by the fact that the students have so few models to emulate. The young grow up by watching and imitating their elders—it is their universal need to be able to revere them; but I submit that in this country today it is quite impossible for a young person to be speeded toward his maturity in this way. (This impossibility contains the key to what has been called "the beat generation.") What the elders have that they can offer the young is the evidence, in their own flesh, of defeats endured, disasters passed, and triumphs won. This is their moral authority, which, however mystical it may sound, is the only authority that endures; and it is through dealing with this authority that the young catch their first glimpse of what has been called the historical perspective.

The authority of which James Baldwin speaks is the moral and intellectual authority of the true teacher and the true parent. The understood child in his later adolescence understands us very well. We are the ones who have taught him caution, a caution he has no desire to emulate. We are the ones who speak of educational reform as a way in which we can put the young through longer stretches of academic material. We are the ones who are calling upon the young for greater effort, higher standards, faster progress.

To which the young reply: Give us by your example the evidence of disasters passed and triumphs won. Give us teachers whose minds are active, whose knowledge is deep and whose character is of a kind we can honestly admire. Earn your authority by showing in your lives that you care about the values of the mind, the qualities of courage, the needs of the world, the ideals of honest effort in the service of others. Understand us, yes. But show us that you also understand the need of the young for ideals and loyalties; convictions and beliefs that can stand up before the pressures of a modern society that asks us to submit to its lesser goals of commercial success and personal security.

When you have done this, then we are ready to do what is asked of us, to find the leadership we seek, to create our own leaders from the ranks of the young, to set to work to solve the problems of the world in which our generation now finds itself.

7-5   THE FOUR FACES OF ABLE ADOLESCENTS

Elizabeth Monroe Drews

Elizabeth M. Drews is professor of educational psychology in the College of Education at Michigan State University. She obtained her B.S. and M.S. at the University of Oregon and her Ph.D. at the University of Michigan. She has taught in public schools in Oregon and Chile, was a psychologist and psychotherapist in Michigan, and served as director of psychological services for public schools in Michigan. She has written extensively for educational and psychological journals. This section of readings emphasizes the complex life faced by American adolescents. It is obvious that parents and the general family unit are in an equally fluctuating state. This concluding essay suggests that the behavior of American adolescents spans a continuum from conformity to nonconformity; that the ideas that concern youth range from few to many. The article has been selected to close this section because of the author's optimistic belief "that human beings, and especially young people, are likely constantly to seek higher values of life."

Although our schools are becoming more skilful at identifying gifted students they still make far too little effort to understand children's potential for intellectual and creative thinking—and we fall far short in applying what we do know.

The tests have improved and, in general, more effective use is being made of test results. It is widely accepted that an intelligence quotient should not be an absolute and final label since the score is apt to vary with the test and the age and condition of the child. Further, educators are asking pertinent questions: Do we measure enough variables? Are our measures broad enough to gauge intelligence? To gauge creativity?

Because even the best of our testing instruments are still rather blunt, the specific strengths and talents of many talented children go unrecognized. These children stand out as superior students but we seldom know how superior and in what ways. This is unfortunate if there is truth in the theory held by some that to be really top-flight in certain fields one has to begin young. Whitehead called it a need for "initial momentum." Tutoring took care of John Stuart Mill in this situation—he was taught Greek at the age of three. Michelangelo, over his father's objection that such work was for artisans, spent his days as a sculptor's apprentice at thirteen and by fifteen shared the company of Lorenzo the Magnificent and his guests, the most able minds in Europe.

Today, development along such unique lines might be thwarted. The tendency is to teach gifted youngsters what they already know and to keep them marking time. And sometimes when they themselves reach for knowledge they need and don't have, they are told to wait, it's too soon, the knowledge is forthcoming in another book, another year.

In the selection of children and adolescents for gifted programs, the guidelines commonly used are achievement measures, teacher judgment, and grades. Beyond this, there are some who are exploring such nonintellectual facets as openmindedness, motivation, tolerance of uncertainty, preference for complexity, high regard for learning, and a

From *Saturday Review*, XLVI, No. 3 (January 19, 1963), 68–71. Copyright 1963 by Saturday Review, Inc.; reprinted by permission of Saturday Review, Inc., and the author.

sense of destiny. These investigators are looking at creativity more closely and at some of the dimensions ascribed to it, such as fluency, originality, spontaneity, and flexibility.

For the past eight years, in a series of studies conducted in the public schools of Lansing, Michigan, and Buffalo, New York, I have been trying to describe superior adolescents by any and all measures available. Almost at the start I found that superior adolescents look disconcertingly alike when viewed in terms of certain group intelligence or achievement tests designed for various grade levels. Yet working with, counseling, and teaching these young people provided ample evidence that they are vastly different from each other. And data beyond achievement and ability scores— showing the varieties of interests, depth and strength of responses, and styles of thinking—also indicate that this group is variable to the widest range of extremes.

Bright children not only have more talents than others but they often have unusual combinations of talents and styles. The boy scientist is sometimes a poet as well, and the May Queen may take computer programming on the side. There are limitless contradictions and inconsistencies.

The years of research included intensive case studies as well as studies of the records, interests, and creative products of about a thousand gifted children. Added to the resultant data were conclusions gathered from reading countless other research studies on such topics as achievement, social acceptance, creativity, and dogmatism. Obviously one cannot talk meaningfully about a thousand different children. A way to reduce and organize the data was essential. My problem was to find some way to depict the disparate styles, tempos, and patterns of the gifted and to bring test data and reality, as I perceived it, closer together.

My search finally resulted in the selection of a formula consisting of four categories of gifted students as a practical method of handling the data. These categories are: the high-achieving studious, the social leaders, the creative intellectuals, and the rebels. The types, of course, are not pure or stable. Many talented children are combinations and many surely will change.

But to test my theory that the formula was practical, I asked 500 superior high school students to indicate which of the types they considered themselves to be and also to describe their personal interests, aspirations, and values. So many times over the years my research had been inconclusive. This time, however, my hypotheses were borne out by the results. The students were dramatically different from one another, and they were able to describe themselves according to the types. There follows an explanation of the four types as the students categorized themselves.

THE HIGH-ACHIEVING STUDIOUS

These students, who think hard work is a good thing in and of itself, have a lot of what the sociologists call "Protestant ethic." Some people call them "grinds," but that seems inappropriate since many of them are girls and such a designation has a harsh, unfeminine sound. Generally speaking, twice as many bright girls are high achievers, at least in the sense of getting good grades, although on achievement tests boys and girls appear to do equally well.

High achievers are attuned to what parents and school (particularly school) expect. They tend to conform to what teachers demand or even to what teachers suggest. Since teachers' expectations, behavior, and attitudes are more often than not at odds with the dominant teen-age culture, this means that these students generally put their school work ahead of pleasure. They are not often school leaders, but they do their work and they turn it in on time. They may not be highly creative and original but many are highly productive in terms of such things as the number of problems completed or the number of words in a theme.

Many of these high achievers want to know just how to do something and when it must be completed, but they are not so interested in knowing the "why" of facts as are some of the other types. They want assignments to be explicit. They prefer to use textbooks and workbooks if given a choice, and they are the one group who do extra work-book exercises just for fun. In college they tend to prefer lectures to discussion groups— they sometimes describe discussion groups as a sharing of ignorance. They do not want the professor to ramble or to digress or to tell funny stories; they want him to lecture from an outline so they can put their own notes in an outline form and memorize them. Their feeling for logic is good; their sense of organization superb.

However, this means that they often reject learning approaches that lack an apparent structure and avoid tasks that are oriented to means rather than ends. They sometimes feel that learning for learning's sake may interfere with getting ahead in the world. For them, education must be instrumental.

In our exploratory research on the students who described themselves as the studious type, we found that they typically said they read to be well-rounded and to help their grades. Among school-year interests, recreation rated lowest (both in relation to all other interests checked and compared to choices made by other groups), and school subjects proved very popular.

Teachers are often favorably predisposed to these boys and girls; some of the teachers were like this when they were young. Besides, it is hard not to respond favorably to those who do everything you tell them to do and who want to know just the way you want things done. Many of the girls will be teachers themselves; others will be secretaries whom even the boss's wife will praise. The studious boys prefer math and science to the humanities and are particularly drawn to engineering.

In their future lives, they want to be hard-working and conscientious, to help others, and to live by the rules. They tend to be deadly serious and sometimes they take themselves that way. However, they are neat and attractive—the girls are often very pretty—and they make fine, upstanding citizens. They will be excellent employees. They may not scintillate at parties but they will shine on their monthly reports. They are punctual and not a little punctilious.

THE SOCIAL LEADERS

A few years ago when education criticism was just becoming a major sport Sloan Wilson of "The Man in the Gray Flannel Suit" was quoted by *Life* as saying that "the schools can't make up their minds whether to make children well adjusted or to teach them something." At that time it was my contention that the children who were doing the very best school work were the best adjusted. (At least adjusted in the popular meaning of the term—well-rounded and well-liked.) A number of recent sociometric studies have supported this point. However, further examination has shown that not all of the gifted children are popular and socially in the groove; only certain ones—whom I term the social-leader type—can really be said to epitomize popularity. These are the ones who shine in personal or social relationships.

The social leaders as a group tend to conform more to teen-age mores than to teachers' expectations. However, they do well enough and sometimes very well academically. It is just that their social interests come first. While the studious are preparing for examinations and the intellectuals are reading about existentialism the social leaders are out electing someone to office or, what is more likely, getting elected themselves.

This interest in and emphasis on social behavior seemingly does not interfere with good grades as much as do certain kinds of intellectual behavior. At least the social leaders consistently get better grades than do the talented "intellectuals." Perhaps schools value and understand sociability more than intellectuality or perhaps these social leaders are able and charming enough to accomplish all that is required academically. They are fluent and persuasive; teachers, as well as students, find them hard to resist.

They are a particularly handsome group, boys and girls alike. Many of the boys are top athletes and mature for their age—"man-type boys" as one girl described them. They tend to be lionized and become campus wheels—very big and neatly rounded. They do not go in for fencing or ping-pong or chess; they are the captains or the quarterbacks of the football teams.

The girls are equally attractive, well-built, and well-coordinated. Many of them become majorettes and cheer-leaders. Some come from homes with money; some do not. All of them like to spend money—on themselves. Clothes are important, a "big thing" in their lives.

The social leaders as a group begin to date early. They attend social functions early and, although some come from average homes, many are quite used to the country club or are beginning to be.

Their parents are often young and handsome, well-educated, and well-connected. Their basic values are materialistic, rounded out with hedonism, but they temper their competitiveness with good-humored togetherness. Neither the parents nor the students are visionaries. They rarely give a second thought to the starving millions in India, but they are community-minded, performing good deeds for the community and according high prestige to the chairman of the committee in charge of the good works. They work for the crusade of the moment but not for an unpopular cause. Other students like them and elect them to office; they're genuinely popular. They probably will become corporation executives, doctors, or lawyers. As one of our intellectual students said, "There isn't a teacher or a minister or a scientist or a real genuine attic-prone artist in the lot of them. They want jobs that pay."

THE CREATIVE INTELLECTUALS

The next group I have called creative intellectuals. As with the other groups, the climate of the community and the ambiance of the school at least partially determine how many one finds among superior students. Of the students involved with this research, about 20 percent called themselves intellectuals and had the proper caste marks. (About 20 percent said they were social leaders; about 60 percent claimed to be studious high-achievers.) In talking to gifted students in some localities, I have felt that the percentage of intellectuals might be higher; in others it is certainly lower. And my guess is that in a few high-ranking liberal arts colleges most of the students lean in this direction.

In general, this group receives lower grades, at least in the conventional Mid-western high schools I studied, than either the studious or the social leaders. However, their achievement test scores are a shade higher than their grades, and there are more highly gifted students in this group. They do not conform to either the teacher's standards or to those set by other students. They are usually not leaders, and they do not want to be, at least in the high school setting. Even in their own groups there are few leaders. Instead, each individual revolves in his own orbit.

On creativity tests they tend to be both fluent and original. The studious high achievers and the social leaders are often fluent but less often truly original. The girls among the intellectuals scored particularly low on dogmatism tests, although teachers related the intellectuals as being more dogmatic than the other groups. In general, girl intellectuals find it hard to be accepted by either fellow students or teachers. As a group, these boys and girls are rather prickly young people, who ask below-the-surface or, for some teachers, below-the-belt questions.

Within this category, there seem to be future scientists (but not engineers), artists, writers, musicians, and scholars-at-large. At the high school stage, many intellectually inclined students have interests in all these areas. They are the ones who delve into extra-sensory perception, read on their own Rokeach's "Open and Closed Mind," and independently become experts on Albert Camus and Thomas Mann.

One sixteen-year-old boy spent last year reading Ibsen and Freud simultan-eously, and assiduously applied Freudian theory to Ibsen passages. Another recently apologized to a psychologist working under a Cooperative Research Grant for not becoming a high achiever after group counseling. He explained: "I've read all of Freud and Shakespeare this year and lots besides, and I'm so busy educating myself that I just don't have time to get more than B's in my school work."

This is a skeptical group. However, they combine skepticism with a deep-seated idealism and a tendency to probe into basic issues. They frequently see the discrepancy between people's expressed beliefs and their actions. And this discrepancy disturbs them. Fortunately, their intense seriousness is usually leavened by a sense of humor that allows their creativity and imaginativeness to come into full play. Their humor is impulsive, subtle, and, above all, zany. They are devotees of shaggy dog stories.

These are students who do not want explicit assignments. They thrive on free choice and although they say "I want to help all I can," they also checked on our questionnaires an item that reads "I want to live my own life and make my own rules." This is in contrast to the high-achieving studious who want to "live by the rules," presumably rules made by someone else.

The intellectuals buy books and read them. Often they read them while the teachers are teaching. In contrast to the social leaders, the boys are fans of comic books, TV, and the sports page, and the girls still read the "series books," such as "Sue Barton." And in contrast to the studious, who read their assignments and occasionally the encyclopedia and current news magazines, the intellectuals read an exotic variety of things: science fiction from the "Fifth Dimension" on out, Russian translations, and French in the original, free verse, classics and plays, philosophy and religion and biographies.

In many ways the intellectuals are an off-beat group. Although they care deeply about mankind, they seldom form teen-age love attachments. They rarely date, especially the budding scientists and philosophers. Some of the scientists never seem to see a girl as a girl until one day—perhaps in graduate school—they see one suddenly on the other side of the test tube. They have more social conscience than social inclination. They are often humanitarian in a broad sense and more concerned with overpopulation and fall-out than with student elections.

Their concern is more with process than product and with internal life than the external effect. Often they do not want or expect rewards. Their eyes are on the ultimate goals rather than immediate tasks. Education is seen as a continuing process and not just a series of grades on report cards. One of them told me, "I would be willing to kill myself for the discovery of one small segment of truth, even if only one other person in the world understood it."

THE REBEL

The rebel is that rare fourth type. More specifically he might be termed an individualistic creative nonintellectual. This group is very small, but it is a definite one with the qualification for admittance being general nonconformity. Nonconformity serves no social or intellectual purpose for these students. It is only a means of showing their dislike for regimentation at all levels.

They are extremely low achievers. Most fall in the moderately gifted range and a few are even brilliant. By definition, they are neither leaders nor followers in school. On the other hand, they may be master minds in a sub-culture that borders on delinquency. Generally, teachers reject the rebels and the rebels reciprocate in kind. Only a few ever become involved in school activities and then only when their teachers are willing to expend much time and effort encouraging them.

Most of the rebels are boys. Their dress is unpredictable; some wear the leather jacket trade-mark, others do not. Elaborate hair styles, leather boots, beltless pants, and open shirts are common exterior signs of the rebel boy.

Rebels measure low in social responsibility and high on delinquency scales. They test higher on the nonverbal than on the verbal sections of intelligence tests. On creativity measures they are not fluent (fluency refers to verbal productivity), yet they are highly original in their ways. Many are very clever with their hands and most are do-it-yourself fans. Their lives appear to be centered around customizing and dragging.

Creative intellectuals, our other non-conformist type, stem from the entire socio-economic range, but rebels are predominantly of lower-class origin. Their parents are often Outsiders; they are not likely to place much value on things either social or intellectual.

Rebels will sometimes be responsive to unusual ideas. An imaginative social studies teacher greeted a class, that was understandably apathetic on a warm fall afternoon, with the comment, "A bomb has been exploded and killed everyone in the world except forty-six people." To one of the students a challenge stirred. He was recognizably a rebel by his pants at half-mast, his "one-button" shirt, and leather boots. After several days and without solicitation he brought the teacher an elaborate plan for evacuation and rehabilitation of the survivors. He not only showed an ability to be precise and take pains, but also revealed a creative flair.

Rebels obviously are at odds with the school and the community, but much of their alienation is a reaction to the kinds of rejection they have experienced. When attempts are made to meet them in ways they understand and when school work "makes sense," they can sometimes be reclaimed. A few will go to college and develop their technical skills, and perhaps become masters of electrical brains. Others may make their mark in the entertainment or sports world. Some will become truck drivers and help to produce a situation such as that noted by a famous psychologist at the end of World War II; viz., the upper quarter of the truck drivers are brighter than the lower quarter of the lawyers.

An inescapable question arises: At high school age, have boys and girls become so molded that the types described are patterned for life? If external conditions (school mores, family values, national goals, etc.) changed, would the students respond and become different in type? Will some even create change, seemingly entirely internally? The striking response of one boy to the challenge of his social studies teacher indicates that change may occur. Some students now categorized in any one group may change to another, but not many.

Change is greater among the rebels than within any other group (in one year, 30 percent of our rebels changed) for theirs is basically a negative reaction to life in general. Yet human beings, given the appropriate conditions, respond by becoming more human; they move in positive directions.

To illustrate the possibility of change, I have constructed a graphic depiction of the types:

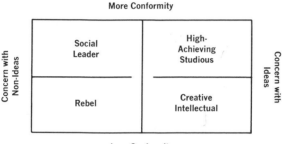

The rebel is not likely to become a high achieving studious, or vice versa. And the creative intellectual and social leader would hardly move into each other's corner. Yet north and south movement and east and west movement of these types not only is possible; we know that it happens.

If it is true, as I certainly believe it is, that human beings, and especially young people, are likely constantly to seek higher values in life—becoming more socially oriented, more creative, and more constructive—then surely there will be movement from one type to another. This possibility is a challenge to those schools committed to greatness.

CONCLUSION

It is obvious that the consanguinal family is rapidly disappearing from the American scene. Except in certain rural areas and ethnic groups and small pockets of religiously orthodox communities, most American families may be considered as conjugal units. Urbanization has caused the family to depend heavily on outside agencies to fulfill functions it once unquestioningly assumed.

As children reach adolescence, both the school and the peer group become increasingly important in identity formation. Those who participate in neither school nor peer group activities forfeit membership in the two institutions readily available to all. Without the experiences achieved through association with these groups, young people have an extremely difficult time in developing what is considered a satisfactory adult identity; anti-social behavior often results. In most cases this behavior is channeled into what is currently described as a teenage subculture in which frivolity and inability to assume social responsibility replace the behavior expected by adults. Those adolescents who do not wish to participate in the so-called "cult of the teenager" sometimes exhibit more serious delinquent behavior. All too often adults do not realize that these overt actions are deliberate attempts on the part of adolescents to delay their entry into the adult world.

American educators must recognize that the school exists both as an academic and a social institution. It must provide a variety of mechanisms through which youth can gain public recognition for their achievements as they move slowly, at their own pace, into the world of adulthood.

ADDITIONAL READING

Harry E. Barnes, "Family and Community Disorganization." *Social Institutions* (New York: Prentice-Hall, Inc. 1946), pp. 601–666. A leader in American sociological thought provides us with some considerations regarding the family and community. Some of the statistics are obviously outdated but the ideas are as pertinent as ever.

Urie Bronfenbrenner, "The Changing American Child," from *Reference Papers for the Golden Anniversary White House Conference on Children and Youth,* 1960, pp. 1–8. A discussion of shifting patterns of socialization and family roles with inferences for the future. Particularly good for class discussion.

James S. Coleman, "The Adolescent Subculture and Academic Achievement," *American Journal of Sociology,* XLV (January 1960), 337–347. Report of a research project that examined the status systems of adolescent communities. Results suggest ways in which rather straightforward social theory could be used in organizing high school activities in order to encourage energies into directions of learning.

Morris E. Eson, "Family Influences," *Psychological Foundations of Education* (New York: Holt, Rinehart and Winston, Inc., 1964), pp. 398–422. The family is the primary force influencing the socialization process. This work examines the effects of various home attitudes and environmental factors upon the developing child.

Ronald C. Johnson and Gene R. Medinnus, "Family Influences on the Growing Child," *Child Psychology* (New York: John Wiley and Sons, 1965), pp. 270–312. "Western culture prescribes general requirements for the role of the parent." Parent attitudes, behavior, personality, and parent-child relationships are thoroughly discussed in this new addition to psychological literature.

Ethel Strainchamps, "The Plight of the Intellectual Girl," *The Saturday Review* (November 19, 1960), pp. 63–64, 81. Does the bright and energetic young female discover early in life that society is not quite certain that the development of maximum intellectual potential is really her role?

8

The Teacher and the Community

INTRODUCTION

The American public school is not only a functional part of American society but also, in a smaller, more intimate way, an integral part of the community it serves. American society has rejected any trend toward a national educational system, relying instead on local and state systems that place the burden of education on local schools. If the school, then, is to serve the local rather than the national community, educators must know the nature of the local community and the best ways to serve it. This section provides insights into the nature of the American community and a method of analyzing it.

Actually, the teacher is a member of several communities. In his professional role he is most concerned with two: the local community in which his school is located and the school's own teacher-student community. He must function effectively in both to be a successful teacher. At times he may have to resolve, for his pupils, conflicts that occur between the school community and the local community. Certainly the esteem in which the local community holds the school will affect his teaching, and the goals that the local community ascribes to the school should coincide with his stated teaching goals.

The philosophy of the modern American school has been affected by the historical tradition of the community-school movement in education. This movement not only envisioned the school as a self-contained community with problems and styles that could be organized and studied by the students themselves but also felt that the school could analyze the local community. Students could use community surveys, interview community leaders, and observe other community institutions. Thus, most schools have accepted the obligation to create citizens who are interested in their communities and who feel they should participate in community government. Consequently, the modern teacher is expected to be interested in community activities himself and to provide opportunities for his students that will lead to their intelligent participation in community affairs.

8-1   THE SCHOOL IN THE CONTEXT OF THE COMMUNITY

John Gillin

John Gillin was research professor of anthropology at the University of North Carolina at the time of his death in 1958. His extensive research had taken him to Algeria, Europe, New Mexico, Northern Wisconsin, British Guiana, Ecuador, the Upper Amazon Valley, Peru, Cuba, Colombia, and Guatemala. His many monographs, such as *Moche: A Peruvian Coastal Community*, reflect this research. In addition he has written such theoretical books as *The Ways of Man* and *Cultural Sociology*. In his essay Gillin suggests the kinds of things a teacher should look for in a community.

This is a sort of outline of what public school teachers and administrators need to find out, rather than what they need to know, about their own schools in the context of the communities where they live. Considering the variety of communities in the contemporary United States, one would find it impossible in a limited space to supply educational personnel with a "handbook" of knowledge about any and all communities in which they might find themselves. On the other hand, I do not think it would be too difficult for them to discover for themselves most of the necessary facts about their particular communities, provided they have the guidance of certain principles and general information regarding American culture and community structure. The present paper aims to suggest the lines of interest public school teachers and administrators might find it rewarding to follow.

It is easy to say that, in cultural terms, it is the function of the teacher to transmit, or at least to attend or assist in, the transmission of culture to the younger generation. But once the public school educator is actually in a concrete situation, he must face up, either consciously or unconsciously, to questions like the following: What culture and what part of it am I transmitting? To whom? The children are not all alike either psychologically, socially, or culturally; what are the significant differences among them from the pedagogical point of view? And who am I in the eyes of my charges and their elders? That is, how is my role defined locally and how am I rated? These are some of the problems that face any teacher. The fact of psychological differences between pupils has long been recognized in advanced educational circles, and sundry methods of determining intelligence and emotional variations are more or less routinely used as a basis for the application of what are considered psychologically appropriate techniques of instruction.

Formulators of educational policy, however, have lately become aware that the psychological approach alone is not enough, and for this reason they ask for added light from cultural anthropology and cultural sociology. In part this is the result of increasingly convincing data that such "psychological" characteristics as the intelligence quotient

Reprinted from *Education and Anthropology*, edited by George D. Spindler, with the permission of the publishers, Stanford University Press. Copyright 1955 by the Board of Trustees of the Leland Stanford Junior University.

(I.Q.) and personality are not entirely innate, but may be culturally and socially conditioned. Likewise, it has been clearly shown on a cross-cultural and cross-community basis that, although certain basic motivations are built into all so-called normal children by their biological heredity, other culturally acquired motivations and attitudes are built into them by their social and cultural background training and experience. Such things as "the desire to learn" and "attitude toward the public school and its personnel" are, so far as modern data go, definitely not biologically transmitted.

One of the first facts the educator must recognize if he is to plan his program in community cultural context is the considerable diversity in pattern among contemporary communities of the United States. Space and time are lacking here to attempt a complete catalogue of variations. Perhaps fundamental from the point of view of cultural anthropology is the fact that the community in which the educator gets a job may be either homogeneous or heterogeneous in culture. The likelihood of obtaining a position in a culturally homogeneous community is relatively slight, because there are comparatively few of them in this country. In general, such communities tend to be small in size (i.e., are rural or small-town) and isolated. There are quite a few such communities, for example, in the Southern mountain region and in the Latter-Day Saints areas of Utah and Idaho. In such a situation the teacher will not be confronted by much diversity in the cultural backgrounds of his pupils. Unless he is a native or long-time resident of the community, however, he may find his own role in the community somewhat anomalous, and he should walk carefully until he discovers from local informants what it is supposed to be. Furthermore, he will find that local ideas of the values of an education may be somewhat "backward" in terms of the general culture, and it is not uncommon that the members want to keep their way of life that way—they prefer backward homogeneity to newfangled perversions from the outside. Finally, one must keep in mind that if he finds himself in such a community, he should not think that cultural homogeneity necessarily means lack of internal conflict and rivalry. It merely signifies that the local citizens know and practice only one set or range of customs for solving life's problems, that they agree on one set of values, and that this local culture is available to all members of the community without the interposition of social distinctions other than those assigned to age and sex. Nevertheless, the community may be divided into cliques or even feud groups, with any one of which the outside teacher would be well advised not to become identified. All members of the community may be agreed, for example, that "lying is bad," but they may not hesitate to accuse each other of committing this sin. Or they may know only a limited range of customs for "attacking a person's character," but use them with great gusto on each other.

More important is the heterogeneous community, for this is the type one may expect to find in the great majority of cases in this country. The condition of cultural heterogeneity is, of course, a matter of degree, and one finds considerable variation in this respect. However, for anthropology such a community is essentially a more or less functionally integrated collection of subcultures. If one finds himself in a population or territory possessing a number of cultures that show no functional integration, he must conclude that he is not dealing with a community, but possibly with several communities in the scientific sense of the term, or even an unorganized and unintegrated congeries of groups with their respective systems of custom. The heterogeneous modern American community consists of a number of socially distinct groups or social categories, each with a system of subculture (including social organization and values) peculiar to itself in the local situation. We call these systems subcultures because, despite their differences, they also all contain certain common or *universal* cultural elements and they all contain patterns of action and organization that permit articulated social relations between the component social groups or categories. Some community universals may be derived from those traits and institutions that are common to all of North American culture, while others may be universal only to the local community. For example, in all United States communities all adults, regardless of their social status and subculture, are required to use English as the language of community-wide discourse and to live with only one spouse at one time. (It is a fact that there are some "foreign" communities on North American soil, such as still unassimilated Indian tribes and immigrant groups. These can be considered North American communities, however, only in the geographical sense.) Likewise there are no communities of United States culture where men do not all wear trousers of a certain pattern with fly front. On the other hand, only in New Orleans is it universal for the whole community to celebrate Shrove Tuesday (Mardi Gras) by participating in street parades and other jollifications of a certain pattern. This is a local universal.

The foregoing are simple examples of patterns that are actually practiced by all sections of the community. One must also consider types of integrating universals that I call value beliefs. They are also sometimes spoken of as moral beliefs, or simply as morals. They have to do with what "should" be done. Sometimes, these value beliefs and the actual practices very nearly coincide. For example, it is universally held in all communities of United States culture that adults "should" be able to read, write, and figure. And the fact is that only a few less than 3 percent of our adult population is illiterate. On the other hand, it is probably a universally held belief in American communities that every voter "should" go to the polls, yet only a fraction of the electorate turns out to register its opinion of, say, a local bond issue. Local universal value beliefs also are often of great interest to the residents. Everyone you talk to in Center City, perhaps, is agreed that the community "should" have a new school plant, but for one reason or another it may be years before this goal is realized, if ever. . . . To sum up, you have to have some general agreements among the members of the population or you do not have a community. Likewise, a functioning community requires certain mechanisms of internal social adjustment. . . .

The *types* of subcultures most commonly found in contemporary North American communities are those associated with social classes, with color castes, and with ethnic groups. The *content* of the subcultures may vary from one community or one region of the country to another. Of course it is not true that all communities have divisions based on all three of these criteria.

It comes as a shock to many good Americans to learn that social classes exist in our country, because according to the national credo "no one is supposed to be recognized as any better than anyone else except through his own efforts and abilities." Perhaps "class" is a misleading word, because the divisions we find in American communities lack the rigid, unpassable barriers that separated them in much of Europe and even England of a former day. Nevertheless, an impressive number of social science studies indicate that probably the great majority of United States communities today contain something like a class system. Even though social mobility is permitted, the structure of the system is "played down," and the average person is not clear about the structure. Evidence from a wide variety of communities in different parts of the country shows that the six-class structure depicted by Lloyd Warner and associates for Newburyport, Massachusetts, is by no means universal. In small, rural centers the "upper group" may be no more than a clique of a few families, such as those of the banker and a half-dozen well-to-do merchants and farmers who have a certain wealth and who have been established in the community for a couple of generations or more. The rest of the populace may be common people, although in small communities there are usually a few families, such as James West reports as "people who live like animals" in Plainville, who are "looked down upon" by almost everyone else.

In the present connection the important points are that each such group or category has cultural characteristics not shared with the others, and that special values, often in the form of invidious comparisons, are attached to these characteristics. Furthermore, these status-cultural categories are hierarchically ranked, with those "higher" on the scale accorded proportionately more privileges and rewards—according to a common scale of values—than those in "lower" position. They usually differ in patterns of family behavior and child-rearing, in occupational range of the breadwinners, in the definition of goals and aspirations and the means of achievement. From this it usually follows that the values they attach to education show some degree of variance. The motivations of the children and the attitudes of their parents are formed by the time the children enter the first grade and tend to be maintained at least during the elementary years while the children are under the family and neighborhood controls of their respective status groups.

Warner points out that a variety of studies in New England, the South, and the Middle West show that about 94 percent of public school teachers are either of the middle class or are upward mobile individuals who have assimilated middle-class culture.[1] If this is true of the country as a whole, and there is reason to think that it is, the average teacher literally does not know from his or her own experience and training what the approved goals of education *are* for those of his pupils who belong either to lower or upper groups. He can find out something about this by background reading and through special courses, and he can get the details in his own community by his personal investigation over a period of time. But once he finds that there are differences in what is expected of education in his community, he is faced with the problem of how to plan his teaching. Should he try to satisfy all comers according to their own class-cultural lights? In cases where the class-cultural expectancies are in opposition to each other, this can only be done by segregating the pupils according to class origin. Should the teacher concentrate merely upon the "common denominators" of the class cultures, leaving the other aspirations of the pupils to be handled by other agencies, such as private schools, clubs, churches, etc.? . . .

What has just been said concerning class subcultures within the total community applies in much the same way to the educational problems of caste and ethnic groups, with certain differences. Color castes and ethnic groups are usually class-stratified within themselves. There is one important difference between them, however. This is that what we call color castes, such as the Negroes and the Nisei, have, class-for-class, practically the same culture as the whites and have taken over parallel class structures. The ethnic groups, on the other hand, in so far as in specific cases they can be considered functioning parts of a community, still preserve significant elements of culture and social organization carried over from their country of origin. I am not

[1] W. Lloyd Warner, *American Life: Dream and Reality* (Chicago: University of Chicago Press, 1953), pp. 176–177.

referring here to ghettos and Little Italies and the like, peopled by recently arrived immigrants or refugees, for such elements cannot be considered to have full function in community culture or social organization until some assimilation has taken place. I have in mind ethnic groups the members of which are "good Americans," but whose sub-cultures and social organizations show some variance from the general community pattern. For example, there are in Savannah and Atlanta groups of highly respected Sephardic Jews whose ancestors came to this country two hundred years ago; in Milwaukee are numerous German families whose forebears left the old country shortly after 1848; in California are Spanish families who trace their lineage back to the *coloniaje*; in the South one finds numerous "old Americans" of Scotch-Presbyterian tradition. These people are Americans all right, but they maintain special relations with members of their own groups and they carry on special traditions and values derived from their ancestral cultures.

The educator who finds one or more such groups in his community is again faced with problems. Should it be the objective of the school to "wipe out" these ethnic differences? There is much to be said against such a course, perhaps the least of which is that it would eliminate yet more of the seasoning and flavor from a standardized American way of life that is rapidly showing signs of becoming monotonous. If the children of ethnic groups are to be educated by the school to the American standard, what standard should be selected? Should they be taught the culture of the upper classes, the middle classes, the lower classes, or what?

The decision of the Supreme Court of the United States in May 1954 declared segregation of the races in public schools to be unconstitutional. During the summer of 1953 a South-wide survey of the possible results of this decision was made with funds provided by the Ford Foundation.[2] This survey indicates that there will probably not be a complete disappearance of segregated schools or pupils, since, because of already existing segregated residential patterns, by "gerrymandering" school districts it will be possible in many cases to send children to schools of their own race. Neverthe-less, a sizable number of schools will inevitably have both Negroes and whites—and the teachers must be prepared to deal with race attitudes which the children carry from the home to the school and also with the fact that Negro children will probably never, in this generation at least, be able to occupy the same status positions in adulthood as their white schoolmates.

In the typical heterogeneous American community, the social relations between the constituent subcultural groups and categories are governed by codes, which in large part are often informal and unwritten. The etiquette, for example, of intergroup relations is not standardized throughout the country. More obsequiousness is required of Negroes in certain parts of the South, for instance, than in other regions of the nation. There is less emphasis on certain symbols of status in the Middle West and Far West than in the Northeast and South. Along with the outward patterns of interaction go internalized ideas, attitudes, and rationalizations of the respective statuses. For example, among many lower-class Negro farm tenants in the South there is acceptance of the "natural superiority" of white people and also of upper-class and educated Negroes, whereas lower-class industrial workers in the North seem to be less inclined to agree with the class attitudes of their "social betters."

The teacher must learn to know what these patterns of subculture interaction

---

[2] Harry S. Ashmore, *The Negro and the Schools* (Chapel Hill, University of North Carolina Press, 1954).

are in order to establish and maintain contact with the various elements of his community. He must also realize that they are the channels, so to speak, of communication and reciprocal action whereby a certain integration is maintained in the community. Were they, or something serving similar functions, not in operation, the subcultural groups and categories within the community would become mutually isolated and the community would lose whatever cohesion it has. Therefore, the teacher and others who would "reform" such patterns must think in functional terms applied to the community as a whole. This does not mean that educators should not participate in movements for reform and betterment of the community or any portion of it, but it does mean that they should try to assess on an objective basis the results of such endeavors in community-wide context.

In order to carry out his role in the community, the educator should be aware of the *power structure*, which usually cuts across subcultural lines. First, of course, one can inform himself fairly easily of the *formal* power structure—the form of local government, the individuals who hold political positions, the shape and make-up of the various administrative and judicial bodies, such as school boards, housing and sanitation commissions, the courts, the tax assessment system, and so on. This sort of information should be passed on to the pupils so that they may become active participants in the democratic process, and it is also necessary to the educator if he is to be an effective teacher or administrator and a good citizen.

Somewhat more difficult to discover is the *informal* power structure and its personnel. The top power group is not usually composed of criminals, but the members prefer "to keep out of the limelight." One excellent study[3] and various other evidence indicate that the members of the small, top power group of the community are not necessarily or exclusively members of the top social status categories. Some, although of upper income, are definitely middle class as far as the status symbols and behavior go. The great majority of such individuals, however, do hold controlling interests or responsibilities in the major financial and economic enterprises of the community. In small communities one may find what I have called the "boss man complex"—a single individual rather than a group that holds effective power. Usually the *ostensible* power holders of the community, including elective and appointive officers of responsibility, are effectively controlled by the informal power group. "Nothing gets done" if it meets the disapproval of these effective power holders—so long as they retain their power—and an effort is made to see that any individual who begins to gain prominence or power himself is either brought into line or effectively hamstrung. It is an oversimplification, and perhaps in most cases untrue, to think of the controllers of this informal power structure as venal. Publicly, they are usually of the highest respectability. One reason, however, that they do not ordinarily advertise their power is that their basic goal is to maintain the local economic system intact and perhaps to expand it. Since this goal might not be rated highest on the list of the population as a whole, or of important segments of it, the counsel of wisdom (from the point of view of the controllers of the economic system) is not to submit the issue to democratic discussion or decision. However, so long as community projects do not seriously interfere with this basic goal,

---

[3]Floyd Hunter, *Community Power Structure* (Chapel Hill: University of North Carolina Press, 1953). Professor Hunter has collected similar information, which seems to check with that in his book, from a series of representative communities throughout the country, for the "power structure" of the nation as a whole. This material is being readied for publication.

the informal power holders will often permit or even encourage them. A paternalistic view of "welfare" is often entertained, so long as it does not cost the wealthy groups too much and does not "upset the applecart."

In this connection it should be noted that there seems to be a tendency for the members of school boards and other control agencies of education to be drawn from the upper groups of status or power, although school board members themselves usually do not belong to the top inner power group, the members of which have "more important" responsibilities. It is rare for the ordinary schoolteacher to have social relations with members of the school board and their families. Or, if social gestures are made by the latter, it is often in a condescending manner. In many communities, I am told, the school board ignores the teacher as an individual and treats him or her as an "employee." The teacher is often a single person without family in the community and lives on a modest salary. For these reasons, even were there no difference in subcultural backgrounds, teachers would seldom be able to reciprocate socially with members of such groups. Furthermore, school board members are often "conservative" in viewpoint, reflecting either their own class-cultural orientations or those of power groups that control them. Teachers themselves, especially when young, are inclined to reflect the more intellectual and "progressive" values of middle-class culture and are therefore constantly exposed to the risk of being dubbed "radical" by their employers.

Thus the teacher in the great majority of American communities is bound to find differences of opinion, and it may be helpful to recognize that these are to a large extent due to differences in subcultural conditioning and controls. It is not surprising, then, that the teacher often either feels insecure in his or her social role or feels guilty of "compromising" his ideals in order to obtain greater solidarity with various local elements. The teacher as perhaps an "advanced" person of middle-class culture is apt to feel resentful of the "pretensions" of the upper-class people, to regard as "stuffy" the sentiments of the more conservative elements of the community, and to find the manners and attitudes of the lower-class students appalling. This is a dilemma of sorts—and dilemmas are not comfortable. What can be done about it?

In solving this problem I believe that the community role of the school administrators is of first importance. It is my impression that in most public school systems of any size, the administrators—superintendents. principals, and the like— have considered their responsibilities to be mainly toward the school board and other control groups in the community rather than to the teachers. They try to identify with the so-called leaders of the community and very little with their teaching staffs. This is accentuated by the fact that the majority of school administrators are men whereas the greater part of the public school teachers—except athletic coaches and instructors in manual training—are women. The top administrators are usually invited to join luncheon clubs and to take leadership roles in charity campaigns, and the like. And they are often in a position to interact on a common social basis with at least the secondary levels of status and power. Such channels, for reasons already mentioned, are not open to the ordinary teacher.

It would therefore seem that school administrators must be brought to a wider conception of their roles. In addition to their purely administrative duties and their function of liaison with the upper status and power groups, they should likewise "face toward" their teaching staffs. They are in a position to interpret the community, or certain aspects of it, to the teachers and to make contacts and to open channels for the teachers into the realities of community life outside the classroom. Such procedures, devoid of authoritarianism, would, I believe, do much to add to teacher *esprit de corps* and ego-satisfaction, and would decrease the alarming rate at which teachers are leaving the profession.

P.T.A.'s and similar groups, of course, form a link between the teachers and the general population. But it is notorious that they are made up principally of middle-class parents. Neither lower-class nor upper-class family representatives usually participate. It would be possible by properly directed effort to enlarge the scope of such groups. In those neighborhoods and communities in which the school becomes a sort of community center in the evenings, the interest and pride of the adult citizens in the institution seem to be increased.

Finally, the teacher should be encouraged to learn the social and cultural realities of the community on her own account. Here again a permissive and constructive attitude on the part of her administrative superiors is desirable. Also some first-rate courses in teacher-training colleges on the community, personality, and culture would help. It is a curious fact that university and college professors are often persons of prominence, although usually not of top power, in their communities, while the schoolteacher is not often listened to outside the classroom. In part, at least, I believe that this is because university and college administrations not only permit, but actually encourage community participation and leadership on the part of their faculties, whereas such administrative attitudes have hitherto been rare in respect to public school teachers. There is no doubt that the average schoolteacher is or could be an "authority" on many subjects of community interest, and he or she should be recognized as such and given the opportunity to participate more in common concerns.

With respect to the content of classroom teaching, there are common denominators running through the content of all the subcultures of a community, there is consensus about certain precepts of morality, there is agreement on certain common goals and the acceptable techniques for realizing them. These at least should form the bases of instruction.

Beyond these, however, rigidity is to be avoided. In a society such as ours, containing many subcultures among which mobility is permitted, the future citizens must be trained to make choices and to see possibilities within the culture as a whole.

8-2   MODELS FOR THE ANALYSIS OF THE EDUCATIVE PROCESS IN AMERICAN COMMUNITIES

Bernard J. Siegel

Bernard J. Siegel has done field work in a Syrian community in Boston, at Taos Pueblo in New Mexico, in Brazil and Portugal, and is now professor of anthropology and executive head of the Department of Anthropology at Stanford University. He was a visiting professor at Tokyo University in 1960–61 and is the author of numerous publications. In this essay Professor Siegel provides a "model" from which to judge the interrelationship of the school and the extra-school community.

INTRODUCTION

In this paper an attempt will be made to raise certain questions about cultural transmission in the American school and community within appropriate frames of reference. The primary objective will be to analyze the forces which tend to maintain or to distort the explicit cultural elements between their entry into teacher-training institutions and their selection and interpretation by children in the classroom.

The term "model" has been used rather loosely by social scientists in recent years as a close approximation to the terms "frame of reference," and "design." The notion of a model has the advantage, perhaps, of connoting structural properties of the phenomena under investigation, *particularly of creating a familiar image* for the consideration of novel or unfamiliar situations which have properties similar to those of known, or hypothecated, situations. It is in this mood, rather than in the technically more accurate sense of a mathematical model, that I shall use the term. It suggests, simply, a convenient way of thinking about the role of the educational system in the training of the young.

The following remarks are largely exploratory. They are not the result of specific researches carried on by the writer, nor do they constitute a critical appraisal of researches by others. Rather, they reflect the reactions of one anthropologist, with cultural and social-psychological orientations . . . . It is hoped that the suggested designs for thinking about these problems will have some constructive value in formulating research projects related to them.

SOME ASSUMPTIONS AND CONCEPTS

For purposes of my argument I shall have to make explicit certain assumptions about the nature of the educational community and clarify whatever concepts may be used in the process. To begin with, we mean by the educational community the *formal* school system—sites and interacting members, stated goals, and the role

Reprinted from "Models for the Analysis of the Educative Process in American Communities," by Bernard J. Siegel; from *Education and Anthropology*, edited by George D. Spindler, with the permission of the publishers, Stanford University Press. Copyright 1955 by the Board of Trustees of the Leland Stanford Junior University.

relations in terms of which the goals are translated into action. These, at least, are the primary elements of the system. It is recognized that in the dynamics of activating this system intrusive or intervening factors distort the intent of the formal blue-print in several respects. Principals and teachers may perceive and use their roles in different ways, in relation partly to personality factors and partly to situational conditions. Concerning the latter, the organization might have grown in size, so that patterns of communication, once successful, now break down at several points. Similarly, varying rates in the turnover in personnel can affect the degree of sharing of common goals and values of the institution. Compensatory adjustments for these and other disturbances within the educational community give rise to informal—or at least unintended—sets of relationships and distortions of the formal system. Our contention is not that such resulting forces are unimportant, but rather that their full significance can best be understood by a prior analysis of the organizational design originally intended for the school. Moreover, it is also suggested that the formal system itself will yield useful insights into the processes of transmission and creative alteration of cultural items within the school. Articulating with the focal educational community, moreover, are two additional and important segments of the total community: (1) the centers of higher learning; (2) class and ethnic family units from which the students are drawn. A third segment, the membership of which is recruited from the above categories, is the school board. Presumably board decisions reflect prevailing community attitudes and sentiments, inasmuch as the positions are elective ones. But since the board has direct face-to-face relationships with school executives and operates more in a leadership capacity, it can be considered as an independent force.

The school, looked at from our point of view, is no isolated organization; its operational structure is continually affected by outside environmental forces. It does not set its own goals, nor can it seek to implement them completely independently of other community agencies. The relationship between the educational community and the community as a whole, however, is reciprocal and interacting. The former is not to be visualized as responding unilaterally and automatically to outside forces which impinge upon it. It obviously must make most of its day-by-day decisions and operate *as if it were* an independent organization. Moreover, its explicit goals (to educate the young for certain purposes and in certain ways) are better and more fully understood by the interacting participants than by outside members of the community as a whole. The educational community has its own culture—albeit a dependent and not an autonomous one—including norms for behavior of participants and values underlying and supporting these norms. What happens in the operation of the school system, moreover, may also be expected to work back to affect the values, sentiments, and operations of the tangential segments with which it interacts, i.e., families and teacher-training centers.

Like any other organization, the educational community exhibits certain regularities in the behavior of its members in carrying on the functions of the group. By charting these regularities we can construct a *structure of alignments*, which will also indicate the varying *characteristics* of the different statuses, or positions within the structure. Individuals who occupy certain statuses, for example, are in a position formally to make decisions and to display authority that affects some or all individuals who occupy other statuses. Conversely, the statuses of some will have built into them few or no rights of leadership and decision-making affecting others. The personnel are

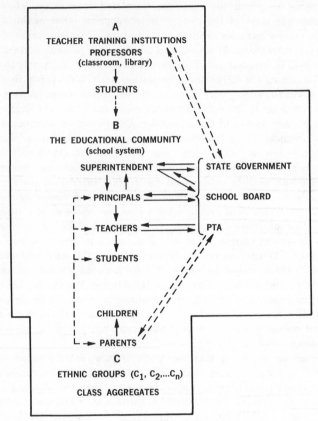

A
TEACHER TRAINING INSTITUTIONS
PROFESSORS
(classroom, library)
↓
STUDENTS
↓
B
THE EDUCATIONAL COMMUNITY
(school system)
SUPERINTENDENT ⇄ STATE GOVERNMENT
↓ ↑
PRINCIPALS ⇄ SCHOOL BOARD
↓
TEACHERS ⇄ PTA
↓
STUDENTS

CHILDREN
↑
PARENTS
C
ETHNIC GROUPS ($C_1, C_2,...C_n$)
CLASS AGGREGATES

LEGEND: 1. Capital letters, A, B, and C, stand for major collectivities
            in interaction and their cultures.
         2. Arrows signify the direction of authority and main powers
            for decision making.
         3. Dotted arrows indicate intercultural relationships.

Fig. 1. Acculturative factors affecting the transmission of cultural materials in the school system.

thus formally organized on a hierarchical (viz., administrator-teacher) and a co-ordinate (viz., teacher-grade) basis.

The school system, conceived as an educational community, has many structural and cultural features in common with other professional communities, viz., the therapeutic community (hospital). Because of the relatively low rank accorded to education as an end-value (in the sense of exciting the young about expanding the frontiers of knowledge), it also differs from the latter. To a considerable extent, education as a value is considered and treated as instrumental to the pursuit of other values (power, wealth, social position). Hence there is much possible ambiguity in the interpretation of its goals and methods within the greater locality. It has different kinds of attractions, interpretations, or repulsions for different segments of the community at large, as well as within the various levels of the educational community itself.

If one accepts these assumed formal characteristics of the school system and its tangential relationships as a point of departure, there are then several possible ways of collecting, organizing, and interpreting data about its operation. We are, of course, particularly interested in how its functioning affects what is taught, and how what is taught is communicated and assimilated. It is the writer's contention—really a guiding hypothesis—that the flow of what is taught is screened, interpreted, and reinterpreted at several levels as a consequence of the carrying networks of role relationships.

One possible model for visualizing the over-all process of transmission would be based upon a theory of organizations.[1] In view of the specific sociological orientation of this framework, and the fact that it only remotely draws upon or contributes to anthropological understandings of the cultural process, I mention organizational analysis only in passing. There are two relevant models, however, which are closely geared to phenomena of cultural transmission as collated and interpreted by anthropologists. One of these is the familiar process of acculturation. The other is a so-called Channels Theory proposed by Kurt Lewin in a study of food habits. In the remainder of this paper an attempt will be made to analyze each of these in terms of the several dimensions of the problem to which it draws special attention.

The acculturation model. For our purposes, we may define acculturation as culture change initiated by the continual interaction of two or more autonomous or quasi-autonomous communities,[2] and their cultures. Strictly speaking, the educational community is not autonomous, for it depends upon other collectivities for the recruitment of its personnel and, in part, for the carrying on of its policies. On the other hand, its teachers and administrative officers largely originate in distant localities, and its day-to-day operations are so extensively independent that we perhaps are justified in speaking of it as quasi-autonomous. It is in this sense that industrial concerns, hospitals, and similar social units have been treated as societies for the purposes of sociocultural analysis. We can therefore think of the school system as an organization standing in apposition to other collectivities to which it must adapt, and which in turn it seeks to influence. These multiple relationships can best be summarized by means of the preceding diagram (Fig. 1), which I shall attempt to explicate in some detail below.

In this schematic presentation only the formal structure of relationships is considered. Informal alignments, such as cliques and less permanent or unrecognized groups, perform important functions for shared needs of individuals arising from the inadequacies of the formal organizations. What these needs are and how urgently they are felt can best be evaluated, it is felt, by prior consideration of formally available channels of cultural transmission.

Each of the collectivities represented by capital letters (*A, B, C*) may be

---

[1]Philip Selznick, "Foundations of the Theory of Organization," *American Sociological Review*, VIII, 25–35; and Philip Selznick, *TVA and the Grass Roots: A Study in the Sociology of Formal Organization* (Berkeley: University of California Press, 1949).

[2]The term "community" is used here in its primitive sense of a group with common interests and common loyalties.

conceived as exhibiting separate subcultures. We are primarily concerned, then, with the way in which *what is meant to be imparted*—the "educational packages"[3]— to the student-child actually reaches him from its point of origin. The educational packages will be limited in our discussion to the formal contents (textbooks, classroom presentations and materials, teachers' manuals, reading assignments, etc.) originating primarily with the teachers of teachers. It is understood that many attitudes and biases—e.g., on sex morality and cleanliness—are consciously or unconsciously betrayed in the classroom as they are in the home, and that their impact is important to assess. In order to establish some control over the content of what is intended to be learned, I have arbitrarily restricted the problem to the transmission of formal materials, or explicit culture.

The way in which content is transmitted, e.g., from level A to level B, is conditioned theoretically by several factors, such as (1) the degree of consistency of the values in each of the subcultures; (2) the extent of agreement of the members of the collectivities on these values; (3) the kinds of role relations established between participants in the several subcultures (these have also been referred to as "intercultural role relations"),[4] (4) the perception of one's own roles and of content intended for transmission. Although no formal content originates in C, the latter is obviously significant as a third force in affecting what reaches the end products (children) and how it is perceived by them. The picture is structurally not unlike political third-force movements in which one national unit stands between two other cultural units and must react continuously to the pushes and pulls exerted upon it from both directions.

Teaching members of the academic community tend to share a distinctive set of values which set them apart from other segments of the population. Among other things, they look upon education not only as providing tools for the pursuance of other values, but also as contributing to long-range satisfactions for the individual, or as an end in itself. They are concerned also with innovating both upon the content of what is transmitted and upon the ways in which this can be done. The process is a continuous one, in that the implications of traditional practice and of innovations are constantly subject to assessment and re-evaluation. Hence the understanding which teachers of teachers will have, let us say, of Dewey's pragmatism in relation to education is based upon a broad intellectual grasp and upon viewing its operation in a wide variety of contexts. The same might be said of their grasp of learning theories, of cultural processes, of child growth phases, etc. If we can assume a rather extensive agreement upon values and understandings, at least among the professional educators of any given institution, we should still need to assess the degree of agreement between any two such training institutions. Failing that, we must confine our investigation to the members and teacher-products of specific centers.

In different geographical regions potential grade school personnel probably

---

[3] The term "educational packages" is not meant to imply unchanging objects or contents that pass ultimately to the child intact. As will become abundantly clear from the text, these packages may change their form and meaning for participants in each of the cultures involved; they may also have different adjustive functions for individuals at different levels and hence be used by them in different ways for varying ends. What is accented in A may be slight in B and in C, or vice versa. They may be identified as specific objects, utterances, and the like, but for the above reasons they become different things to varying categories of individuals who have anything to do with them.

[4] Social Science Research Council Summer Seminar on Acculturation, 1954. "Acculturation: An Exploratory Formulation," *American Anthropologist*, LVI, 973–1002.

come from relatively homogeneous sociocultural backgrounds, although this presumption requires verification. If this is the case, we might hypothesize (1) a rather high degree of consistency in their understandings of values built into the school system, and (2) broad similarities in the way they perceive their own roles and in the way they internalize their training experience. Should their own backgrounds prove to vary more, as they do in the population as a whole, we should expect the contrary to be the case.

In their role as students in the academic setting, school personnel (actual or potential) are brought into contact with only a part of the cultural reservoir of A, and for a limited period of time (or intermittently for limited periods of time). For this reason, and because they enter with a different set of attitudes and orientation to these ideas, they are apt to evaluate them from a limited (from the point of view of A) perspective. This is the nature of intercultural role relations, namely, that they involve the operation of processes of perceptual selectivity.

As a consequence of this selectivity—the adjustment of new learning to previously internalized patterns of thinking, doing, and believing—we can expect alterations in the educational packages by the time they reach the educational community (B). At the latter point, moreover, a similar process occurs whereby students, the ultimate objects of our inquiry, make further choices about what they learn, for what purposes, and with what commitments.

It is common knowledge that grade school children come from as wide a variety of family backgrounds as there are ethnic and class cultures, although this fact is often slighted in discussions about problems of mass education. One well-known study, at least, has indicated certain implications of primary and secondary school education in America for reinforcing the tendency to freeze the inferior occupational roles of ethnic and racial groups. Thus several technical high schools of California steered members of different minority groups—for example Negroes and Mexicans—into specific curricula and occupational training classes which lead to lower class levels of opportunity. Despite widespread opposition of parents, the vice-principal of one large school virtually segregated Mexican-American girls into domestic science courses which emphasize training in cooking, serving, and housework.[5]

In this case there were obvious conflicts of self-conception and conception of others between B and C. The actions of B members cannot be construed as direct applications of marginal participation in A, but rather as special interpretations of what they perceived and selected from it. One might equally wish to know something of the home stresses and motivations which prompt students to elect attending technical high schools in preference to general schools. Several other differences in value orientation and ratings between school and family cultures undoubtedly influence what content is presented in what ways, on the one hand, and how it becomes an object of interest by students, on the other. Among them are conceptions of time—of organizing and economizing time—and of "progressive" self-cultivation, of ranking talents, and so forth.

The cultural (value-interest) forces at work in the contact relations of B and C are several. First, parents and teachers have separate and direct influence upon the children. Second, parent-teacher relations are both formal (P.T.A.) and personal. The intended function of these meetings is to explicate the congruence

---

[5] W. L. Warner, R. J. Havighurst, M. L. Loeb, *Who Shall be Educated? The Challenge of Unequal Opportunities* (New York: Harper & Brothers, 1944).

and conflict of values between the home and schools as they are evidenced in the child's patterns of adjustment. (viz., living up to ideals of conformity in the classroom). How these relations and interpretations are further communicated to the child—and with what effect on his learning tendencies—is an interesting subject for further investigation. Do the mother and teacher, for example, make the same criticisms and appreciate the same strengths in the child, so that their subsequent interaction with him leads to formation of different attitudes and learning readiness? Or are there conflicting reactions and judgments, such that the child is reinforced in basic behavioral tendencies in the home, although these tendencies may already be prejudicial to internalizing educational content in the ways intended by the school?

The agreement or clash of explicit purposes between the school personnel and other public agencies, e.g., the school board, is similarly important to assess, as are consequences of classroom experiences (viz., reinforcement of generational conflict between children and parents). It becomes abundantly clear that an answer to the question, "How well does the school accomplish its objectives?" depends not only upon how well teachers and administrators know these objectives and techniques for achieving them; it depends also upon the dynamic interplay of value systems, interests, and shared self-concepts in contact among the several collectivities involved in the formal transmission process.

Although they have been omitted from this discussion, informal peer groups or relatively unstructured relations with age mates admittedly introduce yet another force—other patterns of values, interests, beliefs, attitudes—affecting the perceptual screening and selective learning of the child. Their very presence is evidence of certain lacks, unsatisfied desires, or frustrations within both home and school. It would therefore be desirable to investigate the areas wherein barriers are erected against acceptance of content transmitted within the school, and the effectiveness of leadership within these associations as well as upon the behavior of non-participant children.

The "channels" model. In 1942 Kurt Lewin directed a project designed to study food habits of a Midwestern town.[6] The general question which he asked was, "How does food get on the table and why?" The answer to this question was conceived in terms of broad and narrow social channels through which food items passed from the points of origin to the table at which they were consumed. The characteristics of the channels and kinds of linkage from one to another were conceptually refined in the process of analysis to account for the adventures of food products, particularly at critical points along the traveled routes. For this purpose, culture was treated as a repetitive process rather than the product of some past history and was conceptualized as being in a state of dynamic equilibrium. "A culture," states Lewin, ". . . is not a static affair but a live process, like a river which moves but still keeps a recognizable form."[7]

It is unnecessary to concern ourselves with the details of this specific study, but the frame of reference utilized may have some possible utility for a consideration of cultural transmission in American school systems. As we shall

[6]Kurt Lewin, "Psychological Ecology," in Dorwin Cartwright (ed.), *Field Theory in the Social Sciences* (New York: Harper & Brother, 1951), pp. 170–187.

[7]*Ibid.*, pp. 172–173.

see, the channels model is related to that of acculturation, and simply constitutes a slightly different—and to some, perhaps a more congenial—way of organizing and looking at the same phenomena. Instead of asking how food gets on the table, however, let us substitute the phrase, "How do educational packages get into the child and why." The student becomes the focal point of inquiry, and we then attempt to trace the channels through which understandings are molded and pushed in his direction, as he proceeds on his way to becoming a formally finished product. We are, in effect, dealing with the *learning habits* of the child, for they represent sets of behavioral tendencies which are created by a variety of converging forces (see Fig. 2).

The incorporation of new learning by a child is in large measure a product of past habit, what reaches him, the role relations (contexts) in which the flow of

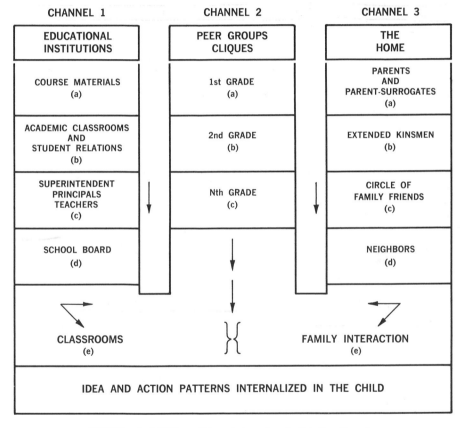

Fig. 2. Channels through which explicit culture reaches the child.

materials occurs, and the values and ways of perceiving which underlie these relations. The effectiveness of one or another channel for the child will depend partly on cultural values. Thus, in families where a high value is placed upon formal learning, greater application and better performance may be expected than in those where education as a value ranks low. In other words, children from families of the former type will make greater use of channel *1* than will children from those of the latter type. They may not only take maximum advantage of what is formally presented in the classroom, but may also seek to go beyond it. From the anthropological point of view we might say that the meaning and functions of learning in channels *1* and *2* are very similar, hence mutually reinforcing.

Many things can happen to the content of what is transmitted in any channel as it passes from one section to another on its way to the child. The "gates" are opened by one or more "gatekeepers." In the academic community the form and meaning of transmitted material enter channel *1* through the teachers of teachers. They control what enters, but not completely what happens to the materials since, as we have seen, student trainees may be expected to interpret cultural items in terms of the values they bring into the learning situation. If the ideology of educational training centers emphasizes the values of individual differences in, e.g., rates of learning, the trainee, on the other hand, may value the disciplinary aspects of the process; or else, he may look upon the ideology in special truncated ways. Merely "putting the packages" in the classroom or in the library will not guarantee that the trainee will retain either their meaning or their intended function in the section of the channel.

The teachers and administrators are the principal gatekeepers of what enters into section *B*—the school system itself. The "keys" which they use to open the gates are their own motivations, consisting in part of the *needs fulfilled* by their professional roles (commitment to education as a way of life, interest in child development, in power seeking, or simply as a job situation), and in part by values which they bring from other collectivities.

Meanwhile, similar processes are at work in channels *2* and *3*. The peer group channel is perhaps the most constant and consistent in the kinds of attitudes and action patterns which it instills. Participation itself in such informal relationships, as has been earlier suggested, is an index of unsatisfied needs or frustrations felt within the school system. Leaders are the gatekeepers and control entry of values and understandings shared by other members. The effectiveness of a teacher in having a student "digest" the understandings with which he is presented, we should expect, will vary inversely with the meaning which peer group ties have for the child.

In channel *3* there is similarly relatively high consistency of understandings between the sections through which cultural objects and patterns flow toward the child. Except for purposes of expediency it would be more accurate, also, to depict the sections as co-ordinate rather than linear, since the hierarchy of values, system of beliefs, and behavior patterns of parents or parent surrogates are usually reinforced by kinsmen and family friends, in so far as the latter have meaningful relations with the children. It is unnecessary for our purposes to review known processes of personality development, socialization, and learning which take place within the home and other primary groups outside the school. An awareness of how they dispose the child to respond to stimuli at the point of contact with the educational community is obviously critical, however, as the problem is viewed in this paper.

In the schools themselves the several social channels converge, thus creating a broad stream of *interacting* (not verging) forces. Congruence or conflict of values now can be studied in the interaction of community representatives (board members, school administrators, teachers, and parents). To continue with our analogy, there are several gatekeepers who control the widened and deepened channel; the flow of *educational* packages must compete with that of others. Explicit culture transmitted in the schools has a different weighting from understandings and orientations acquired outside them. At the final gate of this process, therefore, students will further select what they perceive as needed, desirable, anxiety-reducing, and rewarding in other ways. The classroom situation need not exhibit basic agreement with, e.g., family patterns, in order for maximum transmission to occur; it may accomplish the same end for some children because it is an outlet for rebellion against home constrictions and pressures. It would be desirable to ascertain in which kinds of family cultures the one case prevails and in which kinds the other, if indeed any regularity exists in the matter.

In brief, forms of understanding, their content and order of presentation, are blocked, truncated, or expanded, according to changing interpretations at each gate of the channel sections. Most gates require keys, and the keys are crucial in this process. They consist of cultural perception (viz., terms in which people think about education), values (motivations to acquire, subvert, emphasize, or underplay cultural items), and personality dispositions to behavior.

SUMMARY AND CONCLUSIONS

The foregoing discussion has centered upon the problem of how we can estimate what part of the educational packages—concrete understandings, norms of behavior, and attitudes toward new learning—is actually transmitted to the child in the school system, and with what effectiveness. The sociocultural factors that must be taken into consideration may be conceived a little differently, depending upon the particular frame of reference used for making and organizing observations about the process. In the one case, attention is focused upon the cultures of several communities in interaction: the characteristics of the cultures and the nature of role relations established at points of contact. Backgrounds and contact conditions between the several collectivities constitute the ground and figure, respectively, of the transmission of shared understandings. In the other case, the point of departure is the forces which permit cultural items to move in given forms and with intended meanings and functions through a variety of social agents until they reach the child.

In either event we are concerned essentially with the screening effect of values and learning habits, derived from multiple backgrounds, upon successive reinterpretations and/or reinforcements of behavior patterns. What minimal forms of concrete knowledge, ideology, and behavior norms do academic formulators try to impart to teachers and administrators in training? What functions or consequences for child development do they intend such elements to have as presented, in the light of their own theoretical understandings? To what extend are the intended functions understood and shared in like ways by trainees, and to what extent are they accepted in cult fashion or rejected entirely? The notion of "permissiveness" has certain meanings when interpreted intellectually and critically in terms of psychoanalytic theory (or in terms of some other developmental framework); it may be taken over and subsequently imparted quite differently by teachers with deeply ingrained constricted values. Or, again, teachers of teachers may seek in the same way to transmit concepts of personality adjustment based upon certain social psychological theories, only to have them interpreted and conveyed to the child as conformity toward the middle level.

We may expect the same processes to operate in relations of local agencies, families, and children with the educational community. How do values placed upon specific formal materials and upon education itself coincide or conflict? What rank order does the over-all activity have in each group? And, finally, what use does the child make of his school experience in integrating it with extraschool experiences—previously or currently instilled goal orientations, self-conceptions, and role relations? These are illustrative of the central questions which emerge from the above analysis. Answers to them will be possible only in the course of systematic, long-range research programs, in which comparative case studies of each phase of the process become available.

8-3   SUBURBANISM AND EDUCATION

Dan W. Dodson

Dr. Dodson has been professor of sociology at New York University since 1936. He has directed the Center for Human Relations and Community Studies for the past decade. He has directed numerous neighborhood area and school surveys and is a leading figure in America in the field of educational sociology. In this essay Dr. Dodson suggests that with the emergence of one-class suburban communities, parents and teachers must face the possibility of developing a generation of adults with "tunnel vision": the refusal to see or become involved in the problems of urban and rural society.

One of the profound changes of American life has been accomplished through population mobility in the past decade. It is the emergence of the suburb as the center of cultural dominance in America. By 1950 the 168 metropolitan areas of America contained 54 percent of the nation's population. It is estimated that they grew by 12 million in the next five years. Of this latter growth only 2,600,000 occurred in the inner cities themselves. The remainder was in the suburbs. The pattern of growth is also something to contemplate. New York City and its metropolitan area is the most startling example of the trend, but is different only in degree and not in kind to the others. Between 1950 and 1957 New York City proper lost a middle class white population about the size of Washington, D. C. (about 750,000) and gained an ethnically identifiable Negro and Puerto Rican population, heavily lower socio-economic status, about the size of Pittsburgh, Pennsylvania (650,000), and lost 100,000 population. The suburbs grew by staggering proportions. Long Island, i.e., Nassau and Suffolk Counties, gained about one and one-half million population. Modern technology, transportation, and a

---

From *Journal of Educational Sociology*, XXXII, No. 1 (September 1958), 2–7. © 1958 by the Payne Educational Sociology Foundation, Inc.; reprinted by permission of the Payne Educational Sociology Foundation, Inc.

high level of income have made it possible for more people than ever before to have the home in the country with a garden and sunshine for the children. Heretofore, the inner city dominated its suburbs, but today, what with its loss of middle class leadership and outgrowth of political boundaries, the city and hence the entirety of our society is coming under the cultural dominance of the suburban way of life.

WHAT DOES SUBURBANISM MEAN?

Here, then, is a rich field for sociological and educational research. If this hypothesis has merit it would behoove us to understand it in order to better interpret it to a citizenry, and to better cope with the problems it produces in its wake.

The following characteristics are suggestive of suburbanism as a phenomenon, and are here presented in order to stimulate discussion and research into their implications:

1. Suburbanism is a segregative way of life.

Communities are planned and built by contractors, who use mass production methods, and make the communities large enough to be self-contained. Hence they tend to be homogeneous as to race and socio-economic status. Many are homogeneous as to religious faith. Levittown, N. Y., which our Center for School and Community Service studied, was in 1947 six and one-half square miles of potato fields with 36 children in two class-rooms. In 1954 they had 15,000 houses sheltering 45,000 people with 12,500 children in school and more pre-school children than scholastics. All the families were beginning families. There were few if any grandparents in the community. All were white. Not a single family would have been classified by the census as non-white. All were within a very narrow range of each other as to income.

Levittown is the extreme. It has its smaller counterparts, however, in any one of several other communities in the suburbs. Bethpage, which we next studied, located next door to Levittown, was being built for slightly further advanced families, and instead of the Cape Cod and ranch style architecture was being developed with the more expensive "split level" type home. ("Split level" has become the symbol of upward mobility. Someone humorously remarked that there was a man driving around in a split level Mercury automobile.) Again the segregation as to ethnic background is practically complete. In New Rochelle, N. Y., which was also studied, the new communities in the north end of town were conservatively estimated to be 97 percent Jewish and all of upper socio-economic status.

2. Suburbanism is a homogeneous pattern of life.

Segregation naturally emphasizes cultural homogeneity. However, beyond such socio-economic and ethnic factors of homogeneity are those of the broader bases of culture. One person writing in *Cosmopolitan Magazine* remarked that the families in the development in which he lived were so much alike that had the wives gotten their husbands mixed at the P.T.A. meeting they couldn't have told the difference until they got them home and looked at their drivers' licenses.

Heretofore the suburban couple's interest revolved around the activities of the inner city. Children were brought to the museums and theatres in the inner city.

Today, with the decentralization of the shopping facilities, the television takes the place of the opera or the theatre. The Junior Leagues in some Westchester communities have recently attempted to produce live drama with their local talent, because their children have such small opportunity to see "live" acting. Interest tends to pivot around local neighborhood institutions and concerns. Hence the church becomes a social center in a different sense to what was the traditional pattern. Neighbors' communal concerns are those of husbandry such as keeping up the lawn, getting the garage painted, the attic expanded, or the automobile laundered.

3. Suburbanism is a fragmented way of life.

Perhaps all living is fragmented, but suburbanism accentuates the pattern. Living in segregated, homogeneous neighborhoods is, of course, fragmentation. In addition, however, there are numerous other aspects suggested. One of the first is the fragmentation of family life occasioned by children living in communities where fathers all commute, and their contacts with their children are largely those of the weekend. Then there is the fragmentation occasioned by the separation of children from their larger families, *grosse familie* in sociological terminology. There is the fragmentation occasioned by the fact that political boundaries are completely chaotic. A neighborhood may be in one school district, another recreation district, still a third fire or sewerage unit, and communal programs such as Red Feather are not related to any particular official unit of government. Then there is the separation of industry from community. Most people migrated to the suburbs to escape noise and dirt of industrial proximity. Children often have no conception of the industrial life of the country because of this type of fragmented living. Another aspect of fragmentation is the orientation of the youth to one age group. Levittown is primarily a beginning family community. As the children get older and the parents get more economic status, the tendency is to move to the community with the larger houses. Thus the grouping tends to be that of peers in so far as age is concerned. In planning the school facilities for Levittown as against Bethpage we allowed proportionately more early childhood facilities in the former and more secondary school facilities in the latter. Our greatest miscalculations were that we did not accentuate this trend enough. What this means as to "peer group" domination of the child as he is reared in these "family stage" oriented developments is yet to be assessed. Another dimension of the same phenomenon is what it means to growth and development of children to be reared in developments where there is this "built in" type of mobility. In other words the size of the houses almost guarantees that if a resident has a larger than two bedroom family and economic resource enough to afford it, he will move in the middle of his family developmental stage. The other facet of it is, also, that when the children leave home there is almost the guarantee that the parents will also move from the suburbs back to the inner city. This type of mobility accentuates what is already the American trend of mobility. How to gear education to such mobility is a problem scarcely recognized by school systems at the present time.

4. Suburbanism tends toward conformity.

One aspect of suburbanism is its middle class orientation. "Keeping up with the Joneses" is a familiar part of its behavior pattern. The preoccupation tends to be with how one's status compares with that of the neighbors. Children are pressured to make good in school, not because of academic curiosity, but in order not to embarrass the family. Suburban schools are increasingly faced with the problem of children taking courses not to meet needs, but in order to get in the right colleges. Some join extra-curricular activities not because of interest, but because of desire to have it on record when they apply to college. In many such schools there has developed a climate of anti-intellectualism which is undoubtedly a hostility to working under such pressure.

If proof were needed of the extent to which this type of conformism has pervaded America the Jacob study of college values amply documents it. Of course there is no proof that suburban children are any more conforming than others, but certainly here is an area for study.

5. Suburbanism has "built in" patterns of educational inequality.

A few illustrations from New York City's suburbs will suffice to indicate what is meant. At the peak of their enrollment in Levittown, barring a mass exodus, the community will have a tax base of less than $2,500 per child on which to draw for community services. The reason is obvious. There are no industries in the town. The only non-residential property on which to draw for taxes is that contained in a shopping center. Since the houses are modestly priced and the families attracted to them are of the relatively high cost social welfare type, i. e., they have many children to be educated, and many recreational and other welfare cost needs, the services are meagre. The average child in the average community in New York where the assessment ratio to value is the same as that of Levittown has a tax base of $15,000 for such services.

In contrast the entire county of Westchester has built few residences since the war that sell for less than $18,000 to $20,000. Hence the young families who are just starting, who have the need for services, are either forced to go to the slums of these communities, or else go to the Levittowns of the metropolis.

Another phenomenon is represented in the case of Mahwah, N. J. Here the city fathers signed a contract with the Ford Motor Company for a plant that would employ 5,000 people. As soon as the contract was negotiated they passed an ordinance that no more houses could be built in this northern New Jersey suburb on sites less than one acre in size. This meant that no homes would be erected to sell for less than $20,000. It meant that none of the workers would be able to build in the community. While the community had its tax rolls increased by 50% they will have none of the responsibility for the education and other welfare costs of the families of the people who work there. Some other community must shoulder that burden. The people who live in the community, and commute in large numbers to the inner city, meet the people who work there twice a day as they come and go on the highways between Mahwah and the inner cities of Newark and New York City.

6. Suburbanism is heavily dependent upon "snob appeal" for its stability.

Westchester affords a good example. While studying the racial imbalance in the school system it was clear that such a community, 85% dependent upon residential taxes for support of community services, could not afford too many welfare type families. Their older section had become the bedrooms for the domestics who worked in the surrounding communities of Scarsdale and Pelham. There were approximately 3 women over 14 years of age for every 2 men in the Negro group in the community. The only appeal the community has is the deluxe appeal of its neighborhood schools. Property values would tumble precipitously should this be lost. Hence the board of education had built super-deluxe schools in the upper class neighborhoods, and left the three schools in the low income areas—mostly Negro and Italian background populations—to their own devices in inferior programs as well as facilities.

It is because of this preoccupation with status that the violence erupted in Levittown, Pennsylvania, when the Negro family moved in there in August of 1957.

WHITHER VALUES

As a last issue which concerns this new type of living the question of values is paramount. Can such privilege be enjoyed without attendant concerns for others who are likewise segregated and relegated to inner city ghettoes, or is the sense of alienation which the theologians are beginning to write about the inevitable consequence of the enjoyment of such preferment? Does it make much difference what the schools do to try to produce scientists and other pioneers in behavioral science if the milieu in which the youth are reared is centered on "things," i.e., deep freezers, automobile tail fins, and other symbols of status, and on catching the 8:18 in the morning rather than centered on ideas? Can the dynamic with which to deal with today's world's problems come from a society whose cultural dominance is the conservation of a socio-economic position? It is hoped that these topics here discussed will stimulate further examination of this phenomenon in order that its blessings, which are many, will not be cancelled out by the liabilities.

8-4   THE ROLES OF THE TEACHER

Jean D. Grambs

Jean D. Grambs is associate professor of education at the University of Maryland. She has authored and co-authored many books in education. Her interest in the socio-cultural foundations is reflected in her *Sociology and Education: A Book of Readings* (1965 with J. Raths) and her most recent book, *Schools, Scholars and Society*. In this essay she describes a community's expectations of the teachers in its schools.

In this ... [paper] effort will be made to identify those role-expectations of teachers held by students, parents, the community, and the school itself. Suggestions will be made relative to the extent to which the teacher's role perception produces

---

From *The Teacher's Role in American Society*, Lindley J. Stiles (ed.), pp. 73–93. Copyright © 1957 by Harper & Brothers; reprinted by permission of Harper & Row Publishers, Incorporated.

conflict, low professional morale, and—what may be socially tragic—an institution that changes remarkably little over the decades.[1]

X   In analyzing the attributes desirable for candidates entering the teaching profession, a distinction has been made between "the teacher as a person" and "the person as a teacher."[2] In the discussion here, we are primarily concerned with "the person as a teacher" and the way in which teaching determines how he will feel and act within the institutional framework of the public schools.

How does role behavior develop? What does the teacher do? What is the social function of teaching? When one lists all the possible roles of the teacher two main categories emerge. One category refers to the *teacher as director of learning*. This includes all those activities and concepts that are related to teaching as an *activity* or a *process*. The other category refers to the social function of teaching, the *teacher as mediator of the culture*. Under this category are included those roles that relate to the public nature of the teacher's job, the stake of society in teaching as an aspect of cultural continuity.[3]

THE TEACHER AS DIRECTOR OF LEARNING

Any adult with a group of children acquires certain role relationships that are inherent in the situation itself; parent surrogate, source of authority, giver of affection and punishment, protector, or guide in unknown territory. The teacher, too, partakes of these generalized adult roles with respect to children, because the public school teacher is always older—the adult—in the classroom situation. But for the teacher as a teacher, there are certain more specific roles that the teaching process implies. These are considered below.[4]

1. *The teacher as judge of achievement.* One of the most pervasive elements in determining the relationship between teacher and pupil is the fact that the pupil is being judged by the teacher. Merely observing the differences in relationship and behavior between a child in a classroom situation and in a "Y" youth group sharpens the point. In the one circumstance, the child sees the adult as one who gives "A's" or "F's" and is therefore to be feared, hated, or loved, depending on the degree of success that the child can attain. In the "Y Club," on the other hand, the child views the adult primarily as a helper and adult friend.

The teacher evaluates performance, and by so doing helps to establish certain

---

[1] There is not room here for an extended discussion of role definition. See for example: Willard Waller, *The Sociology of Teaching* (New York: Wiley and Sons, 1932), pp. 321–337; Ralph Linton, *The Cultural Background of Personality* (New York: Appleton-Century-Crofts, Inc., 1945); T. R. Sarbin, "Contributions to Role-Taking Theory, I & II," *Psychology Review*, LVII, 255–270, and LIX, 11–22. An interesting approach from clinical psychology: David C. McClelland, *Personality* (New York: The Dryden Press, 1951), pp. 289–332.

[2] L. G. Thomas, Stanford University, School of Education, mimeographed statement.

[3] See a similar division in W. B. Brookover, "The Relation of Social Factors to Teaching Ability," *Journal of Experimental Education*, XIII, No. 4 (June 1945).

[4] For other role categories and analyses see: Ruth Cunningham and others, *Undeustanding Group Behaviour of Boys and Girls* (New York: Teachers College, Columbia University, 1951), pp. 141–152; Fritz Redl and William Wattenberg, *Mental Hygiene in Teaching* (New York: Harcourt, Brace and Company, 1951), pp. 235–260; Lucien B. Kinney, *Measure of a Good Teacher* (San Francisco: California Teachers Association, 1952).

learning and behavior goals. The teacher who values obedience may tend to judge compliant students as "better," and may give them higher grades; another teacher may value the ability to argue logically; still another may value perfection in solving assigned problems, or neatness of written papers. Since there are few commonly accepted standards regarding what is to be valued and rewarded, each teacher must decide—and usually is unconscious of this process—as to which are valuable pupil achievements and which are not.

As students and parents gain insight into the role of the teacher as judge, recognize its fallibility and its power, one is not surprised to see frustration, contempt, fear, and anxiety influencing the relations of some students and parents to some teachers, as well as contentment, trust, and admiration where the teacher is a wise and beneficent judge.

2. *The teacher as a person who knows.* "Knowledge is power," said Francis Bacon. This is still a key phrase in the analysis of the role of the teacher. He stands as a gatekeeper.[5] He decides what information and skills are important and accordingly lets these selected items through to students. The knowledge that the teacher has of the community, of the children, of the subject matter, is a vital factor in what is explored in the classroom. He selects from a vast body of material that which must be taught; he decides, also, a minimum which must be learned.

As students climb the academic ladder, their respect for the knowledge of teachers changes. The child in the primary grades views the teacher with awe and respect; the teacher knows so much! By the time the student reaches junior and senior high school he has seen that the teacher "knows" a subject field, but in the view of the student this same teacher may know woefully little about the "important" things in life. During the adolescent years academic knowledge may seem least useful. As the student proceeds to college his perspective shifts and he sees that both academic and practical knowledge can be equally important. Since most of the population does not go on to college, the citizen's view of the role of general academic knowledge is the one he took with him when he left high school—often unflattering.

3. *The teacher as one who keeps discipline.* All children expect an adult in their immediate vicinity to interfere when law and order are being violated. In the classroom the disciplinary functions of the teacher are more pervasive, and they differ in quality from those exercised by the ordinary adult with children. . . .

The institutionalizing of disciplinary techniques is a means of ensuring their nonpersonal quality. The discipline the teacher exercises is seen by him as a task performed for the sake of the student. If there is no discipline, students cannot learn. Therefore individuals must be controlled for their own sake.

Both the recipient and the source of disciplinary measures may develop extensive resentment of each other, out of which may come hostility and counter-attack. With a moderately skilled teacher and reasonably compliant students the conflict does not flare into the open. But it may be a source of tension even when overt hostilities are avoided. To live thus for six to eight hours a day for the working year, for a career life of twenty-five years, is bound to produce some compensatory behaviors. One observes

---

[5] The concept of the "gatekeeper" function is well described in B. O. Smith, W. O. Stanley, and J. H. Shores, *Fundamentals of Curriculum Development* (Yonkers, New York: World Book Company, 1950), pp. 682–683.

added sharpness of manner, a cynical view of human nature—particularly in the young—and often a thinly disguised hatred of the teaching situation itself. These behaviors may result from the definition of the teacher's role as one who keeps discipline.

4. *The teacher as one who gives advice, receives confidences.* The child looks upon adults as potential helpers. Since the teacher is a constant element in the world of the child, the helper possibilities are ever present. This role has more overtones of the affectional relationship than any other.

When the teacher accepts the confidences of students, he enters the world of the young person and takes on the role of ally and protector.

As a receiver of confidences, the teacher then may find himself in opposition to parents, against whom many of the complaints of adolescents are lodged. He may also find himself in conflict with his roles as judge and disciplinarian. It is hard to assign a failing grade to a student whose intimate problems one has listened to sympathetically. The student receiving a failing grade may assume that the teacher is not *really* a friend and did not appreciate his problem. The result may be rejection of the teacher by the pupil. Teachers, to avoid such conflicts of roles, may attempt to keep a cold and impersonal barrier between themselves and their students.

The role of confidant is further complicated by factors of personal preference. The mores and values accepted implicitly by the teacher will make some students more sympathetic to him than others. Since he is not trained as a therapist or counselor, he will be able to listen objectively only to certain kinds of exploits and not others.

5. *The teacher as creator of a moral atmosphere.*[6] In the classroom the teacher identifies for the student what is right and wrong in the institutional context. As creator of a moral atmosphere, he makes it clear that cheating is wrong, that the use of obscene words is bad, or that flirting in class is in poor taste. The students expect the teacher to so identify certain acts. Many of the ideas of what is good or bad behavior are often institutional in the sense that they are external to the students and depend on institutional vigilance to be enforced. Likewise the teacher establishes what is good in terms of compliant behavior, defines "acceptable" demonstrations of initiative and "fair play." Finally the teacher establishes what is expected in interpersonal relationships. He establishes a hierarchy of groups of people.

Conflict in moral valuations may occur as a result of differences arising from social class learnings. Other conflicts between teacher concepts of "good" and "bad" groups, individuals, and behavior will derive from the philosophy of education held by a given teacher.

In recent years we have seen a tremendous expansion of the social life officially sponsored by the public school. As such activities multiply, the moral burden on the school personnel becomes greater. Teachers chaperone numerous dances, formal and informal, take students on ski trips, accompany groups for a week at the school camp, or act as sponsor for class and club parties. The etiquette of social situations, the permissible limits to juvenile exuberance, must sooner or later be established by the school authorities. It is easy to see why the community looks with special attention at the behavior of the teacher.

---

[6] John L. Childs, *Education and Morals* (New York: Appleton-Century-Crofts, Inc., 1950); R. Bruce Raup, "The Moral Dimensions in Education," *Educational Theory,* I (May 1951), 35–40.

6. *The teacher as a member of an institution.*[7] Since we are here concerned with the roles of the teacher in the *process* of teaching, we must recognize that the role of the teacher in the classroom is closely related to that he plays in the institution of which he is a part.

Each work type and work situation creates its own culture. The teacher finds his role peculiarly defined because of the nature of the school as an institution. The school establishes appropriate ways of acting on the job in terms of the other employees.

The educational process is unique as a work situation. Prior work experience does *not* fit a teacher for easy adjustment to the school work situation. The fact that there are lengthy and continuous discussions in the professional literature of education as to what constitutes a "democratic" administration-teacher relationship points to one of the contradictions inherent in the situation. Teachers, unlike other workers, do not have a well-developed sense of "the boss." Some teachers, however, do desire strong, often paternalistic, leadership from the administrators with whom they work. How can this expectation be reconciled with mature professional behavior?

The teacher's role behavior is in part determined by his position in the institutional hierarchy. One important functionary in this situation is the administrative personnel. The teacher looks to the administrator for direction. The expected relation between principal and teacher is that of one who gives orders and one who receives orders. Many teachers prefer a "strong" principal, finding it more satisfying to be told what to do than to participate in decision-making themselves. In addition, teachers consider the principal as part of the disciplinary structure of the school—one to be invoked when students defy the limited authority of the teacher.[8]

The principal's word is most powerful in the hiring and firing process. In the eyes of the teacher he is to be placated, cajoled, manipulated. The role of the teacher in relationship to the principal may undergo a change when tenure is achieved. Teachers with tenure sometimes behave as though they were trying to "get even" with administrators. The administrator has power; when the teacher has tenure he too has power—power to ignore an administrative request, to foment community criticism of the administrator, to organize cliques in the faculty who may effectively oppose administrative policies. Many administrators fear and resent older teachers whose power is reinforced by tenure, by length of service, and by outspokenness in faculty meetings. On the other hand, the principal will find that numerous teachers look upon him as a father-confessor, that he must perform a counseling and guidance function for the less mature, more dependent members of his staff.

A final word on the institutional role of the teacher: He is expected to be devoted to the traditions of the school, and a loyal supporter of "the way things are done at dear old Union High." School traditions are to be respected even when they go contrary to personal beliefs or good educational practice. In some systems loyalty to the school is of such importance that careers are ruined and jobs lost by seeming defalcation in devotion.

---

[7] B. O. Smith *et al.*, 1950, pp. 635–640. Max R. Goodson and Gale E. Jensen, *Formal Organization in School Systems* (Minneapolis, Minnesota: Burgess Publishing Company, 1956). See for analysis of school as a social system and the dynamics of change in the institution.

[8] An interesting observation on the necessity for a hierarchy of discipline authority is contained in Fritz Redl and David Wineman, *Controls From Within* (Glencoe, Illinois: The Free Press, 1953), pp. 214, 224.

Summary

We have looked at the kinds of things expected of the teacher in the *process of teaching*. The role expectations are varied and conflicting. While the teacher judges achievement, keeps discipline, establishes a moral atmosphere, at the same time he is confidant and guide, giver of advice and affection. He must have knowledge, and must know how to impart it to individuals of varying talent and interest. He has great power to promote or fail, to facilitate access to knowledge or to withhold it, to establish feelings of comradeship and acceptance, or competition and segregation based on race, intellect, finances, behavior. He is both weak and powerful in the elaborate hierarchy of the school.

These roles provide an almost bewildering assortment of possible behaviors to the teacher. Which shall he choose? How shall he choose? The *final* determinant of which of the classroom roles the teacher emphasizes and which he rejects depends on expectations of parents and the community.

THE TEACHER AS MEDIATOR OF THE CULTURE[9]

The roles of the teacher in this category come primarily from the social function of education. Each culture creates different characterizations of teachers.

The ways in which the community conceives of teachers determine to a large extent the roles he will play. The person who is identified as the "good" teacher may or may not actually be able to "teach." Administrators, guided by community opinion, may tend to select teachers on the basis of factors that have no demonstrable relationship to effective classroom instruction.[10] The teacher has, in years gone by, also experienced the cultural definition of the teacher, for as a student he developed a complicated set of attitudes and anticipations whenever he met or talked with his own teachers.

In the first section we looked at the teacher primarily from the viewpoint of the learner; now we are concerned with the view of the teacher taken by the larger community outside the school—the already schooled adults.

1. *The teacher as a member of the middle class.* The teacher is expected to demonstrate all the virtues of the middle class and avoid all of its sins. He must abide by middle-class standards of behaviors and economic beliefs.

He is considered "soft," clean, religious. Such middle-class virtues are closely associated with the teacher role. He is not thought of as aggressive physically, and socially does not become a competitor for community leadership. For the individual who views teaching as a pathway of upward mobility—as many do—it is essential that he disown himself from the symbols of his own class origin if it is other than middle-class.

2. *The teacher as a model for the young.* The continuous association of the teacher with young people impels the community to invoke the teacher as a standard setter. It is the wish of parents that teachers be adequate to this role. Parents actually have encouraged youngsters to use teachers as models rather than other adults. The

---

[9]See "The Freedom of the Public School Teacher," Washington, D.C., Research Division, National Education Association, mimeographed, August 1951.

[10]W. B. Brookover, 1945.

teacher is the best and most available ally the parent has. At the same time the teacher in his role as confidant may find himself unable to maintain his neutrality and may side with the child *against* the parent; thus the parent can never be sure that the teacher will be a satisfactory surrogate for himself.

3. *The teacher as an idealist.* Because of better education and his special function as a model for the young the teacher is clearly one whose allegiance is to a better way of life than most people can live. He may be considered, therefore, not "practical." He understands theories, not reality. The role of the idealist is often negatively valued by the public. The American emphasis on material success, on being practical and hardheaded, does not provide much room for the teacher.

4. *The teacher as a pioneer in the world of ideas—the teacher as radical.* Closely related to the role of the idealist, and often scarcely distinguishable from it, is the role of the teacher as one-who-is-ahead-of-the-times.

The community thinks that the teacher may be tempted to consider new ways of doing things—revolutionary or radical. The rash of oaths for teachers in recent years is symptomatic of the fear of the teacher-as-radical.[11] The public is seeking some means of controlling the teacher, of keeping him within the bounds of conservative middle-class concepts and policies.

5. *The teacher as a person of "culture."* The teacher is frequently identified with the middle-class culture, particularly its less materialistic manifestations. One of these is an interest in art, music, literature. The teacher has been "abroad" in his education; he is cosmopolitan while the community is provincial. His interests are national and international while the average community participant is more concerned with local affairs.

As a person of "culture," he is also a cultured person. Such a role causes some to feel uneasy in the presence of teachers. As a person of "culture" he has an attractiveness especially to certain high school students. The students who like school are apt to enjoy talking about music, literature, or travel with this teacher. It is to him that they turn in seeking advice on where to go to college. On the other hand, this same evidence of "culture" may make it difficult for students without such interests to approach the teacher so identified.

There is also some ambivalence of the community toward the teacher as a person of "culture." He will be welcome in the community's "little symphony" and will be expected to stimulate boys and girls to take an interest in music and the arts; but this teacher will also be judged to be too "refined" for some circles.

6. *The teacher as participant in community affairs.* The teacher in the community is expected to be interested and helpful but not conspicuously out in front. The teacher belongs at the second layer of community life—taking minor leadership roles: teaching Sunday School; leading some youth group; contributing to charitable drives; belonging to lodges or service clubs; and supporting community-wide programs.

The teacher was once considered an important part of the community's activities and one who did not participate in them was severely criticized. Today's teacher may or may not participate. Often the teacher by his own training has an

---

[11] E. W. Reutter, *The School Administrator and Subversive Activities* (New York: Columbia University Press, 1951).

already well-developed concept of community service. Choosing to be a teacher may be one manifestation of a concept of service. Thus it is not unusual to see teachers seeking ways of becoming identified with the community and meeting community indifference or apathy.

The role as participant in community affairs is apt to be one in which the teacher wishes for more community recognition than he gets. It is less apt today to be a demand made by the community on a reluctant teacher. A *principal* or *superintendent* may move in the upper power circles of a community; the average teacher is expected to keep a more modest role.

7. *The teacher as stranger in the community.*[12] When young teachers start to hunt for a first job, they are often advised not to return to their own home town. Some of their own early teachers, still active there, may view the returning ex-student as a kid rather than a peer. Most teachers find their jobs in new communities.

It takes years of living in a new environment to feel at home in it. Often teachers do not stay long in a job, particularly the first one. The high turnover at the elementary grades means that most of these teachers leave the profession or the community after only a few years. Others who remain in the community develop their own circle of friends, usually among other teachers and individuals in allied professions or avocations. When finally they feel they can call the teaching community home they find that they are in a special part of that community—in it but not of it.

At one time the concern only of the select, "teacher" was duly entertained by the families of the local "400." Today, in this era of mass education, the teacher is the jealous property of all. He therefore is the special concern of none.

The teacher, too, in a more profound sense, must be objective about the community. He must see it as both typical and unique; as a manifestation of the larger culture; and as a locality with problems and concerns of its own. As a student of community affairs for the purpose of guiding young people, the teacher's role as a stranger is a great aid; at the optimum, he behaves as the participant-observer of community processes.

8. *The teacher as the person en route.* For many teachers any given community is merely a way-point. For the men teachers, the young ones in particular, there is hope of moving up the professional ladder.

The route for many women in the educational institution is from maidenhood to marriage to home and out of the profession. The tremendous turnover of younger women teachers in the grades is one of the perennial problems of administrators. Since most of the women who enter education hope to be married, and since a good proportion of them succeed, those who remain several years either are constantly on the alert for a mate or are weighing the marriage potential of another position.

Only after a number of years does the unmarried woman teacher resign herself to her professional celibacy; often an unwilling prisoner of her job. The years of watchful waiting for a more appealing status than that of teacher leave their mark. The unmarried woman teacher comes only lately and reluctantly to accept her role in the community. She tends, even after hope for a marriage is gone, to return to summer schools in far parts of the nation and to go on trips or "conducted tours" to

---

[12] George Simmel, *The Sociology of George Simmel,* translated and edited by K. H. Wolff (Glencoe, Illinois: The Free Press, 1950), pp. 420–428.

foreign countries;[13] in the eyes of the community she is more cosmopolitan than before—in her own soul she is forever seeking a way out.

9. *The teacher as a public servant.* To whom does education belong? And then to whom does the educator belong?

One of the more controversial aspects of the teacher's role is how much control over his behavior, ideas, tenure, and technical skills should be exercised by the body politic. Of all the professions, that of the teacher is most carefully and continually under extensive and intensive public scrutiny.

In recent years with the tremendous pressure on school districts because of increased population and a building backlog, the people have been asked with monotonous regularity to vote more money for education. Thus the attention of the citizen is now continually directed towards the schools by the very nature of the present school crisis.

Happy to have a focus for both his frustrated citizenship and his personal anxieties, John Q. Public is invading the schools. He is visiting classrooms, attending school board meetings, noting the textbooks distributed to students. The teacher more than ever before is being reminded that education is a public trust and he is a servant of the public.

This is not a particularly comfortable role. The public has many faces, many voices. To which shall the teacher respond? Can he be true to *his* concept of good teaching if this is a pattern repugnant to some power group in the community? Is the teacher or the community *right*?

Summary

The roles of the teacher as mediator of the culture are many and contradictory. The generalizations presented here must, of course, be modified in any given situation. Rural and urban emphasis will differ in terms of the expectations of teachers. Variations will exist in socio-economic class, community history, and the traditions of the school. The role behaviors defining the community's expectancies and attitudes are therefore subject to considerable individual interpretation. The factors in one situation will stress some role behaviors and be apathetic to others. But since teachers move from community to community, success requires a nimble personality that can shift and adapt role behavior according to differing community expectations and valuations.

SOME SPECIAL AREAS OF ROLE CONFLICT AND ROLE CONFUSION

"How am I supposed to know what to do?" is one of the recurrent plaints of the beginning teacher. The variety of role expectations leaves them confused and uncertain. Some of this confusion arises from the contradictory expectations met in practice.

1. *The teacher viewed by the parent.* While the parent in part shares the role expectations of the community, he also is intimately identified with his own child. The

---

[13] How many times have we seen in the literature of travel abroad the mention of the two maiden school teachers as more or less stock characters?

ambitions he holds for his own child may be thwarted or facilitated by the teacher. The teacher's gatekeeper function, for example, becomes most crucial to the many parents who have well-articulated ambitions for their children.

Typically, the parent presents school to the child in the terms described by the research of Stendler and Young:

> . . . the school has been presented as a socializing agency. The child has been told that he must behave himself in school, must mind the teacher, must be quiet, must not interrupt, that the teacher takes the place of his mother and is the boss. In some cases, the teacher has been held over his head as a kind of veiled threat, "You'll have to change your ways when you start first grade," "Wait till the teacher sees you acting like that. You won't do it long." Most parents, however, try to present the teacher as a kind of benign socializing agent, "Be nice in school and everyone will be nice to you." "Like the teacher and she'll like you" is the gist of what some children are told.[14]

Probably the parental view of the teacher will be more positive as people who have had more positive school experiences become parents. Today's school generation by and large likes and approves of school. School is less likely to be a repressive, traumatic experience. The rich offerings of the high school, particularly the emphasis on the many social and extracurricular activities, have meant that more and more youngsters stay in school. They stay because they enjoy it.

Another contribution to mutual understanding has been the development of parent-teacher conferences in the lower grades. Teachers are helped to gain insight into the parental role and parents are given aid in seeing what goes on in the school. A fine relationship can develop when teachers recognize parental needs and expectations, and are skilled in working with parents. But it is also true that many teachers fear parents and deal awkwardly with the new human relations problems.

Many parents feel keenly their own insecurity in the parental role. Children, with the sadistic wisdom of the young, have been known to invoke the teacher as the person far more adequate, lovable, and important than the parent. As Gorer says:

> . . . the child can always find in the school teacher an authority who can nearly always be successfully opposed to the parents. The parents keep this acknowledged rival and superior under the closest scrutiny, demanding in her private life standards of conduct and moral rectitude far higher than those they apply to themselves or their neighbours.[15]

Parental expectations and involvements may conflict with community expectations. On the one hand, the values enunciated in verbalizations of American life drama emphasize equality and brotherhood. On the other hand, the parent may find his community unsympathetic to these goals. He will see the school as a potent social force for one side or the other.

The parent seeks and asks for the support of the school and the teacher. He con-

---

[14] Celia B. Stendler and Norman Young, "The Beginning of Formal School Experience," in R. G. Kuhlen and G. G. Thompson, eds., *Psychological Studies of Human Development* (New York: Appleton-Century-Crofts, 1952), pp. 415–422.

[15] Geoffrey Gorer, *The American People* (New York: W. W. Norton & Company, 1948), p. 99.

siders the teacher as an ally. But the teacher, from the child's vantage point, is often thought of as champion and friend. The dilemma is a sharp one. Teachers often find their role as one of liaison between child and parent, interpreting each to the other. This kind of bridging of the generations is one of the basic contributions that teachers can make in supporting stable family situations.

The charge made by some school critics that today's education is "soft" derives in part and receives its pervasive and uncritical support from the anxieties of many people over their own success as parents. Where adults see youngsters blithely ignoring the presciptions of the community, talking "fresh" to the helpless parent, flirting with all the dangers inherent in hot-rods and "the gang," they are inclined to look abroad for a scapegoat. Naturally some think the schools are to blame.

The teacher faces a bewildering role expectation; he feels parental pressure to guide and counsel the child, to take into consideration *his* peculiar personal and family needs—to make the school situation as good and friendly and successful as possible. For such efforts the teacher may find himself the target of bitter complaint. Thus, he may wonder in despair what parents do want.

2. *Differences in role expectations as a function of community, neighborhood, and region.* The roles described in this chapter are generalizations of community expectations. Like any general picture, they define areas of behavior. But within each area the specific kinds of behavior vary greatly. Different groups—ethnic, racial, socio-economic—have differing expectations of the role of the teacher. Children will bring to school different behavior patterns, which in turn pressure the teacher to become stricter, or be more permissive, to emphasize rote learning, or develop "creativity," to extend instruction in cleanliness training, or lead discussions on sex education. Movement from community to community involves often this same need to adjust role behavior. In one community the teacher may be left strictly alone. In a neighboring community he may be invited to take a Boy Scout Troop, teach a Sunday School class, or to join the American Legion. Such a shift in community role expectations can come as a distinct shock.

The gap between community expectancies and the role of the teacher provided by the teacher training institution may plunge the neophyte into a soul struggle from which he emerges cynical and defensive. He is only too apt to yield to community pressures to accept the traditional roles reserved for teachers.

The confusion as to what *are* the teacher's community roles is probably the one most accessible to resolution today because of the social forces now at work. No place is so remote in the United States that the radio cannot be heard; soon TV will be almost as available; every crossroad has its movie house. Since these media usually portray middle-class values in a middle-class urban culture one can expect a general smoothing out of social class and regional differences in role expectations. Variations among individuals or communities will of course still remain, and these will always determine which roles of the teacher will be rewarded and emphasized.

3. *The education of the teacher and role expectations of the community.* Many of the things that the community defines as "the teacher" are of the nature of myths. Generations ago it could be more truly said that the teacher was a person of "culture." He had read more and better books than others, and he valued the arts and literature above more practical and immediate pursuits. Now the teacher is rarely a real intellectual. He may be as scornful of cultural activities as his neighbors. His knowledge

of the world of ideas is often narrow. Today's teacher may be thought to be a prototype of the middle class. That he is a teacher is so often accidental. Thus the teacher as a person often finds himself bewildered and just a bit disturbed when his friends in the community, as their highest form of praise, say, "Why you aren't a bit like a teacher!" He knows he does not fit into the traditional stereotype of the teacher; but he may wonder if some expect him to be.

It becomes a professional problem when the community conserves in its role expectations of teachers a type that was real about fifty or seventy years before. At that time there were fewer schools and fewer teachers. It is probable that those persons who were drawn to teaching were, by a process of cultural selectivity, those who could fit into community expectations.

Those who enter teaching today have developed a view of teaching as *a job*. No longer are they sent out to teach after a few months or a year of normal school education. They are educated in large state colleges or universities where many vocational pursuits are analyzed, discussed, and selected. The prospective teacher also develops an idea of the *job* as a *job*. He does not normally see the educational process in its social setting. Thus the future teacher often is quite unprepared for the community's view of his role.

The educational profession is the largest numerically of all the professional groups. It has increased numerically to take care of expanding enrollments and curricular offerings. This has meant a widening of the selective base. All kinds of jobs are now called teaching: drama coaching; football coaching; nursery school teaching; research; educational testing; counseling. This means that the teacher "type" is bound to be a misnomer. Few common qualities will be found between the head football coach and the head of the English department. Their jobs, their methods of work, their relationships with children, the community's view of them are different.

The gap between the teacher's perception of his job and that of the community has many implications. The teacher is given in his professional training an ideal of the teacher: one who is permissive, helpful, psychologically oriented in interpreting motivations, and is part of a self-respecting, socially important professional group. On the job he finds contrary expectations.[16] Trained to use the most modern insights to guide the methods he uses and to select the content that he teaches, the teacher may find that the community wants none of this. The parent is suspicious of new ways of doing things in anything as intimate and close as the education of his children. The teacher, himself educated in the community's concept of the teacher and the school, finds himself in an acute dilemma. Does he reject the teachings of the university, the authority of research and professors, and accept the usual way of doing things that the community approves? Or shall he snub the community and hold to the vision of his role as provided by his collegiate experiences?

4. *The teacher as a member of a profession*. In the hierarchy of the professions, that of public school teacher is barely above the level of the semi-professions. The teacher may be perceived as middle class in the community's social scheme, but he is barely upper-lower class in the ranking of professional groups. The individual teacher is ambivalent towards his own role. He recognized the value and significance of his

---

[16] Donald McNassor, "Conflict in Teachers Who Try to Learn about Children," *California Journal of Educational Research*, III (September 1951), 144–155.

work (and he is reminded by writers and speakers of how essential is the educational enterprise), but he is treated with cool snobbery by other professional groups.[17] The value of what he does is no protection from community expectations, nor does it keep a roomful of youngsters from creating absolute bedlam if not constantly watched.

In reacting to this neither-fish-nor-fowl position the teacher may behave much like a member of a minority group. He may feel keenly his low professional status and note the "discriminatory" treatment accorded him as a public servant.

The difficulties of recruiting the top level students into the profession have been a recurrent topic of articles in the literature. The research seems to point to some kind of conditioning against teaching as a profession that occurs during the high school years. Children in the sixth grade seem positively oriented towards teachers, but this attitude undergoes a marked negative shift by the time they reach the ninth grade, and continues through high school.[18]

The profession itself further divides teachers into those who are better and those who are not so good. The institutional ladder creates status and role problems; elementary teachers are at the bottom of the heap and university teachers at the top. In order to gain status, therefore, we notice an all too human reaction—modeling behavior after those higher on the respect scale.

This lack of a clear definition of the professional role and the many imbalances that result can be seen demonstrated also in the multiplicity, competitiveness, and seeming lack of common purpose found among professional organizations. The average teacher can join a national and a state teachers organization; he can belong to a subject matter organization with both national and state activities; he can join one of two teachers unions; any special interests he has may involve him in the organizations of those working for the gifted child, for the retarded, for audio-visual education, ad infinitum; and he can, if chosen, be a member of one or more professional honor societies. This multiplicity of organizations is in itself not surprising in view of the many kinds of teaching jobs and the vastness of the system. But what is disturbing to some is the conflicting view of the profession that these different organizations provide their members. Some emphasize the role of the teacher as an expert; some identify the teacher's problems with those of the working class in general; still others play up to his professional self-esteem by being highly selective in membership. And the organizations compete with each other for members and for the participation of members.

REACTIONS TO ROLE CONFLICT

The area of role conflict becomes one of the crucial issues for the teacher as a person and for those educating future teachers. When faced with role conflicts, the individual may react in several ways. He can:

1. Repudiate his role in one of several conflicting groups;

---

[17] Roger G. Barker, "Difficulties of Communication between Psychologists and Educators," *Journal of Educational Psychology* (September 1942), pp. 416–426.

[18] Roderick Langston, "A Study of Attitudes towards Teaching as a Vocation," *Journal of Teacher Education,* II (June 1951), 83–87. See also R. W. Richey and W. H. Fox, "A Study of Some Opinions of High School Students with Regard to Teachers and Teaching," *Bulletin of the School of Education, Indiana University,* XXVII, No. 4 (July 1951).

2. Play off one group against the other;
3. Stall in accepting any given role definition until the pressures subside;
4. Redefine his role so that major conflicts are eliminated;
5. Lead a double life, being a different kind of person in situations which expect different and conflicting behavior;
6. Escape from the field—resign the job or find a new one;
7. Become ill.[19]

As we observe teachers we can see these mechanisms of adjustment at work. For many teachers these devices work well, for others they fail to resolve the basic dilemma. We have noted the ways in which teachers appear dissatisfied with aspects of teaching, and it is time to consider what part role conflict plays in this unrest. By gaining insight into the nature of the conflict in any given community, school, and individual, we may be in a better position to aid the teacher in resolving at a mature level the kind of conflict he faces.

[19]Adapted from Jackson Toby, "Some Variables in Role Conflict Analysis," *Social Forces*, XXX (1952), 323–327.

8-5 THE ROLE OF THE TEACHER IN THE SOCIAL STRUCTURE OF THE HIGH SCHOOL

C. Wayne Gordon

C. Wayne Gordon is associate professor of sociology at the University of Rochester. In this essay he describes the expectations concerning teacher behavior in the teacher-student community.

This paper will examine some of the complexities of the teacher's role in the social structure of the high school.[1] The analysis will be primarily concerned with those aspects of social organization which impinge directly on the teacher in the class-room.

This discussion will rely chiefly on a previously reported study of the social organization of a high school.[2] Wabash is a four-year high school with a student population of 576 in a detached suburb of a midwestern metropolitan community. Lower

From *Journal of Educational Sociology*, XXIX (1955) 21–29. © 1955 by the Payne Educational Sociology Foundation, Inc.; reprinted by permission of the Payne Educational Sociology Foundation, Inc.

[1]The concept of a role used here is that of Talcott Parsons and Edward A. Shils, with the assistance of James Olds, "Values, Motives and Systems of Action," in Parsons and Shils (eds.), *Towards a General Theory of Action* (Cambridge: Harvard University Press, 1951), p. 190; T. M. Newcomb, "Role Concepts in Social Psychology," paper delivered at the 1948 meeting of The American Psychological Association; and Gross and Mason, "Role Conceptualization and Empirical Complexities," paper delivered at the 1953 meeting of The American Sociological Society.

[2]C. Wayne Gordon, "The Social System of a High School," unpublished Ph.D. thesis (St. Louis, Mo.: Washington University, 1952).

middle class members predominate, but all socio-economic levels are significantly represented. There is diversity of socio-economic levels to confront the teacher with a sufficient status range and power system to introduce maximum complexities related to social class which have been reported in other school and community studies.[3] The number of students is sufficiently small to permit the development of a social system in which the members interact sufficiently with one another to establish a clearly defined set of relationships which have a stable character.

Data on the teacher are from three major sources: (1) school records, (2) two hundred personal documents written by upper grade students on their school careers with special reference to classroom performance, (3) the writer's field diary as a participant observer and classroom teacher in the Wabash school system for ten years.

The Structural Context of the Teacher's Role. The Wabash study revealed three major aspects of the high school organization to be relevant to an analysis of the teacher's role. Viewed as systems of expectations which define behavior they are: (1) the formal organization of the school which prescribes learning achievement, (2) the system of student organizations usually referred to as extracurricular activities, and (3) the network of interpersonal relationships defined by the friendship choice referred to here as the informal system.[4]

The chief general finding of the Wabash study was that the dominant motivation of the adolescent was to achieve and maintain a generalized social status within the organization of the school. General social status is regarded as the position held as a consequence of the various specific statuses he achieves throughout his high school career. At the action level, the dominant motivation of the adolescent will be to accept the roles of the informal group. This view suggests that the orientation of the individual is best understood and predicted given his position within the general system of action in the school-wide social system; for instance, the classroom behavior will be conditioned by his relation to his peers which introduces a general tendency to conflict with those performances which the teacher seeks to define. We are not proposing a simple dichotomy between the formal expectations and those of the informal group, rather two definitions of the situation compatible at times between teacher and students and having varying degrees of acceptability among students.

Implication for the Teacher's Role: Sources of Strain. The structural context of the school presents the incumbent of the teacher's role with the task of continuous integration and adjustment of conflicting expectations. There was a significant range of adaptation among teachers in their capacity to harmonize the conflicting tendencies. There also was a great range in the amount of personal anxiety teachers experienced in relation to their efforts to carry on the teaching function. It is further noted that some typical modes of adaptation are made by teachers over a period of years, as they routinize their functions in such a way as to minimize the amount of personal stress which they experience in a situation of endemic conflict.

The institutionally prescribed function of the teacher is to insure the enact-

---

[3]A. B. Hollingshead, *Elmtown's Youth* (New York: John Wiley & Sons, 1949); W. L. Warner, R. J. Havighurst, and M. B. Loeb, *Who Shall Be Educated—The Challenge of Unequal Opportunities* (New York: Harper & Bros., 1944).

[4]The formal-informal distinctions used here are those used by C. I. Barnard in *The Functions of the Executive* (Cambridge: Harvard University Press, 1948), p. 73.

ment of roles related to learning achievement according to a specified range of standards. The range of standards defined by the grading system represents the instrumental goals of the system. Viewed within the achievement-ascription distinction proposed by Talcott Parsons, the high school primarily defines achievement values and roles both as a functioning institution and in relation to the socialization of its members to a technical social order.[5] The task of the teacher is to insure the essential performances. By virtue of his adult status, his personal orientation to knowledge, and as custodian of the institutionally prescribed tasks, the teacher tends to seek performances from the students according to standards somewhat higher than those which the adolescent group will set for itself. There results an incompatibility in the learning output norms which the teacher seeks to resolve.

In spite of the competitive-achievement orientation of the high school, the teacher is confronted with powerful ascriptive tendencies within the system. The Wabash study reveals the same ascriptive influences of the social class system which have been reported by Warner, Hollingshead, and others.[6] The drive for ascriptive rewards operates both at the value level which introduces subjective biases in the grading system and at the power level in which teachers assign rewards and punishments with the awareness that direct and indirect consequences may result from not doing so. Hollingshead demonstrated the tendency for teachers who originated from the local community to be able to ascribe success to members of the higher socio-economic groups because they "understood" the backgrounds of the students.[7] The Wabash data show likewise that the longer a teacher worked in the community the more likely he was to accept the social class controls of the community in his assignment of rewards and punishments. The values of the teacher which define rewards in relation to achievement determine that consciously ascribed success usually is attended by personal conflict.

The clearly defined status system in the informal student group which coincides somewhat with the social class system and extends itself through differential participation also generates potent tendencies for the most prestigeful group to be ascribed success.

A further basis of conflict for the teacher arises in relation to the basic conflict in educational philosophy which expresses the influence of the competitive achievement social order to insist on a product from the high school which can be rated and labeled according to his achievement capacity on the one hand and the influence of educational theory with a concern for the personality development within the learning experience which poses for the teacher the obligation to ascribe minimum success as an investment in the personality development of all students and particularly the least advantaged ones.

The Authority System. Comment on the authority system will be confined to the role of the teacher as intermediate between student and principal. The duty of the teacher is to maintain order both as a condition for learning and because it symbolizes his competence. Teaching competence is difficult to assess, but disorder is taken as a visible sign of incompetence by colleagues, principal, parents, and students. In a situation of conflict the teacher has constant anxiety for his ability to control. A signi-

---

[5]Pattern variable distinctions used throughout this paper are those used by Talcott Parsons in *The Social System* (New York: The Free Press of Glencoe, Inc., 1951).

[6]Warner, *et al.*, 1944; Hollingshead, 1949.

[7]Hollingshead, 1949.

ficant amount of conflict results from the requirements of the two sets of expectations which operate in the classroom, those presented by the teacher and those which the informal system defines.

Interaction within the student group is the most frequent cause of conflict between the authority of the teacher and the expectations of the informal group. The teacher's definition of order makes many of the actions within the student group a threat to authority. Teachers tend to accept noise, confusion, humor and horseplay to a point where it becomes a challenge to authority. Consequently, talking, whispering, inattention, may be viewed as a challenge to authority. In one year there were 81 cases of students being sent from the classroom to the principal's office for discipline. Of these 33 were for disturbance of the group, 27 were for talking without permission, and 14 for talking back to the teacher. The other 7 involved a variety of reasons. The reasons given by teachers are not necessarily the real cause for such action. They are rather symptoms of strain in teacher-individual student or teacher-group relationships. They are both an indication of a mode of adaptation of teachers to the informal group structure and the adaptation of students to the teacher's definition of the expectations of the classroom.

Since eviction from class is a serious crisis in the relationship of students and teachers, eviction is a conservative index of the real conflict which occurs. The classroom situation may be characterized roughly as: (1) conflict of sufficient crisis proportion to result in eviction, with the enlistment of the principal's office to resolve it; (2) conflict of crisis proportions in which the teacher absorbs the conflict without resort to the principal; (3) conflict is minimized or nonexistent as a result of the way in which the teacher articulates the requirements of both the formal and informal groups.

Reasons for absorbing conflict in the classroom have been discussed by Howard Becker in connection with the tri-partitate relations to authority among students, teacher and principal.[8] The extent to which the principal will support the formal expectations of the system by an exercise of authority will determine the kind of authority role the teacher may assume in the classroom. Students and teacher alike seek to avoid the crisis of eviction from the classroom. It affects both the status of the teacher and student in relation to the formal authority system. Student evictions affect student status because they become a factor in grading, establish a formal record of nonconformity, and may result in expulsion from the group. Teacher status is likewise adversely affected. When the burden of classroom control is shifted to the office of the principal, it calls attention to the problems which he usually prefers not to have made public beyond the classroom. Changes in the exercise of authority from the principal's office result in a greater diffusion of power throughout the school system among both teachers and pupils. In Wabash the number of classroom evictions over a three-year period was for successive years respectively 160, 81, and 50. Reduction in the number of evictions was related to the dissemination of a rumor among the teachers that "the principal has a little black book in which he records the number of students which teachers send to the office. When he gets ready to rate your teaching he looks in the little black book and decides your salary increase for the next year." It appeared that the greater the support the principal gives the teacher's authority, the more likely the formal institutional role of the teacher will be utilized to coordinate the

---

[8]Howard S. Becker, "The Teacher in the Authority System of the Public School," *The Journal of Educational Sociology* (November 1953).

classroom. The less willing the principal is to support the teacher's institutional authority, the more likely that the teacher will absorb conflict in his classroom role, and the more likely he will be to resort to personalized leadership, and face a situation of endemic conflict. Waller has pointed out the hazards of personalized leadership because only the virtuoso can sustain it.[9] The personality of the teacher under such a situation will be exposed. An additional consequence is to shift a balance of power into the hands of the students. Here differentials in status among teachers will affect their ability to exercise power and their sense of adequacy since the ability to control is equated with the ability to teach. The Wabash study shows that least secure teachers in tenure are the ones least likely to be supported by colleagues, principal, parents, and the most likely to attack from students.

Teacher Role and the Informal System. In Wabash the teacher role was conditioned by the fact that he faced in the classroom a system of student organization which was differentiated by grade rank, grade achievement, sex, social class, and prestige cliques which were value-differentiated by their participation in both the formally organized and informal student culture. The system as mentioned above exercised a potent influence over behavior. The dominant motivation was to accept the role of the informal group or differentially defined roles within value differentiated cliques or simply the role of subordinate to an overwhelming status system by the unincorporated and incorporated members. There was a consequent muting of action in this direction of teacher-presented expectations.

The teacher perspective of the classroom is one in which behavior is defined according to an ideally conceived classroom situation in which performances approximate the ability and knowledge of the students. According to this perspective discussion operates in ping-pong fashion between teacher and pupils and among pupils limited only by consideration of knowledge and limitations of personality. The teacher accepts the personal limitations of pupils as part of the educational situation. The student understands the teacher's perception of the situation and rules of its operation. However the students of variously rated performance and those of the informal group; namely adolescent in relation to same sex and opposite sex, "dater-nondater," athlete-nonathlete, "brain," "big wheel" or "nonwheels" and "fruits" (derogated group), clique member, and isolate. Each of the above labels defines roles which incorporate expectations counter to those of the teacher. Teacher-defined roles which are not accepted result in strain in the role of the teacher. The teacher with insight into the informal system may articulate both sets of roles in such a way as to fulfill the requirements of the teacher with a minimum of disturbance to the informal group. The unsophisticated teacher may lack the insight and technique or both to harmonize the two systems. He may attack the status system head-on and precipitate conflict.

The informal system with its congeries of ingroups operates as a personalized system of relations significantly motivated by affective response. The teacher as the authority who controls the system seeks to control the system in the direction of affective neutrality. As the co-ordinator of the system, custodian of the formal sanctions, and dispenser of scarce rewards, he tends to increase or reduce the total anxiety of the incumbents of the system by the use of varying amounts of expressive affect in the communication process. The security and protection which students are afforded within

---

[9]Willard Waller, *The Sociology of Teaching*, 1932.

the clique and congeniality groups may be adequate to the needs of the students. Furthermore, it may be disrupted by the way in which the teacher manipulates the reward system. The tension and anxiety is reduced by the manipulation of the symbols or gestures of varying and affective content by the teacher. Thus he will afford the maximum security to students if he expresses and bestows at least a minimum of esteem on every student. Evidence from social class and school studies suggests that teachers display a wide range in the amount of esteem and affective response for various categories of students. The Wabash drop-out of 30 percent appeared to be directly related to the least esteemed and disesteemed students. We are suggesting that an adequate conception of motivation for the teacher is that which has been demonstrated in the studies in industrial sociology. The problem in the teacher's role is that he sometimes accepts the significance of affective response in maintaining student morale and motivation toward his objectives within an institutional framework based on a sanction and reward system of hedonistic psychology. The accompanying ambivalence constitutes a dilemma. He must define goals for students who are widely different in value orientation to his expectations. There is also a discrepancy between the values of the teacher and the students. The teacher will tend to present and express the value of the able minority without impunity from the formal authority system. However, the values of his professional role decree a 100 percent consensus on the goals he presents. If he cares for the consequences, he will have anxiety over the lack of interest on the part of the least motivated group. He will be led to strenuous efforts to sustain the interest of the group with the resulting charge on his physical and emotional resources and the necessity to reduce the stress may be considerable.

TEACHER ROLE IN RELATION TO STUDENT ORGANIZATIONS

We have mentioned the function of participation in student activities as a means for defining the general status of the student in the schoolwide informal system. The result is a status system with a powerful ascriptive tendency. The teacher may accept this system dominated by "big wheels" or he may insist on the achievement values of the institutional system with its narrow deference range admitted in the classroom among superior to failing students. To reject the status system of the students is to risk the sanctions of the informal group.

A second tendency of the system of student organizations which results from the extreme differentials in the amount of participation among most active and least active students is the differential association which is produced among most active students and teachers and least active students and teachers. The differential association results in diffuse affectively toned relationships with some students in contrast to specific affectively neutral relations with the nonparticipants. The result is to particularize with those he knows well in the distribution of rewards and apply universalistic standards with greater affective neutrality in the distribution of rewards and punishment to least active, least known students. For instance, Freshmen make lower grades because teachers know them much less well in addition to the usually accepted fact that they are less sophisticated in the grade-getting culture. We seem to need a distinction between grade getting and grade achievement. By achievement we mean quality of performance and by grade getting the loss of objectivity which accompanies personalizing relationships as well as the student's manipulation of the teacher in the assignment of rewards which accompanies the process.

The more involved the teacher becomes in the student activity program, the more likely he is to be influenced by the particularistic tendencies. When he does he violates the standards of the universalistic or "fair" teacher defined by the institutional values and professional ethics of the teacher. He faces conflict with students in either case.

The teacher who is not involved in the student activity program will be less sensitive to the status differentiation of the informal system and therefore more universalistic with all members. Lacking the personal influence of association he may risk the conflict with the politically potent informal student group. He may likewise gain the esteem of the "underdog status" group.

More attention needs to be given to other than social class factors in teacher-student relationships. For instance, in Wabash Miss Jones was generally regarded to be an able scholar who had high performance expectations of students. She was considered to be "fair," i.e. "just" in her grading by most students. But the reputation of "fair" tended to be qualified by members of different groups. Upper middle class members sometimes thought her "unfair" because she resisted social class ascriptive tendencies. Lower class thought her very "fair" because she practiced a not too subtle form of "underdog" ascription. It should be noted that she was by origin of working class background. Mr. Higby, on the other hand, who affected a manner of rigid universalism, was thought by lower class members to be "unfair" and by all to particularize in favor of more attractive physically mature girls.

TEACHERS' ADAPTATIONS TO THE STRUCTURE

The foregoing discussion of the complexities of the teaching situation adds up to a situation of continuous stress in the teacher's role. An adaptation to the conditions of the situation leads the teacher to seek to adjust the various pressures in order to protect his personality. Adjustments tend to be worked out privately or in intimate congeniality groups. The problems of the classroom are not shared on a colleague-wide basis due to the competitiveness of the status system among teachers. The success ideology of the school states that "successful teachers do not have problems," therefore the most disturbing problems of the teacher tend to be regarded as unique to his situation and therefore are private. His greatest anxieties are not expressed. The teacher perspective with its failure to incorporate the reality of the social structure in which he works prevents him from seeing problems as a consequence of this generic structure. Such a perspective would be necessary in order that teachers define problems as general rather than special and private. Such a solution is necessary to relieve high school teachers of the sources of anxiety in the role and socialize them to the reality of the social structure of the high school within an analytical framework which may replace the current moralistic evaluative one.

8-6   THE ACCULTURATION OF THE SCHOOL TEACHER

George D. Spindler

After attending Wisconsin State Teachers College and the University of Wisconsin, George D. Spindler taught for several years in the public schools of Wisconsin. Later he received his Ph.D. in anthropology from the University of California at Los Angeles. He is now professor of education and anthropology at Stanford University. His publications include *The Socio-Cultural and Psychological Processes in Menomini Acculturation, Education and Culture,* and *Education and Anthropology.* In addition, he and his wife, Louise Spindler, have edited the popular *Case Studies in Cultural Anthropology* and *Studies in Anthropological Method.* Professor Spindler is a major figure in applying anthropological concepts to the field of education. In this essay he suggests the alternatives that prospective teachers face in joining the school community.

... Our culture is one in which conflicts in values, and between goals and the means to them, are present and patterned. And ... teachers, as cultural transmitters, convey these patterned conflicts to children in their classrooms, with the consequence that many professed goals are defeated, or at least obscured. I ... [am] not castigating teachers. They are the agents of their culture ....

Teachers are a special group. They are not selected at random as official culture transmitters; they are trained and accredited to that status and role. They must take courses in educational psychology, the social foundations of education, curriculum design, philosophy and history of education, the methods of education, and must do supervised practice teaching. In short, they must attend teacher-training institutions and graduate with the stamp of approval from the established professional cadre. But professional educational instruction and training consist not alone of courses and training in techniques. Every institution with a history and internal organization, and a specialized personnel, has a culture—or more properly—a subculture. Certain values, symbols, beliefs, and certain basic premises are patterned into the structure and process of the institution. The institutions of professional education—the teacher-training schools and the literature of education—are no exception.

What I am going to try to say now may be misunderstood. I am going to state some generalizations about the subculture of education. Some of my educational colleagues will disagree, but objectively. Others will disagree, and be offended. Some will agree and approve. Others will agree but be unhappy about doing so.

I must refer ... to the traditional and emergent value patterns revealed in the responses of education students to ... values projection techniques.... The traditional pattern included emphasis on thrift, self-denial, faith in the future, a strong emphasis on success and a belief that hard work was the means to it, absolute moral norms, and a

Reprinted by permission of the publishers from George Dearborn Spindler, *The Transmission of American Culture,* pp. 20–28. Cambridge, Mass.: Harvard Universty Press, Copyright, 1959, by the President and Fellows of Harvard College.

strong value placed upon the individual as an end. The emergent pattern included value placed upon sociability, sensitivity to the feelings of others, a relativistic attitude, a present-time orientation, and high value placed upon the group. The modal type of person with respect to these dichotomous value patterns is a mixed type that embraces values from both in varying degrees of coherence.

I believe that many of the conflicts between school boards and educational personnel, between parents and teachers, and between teachers and pupils can be seen as projections of differences in value commitments that represent various approximations to the traditional and emergent positions. But the dynamic process of greatest relevance to us at the moment is the relationship between the culture that the elementary school teacher brings to the professional teacher-training institution subculture, and the patterning of that subculture, the adaptation that the teacher-in-training makes to this patterning, and the consequences in selective culture transmission in the classroom.

This is a complex relationship with many subtle ramifications. I must dissect it with bold and clumsy slashes rather than precise incisions. It is well established that school teachers originate from a middle and lower-middle social class culture. I believe that it can also be demonstrated that the value pattern that I have termed "traditional" is found in this cultural context in its most purely puritanic form. To the extent this is so, it means that whatever selective processes are operating tend to bring many people of traditionalistic value orientation into teacher-training.

The question that the anthropologist raises is—what are the characteristics of the subculture of the teacher-training institution to which these students bring their traditionalist orientations? Analysis of a sample of some of the influential literature of curriculum design for elementary education reveals that there is present a strong values bias that fits in general terms the "emergent" pattern. The literature of child development and educational psychology reveals some of the same trends. Interpretations of the social behavior of boys and girls, intended for educational consumption, provide both implicit and explicit value judgments in the same pattern. The popularity of sociometric techniques is diagnostic of this orientation. The topical content of many of our teacher-training courses suggests it as well.

The basic premise underlying the superstructure of specific emergent values is that what is most important is the social adjustment of the child. His place in the group, the responses of his peers to him, his ability to get along well, to work and play with others are penultimate concerns. I personally do not regard this as all bad. The emphasis on social adjustment is the educator's attempt to meet the demands of a new kind of society, where this kind of adjustment is of vital importance. When balanced by a concern for individual differences, support for the deviating child, for intellectual development and the acquiring of cognitive skills, and when it does not become a form of "groupism," this emphasis on social adjustment is a necessary compensation for what I regard as many of the harshly competitive, egocentric patterns of our culture.

But the point is that however understandable and useful the emphasis may be, this pattern of values incorporated in the ethos of professional education may be at variance with what the new teacher in training brings into the situation. The neophyte in training must reorient his value system wherever the conflict in values is encountered.

This places many new teachers in training in a situation similar to that of acculturating populations all over the world. These populations are attempting to rechannel their emotional and intellectual commitments as they adapt to conflicts between their indigenous culture and the new culture diffused to them or appropriated by them. Anthropological studies of such populations provide the models for characterizations of adaptive consequences for teachers that I wish to make now, but these models are rebuilt in terms of empirical case studies of teachers in classrooms.

When acculturating teachers in training or people in any other acculturating group adapt to sharply disjunctive value systems, essentially four adaptive responses may occur. The individual meets the new value system and feels threatened because it challenges his established, familiar, and comfortable values. He does not, of course, necessarily interpret the experience in these terms. He is more likely to see it as a personal conflict, which heightens the threat. After some exploration in the new dimensions of feeling and belief offered to him by the opposing system, his feeling of threat overcomes him and he seeks refuge in the comforting shelter of his established values. But something has changed. He has been driven back to his "native state" by threat. Therefore he overcompensates, and rigidifies the original system in what may be psychologically termed a reaction formation, or culturally termed a "nativistic reaffirmation." I would call him a "reaffirmative traditionalist" in the framework of this analysis. The teacher of this type will tend to be rigid in his uncompromising projection of traditional values in his classroom behavior.

An alternative adaptive response is represented by the person who encounters the new value system which is sharply disjunctive with his own, likewise feels threatened by the conflict in personal terms, but adapts by overcompensating in the direction of the new system. Perhaps he is more threatened by the possibility of being left behind or out of step than he is by the requirement to change. He uncritically appropriates the new values in their entirety and frequently becomes a strident proselytizer for them. This kind of teacher I term a "compensatory emergentist." His channels of communication with children, and his criteria for their behavior, become narrowed to individual-in-harmony-with-the-group. "Groupism" reigns in his classroom. Individualistic differences and deviations become smothered by group conformity.

The third alternative adaptive response is exhibited by the person who encounters the conflict of value systems and superficially internalizes segments of both but does not rework them into any coherent synthesis. He is a mixed type but quite different from a type that I shall describe shortly. He is usually not particularly thoughtful about the conflicts he encounters and leaves them unresolved, but still a part of his acquired culture. This person as a teacher is likely to vacillate between different modes of group leadership and different modes of interaction with individual children. Obvious discontinuities in his classroom management cause trouble for both him and his students. I term his type, the "vacillator."

The fourth alternative is a happier one than any of the others. This person comes into the acculturative situation with a capacity for adjustment to differences in values and conflicts between them. Usually he is thoughtful and has the ability to combine useful features from more than one system of belief on a rational basis. He does not need to overcompensate as a defense against conflict because he is not threatened by it. He is a mixed type but does not internalize the mixture segmentally. He recombines the aspects from both systems into a creatively coherent synthesis. I have labeled this an "adjusted" type.

As a matter of fact, I believe increasing numbers of students in our senior and graduate education classes are of this latter type. They exhibit workable combinations of what seem to be the best of both the emergent and traditional values. For instance, they accept the need of the individual to be a member of the group but believe that the individual must be self-possessed and self-actualized in order to be a useful participant in any group. They believe that hard work is necessary for success but that there is no point in being unpleasant about it. Whether they represent a shift in the kind of training they receive in the school of education, or whether they represent a change in the culture of generations, or both, I do not know. In any event, I am happy to see them and hope their numbers increase, for I am convinced that large numbers of teachers, at least new ones, are reaffirmative traditionalists, compensatory emergentists, or vacillators.

I make a value judgment here because it seems clear to me that teachers falling into the first two adaptive categories tend to exhibit highly selective biases as culture transmitters. They transmit in narrow channels with few alternatives, due to their reactive rigidity. Without intending to do so, they open some doors to self-cultivating developments for some children but lock them for many others. And the vacillator, though he is not rigid and transmits along many channels, issues only weak signals and produces little but static as a result.

CONCLUSION

In urbanized American society, the community served by the school is drastically different from that served by the country school of yesteryear. During the past decade the largest population growth has taken place in the fourteen largest cities; the country town or rural crossroads community with its homogeneity of cultural and social class membership is rapidly disappearing from the American scene.

Instead, the modern American lives in a megalopolis made up of a variety of communities, none of which is united by the sentiments of the small town. Some urban communities are slums with culturally diverse populations; others are ghettos into which few members of variant groups dare venture. Some are composed of working men's homes and of populations based on socio-economic status; still others are based on religious beliefs. Finally, there are one-class neighborhoods, such as elite suburbs, from which other classes are excluded except in rigidly prescribed social situations.

Since school populations are based upon residence patterns, the school may serve either a culturally distinct community or a culturally diverse community, depending upon its location in the urban area. It is obvious that the teacher must be familiar with the community the school serves in order to provide the best education for the children of that community. His task is complicated by the diversity of subcultures extant in an urban area. However, lacking the required knowledge, the teacher cannot develop an effective program to meet the demands of the community—and the school must meet these demands.

As the size of the community increases, so does the size of the school. The informal interaction patterns of the country school are no longer adequate; instead, they have been replaced by institutionalized behavior patterns. Colleges of education have designed a large number of courses to familiarize the prospective teacher with the various forms which this institutionalized behavior assumes and to help him select the correct educational techniques in terms of the local and school communities' expectations. As indicated in this section, these expectations may conflict with each other to the point that the conflict cannot be completely resolved.

ADDITIONAL READING

John H. Chilcott, "Community Restrictions on Teacher Behavior," *Journal of Educational Sociology*, XXXIII, No. 7 (March 1960), 336–338. A brief description of one community's expectations of the role of the teacher.

Floyd Hunter, *Community Power Structure* (Chapel Hill: University of North Carolina Press, 1953). An excellent analysis of who runs a community and how.

Leo F. Schnell and Harry Sharp, "The Changing Color of Our Big Cities," *Trans-action* (January 1964), pp. 12–14. The non-white population of America's cities increases and the white inhabitants move out; thus, white suburbs surround non-white cities.

John R. Seeley, R. Alexander Sim, and Elizabeth W. Loosley, *Crestwood Heights* (New York: Basic Books, Inc., 1956). A study of the culture of suburban life. Section 8, "The School," is particularly appropriate to an examination of the school's role in a suburban community.

Index of Authors